Acknowledgments

This book has been a long while in the making and owes much to the help, constructive criticism, and good natures of other people. Most of the research was conducted in a number of Mexican archives over the course of the past eight years. I very much appreciate the assistance and unfailing patience of the archivists and staff at the Archivo General de la Nación (Mexico City), Secretaría de la Reforma Agraria (Mexico City, Morelia, and Uruapan), Instituto Nacional de Antropología e Historia (Mexico City), Archivo Histórico del Poder Ejecutivo de Michoacán (Morelia), Registro Público de la Propiedad (Morelia), and Archivo de Notarías (Morelia). Financial support from the John D. and Catherine T. MacArthur Foundation, the MIT Center for International Studies, and Boston College made this research possible.

The book started out as a Ph.D. dissertation in the MIT Department of Political Science, and was shaped through the intellectual support of my thesis committee. My emphasis on the importance of local histories in understanding politics owes much to Charles Sabel, and my thinking on Mexico has been very much influenced by Jeffrey Rubin's work on popular movements, regional politics, and revolutionary state formation. Jonathan Fox, the chair of my committee, has, over the years, taught me a great deal about rural politics and peasants in Mexico, and provided consistently helpful comments and unflagging moral support throughout the course of my dissertation work.

Many people have provided me with insightful comments on various aspects and phases of this work, for which I am enormously grateful. I'd like to thank Christopher Boyer, Lynn Stephen, Jeffrey Rubin, Gilbert Joseph, Ramón Jrade, Betsy Aron, Donald Hafner, Emilio Kourí, Caren Addis, Cathie Jo Martin, Roger Karapin, Annabelle Lever, Stephen Page,

Lourdes Melgar, and Gretchen Ritter. I'm particularly grateful to John Tutino and Mary Kay Vaughan for their careful reading and insightful comments on the entire manuscript. Finally, I want to thank the members of my family, above all my husband, Petri Flint, for their much-tested patience and loving support over the course of this endeavor.

1 ✳ What Makes Peasants Counterrevolutionary?
The Problem of Partisanship in Mexico's
Cristero Rebellion

At some point in the summer of 1926, the Michoacán community of San Juan Parangaricutiro heard the alarming rumor that President Plutarco Elías Calles had ordered that all Mexican churches be closed. One group of residents went to the state capital of Morelia to lodge a protest with the governor. Another traveled to Zamora to consult the bishop. Neither delegation could have returned with reassuring news. The revolutionary state had begun to close Catholic schools and convents, place restrictions on the numbers and activities of parish priests, and prohibit public worship. But it was the episcopate, not President Calles, who had ordered the churches closed, in protest of these and other anticlerical measures. The San Juan peasants may or may not have subsequently learned that the National League for the Defense of Religious (LNDLR or League), an organization of urban lay Catholics, had called for a mass insurrection to begin on 1 January 1927. They certainly did know of the rebellions under way in the neighboring states of Jalisco, Colima, and Guanajuato. In early 1927, residents would later recall, Juan Mincítar, a member of the local council of politico-religious authorities, the *cabildo,* declared that they would "betray themselves, their faith, and the Lord of the Miracles if they did not take up arms as many of their brothers had already done." Shortly thereafter, on 2 February, many of the men from San Juan, under the leadership of Mincítar, headed for the mountains. Other residents sought safe havens in neighboring villages and towns. In declaring themselves in rebellion against the revolutionary state, the peasants from San Juan joined tens of thousands of peasants throughout the center-west region of Mexico in what would come to be called the *cristiada* or *cristero* rebellion of 1926 to 1929.[1]

Two or three days later, armed troops entered San Juan, and, finding

Map 1. Center-west of Mexico. Map by Mark McLean.

the rebels gone, proceeded to burn many of the houses and destroy the seed for the next year's corn crop. A brief shoot-out ensued when some of the San Juan peasants came back to assess the damage. This first military encounter in San Juan did not involve the federal army, however. The troops in question were peasants from the neighboring community of Paricutín.[2] Having previously applied for the restitution of their communal lands through the revolutionary agrarian reform program, the Paricutín peasants offered their political and military support to the state as participants in an *agrarista* militia. Over the course of the rebellion, the state would come to rely on thousands of such peasants in conducting its counterinsurgency campaign against the cristeros, particularly during the more serious military revolts of the period, when the loyal faction of the federal army was engaged in fighting its rebellious counterpart. While some of the agrarista peasants came from outside the center-west, many others were recruited from within the region itself, most notably from Michoacán, where popular support for both the cristiada and the agrarista movement was high.[3]

The conflict between the communities of San Juan Parangaricutiro and Paricutín was but one local manifestation of what Bartra (1985: 37)

calls the "two distinct and clearly antagonistic tendencies" within the Mexican peasantry of the 1920s. Elsewhere in Michoacán, agraristas from the Indian communities bordering Lake Chapala fought cristeros from the neighboring highlands, while agraristas from the Zacapu region were deployed in the Tierra Caliente to battle cristeros from the region of Coalcomán. Revolutionary anticlericalism and agrarianism divided communities as well. Throughout the 1920s and beyond, factional conflicts were expressed in terms of agraristas versus Catholics, reds versus whites, and priest killers versus fanatics. In the Purépecha highlands, the Paricutín agraristas were joined by members and allies of prominent mestizo families from San Juan Parangaricutiro; in Naranja, Tarejero, and especially Tiríndaro, intracommunity hostilities between the agraristas and Catholics sometimes degenerated into astonishing cruelties.

Why, in the context of a conflict between Church and state, did some peasants support the Church and defy the state, whereas others supported the state and defied the Church? Why did some peasants define themselves as anticlerical agraristas, whereas others defined themselves as anti-agrarista Catholics?[4] Why was sustained and large-scale rebellion limited to the states of the center-west, even though the great majority of rural Mexicans considered themselves to be devout Catholics in their religious beliefs and practices?

Nothing inherent in popular Catholicism necessarily entailed opposition to agrarian reform. Nor did support for agrarian reform necessarily entail an attack on the Church, much less on peasants who supported the Church. The Zapatistas of the 1910s had called on divine guidance in their struggle to recover communal lands; like the cristeros, they too carried images of the Virgin of Guadalupe into battle (Knight 1986a: 311). Throughout the 1920s and beyond, many peasant communities organized and applied for land under the revolutionary agrarian reform program without attacking the Church or religious practice and without providing military support to the state. Yet in the center-west region of Mexico in the 1920s, many agrarista peasants explicitly defined themselves as anticlerical, and their personal and political enemies, both elite and popular, as Catholics. Other peasants, in turn, accepted and adopted this Catholic political identity. It came to express their opposition to the anticlericalism of the new state, and in many cases to revolutionary agrarianism, which, though it sometimes increased access to land, also involved a significant increase in the state's role in the regulation of community resources and a subsequent loss of local political autonomy.

The cristero rebellion entailed much more than the defense of the institutional prerogatives of the Catholic Church. At the popular level, it was part of a broader set of struggles between peasants and revolutionary elites over the normative and institutional contours of the new state, involving multiple and competing conceptions of property rights, popular culture, and local political authority. This book is an exploration of how, as Catholics and agraristas, different peasant communities and factions within communities contested and shaped this process of revolutionary state formation in Michoacán. As such, it addresses three broader questions: Was the Mexican revolution indeed a popular revolution? What impact did popular movements and cultures have on revolutionary state formation? and How can we understand the origins and construction of the political identities mobilized in rural collective action? On these matters, the cristeros and agraristas of Michoacán have much to tell us.

The Cristero Rebellion and the Mexican Revolution

One of the central debates about the Mexican Revolution concerns the extent to which peasant grievances and mobilization were decisive in shaping events between 1910 and 1940. Orthodox scholars depict the revolution as a massive and undifferentiated popular rebellion in which the political and economic power of the landed class was destroyed to the benefit of the peasantry at large.[5] Revisionist scholars counter that the revolution was little more than a power struggle between national elites, in which the popular values and aspirations embodied in the Zapatista peasant movement were thoroughly defeated, the revolution thereby constituting little more than the modernization of the *Porfiriato* (1876–1911) (the period of Porfirio Díaz's presidency).[6] What is striking about this debate is how little light it sheds on popular participation in the cristero rebellion. Whether orthodox or revisionist in orientation, most scholars of the revolution treat the cristiada as an instance of church-state conflict, ignoring its popular character altogether, or attributing popular support for the Church to fanaticism and false consciousness.[7] Many scholars, like revolutionary elites, have had a hard time taking popular cultures and religiosity seriously, particularly when it would seem that the cristero peasants were acting against their presumed "class interests" in rejecting the revolutionary agrarian reform. In order to understand peasant partisanship in the cristiada, we need to

take a closer look at what different peasants had to say about revolutionary anticlericalism and agrarianism, and at how these two policies meshed with or violated local values, cultures, and institutions.

Given that orthodox scholars hold that the revolution was unquestionably a popular one, both in its origins and its outcome, and that the state that emerged from the revolution served as the vehicle for the realization of peasant aspirations for land and liberty, popular participation in the cristero rebellion is all but inexplicable, except in terms of false consciousness and the ideological hegemony exercised by the Church.[8] The revolution, for orthodox scholars, had "easily identifiable villains and heroes" (Bailey 1978: 69), and the Church, without doubt, was among the latter. Monolithic, rapacious, and reactionary, the Church kept the peasantry in a state of passivity and poverty, in the name of God and on behalf of its landlord allies and benefactors. Under attack by revolutionary anticlericalism and agrarian reform, the Church responded by mobilizing the peasants most firmly under its ideological domination. In advancing this interpretation, orthodox scholars have echoed the official version of the cristiada, as captured in a 1927 declaration by the national legislature, which, affirming its solidarity with President Calles, condemned the "rebellion of fanatics who have allowed themselves to be misled by the criminal maneuvers of the capitalist reaction conspiring with the high Catholic clergy."[9]

But if there were "many revolutions" in Mexico as students of regional history claim, there were a good number of counterrevolutions as well. The latter, like the former, grew out of both popular grievances and elite political aspirations. The various "counterrevolutionary" movements of the 1910s and 1920s—the *delahuertistas,* Felicistas, Oaxacan *soberanistas,* and cristeros—all appear in the official mythology of the revolution, and in much of the orthodox literature, as reactionary Porfirians, dedicated to restoring the old social and political order at the expense of the peasantry and working class.[10] Yet each movement involved popular groups whose goals could only be considered counterrevolutionary insofar as they deviated from the agenda of revolutionary elites. In rebelling against the new state, the cristero peasants certainly allied themselves with unambiguously reactionary elites, although neither the Church nor the lay Catholic opposition was monolithic in this respect. But the cristeros also advanced popular goals that differed as much from those of their counterrevolutionary allies as they did from those of their revolutionary opponents. As was true during the revolu-

tion of 1910 to 1920, the contradictions between elite and popular agendas became more apparent and more pronounced as the rebellion wore on.

Anticlericalism and agrarian reform were major sources of conflict throughout the period of 1910 to 1940 and beyond. On these issues, there was no simple dichotomy between revolutionary versus counter-revolutionary, or popular versus elite, positions. The Zapatista movement was rooted in ideas about community autonomy in economic and political affairs that differed significantly from the state-led agrarian reform program of the 1920s and subsequent decades. Peasant opposition to that agrarian reform program was based on sometimes different but equally "popular" understandings of property, community, and the state and was quite distinct from the opposition of large landowners.

Revolutionary anticlericalism certainly limited the powers and prerogatives of the Church as an institution, and of the clergy as individuals, but it also constituted an attack on beliefs and practices that were central to popular cultures and the organization of rural social and political life. To explain popular participation in the cristiada in terms of false consciousness is to assume, a priori, that the cristero rebels had no ideas of their own about justice, rights, and legitimacy and is to ignore the extent to which revolutionary agrarianism and anticlericalism could, under some circumstances, constitute a threat to the very values and institutions that were at the heart of the revolution for many peasant communities.[11]

Whereas orthodox scholars depict the revolution as a massive popular insurrection that transformed social relations and political power in Mexico, revisionists see it as an intraelite struggle through which one faction of the bourgeoisie emerged victorious to create a more centralized and authoritarian state capable of fostering a capitalist social order.[12] Given this view of the revolutionary state as profoundly antipopular in character, peasant participation in an antistate movement such as the cristiada is not problematic. Nor, however, is such participation particularly relevant to the revisionist understanding of the outcome of the revolution. In rejecting the orthodox view of the popular character of the revolution (and sometimes even the revolutionary character of the revolution), many revisionists discount the importance of popular movements altogether, be they revolutionary or counterrevolutionary in character, particularly insofar as the formation of the new state is concerned. Focusing on state institutions and intraelite conflict, revisionists have

tended to "relegate popular participation to a subordinate, almost in-consequential role" (Joseph and Nugent 1994a: 7), treating the agrarista movements of the 1920s as cynical efforts to manipulate and control peasants and largely ignoring the cristiada altogether.

J. Meyer's (1973/74, 1976, 1977, 1981, 1991) work constitutes a major exception within the revisionist camp. Challenging orthodox assumptions about the role of Catholic elites, lay and clerical, in the rebellion, he argues that in terms of grievances, leadership, and military and political organization, the cristiada was first and foremost a popular rebellion, directed against a tyrannical state determined to destroy and re-create Mexican society in accordance with a new revolutionary dogma. Meyer's work represents a significant advance over the orthodox interpretation of the cristiada as a conflict between Church and state in which some peasants were induced to act against their own interests by priests and landlords. But it also reproduces, in mirror image, one of the basic flaws of the orthodox literature. For Meyer, "the people" rose up against the revolutionary state, just as in the orthodox view, "the people" rose up against its Porfirian predecessor. Furthermore, given his view of a hostile and authoritarian state bent on the destruction of traditional peasant society, Meyer attributes popular support for the agrarista movement to false consciousness and the coercive power of local agrarista bosses. He sees the agrarista peasants much as orthodox scholars see the cristeros: as the unwitting victims of elite manipulation, control, and deceit (J. Meyer 1973/74c: 50–91).

The cristiada entailed far more than a conflict between Church and state. But neither was it, as Meyer implies, a confrontation between a militantly anticlerical state and a politically and culturally homogenous peasantry. Peasants were deeply divided in their responses to revolutionary state formation. For some communities and factions within communities, the agrarian reform program offered the possibility of reclaiming lost lands, and anticlericalism became a vehicle for displacing despised local authorities. For others, these two policies constituted a threat to community resources, understandings of property rights, and institutions of politico-religious authority. In order to understand partisanship in the rebellion, we need to take a much closer look at what the arrival of the revolutionary state meant for different regions of Mexico and, within regions, for different rural communities and factions within communities.

There is extensive scholarship on the social bases and political dynamics of the agrarista movements of the period;[13] the scholarship on the

cristiada is, in contrast, much sparser, and a good deal of it, as already noted, focuses on urban elites rather than on the peasant rebels. Comparative analyses of the two movements and the peasants who participated in them are all but nonexistent, precisely because so few scholars have considered the cristiada to be a popular rebellion.[14] In the absence of such analyses, assertions about the contrasting socioeconomic attributes of the cristeros and the agraristas are frequently little more than guesswork, deductions based on general theories of peasant behavior but lacking empirical evidence.[15] Explanations of partisanship based on religiosity, meanwhile, are often simply tautological: the cristero peasants rebelled because they were more religious, and the proof of their greater religiosity lies in the fact of their having rebelled.[16] Such evidence as we do have on this point suggests that cristero and agrarista peasants often shared very much the same sets of religious beliefs and practices.[17] Where they differed was in their political identities: the cristeros were not simply Catholics; they were *political* Catholics, "Catholics whose politics were premised on their Catholic allegiance" (Knight 1990b: 299). For many peasants in the 1920s, "being Catholic" came to embody not just opposition to anticlericalism, but a much broader set of understandings about the legitimate role of the state in rural communities. Some of these political Catholics rebelled as cristeros, while many others did not, even as they continued to contest the agrarian and anticlerical projects of the emerging state. Other peasants, who shared much the same set of religious beliefs and practices as the political Catholics, opposed the Church's role in politics and education and supported revolutionary anticlericalism and agrarianism more generally.

The few comparative analyses of peasant partisanship that do exist focus on the unique features of the agrarian structure of the center-west, the one region in Mexico where the mestizo smallholding community predominated over the hacienda and the corporate Indian community.[18] This pattern of social organization, together with the historical strength of the Church as an institution in the region, is taken to have produced a particularly virulent response to the anticlerical and agrarian policies of the revolutionary state on the part of the mestizo smallholders known as *rancheros*. Relatively quiescent during the revolution, the smallholders of the center-west seemed to conform to McBride's (1923: 102) classic characterization of the ranchero: "He is opposed to revolutionary movements of all kinds; and what he desires most is to be left alone, to cultivate his few acres in peace, unmolested by the march of troops or the

raids of rebel bands." This quiescence in the 1910s turned to rebellion in the 1920s, however, in response to increasing economic insecurity; an agrarian reform program that attacked private property; and anticlerical policies that attacked the central spiritual, social, and political institutions of the ranchero communities.[19]

This type of structural analysis, however, is as problematical for the cristero rebellion as it is for the Mexican Revolution more generally. In neither case is peasant partisanship explicable in terms of socioeconomic categories such as ranchero or *comunero* (a member of a corporate Indian community with access to communal land). If the rancheros of the center-west tended to be counterrevolutionary, their counterparts elsewhere figured heavily in the ranks of the revolutionary armies of the 1910s and the agrarista movements of the 1920s. The Maderista rebellion in Guerrero was initiated by prosperous rancheros who sought greater local political autonomy (Jacobs 1982), whereas rancheros in the Sierra Alta of Hidalgo sought to increase their economic and political power through the leadership of local agrarista movements (Schryer 1980). Rancheros also made up much of the rank and file of the agrarista movement led by Saturnino Cedillo in the state of San Luis Potosí (Ankerson 1980; Falcón 1988); some of them were deployed in the state's counterinsurgency campaign during the cristiada. Nor was the center-west simply a region of ranchero communities. Such a characterization greatly exaggerates the social homogeneity of the region, as well as the distinction between mestizo smallholding and corporate Indian communities. Given population growth, the expansion of haciendas, and the extensive privatization of communal lands that occurred in the second half of the nineteenth century, both types of communities often included significant numbers of smallholders, tenants, and landless peasants working for wages within or outside the community.[20] Furthermore, the region was deeply divided politically during the 1920s, and these divisions were by no means reflections of class (or ethnic) lines. The cristeros of San Juan Parangaricutiro had a good deal more in common with the agraristas of Paricutín and Naranja, other Purépecha communities with a history of communal landholding and corporate politico-religious authority, than they did with the cristeros of San José de Gracia, a mestizo smallholding community in which life revolved around the sacraments and the parish priest.

Partisanship in the cristero rebellion, as in the revolution before it, was very much a local affair, rooted in specific histories and cultures that

do not correspond well to class categories, ethnicity, or degrees of religiosity. As Benjamin (1984: 14) argues, there were "many Porfiriatos" in Mexico and it is this that accounts for the many revolutions (and counterrevolutions) experienced at the local level in the early decades of the twentieth century. Benjamin contrasts San José de Gracia, where "life was probably better in 1910 than it had been thirty years before," with Naranja, where the Porfiriato was "a prolonged nightmare." This book argues that it was these very different local historical experiences, rather than differences in class, ethnicity, or religiosity, that account for the emergence of Catholic and agrarista political identities in the two villages in the 1920s: whereas a good many residents of San José de Gracia rebelled against the new revolutionary state as cristeros, Naranja, together with the neighboring communities of Tarejero, Tiríndaro, and Zacapu, was the center of the state's agrarista movement. In linking the specific histories of these and other communities in Michoacán to different popular responses to revolutionary state formation in the 1920s, the book fits within what Joseph and Nugent (1994a) term a postrevisionist synthesis of the orthodox and revisionist approaches to the Mexican Revolution. It combines the former's concern with popular aspirations and movements with the latter's emphasis on the construction of the revolutionary state, while paying much closer attention than either to the diversity of popular cultures and experiences and to the impact of this diversity on state formation.

The Cristiada and Revolutionary State Formation

Peasant movements, especially those that are thoroughly defeated, are rarely considered to have much of an impact on the construction of states.[21] This is particularly true in the case of Mexico, where the dominant image of state formation is one of a coherent, intentional, elite-led project that entailed the gradual but steady expansion of state control over popular groups through the consolidation of a monolithic party with its subordinate corporatist organizations.[22] For many scholars, this "Leviathan on the Zócalo" existed in embryonic form as early as the 1920s, its ultimate shape and nature determined by the functional requirements of dependent capitalist development, or a secular process of political centralization and bureaucratization, rather than by the "messy give-and-take of actual politics involving personal, institutional, regional, and class rivalries and struggles" (Benjamin 1985: 202).[23] This

interpretation of the Mexican state is, as Rubin (1996: 85–86) puts it, both "state-centered and center-centered": the focus on elites and state institutions obscures the importance of popular movements in contesting the terms of power, and the focus on the "center" (geographical, institutional, and discursive) obscures local and regional variations in the presence and form of the central state.

This study of the cristero rebellion presents a different understanding of state formation, holding that no Leviathan, embryonic or otherwise, existed in Mexico in the 1920s. Nor was the nature of the state predetermined by the structural imperatives of capitalism or some internal logic of political centralization. Rather, state formation was a historically contingent process in which different actors, elite and popular, struggled to define the normative and institutional parameters of the new state.[24] This struggle had two interrelated dimensions. The first was the ongoing effort by the center to establish or reestablish control over the periphery, where regional strongmen and state governors, rather than national figures and institutions, prevailed. In the course of this intraelite conflict, both regional and national leaders cultivated popular support in order to advance their own political agendas and careers.[25] The second dimension entailed the relationship between revolutionary elites and their popular allies and enemies. Elites may have envisioned a secular, national, and capitalist society guided by a strong central state, but—facing a mobilized peasantry with very different cultural and political identities and agendas—they were in no position to impose such a state and society "from above." The mobilization of popular support and diffusion of popular opposition required elites to partially accommodate values, practices, and demands that they might well have preferred to ignore.[26] Popular movements were indeed "defeated" in the process of state formation, but the state that emerged from the political conflicts of the 1920s and 1930s was the result of the ongoing "negotiation of rule" (Joseph and Nugent 1994b) between elite actors and diverse popular groups.[27]

Central to these negotiations was the role of the state in the rural communities. "A revolution," as Scott (1994: ix) notes, "is also an interregnum." In the period between the destruction of the old state and the construction of a new one, a "vacuum of sovereignty" prevails, affording local communities a good deal of autonomy in matters of politics, culture, property, taxes, and justice. State formation entails the reassertion of the authority of the central state at the local level, with a concomitant

ing any dichotomous conceptualization of culture as folk versus urban, little versus great, or popular versus elite. Popular receptions of anticlericalism, as with agrarianism, were rooted in previous histories of agrarian and political conflict at the local level, rather than class or religiosity.

Revolutionary state formation in Mexico established both political institutions and "a common discursive framework that [set] out central terms around which and in terms of which contestation and struggle [could] occur" (Joseph and Nugent 1994a: 20). Throughout this process, popular cultures were both transformed and transformative.[35] Popular understandings of land and community, be they rooted in private property or communal holdings, limited the degree to which revolutionary elites could create and impose a new property regime based on state ownership and distribution of use rights through the ejido. Popular religious beliefs and practices, meanwhile, frustrated elite attempts to create a secular society based on a uniform national identity.[36] But the terms of the struggle, the "common discursive framework," were, increasingly throughout the 1920s and 1930s as the revolutionary state took form, set by elite rather than popular actors. Thus the Namiquipans did not "autonomously [choose] the particular issue over which they [struggled]; the issue, and the argument over names and institutional forms, was presented by the projects of a homogenizing state" (Roseberry 1994: 362). Likewise, the peasants of San Pedro Caro rejected the state's offer to grant them land to which they felt they already had legitimate ownership, but contested the state's role in the definition and distribution of property rights in terms of restituciones and dotaciones, procedural categories established and regulated by the revolutionary agrarian reform program. Popular groups continued to contest the role of the state in the local community long after the revolutionary state was consolidated in the 1930s, but in doing so they tended to employ identities, discourses, and institutions established by that state.

The Construction of Political Identities

One of the most perplexing puzzles presented by the cristero rebellion concerns the origins and construction of collective identities. Given that the vast majority of rural Mexicans considered themselves to be devout, why should some Catholic peasants resist revolutionary state formation as political *católicos*, whereas other Catholic peasants supported it, al-

ways in some tension with their elite allies, as anticlerical agraristas? How did the identities of Catholic and agrarista come to embody two distinct sets of popular understandings of property rights, culture, and the legitimate role of the state in the rural community? If class, ethnicity, and religiosity cannot account for the origins and substance of collective identities, then what does?

The problem of identity is central to current discussions of collective action in Latin America, much of which employs the terms, if not the entire conceptual framework, of new social movements theory. But these discussions would seem to be of little relevance to the cristiada, because they do not have much to say about the construction and mobilization of collective identities in peasant rebellions.[37] One of the central claims of new social movements theory is, after all, that the identities involved are quite literally new, based on attributes other than class, and that the movements entail new ways of doing politics, aimed not at the pursuit of class interests, much less at the conquest of state power, but rather at the very construction and affirmation of the new subjectivities themselves. Peasants are clearly not new social actors, and rebellion can hardly be said to constitute a new way of doing politics. New social movements theory also suggests that although we need new conceptual tools for the analysis of "postmodern" identities and noninstrumental forms of collective action, we already have adequate ways of understanding peasant rebellions, in which the actors and their interests can be defined and understood in structural terms.

At the same time, there is a marked dissatisfaction with class-centric and structural analyses among those who study rural politics. With reference to Latin America, Roseberry (1993: 359) maintains that such approaches force complex and diverse rural groups into "models that are historically and sociologically empty," while Stern (1987a: 9) concludes that "[f]or all the advances made in the field of agrarian studies, we are still only beginning to understand the manifold ways whereby peasants have continuously engaged their political worlds." The theoretical disputes generated by Scott's (1976) early work on moral economy, Popkin's (1979) rational choice approach, and Paige's (1975) income-based model of rural collective action were hardly insignificant,[38] but they masked a much more fundamental consensus that peasant rebellions are essentially economic phenomena, explicable in terms of structural transformations and class-based interests. Political identity is a nonissue in this literature: peasants, as political actors, are defined by their structural

and reshaped the symbolic and institutional relationships between property rights, religious practice, and political authority within rural communities and hence the popular understandings of the opportunities and threats involved in subsequent conflicts over revolutionary state formation at the local level.

The nature and duration of these conflicts varied considerably. The cristero and agrarista identities of San Juan Parangaricutiro and Paricutín owed much to a bitter and centuries-long border dispute between the two communities; San Juan's more recent resistance to the privatization of its communal lands, mandated under the liberal reform laws of the nineteenth century, also played a role in the construction of its (predominantly) Catholic and cristero identity. The development of a strong agrarista identity and movement in the Zacapu region, in turn, was the product of failed resistance to the liberal land reform, the near-complete loss of communal lands to neighboring landowners and the state's tax offices, and the concomitant destruction of local institutions of politico-religious authority. And in San José de Gracia, where, before the revolution, "[h]ardly anyone had business with the government or wanted any" (L. González 1968: 133), it was the absence of prior legacies of conflict with either neighboring landowners or the state, combined with the direct threats entailed in revolutionary state formation in the 1920s, that best accounts for that community's participation on the side of the rebels during the cristiada.

In stressing the centrality of legacies of agrarian and political conflict at the local level in explaining partisanship in the cristero rebellion, I do not mean to argue that the cristiada was really about land, even though the peasant rebels thought it was about religion, but rather that peasants understood land, religious practice, and local political authority to be intertwined in ways that depended upon their own local histories.[45] For cristero communities, revolutionary agrarianism and anticlericalism constituted a twofold and simultaneous assault on popular cultures and religious practices, property rights, and local political self-determination. Local allies of revolutionary elites displaced traditional politico-religious authorities and parish priests, attacked and often tried to prohibit religious practice, and, in some cases, monopolized or otherwise threatened community landholdings and other resources. For agrarista communities, the agrarian reform program was an opportunity to recover lands lost in prior conflicts, while anticlericalism provided a vehicle for the displacement of local elites, be they landowners, priests,

or politico-religious elders. Because of the nature of prior conflicts, religion had sometimes lost its symbolic and institutional centrality in agrarista communities, although not its importance as a set of beliefs and practices. Anticlericalism could thus be viewed and used as an attack on the Church and particularly on its unpopular local representatives and allies, rather than as attack on community life and identity.

Stern's distinction between short-term and long-term frames of analysis is helpful in understanding the regional character of the cristiada, as well as local variations in partisanship within the center-west. Given that popular uprisings broke out across Mexico in the context of the "clerical strike" of mid-1926, why was sustained rebellion limited to the center-west states of Jalisco, Michoacán, Colima, Guanajuato, and Zacatecas? Here I argue that a particular combination of historical and conjunctural variables explains the cristiada's regional character: first, the survival of a significant number of communities with their landed bases and traditional institutions at least partially intact; and, second, the existence of a dense network of lay grassroots organizations loosely affiliated with the Catholic Church. Communities did not rebel en masse during the cristiada unless revolutionary anticlericalism and agrarianism attacked local resources, values, and institutions that had been successfully defended until the revolution itself. Communities could not sustain rebellion if theirs was an isolated uprising or if they were detached from the organizational networks that provided the peasant rebels with logistical support, coordination, legitimacy, and some military leadership. Many communities outside the center-west survived the various assaults of the nineteenth century with their landed bases and institutions intact, most notably in the Pacific south states of Guerrero and Oaxaca. The Church and its affiliated lay organizations also had a strong presence outside the center-west, most notably in the center-east region of Mexico. But neither the Church nor its affiliated organizations were strong in the Pacific south, and communities did not survive the Porfiriato in large numbers in the center-east. Furthermore, the distinctive timing and nature of state formation in the center-west come into play here as conjunctural factors that explain the regional character of the rebellion. In contrast to the Pacific south and the center-east, the revolution, as experienced at the local level, was most intrusive and violent in the 1920s in the center-west, just as anticlericalism reached a peak at the national level. This meant that revolutionary state formation at the local level took on a pronounced anticlerical character. It also helped to mobilize

Chapter 4 turns to the cristiada itself, focusing on the question of why sustained and widespread popular rebellion was limited to this region of Mexico. The chapter begins with a narrative account of the rebellion, tracing its development from the initial uprisings that occurred in the context of the clerical strike of 31 July 1926, through its peak as a loosely coordinated but sustained guerrilla war in early 1929, to its conclusion after the episcopate reached an accommodation with the revolutionary state in June 1929 and forbade further rebellion in defense of religious liberty. The chapter then turns from narrative to analysis, examining two competing explanations of why the rebellion was limited to the center-west: the first based on the institutional strength of the Church in the region and the second on the region's agrarian structure. In positing an alternative explanation, I argue that neither class nor ethnicity can account for partisanship and that the institutional strength of the Church provides only a partial explanation of the rebellion's regional character. Lay Catholic organizations were undoubtedly critical in sustaining popular rebellion, insofar as they provided arms, ammunition, logistical support, and some military leadership. But they could not in and of themselves produce it, however grand the schemes of lay Catholic leaders in Mexico City. Sustained popular rebellion required, as further conditions, the survival of large numbers of communities and their constituent institutions related to land, religious practice, and political authority, as well as concrete threats to these institutions in the form of revolutionary state formation. All these conditions were met in the center-west and only in the center-west.

A complete understanding of partisanship requires that we turn to the local level, exploring long-term histories of agrarian and political conflict and the ways in which these conflicts shaped and reshaped the normative and institutional relationships between property rights, religious practice, and local political authority, and hence popular receptions of revolutionary state formation in the 1920s. The fifth chapter examines the Indian communities of the Zacapu region, where the near-complete loss of communal lands in the last quarter of the nineteenth century was accompanied by the breakdown of local institutions linking religious and political authority. Here, in what would become the heartland of the state's agrarista movement in the 1920s, religion had ceased to be a source of popular identity and solidarity. Rather, it generated intense and often grotesquely violent factional conflicts, as anticlerical agraristas attacked and defeated political Catholics within their own communities.

The sixth chapter turns to the central highlands adjacent to the city of Uruapan. In contrast to Zacapu, many of the Indian communities in this region had been far more successful in resisting the state-mandated privatization of their communal land holdings and hence emerged from the Porfiriato with much of their landed bases and local institutions intact. In the highlands, small agrarista movements contended with Catholic majorities who strongly opposed the anticlericalism and agrarian reform program of the new state and who, under certain conditions, rebelled against that state as cristeros. The chapter focuses on San Juan Parangaricutiro, predominantly Catholic and cristero, and its age-old enemy, the agrarista village of Paricutín.

The seventh chapter turns to the predominantly cristero highlands of northwestern Michoacán. The rancheros of this region enjoyed a particularly good Porfiriato, having acquired their smallholdings through the breakup of insolvent haciendas or at the expense of neighboring Indian communities. In rebelling against the revolutionary state as cristeros, they were often joined by the landless members of their communities who, in spite of their landlessness, shared the same historically contingent views of the legitimate relationship between land, community, and the state. The eighth and final chapter returns to the problem of political identity: through a comparative analysis of the cristero rebellion and other popular antistate movements of the revolutionary period, it examines the ways in which long-term legacies of conflict interacted with short-term "strategic" variables, such as allies and resources, to produce the political identities through which peasants participated in and contested the process of revolutionary state formation.

peasant smallholdings known as *ranchos,* at the expense of both hacienda and Indian community. The chapter concludes with an overview
of economic development and social transformation in Michoacán on
the eve of the revolution, providing a context for the discussion of popular responses to revolutionary state formation in subsequent chapters.

Liberals, the Church, and the Hacienda

Mexican liberals considered the Catholic Church to be an obstacle to
state formation on several grounds. It was the Church, rather than the
state, that controlled the registration of births, marriages, and deaths,
and in a profoundly religious society, the refusal to perform the sacraments associated with these life cycle events represented a powerful instrument of social and political control (Sinkin 1979). Félix Díaz, as
governor of Oaxaca, declared in 1869 that the civil registry mandated by
the liberal reform was of "vital importance to the state," affirming "its
independence from all parasitic and foreign powers." Compliance with
the registry law, in his mind, "speaks highly in favor of the civilization of
the citizens of this state, their love for the laws of the reform . . . and the
disappearance, gradual but positive, of pernicious preoccupations with
religion" (Estado de Oaxaca 1869).

Liberals also viewed the Church's role in education as an obstacle to
economic progress and the development of a national identity: individuals would not act rationally in pursuit of their own interests until they
were freed from the dogma and superstitions of Church teachings; nor
would they consider themselves first and foremost as Mexicans, and only
secondarily as Catholics, until society and the state were secularized.[5]
Faith in the transformative power of secular education was quite strong
among many liberals: "[T]he instruction of all classes of society is the
only way to regenerate the spirit of the people, purging them with its
sound doctrines of their vices and passions. . . . [Education] will weaken
their customs, bring order to their unruly habits, and inspire in them a
pure love for occupation and work, a profound respect for law and justice, a rational and dignified obedience of authority, and a pronounced
affection for honor and virtue, the very qualities without which the edi-
fice of a democratic republic cannot be sustained" (Estado de Oaxaca
1869).

Finally, there was the matter of the Church's corporate wealth.[6] Private property rights were central to liberal understandings of individ-

ual liberty, citizenship, and economic development. It was the yeoman farmer who, having acquired his parcel of land through the disentailment of Church wealth, would provide the basis for political peace and economic prosperity in nineteenth-century Mexico.[7] As a liberal newspaper argued in 1851, in the context of the debate over ecclesiastical property, "Each new proprietor will be a new defender of institutions and of stability," and "peace, order, and liberty will have gained" (cited in Hale 1968: 37).

Until the 1850s, the crux of the conflict between liberals and conservatives concerned the degree to which political power should be centralized or decentralized in the emerging state. Anticlericalism did not come to dominate national politics until after the Revolution of Ayutla (1854–55), when liberal forces ousted General Antonio López de Santa Ana and ushered in the period known as La Reforma (Guardino 1996).[8] Once in power, the new liberal government passed a number of anticlerical measures, some of which enjoyed widespread popular support: they abolished the military and ecclesiastical judicial privileges (*fueros*), except in matters pertaining exclusively to military or canon law; limited the clerical fees charged for the performance of the sacraments, abolishing them entirely for the poor; secularized education; mandated the civil registration of births, marriages, and deaths; abolished compulsory services; and, through the Constitution of 1857, provided guarantees for a range of civil and political liberties, including freedom of speech, education, and assembly.[9] It was the 1856 Lerdo Law, however, that was to have the greatest impact on the countryside. Named after the minister of the treasury who wrote it, Miguel Lerdo de Tejada, the Lerdo Law required that almost all property belonging to civil and ecclesiastical corporations be sold to its current tenants or occupants. Unleased property, or property not claimed by tenants or occupants within a period of three months, was to be sold at public auction to the highest bidder. In all cases, corporations were to be compensated through mortgages based on the declared value of the property in question, with interest rates based on current rents. The state was to receive only a tax on real estate transactions.

The ideological rationale behind the Lerdo Law rested on a distinction made between private and corporate property rights. Individual property rights were held to be inviolable, even if the unfettered accumulation of wealth inhibited economic progress, best fostered, the liberals believed, by small and medium-sized producers. As the liberal

Some of these haciendas were broken up only gradually, as their owners attempted to overcome financial difficulties through piecemeal sales of the less productive parts of their properties. Such was the case with two estates near Maravatío in northeastern Michoacán, which were broken up in 17 different sales over the period of 1866 to 1883. In cases where economic circumstances were more dire, properties were subdivided and sold off all at once. The Hacienda of San Bartolo, for example, located in northern Michoacán near Lake Cuitzeo and valued at over half a million pesos, was broken up into 33 units and sold in 1865 (Chowning 1984: 48–50).

The hacienda economy began to recover in the early years of the Porfiriato, and boomed toward the end of the century, as the construction of the railroads, the expansion of other infrastructure, and newly established financial institutions made it possible for landowners to take advantage of growing markets for commercial estate production. Their entrepreneurial efforts were greatly facilitated by sympathetic state governments, particularly in the years of Governor Aristeo Mercado (1891–1911), when, as state historian Romero Flores (1946: 563) would later write, with some exaggeration, "a landowner, however illiterate, corrupt, or untrustworthy he might be, had the ear of the district prefects, who held him in the highest regard, and gave him everything he asked for." Most notably, state officials facilitated the territorial expansion of the haciendas, often at the expense of neighboring communities, through the application, legal or illegal, of the 1856 Lerdo Law, as well as the 1883 and 1894 laws applicable to land lacking legal private title (*terrenos baldíos*) (see the next section). Hacienda expansion remained limited on the eve of the revolution, however, as compared to other regions of Mexico. Furthermore, it was far from uniform across the state: most properties greater than 1,000 hectares were located in just two regions, the Tierra Caliente and the Michoacán Bajío (see chapter 4).

Liberals and the Indian Communities

Many of Michoacán's Indian communities entered the second half of the nineteenth century having preserved, to varying degrees, the central institutions that had regulated local economic, religious, and political life since the early colonial period: the communal property regime, in which land was owned by the community as a whole, even as individual families held long-standing use rights; the offices (*cargos* or *mayordomías*)

and confraternities (*cofradías*) though which religious practice was organized and financed; the *hospital,* with its own confraternity, generally dedicated to the Virgin of the Immaculate Conception; and the council of politico-religious elders, or *cabildo.* Property rights, religious practice, and local political authority were intertwined through these institutions: proceeds from communal property funded civil expenses and religious practice; the cofradía of the hospital cared for the sick and housed visitors, financed regular masses and funerals for all members of the community, took care of church property, and sometimes served as a local source of credit for community members; the cofradías, in which most members of the community participated, usually owned livestock that grazed on communal pasture lands; the performance of the religious cargos, which entailed financing the cult of a particular saint for a one-year period, was a prerequisite for many civil positions and for membership in the cabildo; and the cabildo served as the local political authority, regulated access to communal land, allocated the civil and religious cargos (and hence future political power), mediated disputes, and managed the community's relationship with external actors, including the state.[13]

"Within each community," Espín Díaz (1986a: 254) writes, "there were multiple understandings of property." Cultivated land (*tierras de común repartimiento*) was farmed by individual families with long-standing use rights. It was widely considered to be a form of private property, whether or not it was formally registered with the state as such, albeit one subject to considerable community control, exercised by the cabildo. The entire community had access to the tierras de común repartimiento after the harvest and during fallow years; the land could be cultivated only every other year; residents were prohibited from erecting fences around their plots; and attempts to sell the land to outsiders generated strong communal resistance. The woodlands (*montes*) and pastures (*ejidos*) were used by all members of the community and were clearly considered to be communal property. The cabildo regulated the extraction of wood and often allocated cleared plots in the woodlands to families in need of more land for cultivation. Leased communal holdings called *propios* might be cultivated land, pasture, or woodlands, and their proceeds were used to finance religious and civil expenses. Much more rarely, they were exploited collectively for the same purposes. Finally, the house plots, *solares,* located in the town site, or *fundo legal,* were generally considered to be private property by community members, even if they were, in fact, under corporate title. They included the houses them-

selves, as well as small vegetable gardens and fruit orchards.[14] Access to communal property was by no means egalitarian, particularly with respect to the tierras de común repartimiento, which were occasionally all but monopolized by a few powerful families within the community or by mestizo outsiders. Most community members did have access to the communal pastures and woodlands (and to cultivated plots within the woodlands), however, and community norms constrained what might be done with privatized property and hence limited its concentration and alienation, particularly when it remained registered under corporate title.

Reliable estimates of communal property are almost impossible to make, given the vagueness of colonial land titles, the amount of land subject to ongoing litigation, irregularities in the way such property was registered with the state, and confusion as to what belonged to individuals, the cofradías, and the communities. As of 1869, however, when the Michoacán state government first began to apply sustained pressure on the communities to carry out the division and privatization of their communal property, 166 communities paid property taxes on corporate holdings. Nearly half of these were located in the Purépecha regions of Lake Pátzcuaro (47) and the Uruapan highlands (32). The remainder were in the northern and northwestern districts of Jiquilpan (10), Los Reyes (10), Puruándiro (8), and Zamora (5); the northeastern and eastern districts of Maravatío (16), Zitácuaro (16), and Huetamo (9); the southern district of Coalcomán (8); and the central districts of Tacámbaro (1) and Ario (4).[15]

Many liberals considered communal property to be the main source of the "backwardness" of rural Mexico, its very existence said to be predicated on the belief that Indians were inferior and in need of the state's paternalistic protection. The communal property regime, according to one Michoacán tax official, "served no other purpose than to keep [the Indians] in the state of ignorance, misery, fanaticism, and degradation to which they were reduced at the time of the conquest" (cited in A. Gutiérrez 1984: 20). Only as small proprietors, another liberal argued, would Indians become "true citizens under the tutelage of nobody" (cited in Hale 1968: 227). In Michoacán, district prefects charged with overseeing the disentailment of communal property were instructed to inform the Indians that "the land reform had no other end than their well-being, to provide them with what they needed to be considered real citizens, and to exercise the precious rights that went along with that prerogative" (cited in Knowlton 1990: 7).

The privatization of communal land would create not just citizens, but also wealth, because self-interested individuals, freed from the constraints and obligations of communal life, would be inclined to invest their surplus rather than to squander it on the rituals and fiestas associated with the religious cult. Employing language typical of the liberal discourse of the period, a district prefect in Ocotlán, Oaxaca, reported that the villages under his jurisdiction were "corrupted by drunkenness, and by the custom of mayordomías and superfluous expenses made in the name of religious functions"; "these are the causes," he continued, "of the impoverishment of the pueblos" (Estado de Oaxaca 1872). Along similar lines, in 1869, the municipal president of Zacapu declared:

> The benefits that the privatization of communal land will bring to the Indians themselves and to the whole society . . . are well known and of great importance to the peace and tranquility of the villages: it will bring an end to the laziness and vice of drunkenness into which many of the Indians have fallen, since once this system of communal property, which has deprived them of peace and of occupation, is eliminated, they will dedicate themselves to their own business rather than to the continual fiestas and cargo expenses that have impoverished them and led them into misery and crime.[16]

Viewed as a source of violence, immorality, and sloth, popular religious practice was often condemned by liberals as a wasteful imposition by the cabildo, in the name of the community, on individual community members. Thus the community of Zacapu was said by the same official to have had communal property worth some 100,000 pesos, "the proceeds of which are constantly wasted by a few who control and oppress the others."[17]

Liberal property laws, in fact, tended to treat the Indian community as a landlord from whom the individual peasant was to be liberated. The Lerdo Law, for example, required that "leased" corporate property be sold to tenants, while "unoccupied" property, and leased property not claimed by tenants, was to be sold at public auction. The law could be, and often was, interpreted to mean that peasants were required to explicitly claim and pay for the tierras de común repartimiento they already cultivated under use rights and that outside tenants might claim ownership of the lands they rented from the community. The status of communally exploited woodlands and pasture was even less clear: lacking individual occupants and tenants, it might be subjected to sale at

public auction as unleased corporate property, or "denounced" and claimed by individuals. A further source of confusion lay in which forms of communal land were subject to privatization. The language of Articles 1 through 7 of the Lerdo Law could be interpreted to include all property with the exception of the fundo legal, but Article 8 explicitly exempted from privatization "buildings, *ejidos,* and lands dedicated exclusively to the public service of the towns to which they belong" (cited in Fraser 1972: 633). This clause was a source of ongoing conflict: even as they agreed to privatize the tierras de común repartimiento, community leaders often claimed that pasture, marshlands, and woodlands were not subject to the law.

The ambiguities of the Lerdo Law, and the conflicts generated by these ambiguities, were such as to require countless clarificatory decrees and circulars over the course of half a century. The distinction between leased and unleased communal land proved to be a particular problem for the communities, because few peasants considered themselves to be "tenants" who should apply for ownership of their property and because the law permitted outsiders to denounce and purchase any land not claimed by tenants or occupants after a period of three months.[18] In an early circular of 9 October 1856, Miguel Lerdo de Tejada asserted that because the law was intended "to favor the most humble classes," peasants should receive the lands they farmed under usufruct rights unless they specifically waived their rights to them; all plots valued at less than 200 pesos were to be automatically adjudicated to their occupants for free (Mallon 1995: 98–99).[19] Subsequent circulars consistently upheld the right of tenants to denounce and purchase any lands rented from the communities (Powell 1972: 659). The status of communal pasture and woodlands remained unclear for some time. In some cases, the land was treated much like cultivated land and divided among community members, whereas in others it was declared to be unleased corporate property, and it was either sold at public auction or to whoever denounced and claimed it (Fraser 1972: 640–41).[20] Rooted in an ideology that viewed the community only as an impediment to individual freedom and reflecting a considerable lack of clarity about how communal lands were used in practice, the Lerdo Law thus threatened peasants with the dispossession of a significant part of their holdings, even in the absence of the fraud and coercion that were so often part of the reform process.

The status of communal property was debated throughout Mexico in the constituent assemblies held at the state and national levels in the

years following independence, and many state legislatures, including that of Michoacán, passed laws mandating the privatization of communal lands as early as the 1820s. These laws were not widely implemented, however, given that state governments were far too weak to overcome widespread popular opposition to the land reform (Fraser 1972).[21] Although the Lerdo Law established the privatization of communal lands as a national policy in 1856, most Michoacán communities were able to avoid its implementation throughout the period of the civil wars that followed the promulgation of the 1857 Constitution. It was not until liberals regained control of the state under the Restored Republic that the communal property regime began to be systematically dismantled in Michoacán. The process was accelerated and intensified during the Porfiriato, as a result of land laws and development policies that both increased the commercial value of communal holdings and raised the stakes of community resistance to their division and privatization. The 1883 Terrenos Baldíos Law, for example, authorized surveying companies to measure "unclaimed" or "public" land without private title. One-third of the land surveyed was then granted to the companies and the remainder auctioned off by the government. An 1894 law declared that all land not clearly claimed under a legally recognized title should be considered "public" and hence subject to denunciation. This law was sometimes invoked by landowners and speculators claiming land held under corporate title by the juridically extinct *"ex-comunidades"* of Indians.[22]

In Michoacán, the state government began to apply sustained pressure on the Indian communities to privatize their communal holdings in late 1868. District prefects throughout the state were instructed to convene meetings in all communities with corporate property, in order to explain the legal procedures involved in the land reform and to hold elections for the local privatization commissions, the members of which were to compile a local census, survey and map out all communal lands, and divide them into parcels of equal value for distribution under private title. In order to encourage communities to carry out the land reform as quickly as possible, a new property tax was established on all undivided communal land, at a rate of 10 pesos per 1,000 pesos assessed value. At the same time, state tax officials often doubled or tripled the assessment of lands subject to the new tax.[23] This proved to be a successful pressure tactic, either forcing communities to privatize their lands in order to avoid such onerous taxation or allowing state officials to seize and auc-

nearly all communities claimed that outsiders without rights were included in the census, whereas community members with rights were excluded.[27]

The case of San Pedro Caro, located near Lake Chapala in northwestern Michoacán, was fairly typical with respect to these types of fraud. In 1902, David Méndez, a lawyer charged with overseeing the privatization process, reported that it had been completed "without difficulties, except for a self-interested and insignificant opposition."[28] In spite of his assurances, however, the Ministry of Government in Morelia received numerous complaints of fraud and irregularities from community members. Some claimed that the best and the most land went to peasants who had already sold their shares to outsiders or who had promised to do so after the privatization was completed. In this fashion, the owners of the nearby Hacienda of Guaracha had managed to acquire large tracts of communal land, "100 times better" than that received by the peasants who would not sell, who were left with "land so poor that it isn't even good for pasture."[29] According to other complaints, the parcels were all of equal size, but the land was of vastly different quality; outsiders were included in the census, whereas residents with legitimate rights were excluded; and mestizo families without rights received land, one of their members having served on the local privatization commission. Most important, it was entirely unclear that the marshlands along the shores of Lake Chapala had been divided up, much less divided up equitably: only five or six private titles had been issued, even though the marshlands made up more than half of the community's communal holdings.[30] All of the complaints received by the Ministry of Government were sent to the Jiquilpan district prefect for investigation. An ally of Méndez, he invariably reported back that they were groundless. State officials formally approved the privatization of San Pedro's communal lands in 1903. Disregarding the reported irregularities, the Ministry of Government informed the protesting comuneros that, according to the district prefect, "the privatization was done with equity, since no one with rights to land was omitted, no one without rights was included, nor was any land left undivided and undistributed."[31]

Protests registered by community members after the land reform had been finalized were rarely successful, particularly when powerful landowners had benefited from the process. Many of the rebellions generated by the liberal reform came after years of attempts to rectify fraudulent dispossessions through legal channels.[32] Efforts to delay the land reform,

or to modify its terms in accordance with local norms and institutions, had a much greater chance of success. Repeated requests for delays and extensions were probably the most common way of resisting the implementation of the reform. Given the complexity of the legislation, as well as of property rights and disputes in the villages, countless justifications for such delays and extensions could be found. Another common tactic, and a riskier one, entailed titling communal land in the name of one or more individuals, often through denouncing such land as being without legal title, under the 1894 Terrenos Baldíos Law, or as unclaimed or unleased communal property, under the 1856 Lerdo Law. Although such denunciations were frequently a means through which outsiders gained control over communal property, communities sometimes arranged them with local elites or individual comuneros, in order to secure a legal title to communal lands without altering de facto property rights within the community.[33] This was a particularly risky tactic, because such individuals often proved to be unreliable. The Indian community of San Francisco in Uruapan, for example, carried out a "pretense" of a privatization in 1872, claiming the right to maintain 5,000 hectares of pasture and woodlands as communal property under the terms of the Lerdo Law. Twenty years later, after Díaz had decreed that all communal lands were subject to privatization, forestry companies and external landowners threatened to denounce and claim these lands as untitled property. In order to protect the property from this denunciation, according to community members, "we viewed ourselves as obliged to simulate a sale" of the land to one Agustín Martínez Anaya. Far from conserving communal land rights, however, Martínez began to sell off the 5,000 hectares to outsiders in parcels of various sizes. According to the community's 1916 petition for the restitution of its communal lands, "[o]ur kindhearted benefactor is currently transformed from poverty to opulence, enjoying a life of leisure with the property of the village."[34]

By the end of the nineteenth century, many communities were finally forced to privatize their communal lands, under the combined pressures of property taxes assessed on undivided property, state foreclosures for nonpayment of such taxes, and denunciations or outright seizures by outside landowners. The residents of Tarejero, for example, gave up their decades-long effort to resist the liberal reform in 1896, "as much to comply with the law as to avoid the advances continually made . . . by neighboring haciendas."[35] When forced to implement the reform, however, many communities attempted to retain at least some degree of local

control over the process. In Tarejero, peasants tried, without much success, to protect their claim to lands in litigation with the Haciendas of Cortijo and Bellas Fuentes, among others, through including the disputed properties in the land reform.[36] The residents of nearby Tiríndaro first attempted to delay the land reform until legal decisions had been rendered with respect to lands in litigation with neighboring haciendas and communities. They subsequently claimed that most of their land had long been privatized, "since time immemorial," the ejidos and marshlands remaining communal in accordance with the wishes of the community. Informed by state tax officials that there was no official record of an earlier land reform, residents responded that "making use of the liberties conceded to us by the Supreme Government, we carried out the division of our properties by ourselves."[37] The residents of San Pedro Caro also tried, unsuccessfully, to maintain communal usage of their pasture and woodlands, arguing that their privatization would "in no way be advantageous, and would cause great harm to the community, the land, perhaps, falling into the hands of a single person."[38]

In spite of increasing state pressure to carry out the privatization of communal lands throughout the period of the Porfiriato, however, the implementation of the Lerdo Law remained partial and contested on the eve of the revolution, with significant variations in the degree to which Michoacán Indian communities were able to retain control over their communal holdings. Success was greatest where collective resistance combined with either remoteness or less desirable lands. The all but inaccessible coastal communities of what is now the *municipio* of Aquila were, in many cases, able to avoid the implementation of the reform altogether, as were many of the highland communities around Uruapan, at least with respect to their woodlands. Communities closer to centers of state authority, and with land more attractive to nearby haciendas, were far less successful. By the end of the Porfiriato, many of the communities of the Tierra Caliente, the Zacapu and Lake Chapala marshlands, and parts of the Lake Pátzcuaro region had lost most of their communal lands, through fraud, outright seizures, or property tax foreclosures.

Ranchos and Rancheros in Nineteenth-Century Michoacán

The confiscation of Church property, taken together with the economic devastation of the civil wars of 1858 to 1867, resulted in the breakup of haciendas throughout Michoacán. The application of the Lerdo Law,

and the baldíos laws of 1883 and 1894, allowed haciendas in some parts of the state to reconsolidate and expand at the expense of the Indian communities. Both processes led to a different type of agrarian transformation in nineteenth-century Michoacán: the proliferation of private smallholdings referred to (in central Mexico) as ranchos, which, when congregated, constituted *rancherías* or ranchero communities. Although ranchos sometimes reached up to 1,000 hectares in area, most were small farms, large enough to provide a family subsistence and a small marketable surplus. Well-off rancheros might lease some of their land to sharecroppers and tenants and hire wage labor during peak periods in the agricultural cycle, but most ranchos were worked exclusively by family labor, and some rancheros had to work as wage laborers in addition to cultivating their own land in order to achieve a subsistence (McBride 1923: 82–84).

Although ranchos had existed since the colonial period, it was in the first half century after independence that they began to flourish in the center-west, initially at the expense of the hacienda. Particularly in Jalisco, Michoacán, and eastern San Luis Potosí, large landowners facing severe economic difficulties often leased out portions of their estates to tenants, some of whom were eventually able to buy the land and establish themselves as independent smallholders. The civil wars of the 1850s and 1860s generated a second wave of hacienda bankruptcies, leading to the further expansion of the ranchero economy, a tendency reinforced through the application of the Lerdo Law, which allowed independent smallholders to acquire further communal holdings either through legal purchases or through the various sorts of frauds and coercive measures so commonly associated with the liberal reform (Tutino 1986: 238–39).

Michoacán rancheros were, for the most part, peasant farmers struggling to maintain a subsistence for their families and perhaps achieve a surplus to market, located as they were in the less fertile highlands of the northwest and southern regions of the state. Some certainly took advantage of the new markets and financial opportunities available toward the end of the Porfiriato to expand their wealth, but ranchero communities were far from economically homogenous, including as they did many landless peasants who worked as sharecroppers, tenants, or wage laborers either for their more successful relatives or on neighboring estates. Even though they were based on individual private property rather than corporate property, therefore, ranchero communities, like Indian

communities, were characterized by considerable internal inequalities and social differentiation, mitigated by the solidaristic ties of kinship, godparent relations associated with life cycle events (*compadrazgo*), and participation in community religious life. In contrast to Indian communities, ranchero communities tended to be mestizo in ethnicity and Hispanic in culture; characterized by a more orthodox form of Catholicism rooted in the Church and the sacraments, as opposed to a popular Catholicism revolving around the cult of the saints; and based on the extended patriarchal family, as opposed to the community as a whole, as the crux of social and political life (Tutino 1986: 343).[39] But these differences were more a matter of degree than a question of polar opposites, and in both types of communities, popular understandings of land and property rights were closely linked to religious practice, ideas about community membership and identity, and local political authority, be it vested in the cabildo or the local parish priest.

Ranchero communities were particularly important in two regions of Michoacán: the coastal highlands of the Coalcomán district, and the northwest highlands near Lake Chapala. The rancheros of Coalcomán acquired their holdings at the expense of the Indian community of the same name, which had controlled nearly all of the land in the central region of what is now the municipio of Coalcomán until the land reform was carried out in the summer of 1871. Cochet (1988) estimates that somewhere between 100,000 and 200,000 hectares were affected in the process.[40] The land reform, according to community members who attempted to have it annulled almost immediately, was marred by the usual frauds and irregularities: outsiders were included in the census, whereas some residents were left out, individuals in the community monopolized the best and the most land for themselves, and the local privatization commission sold off some communal lands without community consent and kept the proceeds for themselves. Yet further land was alienated when individuals began to sell off their newly acquired properties at a fraction of their estimated market value.[41] Mestizo colonists, attracted to the region by the prospect of buying up communal lands at rock-bottom prices, established livestock ranchos on parcels purchased from community members who were willing or forced to sell. They then proceeded to seize additional land from those who were not. In this endeavor they had the full support of the district prefect, who refused to investigate either the irregularities associated with the land reform or subsequent complaints about frauds and dispossessions. An 1875 armed

Map 2. Michoacán. Map by Mark McLean.

uprising by community members was squashed by local authorities with the assistance of the region's hacendados and rancheros. Having pacified the area, local authorities then divested the community of its fundo legal in 1881. The community's final attempt to protest the land reform and subsequent dispossessions in 1891 led to a further wave of violence and the loss of what remained of its communal holdings to outside land-owners. By the end of the century, Coalcomán was a region of rancheros. With the complete loss of its communal property and subsequent break-down of local cultural and political institutions, the Indian community of Coalcomán had ceased to exist.[42]

The second major ranchero region, in the northwest corner of the state near Lake Chapala and the Michoacán Bajío, is treated at length in chapter 7. Throughout much of the colonial period and the first century of independence, the region was dominated by the enormous latifundia constituted by the Haciendas of Guaracha, San Antonio, and El Plata-nar, owned, in the nineteenth century, by the Moreno family. Having inherited the heavily mortgaged property shortly after her father's death

in 1845, Antonia Moreno soon faced the usual economic difficulties of the period. These were compounded by gambling debts incurred through her renowned passion for cards. In 1861 to 1863, Moreno was forced to sell off the more mountainous and less productive western half of Guaracha, also known as the Hacienda of Cojumatlán. Some of the property was purchased by well-off residents of the towns of Sahuayo and Jiquilpan, but many of the hacienda's tenants and sharecroppers were also able to purchase holdings of 100 to 1,000 hectares, thus establishing themselves as independent small proprietors. With the peace and economic prosperity of the Porfiriato, the Moreno family fortunes recovered, and the owners of Guaracha began to seize the communal lands of the Indian communities around Lake Chapala. While the hacendados claimed the best of these lands for themselves, the region's rancheros also expanded their holdings at the expense of the Indian communities, providing a partial explanation for the animosities between the agraristas of the lake region and the cristeros of the nearby highlands in the 1920s.

Michoacán on the Eve of the Revolution

In many accounts of the Mexican Revolution, the nineteenth century is depicted as a period in which the hacienda expanded at the expense of the Indian community, through the wholesale appropriation of communal land and the subsequent exploitation of the newly landless labor force. However true this scenario was in some regions of Mexico, it fails to capture the complexity of the agrarian transformations of liberal and Porfirian Mexico, much less the extent to which these transformations and the conflicts associated with them differed across localities and regions. The implementation of national and state policies with respect to property rights, most notably the 1856 Lerdo Law and the baldíos laws of 1883 and 1894, varied widely in accordance with local politics and agrarian configurations, leaving quite different legacies of conflict and institutional change at the local and regional levels. This last subsection consists of a brief overview of economic development and social transformation in Michoacán at the turn of the century, providing a context for the discussion of revolutionary politics and policies that follows.

The state of Michoacán can be divided into four general regions based on both geography and agrarian history. First is the Lake Chapala and Bajío region, a thin and relatively flat band running along the north and northwest part of the state. Predominantly mestizo in ethnicity and cul-

ture, this region was dominated by haciendas in the fertile valleys, and ranchero communities in the more marginal highlands, the latter of which were particularly concentrated in the northwestern part of the region. A small number of Nahuatl-speaking Indian communities existed in the immediate vicinity of Lake Chapala. Many of them lost their communal property to rancheros and expansionary haciendas as the extensive marshlands of the lake region were drained and brought into regular agricultural production in 1909 to 1910. Including some of the best agricultural land in the state and enjoying a relatively ample water supply, this region witnessed considerable economic growth in the latter years of the Porfiriato: once linked via railroad to the Guadalajara and Mexico City markets, the hacendados and rancheros of the Michoacán Bajío and Chapala region entered into the commercial production of livestock, wheat, corn, and garbanzos.[43] Peasants from this region, both indigenous and mestizo, would be among the first to organize and petition for the restitution of their communal lands or for land grants under the Revolutionary Agrarian Reform Law of 1915. Others, however, particularly in the western highlands, battled the revolutionary state as cristeros in the late 1920s.

Michoacán's Purépecha population was (and is) concentrated in the second major region of the state: the central highlands and the adjacent plains of Lake Pátzcuaro and the Zacapu marshlands. There was a great deal of variation in the course and outcome of agrarian conflicts within this region. The Purépecha communities of the Zacapu marshlands, as well as many of those around Lake Pátzcuaro, lost their communal lands to neighboring haciendas and ranchos, either through the liberal land reform or through various deals made between the Porfirian government and the hacendados concerning the drainage and sale of marshlands. The agrarista movement of the 1920s would be centered in this part of the state. The communities of the highlands, in contrast, were much more successful in resisting the land reform: in this region, increasing internal differentiation, conflicts with foreign timber companies, and intercommunity conflicts over boundaries were much more typical than the loss of communal lands to outside landowners.[44] Here, small agrarista movements contended with large Catholic majorities. Some of the latter rebelled against the state and fought their agrarista enemies, as cristeros.[45]

The third major region of the state is the Tierra Caliente. Sparsely populated before and after the conquest, this vast region in the center

and center-east of Michoacán was dominated by large haciendas starting with the colonial period. With irrigation made possible due to the large number of streams throughout the Tepalcatepec and Balsas river basins, Spanish and mestizo colonists engaged in the production of rice, sugar, and livestock. Little was marketed outside of the region, however, until the last quarter of the nineteenth century, when the Italian Cusi brothers arrived as part of a liberal colonization project and purchased several large haciendas, which they then converted to the commercial production of rice and other crops (L. González 1971). Other commercial haciendas were also established in the Tepalcatepec river valley in this period, producing corn, wheat, sugarcane, rice, and sesame and drawing migrant labor from the recently dispossessed communities of the Zacapu and Pátzcuaro regions (Embriz Osorio 1984: 27–28). To some degree, the expansion of large-scale commercial agriculture occurred through the purchase of noncommercial haciendas. The Cusi brothers, for example, bought the 28,000-hectare Hacienda Zanja in 1890, renaming it Lombardia, and the 35,000-hectare Hacienda Ojo de Agua in 1909, renaming it Nueva Italia. But this expansion also occurred at the expense of the existing Indian communities of the region. With the implementation of the liberal land reform laws in the last quarter of the nineteenth century, most of the indigenous peasantry of the Tierra Caliente lost their lands (L. González 1971: 126–29). Although the region served as a battlefield for contending forces during the revolution and the cristiada, its residents were not active participants in either. Only in the 1930s, during the presidential administration of Lázaro Cárdenas, would the resident workers of the haciendas of the Tierra Caliente organize and apply for land under the revolutionary agrarian reform.

Finally, the fourth major region consisted of two distinct zones: the southern highlands and the coastal lowlands of what was formerly the district of Coalcomán. Largely inaccessible until well into the twentieth century, the region contained relatively few haciendas. Those that did exist were concentrated in the lowland region of what is now the municipio of Coahuayana. In the highlands of Coalcomán, ranchero communities predominated, the mestizo colonists having acquired their small-holdings through the legal and illegal dispossession of communal lands after the 1871 implementation of the liberal land reform, as noted earlier. The Nahuatl-speaking Indian communities of the Pacific coast, in contrast, were far more successful in retaining their considerable communal lands under increasing pressure from new mestizo colonists hoping to

establish smallholdings; timber and mining companies; and landowners expanding their production of sugarcane, coconuts, coffee, cotton, and livestock (Brand 1960; Sánchez Díaz 1988). Much of the agrarian conflict along the coast, as in the Purépecha highlands of the center, involved intercommunity disputes over communal boundaries. It was not until the twentieth century, and particularly after 1930, that the communities became involved in extended disputes with the rancheros of the highlands. In the 1920s, both Indian comuneros and mestizo rancheros fought the revolutionary state as cristeros.

Throughout the course of the nineteenth century, liberal theorists elaborated a discourse and practice that linked property rights and the secularization of society to the consolidation of a sovereign state, the creation of a liberal citizenry, and the establishment of the conditions necessary for economic progress. Both the Catholic Church and the Indian communities, privileged corporate entities inherited from the former colonial regime, were understood to be obstacles to the creation of a liberal order, commanding as they did resources, loyalties, and forms of authority that defied liberal understandings of individualism and lay beyond the reach of effective state control. However, the liberal state, and to some extent the Porfirian one, was no more in a position to transform society from above than would be the revolutionary state of the 1920s. Rather, liberal discourses and policies were mediated and modified at the local level in accordance with local agrarian structures, cultures, and configurations of political power. Thus the impact of the liberal reforms, above all the Lerdo Law, varied widely across localities in Michoacán, leaving very different legacies of conflict and transformation. These legacies, in turn, shaped popular receptions of the threats and possibilities entailed in the process of revolutionary state formation, the subject of the following chapter.

3 ✳ State Formation in Revolutionary Michoacán

Michoacán produced no major revolutionary movements in the 1910s. Francisco Madero's 1910 call to overthrow the dictatorship of Porfirio Díaz was heeded by a handful of long-term Díaz opponents, as well as some farsighted Porfirian officials. With few exceptions, the members of both groups feared widespread popular insurrection far more than they desired political or social reforms. Local popular rebellions did occur in the first years of the revolution, but these remained scattered, isolated, and easily repressed, detached as they were from elite opposition or from broader revolutionary movements. Nor did any significant popular movements emerge in the civil wars that followed Victoriano Huerta's 1913 overthrow of Madero. The state certainly produced small groups of Huertistas, Carrancistas, Villistas, and Zapatistas, but for most people in Michoacán, the decade of the 1910s was marked not by active revolutionary participation, but rather by attacks by rebel bands, widespread banditry, prolonged drought, and devastating epidemics.[1]

The decade of the 1920s, in contrast, was characterized by intense social and political conflict, as two radical governors, Francisco Múgica (1920–22) and Lázaro Cárdenas (1928–32), undertook a series of agrarian, labor, anticlerical, and educational reforms that threatened, or promised, to transform the very foundations of Michoacán society. In order to carry out these reforms and to consolidate their own bases of political power, both governors encouraged popular mobilization, organizing and arming peasants so that they might defend themselves from the hired guns of landowners, reactionary elements within the federal army, or hostile local officials. Two other governors, Sidronio Sánchez Pineda (1922–24) and Enrique Ramírez (1924–28) came to office with much more conservative agendas. But facing the military rebellion

led by Adolfo de la Huerta in 1923 to 1924 and the cristiada of 1926 to 1929 respectively, they too found that they needed popular support, the price of which was the partial accommodation of the demands of agrarista peasants. This process of radical reform and popular mobilization certainly sparked a strong reaction on the part of the Church and affected landowners, but it also generated widespread and often violent popular opposition in rural communities that viewed the formation of the revolutionary state as a threat to local resources, institutions, and practices.

The first section of the chapter is an overview of events in Michoacán between 1910 and 1920, the military phase of the Mexican Revolution. The overthrow of Porfirio Díaz in 1911 was followed by two years of tumultuous social conflict, as the popular mobilization generated by Madero's 1910 call to revolution spread well beyond the control of the moderate reformers who had sought to bring the Porfiriato to an end. Huerta's 1913 assassination of Madero led to further civil war, first pitting the reactionary Huertistas against the Constitutionalists of the north and the Zapatistas of the south. Once the Huertistas were defeated in 1914, the Constitutionalists split, generating yet another round of civil war, as the multiclass and reformist Carrancistas fought their former allies, the popular and more radical armies of Villa and Zapata.[2] In order to defeat the Villistas and Zapatistas through expanding their own bases of popular support, military governments throughout states controlled by the Carrancistas began to implement the very moderate Agrarian Reform Law of 1915, encouraging peasant communities to apply for the restitution of their former communal lands or for grants of land based on need. Anticlericalism emerged as a dominant theme in the discourse and practice of the Carrancista revolution at this point as well, in part as a response to the Church's support for Huerta, but rooted much more deeply in the liberal ideology of the nineteenth century. Both agrarianism and anticlericalism were incorporated into the revolutionary Constitution of 1917, written in a convention dominated by radical Carrancistas such as Francisco Múgica.

The second section of the chapter turns to the social and political conflicts unleashed by agrarianism and anticlericalism in Michoacán, when, in the 1920s, the state became one of the "laboratories of the Revolution" (Benjamin 1990: 71) in which state officials, by inclination or by military and political necessity, undertook a series of radical reforms intended to strengthen the links between popular groups and the

state, consolidate state authority at the local level, and eliminate competing sources of identity and authority. However much agrarianism and anticlericalism were "top-down" policies aimed at the consolidation of the revolutionary state, they also responded to and meshed with popular grievances and cultures in some localities throughout Michoacán, while threatening the resources, cultures, and institutions of politico-religious authority in others. This chapter focuses on state-level policies in the 1920s, whereas the case study chapters that follow turn to variations in local responses to those policies.

The Revolution in Michoacán, 1910–20

The revolution began in Michoacán when Salvador Escalante raised the Maderista banner in the town of Santa Clara on 5 May 1911. Until this declaration of armed rebellion, few of the townspeople had heard much of the Maderista movement, initiated the previous November. Some, in fact, misunderstood Escalante's declaration to be part of the traditional Cinco de Mayo celebration of Díaz's 1862 victory over the French in Puebla (Ochoa Serrano 1989a: 74). As the Porfirian subprefect of Santa Clara, Escalante was one of the "last-minute revolutionaries" typical of the center-west states (Knight 1986a: 237). He declared his adherence to Maderismo just a few days shy of Ciudad Juárez's fall to the revolutionary forces of Pascual Orozco and of the subsequent surrender and resignation of Porfirio Díaz. A number of large landowners and well-off rancheros joined forces with ex-Porfirian officials in opposing the crumbling regime: such was the case with Braulio Ramírez and José Rentería Luviano in Huetamo; Jesús García in Tangancícuaro; and Marcos Méndez, who campaigned in Coalcomán, Apatzingán, and Uruapan (Ochoa Serrano 1989b; Oikión Solano 1986). At least some of these landowners declared themselves to be Maderistas with the intention of maintaining, rather than overturning, the existing social order. As the U.S. manager of the Michoacán Power Company wrote in May 1911 with reference to the region around Lake Pátzcuaro: "There has been considerable revolutionary activity . . . and there are a number of bands. In general, the leaders are 'Hacendados' or men of good position in the community and we have heard of no outrage being committed by these bands" (cited in Knight 1986a: 237).

Political expediency certainly led some of the more farsighted Porfirian officials and landowners to declare themselves in rebellion, but the

state's Maderista ranks also included a number of urban and middle-class Michoacanos who had long opposed the Díaz regime. As was true throughout Mexico, the Michoacán middle class had enjoyed considerable economic mobility during the Porfiriato while remaining excluded from political power. Between 1892 and 1912, according to state historian Romero Flores (1946: 581), there were ten state legislatures, "whose deputies were consecutively reelected, only to be replaced when they died or became decrepit." Likewise, Aristeo Mercado, appointed interim governor in 1891 and elected for the first of several four-year terms in 1892, remained in power for 20 years. His first reelection in 1896 sparked scattered elite and middle-class opposition in Zamora and Morelia. Subsequent reelections continued to generate urban political opposition, and, in the context of Madero's electoral campaign of 1909 to 1910, antireelection clubs were established in Los Reyes, Huetamo, Morelia, Jiquilpan, and Zamora (Ochoa Serrano 1989b: 110–11; Romero Flores 1946: 584–85). By the time Madero's call to rebellion reached Michoacán at the end of 1910, many of the state's middle-class professionals, merchants, and rancheros were, as Ochoa Serrano (1989b: 108) puts it, looking for "a new man who would take the state out of the monotonous and tired march that had paralyzed all progress, all forward movement, all things desirable to Michoacanos."

The change of regime in Morelia was brought about through a process of accommodation and negotiation between Porfirians and Maderistas. Once the downfall of Díaz was imminent, both groups were equally concerned with ensuring a smooth political transition, so as to get on with the business of restoring social order. The state's first Maderista governor, Miguel Silva, was initially appointed by the Porfirian state legislature, pending new elections after the ouster of Díaz. Silva's moderate liberal program, and his attempts to subdue local uprisings, gained him the support of many of the state's landowners, businessmen, bankers, and professionals (García Avila 1987: 26). He was subsequently elected as governor in 1912, defeating Primitivio Ortiz of the National Catholic Party (Partido Católico Nacional; PCN).

Social order, however, was not so easily restored. In part, this was due to the nature of Maderismo in the state. Escalante's authority as military commander was challenged by other Maderista leaders, such as Marcos Méndez, and completely ignored by lesser military chiefs (*cabecillas*) operating at the local level. Méndez was arrested by Francisco Múgica, who had been sent to Michoacán by Madero to restore the peace (Knight

1986a: 231–32). The intransigence of the cabecillas, such as the Pantoja family of the Puruándiro region in northern Michoacán, would prove to be a much more enduring problem, both for the Maderistas and for subsequent revolutionary regimes (Pinet 1987). Refusing to subordinate themselves to the central military command of Escalante, or to the civilian government of Silva, many of the cabecillas defied orders to demobilize and disarm their followers after the state's Maderistas and Porfirians had reached their political accommodation, continuing to attack towns and sack haciendas long after the downfall of the Díaz regime. Without the legitimacy conferred by the Maderista banner, these armed groups were considered by state officials to be bandits rather than revolutionaries, at least until they adopted political labels once more, declaring themselves to be Constitutionalists and moving on to Carrancismo or Villismo.[3] The nominal allegiances of the local movements shifted in accordance with state and national military and political dynamics, but their basic character did not: they were antistate movements, rooted in local and regional resistance to the imposition of central political authority in the form of taxes, military conscription, and the designation of local political officials.

Maderista attempts to restore social order were further compounded by increasing levels of agrarian and urban violence. In 1912, under the leadership of Miguel de la Trinidad Regalado of Atacheo, representatives from 20 Indian communities throughout the state formed the Unified Society of the Pueblos of the Indigenous Race (Sociedad Unificadora de los Pueblos de la Raza Indígena), with the objective of providing "moral, practical, financial, and mutual aid" to peasants attempting to recover dispossessed communal lands.[4] Prior to the promulgation of the 1915 Agrarian Reform Law, however, agrarian grievances in Michoacán had more often been manifested in violent, indirect, and sporadic ways: armed peasants from Tototlán and Los Remedios attempted to reclaim lands seized by the Hacienda of Guaracha; Naranja residents attacked mestizo workers from the Hacienda of Cantabria with stones and spears; peasants in Pichátaro assaulted representatives of a lumber company that had, the peasants claimed, dispossessed them of their communal lands; and followers of the Prado family in the Cañada de los Once Pueblos began invading lands held by rich mestizos, as well as by their fellow peasants.[5] Urban violence was often directed against unpopular local authorities, as in the riots in Uruapan, Zamora, and the eastern mining town of Angangueo. In quelling these instances of popular dis-

content, Maderistas joined forces with the Porfirian army and police forces: Angangueo was pacified by Maderistas and the police forces of neighboring Zitácuaro and Maravatío, under the leadership of the federal commander Francisco Cárdenas; Martín Castrejón led Maderista troops in restoring order (and killing two peasants) in Pichátaro; and Múgica, as the Maderista peace commissioner, ended both a riot and a tram drivers' strike in Zamora.[6] In contrast to the revolutionary elites of the 1920s (including Múgica), the Maderistas of 1911 to 1913 had little interest in encouraging or utilizing popular grievances and mobilization. Silva's liberal program called for effective suffrage, checks and balances, education, and the promotion of agricultural production. Hygiene and sobriety, rather than discontent, were to be fostered among the popular classes (García Avila 1987: 26).

Huerta's 1913 overthrow and assassination of Madero unleashed a new wave of armed rebellion in Michoacán. As was true of the Maderistas, the state's anti-Huertista movement was fragmented and decentralized, entailing a loosely coordinated set of local and regional uprisings, the leadership of which only sporadically recognized the authority of Gertrudis Sánchez, the Coahuilan military commander who nominally directed Carrancista operations in Michoacán. After an initial period of fragile unity and military success, the movement was riven by internal conflicts and demoralized by subsequent defeats at the hands of the Huertistas. In this context, local military chiefs began to operate all but independently of Sánchez until Alvaro Obregón's successful drive against Huerta led them to unite again long enough to take over Morelia in August 1914 (Oikión Solano 1987: 88–89). The Carrancistas maintained their control over the state government, albeit precariously at times, until the promulgation of the 1917 Constitution and subsequent election of new state authorities, although Morelia was abandoned on several occasions and temporarily occupied by Villista forces in the spring of 1915 (Aguilar Ferreira 1974: 122–23).

In seeking to establish military and political control, Carrancista governors, in Michoacán as elsewhere, began to promote limited agrarian reform, encouraging peasants to organize and petition for land under the national Agrarian Reform Law of 6 January 1915, which provided for the restitution of communal lands that had been alienated through the misapplication of the 1856 Lerdo Law or the illegal actions of local officials or surveying companies. It also provided for outright grants of land (dotaciones) based on demonstrated need rather than prior owner-

ship and dispossession. Neither restitutions nor dotaciones were intended to re-create the institution of communal property, even as land was adjudicated to groups rather than individuals: according to the 1915 law, "proprietorship to the land will not be vested in the *pueblo* in its corporate capacity but will be parceled out in full dominion . . . with only the limitations necessary to prevent speculators, especially foreigners, from monopolizing such properties" (cited in Simpson 1937: 60). Like their liberal predecessors, moderate Carrancistas saw private property as one of the principal vehicles through which secularization and economic progress would occur.

Shortly after the national Agrarian Reform Law was issued, Gertrudis Sánchez, as Carrancista governor in Michoacán (1914–15), established a Reclamations Office to investigate community claims of dispossession. Miguel de la Trinidad Regalado was appointed as its head in recognition of his military support in the battle against the Huertistas. After a brief interlude of Villista rule in March 1915, Carrancista agrarian reform efforts were resumed under the military governorship of Alfredo Elizonda (1915–17), who established the Local Agrarian Commission (Comisión Local Agraria; CLA) in June of the same year. Throughout the course of 1915, 33 communities solicited the restitution of their former communal lands, while 12 sought dotaciones. Another 27 petitions were filed the following year (Foglio Miramontes 1936: 179).[7] No land was redistributed during Elizonda's two-year tenure as governor, and under the brief administration of José Rentería Luviano (February to August 1917), only the community of Arocutín was successful in its petition for a restitution, while Puácuaro and Teremendo were allocated dotaciones.[8]

The Carrancistas had, in fact, lost interest in agrarian reform shortly after the promulgation of the 1915 law. Once the Villistas and Zapatistas ceased to be a major military threat later that year, Carrancista officials abandoned their attempts to draw popular support through land redistribution, focusing instead on the restoration of agricultural production, which had been devastated through the combined impact of war and drought during the second half of the 1910s.[9] Nor did the Carrancista agrarian reform ever constitute a significant threat to large landholdings. In Michoacán, official protection was granted to haciendas producing staple crops, such as Cantabria in the Zacapu region, or timber for the railways, as was the case with the numerous holdings of Santiago Slade in the Purépecha highlands (Knight 1986b: 467). The

Carrancistas had pledged to support and protect "friends of the revolutionary cause," a category that certainly included large landowners, as long as they weren't actively aiding and abetting the Villistas (Oikión Solano 1987: 91).

The enemies of the revolution were another matter entirely, and first and foremost among this group were the Church and the clergy. Anticlericalism became a dominant feature of revolutionary discourse and practice in 1914 with the military and political ascendancy of the Carrancistas. It would remain so until the end of the Cárdenas presidency of 1934 to 1940. Although Carrancista anticlericalism was in part a product of the Church's support for Huerta, it had much deeper roots in nineteenth-century liberalism. The Carrancistas, like the liberals before them, considered religious faith to be an impediment to economic development, encouraging waste and sloth rather than entrepreneurial investment. Further echoing liberalism, the Carrancistas viewed the Church itself as an obstacle to the creation of the revolutionary citizen and hence to the consolidation of a revolutionary state. As Francisco Múgica declared in the Constituent Assembly of 1916 to 1917, "I am an enemy of the clergy because I consider it the most baneful and perverse enemy of our country. . . . What ideas can the clergy bring to the soul of the Mexican masses . . . ? Only the most absurd ideas—tremendous hatred for democratic institutions, the deepest hate for the principles of equity, equality, and fraternity" (cited in Meyer and Sherman 1987: 543). Or, as Carrancista officials in Nuevo León put it in justifying a number of extreme anticlerical measures, the clergy had "shown themselves to be the implacable enemy of every liberal and progressive movement from that of our National Independence . . . until the present Revolution. . . . [T]he Church has ever striven that light should not shine upon the darkness of the oppressed."[10]

The Carrancistas faced a further dilemma that nineteenth-century liberals had not. By the 1910s, the Church and its affiliated lay organizations had established a network of trade unions, rural cooperatives, and political associations capable of garnering widespread popular support. Thus, after the defeat of the Villistas and Zapatistas, the Church was one of the Carrancistas' main rivals in the construction of the post-Porfirian order. Organized Catholic involvement in social and political issues was rooted in the 1891 encyclical letter *Rerum Novarum*. Issued by Pope Leo XIII in response to the rise of socialism in Europe, the letter condemned class struggle as a violation of the Catholic view of an organic

and harmonious society, but also criticized the immiseration wrought by capitalism. The state, according to the encyclical letter, had the obligation to protect the weak, and the weak had the right to organize. Five years after the letter was issued, Catholics throughout the world were called upon to hold congresses to discuss social ills and establish worker organizations, under the general rubric of Catholic Social Action. The first Mexican congress was held in 1903 in Puebla. Those in attendance recommended the establishment of worker organizations aimed at spiritual development and the diffusion of technical knowledge; the creation of credit societies; and the provision of schools, medical care, and social insurance by Catholic landowners to their resident workers. The 1904 Congress in Morelia emphasized education for the working class; that held in Guadalajara in 1908 focused on wages; and the last Congress, held in 1909 in Oaxaca, focused on the plight of indigenous peoples. Parallel agricultural congresses focusing on the spiritual and material plight of the peasantry were held in 1904, 1905, and 1906, the first two in Tulancingo (Hidalgo) and the third in Zamora (Michoacán).[11] In 1911, there were 25 Catholic Workers Circles, with a total of 8,000 to 9,000 members, linked through the Confederation of Catholic Workers of the Mexican Republic. And by 1913, the number had grown to 50 Circles with 15,000 members (Bailey 1974: 16–17).[12]

After the downfall of Porfirio Díaz in 1911, the National Catholic Party (PCN) was formed by lay Catholics, many of whom had been active in the Social Action movement. Although the PCN opted to support Madero's bid for the presidency in 1912, it competed against the Maderistas for positions in the national and state legislatures, as well as in gubernatorial races. Between 1911 and 1913, PCN candidates won 29 seats in the federal Congress and the governorships of Jalisco, Zacatecas, Querétaro, and the state of Mexico. The party also controlled the state legislatures of Jalisco and Zacatecas. In Jalisco, the PCN government passed a number of social reforms aimed at the working class, both rural and urban, including the legalization of agricultural unions, tax exemptions for worker cooperatives, employer-paid insurance, and a mandatory Sunday holiday (Bailey 1974: 17–19). The legislature also issued a law guaranteeing all rural families a house and a plot of land large enough to provide a subsistence, to be paid for through mortgages assumed by peasants.[13] Critics, contemporary and scholarly, scoffed at the program's optimistic assumptions about social harmony and the willing-

ness of landowners to support structural reform, but the PCN program in Jalisco showed greater concern for popular issues than did that of the Maderistas, many of whom tended to assume that social justice would, at some point, follow the consolidation of liberal political institutions. Whether or not the PCN program would have led to any appreciable gains for workers and peasants in Jalisco is unclear, because its implementation was blocked after Huerta's 1913 overthrow of Madero and Alvaro Obregón's subsequent overthrow of the Jalisco government on behalf of the Carrancistas in 1914 (Quirk 1973: 32–33). What was clear from the electoral competition of 1912 to 1913, however, was the capacity of a Catholic political party to gain widespread popular support, in certain regions of the country including but not limited to the center-west, and to address, however partially, popular grievances and concerns.

After the defeat of the Huertistas in 1914, state-level Carrancista military governments began to enact the type of anticlerical measures that would later be incorporated into the 1917 Constitution and enforced, with such devastating effect, in the mid-1920s. In Nuevo León, the Carrancistas expelled all foreign priests (a common measure), as well as any Mexican priests deemed to have meddled in politics; limited church hours from six in the morning to one in the afternoon; and allowed church bells to be rung only in celebration of patriotic holidays and Carrancista military victories.[14] Churches in the city of Zacatecas were closed, and members of the clergy were held for ransom. To avoid that fate, the bishop of Zacatecas fled to San Antonio, Texas.[15] The Carrancista governor of Veracruz expelled all foreign priests, and he authorized only a limited number of Mexican priests to officiate in accordance with population density.[16] In Mexico City, according to the vicar general, some 32 priests had been arrested and two killed, during the period between the fall of the Huerta regime in July of 1914 and November of the same year.[17] Meanwhile, in Michoacán, the Carrancista governor Gertrudis Sánchez imposed a forced loan on the Morelia clergy, and confiscated property belonging to the Church as an institution and to the clergy as individuals. These properties, as well as those belonging to other "enemies of the revolution," were placed under the control of the Commission for the Administration of Rural and Urban Properties and were used to finance the Carrancista government and war coffers.[18]

At the local level, anticlericalism was often experienced as part of the

depredatory repertoire of Carrancista soldiers. San José de Gracia's introduction to Carrancismo, in the person of General Francisco Murguía, was not uncommon:

> He came with an army of thousands, taking three days to pass through San José. On the first day, he began to plunder the church, and the priests, who fled in panic, were pursued with gunfire for many leagues. The intimidated populace provided food for Murguía's men and their horses. Aside from stuffing themselves and robbing the church, they committed no outrages. They were either on their way to or returning from a skirmish with Pancho Villa. (L. González 1974: 128)

Carrancista troops often raised funds through the ransom of priests, as in Sahuayo, where, in June 1914, Eugenio Zúñiga entered town with 700 men, ordered the arrest of some 13 priests, and offered to ransom them to the local population for a sum of 40,000 pesos (L. González 1979: 144–45; Ochoa Serrano 1978: 147). Such actions sometimes generated rebellions as well as ransoms and resignation on the part of affected populations, particularly when linked to more egregious abuses of power. The Carrancista general Joaquín Amaro was particularly hated in Michoacán, a sentiment that would only intensify when he directed military operations in the state against the cristeros in the 1920s. After seizing Zamora in August 1914, "[t]he fierce cabecilla imposed his will for twelve months, throughout the whole region: church bells silenced, places of worship sacked, townspeople hanged, old papers burned, families hiding in their houses, forced loans, rash shootings of the well-to-do." In response to these outrages in Sahuayo, a group of men took up arms against Amaro at the end of 1914. Given that their rebellion was directed against the Carrancistas, they, like countless other groups in a similar position, adopted the banner of Villismo (L. González 1979: 145–46).

Revolutionary anticlericalism and agrarianism were both incorporated into the Constitution of 1917, written in a convention dominated by the more radical Carrancistas, including Francisco Múgica. Article 27 declared all land to be the property of the nation, and it vested the state with the power to allocate property rights. Unlike the liberals of the nineteenth century, revolutionary state makers considered private property rights as well as corporate ones to be a concession of the state, which could allocate or revoke them in accordance with the public interest. The same article also established the constitutional obligation of the state to

redistribute land to those in need, either in the form of a restitution, in cases where peasants could prove both prior ownership and illegal dispossession, or in the form of a grant, in cases where they could not. As was true of the 1915 law, Article 27 was not intended to re-create the communal property regime, nor to restore control over the allocation of property rights to rural communities. The Constitution stipulated that communities who had "conserve[d] their communal character" should have "the legal capacity to enjoy in common the waters, woods and lands" that they had retained as communal property or which were restored to them under the 1915 Agrarian Reform Law through the procedure of restitution, "until such time as the manner of making the division of the lands shall be determined by law" (Simpson 1937: 69). But land was to be returned or redistributed in the form of an *ejido,* a property regime in which peasants received use rights to the parcels they cultivated, with ultimate ownership and control of the land remaining vested in the state.[19]

Many state officials saw little distinction between the procedural categories of restitución and dotación, sharing, perhaps, the view widely held among social scientists that peasants, as a class, simply wanted land and that any land sufficient to provide a subsistence would do. Because it was almost always impossible for communities to prove both prior ownership and illegal dispossession, agrarian reform officials routinely denied petitions for restitution as soon as they were received, treating them instead as petitions for dotaciones. Even the most sympathetic of state officials was at a loss as to why this should outrage peasants as often as it did, because the land granted through a dotación might well be of superior quality and greater extent than that claimed through the category of restitution. For many peasants, however, the difference was a moral and political one, rather than semantic or practical. Whereas a restitution constituted recognition by the state of a community's claim of legitimate ownership and unjust dispossession, a dotación was simply a grant bestowed by a paternalistic state, with a good many strings attached at that.[20] As the residents of San Pedro Caro put it in explaining their insistence on a restitution rather than a dotación, they had not solicited a grant of land, because they believed that they already owned it, and were simply asking that the state recognize that ownership.[21] "[T]he *pueblo,*" the residents wrote, "considers its right to restitution to be fully proved, and awaits only the official sanction that will decree it symbolically."[22] The revolutionary agrarian reform, far more than the liberal land re-

form, entailed a significant increase in the state's role in rural communities, in regulating and distributing property rights, and in establishing the organizational forms and legal procedures through which newly created agrarian reform communities would relate to the state. Popular receptions of that reform varied considerably, including outright rejection, negotiated accommodation, and an enthusiastic embrace, depending on prior legacies of agrarian conflict and conjunctural alliances made among community members, state officials, and counterelites.

Revolutionary anticlericalism also entailed an expanded role for the state in rural communities, particularly insofar as it attempted to transform popular cultures and religious practice. Patriotic holidays were to replace religious ones, homage to the heroes of the independence wars, the War of the Reform, and the revolution supplanting the cult of the saints and the liturgical calendar. Even life cycle sacraments were appropriated, as revolutionaries held "socialist baptisms" and bestowed patriotic names upon their children. Anticlericalism profoundly affected the central institutions of community life: parish priests and cabildo members were displaced as local political authorities; Catholic schools, the only source of education for many communities, were closed; and the activities of the cofradías and other forms of local religious organization were severely curtailed. Given the tight interweaving of economic, religious, and political institutions in many rural communities, revolutionary anticlericalism left almost no aspect of everyday life untouched. This caused a great deal of anguish for many peasants, as indicated in the following letter written by Jacinto Espinosa of Jacona to Governor Lázaro Cárdenas: "The indigenous people of Jacona, obeying old traditions, very respectfully ask that you grant us a special dispensation in this case, to take an icon into the fields, in order that the scarcity of rain be remedied, since our crops, the sustenance of our children, are being lost, and since the institutions of the Supreme Government, to which we offer obedience in the presentation of the people, will not be prejudiced in any way."[23]

Permission to carry an icon into the fields was denied, on the grounds that it would constitute a violation of the law banning public worship outside of church buildings.[24] Implicit in Espinosa's letter were both the recognition that such a ban was viewed by state officials as necessary for the consolidation of state institutions and the countervailing claim that religious belief and worship need not interfere with the rights and duties of citizenship.

Until 1920, the constitutional provisions pertaining to agrarian reform and anticlericalism had received scant attention in Michoacán. Francisco Múgica, having undergone a transformation from a Maderista peacekeeper to a radical Jacobin, lost the 1917 gubernatorial elections to a far more moderate Carrancista, Pascual Ortiz Rubio, who had little interest in either redistributing land or attacking the Church. Three years later, however, Múgica assumed power through a combination of disputed elections, popular uprising, and the assistance of then state military commander Lázaro Cárdenas. Múgica was on political principle a radical reformist and hence inclined to mobilize popular support to advance a set of labor, educational, agrarian, and anticlerical reforms. His need for popular support, and hence willingness to accommodate popular demands, was further reinforced by his precarious relationship with the central state, and the presence in Michoacán, for much of his term in office, of reactionary military commanders firmly allied with the state's most powerful landlords. Múgica's brief tenure as governor, lasting only eighteen months, sparked conflicts and confrontations that would continue to define Michoacán politics for at least two decades.

Center, State, and Popular Movements:
Michoacán in the 1920s

In 1920, Venustiano Carranza tried to impose his own handpicked successor, Ignacio Bonillas, as president, over the more popular revolutionary general Alvaro Obregón. To this end, he sent federal troops to Sonora, Obregón's home state and main source of support, over the objections of Governor Adolfo de la Huerta. Citing this violation of sovereignty, the Sonoran legislature declared the state in rebellion against the central government, in what became called the Plan of Agua Prieta. Shortly thereafter, Carranza was overthrown through the joint efforts of de la Huerta, Obregón, and the majority of the military high command.[25]

As Benjamin (1990: 71–73) notes, the rebellion of Agua Prieta established a political framework that both recognized and accommodated the power and autonomy of regional military strongmen (*caudillos*) and state governors, be they radical or reactionary, vis-à-vis the central government. In contrast to Carranza's more precipitous attempts to assert the authority of the center, Obregón pursued a policy of "cautious centralization," supporting civilian governors so as to offset his dependence on regional military chiefs, while at the same time building his own base

of support among workers and peasants outside the control of either. Calles would continue this process, albeit with far less tolerance for either reformist governors or independent agrarista leaders (Benjamin 1990: 80). For the duration of the 1920s, however, some state governors retained enough autonomy to carry out a wide range of radical reforms, as long as they were able to deliver agrarista military support to the center during the military rebellions of 1923 to 1924, 1927, and 1929 and the cristiada of 1926 to 1929.[26]

Múgica's freedom of maneuver as governor of Michoacán was limited at the onset by his only reluctant support of Obregón in the 1920 rebellion against Carranza. Ortiz Rubio had led the Revolutionary Movement of Legality (Movimiento Revolucionario de la Legalidad) in Michoacán, joining the Obregonistas with some 200 armed men after the Plan of Agua Prieta was declared.[27] Múgica, in contrast, remained loyal to Carranza until almost the end of the rebellion. However, with the support of Lázaro Cárdenas as the state military commander, as well as that of contingents of armed peasants, Múgica assumed the governor's office on 22 September 1920, taking over the government palace by force and thus ending a period of dual government and political stalemate that had followed the hotly contested elections of the previous July.[28] Although Cárdenas had violated the spirit, if not the letter, of interim president de la Huerta's orders in allowing Múgica to do so, the center did not intervene. Múgica had "a certain amount of local military support," as the U.S. chargé d'affaires noted, and, consequently "it [might] not be easy to oust him and at the same time mollify him."[29] Some eighteen months later, after a period of intense social and political conflict unleashed by Múgica's agrarian, anticlerical, and military policies, Obregón decided to oust him without worrying much about mollifying him.

Facing significant internal challenges from the better-organized Liberal Party of Ortiz Rubio and enjoying only the reluctant support of the center, Múgica set about building a base of popular support through the organization of a statewide peasant movement and the promotion of agrarian reform. As already noted, the Michoacán peasantry was by no means entirely quiescent prior to 1920: sporadic agrarian uprisings punctuated the 1910s, individual communities had begun to petition for land, and some extralocal organization was attempted through the short-lived Sociedad Unificadora de los Pueblos de la Raza Indígena under the leadership of Miguel de la Trinidad Regalado.[30] But the emer-

gence of an agrarista leadership and an organized movement in Michoacán owed more to state patronage and military support than to such "impulses from below" (Tobler 1988: 502). Shortly after assuming office, Múgica established the Office for the Promotion of Indian and Worker Affairs within the state's Local Agrarian Commission to encourage communities to apply for land under the national Agrarian Reform Law and to assist them in navigating its tortuous legal proceedings.[31] He also created the Michoacán Agrarista Party as a vehicle for organizing peasant political support and promoted the formation of the Union of Agrarian Communities (Sindicato de Comunidades Agrarias), which, after Múgica's ouster in 1922, grew into the state's most important peasant organization, the League of Agrarista Communities and Unions of Michoacán (Liga de Comunidades y Sindicatos Agraristas de Michoacán).

Múgica also distributed arms to agrarista peasants organized in local defense forces, in order to counteract the repressive capacity of landowners and elements in the federal military.[32] Landlord violence had long been one of the main obstacles to peasant political action in Michoacán. This was particularly true in the 1910s, when many landowners formed private defense forces with the encouragement of the Huerta government. In the 1920s, these hacienda armed guards were augmented by federal units operating under the orders of antireform officers such as Enrique Estrada, first as minister of war and subsequently as divisional commander of the northwest.[33] Throughout Múgica's tenure in office and beyond, federal soldiers and hacienda guards prevented peasants from occupying land they had been adjudicated under the agrarian reform program, and they forcibly disarmed the peasant militias created by the state government.[34]

Much of the violence that occurred during Múgica's tenure as governor grew out of his attempts to deploy the agrarista militias in the enactment of his political program and from the response of the federal military to that violation of its monopoly on the use of state-sponsored force.[35] Operating under orders from Múgica, local agrarista militias attacked and killed Spanish landlords and hacienda administrators in Tacámbaro, Curimeo, and Ziracuarétiro, after his attempts to distribute land through legal channels were blocked by the state's chief of military operations (Fowler-Salamini 1980: 180). Near the very end of his administration, some 300 armed agraristas were preparing to attack haciendas in Puruándiro in order to enforce the implementation of the Agrarian Reform Law.[36] Mugiquistas in Jacona killed the chief of police, wounded

several other local authorities, and seized the municipal palace. An armed group from Zamora attempted to expel them, but were, according to the U.S. chargé d'affaires, stopped by federal troops under the state military commander Alfredo García, who had "stringent orders from Estrada to disarm the civilian population of Michoacán, regardless of their political persuasion."[37] Several months later, five Jacona agraristas were assassinated by members of the defense force of a hacienda recently affected in an agrarian reform grant. Their bodies were hung from the trees in the central plaza as a warning to other would-be petitioners.[38] Fifty federal soldiers entered the town of Undameo with the object of disarming its agrarista defense force. The one leader who had not fled was beaten, as was the wife of another.[39] A similar incident occurred in Tiríndaro: although the agrarista leaders had left prior to the arrival of 20 federal soldiers, the latter seized the wife of one of them as well as legal documents pertaining to the community's agrarian petition, having been directed to the relevant houses by the municipal president of Zacapu.[40]

Múgica's radical anticlericalism also unleashed considerable social conflict, as in Uruapan, where a group of Mugiquistas hung a socialist flag in the church, after which, as Santiago Slade reported, "the people of all classes rose against the small party of bolsheviks, and forced them to leave town."[41] The events in Morelia between May 8 and 12 were the most serious, mobilizing considerable Catholic opposition to the state and furthering Obregón's doubts about Múgica's desirability as governor. A group of Mugiquistas led by the municipal president of Morelia had entered the cathedral on 8 May, attacked a priest, desecrated an image of the Virgin of Guadalupe, and hung the usual socialist flag from the bell tower. Some 10,000 people turned out four days later in protest, and they were fired upon by the local police and several members of Múgica's Socialist Party. Between 15 and 50 Catholic protesters were reported to have been killed, as were five Socialists, including Isaac Arriaga, the head of the Local Agrarian Commission. A group of Mugiquistas took over the Chamber of Deputies in Mexico City the next day in protest of Arriaga's death, where, according to a hostile observer, they "listened with applause to the subversive harangues delivered by their hosts and leaders." Obregón shortly thereafter sent letters to all of the state governors, condemning the events in Morelia and Mexico City and urging them to restore order. Mexicans had no right to incite rebellion by

hanging banners, nor to invade places of worship, he wrote, given that "it has not been the purpose of the revolution to establish anarchy."[42]

Throughout his administration, Múgica protested the role of the federal army in repressing organized peasants and obstructing the implementation of the agrarian reform program. The chief of military operations within the state was replaced five times at his request, always on the grounds that the federal army had allied itself with landowners and clerics in opposing the administration's program of radical reform.[43] Múgica further demanded that the federal army be used only to support legitimate state authorities, especially in the delivery of agrarian reform titles, and that he, as governor, have exclusive control over the agrarista militias.[44] Radical agrarianism and anticlericalism might be tolerated in the context of the evolving relations between the states and the center in the 1920s. Unbridled popular violence and interference in the prerogatives of the federal army were not.[45] In February 1922, Francisco Cárdenas, commander of the Morelia garrison, declared himself in rebellion against the state administration, allegedly in response to antimilitary articles published in the Mugiquista newspaper *El 123*.[46] He was joined by forces under the command of José María Guízar, the municipal president of Pátzcuaro, Ladislao Molina, later a cristero chief, and Trinidad Rodríguez, an ally of Molina in Tacámbaro. All were said to be motivated by their opposition to Múgica's agrarian reform program.[47] Shortly thereafter, Obregón ordered the arrests of key Mugiquistas, including Jesús Corral, author of the offending articles; two directors and an editor of *El 123*; four state deputies and several municipal presidents; Jesús Bermúdez, president of the CLA; and José Sobreira, Múgica's private secretary. He then instructed Luis Gutiérrez, as chief of military operations in Michoacán, to evacuate the ostensibly loyal federal soldiers remaining in Morelia, thus leaving the state government defenseless against the Cárdenas rebellion.[48] On 10 March, Múgica submitted a letter of resignation to the state legislature, which rejected it, granting him instead a year's leave of absence and appointing Sidronio Sánchez Pineda as interim governor. Those leading Mugiquistas who had previously avoided arrest by Obregón were soon ousted from the state administration.[49]

In spite of his commitment to agrarian reform, Múgica managed to distribute little land during his brief tenure in office, even to the agrarista peasants who constituted the core of his popular support. A provisional

(state-level) possession granted to the agrarian committee of Opopeo was blocked after the assassination of agrarista leader Felipe Tzintzún by Ladislao Molina, and the peasants of Angangueo, Ocampo, and Asoleadero could not take possession of their ejidos because of legal injunctions obtained by the affected landowners. In Zacapu, the heart of Michoacán agrarianism, agrarista peasants were continually frustrated in their attempts to secure ejidos by the hired guns of the Hacienda of Cantabria, and the legal maneuvers of its owners, Alfredo and Eduardo Noriega.[50] Múgica did leave, however, a legacy of popular mobilization, which produced, after he was ousted from office, one of the strongest and most radical of the state-level agrarista organizations in Mexico. Both Sánchez Pineda (1922–24) and Enrique Ramírez (1924–28) came to office intending to restore social order through the repression of popular mobilization.[51] But the Michoacán agrarista movement had become strong and independent enough to survive the loss of its allies in the state apparatus. Furthermore, Sánchez Pineda and Ramírez both found that their own political fortunes depended on their ability to deliver agrarista support to the central state during the rebellions that occurred during their administrations and so were forced to make concessions they might well otherwise not have considered.[52]

The League of Agrarista Communities and Unions of Michoacán (hereafter the Agrarista League) was established in December 1922 under the leadership of Primo Tapia of Naranja.[53] The main thrust of its political program consisted of support for the collective organization of land distributed under the agrarian reform program, rather than its parcellation to individual ejidatarios, and the inclusion of resident hacienda workers among the groups of peasants eligible to apply for land grants.[54] The Agrarista League encouraged communities to petition for restitutions and dotaciones, and it provided some support in navigating the convoluted agrarian bureaucracy. It also established Agrarian Women's Unions (Sindicatos Femeninos Agrarios) in numerous communities, intended to counteract the Church's capacity to mobilize women in opposition to anticlericalism.[55] In its discourse and practice, the Agrarista League itself was profoundly anticlerical and sometimes anti-Catholic. In many agrarista communities, the clergy had condemned peasants who accepted land through the agrarian reform program to eternal hellfire, and factional conflicts within communities, whatever their actual substance, had already come to be defined in terms of agraristas versus Catholics. Thus agrarista peasants attacked their personal and political

enemies, elite and popular, as Catholic fanatics in cahoots with the reactionary Church and disloyal to the ideals and institutions of the revolution, particularly when writing to state officials known to be sympathetic to such claims.[56]

Lacking powerful allies in the state government between Múgica's ouster in 1922 and Cárdenas's election in 1928, the political fortunes of the Agrarista League varied in accordance with how much state officials needed popular support during the military revolts and popular rebellions that punctuated the decade of the 1920s. The first such episode was the delahuertista rebellion of 1923 to 1924, in which over half the federal military rebelled under the leadership of Adolfo de la Huerta, in opposition to Obregón's attempt to impose Plutarco Elías Calles as his successor in the presidency. According to the U.S. chargé d'affaires, support for Calles came from "the unruly agrarian and labor organizations and the rowdy elements generally," whereas de la Huerta was said to have the backing of the more reactionary elements within the federal military. As was the case with other "counterrevolutionary" movements of the period, however, the delahuertistas included a wide range of political actors, united only by their opposition to Obregón and Calles and their rejection of the policies of the central state. Thus the same diplomat noted that the revolutionary generals Salvador Alvarado and Antonio I. Villareal, who had joined de la Huerta, were "bitterly hostile to the Administration and yet distinguished by more radically socialist doctrines and practices than are generally characteristic of the leaders of the rebellion." The governor and the chief of military operations in Oaxaca also declared themselves in rebellion, even though they did not espouse the goals of delahuertistas elsewhere and announced "somewhat original political objectives."[57]

The autonomy and power of the agrarista governors and caudillos were greatly affected by their ability to deliver support to Obregón and Calles throughout the course of the rebellion. Adalberto Tejeda and Ursulo Galván of Veracruz, Tomás Garrido Canabal of Tabasco, and Saturnino Cedillo of San Luis Potosí all succeeded in mobilizing significant agrarista militias, and, as a result, strengthened their bargaining position with central authorities after the rebellion was defeated, retaining their ability to carry out radical reforms, even as Calles moved away from his support for agrarianism once in the presidency.[58] In contrast, Felipe Carrillo Puerto, the radical governor of Yucatán, had been unable to mobilize agrarista support, and was executed by delahuertista soldiers

during the rebellion (Benjamin 1990: 74–79).[59] The position of the Michoacán agraristas was complicated by Múgica's ongoing conflict with Obregón. De la Huerta had been one of Múgica's main sources of political support in February and March 1922, and the Mugiquistas initially supported the rebellion in return for de la Huerta's promise to back an agrarista candidate for governor once the rebellion was successfully concluded. Múgica was arrested by federal authorities in December 1923, however, as he attempted to retake the governor's office,[60] and the state's agraristas, after a period of great indecisiveness, eventually threw their support behind Sánchez Pineda and Obregón, at the same time using the arms distributed to them by the government to deal with personal and political enemies in their own communities.[61]

Neither Sánchez Pineda nor Ramírez was inclined to respond to the demands of the Agrarista League in the absence of military or political crises. Sánchez Pineda's conservatism in this respect was strengthened by the agraristas' vacillation during the delahuertista rebellion. Primo Tapia, the leader of the Agrarista League, had managed to switch sides seven times before throwing his support behind the government (Friedrich 1977: 109), and Sánchez Pineda would later retaliate, ordering Tapia's arrest in mid-1924, on the grounds that he was a "divisive element" and one of "the agraristas in the state who took part in the armed rebellion led by [delahuertista leader Enrique] Estrada."[62] Ramírez escalated state repression of the Agrarista League, ordering the torture and assassination of Tapia in April 1926 and cracking down on the movement more generally. Even as the Agrarista League was weakened within the context of state politics, however, that same year it joined forces with 10 other state-level organizations representing some 300,000 agraristas, forming the National Peasant League (LNC, Liga Nacional Campesina), which soon became the strongest peasant organization operating at the national level (L. Meyer 1978; Rivera Castro 1988). Furthermore, however opposed Ramírez might be to radical agrarianism, he found that he needed the political and military support of the organized agraristas in order to deal with the armed uprisings of the cristeros.

With the advent of widespread and sustained popular rebellion in the spring of 1927, the minister of war ordered state governors to form and arm agrarista militias to supplement the federal army in its counterinsurgency efforts against the cristero peasants.[63] At the same time Calles instructed governors to resolve pending agrarian reform cases as rapidly as possible, in order to counteract the discontent being sown among

peasants by "enemies of the current regime."[64] In response, Ramírez was able to inform Calles that "the agrarista element in this state is fully identified with the government of the Union as well as with that of this state, and in response to the uprisings provoked by the fanatics has offered its military support."[65] Senator Jesús Cuevas, who had come to Michoacán to organize agrarista and workers' unions on behalf of the Regional Confederation of Mexican Workers (Confederación Regional de Obreros Mexicanos; CROM), noted similar agrarista support for the state, citing a demonstration of some 3,000 peasants in Pátzcuaro "who apart from manifesting themselves supporters (*adictos*) of the CROM have offered the citizen President of the Republic, General Plutarco Elías Calles, their unconditional services in whatever form he might wish."[66]

Lázaro Cárdenas became governor of Michoacán in 1928, in the midst of the cristero rebellion.[67] At the same time, he served as chief of military operations in the state. Unlike Múgica, therefore, Cárdenas controlled the federal forces stationed in Michoacán and did not face constant military threats to his program of radical reform and popular mobilization. Almost immediately after assuming the governorship, Cárdenas took a leave of absence to lead the counterinsurgency campaign, and, through a combination of negotiation and repression, he managed to pacify the state, a task made much easier by the June 1929 accord reached between Church and state and by the episcopate's subsequent condemnation of armed rebellion.

Given the existence of widespread elite and popular resistance to the formation of the revolutionary state, as expressed through the cristero rebellion, Cárdenas, even more than Múgica, was concerned with establishing strong political and military ties between local communities and the state. Thus throughout his tenure as governor, he focused on creating a strong statewide agrarista organization closely linked to his administration and on consolidating alliances with local and regional leaders, be they agraristas, mestizo elites, or ex-cristero rebels. The pacification of the Coalcomán region, for example, was achieved through negotiations with the Guillén brothers of San José de la Montaña, cristero chiefs who agreed to lay down their arms in exchange for considerable power and autonomy at the local level. In San Juan Parangaricutiro, Cárdenas established an alliance with the Anguiano family, which had led the agraristas of Paricutín against the cristeros of San Juan and which was in the process of defrauding the community of its communal lands. Throughout the Purépecha highlands, Cárdenas allied with and sup-

ported agrarista minorities, thus exacerbating factional conflicts between agraristas and Catholics that had remained somewhat muted throughout much of the 1920s (see chapter 6). The Prado family of the Cañada de los Once Pueblos used the political power it had gained through its alliance with Cárdenas to seize lands belonging to its political enemies, many of whom were other peasant smallholders. These alliances were consolidated through the creation of the Revolutionary Workers' Confederation of Michoacán (Confederación Revolucionaria Michoacana del Trabajo; CRMDT) in 1929, which linked local agrarian committees and served as a conduit through which Cárdenas's agrarista allies obtained political office at the municipal and state levels (Rivera Castro 1988: 83–85). Highly dependent on the financial and political support of the state, the CRMDT replaced the more independent Agrarista League as the main statewide peasant organization in Michoacán, headed by new agrarista leaders whose principal loyalties lay with Cárdenas (Embriz Osorio and León García 1982: 97).

In the Mexico of the 1920s, there was no "Leviathan on the Zócalo." Revolutionary state formation was, throughout the decade and beyond, a highly contested process in which complex and often conflictual alliances were formed between elite and popular sector groups in order to advance different understandings of the legitimate role of the state in Mexican society. In Michoacán, revolutionary elites, by inclination or under force of circumstance, allied with agrarista peasants in order to counter multiple challenges to the consolidation of state authority. The price of that alliance, for elites, was the partial accommodation of popular demands for land and local political and military power. For popular groups, it was the partial loss of autonomy in the definition and distribution of property rights and of local authority. Some agrarista peasants embraced revolutionary anticlericalism and agrarianism with enthusiasm. For the agraristas of the Zacapu region, for example, revolutionary state formation afforded the opportunity to recover lost lands, to undermine the power of a much despised local priest and the landowners with whom he was allied, and to defeat personal and political enemies in their own communities.

In other cases, the alliance between revolutionary state makers and peasants was a much more partial and contested one, as in San Pedro Caro, where peasants demanded that land be returned to them in the form of a restitution, rather than granted to them through a dotación. The San Pedro agraristas participated in the political organizations cre-

ated by state authorities, but appear not to have provided much if any military support during the rebellions of the 1920s. Nor did they embrace anticlericalism to the same degree as the agraristas of Zacapu; they denounced antireform priests but otherwise refrained from wholesale attacks on either the Church or other peasants as Catholics. Yet other communities, such as Zacán in the Purépecha highlands, applied for the restitution of their communal lands under the agrarian reform program, while attempting to keep the state at arm's length, participating only reluctantly if at all in the agrarista political organizations and refusing to provide any military support during the cristiada. Finally, there were communities and factions within communities that rejected anticlericalism and agrarianism entirely, allying themselves not with revolutionary authorities but rather with counterrevolutionary elites in resisting the consolidation of the new state. In the Indian community of San Juan Parangaricutiro, as in the mestizo ranchero community of San José de Gracia, anticlericalism and agrarianism constituted threats to both local resources and the local institutions that regulated property rights, religious practice, and political authority. The next chapter turns to popular resistance to the formation of the revolutionary state and to the partial and sometimes reluctant alliances formed between peasant rebels and elite lay Catholics.

4 ❋ The *Cristiada:* Elites and Popular Groups in Rebellion against the Revolutionary State

On 31 July 1926, the Mexican episcopate ordered that all Catholic churches be closed and public worship suspended, in protest of a recent intensification of revolutionary anticlericalism. Attempts by local authorities to take charge of the churches and inventory their property, as required by law, sparked violence throughout Mexico. Over the course of the next few months, U.S. and British consular officers noted a rapid increase in banditry, at least some of which they believed to be motivated by opposition to the new state. In diplomatic circles, rumors abounded as to an imminent revolution (or counterrevolution, as Mexican officials would have it), the only question being who among the officer corps or the ranks of prominent Mexico City Catholics would be likely to take charge. Adolfo de la Huerta's name was often mentioned in this regard. He was indeed in the United States planning a second rebellion, but declared himself to be a liberal and hence unable to form an alliance with reactionaries intending to restore the prominence and privilege of the Catholic Church in Mexican society.[1] However, the National League for the Defense of Religious Liberty (Liga Nacional Defensora de la Libertad Religiosa; LNDLR or the League), an organization of lay Catholics centered in Mexico City, noted both the prevalence of armed uprisings in the countryside and the failure of its own economic boycott, and it began to contemplate the possibility of rebellion.

In early December, the League issued a call for a mass insurrection against the revolutionary state, to begin on 1 January 1927. On or around the appointed day, members of the League joined forces with young men from the Catholic Association of Mexican Youth (Asociación Católica de la Juventud Mexicana; ACJM) in leading small uprisings throughout Mexico, from Coahuila in the north to Oaxaca in the south.

By the spring of 1927, however, widespread rebellion was sustained only in Jalisco, Michoacán, Colima, Guanajuato, and southern Zacatecas, states in which popular uprisings either predated the League's manifesto or broke out several months after it had been issued. In contrast to the urban Catholics of the League and the ACJM, popular rebels, especially those in the countryside, responded much more to local conditions, grievances, and leaders than they did to League pronouncements and schedules.

This chapter explores the regional character of the cristiada: why was sustained popular rebellion limited to the five states of the center-west, even though the vast majority of Mexicans considered themselves to be Catholic in terms of their religious beliefs and practices? The first section is a narrative account of the cristero rebellion, examining the timing of its outbreak in different states and the relationship between the rural rebels and elite lay Catholics organized in the League and the ACJM. The second section turns to analysis, evaluating two prevailing explanations of why the cristiada was limited to the center-west. The first argues that it was the institutional strength of the Church in the center-west that accounts for the rebellion's regional character, whereas the second focuses on the (sometimes presumed) class characteristics of the rebels. After assessing these two explanations, I propose an alternative, arguing that three conditions were necessary for sustained rebellion and that all three existed only in the region of the center-west in the 1920s: the survival of a significant number of communities with their landed bases and local institutional arrangements more or less intact; the presence of a dense network of grassroots Catholic organizations capable of offering military and logistical support to the peasant rebels; and direct experience of revolutionary state formation at the local level, through the implementation of anticlerical policies and the agrarian reform program.

The Cristiada of 1926 to 1929

Once in power in the presidency, neither Venustiano Carranza (1917–20) nor Alvaro Obregón (1920–24) had much interest in enforcing the anticlerical provisions of the 1917 Constitution. Obregón had, in fact, begun to reestablish a relationship with the Vatican, authorizing the presence of a papal delegate in Mexico. In exchange, the Vatican pledged to concern itself only with spiritual matters and to appoint apolitical bishops and archbishops as positions became vacant in the Mexican

episcopate.[2] In contrast to Carranza and Obregón, Plutarco Elías Calles (1924–28) came to the presidency with a well-deserved reputation as being militantly anticlerical, having placed stringent restrictions on the Church and religious practice when he was governor of Sonora.[3] According to the French chargé d'affaires, Ernest Lagarde, the conflict between Church and state was, in Calles's mind, "a battle without quarter between religious and lay ideas, between reaction and progress, between light and shade[.]"[4]

In February 1925, Calles directed a memorandum to the governors, reminding them that it was the responsibility of state and municipal authorities to oversee Church activities and ensure that they remained confined within the narrow limits allowed by the Constitution.[5] In response, several state governments began to place tight restrictions on religious worship. Later that month, Calles encouraged the formation of a schismatic movement, under the leadership of two dissident priests and members of the CROM, the latter constituting Calles's main base of organized popular support. On the night of 21 February, the two priests, "recruited from the worst of the clergy," seized a church in Mexico City, Nuestra Señora de la Soledad, and declared the establishment of a Mexican Catholic Church independent of the authority of the Vatican. Members of the CROM, meanwhile, occupied smaller churches throughout the country. The schismatic movement died out quickly, having virtually no support among the clergy or the vast majority of lay Catholics. It did convince many Mexicans, however, that Calles had set out to destroy the Catholic Church.[6] In response, urban lay Catholics joined together to form the LNDLR in March 1925. Many had prior experience in Catholic political organizations, including the then defunct National Catholic Party (PCN) and the ACJM, the latter created by the Church during the Madero administration to coordinate Catholic Social Action projects aimed at improving the spiritual and material well-being of workers and peasants.[7]

The conflict between the episcopate and the Mexican state escalated dramatically in early 1926, when José Mora y del Río, archbishop of Mexico, condemned restrictions placed on religious worship in Hidalgo, Chiapas, Colima, Jalisco, Tabasco, and Yucatán and instructed the clergy to disobey any laws that contravened religious freedom (Bailey 1974: 62). After the archbishop's statement was printed in the Mexico City newspaper *El Universal* on 4 February, Adalberto Tejeda, minister of the interior and, according to Lagarde, "one of the most implacable and

malignant enemies of the Catholic religion," ordered Mora y del Río's arrest. The archbishop quickly retracted the statement, and the arrest order was dropped.[8] Tension between Church and state continued to rise after this incident, however: a number of Spanish priests were expelled on 10 February; Tejeda ordered all monasteries and convents closed on 17 February; and, a day later, La Sagrada Familia, a Mexico City church, was occupied by federal soldiers, on the grounds that it was built after 1917 and therefore required state permission to operate as a house of worship. The latter incident led to a riot in which seven protesters were killed.[9] Finally, at the end of February, Tejeda instructed all state governors to take immediate steps to enforce the anticlerical provisions of the Constitution, particularly as these pertained to the expulsion of foreign priests.

State-level compliance with Tejeda's order "varied greatly with the temperament and mentality of the governors," as did subsequent efforts to restrict religious practice.[10] The governments of Tabasco and Yucatán were among the most extreme. In Tabasco, "the contemptible tyrant" Tomás Garrido Canabal first limited the number of priests allowed in the state to six, then mandated that they all be over 40 years of age and married. As a result, the clergy left the state and the Church ceased to function there.[11] The state government in Yucatán also placed restrictions on the number of priests (40 statewide), and passed a set of so-called sanitary laws with the obvious intention of limiting religious worship. Corpses were not allowed in churches, thus barring funeral masses (which could not be held outdoors either); the use of holy water was banned; and people were prohibited from kissing icons or other sacred items. The use of religious images outside of churches, an important aspect of rural popular culture, was also declared to be illegal.[12]

Efforts to restrict the numbers and activities of parish priests generated considerable violence in some states, most notably Nayarit and Colima. In Nayarit, U.S. consul William Blocker reported:

The Secretario de Gobernación of the state, Rafael Sánchez Lira, personally entered the main cathedral in the city of Tepic on February 28th during Mass and with pistol in hand ordered the Spanish priest to leave the building and prepare for departure from the country. Hardly had the Secretario de Gobernación finished his words when a mob consisting of some of the high society and the Indian women pounced on him and had it not been for the appeals of some of

the ladies of the higher class who did not wish a crime to be committed within the Church, it is very possible he would have been murdered on the spot. As it was, he was carried from the church unconscious and his body was terribly beaten. He is now confined to bed and may die.[13]

Congressional deputies attempting to expel priests from rural villages were killed outright. "It was," Blocker continued, "a different class of people consisting of Indians and peons who pounced on them with knives, pistols, and clubs."[14] Elsewhere, including Puebla, Querétaro, Michoacán, and San Luis Potosí, members of the episcopate and state governors were able to negotiate "tolerable arrangements," as Lagarde put it, although this did not completely eliminate conflicts at the local level.[15]

The conflict between Church and state at the national level came to a head with the promulgation of what became known as the Calles Law on 2 July 1926, consisting of a set of regulations necessary for the implementation of the anticlerical provisions of the Constitution. The Calles Law repeated and expanded upon those provisions and established penalties for their violation: foreigners were prohibited from acting as members of the clergy; education, whether public or private, was to be completely secular in content; monasteries and convents were abolished; the clergy were prohibited from making any statements in opposition to existing laws and institutions; religious publications could include no political commentary; no political organization could bear a name including any religious references; political meetings could not be held in church buildings; all religious worship was to take place in churches under the supervision of local authorities; religious clothing could not be worn in public; and the Church was prohibited from owning all forms of real estate. This last provision applied to church buildings, all of which were declared to be the property of the nation, their use as places of worship subject to government approval. Convents, parish houses, and other church annexes were to be appropriated in the name of the revolution and turned over to trade unions and peasant leagues. Finally, local authorities were charged with implementing the Calles Law, in conjunction with neighborhood committees created to oversee and administer church property. The law was to go into effect on 31 July 1926.[16]

After the law was published in early July, the League and the episcopate encouraged Catholics to engage in nonviolent forms of resistance,

including a boycott on all nonessential goods, the nonpayment of taxes, and a petition drive to amend the relevant articles of the Constitution.[17] The Vatican, meanwhile, attempted without success to negotiate a compromise with the Calles administration. On 25 July, shortly after those negotiations broke down, the episcopate declared that all priests would withdraw from their churches on 31 July, the day the law went into effect, and that the churches would remain closed until the state reached an accommodation with the Church.[18]

Popular reactions to the church closures varied considerably, in large part depending on the degree of antagonism between local officials and Church representatives. In Sinaloa, the U.S. consul reported that "Mazatlán appear[ed] as gay as ever," largely because the governor handled the religious question very carefully, instructing all municipal presidents to consult with parish priests before appointing the neighborhood committees placed in charge of the churches. Having learned from the events of the previous February, the governor of Nayarit was equally discreet.[19] In Torreón, Coahuila, hundreds of people, "mostly of the poor class and all dressed in mourning," rioted in response to the closure of the churches. Armed with stones, knives, and bags of pepper to throw in the eyes of the police, they were no match for federal soldiers who, instructed to fire into the air, fired into the crowd instead, "with deplorable consequences."[20] Violent conflict was also reported in Guerrero, most notably in the town of Chilapa, where the municipal president was stoned to death by local women while attempting to take an inventory of church property in August.[21] Attempts by federal soldiers to inventory church property resulted in considerable violence in several towns and villages in Jalisco as well, with casualties on both sides. After this inauspicious start, local authorities in much of the state ceased their attempts to take over church property, and, where possible, appointed prominent Catholics to the neighborhood committees charged with the oversight of the churches. In Guadalajara, however, local authorities seized a church named Santuario de Guadalupe, in the process taking 500 protesters as prisoners; 420 were eventually released, but some of the remaining 80 were reported to have been executed.[22]

The Initial Uprisings of August to December 1926

During the last five months of 1926, what would eventually come to be called the cristero rebellion consisted of sporadic, disorganized, and short-lived violence and uprisings, many of which were connected to the

seizure of churches by federal troops. There was no central leadership, no military coordination, and, until late 1926, no declaration of rebellion or statement of principles. Urban lay Catholics in the League and ACJM had begun to give some consideration to armed rebellion, but most of their activity was focused on building popular support for the economic boycott declared in July.[23] Referring to rumors of a revolutionary plot by "prominent Mexico City Catholics," Arthur Bliss Lane, chief of the Mexican Desk in the U.S. State Department, assured the secretary of state in August that "[t]he consensus of opinion of intelligent and unbiased persons . . . is to the effect that the Mexican people are submissive by nature and that this trait will effectively prevent any serious revolutionary movement, particularly as long as the United States government maintains the embargo on arms and ammunition." The federal army, Lane continued, was doing little other than "assiduously disarming agraristas."[24]

Meanwhile, Alexander Weddell, the U.S. consul general, reported that the Mexico City police were engaged in "feverish activity," smothering plots that, in his opinion, existed only in their imaginations. Given that the military remained united, Weddell saw no prospects for a successful uprising. He did note "religion-related disturbances" in Guadalajara, Torreón, Durango, Colima, and Saltillo, but he considered the agraristas to be the military's primary concern, in light of their "pernicious activities" in Jalisco, Colima, Michoacán, and other states and the numerous reports of illegal acts by agraristas "to the prejudice of American property rights."[25]

By early September, however, reports of isolated uprisings did begin to filter in from the provincial consulates. In an "uprising planned and fostered by the Catholic Church," according to one such report, 60 men tried to burn a railroad bridge near Acaponeta, Nayarit.[26] Residents of Chilapa, Guerrero, where the municipal president had been killed in August, declared themselves to be in rebellion as of 27 September. The Chilapa insurgents fled when federal soldiers arrived and arrested 10 priests.[27] U.S. vice consul E. W. Eaton noted a distinct rise in banditry in Colima in September. The individuals in question, "all of whom call themselves rebels and claim to be in arms against the Federal government," were in Eaton's mind, bandits "pure and simple . . . as they are composed of this class of men and under the leadership of men of the same type." Bandits or rebels, they most likely were peasants, as Eaton would not have confused the middle-class urban Catholics of the League

or ACJM with "this class of men." He also reported that bandits in southern Jalisco had murdered some men known to be "loyal to the federal government and against a revolutionary [i.e., Catholic] movement."[28]

The U.S. vice-consul in Tampico, Veracruz, had no doubt that he was seeing rebels rather than bandits in early October: "That there exists a widely organized plan to attempt to overthrow the present government at the first opportunity cannot be doubted by the most casual observer," he reported, the revolution to be sponsored by unnamed ex-Porfirian military officials who sought the restoration of law, order, and respect for property.[29] By mid-November, small uprisings were also reported to be increasingly common in the region around Guadalajara. General Ferreira, chief of military operations in Jalisco, called them the work of "fanatics" and "militant elements of the clerical party." Dudley Dwyre, the U.S. consul, attributed increased rioting and banditry to the dearth of federal troops in the state, as the bulk of the military was deployed in fighting the Yaqui insurgency in Sonora.[30] At the end of 1926, he reported that the rebel bands had grown much larger: 200 to 300 "revolutionaries" had killed an entire garrison of federal soldiers in Colotlán.[31]

As it became apparent that the economic boycott would achieve no discernible results, League leaders began to take the idea of rebellion more seriously. The armed uprisings of the fall encouraged them to believe such a rebellion would receive widespread popular support. A military command structure was duly created, and René Capistrán Garza, the president of the ACJM, was appointed by the League to lead the rebellion, in spite of his total lack of military experience and the fact that he was then in the United States, trying to drum up financial support.[32] League leaders then met with the episcopate in an attempt to secure ecclesiastical approval. The episcopate declined to authorize the rebellion, but agreed, in principle, that rebellion was in some cases justified on theological grounds. This tacit approval was sufficient for the League, which in its 10 December 1926 "Manifesto to the Nation," called for a mass insurrection to begin on 1 January 1927, with the aim of overthrowing the existing political order, abrogating the constitutions of 1917 and 1857, and adopting a new Constitution that would be based on elements of both, while eliminating any semblance of anticlericalism or socialism.[33]

Widespread Popular Rebellion: 1927 to 1929
Responding to this call for insurrection, members of the League and the ACJM organized uprisings throughout Mexico in the initial weeks of

1927. Some 9 to 35 members of the ACJM, many of them boys, burned railroad bridges and briefly incarcerated the municipal president in Parras, Coahuila. All but one were taken prisoner and summarily shot.[34] Across the state, around Saltillo, bands of armed men began to form "because of dissatisfaction over religious matters." Six hacienda workers "gave notice that they were abandoning their work to join the revolutionary movement" and "commended their families to the care of their employers." Two other groups of workers rebelled near the town of Agua Nueva. All three groups were said to be poorly armed and lacking in military leadership.[35] In the city of Saltillo itself, 30 ACJM members rebelled under Antonio Acuña Rodríguez, the local League delegate. Instructed by the League to take over both Parras and Saltillo, the rebels were quickly defeated by federal forces (Olivera Sedano 1966: 168). According to official reports, Acuña Rodríguez was captured with "ample documentation proving the connivance of the clergy," and the ACJM rebels were said to be under the influence of "fanatical hacendados."[36]

In the northern Zacatecas town of Concepción del Oro, 150 miners, led by the local president of the ACJM, opened up the jails on 1 January, requisitioned money from local businessmen, and stole horses and dynamite from the Mazapil Copper Company.[37] That same day, 50 to 60 miners in the nearby town of Aranzazu declared themselves in rebellion, stole five horses in the morning, attended mass at noon, and then joined up with the miners of Concepción, where they seized more dynamite and clothes.[38] The Mazapil Copper Company was informed by one of the rebels that "they had been contemplating this movement for some time, and that every miner had instructions to take away as much dynamite and fuse and caps that they could get a hold of for the past thirty days."[39] Federal reinforcements soon arrived from Saltillo, and Concepción del Oro was placed under martial law.[40] The U.S. consul in Mazatlán, meanwhile, reported a significant increase in banditry in both Sinaloa (Mazatlán, Culiacán) and Nayarit (Acaponeta, Ixtlán, and Tepic), the response of the government being "to find a peon and hang him near the site of the crime, thus creating hatred among the people and expanding the rebel ranks."[41]

Isolated uprisings were also reported in Veracruz, Oaxaca, Guerrero, Puebla, Mexico State, Querétaro, Durango, Hidalgo, Morelos, San Luis Potosí, Tabasco, Tamaulipas, and the Federal District.[42] In contrast, the League had little success in promoting rebellion in Chihuahua, even though it was one of the states in which it had developed a strong orga-

nizational presence. Few if any uprisings appear to have occurred in Sonora, Nuevo León, Campeche, Yucatán, Baja California, or Quintana Roo.[43] In Sonora, according to the U.S. consul, religious apathy was so high, and hatred of the Yaquis so intense, that non-Yaquis were unlikely to engage in a "sympathetic or concurrent revolt." Disregarding the Yaquis entirely, he concluded that "[t]he religious controversy seems to have had almost no effect on the residents of this consular district in their political or economic life."[44]

By mid-January, the U.S. military attaché had reported that there were 14 "very active" centers of rebellion with an estimated 3,000 rebels in arms, excluding the Yaquis of Sonora.[45] At the end of the month, U.S. consul general Alexander Weddell somewhat more dramatically announced that "the Specter of Revolution is to be observed in all directions, seemingly hydra-headed, despite savage repression by the government."[46] But nearly all of the uprisings of the early days of 1927 involved League and ACJM members acting on their own or with the support of small groups of workers and peasants, as was the case in the mining towns of northern Zacatecas. Even in states where the League was well organized, such as Chihuahua, Puebla, and the Federal District, sustained rebellion proved impossible in the absence of widespread popular support. Uprisings that occurred solely in response to the League's manifesto were easily repressed or dispersed, and defections were particularly common among "the inexpert and passionate youth of the ACJM" (Olivera Sedano 1966: 181). By the spring of 1927, sustained rebellion was limited to the center-west: Jalisco, Michoacán, Colima, Guanajuato, and southern Zacatecas. And in these states, uprisings began either well before or well after the League's manifesto. The cristeros of the center-west often allied themselves with the League in some fashion and at some point, but the timing and nature of their rebellion were the products of local circumstances outside of the League's direction and control.

In Jalisco, U.S. consular officials had reported small-scale uprisings as early as September 1926. Large-scale rebellion began in the Los Altos region around Lake Chapala in December 1926, where it quickly intensified, spreading to the northeast corner of the state. By mid-January, 1,500 to 2,000 rebels operated in Jalisco, their numbers growing to 6,000 by the end of February. U.S. consul Dudley Dwyre, prone to some exaggeration, reported that the entire population of Jalisco supported the rebels, except for the "federal and state governments, police, and radical labor and agrarian groups."[47] In response to the spread of re-

they wish to conform to its idea of military discipline, preferring, whenever possible, to return home to plant their fields and harvest their crops. The League thus faced the same problem that revolutionary generals had before them: rebel groups might adopt national names and banners, but they continued to adhere to local and regional logics and leaders.

Guerrilla warfare did not accomplish much in military terms, but it proved quite difficult to eradicate. As the British chargé d'affaires put it:

> I hear of good authority that these movements are mostly the work of small roving bands, whose mobility and local knowledge make them difficult for the trained troops to catch, while they draw reinforcements as required from among local sympathizers. The latter, when their particular enterprise has been attempted or contact is made by Federal columns, simply disperse and endeavor to regain their homes. For this reason, the authorities themselves probably cannot estimate the real numbers of their armed opponents, while generally well-informed people offer the most diverse estimates, varying from 1000 to 20,000.[56]

This situation began to change in August 1927, however, when two League-appointed leaders began to reorganize and coordinate the actions of the many local groups operating in the center-west. Jesús Degollado y Guízar was appointed chief of operations in southern Jalisco, Colima, Nayarit, and western Michoacán, while Enrique Gorostieta was placed in charge of organizing the rebels of central and northeastern Jalisco. Gorostieta's scope of authority increased over the following year, and in August 1928 the League designated him as the first chief of the liberation army.

Born in Michoacán, Degollado y Guízar lived and worked in the Los Altos town of Atotonilco as a pharmaceutical dealer. A long-standing member of the ACJM, he also belonged to the U, a secret Catholic society that appears to have included some of the local and regional cristero leaders of northwestern Michoacán and Jalisco.[57] Degollado's ties with the U may have accounted for his acceptance by the cristeros, because he had no military experience and was quite unfamiliar with the countryside and its inhabitants. Such acceptance was by no means complete, however: Prudencio Mendoza nearly had him shot when he came to Cotija to present his credentials as chief of military operations in western Michoacán.[58] In spite of his lack of experience, Degollado was able to

achieve some level of organization and coordination in the areas under his control.

Enrique Gorostieta was far more successful in gaining the respect of the cristeros, in part because of his military experience in the federal army under Victoriano Huerta (1913–14). More important, he formally recognized the authority of the local and regional cabecillas, who had always constituted the de facto leadership of the rebellion, regardless of who might be named as such in the League records in Mexico City. Gorostieta was aware of the limits to which locally based peasant rebels could be induced to act as a national (or subnational) army. As the U.S. military attaché put it, "Gorostieta's control is not strong, but the leaders of various bands do recognize him as chief, and obey him in important matters."[59] Although he managed to get along well enough with the peasant rebels, he soon came into conflict with the League, over the latter's interference in military matters and the disruption of supply lines that occurred as the result of its conflicts with other Catholic organizations.[60]

By late 1927, the cristeros had the capacity to coordinate and carry out large-scale attacks that involved the participation of groups from different regions and states. With reference to Zacatecas, Jalisco, and Michoacán, the U.S. chargé d'affaires noted, in some confusion, that "rebel groups pass so frequently from one to the other State that it is very difficult to determine whether they are actually operating in one State or another."[61] On the night of 9 October, for example, a "battle of considerable proportions" broke out in Tizapan El Alto, in the Los Altos region of Jalisco. Local agraristas battled cristeros under the leadership of Anatolio Partida and Father Federico González Cárdenas, both of San José de Gracia.[62] A month later, some 800 rebels from northwest Michoacán and the Los Altos region attacked a major federal garrison stationed in Jiquilpan. Some 200 cristeros occupied the north central town of Ixtlán on 13 November, obliging local authorities to hand over the public treasury, such as it was.[63] Military action continued unabated during the first few months of 1928 throughout western Michoacán: Jiquilpan was attacked once more and the federal garrison of 80 men reportedly annihilated, and an attack on 400 soldiers stationed in Zamora resulted in the deaths of 100 federal troops, including most of the officers. In mid-March, a group of cristeros unsuccessfully attempted to take control of Zamora; a few days later, 200 rebels attacked a hacienda in Yurécuaro.

In southwestern Michoacán, 700 cristeros combated federal troops in the Cerro Verde, and Coalcomán was successfully held by the rebels after an attack by federal soldiers in January. In March in the same region, 400 cristeros fought federal soldiers in Aguililla, and 650 cristeros attacked the municipal seat of Chinicuila, Villa Victoria.[64]

In addition to improved military leadership and coordination, national politics and conflicts within the federal military also affected both the scope of the rebellion and the capacity of the cristeros to undertake larger-scale military actions. A struggle over the presidential succession began in May 1927: according to the Constitution, Calles could not be reelected for a second term in 1928, and although Obregón's position as a former president was somewhat ambiguous, the "no-reelection" provision was widely believed to apply to both incumbent and ex-presidents. General Arnulfo Gómez declared, in May, that Obregón would not run for president, and shortly thereafter was himself nominated as the candidate of the Antireelection Party. Another general, Francisco Serrano, was nominated by the National Revolutionary Party, and the Socialist Party of the Border States declared Obregón as its candidate.[65] Calles opted to throw his support behind Obregón, intending, perhaps, to alternate with him in the office of the presidency. In response, Gómez and Serrano declared themselves in rebellion against Calles and Obregón, and whereas Serrano was captured and executed by loyal soldiers almost immediately, Gómez continued to fight in Veracruz with the support of about 2,000 federal troops, until he was finally defeated by General José Gonzalo Escobar on 5 November.[66]

The Serrano-Gómez rebellion had the short-term effect of reducing the presence of the federal army in the center-west. The previous May, the U.S. ambassador noted that "exceptionally strong forces [had been] mobilized under the command of General Amaro, the Secretary of War" to fight the *cristeros,* particularly in Jalisco and Zacatecas.[67] In October and November, however, many of the troops were transferred out of the region to fight Gómez in Veracruz, thus facilitating cristero attacks against the agrarista militias, the remaining federal forces, and the major towns. Once Gómez was defeated, the troops returned to the center-west, and the state intensified its counterinsurgency campaign, setting up concentration zones in southern Zacatecas, Jalisco, and western Michoacán and declaring anyone found outside those zones to be subject to summary execution. Rather than reducing popular support for the cris-

Table 4.1   U.S. War Department Estimates of the Number of Active Rebels in Mexico, 1927 and 1928

1927	Number of Rebels	1928	Number of Rebels
July	7,000–8,000	January	23,400
August	7,000–8,000	February	24,650
September	9,000	March	21,750
October	10,700	April	15,725
November	15,000	May	11,500
December	17,000–20,000	June	5,000

Source: DS 812.00/29215.5, Dwight Morrow, U.S. Ambassador to Mexico, to U.S. State Department, 16 July 1928.

Note: These figures refer to all "rebels" and thus include, among others, the federal soldiers involved in the Serrano-Gómez rebellion. The bulk of the rebels were cristeros, however, as the Yaqui rebellion was winding down and there were no other significant rebellions in Mexico at this point.

teros the brutality of the new policy generated yet further resistance to the state, and the ranks of the rebels swelled accordingly.[68]

As shown in table 4.1, the number of active rebels in Mexico increased from 7,000 to 8,000 in July 1927, to a high of 24,650 in February 1928, then declined to a low of 5,000 in June. The U.S. military attaché attributed the rapid increase in the fall and winter of 1927 to 1928 to the transfer of troops to Veracruz and the subsequent adoption of the concentration zone policy. "It may be said," he wrote, "that the government barely held its own during January and February." The subsequent decline in rebel strength, he reported, was the result of better coordination and cooperation between the federal military officers operating at the state and regional levels, as well as the onset of the rainy season, which made military action difficult for both sides and led many peasants to return home to tend to their fields.[69] The number of active rebels increased again during the fall and winter of 1928 to 1929, although not as dramatically as the previous year. In May 1929, the U.S. military attaché estimated that there were a total of 21,000 federal troops fighting some 10,230 rebels.[70]

The Serrano-Gómez rebellion only temporarily reduced the numbers of federal troops stationed in the center-west, but it had another, longer-

lasting impact on the cristiada as well in that the state began to rely much more heavily and systematically on the agrarista militias in fighting the cristero rebels. Prior to the Serrano-Gómez rebellion, the federal army had been involved in a long and extremely conflictual process of disarming the agrarista militias created during the delahuertista rebellion of 1923 to 1924, often in support of landowner interests, and more rarely because the agraristas used their weapons to abuse their personal and political enemies.[71] Furthermore, until the spring of 1927, state officials did not see the need for armed agrarista support. In October 1926, for example, the local political authority (*jefe de tenencia*) of San Juan Tumbio, Michoacán, offered the armed services of himself and 65 others, as "campesinos and Aggristas [*sic*]" to fight the "gang of Catholics" operating in the area. Calles thanked him for his offer but declined, saying that "currently the Government of the Federation is well prepared to counteract any attempt at rebellion."[72] Other offers of armed support came from agrarista communities in the municipios of Maravatío, Acuitzeo, Zitácuaro, and Angangueo, all in the northeast and east of Michoacán, and were likewise turned down by the state officials.[73]

Many who observed the armed uprisings of January 1927 assumed that the workers and peasants involved were agraristas. Such was the case with an official at the Mazapil Copper Company in Concepción del Oro.[74] Likewise, E. W. Eaton believed the uprisings that occurred in the fall of 1926 in Colima to be the work of agraristas, denying that the rebellion was related to the "religious question" for two months, at which point he settled on the term *bandits*.[75] Foreign observers may have confused cristero and agrarista peasants because they were, as Eaton would have put it, of the same "class of men." But state officials were none too sure they could make the distinction either, and, early on, feared that armed agraristas might themselves rebel in support of the Church. Thus the 2,000 carbines sent to arm agraristas in Jalisco in January 1927 were distributed instead to urban workers because "the state government felt that arms in the hands of agrarians would be used against the state government as these are country people and their religion comes first and they will be more inclined to support the revolution [i.e., oppose the state] than go against it."[76]

In April 1927, with the escalation of rebellion in the center-west and the bulk of the federal army off fighting the Yaquis of Sonora, Minister of War Joaquín Amaro sent arms to the state governments, instructing

them to distribute them to "residents interested in defending their lives and interests, and to people knowledgeable about the area."[77] Until the fall of 1927, however, the agrarista militias that received the arms acted as local defense forces, defending their own communities against rebel attacks and on occasion going on the offensive against cristeros in their immediate vicinity. The Serrano-Gómez rebellion forced the state to shift its strategy, given the reduction of federal troops in the center-west and the questionable loyalties of members of the divided officer corps. In addition to relying more heavily on the agraristas of the center-west, the state also began to deploy large numbers of agrarista peasants from outside the region. Thus Calles had 4,000 rifles and thousands of rounds of ammunition sent to the agraristas of Puebla, along with military officers to train them, on the grounds that he did not "trust the federal forces in the state in the aftermath of the Serrano-Gómez rebellion." The loyalty of the governor was in doubt as well. A week later, thousands of rifles were sent to arm agrarista militias in the state of Mexico, the Federal District, and Veracruz.[78] At the same time, Calles instructed the state governments to take all measures necessary to resolve agrarian reform petitions pending before the state-level Local Agrarian Commissions.[79]

The state continued to rely on the agrarista militias after the end of the Serrano-Gómez rebellion, as the ranks of the rebels continued to grow in the winter and spring of 1928 in reaction to the increasing brutality of the counterinsurgency campaign. Agraristas from San Luis Potosí were deployed in Jalisco and Zacatecas, under the military command of Saturnino Cedillo, while in Michoacán, some 300 to 400 men from the Zacapu region were sent to the Tierra Caliente to fight cristeros from the southwest.[80] When General José Gonzalo Escobar, then chief of military operations in Coahuila, staged his own rebellion in March 1929, the state began to mobilize agraristas in the thousands, first to join the loyal faction of the military in fighting the Escobaristas in the north and subsequently to fight the cristeros of the center-west.[81] The great majority of the agraristas came from San Luis Potosí, where 20 battalions of peasants were incorporated into the federal army to assist in putting down the Escobarista military rebellion. Some 8,000 of these would then be deployed under Cedillo's command in the center-west once Escobar was defeated. By May 1929, Cedillo commanded 35,000 men, both agraristas and federal soldiers, in his counterinsurgency campaign against the cristeros (L. Meyer 1978: 311).

The Accord between Church and State

The situation might have remained one of a military stalemate had it not been for two events. First, Gorostieta was killed in an encounter with federal troops on 1 June 1929. Degollado y Guízar took his place as supreme commander of the rebellion, but never was able to command the same respect as his predecessor. Second, and more important, having reached an agreement with state authorities at the end of June, the Mexican episcopate explicitly condemned armed rebellion and ordered the cristeros to lay down their arms. The accord (*los arreglos*) was the result of two years of negotiations between the clerics and the state, mediated by the U.S. ambassador Dwight W. Morrow. The key stumbling block on both sides had been the constitutional authority of state governments to limit the numbers of priests and require their registration with the state. As Morrow finally convinced Calles, this provision did, in fact, represent a real threat to the integrity of the Church as an institution, inferring that the state had the right to designate individuals as members of the clergy. After much effort, Morrow finally produced an agreement acceptable to both the episcopate and Calles, at this point the jefe máximo wielding power through the presidential administration of Emilio Portes Gil. On 21 June 1929, a joint statement was issued in which

> Portes Gil agreed that the enforcement of the registration law did not mean that his government could register priests who had not been designated by their hierarchical superiors, that the laws regarding religious education did not prevent the teaching of children and adults within church confines, and that the constitution, as well as the laws of the land, guaranteed to all citizens the right to petition for the reform, repeal, or passage of any law. In turn, the apostolic delegate announced that the Mexican clergy would restore religious services "in accordance with existing laws." (Quirk 1973: 244)

Once the agreement was reached, Archbishop Ruiz y Flores of Michoacán issued a condemnation of the rebellion, ordered the League to cease all its political and military activities and to change its name, and commanded the rebels to surrender themselves and their arms to state authorities and to refrain from any criticisms of the accord.[82]

The agreement between Church and state did not reform or modify any of the existing anticlerical laws or constitutional provisions. Nor did the state provide any guarantees that religious practice would be tolerated within the narrow confines allowed by law, even as the Church

agreed to register priests, the one provision it had declared itself unable to live with three years earlier. The bishops' condemnation of rebellion, therefore, caused great bitterness among the cristero rebels. As one cristero leader complained in writing to a local priest:

> Can it be possible that our spiritual superiors, who know that their authority is strictly limited to the spiritual realm, entertain the hope of doing to us what the tyrants themselves were unable to do? The tyrants, after three years of an unequal and hazardous struggle, have not been able to get their hands on us, and yet our kindly prelates and priests . . . are undertaking the shameful task of delivering us up to them. . . . Why do you want to humiliate us in front of friends and enemies, when the enemy has not been able to humiliate us by force?[83]

In condemning the rebellion, however, the episcopate had the support of the pope, and gradually and quite reluctantly, the great majority of the rebels surrendered themselves and at least some of their arms, and, under a general amnesty, returned to what remained of their communities.

Explaining Partisanship in the Cristiada

This section turns from narrative to analysis, addressing the question of why popular rebellion was sustained on a large scale only in the center-west states of Jalisco, Michoacán, Colima, Guanajuato, and Zacatecas. Explanations of the cristiada's regional character tend to fall into one of two categories. The first focuses on the institutional strength of the Catholic Church in the center-west, and argues either that priests and prelates played a key causal role in instigating the rebellion, or that the institutional Church was of particular importance in the daily lives of center-west peasants, as compared to peasants elsewhere in Mexico. The second focuses on the agrarian structure of the center-west, and explains partisanship in terms of the class characteristics of the region's mestizo smallholding peasants (or rancheros), who were presumably unable to take advantage of the agrarian reform program and, by virtue of their structural location, particularly prone to conservative politics.[84]

The institutional strength of the Church is important in accounting for partisanship, but it provides only a partial explanation. It undoubtedly contributed to the development of a Catholic political identity among the peasant rebels, and lay Catholic organizations helped to sustain the rebellion through the provision of military and logistical sup-

port. Both the lay organizations and the Church were strong in regions that experienced no rebellion, however, as well as in regions where active popular support for the revolutionary state was quite high. Likewise, the agrarian structure of the center-west does come into play in explaining partisanship, but hardly in a way that can be collapsed into simple class categories or a mechanistic connection between class and political behavior. Legacies of agrarian and political conflict at the local level were such that a significant number of communities in the center-west survived the Porfiriato only to be threatened by the formation of the revolutionary state in the 1920s. But a similar pattern is evident in other states as well, and these communities did not rebel in large numbers or a sustained fashion during the cristiada. Rather, the regional character of the rebellion is a product of both the presence of the Church and its affiliated lay organizations, and a particular pattern of agrarian and political conflict, taken together with the timing of revolutionary state formation in the center-west.[85]

The Catholic Church and Affiliated Lay Organizations

The Catholic Church undoubtedly had a very strong institutional presence in the center-west, but it was also quite strong in other states and regions that either witnessed no rebellion or that developed revolutionary and agrarista movements with significant popular support and participation. Table 4.2 presents one measure of the Church's institutional presence at the state and regional levels: the ratio of population to church buildings in 1900. The regions here, it should be noted, refer to widely-used census and statistical categories, and the census "center-west" is not the same as the cristero "center-west" of Jalisco, Michoacán, Colima, Guanajuato, and Zacatecas. The density of churches was actually lower in the cristero center-west (1,300 people per church) than it was in the center-east (760), a region in which large numbers of peasants supported the revolutionary movements of the 1910s and the agrarista movements of the 1920s, but few participated in the cristiada. Churches were also fairly numerous in relation to population in much of the Pacific south, a region that produced popular revolutionaries and counterrevolutionaries in the 1910s, but (with the exception of Colima, which falls into the cristero center-west grouping) very few cristeros in the 1920s.[86]

In response to liberal anticlericalism, the Catholic Church devoted considerable resources to the construction of new church buildings during the Porfiriato, in order to decrease the size of parishes and increase

Table 4.2   Ratio of Population to Churches, 1900

Region/State	Population/Church	Region/State	Population/Church
Center-east	760	*North*	2,203
Federal District	1,944	Chihuahua	1,582
Hidalgo	684	Coahuila	3,373
Mexico State	612	Durango	1,645
Morelos	556	Nuevo León	3,451
Puebla	810	San Luis Potosí	2,581
Tlaxcala	611	Tamaulipas	5,265
		Zacatecas	1,531
Center-west	1,243		
Aguascalientes	1,819	*Gulf*	1,275
Guanajuato	889	Campeche	462
Jalisco	1,727	Quintana Roo	—
Michoacán	1,482	Tabasco	1,415
Querétaro	918	Veracruz	2,373
		Yucatán	630
Pacific south	806		
Chiapas	932	*Pacific north*	2,416
Colima	1,971	Baja California	4,254
Guerrero	857	Nayarit	1,995
Oaxaca	719	Sinaloa	2,738
		Sonora	2,181
		Mexico (Country)	1,106

Source: Secretaría de Economía Nacional 1956: 13–14, 133–34.

Note: This table is based on the total Catholic population of each state and region, divided by the total number of Catholic churches in each state and region. In the 1900 census, 99.6 percent of the population identified themselves as Catholic.

the influence of the clergy over the laity. Both Jrade (1980) and Foley (1979) consider this program to be important in explaining high levels of popular support for the cristiada in Jalisco and Colima respectively, because it entailed the mobilization of entire communities in the construction of the church buildings and strengthened the institutional presence of the Church at the local and regional levels. The church-building program, however, was by no means limited to the cristero center-west.[87] Of the cristero states, data for the entire period of the Porfiriato are available only for Colima and Jalisco, where the number of church build-

and to the development of a Catholic political identity, but it cannot be seen as a direct cause of the rebellion.

Of the 38 bishops and archbishops that comprised the Mexican episcopate, 4 actively supported the cristiada, 10 actively opposed it, and the rest were indecisive for much of the period between 1926 and 1929. The prorebellion prelates included Bishop José de Jesús Manríquez y Zárate of Huejutla (Hidalgo), Archbishop José María González Valencia (Durango), Bishop Leopoldo Lara y Torres of Tacámbaro (Michoacán), and Archbishop Francisco Orozco y Jiménez of Guadalajara (Jalisco). The most active high-ranking opponents of the rebellion were Archbishop Pedro Vera y Zuria (Puebla), Archbishop Antonio Guízar Valencia (Chihuahua), Archbishop Leopoldo Ruiz y Flores (Morelia, Michoacán), and Archbishop Miguel de la Mora (San Luis Potosí).[89] The bishop of Huejutla and the archbishop of Guadalajara were among the most vehement supporters of the cristiada, yet Hidalgo witnessed no sustained rebellion and Jalisco did. The archbishop of Durango, however much he supported armed insurrection, could not produce one in the absence of widespread popular support. The bishop of Tacámbaro advocated rebellion, but his superior, the archbishop of Morelia, strongly opposed it, which did not prevent Michoacán from producing the largest number of cristero rebels after Jalisco.

Anecdotal evidence suggests that the attitudes and behavior of individual priests do not account for peasant partisanship any better than does that of the prelates. A handful of priests acted as military leaders at the regional level, including José Reyes Vega and Aristeo Pedroza of the Los Altos region of Jalisco, José María Martínez of Coalcomán, and Federico González Cárdenas of San José de Gracia. Others undoubtedly offered their services as chaplains without playing a military role, because the sacraments were performed with regularity in many cristero military camps. But Father García Morfín of San Juan Parangaricutiro took the far more usual course, fleeing the community for the relative safety of a provincial town and declaring to local authorities that he was not in any way associated with or connected to the rebels of San Juan.[90] Many such priests were a grave disappointment to the cristeros, who expected them, at the least, to provide the rebels with solace and the sacraments. A typical complaint came from a cristero rebel in the Coalcomán region of Michoacán: the parish priest of Arteaga, he said, preferred to live "surrounded in luxury," looking after his own interests, rather than fighting alongside the cristeros in a cause for which he should

be willing to martyr himself.[91] Martyrdom was, in fact, a real possibility for priests who remained in the countryside, because it was the policy of the federal army to summarily execute them, on the grounds that they wouldn't be there unless they were rebels. Priests who took up residence in provincial towns and cities, in contrast, were a good deal safer, particularly if they registered with the state and refrained from any semblance of political activity.[92]

In contrast to the clergy, lay Catholic organizations loosely affiliated with the institutional Church did play a key role in sustaining the cristiada, providing the peasant rebels with arms, ammunition, logistical support, and some military leadership. One would expect these organizations to be particularly strong in the center-west, and they certainly were. But several, most notably the League and the ACJM, also had a well-established presence in other states and regions that experienced little or no rebellion during the cristiada.[93] The League, formed in 1925 in response to the schismatic movement facilitated by Calles, claimed to have 30 state and 145 local chapters by 1926, the distribution of the latter shown in table 4.4. The League was relatively well organized in the cristero states of Jalisco (17 local chapters), Michoacán (16), and Guanajuato (16), but also in the non-cristero states of Chihuahua (16) and Durango (15), as well as in the Federal District (18). In the cristero states of Colima and Zacatecas, there were relatively few local chapters, with 5 and 6 respectively. Formed in 1918 to 1919 to coordinate the Catholic Social Action movement in Mexico, the ACJM had state chapters in Baja California, Coahuila, Durango, Tamaulipas, and Querétaro. Its organizational density was greater in other states, which had both state and local chapters (the number of the latter in parentheses): Colima (4), Guanajuato (7), Jalisco (34), Mexico State (2), Michoacán (16), Nuevo León (2), Oaxaca (1), Puebla (5), San Luis Potosí (3), Tlaxcala (1), Veracruz (2), and Zacatecas (4) (Olivera Sedano 1966: 85–86).

Many of the uprisings of early January 1927 occurred in areas where the ACJM and/or the League had a strong organizational presence. Lacking significant popular support, however, these were easily and brutally suppressed by the federal army. Such was the case in Parras (Coahuila), Saltillo (Coahuila), and Concepción del Oro (northern Zacatecas). In the center-west, where the rebellion did have widespread popular support, conflicts between League-appointed military leaders (many of them members of the ACJM with no military experience) and locally recognized leaders were a frequent and sometimes violent event, particularly

Table 4.4   Distribution of League Local Chapters, 1925

Region/State	Number of Chapters	Region/State	Number of Chapters
Center-east	35	*North*	42
Federal District	18	Chihuahua	16
Hidalgo	7	Coahuila	5
Mexico State	5	Durango	15
Morelos	1	Nuevo León	0
Puebla	3	San Luis Potosí	0
Tlaxcala	1	Tamaulipas	0
Center-west	51	Zacatecas	6
Aguascalientes	0	*Gulf*	5
Guanajuato	16	Campeche	0
Jalisco	17	Quintana Roo	0
Michoacán	16	Tabasco	1
Querétaro	2	Veracruz	3
Pacific south	8	Yucatán	1
Chiapas	0	*Pacific north*	4
Colima	5	Baja California	0
Guerrero	3	Nayarit	2
Oaxaca	0	Sinaloa	2
		Sonora	0
		Mexico (Country)	145

Source: Olivera Sedano 1966: 115–17.

in Colima and Michoacán, where a strong peasant leadership emerged independently of the League. Such conflicts were indicative of the limited ability of urban Catholic organizations to control recalcitrant and largely autonomous regional movements with very distinct military styles and agendas. The Maderistas and Carrancistas faced quite similar problems in the 1910s.

The career of Luis Navarro Orígel is illustrative of the League's more general dilemma. Navarro was, according to one history of the cristiada, "one of the most virtuous and noble Catholics in Mexico" (Ochoa 1961: 262). President of the League in Pénjamo, Guanajuato, and a member of the ACJM, Navarro declared himself to be in rebellion on 28 September 1926, along with three of his brothers.[94] Forced to flee Guanajuato by

federal forces, Navarro was appointed military chief of northwestern Michoacán by the League. The rebels of that region, however, recognized the military leadership of the Cotija-based cacique Prudencio Mendoza, and they refused to acknowledge Navarro's appointment. The League subsequently appointed him military commander of Coalcomán, Apatzingán, and Arteaga in southwestern Michoacán, "a region that Luis Navarro did not know, but to which he traveled in order to carry out his mission" (Trueba 1959: 59, 111–12). Upon his arrival, however, Navarro immediately came into conflict with the locally recognized leaders, Father José María Martínez of Coalcomán and the Guillén brothers, rancheros from San José de la Montaña. The main source of the conflict concerned military discipline within the rebel ranks: Navarro wanted to form a proper army, but found himself surrounded by rebels who fought close to home, when the agricultural season allowed and under the orders of local and regional leaders. He objected to the presence of peasants who "join the forces of the National Liberation Army [the cristeros] when they want, where they want, and for the time they want." He tried, he said, to "prevent the dissolution and weakening of our ideas," to "form an army in the midst of chaos, to establish order, honor, and discipline in the midst of disorder and anarchy." After he shot two local rebel leaders, Jesús Sánchez Macías and Jacinto Arreola, for insubordination, Navarro's troops mutinied and would have killed him had it not been for the intervention of Martínez.[95] Navarro's League-appointed successor, Luis Guízar Morfín, fared even worse than his predecessor. After Guízar Morfín shot two leaders of the mutiny against Navarro, the League decided to transfer him to Colima, but prior to his departure, he was killed by "Indians from the coast," cristero rebels from the Indian communities of the municipio of Aquila.[96]

Appointed as military commander of Jalisco, Colima, and Michoacán in 1927, Jesús Degollado y Guízar had somewhat better luck in establishing his authority with the cristero rebels, with the notable exception of Prudencio Mendoza. This may well have been because of his membership in the secret society known as the U, as well as his contacts with the Popular Union (Unión Popular; UP) of Guadalajara, a lay Catholic organization with a well-developed network of local "cells" throughout Jalisco and western Guanajuato. Relatively little is known about the U. It is believed to have been founded in 1920 by Luis M. Martínez, the auxiliary bishop of Morelia, and to have spread rapidly throughout parts of the center-west prior to the League's creation in 1925, its members infil-

trating other lay Catholic organizations (Olmos Velázquez 1991: 248–49). In his memoirs, Degollado (1957: 12–13) wrote that he was invited to join the U by a priest in Guadalajara, his first meeting taking place in a parish house, "where forty of the most distinguished people of the area were united," including UP leader Anacleto González Flores. According to Degollado (1957: 21), the U developed an extensive network of local groups in Michoacán and Jalisco during the first half of the 1920s, but did not spread far beyond those two states: "The time passed and the U continued organizing; there wasn't a town, congregation, hacienda, or settlement where there were no members of this group. The same thing happened in Michoacán. Unfortunately in other places it did not happen this way. If the U had existed in the entire Republic, all of the states would have had [rebel] contingents equal to those in Jalisco and Michoacán and the result of the struggle could have been different."

The U and the League were in conflict throughout the course of the cristiada, in spite of the fact that leaders such as Degollado y Guízar and González Flores were members of both groups, because the U insisted on retaining its organizational autonomy and leadership structure. In 1928, a special subcommittee of the League reported to its president that "the secret and half-sinister" group known as the U had appointed military leaders without the League's consent, thus "undermining the work of the League in order to make the work of the tyrants easier."[97]

The organizational networks of the U undoubtedly helped sustain the cristero rebellion in the center-west, particularly in Jalisco and northwestern Michoacán. So too did the Women's Brigades (Brigadas Femeninas), a military organization founded in Guadalajara in June 1927. Initially composed of a single group of 17 women, the Women's Brigades soon grew to include some 25,000 members in 56 groups, many of which were based outside of the center-west.[98] The Women's Brigades procured and manufactured much-needed ammunition, and they set up and operated complex supply lines to deliver it to the cristero rebels. As was true of the U, the Women's Brigades refused to subordinate themselves to the direction and leadership of the League, leading to conflicts between the two organizations that temporarily disrupted the ammunition supply lines, which in turn created conflicts between the cristero military leadership, especially Enrique Gorostieta, and the League (Bailey 1974: 235–36).

Referring to the reaction of lay Catholic organizations to the 1926 Calles Law, French chargé d'affaires Ernest Lagarde wrote: "The vio-

lence and the unexpectedness of the action of the public authorities has stupefied the clergy. In Catholic circles, the confusion was complete. Between the various associations—the Knights of Columbus, the National League for the Religious Defense, the Union of Catholic Ladies, the Catholic Labor Confederation, the Mexican Association of Catholic Youth, the National Association of Heads of Family—there was less cohesion than rivalry, the Catholic forces were unorganized and weak, unfit and not prepared for resistance."[99] His assessment was accurate, if somewhat exaggerated, for the League and the other lay Catholic organizations centered in Mexico City. The League's main contribution to the rebellion was the appointment of Enrique Gorostieta as the military commander-in-chief, and Gorostieta was experienced enough to know that he was leading not an army but a wide array of local and regional movements only marginally susceptible to centralized command and coordination. Within this framework, Gorostieta's leadership was widely acknowledged to be effective.

Regional lay Catholic organizations, such as the U, the UP, and the Women's Brigades, had a much stronger presence, deeper popular roots, and less ambitious national political agendas. Although unevenly spread throughout the center-west, they clearly did help to sustain the rebellion, providing arms, ammunition, logistical support, and military leadership. They cannot be said to have caused the rebellion, however, given that many cristero communities, particularly those outside of Jalisco, western Guanajuato, and northwestern Michoacán, had no contact with them prior to the outbreak of the cristiada. The role of the regional lay Catholic organizations in instigating the rebellion was probably greatest in Jalisco, where many of the rebel leaders were members of the U or the UP or both. In northwestern Michoacán, the U seems to have existed before the rebellion, but so little is known about it that it is difficult to estimate its causal importance. It can be said, with a fair degree of certainty, that the U did not exist in Coalcomán, San Juan Parangaricutiro, or Aquila, as the cristeros of these regions remained isolated even during the peak of military coordination under Gorostieta's leadership. Because of their proximity to the Los Altos region of Jalisco, the rebels of northwestern Michoacán probably did have contact with the U preceding the outbreak of the rebellion. Although the UP was quite well organized in Jalisco and western Guanajuato, it does not seem to have been a factor in Michoacán, Colima, or Zacatecas. The existence of these regional organizations was, in sum, a necessary but insufficient condition for sustained popular

rebellion. They provided essential support to the rebels, fostered a Catholic political identity among many peasants who opposed the state, and help explain why the rebellion was sustained in the center-west and no other region of Mexico. But their existence cannot explain why communities in the center-west rebelled in the first place, much less why some communities supported the Church whereas others defended the state.

Class and Peasant Partisanship in the Cristiada

The class-centric and structural analyses of peasant rebellion that have dominated the scholarship on rural politics until recently suggest that class position, class consciousness, and class-based grievances ought to tell us a good deal about peasant partisanship in the cristero rebellion. The usual suspects in a counterrevolutionary rebellion would include smallholders, held to be inherently conservative and incapable of solidarity with their less fortunate brethren, and/or resident hacienda workers, whose complete dependence on and paternalistic relationships with landowners ostensibly foster false consciousness and hence the inability to define, much less act upon, class interests.[100] And, in fact, many accounts of the cristero rebellion, to the extent that they raise the issue at all, argue that the rebels were either resident hacienda workers or rancheros, the mestizo smallholding peasants that were so numerous throughout the center-west. Hellman (1983) and Huizer (1970) attribute popular opposition to the revolutionary state to peons or resident workers who could neither benefit from the agrarian reform program nor escape the ideological hegemony exercised by their landlords and priests. Likewise, in a study of the cristero rebellion in the region of Coalcomán, Sánchez Díaz and Carreño (1979) conclude that the cristeros were landless workers recruited by hacendados to serve the latter's own ends. With considerably more empirical evidence and careful analysis, scholars such as Díaz and Rodríguez (1979), Fábregas (1979), Jrade (1980), Rueda and Smithers (1981), and Tutino (1986) argue that the cristero rebels were predominantly rancheros for whom the agrarian reform was either irrelevant or an active threat to their smallholdings.

Some resident hacienda workers certainly did participate in the cristero rebellion. But at least in Michoacán, they were the least important popular rural group to do so. In both absolute and relative terms, the numbers of resident workers in the cristero regions of Michoacán were quite low. Census data indicate that there were no resident hacienda workers in the cristero municipios of San Juan Parangaricutiro and

Aquila and that there were relatively few in Coalcomán (4 percent of the municipio's total population), Cotija (2 percent), and Cojumatlán (2 percent). The municipios with relatively large numbers of hacienda workers (up to one-fifth to one-half of the total population) were located primarily in the Bajío region of north-central and northeastern Michoacán, and the Tierra Caliente, which includes parts of the southwest, center, and southeast. Neither the Michoacán Bajío nor the Tierra Caliente produced significant uprisings, although both served as battlegrounds for cristeros from other regions, agraristas, and federal forces.[101]

The claim that resident hacienda workers made up the bulk of the rebel ranks is based on the assumption that landowners actively supported the cristiada as a counterrevolutionary movement aimed at restoring the economic and political power they enjoyed during the Porfiriato. Landowners, in this analysis, colluded with their clerical allies in encouraging their dependent workers in rebelling against the revolutionary state and thus in unwittingly violating the workers' own (unrecognized) class interests. Apart from the facile assertion of false consciousness entailed in this argument, there is little evidence to suggest that many large landowners participated in or voluntarily supported the cristiada, and there is much to suggest that they opposed it. The remarks of the U.S. consul in Chihuahua were equally applicable to the rest of Mexico, including the center-west: "My observation of the sentiment of Roman Catholics of the well-to-do or so-called better classes in Chihuahua, of which class the Liga de Defensa Religiosa is composed, is that from intense indignation of legislation detrimental to their church their feelings have subsided to a state of apathy, and I doubt very much if there is any real enthusiasm for a revolution in which they themselves are to take an active part."[102]

Some members of the League clearly believed that landowners would help finance their revolution. The (otherwise unidentified) chief of the division of the east informed the landowners of Puebla and Tlaxcala that he had assigned each a set sum of money that they were to contribute "to help cover the indispensable costs of the Liberation Army in its entire scope of military operations." "I believe, Señores Hacendados," he continued, "that convinced of the urgent necessity . . . you will accept this, your highest duty . . . and agree to pay the assigned contribution."[103] Voluntary contributions were not forthcoming, however, and the cristeros attacked haciendas and mining companies throughout the course of the rebellion, seizing supplies and extracting forced loans. According

to U.S. consul Dudley Dwyre in Guadalajara, it was a common rebel practice to occupy haciendas, forcing their owners to provide food, horses, and "loans" as high as 5,000 pesos.[104] Ransoms were extracted as well. The manager of the Chapala Electric Plant in Jalisco was kidnapped by rebels and held for a 20,000-peso ransom in March 1927. The ransom was apparently not paid, and his body was found a few days later.[105] That same month, cristeros stole 10,000 pesos from a British mining company in Zacatecas, threatening to destroy the mine and taking an employee as hostage.[106] And after his 147,000-hectare hacienda was occupied by cristeros in 1927, a British citizen by the name of B. Johnson complained: "The towns are well-guarded but the rebels do not inhabit the towns, but rather stay and rob the Haciendas."[107] Agrarista peasants were often deployed to protect mines and haciendas from cristero attacks, the inadvisability of which was noted by P. G. Holmes, British vice-consul in Guadalajara: "It is manifest that Agrarista troops, who are irregulars and not Federal Troops, are scarcely to be depended upon for the defence of large foreign estates, since they are constitutionally opposed to the theory of large land holdings, and they are usually not well affected toward foreigners."[108]

The federal army extracted forced loans as well, thus forcing landowners (and other wealthy individuals) to contribute to the coffers of both sides of the rebellion. In late 1926, a landowner in Durango noted that "if one will agree to pay the rebels as well as the Federals, one may continue to work."[109] In Torreón, Coahuila, it was observed "the people feel that as they are robbed by both sides, it doesn't make any difference to them who does it."[110] Nor was the federal army above extortion: in Guadalajara, Generals Amaro and Ferreira invited 40 prominent businessmen to military headquarters and demanded 60,000 pesos in exchange for protecting the city against rebel attacks.[111] The financial support given to the state by wealthy Catholics, voluntary or otherwise, caused great bitterness among the cristero rebels. According to an unsigned letter published by the League, "[t]he rich are helping the treacherous, thieving, and tyrannical government in exterminating us. . . . Destruction and ruin do not figure in our program, nor do our ideals include robbery and pillage; but just as we have been obligated to assault trains . . . so can we ruin the properties of the rich who help the government with money, arms and people, and we promise to do it thus, punishing the infamy that they are committing against us."[112]

If there is little evidence to support the claim that landowners sup-

ported the cristiada and induced their resident workers to participate in it, rancheros certainly were involved in large numbers. The agrarian structure of the center-west was, in fact, notable for the prevalence of mestizo smallholdings communities (rancherías), as opposed to Indian communities and haciendas. But class categories, particularly when extracted from their social, cultural, and historical contexts, cannot explain partisanship in the rebellion. Three points need to be made with respect to the characterization of the cristiada as a ranchero rebellion. First, the distinction between ranchero communities and Indian ones is often overdrawn: given population growth, the expansion of haciendas, and the extensive privatization of communal lands that occurred in the second half of the nineteenth century, both types of communities usually included significant numbers of smallholders, tenants, and landless peasants working for wages within or outside the community. Second, Indian communities did not predominate in the center-west, but they did exist in significant numbers, and some participated in the cristiada, most notably in Michoacán, but also in Nayarit and Colima. Third, ranchero communities existed in large numbers outside of the center-west, and their political behavior varied considerably in the 1910s and 1920s.

Many analysts who attribute the regional character of the cristiada to the agrarian structure of the center-west and the prevalence of smallholders assume that the agrarian reform program was at best irrelevant and at worst a threat to the peasants of the region.[113] But within the ranchero communities, there were many landless and land-poor peasants who were eligible to apply for land under the agrarian reform program. In the 1920s, the agrarian code required that a minimum of 20 families be in need of land in order to file a petition, that the community involved have at least 50 families overall, and that there be affectable, land that is, a hacienda, within a seven-kilometer radius of the petitioning community. Based on the first two criteria, Sanderson (1984: 45) calculates that 43 percent of the rural communities in Guanajuato were eligible to apply for land under the agrarian reform, 41 percent in Zacatecas, 34 percent in Michoacán, 25 percent in Colima, and 23 percent in Jalisco. As indicated in table 4.5, the percentage of communities eligible to apply for ejidos in these center-west states was much lower than in the center-east, but was about the same or higher than most states in the north, Pacific north, and gulf regions.

Sanderson's calculations do not include the criteria of affectable land within a seven-kilometer radius, and it might be argued that given the

Table 4.7   Relative Distribution of Agricultural Properties by Size in the
Center-West: Size Category as Percentage of Total Properties by State, 1923

Property Size (Hectares)	Aguas-calientes	Guanajuato	Jalisco	Michoacán	Querétaro
Less than 1	20.7	21.7	28.0	31.6	32.3
1–5	34.7	26.4	38.4	41.6	38.5
6–10	12.9	11.5	10.2	9.6	9.2
11–50	21.0	21.7	16.8	11.7	13.0
51–100	4.5	6.3	3.0	2.0	2.7
101–200	2.2	4.0	1.6	1.2	1.7
201–500	1.9	3.6	1.1	1.1	0.9
501–1,000	0.7	2.3	0.4	0.4	0.5
1,001–5,000	1.0	2.1	0.4	0.6	0.8
5,001–10,000	0.2	0.3	0.1	0.1	0.2
Over 10,000	0.2	0.1	0.0	0.1	0.2

Source: Tannenbaum [1929] 1968: 484–85.

Table 4.8   Relative Distribution of Agricultural Properties by Size in the Pacific
South: Size Category as Percentage of Total Properties by State, 1923

Property Size (Hectares)	Chiapas	Colima	Guerrero	Oaxaca
Less than 1	7.3	0.1	4.9	13.8
1–5	34.2	6.7	32.3	33.9
6–10	11.3	5.9	12.5	24.7
11–50	21.4	33.4	20.3	21.3
51–100	5.9	12.7	7.6	2.6
101–200	5.1	13.2	6.8	1.6
201–500	6.3	10.7	6.4	1.2
501–1,000	3.6	6.7	3.9	0.4
1,001–5,000	4.4	7.5	4.1	0.4
5,001–10,000	0.3	1.2	0.7	0.1
Over 10,000	0.2	1.9	0.5	0.0

Source: Tannenbaum [1929] 1968: 484–85.

Table 4.9   Relative Distribution of Agricultural Properties by Size in the
Center-East: Size Category as Percentage of Total Properties by State, 1923

Property Size (Hectares)	Hidalgo	Mexico State	Morelos	Puebla	Tlaxcala
Less than 1	49.0	16.3	55.6	45.7	7.5
1–5	38.7	64.7	36.0	36.2	33.1
6–10	4.5	7.9	3.7	5.0	14.5
11–50	5.6	7.4	3.7	6.9	19.9
51–100	0.8	1.2	0.5	1.7	4.2
101–200	0.4	0.7	0.3	1.3	4.7
201–500	0.4	0.7	0.1	1.2	6.0
501–1,000	0.2	0.4	0.1	0.8	4.6
1,001–5,000	0.3	0.5	<0.1	1.0	5.2
5,001–10,000	0.1	0.1	—	0.1	0.2
Over 10,000	0.0	0.1	—	0.1	0.1

Source: Tannenbaum [1929] 1968: 484–85.

in the cristiada. Legacies of agrarian and political conflict, like the institutional strength of the Church, constitute only a partial explanation of partisanship in the cristero rebellion.

The Regional Character of the Rebellion

Three conditions were necessary for sustained popular rebellion during the cristiada, and all three existed only in the center-west in the 1920s. The first condition was the survival of a significant number of communities with their landed bases and local institutions more or less intact. The second was the presence of a strong grassroots network of lay Catholic organizations capable of supplying the peasant rebels with at least some arms, ammunition, logistical support, and military leadership. And the third was direct experience with revolutionary state formation at the local level in the 1920s, through the implementation of anticlerical policies and the agrarian reform program. Many communities in Oaxaca survived the various onslaughts of the nineteenth century, but the lay Catholic organizations so critical to sustained rebellion were weak in the Pacific south, and the most intrusive phases of revolutionary state forma-

tion, as experienced at the local level, occurred in the 1910s and the 1930s, rather than the 1920s.[114]

In the center-east, both the Church and its affiliated organizations were quite strong, but few rural communities emerged from the Porfiriato with either their landed bases or their local institutional arrangements intact. Many of the communities of this region were active participants in the revolutionary battles of 1910 to 1917, and the center-east provided a good number of the agrarista irregulars deployed against the various enemies of the revolutionary state in the 1920s. But few center-east peasants participated in the cristiada. In the center-east, urban lay Catholics tried to organize uprisings in support of the Church in early 1927, but these were easily defeated in the absence of widespread popular support, as many of the young men of the ACJM found out at great cost. Only in the center-west did a dense network of lay Catholic organizations coincide with the existence of a significant number of communities attempting to defend their landed bases and local institutions against the immediate threats entailed in revolutionary state formation in the 1920s, and it was only in the center-west that widespread popular rebellion was sustained throughout the course of the cristiada. In order to explain intraregional variations in peasant partisanship, however, we need to take a closer look at conflicts over revolutionary state formation at the local level. The next three chapters consist of case studies of (predominantly) agrarista and cristero communities in Michoacán, and they link historical experiences of agrarian and political conflict at the local level to subsequent struggles over revolutionary anticlericalism and agrarianism in the 1920s.

5 ✴ The *Agraristas* of the Zacapu Region

The agrarista heartland of Michoacán lay in Zacapu.[1] With support from Mugiquista state officials, and under the leadership of Primo Tapia of Naranja, the municipio's three largest Purépecha communities formed the nucleus of the state's agrarian movement, first through the Union of Agrarian Communities of Naranja, Tiríndaro, and Tarejero, and later through the statewide League of Agrarista Communities and Unions of Michoacán. Together with the Cañada de los Once Pueblos, Zacapu provided many of the agrarista irregulars recruited by state officials as part of the counterinsurgency campaign against the cristeros. With the exception of the agrarista leadership, the great majority of Zacapu peasants were devout and practicing Catholics. Until the 1920s, when the agraristas obtained political power at the local level, the content of religious practice was much the same in Zacapu as it had been since the colonial period. However, the symbolic and institutional relationships among religious practice, property rights, and local political authority had changed dramatically in the course of agrarian conflicts in the decades prior to the revolution. By the end of the Porfiriato, the Zacapu communities had lost almost all of the land they had held under communal title to neighboring haciendas and ranchos. The loss of this land was accompanied by a shift in political power at the local level, from the politico-religious authorities of the cabildo to mestizo and Spanish landowners within and outside the communities. Religious practice, in turn, became detached from the local institutions that had regulated property rights and local political authority, and became more closely associated with the institutional Church and the sponsorship of mestizo and Spanish elites. Throughout the 1920s and beyond, religion came to divide rather than unite the Zacapu communities.

This chapter begins by outlining the basic social and political organization of Purépecha communities, much of which applies to the Uruapan highlands (the subject of chapter 6) as well as Zacapu. The second section of the chapter relates the history of agrarian conflict in Zacapu, focusing on the second half of the nineteenth century, when the communities struggled unsuccessfully to protect their holdings from expansionary haciendas and state tax officials. By the time the region's most powerful landowners, Eduardo and Alfredo Noriega, finished draining the Zacapu marshlands in the 1890s, the communities had lost nearly all of the lands they held under communal title. The discussion then turns to the ways in which this loss altered the symbolic and institutional relationships between property rights, religious practice, and local political authority. The third section examines the construction and mobilization of an agrarista political identity in Zacapu. However much it owed to state sponsorship under Francisco Múgica, and later Lázaro Cárdenas, the Zacapu movement was not simply created from above in order to fulfill the political agendas of revolutionary officials. Elite efforts to mobilize popular support through state-supported agrarianism succeeded only to the extent that they responded to and meshed with local grievances and aspirations. In Zacapu, state officials found ready allies at the local level, who employed the revolutionary agrarian reform program to carry on the decades-long struggle to recover communal lands and who adopted anticlericalism as a means of discrediting and displacing local elites, including mestizos within the communities, outside landowners, and the clergy. In the process, however, the anticlericalism of the agrarista leaders alienated significant numbers of peasants in their own communities, setting off intense and often brutally violent factional conflict in which the agraristas defined their political enemies as Catholics, fanatics, and reactionaries. The struggle to obtain the ejidos thus entailed the political defeat of Catholics within the communities, as well as the large landowners and their allies outside of the villages. The Catholics of Zacapu did not rebel as cristeros: they were defeated, killed, or dispersed well before the cristiada began.[2]

Property Rights, Religious Practice, and Political
Authority in Purépecha Communities[3]

Until the end of the nineteenth century, Purépecha communities, like their counterparts elsewhere in indigenous Mesoamerica, were char-

acterized by a close integration of the material, cultural, and political realms. Three interrelated institutions regulated community life: the communal property regime, in which land was often held and viewed as de facto private property but remained under corporate title and subject to some degree of communal control; the cargo system, through which individual families served in a two-sided ladder of civil and religious offices; and the cabildo, or council of politico-religious elders, which allocated cargos, defined and distributed use rights to communal property, and acted as the de facto political authorities within the community. Two other institutions were also of importance in many Michoacán communities: the cofradías, religious associations that owned property dedicated to the worship of particular saints, and the hospital, which took care of the church as well as the sick, and was administered by a cofradía invariably dedicated to the Virgin of the Immaculate Conception.

The communal property regime had its origins in the early colonial period, when the Crown, intending to offset the power of the Spanish colonists, decreed that each *pueblo de indios* should have lands of its own, inalienable and held under corporate title. Such land was used in four ways: the fundo legal, or town site, which included the houses, gardens, community and commercial buildings, and central plaza; the tierras de común repartimiento, arable land cultivated under use rights by individual families; the ejidos, or communal pastures and woodlands (the latter referred to as montes in Michoacán); and the propios, communal land that was rented to tenants, the proceeds used to finance civil expenses and religious practice. In addition, the hospital and cofradías sometimes owned land, although their property more often took the form of gold and livestock. The Indian community of Zacapu, for example, had three cofradías, each with cattle, sheep, and horses that were pastured on the communal ejidos (Bravo Ugarte 1960: 48).

Much of the communal land owned by the Purépecha communities was widely understood by comuneros to be a form of private property held by individual families. This was certainly the case with the house sites and gardens (solares), and the tierras de común repartimiento. The ejidos, montes, and propios, in contrast, were usually considered to be communal property, even as individual families sometimes cleared and cultivated plots in the woodlands.[4] The concept of "private property" within the communities did not, however, necessarily correspond with liberal or legal definitions of the same term. Cultivated lands in particular might be considered the private property of individual families, but

they were subject to considerable communal control, wielded by the members of the cabildo: such lands reverted to common usage after the harvest and during the biannual fallow period; because they were used for communal pasture they could not be fenced; and individual families were prohibited (more or less successfully) from selling them outside of the community. In use and in popular understanding, then, the distinction between private property and communal property was a blurred one. Nor were clear-cut distinctions made between the property of (or membership in) the community and the various cofradías and the hospital.[5]

The close interrelationship of religious and civil offices in the cargo system was a product of the late colonial period. Earlier, cargos were purely civil in nature, consisting of the political offices created by the Spanish under the Castillian municipio system (Greenberg 1990: 97). Religious practice, in contrast, was organized and financed through the cofradías and hospital, supplemented with funds raised through the rental of communal lands. As communities lost land to expanding haciendas throughout the colonial period, however, religious practice gradually became the responsibility of individual families, who, in accepting a religious cargo, agreed to organize and finance the cult of a particular saint for a year (Chance 1990).[6] In this process, the cargo system became a two-sided ladder of religious and civil offices. Families with the resources and political clout to do so worked their way up this ladder, alternating civil and religious cargos and ultimately assuming local political power as members of the cabildo. The cabildo, in turn, regulated access to communal resources, managed the proceeds derived from the propios, distributed cargo positions (and hence determined future membership in the cabildo), and arbitrated conflicts within the communities (Espín Díaz 1986a). With the consolidation of a central state during the Porfiriato, the cabildo often lost its capacity to regulate access to political offices, which came under the control of the district prefects and other state officials. Even so, the cabildo often remained the de facto source of local political authority, and in control of access to communal resources, until the consolidation of the revolutionary state in the 1920s and 1930s.[7]

Religious practice in Purépecha communities included elements of both orthodox and popular Catholicism, the former revolving around the priest, the sacraments, and the rosary, and the latter revolving around the cult of the saints and including beliefs and rituals that were local in

origin.[8] Thus Christ is sometimes seen as the son of God and a member of the Trinity, in accordance with orthodox Catholicism, and sometimes as a brother to other saints. Different Christ-saints were associated with different communities. The Lord of the Miracles (*Cristo de los Milagros*), for example, was a central source of identity for the residents of San Juan Parangaricutiro, and of ethnic solidarity as well, revered as he was throughout the central highlands. Each Purépecha community worshipped a patron saint, as well as a number of others associated with different occupations and agricultural activities. The rituals and fiestas that made up the cult of the saints followed the liturgical calendar of the Catholic Church, but also included popular elements, such as dances, dramatizations, and music, that often obscured their orthodox content (Carrasco 1976: 62). Such was the case with the Tacari fiesta held in Naranja on 15 December, as described by Friedrich (1977: 29–31). Named after a highlands grass held to be particularly full of symbolic energies, the fiesta began with a procession that included the individual charged with organizing the annual cycle of fiestas, the *prioste,* village girls, and a burro carrying the *tacari* grass and a Christ child. While the procession "normally provoked great hilarity and provided an opportunity for amorous advances," it was supposed to end on a more solemn note, as the participants requested lodging for the Christ child at the church door. This was then followed by eight nights of fiestas, including the Dance of the Little Old Men, characteristic of the Purépecha region as a whole. With reference to the orthodox elements of the Tacari fiesta, Friedrich (1977: 31) notes: "The request for lodging for the Christ Child, technically the main point of these rituals, was often omitted in practice, just as little attention was actually paid to the infant Christ during the Tacari [procession]."

Few fiestas were purely religious in content.[9] The annual fiesta dedicated to a patron saint or a significant local Christ or Virgin, for example, had commercial, ethnic, and religious dimensions, serving as a source and reaffirmation of communal and ethnic identity and as an opportunity to trade goods and news with neighboring, and sometimes far-flung, Purépecha communities. The organization of Naranja's annual fiesta for its patron saint, Nuestro Padre Jesús, involved almost the entire community in one way or another: the cabildo, cofradía, and sacristan were responsible for collecting the funds necessary to pay for the fiesta, and all community members were expected to contribute money and labor in the preparations. It also strengthened Naranja's ethnic, reli-

gious, and commercial ties with other communities, as people came from all over Purépecha Michoacán to participate in the fiesta (Friedrich 1977). Likewise, the annual fiesta dedicated to the Lord of the Miracles in San Juan Parangaricutiro was a religious, commercial, and social event, drawing thousands of visitors from across the state (Lumholtz 1902).

Throughout the colonial period and first century of independence, the precise relationships between property rights, religious practice, and local political authority changed in Purépecha communities, most notably as religious practice became the responsibility of individual families on a rotating basis, and as the cabildo lost its official political functions, although not always its de facto ones, to appointees of the central state. But even as religious practice lost some of its communal character, it remained tightly intertwined with local political authority through the cargo system and cabildo, and it served as a source of communal and ethnic identity and solidarity. This began to change, in some communities but not others, in the second half of the nineteenth century, as the liberal and Porfirian states attempted to redefine and redistribute property rights within the Purépecha communities, at the same time transforming political authority at the local level and with it the connection between land, politics, religion, and local identity.

Prerevolutionary Agrarian and Political Conflict in Zacapu

Throughout the colonial period, Zacapu was dominated by the Hacienda of Bellas Fuentes, with its "enormous herds of cattle and horses, massive fields of irrigated wheat, rainfed corn, and other crops, and large numbers of tenants who independently cultivated their own fields" (Bravo Ugarte 1960: 45). The hacienda began to encroach upon the communal lands of Zacapu's Indian communities early on in the colonial period, as did others in the region. The Indian community of Zacapu, for example, had applied for and received a settlement title (*título de composición*) in the early seventeenth century, confirming its possession of some 20,000 hectares of land.[10] Some of this land must have been lost by the end of the eighteenth century, however, because the community had at that point been engaged in long-standing litigation with the Haciendas of Bellas Fuentes, Zipimeo, and El Cortijo.[11] Visiting the region toward the end of the colonial period, a royal inspector noted that one Don Diego Sánchez Piña Hermosa had seized the best of the communal lands

for the expansion of his hacienda, leaving the Indians with the least productive lands furthest from the town, actions that had resulted in "incessant disagreements and repeated outrages, even violence." The same inspector noted, however, that Zacapu's 187 Purépecha families retained enough communal property to support religious practice, a school, a teacher, and a priest, as well as the substantial livestock holdings of the community's three cofradías (Bravo Ugarte 1960: 49).

The Indian communities of Naranja, Tiríndaro, and, especially, Tarejero did not fare as well. The 99 Purépecha families of Naranja still retained some communal lands at the close of the eighteenth century, but had to rent additional land for cultivation from Bellas Fuentes. Nor were Naranja's communal pastures sufficient for the livestock of its single cofradía, dedicated to the Virgin of the Immaculate Conception and associated with the hospital, and so the community had to rely on marshlands claimed by Bellas Fuentes, in exchange providing the unpaid labor of 80 individuals for five days every year. A similar arrangement held in Tiríndaro, where the comuneros claimed that Bellas Fuentes had usurped much of its land. While Naranja and Tiríndaro both retained control of some communal lands at the end of the colonial period, Tarejero was almost completely landless, its much reduced population of 69 families forced to work as peons at Bellas Fuentes (Bravo Ugarte 1960: 46–51).

Bellas Fuentes was the first ecclesiastical property in the region to be affected by the liberal land reform: nationalized in 1859 in the context of the War of the Reform, part of the hacienda was sold to Luis G. Obregón, who paid half its deflated purchase price in uniforms and military equipment to be used in the liberal war effort. Later sales led to the creation or expansion of other haciendas, including Copándaro, El Cortijo, Buenavista, Tariácuri, Zipimeo, and Los Espinos. Indigenous land claims were not taken into account in the parcellation and sale of the nationalized Bellas Fuentes, complicating and perpetuating disputes and litigation between the haciendas and the communities. The comuneros thus continued to work, as sharecroppers, tenants, and peons, on hacienda land, some of which they claimed as their own (Embriz Osorio 1984: 41–47).

Little was done to implement the liberal reform in the Indian communities until early 1869, after the liberals regained power in the Restored Republic. At that point, the district prefect convened meetings in all of the Zacapu communities with title to corporate property, in order to

explain the state and national laws that mandated its privatization, secure their consent to the proceedings, and elect the local committees charged with the preparation and distribution of individual private titles. The issue of consent was not a complete formality: liberal officials did wish to convey, through these proceedings, the economic, social, and political advantages they expected the Indians to enjoy as small proprietors, and, on occasion, they were willing to address popular concerns that the process would be unfair, fraudulent, or disadvantageous to the community and its members. It was also made clear, however, that the unpersuaded would be subject to the coercive authority of the state. As the Zacapu district prefect put it with reference to the comuneros of Naranja, who met with local officials on 9 January 1869, "[t]he President of the Ayuntamiento sought to instill in them the benefits that would come from the division of their lands, and the harm that would come from any opposition to the laws."[12]

In Zacapu, as throughout Michoacán, popular responses to the liberal reform entailed a complex mixture of accommodation, negotiation, and resistance, as communities tried to retain local control over the privatization process, carry it out in accordance with local norms and institutions, minimize the amount of land alienated to outsiders, and include in the process lands subject to disputes and litigation with neighboring communities and haciendas. Indian communities were often willing to privatize their tierras de común repartimiento, because these were already cultivated by individual families and widely viewed to be a form of private property, albeit one subject to a degree of communal control. Resistance was much greater to the privatization of communal woodlands, pasture, and, in the case of the Zacapu communities, marshlands, because these were exploited by all comuneros and considered to be the property of the community as a whole. Liberal land laws, especially the Lerdo Law, contained enough ambiguities and contradictions to allow communities to claim, with some justification, that they were required to privatize their cultivated lands but permitted to retain communal ownership and use of the ejidos and montes, in accordance with longstanding local practice.

Thus, when instructed to privatize their lands, the comuneros of Naranja replied that they done so long ago, leaving only "a bit of marshland" undivided. State officials agreed that Naranja's lands had, in fact, been divided up among its residents "through an agreement reached between themselves" but that the privatization (*reparto*) was not valid,

because it had not been carried out in accordance with the law, nor had state officials approved it. Furthermore, the parcels in question were neither registered nor taxed as private property. Until the state decreed the property to be private, collecting the relevant fees and taxes and generating the necessary forms, the land was to be considered communal and taxed as such.[13] The residents of Tiríndaro made a similar claim: "Making use of the liberty granted to us by the Supreme Government," their legal representative wrote, "we carried out the division of our communal lands by ourselves." As was the case with Naranja, state tax officials replied that the land would be taxed as communal property until such time as its division was carried out in accordance with the law, and the newly privatized parcels were registered with the state and taxed as private property.[14]

Negotiations over the terms and implementation of the reparto dragged on for several decades. Comuneros were concerned that the privatization of their communal lands would entail the definitive loss of lands in litigation with neighboring haciendas and villages, because these could not be included in the process until a legal decision had been rendered. There was also fear that the reform would mean that the community, having lost its juridical personality, could no longer pursue its land claims through the courts. In the last quarter of the nineteenth century, the Indian community of Zacapu was engaged in boundary disputes with the municipal government of Purépero; the Indian communities of Ichán, Tacuro, Carapan, and Cherán; and numerous owners of nearby ranchos and haciendas.[15] Residents were concerned that the reform would allow long-term tenants to claim ownership of rented lands (propios) and that it would legitimate previous unauthorized alienations of communal land by individual comuneros to outsiders.[16] Community members were also worried that their mestizo neighbors would acquire further communal land, by claiming to have rights to lands privatized in the reform as residents of the town of Zacapu.[17] Finally, expense was a significant issue. Although comuneros did not have to pay for the land itself, under the terms of the 9 October 1856 circular, outsiders appointed by the government to the local privatization commission often charged substantial fees for their work in compiling the census, surveying the lands, and preparing and distributing the new private titles. The state government also required a small but often onerous fee for processing the titles.[18]

In both Zacapu and Naranja, the liberal land reform generated deep

and sometimes violent factional conflict, pitting members and allies of the cabildo, who up until the reparto had controlled access to and use of communal lands, against local mestizo families allied with outside land-owners, who hoped to benefit from the many frauds and illegal transactions that were so commonly part of the reform process.[19] In Zacapu, the cabildo, represented first by Benito Martínez, and subsequently by his son Eduvirgis together with Sacramento Torres, maintained control over the local privatization commission for much of the period between 1869, when the state first began to apply pressure on the communities to carry out the reform, until 1904, when private titles were finally distributed in Zacapu. Without ever openly opposing the law, the Martínez faction managed to delay its implementation for decades, through long periods of inaction, as well as repeated requests for extensions and various sorts of authorizations. The central objective of this faction, which had the apparent support of the majority of the comuneros, was to recover lands lost through prior sales, rental agreements, mortgages, and dispossessions prior to the implementation of the reparto, and to prevent outsiders from benefiting from the process.[20]

A much smaller faction in the community, allied with mestizo elites living in Zacapu and outside landowners, fought for the immediate implementation of the reparto, in order to gain access to lands that had been previously, if partially, protected by the communal property regime. Represented initially by Severiano Valencia, and later by José Dolores Heredia, this faction challenged that led by Martínez for control over the local privatization commission, without much success until the turn of the century. Meanwhile, its members appropriated communal lands for themselves, and alienated it to their outside allies through illegal or fraudulent sales, rental agreements, and mortgages. Thus Rafael García Jaso, owner of a nearby rancho and a party to a long-standing legal dispute with the community, acquired land valued at 40,000 pesos, after the community failed to repay a 1,500-peso "loan" arranged by the Valencia/Heredia faction. The faction also managed to appoint García Jaso as the community's legal representative, and he used his powers of attorney to arrange a number of rental agreements that violated local norms with respect to access to communal pastures and woodlands. Noting García Jaso's many abuses, a visiting tax official reported that "the Indians have been the victims of the bad faith of their legal representative, because far from promoting their interests he has used his legal powers to extract from them as much as possible, and retain for himself

the best of their property."[21] By the time the reparto was finally carried out in 1904, the community had far less land to privatize than it did in 1869, in large part because of the alienations arranged by the minority faction.

Factional conflict in Naranja entailed the same ethnic dimension. Until the late nineteenth century, the mestizo Mata and Torres families shared local political power with the community's leading Purépecha families, most notably that of Ambrosio de la Cruz (Friedrich 1977: 47). In the course of conflicts over the liberal reparto, however, the Mata and Torres families allied themselves with Eduardo and Alfredo Noriega and other hacendados, and they attempted to gain control over the local privatization committee in order to claim land for themselves and alienate it to their outside allies. In this effort they confronted Joaquín de la Cruz, the son of Ambrosio and by the end of the century the leader of Naranja's struggle to protect its holdings against the encroachments of the Noriega brothers and other landowners. The de la Cruz faction, complaining to state officials about the actions of the Mata family, attempted to assert the claim that the mestizos had no rights to land divided in the reparto as they were not members of the community. "These gentlemen," some Naranja residents wrote in 1899, "are residents of this place without being Indians, and for that reason we do not believe that they have the same rights as us with respect to our community property." "Before the Mata family got involved in village affairs," they continued, "we enjoyed complete peace."[22] A few years later, in 1902, Mauricio Mata obtained power of attorney as Naranja's legal representative, giving him the right to rent and sell its communal lands.[23] He promptly took advantage of this right, alienating Naranja's holdings in the Zacapu marshlands to Eduardo and Alfredo Noriega.

The process through which the Zacapu communities were divested of their communal holdings culminated with the drainage of the marshlands, undertaken by the Noriega brothers with significant economic incentives and political support provided by state officials. The state government had offered property tax exemptions, without success, to any landowners willing to undertake the drainage project, first in 1864 and then again in 1884. The region's landowners did embark on the project under a federal concession in 1886, but ran out of capital partway through, abandoning the work and losing thousands of pesos in the process. The federal concession was then passed on to Eduardo and Alfredo Noriega, and the brothers reached agreements with all of the

hacendados with land in the marshes in 1896, whereby they would receive a third of all the land they drained.[24] With the completion of the project, the Noriegas used their 4,000-hectare share to establish the Hacienda of Cantabria, one of the largest in the region.

While respecting the land claims of their fellow landowners throughout the course of the project, the Noriegas violated those of the communities, gaining control over communal property in the marshlands with the connivance of their allies within the communities and state tax officials. In Zacapu, José Dolores Heredia, Teófilo Medina, Nicolás Orozco, and several other members of the minority faction sold "shares" in the communal marshlands to Nicolás Luna and Miguel Guido in 1897, the land itself to be acquired once the privatization had been finalized. Luna, and probably Guido, bought the rights on behalf of Eduardo Noriega, whose lawyer proceeded to press state officials to finalize the reform so that his client might make use of his newly acquired rights.[25] The Noriegas acquired a further 900 hectares of Zacapu's marshlands in 1900, seized by state tax officials the previous year and sold at auction to cover accrued property taxes.[26]

Tarejero lost what little remained of its communal lands in the same fashion. Pressed to implement the Lerdo Law for several decades, the comuneros finally agreed to do so in 1896, "as much to comply with the law as to avoid the continual advances made . . . by neighboring hacendados."[27] They had been engaged in long-standing conflicts over land in the marshes with the owners of Bellas Fuentes, Copándaro, and El Cortijo, and these conflicts intensified with the prospect of rising land values once the drainage project was completed. Thus Francisco Elguero, the legal representative of the owners of Copándaro, protested that the comuneros had obstructed the construction of canals on land claimed by both the hacienda and the community, writing that "the Indians of Tarejero, like all those of their race, do not miss a single opportunity to harass the neighboring landowners, opposing the work on the pretext that it invades their possessions."[28] Some months later, he lodged a similar complaint on behalf of the owners of El Cortijo. The Indians, he said, believed that through the reparto "they would get possession of the entire marshland, and this has greatly encouraged, naturally, the abuses and dispossessions they are already inclined to carry out on their own."[29] In preparing the titles for distribution to individual comuneros, the local privatization commission had, in fact, included lands subject to litigation with the Haciendas of Bellas Fuentes, El Cortijo, and Copándaro.

On these grounds, after numerous complaints from the affected land-owners and reports of land invasions by the comuneros, the Ministry of Government refused to approve the reparto, while noting that this refusal did not in any way exempt the community from back taxes owed on its property.[30] At the end of 1896, tax officials impounded almost all of Tarejero's communal lands, including 535 hectares in the marshlands and 200 solares, the garden plots adjacent to the houses in the town site, to be auctioned off to cover the community's tax debt of more than 6,500 pesos. The community would not be able to carry out the reparto, its legal representatives complained, "for lack of any land to divide."[31]

The loss of communal lands through the drainage of the Zacapu marshlands radically altered the nature of political authority in the region's Indian communities, and, without changing the content of religious practice, transformed the relationship between religion, politics, and community identity. Friedrich (1977) discusses these changes in Naranja. Prior to the drainage project undertaken by the Noriega brothers, the community was divided into several political groupings based on extended families and ceremonial kinship. Each group was represented in the cabildo, which regulated access to communal resources, organized religious practice, and, unofficially, appointed the occupants of local political offices. The most powerful family, in political terms, was that of "the forceful and prolific Ambrosio de la Cruz" (Friedrich 1977: 47), followed by the Mata and Torres families. The latter two were mestizo, but spoke Purépecha and participated fully in the community's social and ritual life. With the loss of communal property in the marshlands, political power in the Indian communities shifted from the Purépecha-dominated cabildos to mestizos allied with outside landowners, especially Eduardo and Alfredo Noriega, who, with the establishment of Cantabria as a thriving commercial hacienda, became the region's most powerful economic and political elites. In Naranja, the Mata and Torres families "disassimilated" themselves from Purépecha culture, and they began to associate and identify with their mestizo relatives in Zacapu. With the backing of the Noriegas, the two families were able to monopolize political power in Naranja until 1920, alternating political office and control over the local defense force (Friedrich 1977: 47). The agrarista movement in Naranja would be led by members of what had been, prior to the breakdown of the communal property regime, the community's most powerful Purépecha family, that of Ambrosio de la Cruz.[32]

The impact of the loss of communal lands on religious practice was

less obvious but still profound. Zacapu comuneros, as impoverished as they were, continued to sponsor the cult of the saints as office holders (*cargueros*), often migrating to the Tierra Caliente to find seasonal work in order to do so. But as the cabildo lost its symbolic and institutional centrality within the communities, mestizo and Spanish landowners began to play the primary role in organizing religious worship and supporting the Catholic Church (Friedrich 1977: 48). Thus religious practice became associated with the patronage of local elites, and, after the revolution, came to constitute a source of intense conflict in the communities. In the 1920s, agrarista peasants would use anticlericalism to attack the mestizo families who had allied themselves with external landowners to defraud the communities of their holdings in the marshlands. In the context of the cristero rebellion in 1927, for example, Naranja agraristas "denounc[ed] the seditious activities" of Rafaela Aviles Vda. de Torres and Estefania Torres, then living in Zacapu, accusing them of violating the laws prohibiting public worship, of shouting "¡Viva Cristo Rey!" (the cristero slogan) in the streets, and, in general, of "stirring things up, engaging in subversive activities, and attempting to turn people into fanatics, like the people [of Naranja] used to be."[33] At the same time, agrarista leaders directed their anticlericalism against fellow Purépecha peasants as well, attacking their personal and political enemies as *fanáticos* allied with landowners and clerics against the revolutionary state. The Zacapu communities remained profoundly religious after the loss of their communal lands, in terms of the beliefs and practices of the majority of their inhabitants, but religiosity became a source of intracommunity violence, symbolizing divergent responses to the state-building activities of the new revolutionary state, rather than local identity and solidarity.

The Agrarista Movement in Zacapu

The Zacapu communities experienced the early years of the Mexican Revolution in much the same way as countless other places in Michoacán. A few individuals joined forces with revolutionary bands operating outside the region, as was the case with Juan Cruz de la Cruz of Tarejero, who fought with the Maderistas under Salvador Escalante, and Joaquín de la Cruz of Naranja, who, as a Carrancista, fought the Huertistas alongside Miguel de la Trinidad Regalado of Atacheo (Guzmán Avila 1986; Friedrich 1977). Some of the region's landowners joined the ranks

of Michoacán's "last-minute revolutionaries," their political allegiances shifting with the changing fortunes of Madero, Huerta, Villa, and Carranza. As the Naranja agrarista leaders would later write of Alfredo and Eduardo Noriega: "They have always been against honorable revolutionaries: they were Villistas against Carranza, and before that Huertistas against Madero. The nephew, Ruiz Noriega, who was a high-level Villista, brought people to oust the Carrancistas from the Hacienda— later they were Carrancistas against Obregón . . . and today they are plotting and just waiting to aid some other subversion, with the object, no doubt, of saving the hacienda."[34] For most of the region's residents, however, the early years of the revolution brought only the occasional attack by armed groups calling themselves Carrancistas, Zapatistas, or Villistas, compounded by fears of the great brutalities inflicted by the bandit gang of José Inés Chávez García.[35] There were a few notable incidents of violence motivated by agrarian grievances, but these remained sporadic and disorganized, detached from any revolutionary movements and only loosely connected to the decades-long struggle to recover dispossessed communal lands.[36]

Once the Carrancistas issued their Agrarian Reform Law in 1915, however, agrarian discontent in Zacapu began to assume a more organized form. In Naranja, the law provided Joaquín de la Cruz a new vehicle through which to pursue the community's land claims, an effort in which he had been engaged since the 1890s as the community's legal representative in matters dealing with the liberal reparto. Working with Miguel de la Trinidad Regalado in the short-lived Sociedad Unificadora de los Pueblos de la Raza Indígena, Joaquín de la Cruz continued to represent Naranja until his assassination in 1919 by bodyguards bribed by Alfredo and Eduardo Noriega (Friedrich 1977: 52–56). After his death, a second generation of agrarian leaders emerged, including Primo Tapia de la Cruz, Juan Gochi de la Cruz, and Crispín Serrato, all descendants of Ambrosio de la Cruz. In Tarejero, Tiríndaro, and Zacapu, this younger generation of leaders emerged a few years earlier. Under the leadership of Juan Cruz de la Cruz, Severo Espinosa, and Ramón Aguilar respectively, these communities formed agrarian committees and submitted petitions for the restitution of their communal lands in 1915.

Agrarian officials transmitted the petitions of Tarejero and Tiríndaro as dotaciones rather than restitutions, on the grounds that neither community could prove, as required by law, both legal ownership and illegal dispossession of the land in question.[37] Naranja's first recorded petition,

submitted in 1921, was also for a dotación.[38] Zacapu was a somewhat different case: given the amount of documentation submitted by both sides as to the ownership of the land and the means through which the community lost control of it, the case proceeded as restitution until 1921, at which point the state-level Local Agrarian Commission recommended that Zacapu be granted a dotación, without ever formally terminating its petition for a restitution.[39]

In contrast to other communities in Michoacán, the Zacapu agraristas did not continue to press for restitutions, which would have recognized the validity of their prior land claims, in place of dotaciones, which did not. Perhaps this was because the ejidos created through the dotaciones consisted almost exclusively of former marshlands, much of the land taken from the haciendas of Alfredo and Eduardo Noriega. Although the Zacapu communities had lost cultivated land, pasture, and woodlands over the course of centuries, the agraristas of the 1920s, in recounting their grievances with the landlords of the region, focused almost exclusively on the powerful and much-hated Noriega brothers and the more recent dispossession of their communal lands in the Zacapu marshes. The drainage project, the agraristas recalled, could only be carried out with the assistance of federal forces and hacienda white guards, who "stifled and smothered the clamor of the poor indigenous people of the region, so constantly and perseveringly had we opposed the dispossession of our lands through concessions of the Porfirian government to foreign companies." In 1896, they continued, the year the Noriegas received the federal concession for the drainage project, "there began the period of hatred toward the Noriegas . . . stemming from the fact that their properties have been formed by means of bayonets and the violent dispossession of our villages; and they have been sustained in the same way up until now."[40]

When their ally Francisco Múgica assumed the governor's office in 1920, the Zacapu agraristas were able to oust local mestizo elites, gaining control over local political offices and, more important, the arms of the local defense forces. With Múgica's support, they then used their new political and military power to press their land claims against neighboring landowners who, in turn, employed federal troops and private guards against them. In October 1921, for example, 20 federal soldiers entered Tiríndaro, searching for the agrarista members of the local defense force. Forewarned, the agraristas had already left the community, and the frustrated soldiers "[took] out their wrath on the defenseless

families of the civil defense members." Irene Miguel de Espinosa, the wife of Félix Espinosa, was briefly incarcerated, while soldiers searched her home, and that of her brother-in-law Severo, seizing documents related to the community's agrarian reform petition. According to Félix Espinosa, the soldiers were accompanied by the municipal president of Zacapu, who identified the relevant houses, and "some enemy neighbors of this peaceful and honorable town."[41] Naranja suffered similar attacks by federal soldiers during the same time period.[42] As Jesús Corral, then secretary of the state-level Local Agrarian Commission, put it in a letter to Obregón, federal attacks on the local defense forces "leave the impression that the federal forces are aiding the hacendados against the indigenous people," because "disarming the groups leaves them at the mercy of forces hired by the hacendados."[43]

In one of his last acts as governor, in the midst of the military rebellion through which he lost power, Múgica signed acts granting provisional possession of ejidos to the communities of Tiríndaro, Tarejero, and Naranja.[44] Tiríndaro was granted 690 hectares, 50 of which were to be expropriated from El Cortijo, its long-standing partner in litigation, and 640 from Cantabria, the hacienda created by Alfredo and Eduardo Noriega through the drainage of the Zacapu marshlands. Tarejero, with its smaller population, received 450 hectares, all former marshland, 200 hectares to come from Bellas Fuentes, 200 from Cantabria, and 50 from El Cortijo. Naranja, finally, was allocated 540 hectares, 300 from the Cantabria marshlands.[45] Zacapu's provisional possession was delayed until 1924, in part because of the extent of the documentation presented by both sides, and in part because it had the political status of town (villa) and hence was technically ineligible to receive land under the prevailing agrarian code.[46] None of the communities was able to take possession of the ejidos in 1921, however, because the affected landowners immediately obtained legal injunctions (amparos) preventing them from doing so, setting off several years of violent conflict between the agraristas and the landowners and their allies.

Múgica's loss of power affected his agrarista allies as well: in Naranja, for example, J. Natividad Torres regained control of the local defense force, leaving the agraristas unarmed and all the more vulnerable to attacks by federal soldiers and hacienda guards. The conservative revival was short-lived, however, even though the Mugiquistas failed to regain power at the state level. In July 1923, Naranja's mestizo jefe de tenencia reported an "uprising" by Juan Manuel Gochi, Eleuterio Serrato, and

Herculano Gochi, who, to the cry of "Viva Múgica," fired pistols first into the air and then at the jefe. The latter survived to tell the tale, but the widely despised J. Natividad Torres did not. Similar incidents occurred in Tiríndaro around the same time.[47]

These conflicts over local political power did not simply reflect class or ethnic lines. Local mestizo elites certainly opposed the agraristas, as did many poor mestizos who worked for their better-off relatives or on neighboring haciendas. But many poor mestizos also supported the agrarista movement, while landless Purépecha comuneros opposed it. Some of this opposition might be attributed to the ideological dominance of landlord and clergy. Father Trinidad Cruz, the parish priest of Zacapu, certainly lost few opportunities to condemn the agraristas to eternal hellfire from the pulpit. As an agrarista resident of Zacapu recalled in 1984: "The priests persecuted and condemned us. There was one in particular: Trinidad Cruz, who in his sermons said that he who seized [agarrar] land was condemned. On one occasion, when some stubble in the fields was being burned, he said this is what would happen to those who accepted land[.]"[48]

Popular opposition to the Zacapu agrarista movement, however, was also a product of the extreme anticlericalism of the agrarista peasants themselves, and of their allies among revolutionary elites. Joaquín de la Cruz, as Friedrich (1977: 56) points out, was highly respected by both conservative Catholics and radical agrarians, whereas the anticlerical actions of agrarista leaders such as Primo Tapia and Severo Espinosa continued to divide communities for decades after the events of the 1920s. In Naranja, at some point in 1923, agraristas seized the church, confiscated its property, and used the building to hold their meetings. Severo Espinosa, as was typically the case, accomplished much the same thing with a great deal more brutality: under his leadership, the Tiríndaro agraristas stormed the church, killed five residents who happened to be inside it, desecrated sacred objects, and then proceeded to break into the homes of five "fanatics," seizing their bibles and religious images. Much to the dismay of the majority of the comuneros, there were no priests left to perform the sacraments in Naranja, Tiríndaro, or Tarejero by the end of 1923 (Friedrich 1977: 120–21).

The delahuertista rebellion of 1923 through 1924 provided new opportunities for the agraristas to attack their enemies and consolidate their hold on local political and military power. Backing Obregón against de la Huerta, Governor Sidronio Sánchez Pineda was forced to

call upon the military support of the state's organized agraristas. Such support was not immediately forthcoming in Zacapu: de la Huerta had been one of Múgica's most ardent supporters in the latter's conflict with Obregón, and, given that half of the federal army had joined the rebellion, it was by no means clear who would emerge the victor. In early 1924, the Zacapu agraristas struck a deal with the delahuertistas who, at that point, occupied Morelia; supplied with arms, Primo Tapia and about 100 others were sent to the Cañada de los Once Pueblos to fight the agraristas of that region. Somewhere along the way, Tapia and the other leaders decided to place their bets with Obregón and Calles once more, and instead of going to the Cañada, headed home to use the arms against their own political enemies. On 2 February 1924, the agraristas staged an attack on the "Catholics" of Tiríndaro, summarily executing 15 men who had surrendered after the battle had been won. Referring to these events, Primo Tapia, Crispín Serrato, and Tomás Cruz of Naranja declared:

> In all of the communities surrounding Cantabria, the Noriegas have people who defend their interests and men whose sole job it is to sow discord among the workers, such as one Dr. Dolores Torres, in Naranja, the family doctor of the Noriegas; one Miguel Mercado in Tarejero; one Ramón Chávez and Cipriano Baltazar in Tiríndaro, and the wicked Trinidad Cruz, parish priest of Zacapu. . . . Thanks to the tenacious opposition that the Noriega *latifundistas* and the clergy encountered in the region, in the persons of our leaders who have never backed away in the face of the powerful and numerous forces of the enemy, as was the case in Tiríndaro last February, the REACTION bit the dust in defeat.[49]

Conflicts between agraristas and Catholics in Naranja were more violent yet. With the end of the delahuertista rebellion, the agraristas turned their attention to their opponents within the community, "killing by ambush, dragging men from their houses by night, and robbing the 'reactionaries' by collecting a civic tax at gun-point. Occasionally the female relatives of enemies were violated" (Friedrich 1977: 114). In the context of this violence, some 100 families were forced to leave Naranja. Many were allowed to return eventually, on the condition that they sign a second agrarian census and pay a "fine" of 10 to 30 pesos, the prevailing daily minimum wage being 1 peso at the time. About half of the families never returned to Naranja, however, taking up residence in the

town of Zacapu or the neighboring Purépecha village of Cherán. As Primo Tapia put it after the defeat of the political Catholics in 1924, "I succeeded in reuniting the town, except for two or three who don't count, and an armistice was written up. I hold the town united" (Friedrich 1977: 114).[50]

The agraristas of Naranja, Tiríndaro, and Tarejero received definitive possession of their ejidos in presidential resolutions of 20 February 1924, at the height of the violence within the communities and just as the delahuertista rebellion was coming to an end. The injunctions obtained earlier by the landowners were not overturned until April 1925, however, and so the status of the land remained in question, at least in the minds of the affected landowners, who continued to harass and repress the agrarista peasants with assistance from the federal military. In May 1924, Alfredo and Eduardo Noriega employed federal troops to oust peasants from Cantabria lands they had been granted in the presidential resolution. Although the peasants regained possession of the property with the assistance of the state CNA delegate and the *procurador de los pueblos,* federal soldiers and hacienda guards returned in December with trucks provided by the Noriega brothers to cart off the harvested corn crop. In the course of doing so, they incarcerated several agraristas; hanged two local officials, Andrés Ramírez and Raymundo Espinosa, cutting them down just before they died; and beat Valentina Neves, María de la Cruz, María Salud Morano, Isadora Serrato, and Andrea de la Cruz, all wives of agrarista leaders.[51]

The landowners' injunctions were finally overturned in April 1925, thus granting the agraristas full legal rights to the ejidos obtained through the presidential resolutions of the previous year. Six months later, the agraristas of Zacapu finally received definitive possession of their ejido as well, prompting Ramón Aguilar to pledge their full support and assistance to President Calles, whenever he might need it: "The pueblo, together with all of the rural workers, send you the most intense gratitude, and are ready to defend, within the revolutionary laws that rule us in the country of our magna carta, the ideals for which we have been struggling and for which we will continue to struggle until we obtain the complete improvement of all the working classes, socialists and workers."[52] Inviting Calles a few days later to visit the ejido, Aguilar wrote that the agrarian reform had freed the communities from "the ignominies of the landowners"; without it, they would have remained "the slaves of the capitalists, . . . living in the most frightening misery,

because of the marked oppression that they exercised over the peasant class."[53]

Anticlericalism continued to dominate local politics after the Zacapu communities received definitive possession of their ejidos. This was particularly true in Tiríndaro, where Severo Espinosa used anticlericalism as a vehicle through which to set himself up as a local political boss (*cacique*). Upon receiving possession of the ejido, Espinosa required that all peasants who wanted access to the land had to renounce the Church. Only 108 were willing to do so, leaving close to 300 families, designated as beneficiaries in the presidential resolution, without land. Having deprived so many Catholic families of the land they should have received, Espinosa maintained his hold on power with the utmost brutality. In 1929, for example, he and several followers massacred an entire "Catholic" family with machetes, including the pregnant mother and her two small children (Friedrich 1986: 146). And throughout his tenure as a local cacique, Espinosa refused to allow religious worship in Tiríndaro. Writing in the context of a devastating local epidemic in 1930, Tiríndaro residents, on behalf of "372 women and a greater number of children," directed themselves to the President of the Republic: "We lament the great epidemic that has attacked our town—fever, smallpox, and scarlet fever. And we lack a priest to perform last rites for those who are dying because of this epidemic, because the Agrarista Party of this place opposes it. We direct ourselves to you, Señor President, with all due respect, asking that justice be made to shine in our town . . . here, the majority are believers."[54]

When the cristero rebellion broke out in Michoacán in 1927, the agraristas of the Zacapu region provided a significant number of the irregular troops used to supplement the federal army. Juan Gochi, of the Naranja Gochi family, led a regional militia of some 300 men to fight the cristeros in the Tierra Caliente; 400 men from the region later fought in Jalisco. Very few peasants from the region participated as rebels in the cristiada, regardless of their religiosity or their opposition to agrarista anticlericalism. The one rather remarkable exception was Ramón Aguilar, the agrarista leader from Zacapu who, having passionately pledged his assistance to Calles upon receiving title to the Zacapu ejido in 1925, joined the cristero rebellion with 27 other men from the region in mid-1927. There are various accounts of why he became a cristero leader, none of them neutral. Some say he broke with Primo Tapia because of the latter's vacillation during the delahuertista rebellion, and with the

revolutionary state more generally due to the lack of support given to ejidatarios once the land had been delivered. Others say he stole ejido funds, and joined the cristeros in order to avoid prosecution by the authorities (see Olivera Sedano 1996, 1970a). Aguilar himself claimed that federal soldiers stationed at Cantabria stole the money, proceeds from the corn crop which had been set aside to pay taxes.[55] Whatever his motivation for joining the cristero rebellion, it was apparently not religious. The League military leader Degollado y Guízar writes of an encounter with Aguilar and his followers in the headquarters of cristero leader Maximiliano Barragán in the sierra around Cotija in May of 1927. According to Degollado y Guízar, "[Aguilar] was an agrarista and because of difficulties with the people from the union he resolved to take up arms together with the other compañeros." During this meeting, a chaplain offered to hear confessions:

> Captain Aguilar came over to me and asked me:
> "What, is confession obligatory?"
> "No," I answered. "Confession, if it is not done voluntarily and out of regret for your sins isn't worth anything, because it wouldn't have the right effect."
> "In that case I won't confess," he answered, "I don't believe in it."
> (Degollado y Guízar 1957: 49)

Aguilar's rebellion against the revolutionary regime lasted almost 10 years: he took part in the "second cristiada," a far less organized and smaller-scale set of rebellions that occurred in many of the same regions of the center-west as the first cristiada, in response to the "socialist education" programs of President Lázaro Cárdenas.[56]

In the Purépecha communities of the Zacapu region, efforts by revolutionary elites to consolidate the authority of the state at the local level meshed with local aspirations to recover lost lands and dislodge mestizo elites, landowners, and the clergy from positions of power and authority, thus producing one of the state's strongest and longest-lasting agrarista movements. These local aspirations, in turn, were the product of prior legacies of agrarian and political conflict, through which the Zacapu communities gradually lost their communal lands to neighboring landowners, and, in the process, witnessed the destruction of local institutions through which religious practice was organized and political power allocated and exercised. State makers found ready allies in the descendants of the members of the cabildo who had lost political power

in the course of the transformations that occurred in the late nineteenth and early twentieth centuries. Even as they responded to popular aspirations in Zacapu, revolutionary anticlericalism and the agrarian reform program generated popular resistance as well. Agrarista leaders such as Primo Tapia and Severo Espinosa employed the anticlerical rhetoric and practices of their Mugiquista allies in order to attack the alliance between the region's landowners and the clergy, and, in the process, alienated and attacked many of their fellow peasants as well, defining them as fanatical and reactionary Catholics. These identities of Catholic and agrarista, forged in the conflicts of anticlericalism and agrarian reform in the 1920s, continued to dominate factional conflict well into the 1930s.

In contrast to Zacapu, many of the Purépecha communities in the highlands around Uruapan entered the twentieth century having preserved, to varying degrees, the central institutions which regulated community life: the communal property regime, the cargo system and cofradías, and the cabildo. Whereas the descendants of traditional Purépecha elders led the agrarista movement of Zacapu, it was the traditional authorities themselves in the highlands that led the resistance to state intervention in community life. The predominantly Catholic communities of the highlands are the subject of the next chapter.

6 * Catholics, *Cristeros,* and *Agraristas*
in the Purépecha Highlands

In 1943, the volcano of Paricutín erupted, its lava gradually covering the highland communities of San Juan Parangaricutiro and Paricutín. Today, only the church steeple of old San Juan is visible, rising above the black volcanic rock and covered with graffiti. Enemies since the colonial period, the residents of these two Purépecha communities had quite different explanations for the eruption of the volcano: according to the people of San Juan Parangaricutiro, "the fault lay with the inhabitants of Paricutín, for being agraristas, sacrilegious, and without fear of God"; in Paricutín, it was argued that God wanted to stop the sponsorship of religious fiestas, because they only served to impoverish the peasantry.[1] Once the town sites of both communities were reconstructed elsewhere in the highlands, San Juan and Paricutín resumed the centuries-long border conflict that was such an integral part of local identities: to be of San Juan Parangaricutiro was to be an enemy of Paricutín and vice versa. As Celedonio Gutiérrez, a resident of Nuevo San Juan put it, "with Paricutín, the people of San Juan have always been like cats and dogs."[2] This intercommunity dispute explains, in part, why residents of San Juan Parangaricutiro identified themselves as Catholics and rebelled against the new revolutionary state as cristeros, while residents of Paricutín identified as agraristas, and fought alongside the federal army during the cristiada. The land claimed by Paricutín in the restitution petition submitted in 1916 under the revolutionary agrarian reform program was that which it had unsuccessfully contested with San Juan Parangaricutiro over a period of several hundred years.

San Juan Parangaricutiro's participation in the cristero rebellion was also a product of a more recent conflict between a majority of the com-

munity's residents and state officials, both Porfirian and revolutionary. In contrast to the Zacapu region, San Juan Parangaricutiro, along with a number of other highland communities, managed to resist the complete implementation of the nineteenth-century liberal reform law, retaining its substantial holdings in the mountainous woodlands and some of its cultivated land under communal title and the control of the cabildo. Throughout the last two decades of the Porfiriato, local mestizo elites within the community appropriated small tracts of cultivated land under private title, but unlike their counterparts in Zacapu, they lacked powerful external allies among state officials or outside landowners. Thus they were limited in the extent to which they could claim land for themselves or alienate it outside the community. On the eve of the revolution, therefore, much of San Juan's landed base and its institutions of politico-religious authority were essentially intact. Although mestizo elites dominated the official political offices of the municipal government (*ayuntamiento*), much de facto political power remained vested in the cabildo, which defined and allocated use rights to communal property, oversaw the organization of religious practice through the distribution of the cargos, and mediated disputes within the community and between it and its neighbors. Furthermore, religious practice, particularly the cult of the Lord of the Miracles, remained a strong and vital source of community identity and solidarity, linking San Juan Parangaricutiro to other Purépecha communities throughout Michoacán and serving as the vehicle through which communal consensus was expressed in conflicts with outsiders.

Having survived the Porfiriato, San Juan Parangaricutiro then confronted the revolutionary state. In the Zacapu region, revolutionary agrarianism and anticlericalism responded, at least in part, to popular needs and aspirations, allowing agrarista peasants to acquire land and displace local elites allied with the region's most powerful landowners. Agrarian conflicts in the highlands, in contrast, were only exacerbated by the revolutionary agrarian reform program, given that they entailed disputes within and between communities, rather than disputes between communities and haciendas. Seeking out allies at the local level, state officials nevertheless encouraged the formation of agrarian movements in the region, encouraging agrarista peasants to lay claim to communal property or to the smallholdings of their better-off neighbors. Revolutionary anticlericalism, meanwhile, served as a vehicle through which

agrarista peasants undercut the power of the politico-religious authorities of the cabildo. Given the centrality of religious practice in the highlands, and its close links to both communal land claims and local identity, anticlericalism was also perceived as an attack on the communities themselves and on local popular cultures, rather than as a conflict between the Catholic Church and the new revolutionary state. Whereas the descendants of powerful cabildo members such as Ambrosio de la Cruz led the agrarista movements of the Zacapu region, it was a member of the cabildo itself, Juan Mincítar, who led popular resistance to the revolutionary state in San Juan Parangaricutiro. Furthermore, although local mestizo elites in Zacapu allied themselves with large landowners in opposition to the revolutionary agrarian reform program, their counterparts in the highlands often allied themselves with revolutionary authorities, assuming the role of the agrarista leadership and, with their newfound political and military power, appropriating communal resources for themselves.

The construction of agrarista and Catholic identities began in the 1920s throughout the highlands: political factions explicitly referred to themselves and to each other in these mutually exclusive terms. Substantial Catholic factions existed in almost all of the region's communities, but only the residents of San Juan Parangaricutiro rebelled en masse during the cristiada. Elsewhere, agrarista attacks on traditional institutions and authorities did not peak until the presidential administration of Lázaro Cárdenas in the 1930s, at which point Catholic resistance to the state and its local allies was channeled through the *sinarquista* ("with order") movement. Only San Juan Parangaricutiro experienced a dual and simultaneous attack on its landed base and its religious practices and institutions in the 1920s, when the mestizo Anguiano and Equihua families allied themselves with revolutionary authorities, and, as the self-proclaimed agrarista leadership in the community, monopolized large tracts of communal property under private title, something they had been unable to do throughout the course of the Porfiriato. It was Hermenegildo Anguiano and his brother-in-law Espiridión Equihua who led the agrarista peasants recruited from Paricutín and Corupo against the cristeros of San Juan Parangaricutiro.

This chapter begins with an exploration of the relationship between land claims, religious practice, and community identity in San Juan Parangaricutiro, as expressed through local histories dealing with the appearance of the Virgin of the Immaculate Conception and the Lord of the

Miracles in the community. It then turns to an analysis of the liberal reparto in the region: in the highlands, state efforts to privatize communal lands generated and exacerbated long-standing conflicts between communities and led to increasing social differentiation and factional conflict within communities. As in Zacapu, the outcomes of these conflicts are critical in understanding the emergence and construction of agrarista and Catholic political identities in the 1920s, the subject of the third section. The chapter concludes with a brief overview of San Juan Parangaricutiro's ongoing attempts to gain state recognition of its communal land holdings after the cristiada, a struggle it finally won in 1991 when, through a presidential resolution granting the "Recognition and Titling of Communal Property," the state acknowledged the San Juan Parangaricutiro comuneros' claim to more than 14,000 hectares of land.

Land, Religion, and Community Identity in San Juan Parangaricutiro

At some point in the mid-sixteenth century, a member of the secular clergy, referred to in historical accounts as the "bachiller Fuenllana," arrived in the Itzcuaro valley in the central highlands, charged by Don Vasco de Quiroga, the bishop of Michoacán (1538–65), with the conversion of souls in the newly created parish of Santa Ana Tzirosto (later Zirosto). Like his Franciscan and Augustinian counterparts elsewhere in Michoacán, the bachiller Fuenllana proceeded to establish new communities through the congregation of people living in dispersed settlements, assigning each locale a patron saint and an economic specialization, and overseeing the construction of churches and hospitals.[3] As Celedonio Gutiérrez (1972: 9), a resident of Nuevo San Juan, recounts:

> The friars, who were in charge of founding these towns, began with the town of Uruapan, dividing it into several barrios each with a chapel and a saint who would be honored when the feast day arrived. . . . They did the same thing in the Sierra. In San Juan Parangaricutiro they assigned San Juan as patron, and the destined work of the Indians was to make blankets. Angahuan was given Santiago as patron and the destiny of tilling the soil. Corupo had San Francisco as patron and its people were designated as musicians and hat makers. Zirosto was given Santa María and the destiny of being musicians and other things.[4]

The Purépechas who formed San Juan Parangaricutiro most likely lived in a number of smaller settlements scattered throughout the highlands above the Itzcuaro valley prior to their congregation, although local accounts most often refer only to a site called Pantzingo (also known as Pueblo Viejo). Many twentieth-century residents of San Juan Parangaricutiro consider the congregation and conversion of their ancestors to be the starting point of their history: in relating the work of clergy, Gutiérrez refers to the "conquest of the brutish Indians" as if they were another people altogether; others say the residents of Pantzingo were "people without reason" who "lived like animals in caves without knowledge of God."[5] But Pantzingo remains an important source of both community identity and factional conflict: local histories combine a religious miracle with a land claim in such a way as to demonstrate what Moheno (1985: 16) means when he writes that "the rural culture that was created in the world of San Juan Parangaricutiro did not separate material life and religious life, or work and religious beliefs."

According to oral histories, a sixteenth-century peasant from the newly created community of San Juan Parangaricutiro returned to the abandoned settlement in Pantzingo to collect wood. As he did so, the Virgin of the Immaculate Conception appeared to him, standing next to a spring. The peasant took the image of the Virgin back to San Juan and built a chapel for her, but she refused to stay, returning to Pantzingo each and every time the residents of San Juan brought her back to her chapel. Finally the people begged the Virgin to stay in San Juan, and she agreed to do so, as long as they promised to always bring her water from the sacred spring at Pantzingo. This, then, was the account of San Juan Parangaricutiro residents as to the origins of the community's first cofradía, that dedicated to the Virgin of the Immaculate Conception: "According to them, it was necessary to create the mayordomías to take care of and administer the cofradía with the end of serving and complying with the wishes of the Virgin; if it were not so, she would have abandoned them once more." The cult of the Virgin entailed a claim to the lands around Pantzingo, which the residents of San Juan Parangaricutiro had occupied before the congregation: "With the legend was born the commitment never to forget those lands in which their roots were to be found" (Plá 1989: 274). Among the lands appropriated by mestizo elites at the end of the nineteenth century were those located in Pantzingo, claimed as private property by members of the Anguiano and Ortiz families.[6]

If the Virgin of the Immaculate Conception had to be convinced to stay in San Juan Parangaricutiro, the Lord of the Miracles chose the community himself and refused to leave. According to the history related by Nuevo San Juan resident Jesús Saldaña to Plá (1989: 275–76), a muleteer arrived in San Juan Parangaricutiro and was given lodging by a peasant named Maricho, who was unable to walk. The next day, the muleteer reloaded his cargo, but found that two small boxes had become so heavy that he was unable to lift them. So he left them with Maricho, saying that he would return for them. But the muleteer did not return, and Maricho, a year later, opened the boxes, having first asked permission from the cabildo. Inside, he found two icons of Christ, their beauty so great that he was reported to have cried, "little Christ, if you cure me I will dance for you." Maricho was immediately cured, and he danced before the icons. Maricho kept the smaller of the two icons in a chapel in his house, while the other one was moved to the church, where people prayed for favors that were granted only if they danced before it.[7] It was this icon that became known as the Lord of the Miracles, far surpassing San Juan Parangaricutiro's patron saint as an object of reverence and source of solidarity and identity.[8]

The Lord of the Miracles was also a symbol of a broader ethnic identity: each year, on 14 September, thousands of Purépechas from communities throughout the highlands and beyond came to San Juan Parangaricutiro to celebrate its feast day, participate in the regional market, and partake of various types of entertainment. Lumholtz (1902: 377), who visited San Juan in 1895, describes the event with some dismay, noting what he considered to be an idolatrous form of worship, and the prevalence of alcohol, gambling, and other profit-making activities: "Prices of the necessities of life were four times as high as before, to the great delight of the natives. Women who were the happy possessors of cows combined to make a corner in milk and manipulated the market with the cleverness of experienced stockbrokers. A troop of soldiers arrived to guard public safety, for fights and homicides must be expected, and a good deal of thieving and swindling was going on all the time."

As important as the market and the entertainment were, however, the main point of the day was to express reverence for the Lord of the Miracles, dancing before the icon as tradition dictated and requesting that special favors be granted. An "endless file of humanity" came to the church, Lumholtz (1902: 377–78) writes, the poor on their knees and

the wealthy, on occasion, accompanied by musical bands. Upon entering the church himself, Lumholtz continues:

> I was not a little surprised to find [it] chockful of people dancing la danza up and down with lighted tapers. I could only dimly perceive them in the dense cloud of dust in which they were enveloped, and the hundreds and hundreds of flickering lights seemed to be so many will-o'-the-wisps. There must have been upwards of a thousand persons in that church, endeavouring to reach the image on the high altar, and then retreating dancing backward. To complete the tour took about an hour, on account of the denseness of the crowd, but nevertheless there were many whose religious zeal prompted them to repeat the ceremony several times.

According to the accounts of San Juan Parangaricutiro peasants, worship of the Lord of the Miracles distinguished Purépechas from non-Purépechas, and popular religious practice from the sacraments of the Catholic Church. San Juan Parangaricutiro's Christ did not perform his miracles before Spaniards or mestizos; nor did he do so in front of the clergy, unless the latter attempted to replace him with more acceptable objects and forms of worship (Plá 1989). Lumholtz (1902: 383) recounts one version of an encounter between the Lord of the Miracles and a priest who banned dancing before the icon:

> The story goes that one padre made up his mind to put an end to this pagan mode of worship, and the people coming to the church found its doors locked. Before daybreak, nevertheless, the priest was awakened by his sacristan with news that the dancing was going on in spite of him. The two repaired to the church, where to their consternation they perceived hundreds of little lights dancing. The dust was there too and they heard the noise of shuffling feet, but they could see no people. At this the padre became frightened and ordered the church-doors to be thrown open. And since then no padre has been able to stop the dancing, nor will there ever be one who can do it the people declare.

Well after the revolution, community consensus was still expressed through the actions and decisions attributed to the Lord of the Miracles (Plá 1989). According to local accounts, for example, it was the Lord of the Miracles, rather than state agrarian authorities, who chose the com-

munity's new town site after old San Juan was covered with lava from the volcano of Paricutín, in the process defying a bishop, several priests, and ex-president Lázaro Cárdenas.

Throughout the colonial period and the first century of independence, religious practice remained firmly intertwined with property rights and local political authority in San Juan Parangaricutiro, through the institutions of the cabildo, the cargo system and cofradías, and the communal property regime. The cabildo, under the leadership of the *mandón,* periodically redistributed use rights to the community's cultivated lands, and regulated access to and exploitation of the communal woodlands and pastures.[9] The cabildo also allocated the cargo positions through which individual families fulfilled civil obligations and organized the cult of the saints. Religious practice was further organized and financed through the cofradías, in which many members of the community participated. The most important was that of the Virgin of the Immaculate Conception, which ran the hospital, caring for the sick as well as organizing the cult of the Virgin. The hospital cofradía was relatively wealthy at the end of the colonial period: according to a royal inspector, it owned 25 cows and 27 sheep, which grazed on communal lands, and a treasury of some 456 pesos. The same inspector noted that San Juan Parangaricutiro had enough communal property to provide arable lands for its members' use, to finance a school, and to meet civil expenses (Bravo Ugarte 1960: 91–92).

In contrast to their counterparts in the Zacapu region, the highland communities faced little pressure from expanding haciendas, either during or after the colonial period. With little potential for large-scale agricultural production and no mineral wealth, few Spaniards or mestizos arrived in the region to lay claim to communal resources. As Fray Diego Muñoz wrote in 1603: "These were lands only for the Indians who were born there and experienced in using them . . . the Spaniards own very little because of the harsh weather, the coldest in Michoacán, and because the vegetation is rough and useless for livestock" (cited in Aguirre Beltrán 1952: 86). By the end of the colonial period, there were but 12 "families of reason" in San Juan Parangaricutiro, as compared to 188 Purépecha families. Both groups were engaged in similar economic activities: subsistence agriculture, muleteering, and the production of cotton bedspreads and blankets. The Spanish and mestizo population of San Juan's immediate neighbors was even smaller yet: there were only

two non-Purépecha families in San Francisco Corupo and none at all in San Felipe de los Herreros, Santiago Angahuan, and San Salvador Paricutín (Bravo Ugarte 1960: 88–93).

Although there was little conflict between the highland communities and external landowners, boundary disputes between communities were extremely common, due in large part to the vagueness and inconsistency of colonial land titles. These disputes were often exacerbated, rather than resolved, by the periodic royal decrees that required the communities (and other landowners) to apply and pay for títulos de composición. In 1715, San Juan Parangaricutiro applied for a composición in hopes of gaining control over lands in dispute with the neighboring (and politically subordinate) communities of Paricutín and Angahuan. Colonial authorities supported San Juan Parangaricutiro's claims against its two neighbors in a title issued in 1720, but the decision did little to resolve the conflict between the communities. San Juan Parangaricutiro sought and received another composición in the 1760s, which reaffirmed the boundaries established in the 1720 decision. Paricutín continued to invade the land awarded to San Juan Parangaricutiro, however, and in a court case decided in 1786, colonial authorities once more decided in favor of San Juan, ordering Paricutín to leave the disputed lands and to abstain from further invasions.[10]

Elsewhere in the highlands, the community of Quincio, claiming to hold the oldest title in what became the state of Michoacán, was embroiled in a long-standing dispute with the community of Paracho.[11] San Bartolo Uren claimed lands held by Cherán, Tanaco, and Tanaquillo.[12] Nahuatzen, in the restitution petition submitted under the revolutionary agrarian reform program, argued that the community of San Angel Zurumucapio had invaded its communal lands over the course of the previous 400 years; San Angel, in turn, accused Nahuatzen of similar dispossessions.[13] Nahuatzen, Cherán, and Arantepacaura, meanwhile, were engaged in a boundary dispute of such duration and complexity that an official of the Ministry of Government, Gabriel Avila, attempted to resolve it in 1907 by suggesting that the three communities simply divide up the contested land. None of the communities had valid titles, Avila wrote: that of Cherán, ostensibly signed by Hernán Cortés in 1533, was a clear forgery, while Arantepacuara offered a royal title dated 1519, "an epoch in which the conquest of Mexico had not yet been undertaken."[14] All of these disputes, and many others, were exacerbated in the course of conflicts over the nineteenth-century liberal reparto, which,

like the composiciones of the colonial era and the revolutionary agrarian reform of the twentieth century, threatened to recognize one community's claim to disputed land at the expense of another.

The Liberal Reparto in San Juan Parangaricutiro

State officials convened a meeting in San Juan Parangaricutiro in early 1869, to secure the agreement of the community to the liberal land reform and to elect the commission charged with the preparation and distribution of private titles to those individuals with rights to communal property. Having had the relevant laws "explained to them in intelligible words," the residents of San Juan Parangaricutiro discussed the matter for some three days, and finally declared themselves to be "convinced of the benefits bestowed upon them by the Supreme Government" and therefore unopposed to the privatization of their communal lands. They did, however, request an extension of nine months, in order to resolve their many border disputes with neighboring communities.[15]

A few months later, legal representatives from San Juan Parangaricutiro and other highland communities requested an indefinite extension, employing, as was usual in this type of correspondence, formulaic expressions of respect for state authorities, and asserting the peasants' willingness to comply, eventually, with the terms of the law:

> If we were to heed only [the Indians'] wishes, we would ask that the legislature repeal this law which prohibits the existence of the communities and mandates the division of their property. There may be many reasons for such a request, but these have already been examined and rejected many times, it being determined that the reform is in the public interest, and in the private interests of the Indians. . . . [The Indians] respect this decision, and do not in any way wish to frustrate the aims of the legislation, and in spite of their desire to continue as communities, they have decided to request only a sufficient period of time to divide their lands in a beneficial way.[16]

Little, if anything, was done about the reparto in San Juan Parangaricutiro for another two decades, however, and the community continued to pay property taxes on undivided communal property. The archival record gives no indication of who made up the local privatization commission at this time, if, in fact, one existed at all. The cabildo continued to exercise de facto control over communal resources, and remained

opposed to their privatization, as evidenced in a letter written by a group of pro-reparto residents to the Uruapan district prefect, soliciting his assistance in the implementation of the reform:

> [T]he disorder and irregularities with which the elders of the community administer the property that belongs to all of us, obliges us, contrary to the opinions of the elders, to request that this High Office put into effect the laws and dispositions with respect to the division of communal property. . . . All of the efforts of the current government, and previous ones, to carry out the reparto have been dashed before the Oligarchy that the old ones called the cabildo exercise over the young.[17]

After the Terrenos Baldíos Law of 1894 was passed, state officials once more pressured the residents of San Juan Parangaricutiro to comply with the terms of the liberal land laws, and at this point, two factions emerged.[18] One consisted of local mestizo elites, most notably members of the Ortiz, Equihua, and Anguiano families, together with their allies within the Indian community. These mestizo elites already controlled the local political offices of the ayuntamiento, or municipal government, and enjoyed the unwavering support of the Uruapan district prefect. Their political power and connections allowed them to appropriate much of the cultivated land closest to the town site in the last quarter of the nineteenth century, although they often did not register this land as private property until shortly before or after the revolution.[19] With the support of the district prefect, they also managed to place close allies such as Luis and Felipe Cuara on the local privatization committee, with an eye toward acquiring control over the community's vast woodlands, through the various types of frauds and illegal sales so often made possible by the reparto process.[20] In contrast to their counterparts in Zacapu, however, the Ortiz, Equihua, and Anguiano families of San Juan did not have sufficient power or political connections to overcome the resistance of the majority of community members to the privatization of communal lands, particularly given the willingness of officials within the state Ministry of Government to investigate and mediate the conflicting claims of the two opposing groups.[21]

The complex role played by state officials in the course of the struggle over the liberal reparto is manifested in a legal dispute that began in 1895, when Gonzalo Chávez, as a resident of San Juan and member of the Indian community, claimed rights to the community's extensive

woodlands under the 1856 Lerdo Law, which specified that corporate property not claimed by its occupants within a specified period of time might be sold to whoever denounced it.[22] The denunciation had considerable support within the community, because many residents believed that it would provide a safe and legal title to the lands in question, protecting them from both mestizo residents of San Juan Parangaricutiro and the claims of neighboring communities without altering de facto communal control or customary usage. The pro-reparto faction, led by Felipe Cuara, an ally of the three mestizo families, adamantly opposed the denunciation and pushed for the implementation of the reform.[23] The denunciation was also immediately opposed by the Indian communities of San Lorenzo, Angahuan, and Paricutín, among others, since it included lands they disputed with San Juan Parangaricutiro.[24]

Elections for a new privatization commission were held in March 1896, possibly in response to the denunciation and the divisions it caused (and reflected) within the community. According to the municipal president, an ally of the mestizo families, "the denouncer Chávez has worried the Indians . . . it being said that the reparto is entirely contrary to the interests and well-being of the village." Chávez, he reported, had the support of 30 comuneros, while 81 supported Felipe Cuara's petition to proceed with the reparto.[25] The new commission consisted of Anastasio Anducho, Francisco Gallegos, Nicolás Anguiano, and Antonio Morales, all of whom were involved in the appropriation of communal lands at the end of the nineteenth century and in the first several decades of the twentieth.

State officials were quite aware of the motivation behind Chávez's denunciation, because he himself informed them that "the denunciation was not made with the object of benefiting himself, but rather in favor of the ex-community, with the objective of protecting the land from external ambitions."[26] A few even supported it, as long as Chávez was willing to agree to a set of conditions designed to protect community rights to the lands in question. As one Ministry of Government official wrote:

> It should be noted that in this case it would not be unsuitable to adjudicate the community's lands to Señor Gonzalo Chávez, as long as the Indians themselves want this to be done, in order to obtain a valid title that would protect the property and avoid the continual conflicts that arise as a result of the boundary disputes between neighboring villages, conflicts that cannot be resolved juridically, because

the communities, having been extinguished in legal terms, lack juridical standing.[27]

Faced with both the denunciation and the petition to proceed with the reparto, state officials were unsure as to how to proceed, and therefore sent the matter to the Ministry of Finance in Mexico City for clarification of the legal issues involved, particularly with respect to the question of who, if anyone, had the right to denounce communal land under the 1856 Lerdo Law.[28] The decision of the Ministry of Finance, made in the name of President Díaz, reveals something of the complex and often contradictory nature of the struggle over property rights during the Porfiriato. Communal lands, according to the ministry, were not subject to denunciation under the 1856 Lerdo Law. Although tenants had the right to purchase lands they rented from the communities, all unleased land was to be divided among the residents of the community, whether or not they had explicitly claimed it as occupants.[29] Thus although the 1894 Terrenos Baldíos Law had facilitated the alienation of undivided communal lands to speculators, surveying companies, and landowners, state officials at least sometimes continued to interpret the 1856 disentailment law in such a way as to protect the communities from denunciations, most often made by outsiders.[30]

The Ministry of Finance rendered its decision in 1900, denying Chávez's right to denounce communal land, given his status as a community member rather than as a tenant, and instructing the Ministry of Government in Morelia to proceed with the reparto in San Juan Parangaricutiro.[31] Faced with this setback, Chávez simply absconded with the legal documents, hiding from state officials for almost two years. After Chávez was finally found, a new privatization commission was chosen in San Juan, its members once more allies of the three leading mestizo families.[32] In spite of the support of the district prefect, however, the privatization commission was unable to carry out the reform, and the bulk of San Juan's communal holdings remained undivided on the eve of the revolution.

In his well-known history of San Juan Parangaricutiro, Moheno (1985) argues that mestizo elites controlled much of community life by the end of the nineteenth century, monopolizing communal land and political power, and legitimating their dominance through ritual kinship (compadrazgo) and participation in the cofradías that organized and sponsored religious practice. In this analysis, San Juan's Indian residents

were reduced to the status of dependent sharecroppers and laborers on their former communal lands, servile clients of their mestizo *patrones*. This picture, however, is contradicted by subsequent events in San Juan, many of them eloquently narrated and analyzed in Moheno's own work, as well as by archival evidence related to twentieth-century conflicts between self-identified comuneros seeking state confirmation of their communal holdings and smallholders claiming the same land as private property.[33]

Descendants of the Anguiano, Equihua, and Ortiz families and their allies would certainly claim, nearly a century later, that the reparto had indeed been carried out in San Juan, to the benefit of their parents and grandparents. In 1992, for example, Anselmo Martínez Angeles, Bertha Cuara Murguia, and Carolota Campoverde Anguiano informed President Carlos Salinas de Gortari that the land they claimed as their own was private property that had "originated in the legal and constitutional framework of 1856 to 1917." During this time, they continued, "the communities did not exist either in fact or in law, and we are descendants of the Indians and *parcioneros* [individuals who received title to privatized land under reparto] of the village buried by the volcano of Paricutín, whose smallholdings were acquired by our ancestors through the division ordered in accordance with the law of 1856, the [1857] Constitution, and all of the legal decrees of the period."[34] Prior to the revolution, however, the ownership of much of the community's cultivated land near the town site remained hotly contested: mestizo elites might claim it as private property, but they often had not registered it with the state as such, in part to avoid paying property taxes and in part because of the dubious legality of the appropriations. A 1907 map produced by state officials supported the comuneros' later claim that the reparto had never been carried out in San Juan Parangaricutiro, confirming that the community as such still owned a total of 21,106 hectares of land under corporate title, far more than had been recognized in two eighteenth-century títulos de composición.[35]

Furthermore, the majority faction within the community was able to prevent the three leading mestizo families from leasing the communal woodlands to a U.S. timber company in the years immediately preceding the revolution. In 1907, Luis Cuara, allied with the mestizo elites and at that time the community's designated legal representative, signed a rental contract with Santiago Slade, owner of several timber companies. According to the terms of the contract, Slade was granted the right to

extract timber from the woodlands over a 30-year period for a rent of 215,000 pesos, 8,000 of which were to be paid immediately to the community. San Juan comuneros were to retain the right to extract wood for domestic use and to graze their cattle on the land leased to Slade, but in contrast to previous agreements with other timber companies, they were prohibited from cultivating crops on cleared parcels in the woodlands.[36] Because of this violation of traditional usage, the majority of comuneros opposed the agreement arranged by the mestizo families, and they refused to either recognize its validity or to accept any part of the 8,000-peso down payment. The conflict between the two factions reached a peak in 1909, when the district prefect of Uruapan, a close ally of the mestizo families, ratified the contract over the objections of the majority. Over half of the houses in San Juan Parangaricutiro were burnt that year, in an unsuccessful attempt by the mestizos to force the community to accept the contract. In the end, the majority won, at least as far as Santiago Slade was concerned: the conflict ended some 8 to 10 years later when, as one resident of Nuevo San Juan put it, "the American decided to go back to his own country, without our ever knowing why" (Moheno 1985: 122).

The liberal land reform, though never fully implemented in San Juan Parangaricutiro, certainly increased agrarian and political conflict within the community. It also intensified border disputes between San Juan and its neighbors, particularly the community of Paricutín. In 1859, at the request of San Juan, state officials drew up a survey map to establish the boundaries between that community and Angahuan, Corupo, Zacán, Zirosto, Tancítaro, and Paricutín. With the exception of Zirosto and Angahuan, all of the communities formally agreed to respect the boundaries established by the 1859 survey. Border disputes continued unabated throughout the liberal and Porfirian eras, however, as communities attempted to include long-disputed land in the reparto (or related maneuvers) in order to consolidate their claims to it.[37] Thus the residents of San Lorenzo protested that some of their communal land was included in the denunciation made by Gonzalo Chávez, the land having been seized by San Juan Parangaricutiro peasants some time before.[38] In 1896, Rafael Urtiz, owner of the Rancho of Tierras Blancas, charged that his property, purchased from Paricutín two years earlier, was subject to continual invasions by San Juan Parangaricutiro comuneros, who came "in enormous gangs, and well armed, for which reason any reclamation was dangerous."[39] San Juan Parangaricutiro, in turn, claimed that Paricutín

had no right to sell the land in question, because it was part of San Juan Parangaricutiro's own communal property. Both communities routinely accused the other of invading and sometimes selling its land. None of these conflicts had been resolved by the time the revolutionary state arrived in the highlands in the 1920s. Rather, comuneros from different communities continued to fight them as agraristas and Catholics, finding new allies within the state and among counterelites.

The Construction of Political Identities in the Highlands: Agraristas, Catholics, and Cristeros

The revolution of 1910 to 1920 followed much the same course in the highlands as it did in the Zacapu region: soldiers marching under the banners of Carranza, Villa, and Zapata made the occasional appearance, as did the far more destructive bandits of José Inés Chávez García and other gangs. Cherán suffered the most from banditry, being all but burned to the ground on two occasions. Hundreds of residents died in the fighting or through starvation, while many others fled the highlands, eventually migrating to the United States (Beals 1946: 12). Charapan was also attacked twice by different armed groups, which may have been bandits or revolutionaries, the difference between the two often indiscernible. For a period in 1914, only 10 families and the parish priest remained in the community, most of the other residents having fled in search of safer havens. A few men from Charapan fought alongside the Villistas, "for no reason other than adventure," while others joined forces with the different bandit gangs operating in the highlands (García Mora 1981: 72–74).

Francisco Madero was popular with many of the residents of San Juan Parangaricutiro, because, as they would later recount to Moheno (1985: 123), "he proclaimed his love for liberty and justice, so that people could live in peace," but for them, "Villa and Zapata did not exist." In the 1980s, nearly everyone in San Juan Parangaricutiro could recall the cristiada in great detail or knew its history through their parents and grandparents, but only one elderly man had a vague recollection of the revolution of 1910 to 1920: "I remember another war, but I can't say much about it, I only remember that [soldiers] arrived on their horses and attacked everything, demanding that tortillas be made, if there were hens, they ate them, if there were pigs, they killed them. . . . When it was all over, I still didn't understand this war, the people were killed,

nothing more, they were found on the road and they were killed" (Plá 1989: 280).

The second half of the 1910s stood out more clearly in popular memory, the residents of Nuevo San Juan Parangaricutiro recounting three "disgraces" (*sambenitos*): epidemics and drought, banditry, and the creation of a rural defense force led by Hermenegildo Anguiano. Between them, the epidemics and drought killed all the cattle and many of the people. Once those calamities had passed, the bandits arrived, and "one could not put on a hat, or new shoes, or anything, they stole everything from you." The rural defense force would prove to be the most enduring problem, however: created to fight banditry, it soon became the private army of Anguiano and other mestizos in the community, who wielded it in their ongoing battles against the cabildo and allied comuneros, as the self-proclaimed agrarista leadership of San Juan Parangaricutiro.[40]

Throughout the highlands, revolutionary agrarianism responded far more to the needs of state makers than it did to popular aspirations. In contrast to Zacapu and other regions of Michoacán, the agrarista movements of the highlands, with a few exceptions, were top-down creations, intended to establish the authority of the central state at the local level, build a base of agrarista military and political support, and displace traditional authorities and institutions, including parish priests, the *principales* of the cabildo, and, sometimes inadvertently, the communal property regime. Given the absence of haciendas in the region, highland agraristas invariably claimed private smallholdings belonging to their better-off neighbors, larger properties rented to peasant sharecroppers, or communal property belonging to their own or other communities (Carrasco 1976: 53). As in Zacapu, highland agraristas employed anticlericalism, but they usually did so in order to wrest control over communal property from the politico-religious authorities of the cabildo and to consolidate their own political and military power at the local level. Revolutionary officials and their agrarista allies defined their opponents as Catholics and hence by definition counterrevolutionaries; the terms were quickly embraced throughout the highlands, by peasants who opposed revolutionary agrarianism and anticlericalism as assaults upon local values, cultures, and institutions.

State officials promoted revolutionary agrarianism most actively during Lázaro Cárdenas's tenure as governor in Michoacán (1928–32), and throughout much of his presidential administration (1934–40). One of their key objectives was to build a base of political support within the

highland communities, linking them first to the state-created Revolutionary Workers Confederation of Michoacán (CRMDT), and, subsequently, to the National Peasant Confederation (Confederación Nacional Campesina; CNC), the latter created by Cárdenas in 1938. At the local level, agrarista political power peaked in the 1930s, when agrarista minorities gained control over municipal offices throughout the highlands with the support of Cardenista officials. But the agrarian movements of the highlands were dependent on such support, and once Cárdenas left office in 1940, political Catholics regained power in most of the region's municipalities.[41]

Although much of the overt conflict between highland agraristas and Catholics occurred in the 1930s, these two political identities emerged much earlier, initially in response to the intense anticlericalism of the Múgica administration (1920–22). The precise nature of the conflicts depended on specific local histories, as did the extent to which political Catholics actively rebelled against the state as cristeros. In Charapan, where the liberal reparto was carried out in the 1890s, the barrios of San Bartolomé, San Miguel, and San Andrés divided up their lands in a relatively egalitarian manner, whereas the barrio of Santiago lost all of its land to a family living in Tangancícuaro.[42] The residents of Santiago petitioned for the restitution of their communal lands in 1921, claiming not the land they lost to outsiders, but rather that belonging to peasant smallholders in the other three barrios, above all San Andrés, the traditional political, religious, and commercial center of Charapan. The Santiago agraristas, referring to themselves as "reds from below" (*rojos de abajo*) defined their personal and political enemies in Charapan as Catholics and "whites from the center and above" (*blancos del centro y arriba*).[43] Neither the agraristas nor their leaders, the relatively well-off Ruiz family, are well-remembered outside of Santiago: according to local accounts, the members of the Ruiz family were "power hungry," "opportunistic," and engaged in "tricks and funny business," including cattle rustling. Inevitably and possibly accurately, one of the sons was held to be a Chavista bandit (García Mora 1981: 74–76).[44]

Charapan's local defense was headed by Luis Rodríguez and included only men "from above." Run out of town by the Ruiz family in the early 1920s, Rodríguez regained local power a few years later, and, even though he was identified with the Catholic faction, led the local defense force in fighting the cristeros of San Juan Parangaricutiro and other highland communities, for which service Lázaro Cárdenas granted him

the military rank of colonel. At the same time, Rodríguez used the local defense force to defeat the Ruiz family and the Santiago agraristas. Anticristero and an ally of the revolutionary state, Rodríguez nonetheless did not represent a threat to local norms and institutions, and few Catholic peasants from Charapan joined forces with the cristeros. Intracommunity conflict between agraristas and Catholics intensified greatly in the 1930s, when a new agrarista committee was formed, under the leadership of the González brothers, who, although coming from a wealthy family *de arriba* (from above), were staunch Cardenistas affiliated with the CRMDT. They initiated a second petition for the restitution of Santiago's communal lands in 1932. Shortly thereafter, Rodríguez was assassinated, and although the agraristas claimed to have nothing to do with it, the anti-agrarista municipal president had three of the five González brothers tortured and killed by the local defense force.

Few people from Cherán participated in the cristiada either, even though the majority defined themselves as Catholics in the political battles of the 1920s and beyond.[45] In the 1930s, Cherán came under the control of an agrarista minority of some 30 men, with the support of the Cardenistas. As elsewhere in the highlands, the agraristas were dislodged from power by federal troops once the Cárdenas administration came to an end, after a decade of violent conflict with the local Catholic opposition. Until it received the support of Cardenista state officials in the late 1920s, however, revolutionary agrarianism in the immediate area around Cherán remained quite weak. State officials installed agrarista peasants in political office and the local defense force during the cristiada, but the agraristas could not count on much support either within Cherán or from nominally agrarista peasants in neighboring communities. In the matter of tracking down and arresting a local priest, Father Esteban Avila, Cherán's agrarista defense chief complained that "instead of dedicating itself to carrying out its duty of pacification, assisting the government which rules us, the members of the [Tanaco] defense dedicate themselves to guarding the priest." He made the same complaint about the local authorities and defense forces of Paracho and Pichátaro. Cherán's agrarista municipal president continued to complain about the priest after the cristiada ended, indicating the strength of the Catholic opposition. The presence of the priest was truly "unbearable," he wrote, "given that he constantly provokes the religious organizations to be insubordinate to the authority that I represent." At a recent fiesta, in fact,

"the Franciscans" became drunk and "provoked all sorts of scandals," shouting "Viva Cristo Rey" and "Death to the Authorities."[46]

Throughout much of the highlands, communities remained relatively neutral throughout the cristiada, although local officials might take the side of the state, and the majority of the residents might secretly continue religious practice and, perhaps, sympathize with the rebels. Largely because the agrarista movements of the highlands were the creation of Lázaro Cárdenas in the late 1920s and 1930s, agrarismo did not constitute an attack on community institutions until the 1930s. When agraristas did achieve power in the highlands, Catholic opposition was often channeled through the sinarquista movement, rather than through armed rebellion. San Juan Parangaricutiro would certainly support the sinarquistas in the late 1930s and early 1940s. But San Juan Parangaricutiro also rebelled in the cristiada, the first Michoacán community to do so. Agrarismo was a direct threat to traditional community institutions in the 1920s, in part because of the alliances made between mestizo elites and revolutionary authorities and in part because Paricutín applied for the restitution of its communal lands (those it contested with San Juan Parangaricutiro) as early as 1916. The threat posed by agrarismo was compounded by the anticlericalism of the new regime, which was viewed as an assault on the Lord of the Miracles in particular, and religious practice in general, and hence as an assault on the community itself.

Mestizo elites began to appropriate communal land in San Juan Parangaricutiro during the last quarter of the nineteenth century, but they usually did not register it with the state as such or attempt to alienate it outside of the community. The ownership status of the appropriated land thus remained ambiguous and contested within the community itself. As the mestizo elites developed alliances with revolutionary state officials in the late 1910s and 1920s, they began to appropriate larger tracts of communal land, to register it as private property acquired through sales or inheritance, and to sell it to nonresidents. Thus Victoriano Anguiano, his son Hermenegildo, and other members of the Anguiano family received private title to property in Teruto, Tejamanil, Guaritzio, Falda de Cutzato, Pantzingo, and other locales between 1908 and 1933, Pantzingo being the site of the sacred spring of the Virgin of the Immaculate Conception.[47] The Equihua family was even more acquisitive, its various members claiming private property in Tejamanil, Las Ampolas, Agua Blanca, Rancho de los Lobos, Teruto, El Rosario,

of San Juan Parangaricutiro. Corupo, like Paricutín, was a politically subordinate tenencia of San Juan Parangaricutiro and had been long engaged in land disputes with it. In May 1928, in the midst of the rebellion, Corupo residents requested that the community be designated as a tenencia of Charapan, citing "the crazy undertaking of those who rebel only to carry out acts of revenge, murders, robberies, etc." Once the transfer was made, the Corupo agraristas fought the cristeros of San Juan under the leadership of Luis Rodríguez of Charapan.[54]

If the agraristas of Paricutín offered military support to the state in hopes of gaining the restitution of land in dispute with San Juan Parangaricutiro, they acted in vain, because their petition was not even acted upon until 1933 and was shortly thereafter denied, causing at least some residents to regret their loyalty during the cristiada. As community representatives wrote in 1935 with reference to the residents of San Juan Parangaricutiro: "They have always attacked us, and we do not consider it just that the Community of Parangaricutiro is usurping our rights, given that [Paricutín] has always demonstrated its submission and obedience to the laws of the Supreme Government, while in contrast the Community of Parangaricutiro has always been undisciplined . . . violating the laws and dispositions of the Government."[55]

The community of Zacán, in contrast, was offered a dotación without its ever having asked for one, by state officials hoping to recruit more peasants to local agrarista militias. In 1922, Zacán submitted a petition for the restitution of communal lands dispossessed by one José María Huanosto. Governor Sánchez Pineda approved the restitution in 1924, and sent the matter on to the National Agrarian Commission for its decision, and ultimately that of the president. The CNA took no action until 3 December 1927, at which point it declared Zacán's titles to be invalid, denied the restitution, and terminated Zacán's case. Shortly after Hermenegildo Anguiano was killed in a January 1928 battle between agraristas and cristeros in the highlands, however, President Calles issued a resolution granting Zacán the definitive possession of 780 hectares of land as a dotación. When CNA representatives arrived in Zacán to deliver the land in question, the peasants could not have been more surprised. According to Zacán resident Eliseo Aguilar:

> We had never asked for this ejido, nor did we know what it was. For this reason, when the government officials arrived, we thought once again that they were looking for cristeros, we believed nothing, noth-

ing they said and we didn't want to accept this business of ejidos. . . . But they talked and talked, declaring it done, saying that the government was this, and that the government was that. . . . Two or three days they stayed and they gave us the papers.[56]

State officials found no military support in Zacán, however: as Aguilar explained, "We, the people of Zacán, prayed that those in the hills would win, and when they needed to pass through our village, if they were being pursued, we would hide them in the eaves or under the beds. But nobody from Zacán went to the hills."[57] The state was forced to rely on the agraristas of Paricutín, now under the leadership of Victoriano Anguiano Equihua, the son and successor of Hermenegildo.

The Lord of the Miracles plays an important role in local accounts of the cristiada, as in all of the important episodes of San Juan Parangaricutiro's history. In February 1928, according to accounts related to Plá (1989: 281), the San Juan rebels were concerned that their religious icons would be destroyed, the community being completely deserted after an attack by federal forces and highland agraristas. Two men, José María Cuara and Cayetano Antolino, returned to San Juan, retrieved the icon of the Lord of the Miracles, and hid it in the nearby mountains. They were soon captured by federal troops, who tortured them in an attempt to force them to reveal the hiding place of the icon. Both refused, and Antolino was hanged. The soldiers were on the verge of hanging Cuara as well, when, according to local residents, a miracle occurred: the federal officer in charge changed his mind and ordered the release of Cuara, thus making the recovery of the Lord of the Miracles after the cristiada possible, because no one else knew where the icon was hidden. Plá (1989: 281) writes with reference to these oral histories: "Cayetano Antolino became a martyr of the cristiada and a hero who saved that which unified and protected the community, the Lord of the Miracles. The community and the Christ were the same thing. If the icon was attacked, the people were attacked too, and if aggression was directed against the people, the Christ suffered as well."

The behavior of the local representative of the Catholic Church was not as valiant; nor is he mentioned in local accounts of the rebellion: Father José García Morfín left San Juan Parangaricutiro in September 1927. A year later, he explained to the Ministry of Government that he did not wish to be associated with the rebels nor blamed for their rebellion, but simply requested the return of his clothes and books, seized

by the Uruapan defense force in an unsuccessful search for seditious materials.[58]

The Reconstruction of Identity in San Juan Parangaricutiro

Neither the conflicts within San Juan Parangaricutiro, nor those between San Juan and Paricutín ended with the cristero rebellion. The Anguiano and Equihua families continued to appropriate communal resources under private title, as did their allies within the community in smaller amounts. State officials, meanwhile, finally took action on Paricutín's petition for the restitution of its communal lands, which, though it was eventually denied, exacerbated tensions and violence between the two communities, as agrarian authorities attempted to survey the land in question and determine who had rights to it.[59] But although the substance of these conflicts changed little after the cristiada, the political identities articulated by the different actors involved in them did, in response to the changing political and institutional environment in which collective action took place. Above all, changes in the agrarian code with respect to property rights afforded new possibilities of defending interests and making claims on the state. Thus the political Catholics of San Juan Parangaricutiro, who rebelled against the state as cristeros, sought and achieved state recognition of their communal land claims as self-identified comuneros, members of a *comunidad agraria,* an institution whose legal status was gradually recognized by the state beginning in the 1930s.

Although the cabildo had lost much of its power at the local level by the 1930s, religious practice and communal land claims remained firmly intertwined in San Juan Parangaricutiro, and a central source of identity for many residents, as evidenced in local histories of the Paricutín volcano and the relocation of the community in Los Conejos. In February 1941, in an attempt to reconcile San Juan Parangaricutiro and Paricutín, several priests held a mass on a nearby mountain, the service attended by thousands of people from the highland communities and beyond. After the mass, a cross was left on the mountain, in remembrance of the service. Several days later, however, Paricutín peasants destroyed the cross, believing it to be a boundary marker and hence a claim by San Juan Parangaricutiro on land contested by the two communities.[60] After this sacrilege, according to Celedonio Gutiérrez (1972: 11–14), everyone in the region feared divine retribution, which did, in fact, manifest itself in

short order: in February 1942, "there appeared a plague of locusts so thick that they almost obscured the sun," and a year later, the volcano of Paricutín erupted, its lava gradually spreading over the town sites of Paricutín and San Juan Parangaricutiro over the course of more than a year. The residents of Paricutín were evacuated and resettled in June 1943. As they left the old site, Gutiérrez recounts, "[m]any families fought back their tears in order to hide their feelings before the whole world . . . that blamed them for the punishment which came because of the destruction of the Holy Cross by some of the men from the village" (C. Gutiérrez 1972: 27).

Most of the residents of San Juan Parangaricutiro refused to leave, however, even as agrarian authorities, and then minister of defense Lázaro Cárdenas, prevailed upon them to do so, offering to resettle them with new lands in the municipios of Ario, Apatzingán, Nueva Italia, and Parácuaro.[61] The annual fiesta for the Lord of the Miracles was held on 14 September 1943, attended by thousands of pilgrims, who knew it would be the last to be held in the place that the icon had chosen to stay several centuries back: "All who sought help for their needs were easily given help, and for this reason His sons cried bitterly and without consolation, not because Christ would no longer be with them, but because his image was to be taken from them" (C. Gutiérrez 1972: 36–37).

Fearing for the San Juan residents' safety, the bishop of Zamora instructed several priests to take the icon to Corupo, thus prompting a mass exodus in its wake. Shortly thereafter the bishop decided that he had made a mistake, and so ordered the icon returned to San Juan. Once again, however, the Lord of the Miracles expressed the community's displeasure with ecclesiastical interference in its affairs: whereas the bishop and priests found the icon too heavy to be moved, members of the cabildo lifted it without any problem and carried it back to San Juan Parangaricutiro. Several months later, in April 1944, when the residents of San Juan Parangaricutiro were forced to flee the approaching lava, they followed the Lord of the Miracles in a procession through the nearby highlands, finally stopping in a place called Los Conejos, where the icon, having arrived where it chose to stay, made itself too heavy to move.[62] Agrarian authorities tell a somewhat different story about the relocation: the choice of Los Conejos was a disruptive one, necessitating the expropriation of land that had already been granted to the Ejidos of San Francisco and Quinta, as well as a number of private properties. But the choice of Los Conejos for the new town site allowed the San

Juan comuneros to be close to the forests and cultivated lands they still claimed as communal property, even though much of it was under the control of mestizo families, most notably the Anguianos and Equihuas.[63]

The legal status of communal property remained ambiguous for several decades after the revolution. The 1917 Constitution specified that rural communities that had preserved their "communal status" might continue to enjoy in common the lands they retained or recovered through restitution, but Indian communities had no clear legal status, either in the Constitution or in the prevailing agrarian code. In 1937, President Lázaro Cárdenas had the Constitution amended in order to place matters related to communal property under federal jurisdiction, but his administration remained wary of creating a new property regime or a new subset of rights for indigenous peasants. These legal ambiguities, however, generated numerous conflicts between ejidatarios, private landowners, and peasants claiming land as comuneros, and so, in 1958, regulations were issued for a new agrarian procedure called the Recognition and Titling of Communal Property (*Reconocimiento y Titulación de Bienes Comunales*) through which peasants could petition for the state's confirmation of their rights to and possession of communal property. Finally, a 1971 article added to the federal Agrarian Reform Law explicitly recognized, for the first time, the comunidad agraria as a corporate entity with juridical status, and distinguished between the rights of comuneros and ejidatarios (Vázquez León 1992: 113–14).

These legal and institutional changes afforded new opportunities for San Juan residents to defend claims advanced since the liberal reparto of the late nineteenth century: the comunidad agraria, in contrast to the ejido, allowed for local control over the definition and distribution of property rights within the community, ownership being vested in the community as a corporate entity rather than in the state. The reconocimiento process, meanwhile, provided a means through which community members could recover lands previously appropriated by individuals as private property. In theory, the process applied only to lands "in the quiet and peaceful possession of the community since time immemorial," but in practice agrarian authorities inevitably recognized the claims of one party or the other in the course of preparing communal titles. Thus in 1991, the 1,229 self-identified comuneros of San Juan Parangaricutiro received a presidential resolution recognizing their possession and ownership of 14,068 hectares of land as communal property. Another 4,070 hectares remained subject to disputes between the co-

muneros and small proprietors living within the boundaries of the community, and so were left out of the resolution, both parties instructed to respect each others' rights until the matter might be resolved.[64]

In the Purépecha regions of Michoacán, revolutionary agrarianism and anticlericalism generated intense and often violent conflicts within and between communities, pitting allies of the new revolutionary state against peasants (and nonpeasants) who defended local values and institutions they perceived to be under external attack. In the political context of the 1920s and 1930s, popular opponents of the state identified themselves, and were identified by others, as Catholics, the term having come to embody a broad understanding of the legitimate role of the state in rural society. The precise nature of conflicts between Catholics and agraristas, and the degree of popular support enjoyed by either group, depended on specific local histories, as did the extent to which political Catholics mobilized and rebelled as cristeros. In the Zacapu communities, local institutions had been destroyed prior to the revolution, with the loss of communal lands throughout the course of the struggle over the liberal reparto and the concomitant shift of local political authority from the cabildo to local mestizo elites, the parish priest, and neighboring landowners. The agrarista movements of Zacapu thus had considerable popular support, even as they encountered resistance from political Catholics, wary of the state or under the blandishments of the clergy, who opposed revolutionary anticlericalism and the agrarian reform program. Religion had come to divide the Zacapu communities, and, though identifying themselves as political Catholics, the anti-agrarista peasants did not rebel as cristeros, many of them having been exiled from their communities prior to 1926.

Many highland communities, in contrast, survived the Porfiriato with their land and their institutions intact, their communal property remaining under the control of the cabildo. With the sponsorship and support of state officials eager to find local allies, small agrarista movements did develop in the region, but they faced considerable opposition from Catholic majorities, particularly when they monopolized communal resources for themselves. In most of the highland communities, conflicts between agraristas and Catholics did not peak until the governorship and later presidency of Lázaro Cárdenas. Throughout much of the 1920s, Catholic peasants in these communities opposed revolutionary anticlericalism, but they did not actively rebel as cristeros. In San Juan Parangaricutiro, in contrast, revolutionary anticlericalism and agrarian-

ism constituted a simultaneous and two-pronged assault on local resources and institutions in the 1920s: mestizo elites formed political and military alliances with revolutionary officials, and they used their newfound power to monopolize communal resources and dislodge the politico-religious authority of the cabildo, at the same time attacking local popular culture and identity through anticlericalism. Meanwhile, San Juan Parangaricutiro's age-old enemy Paricutín applied for the restitution of communal lands it had unsuccessfully contested with San Juan since the early eighteenth century, offering its political and military support to the new revolutionary state. Almost alone among the highland Catholics, residents of San Juan Parangaricutiro rebelled against the state as cristeros, fighting the Paricutín agraristas led by the Anguiano and Equihua families.

San José de Gracia and Cojumatlán appear, at first glance, to have had relatively little in common with San Juan Parangaricutiro and the other Purépecha communities of the central highlands. Located on a plateau in northwestern Michoacán, both were ranchero communities, predominantly mestizo in ethnicity and Spanish in culture, and characterized by private smallholdings and an orthodox religious practice that revolved around the mass, the rosary, and the sacraments. Political authority was vested in the parish priests, rather than a cabildo, who were consulted on most matters, large and small, well into the twentieth century. Differing greatly in their economic, social, and cultural attributes, the residents of the two ranchero communities did have one thing in common with those of San Juan Parangaricutiro: many rebelled against the revolutionary state during the cristiada, in response to policies that violated local norms and threatened local institutions which regulated property rights, religious practice, and local political authority.

The residents of San José de Gracia and Cojumatlán did not have long histories of conflict with the state, be it colonial, liberal, or Porfirian. Prior to the period of revolutionary state formation in the 1920s, in fact, they had relatively little contact at all with state officials. There were, as Benjamin (1984: 14) notes, many Porfiriatos in Mexico, and most people in San José de Gracia and Cojumatlán had particularly good ones. Having acquired private smallholdings through the breakup of an insolvent hacienda and at the expense of neighboring Indian communities, the rancheros of the plateau were well positioned to participate in the economic boom of the late Porfiriato, as the construction of the railroads and the provision of steamship service on Lake Chapala connected them to expanding markets in Guadalajara and Mexico City.

The revolution, in contrast, brought little but difficulties to the region, the 1910s marked by the abuses of Carrancista soldiers and officials, severe drought, and widespread and particularly vicious banditry. Conditions began to improve in the 1920s, when two large landowners in the region divided and sold part of their properties to residents of San José de Gracia and Cojumatlán in anticipation of the agrarian reform. It was at this point that the full power of the central state was first felt on the plateau: revolutionary officials threatened to overturn the sales of hacienda property, while attacking the Church and its affiliated organizations, through which community social, cultural, and political life were organized. On 9 July 1927, after much consultation with their parish priests and under the leadership of Father Federico González Cárdenas of San José, groups from both communities declared themselves to be in rebellion against the revolutionary state, joining forces with Prudencio Mendoza and his many followers in nearby Cotija. This chapter accounts for the construction of a Catholic political identity in San José de Gracia and Cojumatlán and for its mobilization during the cristero rebellion.

The Ranchero Communities of the Plateau

San José de Gracia and Cojumatlán are located on a plateau rising above the southern edge of Lake Chapala in northwestern Michoacán. To the east lie the valleys of Jiquilpan, site of the region's largest and most prosperous haciendas prior to the revolution; to the north lie the former marshlands of Lake Chapala, first drained and brought into regular agricultural production in 1909 and 1910. Upon arriving in Michoacán, the Spanish found a number of Nahuatl-speaking Indian communities along the shores of the lake, tribute-paying subjects of the Purépecha empire centered in Tzintzunzan. The plateau, in contrast, was all but unpopulated: with its poor soils and rocky terrain, it served as a military buffer zone between the warring Purépechas of Michoacán and the neighboring Sayultecas of what is now the state of Jalisco. Early on in the colonial period, the Spanish established enormous cattle haciendas in the region, the most notable being those of Guaracha, Cojumatlán, and El Monte. In the highlands, landowners rented out much of their property to tenant families, who took care of the livestock and engaged in subsistence food production (L. González 1974: 8–16; Reséndez Torres 1986: 227–30).[1]

Over the course of the next two centuries, the highland population of

western Michoacán grew steadily, comprising tenant families living in small communities called rancherías and *congregaciones* within the boundaries of the haciendas. Beginning in the late seventeenth and early eighteenth centuries, many such communities petitioned colonial authorities for the politico-administrative status of pueblo, so that they might solidify their claims to the lands they rented, elect their own local authorities, and achieve a degree of political autonomy from the haciendas of which they formed a part. After independence in 1821, many highland tenants were able to acquire private title to the lands long occupied by their families, either through the implementation of the 1856 Lerdo Law on properties owned by the Catholic Church or through the partition and sale of insolvent haciendas by landowners faced with the economic destruction and social dislocation of the independence wars and, half a century later, the War of the Reform (Chevalier 1982: 4–8).[2]

The rancheros of San José de Gracia and Cojumatlán acquired their holdings through the latter route. Antonia Moreno, the owner of the Hacienda of Guaracha in the mid-nineteenth century, faced the usual economic difficulties of the times, compounded by large debts incurred through gambling. On the verge of bankruptcy, she was forced to partition and sell the western and far less productive half of her property, known as the Hacienda of Cojumatlán, a process completed in 1863. At the time of the sale, most of the land in question was leased to José Dolores Acuña, who used part of it for his own cattle hacienda and rented out the rest to subtenants. He bought the largest number of shares, acquiring the best land around Lake Chapala and the hacienda residence. Another 4,000 hectares were purchased by Manuel Arias to form the Hacienda of Sabino. Finally, many of Acuña's tenants were able to purchase parcels ranging from 100 to 1,000 hectares, albeit on the worst of the land located on the plateau, thus forming the nuclei of what would become the ranchero communities of San José de Gracia and Cojumatlán.[3]

Throughout the colonial period, the Indian communities of Lake Chapala were engaged in land disputes and litigation with each other and with neighboring landowners. San Pedro Caro, for example, requested and received three títulos de composición in the eighteenth century, confirming its claims against the Haciendas of Cumuato and Guaracha and the Indian community of Pajacuarán. Most notably from the community's point of view, the Spanish Crown confirmed San Pedro Caro's claim to communal holdings in the marshlands and fishing grounds of the lake, which would later become a source of great conflict with both Porfirian

and revolutionary state authorities. Some of San Pedro Caro's land was leased to neighboring hacendados in order to finance civil expenses and religious practice, but the community repeatedly refused to rent any land to the owner of the Hacienda of Guaracha, because "he wanted to incorporate the communal lands into the hacienda, as [had] already occurred with the pueblos of Pajacuarán, Guaracha, and Jaripeo."[4] In the nineteenth century, disputes over communal land increasingly involved the region's rancheros as well as its hacendados, as the former augmented the holdings they acquired from the latter through appropriating the communal lands of the Indian communities, through purchase and through frauds perpetuated during the course of the liberal land reform.

At the turn of the century, for example, Wenceslao del Toro protested that mestizos from Cojumatlán and Sahuayo had invaded communal lands belonging to the *ex-comunidad de indígenas* of Cojumatlán. Supporting the claims of the rancheros, the Sahuayo municipal president and Jiquilpan district prefect informed the Ministry of Government that the land in question had always belonged to the Hacienda of Guaracha, and was now in the legal possession of individuals who had acquired it in 1863 when the western half of the hacienda was subdivided and sold by Antonia Moreno. "No property is known, or has been known, to belong to the Indians of that village," the district prefect continued, "and for that reason, no reparto of any lands they claim to own has been initiated."[5] The Indian community of Sahuayo, in turn, complained that the family of José Trinidad Barragán had employed illegal and fraudulent means to acquire newly privatized parcels from individual comuneros in order to form the rancho of El Salitre.[6] And in San Pedro Caro, residents claimed that the local privatization committee had arranged matters so that the best of the community's communal land was allocated to individuals who had agreed to sell their shares to neighboring rancheros and hacendados, most notably the owners of the Hacienda of Guaracha.[7]

The rancheros of the municipios of Cojumatlán, Sahuayo, and Jiquilpan flourished during the Porfiriato, as did the region's hacendados, after the completion of the Mexico City–Guadalajara railroad allowed them to take advantage of growing markets in both cities. The Hacienda of Guaracha became one of the most important commercial enterprises in Michoacán, as Diego Moreno, the younger and more entrepreneurial brother of Antonia, invested heavily to modernize sugar production and improve local transportation infrastructure. Although livestock continued to dominate the regional economy, there were also significant

increases in the production of corn, wheat, barley, sugar, alfalfa, and bean production during this period. Sahuayo, meanwhile, grew into a major manufacturing and commercial center.[8] As the regional economy boomed, landowners sought more land to bring into commercial agricultural production, their sights turning to the 50,000 hectares of marshlands lying along the edge of Lake Chapala. Although the marsh soil was exceptionally rich, the region's rancheros and hacendados employed the marshland only for pasture, because periodic flooding by the lake prevented its exploitation for commercial production. The Indian communities, in turn, depended on their holdings in the marshlands for subsistence agriculture, suffering recurrent crop losses, as well as for fishing grounds and a source of reeds and other plant materials used by artisans.[9]

In 1909, on the eve of the Mexican Revolution, Porfirian officials signed a contract with Manuel Cuesta Gallardo, related by marriage to Diego Moreno of the Hacienda of Guaracha, granting him the concession to drain the marshlands and to sell his share of the land, in theory in parcels of up to 500 hectares with no more than one parcel sold to any individual. The central state was to receive 12,000 hectares of the drained land as national property. The region's landowners benefited enormously from this arrangement, although Cuesta Gallardo was unsuccessful in his first attempt, made in 1909–10, to prevent the marshlands from flooding. The Indian communities of Sahuayo, San Pedro Caro, and Pajacuarán, in contrast, lost much of what remained of their communal holdings in the marshes, because both Cuesta Gallardo and the officials of the Ministry of Finance and Development ignored their long-standing land claims throughout the course of the project and subsequent sales of the drained marshland (Vargas González 1989).[10] The drainage project, and subsequent alienation of communal lands to neighboring landowners, would be the basis of restitution claims made by the communities under the revolutionary agrarian reform program in the 1910s and 1920s.

The ranchos formed through the subdivision of the Hacienda of Cojumatlán were scattered throughout the plateau in small settlements called rancherías, each settlement constituting a politically subordinate unit of the tenencia of Cojumatlán, which was itself subordinate to the municipal seat of Sahuayo and the district of Jiquilpan. In the mid-1880s, however, some of the plateau rancheros organized to form a new community, in large part so as to obtain a church and the services of a

resident priest. In this effort they had the support of a priest from Sahuayo, who first organized a meeting with the bishop of Zamora to obtain his approval for the creation of a new vicariate, and later met with President Porfirio Díaz to petition for the creation of a new tenencia, with the recently established San José de Gracia as its political seat.[11] These efforts succeeded in 1909, with the establishment of the tenencia of Ornelas, which, like Cojumatlán, formed part of the municipio of Sahuayo.[12]

The desire of the rancheros to form a new vicariate corresponded with a broader movement on the part of Church authorities to expand the institutional presence of the Church at the local level, to combat both liberal anticlericalism and the prevalence of unorthodox forms of religious worship. With the encouragement of Clemente de Jesús Munguía and Pelagio Antonio de Labastide y Davalos, the archbishops of Michoacán and Puebla who had been exiled by the liberals in 1856, Pope Pious IX authorized the creation of a new diocese in Zamora in 1862, with jurisdiction over all of western Michoacán, including the Chapala region. Three years later, the Zamora seminary was established as well, soon to become one of the most important centers of higher education in the state, for members of the clergy and laity alike. During the tenure of the first two bishops of Zamora, Antonio de la Peña Navarro (1865–1877) and José María Cázares y Martínez (1878–1909), the Church's presence in the daily lives of the region's residents increased greatly, with the creation of new parishes, the promotion of lay participation in devotional societies, the development of social assistance programs and workers' clubs, and the exercise of stricter ecclesiastical control over the worship of local patron saints (Becker 1995; Tapia Santamaría 1986).

L. González's (1968, 1974) history of San José de Gracia vividly portrays the centrality of religious practice and authority in the daily lives of the rancheros and their extended families. With the arrival of the parish priest, Father Othón Sánchez, in 1890, the passage of the day was marked by religious worship: daily mass was followed by morning prayers, the noontime recitation of the Angelus, the evening Rosary and Litanies of the Virgin, and yet further evening prayers. The residents of San José also actively participated in two devotional societies established by the priest, the Apostles of Prayer, for the men of the community, and the Daughters of Mary for the young women. The role of the Catholic Church in the community extended far beyond the religious realm, however. A school for young children and older girls was established by the

bishop at the end of the century and staffed by nuns. Older boys were instructed by the parish priest, and many of them went on to study at the seminary in Zamora. Local political authorities, meanwhile, appointed by the tenencia of Cojumatlán until 1909, consulted with the priest on virtually all matters having to do with the administration of the community's affairs. The creation of the tenencia of Ornelas in 1909 with San José de Gracia as its seat gave local authorities greater autonomy within the political structure of the municipio of Sahuayo, but did not alter their habit of deferring to the priest in civil and political matters.

By the end of the Porfiriato, the ranchero communities of northwestern Michoacán were characterized by four central institutions: a property regime based on smallholdings acquired through purchase or inheritance; orthodox religious practice organized by the institutional Church and its local representative, the parish priest; and a system of local political authority in which officials designated by state authorities generally deferred to the priest, who held de facto political power in the communities. These institutions, and the normative understandings of property rights, popular culture, and political authority upon which they were based, all came under attack as the revolutionary state attempted to assert its authority at the local level through anticlericalism and agrarianism.

Revolutionary State Formation in Northwestern Michoacán

When asked to supply the state historian with information on local experiences during the revolution of the 1910s, the Cardenista municipal president of Cotija provided the following account, fairly typical for the western region of Michoacán as a whole. In 1910 to 1911, he wrote, Maderistas took over the town without resistance and "with the general applause of the residents who sympathized with the revolutionary movement"; the arrival of the Carrancistas in 1914 generated no hostilities but some confusion, as a member of the local defense force accidentally discharged his gun, leading to a shoot-out of several hours. Throughout 1915 to 1916, Villistas and Carrancistas periodically entered Cotija, there being little violence between them except for one incident, in which the Villista Manuel Guízar Valencia carried out a surprise attack, taking over the Carrancista barracks, "more by shrewdness than by military force," and killed nine soldiers. And in 1917, 300 well-armed Zapatistas attempted to take over the town, but were defeated, with many casu-

alties on both sides, by the Carrancistas. The very worst times of the revolution arrived in 1918, however, in the person of the bandit leader José Inés Chávez García and his followers. Finding only the 80 men of the local defense force to defend the town, the Chavistas burned down some 70 houses in the center, committed countless robberies and a number of murders, and took off the next day.[13]

The Chavista bandits plagued the western region of Michoacán throughout the 1910s, killing both rich and poor, burning entire towns, and committing grotesque, and gratuitous, acts of violence (Olivera Sedano 1981: 107). Their origins were not atypical, even if the intensity of their violence was. Chávez García, a native of Puruándiro, had fought the Huertistas under the leadership of Anastacio Pantoja. After the latter was killed by his fellow Carrancistas, Chávez, along with some 9,000 of Pantoja's troops, adopted the banner of Villismo. After Villa's 1915 defeat in the Bajío, however, the Chavistas gradually turned to banditry, attacking, among other places, Sahuayo, Cotija, Jiquilpan, San José de Gracia, and the Hacienda of Guaracha. The federal garrison stationed in San José fled in the face of the 800 attacking Chavistas, leaving only the local civil defense force under Apolinar Partida to protect those residents who had been unable to escape. The incident did little to bolster the reputation of the new revolutionary state, although it did much for that of Father Federico González Cárdenas whose intervention prevented the execution of several San Joseans by Chavista troops (L. González 1974: 131–36; Olivera Sedano 1981: 107–8).

The Puntada bandit gang also operated in the highlands of northwestern Michoacán, under the leadership of an ex-Villista named Eliseo Zepeda and including men from Cojumatlán, Sahuayo, Jiquilpan, and some of the rancherías in the tenencia of Ornelas. In contrast to the Chavistas, the Puntada bandits called themselves revolutionaries and concentrated their attacks on the wealthier rancheros of the region. The main opposition they faced in this endeavor came from the followers of Prudencio Mendozo, himself an ex-Villista (by virtue of his anti-Carrancismo), and soon to be military leader of the cristeros in northwestern Michoacán (González 1974: 130–32; Ochoa Serrano 1978: 152).

With the reassertion of some semblance of state authority during the presidential administrations of Venustiano Carranza and Alvaro Obregón, wide-scale banditry was gradually eliminated in the northwestern highlands, as in other regions of Michoacán and the center-west more

generally. Revolutionary state formation entailed its own set of opportunities and threats, however, the precise mix depending on prior legacies of conflict and transformation at the local level. For the Indian communities alongside Lake Chapala, the revolutionary agrarian reform program offered a new vehicle for the reclamation of communal lands lost over the course of centuries to neighboring haciendas and ranchos. In contrast, the rancheros of the region faced a threefold assault on local values and institutions: personal and political enemies assumed positions of local political power as the agrarista allies of revolutionary state officials; revolutionary anticlericalism attacked both the parish priest and religious practice itself, the central institution through which daily life was organized and understood; and, finally, many rancheros faced the prospect of losing their land, either to neighboring agrarista committees or through the nullification of subdivisions and sales carried out by large landowners in anticipation of the agrarian reform.

In the municipal seat of Sahuayo, Crisóforo and Eufemio Ochoa acquired local political and military power as agrarista leaders. Eufemio was appointed commander of the local defense force of Sahuayo, thus affording him the arms with which to harass his family's many personal and political enemies throughout the municipio. Crisóforo, in turn, led the town's small agrarista movement, in 1917 submitting a petition for the restitution of El Salitre as the communal property of the Indian community of Sahuayo, dispossessed by the family of José Trinidad Barragán in the context of the liberal reparto. The Trinidad Barragán family countered that it had acquired various smallholdings through a series of legal purchases made between 1878 and 1913, the latest parcels having been purchased from eight members of the Ochoa family, including Crisóforo.[14] Threats posed by local agraristas increased when Francisco Múgica assumed power as governor of Michoacán in 1920. With support from Mugiquista state officials, agrarian committees in several communities around Lake Chapala petitioned for the restitution of communal lands seized by neighboring haciendas and ranchos. Few were successful, given the degree of legal proof required in the restitution procedure, but state officials did usually grant dotaciones instead, expropriating land, for the most part, from the smaller haciendas of the lake region.[15]

The ranchero communities of San José de Gracia and Cojumatlán remained largely untouched by revolutionary agrarismo until the mid-1920s. None of the residents of San José formed an agrarian committee

to apply for land in the 1920s, in spite of the fact that two-thirds of the community's residents were landless at the beginning of the decade. It was not a question of eligibility: the number of landless families far exceeded the minimum of 20 required to form an agrarian committee, San José was neither too large nor too small to qualify for land under the prevailing agrarian code, and, with the 4,232-hectare Hacienda of Sabino nearby, there was certainly affectable property within a seven-kilometer radius as required by law. The local clergy undoubtedly played a role in this, given that San José's Father Federico González Cárdenas did not approve of agrarismo and that Father José Trinidad Barragán of the neighboring town of Sahuayo, influenced both by the teachings of the Church and by the threats it posed to his family's property, passionately denounced agrarismo, begging God, on one occasion, to open up the ground and swallow up all of the region's agraristas (L. González 1979: 158).

But the real issue was one of property rights and how they might be acquired. For the landless residents of San José de Gracia, according to L. González (1974: 144), the private ownership of property was central to community understandings of personal and familial strength, purchase and inheritance constituting the only legitimate and secure ways of obtaining it. Both had been possible in the past: the rancheros who formed San José de Gracia as a new parish had acquired their property through the subdivision of the Hacienda of Cojumatlán in 1862, and to the extent that land ownership increased over the following decades it did so through inheritance or through the purchase of land, often from nearby Indian communities. The revolutionary agrarian reform program offered only use rights to land owned by the state, which also retained the prerogative to intervene in how such land was used and allocated within the ejidos.

In the mid-1920s, about half of the landless residents of San José de Gracia had the opportunity to purchase the private smallholdings they desired. María Ramírez Arias, owner of the Hacienda of Sabino, decided, in consultation with Father Federico González Cárdenas, to subdivide and sell most of her property, having learned that the Local Agrarian Commission in the neighboring state of Jalisco was about to expropriate part of it in a provisional grant made to the community of Paso de Piedras. Under the direction of the priest, Sabino was divided up into 206 parcels of 7 to 15 hectares, and 12 larger ranchos of 40 to 150 hectares. These were then sold through a lottery system at 50 pesos per hectare, to be paid over a 10-year period. Most of the parcels were sold

to the landless residents of San José de Gracia, about half of whom became small proprietors when the subdivision was completed in 1926 (L. González 1968: 141–42).

The Sabino subdivision was immediately challenged by Rafael Picazo, the agrarista municipal president of Sahuayo, and Eufemio Ochoa, the commander of the local defense force, on the grounds that it violated a provision of the agrarian code that prohibited landowners from selling their property after it had been cited as subject to expropriation in a petition published in the *Periódico Oficial del Estado*. This provision was intended to prevent the common practice of arranging simulated sales of hacienda property to family members in order to avoid expropriation under the agrarian reform program. María Ramírez Arias did subdivide her property to avoid expropriation, but the sales were very much real, benefiting a significant percentage of the landless population of San José de Gracia and allowing them to claim property rights in accordance with local norms and institutions.

A similar subdivision was challenged in neighboring Cojumatlán, where a much smaller group of local residents benefited from sales arranged in 1924 by Francisco Arreguí, owner of the Hacienda of Cojumatlán. Much of the property was registered under the names of Arreguí's children, suggesting that they were simulated in order to avoid expropriation. Smaller parcels were also sold to other families in Cojumatlán, however, allowing them, like their neighbors in San José de Gracia, to become small proprietors in a way sanctioned by the norms and institutions of the ranchero community. Shortly after these sales occurred, however, a small group of Cojumatlán residents applied for a land grant under the agrarian reform program, citing the newly subdivided Hacienda of Cojumatlán as subject to expropriation. Upon the publication of the petition on 21 March 1926, the affected landowners, some of them truthfully, claimed that they were smallholders, but the Cojumatlán agrarian committee charged that the entire subdivision had been simulated, in an attempt to avoid an expropriation.[16] State officials did not grant the Cojumatlán committee a dotación until the 1930s, nor did they annul the subdivision of Sabino, but ranchero families faced the prospect of losing their newly acquired properties in 1926, just as tensions were escalating between the revolutionary state and the Catholic Church.

Opposition to revolutionary anticlericalism was not a new phenomenon on the plateau: recurrent Carrancista attacks on churches and clergy

tion in the rebellion increased considerably in the fall of 1927, after the federal military bombed the plateau, as part of a scorched earth counterinsurgency campaign. The campaign was largely unproductive, generating only more refugees and rebels: after San José de Gracia was burned to the ground, its rebel contingent increased to 300 men, well over half of its male population (L. González 1968: 148–57, 162–63).[24]

Once augmented, the cristero rebels stepped up their military activities, seizing control over the town of Jiquilpan in late October 1927, and holding it for several weeks, until 3,000 federal soldiers arrived to dislodge them.[25] Throughout 1928, the cristeros controlled all of northwestern Michoacán, with the exception of the largest towns: in the summer of that year, U.S. consular officials estimated that there were 3,000 armed rebels operating in the region between Tizapán and La Palma, Cojumatlán and its environs standing out as a center of rebel activity. Conditions near Lake Chapala, meanwhile, were said to be so "badly disturbed" that cargo boats could not operate, thus bringing "commercial and agricultural activity in the region to a standstill."[26] Cristero activity intensified in March 1929, as loyal federal troops were transferred north to fight the Escobarista rebels. But several months later, the cristiada came to a close, with the accord reached between the Mexican episcopate and the Portes Gil administration, and the rebels of San José de Gracia and Cojumatlán reluctantly accepted the state's offer of a general amnesty. Only Father Federico González Cárdenas was prohibited from returning home, because of his active participation in the rebellion.[27]

Conflicts between agraristas and political Catholics continued on the plateau throughout the 1930s, particularly during the Cárdenas administration of 1934 to 1940, when state officials pursued both revolutionary agrarianism and anticlericalism with great vigor in the region. The Local Agrarian Commission finally acted on the dotación petition submitted by the agraristas of Cojumatlán, granting them the provisional possession of 994 hectares on 21 October 1931. Disputes between the ejidatarios and the affected landowners continued well after the definitive possession of the ejido was awarded in a presidential resolution of 1938, however, as the latter insisted that they had obtained their holdings legally, through the subdivision of the Hacienda of Cojumatlán, subsequent sales, and inheritance.[28] An agrarista movement also developed in San José de Gracia, albeit with less success. With the political support of Lázaro Cárdenas, first as governor and then as president, the

San Josean agraristas assumed power in the tenencia of Ornelas at various points in the 1930s, leading to considerable conflict with the political Catholics and to periods in which civil authority was replaced by military rule (L. González 1968: 183–202). San José's agrarista movement never achieved widespread support in the tenencia, however, given the centrality of private property to personal, familial, and community identity. The local agrarian committee submitted petitions for land grants first in 1933 and subsequently in 1950, but neither one generated significant interest among San Joseans, nor did state officials respond favorably to them, citing the lack of affectable property in a region characterized by smallholdings and cattle ranches protected from expropriation under the agrarian code.[29]

San José de Gracia and Cojumatlán represent one type of community involved in the cristero rebellion. In the case of San José, the very origins and identity of the community were rooted in its strong ties with the Catholic Church, in that it was first established as a parish in the Church's drive to increase its institutional and spiritual presence at the local level in the wake of liberal anticlericalism. Bordering Jalisco with its strong network of lay Catholic organizations, San José de Gracia and Cojumatlán were also connected to the Catholic Association of Mexican Youth, the National League for the Defense of Religious Liberty, and the secret society called the u. But thousands of communities throughout Mexico were characterized by such close ties to the Church, and relatively few of these participated in the cristero rebellion. Other communities, such as San Juan Parangaricutiro in the Purépecha highlands of Michoacán, had few ties to the institutional Church or its affiliated lay organizations, and they did rebel against the state as cristeros. In both cases, local histories of agrarian conflict and transformation in the decades and centuries prior to the revolution played a key role in determining partisanship in the cristiada.

Many residents of San José de Gracia and Cojumatlán prospered during the Porfiriato, having acquired smallholdings through the subdivision of the Hacienda of Cojumatlán and at the expense of neighboring Indian communities. With the expansion of transportation infrastructure at the end of the nineteenth century, they were well positioned to profit from expanding markets for food in Guadalajara and Mexico City. With this new affluence came the development of an active community life revolving around the Church, the parish priest, prayers and the sacraments, the expansion of Church schools, and participation in

lay devotional societies. The growth and prosperity witnessed in San José de Gracia were such as to qualify the community for the politico-administrative status of tenencia in 1909, giving it greater political independence and a larger role within municipio politics.

The revolution, in contrast to the Porfiriato, brought near ruin to the plateau. The residents of San Juan Parangaricutiro recalled three "disgraces" suffered by the community in the 1910s: banditry, drought and epidemics, and the local defense force. The plateau communities suffered from two of them: the depredations inflicted by the Chavista and Puntada bandit gangs were followed by a prolonged drought that destroyed food production and forced a good number of residents to leave the region, finding new homes elsewhere in Michoacán or migrating to the United States. Conditions began to improve with the subdivisions of Sabino and Cojumatlán, but it was at this point that revolutionary state formation first began to have a profound and negative impact on the lives of many plateau residents: personal and political enemies such as Crisóforo and Eufemio Ochoa assumed positions of political and military power in the municipio, and they attacked and attempted to overturn the subdivisions. At the same time, the implementation of the Calles Law in 1926 led to the closure of the churches, attacks on the clergy and on Church property, and severe restrictions on the religious practices that were so central to community life. San Joseans "were in the habit of expecting only trouble from the authorities," as L. González (1974: 144) writes, and they and their neighbors in Cojumatlán certainly found it in revolutionary agrarianism and anticlericalism, violating as they did local values and threatening to undermine local institutions with respect to property rights, religious practice, and local political authority.

8 ✳ Popular Groups, Political Identities, and the State in Mexico: The *Cristiada* in Comparative Perspective

Long treated as one episode in a long-standing conflict between Church and state, the cristiada of 1926 to 1929 was also the last major popular rebellion in Mexican history. As such, it was part of a broader set of struggles through which popular and elite groups contested the normative and institutional contours of the revolutionary state, articulating diverse and often contradictory notions of legitimate property rights, culture, citizenship, and political authority. The central concern of this book has been to explain peasant partisanship in the cristero rebellion, in terms of the formation, substance, and mobilization of the political identities of agrarista and católico. Across Mexico and within the region of the center-west, peasants were deeply divided in their responses to revolutionary state formation. How can we explain these divisions? What do they tell us about the relationship between agrarian structures, popular cultures, and politics in accounting for political identities and behavior?

Revolutionary agrarianism and anticlericalism were, in part, state-building policies, intended to consolidate the authority of the central state at the local level, through the creation of new forms of property rights that linked peasant beneficiaries directly to the state, new cultural identities and practices through which local patron saints and communal ties would be replaced by secular heroes and a national identity, and new forms of local political authority, through which allies of the new revolutionary state would hold state-created and regulated political offices, displacing parish priests, landlords, and politico-religious elders. Given that they sought to refashion the very symbolic and institutional fabric of rural life, such policies inevitably and invariably created new conflicts and intensified old ones, within communities, between communities, and between communities and the state. But they also provided possibilities

for new alliances between popular and elite actors and for the partial realization of popular demands and agendas.

Popular responses to revolutionary state formation varied in accordance with the extent to which agrarianism and anticlericalism meshed with or violated popular understandings of property rights, religious practice, and local political authority. These understandings, in turn, were products of previous histories of agrarian and political conflict and accommodation at the local level. For some communities, and factions within communities, revolutionary state formation offered the opportunity to gain or recover land, displace abusive local authorities, and settle long-standing agrarian and political grievances with rival pueblos and much-despised hacendados. According to Ramón Aguilar, an agrarista leader in Zacapu, the agrarian reform had freed the communities from the "the ignominies of the landowners"; without it, they would have remained "the slaves of the capitalists," "living in the most frightening misery, because of the marked oppression that they exercised over the peasant class."[1] For Primo Tapia of Naranja, revolutionary anticlericalism allowed the agraristas to seize political power from "the Noriega latifundistas and the clergy," above all "the wicked Trinidad Cruz, parish priest of Zacapu."[2]

Elsewhere, these same policies constituted a profound threat to community resources, norms, and institutions, attacking the religious practices that served as the core of popular culture and local identities and allowing minority factions or rival pueblos to seize land and local political authority. As residents of Nuevo San Juan Parangaricutiro wrote, in the course of later conflicts between comuneros and the small proprietors who had taken advantage of their alliances with revolutionary officials to appropriate communal land, "this community, that for centuries maintained its unity and integrity, that endured the attacks of the [reparto] laws, that was able to survive the agrarian policies of Porfirio Díaz, has been almost completely dismembered by those who have personified the authority of the revolutionary governments" (cited in Moheno 1985: 132). For the landless residents of San José de Gracia, the revolutionary agrarian reform program offered only an ejido, viewed as an illegitimate and insecure form of property rights; local agrarista leaders and state officials, meanwhile, threatened to annul the subdivision of the Hacienda of Sabino, through which half of those residents had acquired private smallholdings. Revolutionary anticlericalism, mean-

while, was perceived as an attack on Father Federico González Cárdenas, who had contributed so much to the well-being and prosperity of the community, and on religious practice itself, the central institution through which daily life was organized and understood.

Throughout the book, I have argued that peasant partisanship in the cristero rebellion is best understood in terms of the interaction between historical legacies of conflict and transformation at the local level, and the political and strategic context of revolutionary state formation in the 1920s. I looked at how the agrarian and political conflicts in which peasants were engaged in the decades, and sometimes centuries, before the revolution shaped and reshaped the normative and institutional relationships among property rights, religious practice, and local political authority in rural communities. I then linked these local historical legacies to divergent popular responses to the threats and opportunities entailed in revolutionary state formation at the local level, as embodied in the policies of agrarianism and anticlericalism. This approach thus combines a concern for structural change, popular cultures, and political alliances and institutions, paying particularly close attention to how people understood and interpreted transformations in land tenure in relationship to religious practice, local political authority, and broader notions of justice and legitimacy. In so doing, it suggests that neither the literature on peasant rebellion, nor that on new social movements theory, adequately conceptualizes the relationship between the economic, cultural, and political facets of identity construction, or the relationship between the construction of political identities and the historical, political, and institutional context in which collective action takes place.

The structural and class-centric approaches that have dominated the literature on peasant rebellion suggest that political identity is a non-issue: as political actors, peasants are defined by their structural location as subsistence producers with precarious control over scarce resources. Peasant rebellions, in turn, are explicable in terms of general economic processes and transformations that expose individuals, communities, and/or rural classes to new and increasingly severe economic insecurities. New social movements theory, in contrast, is quite concerned with the "constructedness of political identity" (Starn 1992: 92). But one of its central claims is that new social movements, as opposed to old ones, involve political actors who are not defined by class or economic interests, but rather by gender, religion, generation, sexuality, ethnicity, or region.

Such identities are said to be forged through expressive action and the creation of new meanings and discourses, processes almost completely divorced from economic structures and political institutions. Both literatures, in other words, posit a fundamental dichotomy between an economic and a noneconomic realm of existence in the formation, substance, and mobilization of political identities in collective action.

Peasant partisanship in the cristiada is simply not explicable in purely economic terms. The ranks of both the cristero rebels and the agrarista militias included landless peasants, smallholders, sharecroppers, tenants, and members of corporate Indian communities. Agricultural production was certainly hard hit by years of warfare, banditry, and recurrent drought, but economic insecurities were hardly limited to the center-west, much less to the cristero communities of the center-west. Nor can economic insecurities explain why so many landless peasants, such as those in San José de Gracia, rebelled against a state that offered them significant material incentives through the revolutionary agrarian reform program, or why others, as in San Pedro Caro, rejected a land grant (dotación), insisting that their land claims be recognized and respected through the much more difficult process of restitution. The cultural variables suggested by new social movements theory hardly offer a better explanation of partisanship: the Catholic Church and religious practice were certainly of central symbolic and institutional importance in cristero communities, but this was also true of the vastly more numerous communities that neither rebelled against the anticlerical state, nor actively supported it through the agrarista movement. Most agrarista peasants were devout Catholics as well, although religious practice had often become divorced from other local institutions and sometimes constituted a profound source of factional conflict in the context of revolutionary state formation in the 1920s.

Land was, of course, important to the cristero rebels, as were religious practice and the Catholic Church. But these peasants did not see land and religious practice as distinct spheres of life, nor can we understand their actions if we abstract economic interests or cultural identities from the normative and institutional fabric of rural life. Rather, peasants understood land, religious practice, and local political authority to be intertwined in ways that depended upon their own local histories of conflict and accommodation, and these understandings, in turn, produced divergent responses to the conflicts over revolutionary agrarianism and

anticlericalism in the 1920s. Although the nature of local agrarian and political conflicts varied considerably within both the cristero and the agrarista camps, there is a general pattern to their outcomes. The predominantly Catholic communities of the Pacific coast and the central, northwestern, and southwestern highlands survived the Porfiriato with their landed bases and local institutions more or less intact. The Catholic Indian communities of the central highlands and Pacific coast had been able to retain local control over communal property rights in the course of struggles over the implementation of the liberal land reform, while the ranchero communities of the northwestern and southwestern highlands expanded private property ownership through the fragmentation of haciendas and the legal and illegal acquisition of land from neighboring Indian communities. In all cases, religious practice remained a central source of community identity and solidarity, closely intertwined with institutions of local political authority, be such authority vested in the parish priest or the politico-religious elders of the cabildo.

In the predominantly agrarista communities of Zacapu, the Lake Pátzcuaro region, and northeastern Michoacán, the agrarian and political conflicts of the second half of the nineteenth century resulted in the near-complete loss of land, through the liberal reparto, the Porfirian Terrenos Baldíos Laws, illegal sales, foreclosures by state tax authorities, and outright seizures by neighboring hacendados and rancheros. In many cases, this represented an intensification and acceleration of processes under way since the colonial period. In Indian communities, such as those of the Zacapu region, the alienation of land was accompanied by the transfer of local political power from the politico-religious authorities of the cabildo to mestizo elites and parish priests allied with neighboring landowners. Religious practice did not necessarily change in content, but its relationship to other community institutions generally did. No longer financed by communal resources or regulated by the cabildo, religious practice ceased to be such a strong source of community identity and cohesion, associated as it increasingly was with the sponsorship of mestizo elites and more closely linked to the institutional Church and the parish priest. Particularly in the 1920s, religion caused deep divisions and intense factional violence within communities, as agrarista peasants employed revolutionary anticlericalism to displace competing sources of political authority (and a good number of personal enemies) at the local level.

As a popular movement asserting local claims and identities vis-à-vis a central state, the cristiada of 1926 to 1929 had ample precedent in Mexican history. It falls within that broad and eclectic category of events that Knight (1986b: 115–27) calls serrano rebellions: multiclass movements with a significant popular base, directed against an expanding and centralizing state intent upon establishing political authority at the local level. Such rebellions were particularly common when the state was both weak and intrusive. This was the case in the tumultuous decades of the 1850s and 1860s, when state makers attempted to fashion a new liberal economic and political order, through a series of reforms aimed at the transformation of property rights, popular cultures, and understandings of citizenship within Mexico's Indian communities. It was most certainly the case between 1915 and 1930, between the destruction of the old state, marked by the Constitutionalists' defeat of the Huertistas and the consolidation of a new one during the latter years of Calles's *maximato* (1928–34) and the presidential administration of Lázaro Cárdenas (1934–40). This period was marked by a partial "vacuum of sovereignty" (Scott 1994: ix) that afforded popular groups a good deal of room for negotiation and resistance in matters of property rights, taxes, conscription, local political authority, and justice. Antistatist movements of the type described by Knight were rife throughout the period, particularly in southern and center-west Mexico. But if popular antistatism was ubiquitous prior to the consolidation of the revolutionary state under Cárdenas, why then was it expressed through a Catholic political identity in the 1920s in the center-west, and not at other times or in other regions in Mexico?

Here the relationship between long-term local histories and short-term conjunctural factors (Stern 1987a: 11) comes most clearly into play. The Catholic political identity of the cristero rebels was a product of long-term legacies of political and agrarian conflict at the local level (the historical component of identity), and of the political and strategic context in which collective action took place in the center-west in the 1920s (the conjunctural component). This context included concrete and immediate threats to local institutions regulating access to land, religious practice, and political authority, in the form of revolutionary anticlericalism and agrarianism. It also included the existence of a strong grassroots network of lay Catholic organizations capable of providing anti-

state peasants with logistical, military, and political support. Such a combination of historical and conjunctural factors existed only in the center-west in the 1920s, and only in the center-west was there sustained and widespread popular rebellion during the cristiada. Other regions certainly experienced antistate rebellions with strong popular support. But given different political and strategic contexts in those cases, popular antistatism was expressed through quite different political identities.

Carrancista efforts to reestablish the authority of the central state sparked numerous counterrevolutionary rebellions in the period between 1914 and 1920, particularly in southern Mexico. Having overthrown Victoriano Huerta in 1914, the Constitutionalist forces led by Venustiano Carranza began to battle their former allies in northern and central Mexico, the popular armies of Francisco Villa and Emiliano Zapata. In the south, the Carrancistas attempted to establish control in a region as yet little touched by revolutionary activity, through military occupation and a set of structural, social, and political reforms aimed at undermining the power of landlords and clergy, and building a base of popular support among workers and peasants. Such efforts were widely resented, however, by popular groups and elites alike, as unwelcome intrusions in local affairs, particularly when they entailed new taxes, emergency war contributions, conscription, anticlericalism, and corruption.

In Oaxaca, such resentment was manifested in the Oaxacan Sovereignty Movement of 1915 to 1920, described by Garner (1990: 163–65) as "a vehicle for a broad spectrum of both popular and provincial opposition to the form of political centralization that Constitutionalism attempted to impose upon the state after 1915."[3] Although it certainly included Porfirian elites dedicated to the restoration of the old social and political order, the social bases of the Oaxacan Sovereignty Movement lay in the indigenous peasantry of the Sierra Mixteca and Sierra Juárez, whose participation was, according to Garner (1990: 165), "founded upon the protection and promotion of local, community, and regional autonomy, threatened by the imposition of an encroaching, alien, and central political authority."

As in the Purépecha highlands of Michoacán, much of the agrarian conflict in the central valleys and highlands of Oaxaca grew out of centuries-long border conflicts between rival pueblos. Along similar lines, peasants had engaged in a complex process of negotiation and accommodation with state officials during the second half of the nineteenth century, through which they attempted to either avoid the liberal

land reform altogether, or to implement it on their own terms, in keeping with local norms and institutions. For the most part, they did this, in the time-honored tradition of Oaxacan peasants, through the instigation of litigation against rival communities and encroaching landowners, and the pursuit of legal injunctions against the actions of state officials (Purnell 1997). Given these legacies of local agrarian and political conflict, many communities in central Oaxaca, like their counterparts in parts of Michoacán, emerged from the Porfiriato with their landed bases, popular cultures, and institutions of politico-religious authority intact.

Motivated by specific Carrancista abuses, the Oaxacan Sovereignty Movement drew upon identities forged through a long history of intermittent conflict between the regional caudillos of the highlands and the representatives of the central state in the valleys, mobilizing peasants through kinship, patronage, and clientelism, central characteristics of nineteenth-century serrano society (Garner 1990: 165). In Oaxaca, therefore, popular antistatism was expressed through the political identities of soberanista and serrano in the second half of the 1910s, the construction and mobilization of these identities products of local historical experiences, the availability of allies among the serrano caudillos and the Porfirian aristocracy of the central valleys, and the timing and nature of revolutionary state formation, in the form of military occupation by Carrancista state makers.

Carrancista efforts to establish military and political control in the south generated other rebellions in 1914 and 1915, often framed within a discourse of "states' rights" and drawing variable levels of popular support.[4] The Carrancistas arrived in Chiapas in the fall of 1914 and promptly set out to assert their control by undermining the power and prerogatives of landed elites and the Church: they abolished debt peonage, expropriated ecclesiastical property, shut down convents, and initiated a land reform program. Not surprisingly, such efforts generated a landlord rebellion by the end of the year. Even though it was aimed at the restoration of the Porfirian order, the rebellion drew considerable popular support, on the part of estate workers and Indian peasants whose opposition to external interference in state and local politics exceeded the class and communal conflicts that divided them from each other and from the landed elite. Francisco Múgica brought the Carrancista revolution to Tabasco with similar results. In a preview of his later tenure as governor of Michoacán (1920–22), Múgica introduced educational and agrarian reforms, anticlericalism, and feminist congresses to highly resis-

tant Tabascans. "Radical this may have been," as Knight (1986b: 246) writes, "popular it was not."

Southern resistance to Carrancista efforts to establish the authority of a recreated central state coalesced in the period of 1916 to 1920 under the banner of Felicismo. Félix Díaz, nephew of Porfirio and former ally and coconspirator of Victoriano Huerta, provided the southern rebels with a common name, a modicum of logistical coordination and military leadership, and an ideological program vague enough to encompass a wide range of local grievances with the central state. The Felicistas rejected the revolutionary constitution of 1917, embraced the liberal one of 1857, and called for an end to the corrupt, authoritarian, and arbitrary rule of the Carrancistas. Their common name and program, however, represented only tenuous political and military alliances between movements that remained rooted in local identities, leadership, and grievances against the central state. As Knight (1986b: 383) argues, "[the] common denominator which loosely united the varied Felicista forces—and for which the proclaimed adherence to the 1857 Constitution was a kind of political shorthand—was a rejection of alien, northern interlopers (whose generals were callous and whose troops ill-behaved) and an assertion of local opposition and resistance."

In the northwestern state of Sonora, the Yaquis periodically battled the Carrancistas between 1915 and 1920, drawing upon their long history of resistance to the authority of the central state—colonial, liberal, Porfirian, and revolutionary.[5] In the twentieth century, as before it, the Yaquis attempted to maintain complete control over their traditional territories in the Yaqui river valley and to defend the autonomy of their institutions of local politico-military authority in the face of a centralizing state. Between 1828 and 1833, the Yaquis rebelled in response to decrees that made the Yaqui pueblos subordinate to a non-Yaqui (*yori*) town, mandated the privatization of lands cultivated by the Yaquis, promoted the colonization of uncultivated Yaqui land by non-Yaquis, and drafted Yaqui soldiers into the state militia. Temporarily quelled, the Yaquis rebelled periodically over the course of the next 30 years, whenever afforded the opportunity to do so by political crises and civil wars, forming alliances with whatever yori faction seemed most likely at the time to advance the Yaqui agenda. Most notably, the Yaquis allied first with Mexican conservatives and subsequently with the French army of occupation, in response to attempts by the Juarista governor Ignacio Pesquerira to implement the liberal program in Yaqui territory. With the

consolidation of the central state during the Porfiriato, the Yaquis were forced to resort to guerrilla warfare and sporadic raids on yori towns. Porfirio Díaz eventually achieved pacification, but only through the large-scale deportation of Yaqui civilians to southern Mexico.

Once Díaz was overthrown at the onset of the Mexican Revolution, the Yaqui deportees returned home, fighting the Huertistas and then the Carrancistas alongside the Villistas. After the defeat of the Villistas in 1915, the Yaquis continued to battle the Carrancistas, readopting the guerrilla warfare strategies and modes of military leadership they had developed over the course of the nineteenth century. In the aftermath of the Agua Prieta rebellion of 1920, the Yaquis reached a peace accord with Adolfo de la Huerta, then the provisional president, which afforded them partial political autonomy. The peace was short-lived, however, because neither Alvaro Obregón nor Plutarco Elías Calles was willing to tolerate Yaqui political autonomy or control over the potentially rich lands of the Yaqui river valley. The Yaquis rebelled once more in 1926 and 1927, citing religious grievances as well as their traditional concerns with land and the preservation of the political institutions of the pueblos. Such grievances led U.S. diplomatic observers to link the Yaquis with the Catholic Church and the early, disorganized uprisings of the cristero rebellion. As the U.S. consul in Mazatlán (Sinaloa) put it:

> The Indians have sent word out that they are in revolt demanding their priests, a change of administration of the state of Sonora, and the return of their lands on the Yaqui river. . . . There seems to be a general belief that the Yaqui revolt is not local, nor purely an Indian uprising, but is the beginning of a general revolt across the country, headed by the Catholic Church with an unknown leader. It appears to be well-organized and directed by other than the brains of an Indian.[6]

This final antistate rebellion of the Yaquis was distinct from that of the cristeros, however, completely disconnected from the League for the Defense of Religious Liberty and other lay Catholic organizations, and rooted firmly in centuries-old Yaqui traditions and mechanisms of resistance. It came to an end in 1927, the aerial bombardment of the Yaqui pueblos proving to be much more effective than previous state counterinsurgency tactics (Knight 1986b: 374–75).

The major military revolts of the 1920s were, in large part, power struggles between contending factions of a heterogeneous revolutionary elite, as when Adolfo de la Huerta rebelled against Alvaro Obregón's

installation of Plutarco Elías Calles in the presidency. But they also involved—and generated—struggles over the nature of the emerging central state. Although revolutionary orthodoxy holds that the losers were invariably counterrevolutionaries intent upon the restoration of the Porfiriato, the military rebellions of the 1920s, like the antistate movements of the 1910s, included a broad range of political and ideological agendas, and provided numerous opportunities to address local grievances through establishing alliances with national political actors. The delahuertistas of 1923 and 1924 certainly included in their ranks many of Mexico's most reactionary generals and politicians. But they also had the support of ex-Villistas, such as Nicolás Fernández, Hipólito Villa, and Manuel Chao in Chihuahua and Durango (Wasserman 1990a: 221), and of reformist Carrancistas, such as Salvador Alvarado, the former governor of Yucatán. Referring to the ideological heterogeneity of the delahuertista ranks, the U.S. chargé d'affaires noted the Alvarado was "bitterly hostile to the [Obregón] Administration, and yet distinguished by more radically socialist doctrines and practices than are generally characteristic of the leaders of the rebellion."[7]

The Mugiquistas of Michoacán initially sided with the delahuertistas as well. De la Huerta had earlier supported Francisco Múgica in the latter's ongoing conflict with Obregón, and he promised to install an agrarista governor in the state once Obregón and Calles were overthrown. Múgica was arrested by loyal federal troops when he attempted to take control of the governor's palace in December 1923, but his many followers continued to vacillate between de la Huerta and Obregón for some time.[8] Primo Tapia, the agrarista leader of Naranja, managed to switch sides some seven times over the course of the rebellion (Friedrich 1977: 109). This was not a question of ideological inconsistency, but rather of difficult and shifting political and military calculations as to which side had the best chance of winning and advancing local agendas.

Although subjected to military incursions and widespread banditry in the 1910s, the region of the center-west was a relative latecomer to the revolution. As in southern Mexico in the 1910s, state officials attempted to carry out a revolution from above in the center-west in the 1920s, combining structural, social, and political reforms with a concerted effort to mobilize peasant and worker support through the creation of state-sponsored (and sometimes armed) peasant and worker movements. In these "laboratories of the new state" (Benjamin 1990: 71), revolutionary state makers such as José Guadalupe Zuno, governor

of Jalisco (1922–26), and Francisco Múgica, governor of Michoacán (1920–22), articulated a strong link between anticlericalism and agrarianism as two sides of the same revolutionary coin, defining their opponents, elite and popular, as fanatical and counterrevolutionary Catholics.[9] Popular resistance to revolutionary state formation was expressed in much the same terms, the defense of local agrarian, cultural, and political agendas linked to support for the Church vis-à-vis an anticlerical state.

At the same time, the intensification of revolutionary anticlericalism at the regional and national level led lay Catholic elites to organize and mobilize through the National League for the Defense of Religious Liberty, the Catholic Association of Mexican Youth, the Popular Union, and the secret society known simply as the U. These organizations helped to sustain the cristiada in communities and regions where the rebellion had strong popular support, through the provision of arms and ammunition, military leadership, and logistical support. The alliances forged between these organizations and the rural rebels also contributed to the latter's Catholic political identity and discourse. Both the Catholic Church and its affiliated lay organizations mobilized against revolutionary anticlericalism outside of the center-west, but it was only in the center-west that a strong network of Catholic organizations coincided with the existence of a significant number of communities faced with concrete and immediate threats to their norms and institutions in the form of revolutionary agrarianism and anticlericalism in the mid-1920s.

In a broad sense, the grievances involved in the antistate popular movements of the 1910s and 1920s were quite similar, in Oaxaca and Sonora, as in Michoacán and Jalisco: local norms, resources, and institutions were threatened by revolutionary state formation, as manifested in church closures, restrictions on religious practice, new taxes and military conscription, the imposition of local authorities, secular (and eventually "socialist") education, graft and corruption, and the loss of local control over property rights. The political identities through which these grievances were expressed differed considerably, however, over time and across regions: in the south, antistate peasants rebelled as serranos, felicistas, and soberanistas; in Sonora, they identified the enemy as yori and rebelled as Yaqui guerrilla fighters (broncos); and in the center-west, they called themselves católicos, libertadores, and, eventually, cristeros. These different political identities, in turn, were products of local and regional histories and patterns of sociopolitical organization (the histor-

ical component of identity), the timing and dynamics of revolutionary state formation, and the availability of political and military alliances and legitimating discourses (the conjunctural components). Thus the soberanistas of Oaxaca drew upon a historical legacy of adamant federalism and a social organization based on caudillismo, kinship, and clientelism; their rebellion was sparked by the Carrancista military occupation of 1915 to 1920. The Yaquis of Sonora took advantage of the overthrow of Díaz and subsequent civil wars between contending revolutionary armies to press long-standing claims with respect to their territorial and political autonomy. In battling the Carrancistas during the second half of the 1910s, they drew upon identities and repertoires of resistance developed over the course of nineteenth-century revolts against liberal and Porfirian state makers. The Catholic political identity of the center-west rebels, in turn, reflected the historically strong connection between property rights, religious practice, and political authority in many communities, the cristero rebellion having been sparked by the extremely anticlerical nature of revolutionary state formation in the center-west in the 1920s and sustained by a dense network of lay Catholic organizations at the regional level.

Popular Movements and State Formation

The state that emerged from the Mexican Revolution of 1910 to 1940 is not the democratic vehicle for the realization of popular aspirations and social justice envisioned by orthodox historians. Nor, however, is it a "Leviathan on the Zócalo" (Benjamin 1985: 202), its nature determined by the functional requirements of dependent capitalist development or the logic of some secular process of political centralization, as argued by revisionist scholars. Rather, as I contend throughout the book, the Mexican state is the product of historically contingent struggles between diverse elite and popular groups, entailing multiple areas of contestation and negotiation. Popular groups can hardly be said to have won the war, but they certainly succeeded in shaping the state, insofar as elites were forced to accommodate values, practices, and institutions that ran contrary to their understandings of a modern, secular, capitalist society (Knight 1990b). Popular understandings of land and community, be they rooted in private property or communal holdings, limited the degree to which revolutionary elites could create and impose a new property regime based on state ownership and distribution of use rights through the

ejido. Popular religious beliefs and practices, meanwhile, frustrated elite attempts to create a secular society based on a uniform national identity.

State formation, as Joseph and Nugent (1994a: 20) argue, involves the creation of institutions of rule, as well as a "common discursive framework that sets out central terms around which and in terms of which contestation and struggle can occur." Popular groups continued to contest the role of the state in rural communities long after the consolidation of the central state under Lázaro Cárdenas, but in doing so, they increasingly employed the identities, discourses, and institutions established by revolutionary state makers.[10] Sometimes, peasants simply rejected official names and histories. When the residents of Paricutín were relocated, state officials insisted on naming the new town Caltzontzin, part of a broader effort to change place names to honor secular heroes or the precolonial indigenous past. The residents never adopted the new name, however, referring to themselves as the comunidad indígena of Paricutín, a term that had no juridical meaning but which was part of their long-standing efforts to win state recognition of their claims to communal land.[11] In the oral histories of the "volcano years," the residents of Nuevo San Juan Parangaricutiro rarely refer to the considerable efforts of agrarian officials to find them a new town site; the legitimacy of their new location rests on its having been chosen by the Lord of the Miracles (expressing the will of the community), not on the benevolence of the state. Even the use (and misuse) of hegemonic discourses afforded plenty of opportunities for contesting power relations, however, through the assertion of counterhegemonic claims. Having received an ejido, for example, the peasants of Zacán consistently insisted on calling themselves comuneros rather than ejidatarios, and on electing a representative of communal property (*representante de bienes comunales*) rather than the ejido commission required by law (Moheno 1985: 145).

The impact of state formation on popular movements is apparent in the ways popular identities, strategies, and grievances are shaped by the political and institutional context in which collective action takes place. On a more subtle but very real level, popular movements have continued to shape the state itself in Mexico, stretching interpretations of state-sanctioned discourses and employing state laws and institutions to gain recognition of popular identities and claims that the state did not necessarily intend to recognize in the creation of those laws and institutions. Consider the case of San Juan Parangaricutiro. Taking advantage of their local political power and alliances with revolutionary state officials, mes-

tizo elites in San Juan continued to appropriate and alienate communal land after the defeat of the cristeros. Whereas state officials recognized San Juan's possession of 21,106 hectares of communal land in 1907, by 1943 the community was in possession of only 3,390 hectares, much of which was claimed by Paricutín in its restitution petition.[12] This ongoing conflict led many members of the majority faction within the community to support the sinarquistas, a conservative Catholic movement that emerged in 1937 in response to a renewal of anticlericalism during the presidential administration of Lázaro Cárdenas, most notably the "socialist education" campaign aimed at eradicating the Church's role in primary education. The movement reached a peak in 1940 and 1941, in the context of widespread popular discontent with the election of Manuel Avila Camacho as Cárdenas's successor in the presidency, and then declined throughout the second half of the 1940s.[13]

In Michoacán, the sinarquistas garnered considerable popular support in regions that had been predominantly Catholic and cristero in the 1920s. The movement's popularity in San Juan Parangaricutiro, as elsewhere in the Purépecha highlands, was a product of both its support for the Church and its attacks on revolutionary agrarianism, above all the institution of the ejido. According to sinarquista propaganda, the revolutionary agrarian reform program entailed little more than a change of *patrón,* from the landlord to the state; only through the private ownership of property could peasants ever hope to be truly free. This emphasis on private property certainly had great appeal in the ranchero communities of the northwestern and southwestern highlands of Michoacán, but it also appealed to residents of the Indian communities of the Purépecha highlands, insofar as it constituted an attack on state control over the definition and distribution of property rights at the local level. According to oral histories, San Juan residents saw the National Sinarquista Union (Unión Nacional Sinarquista; UNS) as a vehicle through which they might defend local interests vis-à-vis the central state. Referring to the sinarquistas, a resident of Nuevo San Juan told Plá and Moheno (1981: 74–79): "They were defenders of themselves, of their own villages, people who could defend themselves better united. They wanted the government to listen to them, to pay attention to them, to support them, in a word. . . . [I]n San Juan, people wanted to belong to the UNS to make sure that the government would pay attention to them."

The sinarquistas could do little to stop the appropriation and alienation of San Juan Parangaricutiro's communal land. Gradually, however,

over the course of several decades, changes in the legal and institutional framework governing rural property rights afforded the residents of San Juan a new political identity and weapons with which to fight their long-standing battles with mestizo elites within the community, and their age-old rival, the neighboring community of Paricutín. Taking advantage of these new political possibilities, the católicos of San Juan Parangaricu-tiro began to identify themselves as comuneros and demand that the state recognize their right to the communal lands granted to them by the Crown during the colonial period.

The revolutionary Constitution of 1917 certainly recognized the existence of communal land, but clearly intended it to be a transitional form of property, stipulating that communities that had "conserve[d] their communal character" should have "the legal capacity to enjoy in common the waters, woods, and lands" that they had retained as communal property, "until such time as the manner of making the division of land shall be determined by law" (Simpson 1937: 69). The old comunidad indígena, juridically "extinguished" under the liberal reforms, had no distinct legal status, either in the constitution or the agrarian code. However, the redistribution of land under the revolutionary agrarian reform program generated new conflicts between ejidatarios, large and small private property owners, and peasants claiming rights to communal land, leading state officials to gradually clarify the status of communal property. In 1958, regulations were issued for a new agrarian procedure called the Recognition and Titling of Communal Property, through which peasants could petition the state for confirmation of their de facto, and presumably "quiet and peaceful," possession of communal lands "since time immemorial." And in 1971, through an amendment to the agrarian code, the state explicitly recognized, for the first time, the co-munidad agraria (successor to the *comunidad indígena*) as a corporate entity with juridical status distinct from that of the ejido, and distinguished between the rights of comuneros as opposed to ejidatarios (Váz-quez León, 1992: 113–14).

These legal and institutional shifts were not intended to create new rights, much less to redistribute property. Rather, they were simply meant to clarify existing property rights within the countryside, identifying and recognizing communal lands held by peasants since the colonial period, so as to resolve conflicts between those peasants and neighboring ejidatarios and small proprietors. But the clarification of existing property rights has never been a simple matter in the Mexican countryside,

as neoliberal reformers have found to their dismay in the 1980s and 1990s.[14] Many peasants have been able to use the reconocimiento procedure to pursue decades and centuries-old claims against individual landowners and rival pueblos, in some cases recovering long-disputed land through the newly state-sanctioned identity of comunero. Thus, as self-identified comuneros, the former Catholics and cristeros of San Juan Parangaricutiro employed the new laws and institutions with respect to communal property to regain control over land that had been appropriated and often sold by the mestizo families throughout much of the twentieth century, and they consolidated their long-standing claims against Paricutín, by obtaining a presidential resolution recognizing and titling over 14,000 hectares of communal land in 1991.[15]

The state's gradual recognition of the communal property regime generated new possibilities for political organization and collective action across Michoacán. In the 1980s, the Emiliano Zapata Comunero Union (Unión de Comuneros Emiliano Zapata; UCEZ) emerged as one of the strongest peasant organizations in the state, second only to the official National Peasant Confederation (Confederación Nacional Campesina; CNC) and representing some 150 ejidos and comunidades agrarias.[16] Engaged in the defense of community land rights vis-à-vis private mining and forestry companies, the UCEZ has also attempted to reaffirm and sometimes re-create the corporate Indian community, through the defense and recuperation of communal lands. As Gledhill (1988: 264) argues with respect to UCEZ, "[i]ts *indigenista* orientation is not exclusionary and it is not a romantic or 'backward-looking' movement: everyone concerned is aware that they are trying to *re-create* their lives on the basis of reconstructed social relationships and a reconstructed culture by obtaining possession of economic resources." Although the membership of the organization is spread throughout Michoacán, the most active and militant communities are located in the former Catholic and cristero regions of the Pacific coast and the Purépecha highlands.

Within the Indian communities of the coast and highlands, the political identities of Catholic and comunero have expressed quite similar understandings of the interrelationships between property rights, popular cultures, and political authority. As Reinaldo Lucas Domínguez (1991: 46), an activist in the contemporary comunero movement, puts it: "One may ask why we insist so much on the communal ownership of the land; for us it is important, given that the communal ownership of the land allows us to maintain our unity, to maintain our culture, our indige-

nous traditions such as language; it is the basis of the development and the subsistence of our communities." Both identities have also expressed similar understandings of citizenship and legitimate state-community relationships, in which the state recognizes and respects local norms, practices, and institutions. What has changed is the political and institutional context in which political identities are constructed and collective action takes place. Each time the Mexican state has attempted to redefine the relationship between peasant communities and the state, it has added a new layer to local legacies of agrarian and political conflict and has created possibilities for new alliances, new claims, and new identities.

Notes

1 What Makes Peasants Counterrevolutionary?

1   San Juan's entry into the cristero rebellion is described by Moheno (1985: 141–43) and Meyer (1973/74a: 189). The quote is from an interview conducted by Moheno with an unidentified resident of San Juan. The Lord of the Miracles was San Juan's most important Christ-saint and was venerated throughout the Purépecha highlands (see chapter 6). Most sources estimate that the number of active rebels ranged from 20,000 to 50,000. In March of 1928, the National League for the Defense of Religious Liberty (LNDLR, or League) claimed to wield an army of 50,000 rebels, almost half of them in the states of Jalisco and Michoacán (INAH, CR, Reel 16, LNDLR special bulletin, March 1928). Enrique Gorostieta, the chief military commander of the cristeros, estimated that he had 20,000 rebels under his command in mid-1929 (INAH, CR, Reel 30, Enrique Gorostieta to "Val," 16 May 1919). U.S. diplomatic and military intelligence sources reported that the number of rebels ranged from a low of 5,000 to a high of 25,000 in 1927 and 1928 (DS, 812.00/29215.5, Dwight Morrow, U.S. Ambassador to Mexico, to U.S. State Department, 16 July 1928; USMI, U.S. Military Attaché, Mexico, to U.S. War Department, Reports on Stability of the Government, 17 April, 22 May, 7 August, and 14 August 1928).

2   This incident is described in *David*, 22 June 1959, p. 179, a magazine produced by veterans of the cristiada between 1952 and 1968.

3   The term *agrarista* will be used here to refer to peasants who gave active political or military support to the state or to individual revolutionary leaders. These would constitute only a minority of those peasants who had applied for either land grants or for the restitution of communal lands under the agrarian reform program. The mobilization of agrarista peasants varied according to military necessity; J. Meyer (1973/74a: 159–60) estimates that their numbers ranged from 5,000 to 20,000 over the course of the rebellion.

4   The term *cristero* was not employed until 1929, when the government began to use it in a pejorative sense to imply that any military movement led by Christ

was doomed to fail. Although rebel veterans later adopted the name, throughout the course of the rebellion they usually referred to themselves as Catholics, as did many people who opposed the regime but did not actively participate in the rebellion.

5   Most notably, see Tannenbaum [1929] 1968, [1933] 1966; Gruening 1928; Simpson 1937; Weyl and Weyl 1939; and Brenner 1943.

6   See, among many others, J. Meyer 1973/74a,b,c, 1976, 1977, 1991; Ruiz 1980; and Womack 1991.

7   Several of the major works on the cristero rebellion itself treat it as a conflict between Church and state and focus almost exclusively on elite actors, aspirations, and organizations. Quirk's (1973) analysis centers on the actions and interactions of the Mexican episcopate, revolutionary officials, and U.S. diplomats; he argues that few peasants came to the support of the Church, because the clergy and the sacraments were all but irrelevant to peasant lives and their practice of popular Catholicism. Bailey (1974) focuses on the urban, lay, middle-class Catholics of the LNDLR; although he acknowledges that most of the rebels were peasants, he considers them peripheral to the political competition between Catholic and revolutionary elites. Olivera Sedano (1966) also centers her analysis on the League, but is somewhat more careful in distinguishing between the goals of the urban *ligueros* and the rural rebels.

8   Some orthodox scholars simply deny the popular character of the rebellion altogether. Gruening (1928: 328), for example, writes that "[t]he Calles government properly made light of the Catholic rebellion. It had no popular following." Likewise, Brenner (1943: 78) claims that the Mexican peasantry as a whole rejected the Church, choosing instead to support a revolutionary regime that promised to fulfill their demands for land.

9   DS, 812.00/28411, James Sheffield, U.S. Ambassador to Mexico, to U.S. State Department, 6 May 1927.

10   See chapter 3 on the delahuertista (named after Adolfo de la Huerta) rebellion of 1923 to 1924. On the Felicistas of the 1910s (named after Félix Díaz, the nephew of Porfirio Díaz), see Knight 1986b. On the Oaxacan Sovereignty Movement of 1915 to 1920, whose adherents were the *soberanistas,* see Ruiz Cervantes 1983, 1993 and Garner 1990.

11   Although I would not go as far as Scott 1990 in rejecting the concept of false consciousness altogether, I would argue that it should be used much more judiciously and with a stronger empirical foundation, rather than being broadly applied to behavior that does not appear to correspond with our theoretical expectations of how people should act.

12   On revisionism, see, among many others, Bailey 1978; Carr 1980; Fowler-Salamini 1993; and Joseph and Nugent 1994b.

13   On Michoacán, see Boyer 1997; Embriz Osorio 1984; Embriz Osorio and León García 1982; Espín Díaz 1986b; Fowler-Salamini 1980; Friedrich 1977, 1986; García Mora 1981; Guzmán Avila 1986; Huizer 1970; Múgica Mar-

tínez 1982; Ochoa Serrano 1989a; and Vargas González 1989. On agrarista movements elsewhere during the 1920s, see, among others, Ankerson 1980; Bartra 1985; Benjamin 1990; Buve 1980; Craig 1983; Falcón 1988; Fowler-Salamini 1971; Rivera Castro 1988; Schryer 1980; and Tobler 1988.

14 Jrade 1980, 1985 is an important exception. This work is a careful comparison of agrarian structures, forms of social organization, and political conflicts in agrarista and cristero communities in Jalisco.

15 Shadow and Rodríguez-Shadow (1994) make a similar point in their assessment of Meyer's religiosity argument. Many analysts have simply asserted that the cristero rebels were resident hacienda workers who, unlike the free villagers of the corporate indigenous communities, could neither benefit from the agrarian reform program under the prevailing agrarian code, nor escape the ideological constraints imposed by the landlords and priests (e.g., Brenner 1943, Huizer 1970, and Weyl and Weyl 1939).

16 A similar tautology is often applied to the center-west as a region. The center-west of Mexico was "more religious" than other regions in terms of the institutional strength of the Church. This institutional presence at the regional level cannot, however, explain divergent partisanship within the center-west. Nor was the center-west unique with respect to the presence of the Church: as an institutional force, the Church was also quite strong in a number of other states, particularly in the center-east, that witnessed sporadic violence in the context of the Church-state conflict but no sustained popular rebellion. See the discussion that follows in the text and in chapter 4.

17 As J. Meyer (1973c: 79) notes with respect to his own surveys of and interviews with survivors of the period, "it is surprising to see that the *agraristas* were as Catholic as the *cristeros.*"

18 Sporadic popular uprisings in support of the Church occurred throughout Mexico in the second half of 1927, from Coahuila in the north to Oaxaca in the south. During the period of 1926 to 1929, however, large-scale rebellion was sustained only in the center-west states of Jalisco, Michoacán, Colima, Guanajuato, and Zacatecas. The state of Nayarit, adjacent to but not usually considered part of the center-west, also experienced significant popular uprisings. The center-west is frequently, but erroneously, referred to as the Bajío, with which it overlaps. A relatively flat agricultural basin with a distinct social and agrarian history, the Bajío corresponds roughly to the states of Guanajuato and Querétaro and includes part of northern Michoacán.

19 Tutino (1986: 345), for example, claims that "[f]or the rancheros and sharecroppers of west central Mexico, a regime claiming to be revolutionary was threatening the landed and religious foundations of already difficult lives." Other analyses that view the cristiada as a ranchero rebellion include Díaz and Rodríguez 1979; Fábregas 1979; and Rueda Smithers 1981. See also Jrade 1980, 1985, who links conflicts over revolutionary state formation in Jalisco to local agrarian structures. On ranchero communities more generally, see

Barragán López 1990 and Barragán López et al. 1994. The question of class is discussed further in chapter 4.

20　The image of the center-west as a region of rancheros has developed in part because of the use of census data in delineating agrarian structures. The census category of rancho did not entail ethnic or agrarian connotations, but simply referred to villages too small to constitute pueblos. Villages designated as ranchos in the census might therefore be mestizo smallholding communities or corporate indigenous communities.

21　Exceptions include Guardino 1996; Joseph and Nugent 1994b; Mallon 1995; Rubin 1997; and Stern 1987a.

22　See, for example, the essays in Reyna and Weinert 1977 as well as J. Meyer 1976. Huntington (1968) presents much the same view of the Mexican state from a very different normative perspective.

23　See Benjamin 1985. Knight (1985: 12) points to the teleological nature of this view of the 1920s, which, he argues, greatly exaggerates the power of the pre-1940 state.

24　This view of state formation draws on the essays in Benjamin and Wasserman 1990 and, especially, Joseph and Nugent 1994b.

25　As Wasserman (1990c: 9) argues, neither Alvaro Obregón nor Lázaro Cárdenas could have established central state control over the regions without the support of significant numbers of organized peasants and workers. "The crucial struggle to form the Mexican state was, therefore," he concludes, "inseparable from the popular aspect of the revolution."

26　See Knight 1990b, 1994.

27　See also Becker 1995; Rubin 1997; and Vaughan 1997.

28　See Mallon 1994, 1995 for a similar argument.

29　The *ejido* is a form of property created under the revolutionary Agrarian Reform Law of 1915. Land grants were made to groups of peasants in the form of an ejido; the peasants, or *ejidatarios*, had use rights to the land, which was most often farmed individually, the ultimate ownership of which was retained by the state.

30　AGN, Papeles Presidenciales, Obregón-Calles, 818-N-12, Anexo 3, Ramón Aguilar, Zacapu, to President Calles, 19 October 1925.

31　ASRAM, San Pedro Caro, exp. 57 (dotación), "Breve exposición que formula todo el pueblo de San Pedro Caro a la honorable Comisión de Ingenieros encargada de ejecutar la ilegal resolución del Gobierno de este de Michoacán de Ocampo, declarando improcedente la restitución de tierras de ciénaga solicitada por este pueblo desde el veinte de enero de 1922," 30 March 1923.

32　AGN, Papeles Presidenciales, Obregón-Calles, 818-N-12, Anexo 3, Primo Tapia, Crispín Serrato, and Tomás Cruz to President Plutarco Elías Calles, 4 September 1925. See also the interviews conducted by Domínguez (1989).

33　ASRAM, San Pedro Caro, exp. 57 (dotación), Municipal President, Sahuayo, to CNA Delegation, Morelia, 28 February 1928.

34　Rockwell (1994: 202) refers to such practices as "popular appropriations of the revolution." Her central thesis with respect to education in Tlaxcala is that "the development of rural schools in the post revolutionary years owed as much to popular claims and resources as to any 'rational' designs of the newly forming state" (Rockwell 1994: 191). On the politics of culture and education in the revolutionary period, see Vaughan 1997.

35　See Hall (1981: 228), who argues that popular cultures are situated within a "larger field of social forces and cultural relations" and subject to contestation between subordinate and dominant groups.

36　See Becker 1995 and Knight 1990b.

37　See, for example, Escobar and Alvarez 1992 and Foweraker and Craig 1990, as well as Haber's (1996) analysis of recent trends in the literature on social movements in Latin America. For a critique of this literature with respect to peasant politics, see Starn 1992.

38　For a review and analysis of these disputes, see Skocpol 1982.

39　Much of the more recent work on peasant politics shows a similar concern with the broader political agendas advanced by peasants, particularly in the context of state formation. For example, Scott (1985, 1990) examines the far-reaching economic, political, and normative claims asserted by subordinate groups through popular cultures and everyday forms of resistance. The essays in Stern's edited volume stress the "innovative political engagement of the state by peasants" (1987a: 9) in Andean rebellions spanning the eighteenth through the twentieth centuries. Mallon's (1995) comparative analysis of nineteenth-century Mexico and Peru examines the ways peasants actively shaped liberal discourse and practice with respect to nationalism, citizenship, democracy, and property rights. See also Guardino 1996 on peasants and state formation in Guerrero in the first half of the nineteenth century. Finally, many of the essays in the volume edited by Joseph and Nugent (1994b), as well as Becker 1995, Rubin 1997, and Vaughan 1997, highlight the ways in which rural popular groups contested state formation in revolutionary Mexico in the arenas of political authority, property rights, culture and religious practice, education, and gender.

40　On the dubiousness of that distinction, see Boschi 1984; Cohen 1985; Haber 1996; Knight 1990a; Rubin 1990; and Starn 1992.

41　As Munck (1990: 25) writes with reference to the identity-oriented approach, "The processes whereby identities are formed, whether class-based, gender-based, or whatever, are seen as central questions." See also Starn 1992.

42　The terms derive from Cohen's (1985) discussion of the literature on social movements in the United States and Europe.

43　As Hindess (1983: 270–71) maintains, "Actors' ends and their forms of thought do change, partly as a function of what is available to choose from, and the point of several forms of political activity is to try to change them in a particular direction." See also Przeworski 1985.

44 "Popular politics," as Foweraker (1990: 44) maintains, "can only occur at all in intimate interrelation with state laws and institutions." See also Craig (1990), who argues that landless agricultural laborers in the Laguna region in the 1930s developed a collective identity as workers rather than as peasants, even though land was central to their claims, in large part because of "strategic" variables such as the prevailing agrarian and labor codes and the organizing efforts of the Mexican Communist Party.

45 Nor does it make sense to talk about cultural versus economic grievances (cf. Knight 1990b), because these were so thoroughly interwoven in the symbolic and institutional life of many rural communities.

46 Joseph and Nugent (1994a: 12) aptly refer to this approach as "bringing the state back in without leaving the people out."

47 See Hale 1968 on this tension in nineteenth-century liberalism.

2 Liberals, Indians, and the Catholic Church in Nineteenth-Century Michoacán

1 During the colonial regime, the Church was essentially part of the state: under the agreement (the *real patronato*) established at the time of the conquest, the pope granted the Spanish Crown control over all aspects of Church functioning, except for matters of dogma and clerical discipline, in exchange for converting conquered peoples to Catholicism. If this arrangement gave the state considerable powers, such as that of making appointments to the ecclesiastical hierarchy, it also meant that the Church could rely on state coercion in the enforcement of matters such as the tithe and the fulfillment of monastic vows. Given this history, the relationship between Church and state was inevitably a source of conflict after independence (1821), as liberals and conservatives struggled over the contours of the new state. See Farriss 1968 on the issue of ecclesiastical privilege in late colonial Mexico, and see Costeloe 1978 on the debate over patronage in the first decades after independence.

2 Indian community is used here to refer to rural communities that held corporate title to property by virtue of their status as *repúblicas de indios* during the colonial period. Such communities differed greatly in the extent to which they retained indigenous cultural practices, including dress, language, and forms of religious and political authority.

3 On the role in popular groups of nineteenth-century state formation in Mexico, see di Tella 1996; Guardino 1996; and Mallon 1995.

4 Given its brevity, my treatment of nineteenth-century liberalism obscures the importance of regional variations in liberal discourse and practice, these variations in part a result of the active role played by diverse popular groups in the liberal movement. On these regional variations, see Hamnett 1996.

5 See Bailey 1974: 9–10; Hale 1968: 125; and Sinkin 1979: 119.

6 Liberals differed greatly in their estimates of Church wealth, as do twentieth-

century scholars. Miguel Lerdo de Tejada, the author of the 1856 Disentailment Law, estimated Church wealth, including land, urban real estate, and properties to which ecclesiastical institutions held mortgage, to be 275 million pesos in 1857, or 21 percent of the total national wealth of 1.3 billion pesos. Other liberals, looking at the gold, silver, and religious art not included in Lerdo's estimate, considered 620 million pesos, or half of the national wealth, to be closer to the mark (Sinkin 1979: 117–18). Bazant's (1971: 13) research supports Lerdo's relative assessment, estimating that the total value of all of the productive and unproductive assets of the Church and its affiliated institutions was 100 million pesos, or one-fifth to one-quarter of the national wealth. For further discussions of the magnitude and sources of Church wealth, see Costeloe 1967 and Knowlton 1976.

7 See Hale's (1968) discussion of the relationship between property rights and politics in liberal ideology.

8 In 1833 to 1834 the liberal Valentín Gómez Farías, as acting president, passed a number of anticlerical laws that limited the political activities of the clergy, secularized education, abolished the mandatory tithe, and gave the state the right to make ecclesiastical appointments. This early attempt at reform was aborted almost immediately when Santa Ana ousted Gómez Farías, dissolved the Congress, and annulled most of the legislation. According to Guardino (1996), Gómez Farías had little support from other liberals (or federalists as Guardino calls them in this context) for his extreme anticlericalism.

9 The degree of popular support for and opposition to liberalism remains a source of debate, particularly in the period prior to the Porfiriato. Fraser (1972), Powell (1972), and Tutino (1986, 1988) all depict a liberalism aimed at the deliberate destruction of the landed bases of the Indian communities and popular resistance and rebellion; Mallon (1994, 1995) and Thomson (1991a, 1991b) argue that Mexican liberalism generated widespread popular support, and they highlight the extent to which peasants actively participated in defining and shaping its discourse and practice. Mallon, in particular, argues that peasants actively embraced the land reform prior to the Restored Republic, interpreting the Lerdo Law and related circulars and decrees to support their claims to a more just and equitable distribution of resources and to imply that the state had an obligation to protect the communities from the encroachments of haciendas and speculators.

10 Together with Guanajuato to the north, Michoacán suffered considerable economic destruction and social dislocation in the independence wars of 1810 to 1821. This was particularly true in the Tierra Caliente and Bajío valleys, regions where most of the state's haciendas were concentrated. Michoacán landowners, therefore, faced particularly trying times once the wars were over, and many, finding their property in ruins and their workers gone, were unable to meet interest payments on debts owed to the Church. Throughout the course of the 1820s and 1830s, some 21 of the state's largest landowners provided the

Church with proof that their estates had earned no income whatsoever, in order to secure deferrals on interest payments. Many landowners were finally forced to default, and the Church acquired their properties through foreclosure (Chowning 1984: 71–80). Bad times for *hacendados* could be good news for other agrarian classes: as Tutino (1986: 228–41) notes, landowners often responded to economic difficulties by leasing out more of their land to tenants and sharecroppers, thereby benefiting subsistence peasants and ranchero smallholders.

11 Once Juárez decreed the nationalization of Church property, the episcopate declared that any Catholic who purchased such property from the state would be excommunicated, even if this was done with the intention of supporting the Church; in practice, however, dummy sales were sometimes arranged, allowing the Church to retain de facto control over some of its property (Knowlton 1965: 523–24).

12 Chowning notes that these figures exclude divisions through inheritance, which led to the further fragmentation of haciendas in the state.

13 On the cargo system and the cofradías, see Bechtloff 1993, Brading 1994, and Stephen and Dow 1990b. On the cabildo, see Carrasco 1976 and Espín Díaz 1986a. The cofradías were by no means limited to Indian communities; as Brading (1994: 137) notes, they were common to all classes and races in Mexico. Some were dedicated to the celebration of the feast days of the liturgical calendar, some functioned as burial societies, and others were dedicated to the patron saints of particular communities and occupations. It was in the Indian communities, however, that the cofradías constituted an integral part of community organization and identity. With respect to the Indian communities of Michoacán, Brading (1994: 134) writes: "The distinction between hospital, mayordomía, confraternity, and the community at large was by no means clearly defined."

14 On the use and categories of communal property, see Carrasco 1976 and Espín Díaz 1986a.

15 See A. Gutiérrez 1989: 46. In some districts, such as Puruándiro, the small number of communities meant that there was little communal land; in others, the few existing communities held considerable amounts of property, as was the case with the coastal communities in the Coalcomán region.

16 AHPEM, Hijuelas, District of Zacapu, vol. 4, Municipal President, Zacapu, to Ministry of Government, Morelia, 26 February 1869.

17 Ibid.

18 In a 1902 letter, the Ministry of Finance acknowledged that the Lerdo Law had generated considerable conflict and confusion insofar as it did not provide clear instructions about the privatization of unleased communal properties, thus allowing outsiders to denounce and claim such land. It was the position of the ministry at that point that outsiders other than tenants could not denounce and claim communal land; any unleased land and rented land not claimed by

tenants was to be divided among the members of the community (AHPEM, Hijuelas, District of Uruapan, vol. 23, Ministry of Finance, Mexico City, to Governor of Michoacán, Morelia, 3 August 1902).

19 Lerdo's decree did not eliminate the small but often onerous fees and taxes imposed by state governments, including that of Michoacán, as part of the privatization process.

20 The questions raised by Article 8 were only gradually resolved: circulars issued in 1889 and 1890 affirmed that all communal lands were subject to privatization, to be distributed to community members unless claimed by current tenants (Simpson 1937: 29).

21 The Michoacán state legislature passed two land reform laws, one in 1827 and a second in 1851, neither of which was widely implemented. Both laws clearly exempted the fundo legal from privatization, and the 1851 law also exempted the ejido; both also included restrictions on selling and mortgaging parcels for four years after their privatization. On the history of land reform legislation in Michoacán, see Mendoza 1986 and Sánchez Díaz 1988 and 1989.

22 The degree to which communal lands were alienated through the terrenos baldíos laws of the Porfiriato is subject to dispute. Simpson (1937: 27) articulates the orthodox position on the subject in writing that the 1883 law "started an era of land grabbing and speculation which in a few years reached enormous proportions." Recent work by Holden (1994) contradicts this view, arguing that Porfirian officials tended to respect community land claims in the implementation of the baldíos laws. The care with which state authorities treated a denunciation of communal lands in San Juan Parangaricutiro (see chapter 6) suggests that, at least in some cases and under some conditions, peasant claims were, in fact, taken seriously during the Porfiriato.

23 In 1904, for example, the tax assessment on the communal lands of the coastal village of Pómaro was increased from 19,250 to 70,000 pesos. A state tax official wrote that the property in question was "very good, because it is covered by extensive forests in which one can find incredibly valuable wood, and they have, in addition, very good pasture and cropland" (AHPEM, Hijuelas, District of Coalcomán, vol. 2, Administrator of Revenues, Morelia, to Governor of Michoacán, Morelia, 3 February 1904). Not coincidentally, U.S. forest companies had recently expressed interest in exploiting the woodlands of the region.

24 See Sánchez Díaz 1988: 31–32. State authorities in Michoacán did little to enforce the Lerdo Law until late 1868; the process took three years because the community lacked funds for the necessary fees and taxes. Other communities carried out a partial division of their communal lands in response to an 1827 state law, which, given the weakness of the state in the early years after independence, suggests some support for privatization.

25 The status of mestizos in the land reform process was often a source of conflict. The Indian community was a juridical and political entity rather than a ter-

40 Cochet (1988) notes that neither the communal lands of the Indian community nor those of neighboring haciendas had boundaries established by accurate measurements or surveys. Until the mid–nineteenth century, however, there were no records of private property (either haciendas or ranchos) in the central region of the current municipio; only the northwest region of the municipio was incorporated into a hacienda.

41 AHPEM, Hijuelas, District of Coalcomán, District Prefect, Coalcomán, to Ministry of Government, Morelia, 1 November 1871.

42 See Brand 1960: 109–10; Cochet 1988: 217–80; and Sánchez Díaz 1988: 66–78.

43 See Chowning 1984; Embriz Osorio 1984; Estado de Michoacán 1958; and L. González 1968, 1974.

44 Much of the foreign investment in the state was concentrated in mining in the eastern part of the state and timber in the central highlands and Pacific coastal region. On the eve of the revolution, the American Smelting and Mining Company exploited relatively insignificant gold and silver mines in the eastern municipio of Angangueo; the French company of Dos Estrellas operated mines in Tlalpujahua. The various companies of Santiago Slade obtained timber concessions from the indigenous communities in the highlands around Uruapan, whereas the Pacific Timber Company operated in the southern part of the state, until it abandoned its concessions with the onset of the revolution.

45 Carrasco 1976; Estado de Michoacán 1958; and García Mora 1976, 1981.

3   State Formation in Revolutionary Michoacán

1 As the municipal president of Cuitzeo put it, in response to a request by the state historian for information on local experiences during the revolution, nothing much happened until bandits occupied the town for several months in 1918, after which "various groups passed by on their way to somewhere else" (AHPEM, Gobernación-Religión, caja 7, Municipal President, Cuitzeo, to Ministry of Government, Morelia, 19 February 1930).

2 There is a substantial literature on the social composition and political agendas of the Maderistas, Carrancistas, Villistas, and Zapatistas. For brief analyses, see LaFrance 1990 and Tutino 1990. See also the fuller treatments in Brading 1980; Katz 1981; Knight 1986; and Tutino 1986.

3 Thus the Pantoja brothers, together with some 300 of their sharecropper and ranchero followers, sacked and burned the town of Puruándiro in 1912, in response to an attempt by Maderista officials to take a census to be used for military conscription. See Pinet 1987: 16–23. These local movements correspond to Knight's (1986a) category of *serrano* rebellions, multiclass movements aimed at defending or establishing local autonomy vis-à-vis the central state. The revolution, as Knight (1986a: 368–69) notes, was both a product and a source of such rebellions; the many abuses of the Carrancista regime, in

particular, generated an entirely new generation of local serrano revolts in Michoacán, often (being anti-Carrancista) adopting the banner of Villismo. At least some of these local rebellions would continue as part of the cristiada: Prudencio Mendoza of the Cotija region, for example, led a contingent of rancheros first against the Carrancistas (as a Villista) and later against the Calles administration (as a cristero).

4 The organization did not survive the overthrow of Madero, however, although at least some of its members joined the anti-Huertista forces of Gertrudis Sánchez, based on his promises to restore their communal lands. See Ochoa Serrano 1989a.

5 See Friedrich 1977: 51; Knight 1986a: 219–21; Ochoa Serrano 1992: 119–20; and Ramírez 1986a: 127.

6 See García Avila 1987: 27–28; Knight 1986a: 213, 231; and Pérez Escutia 1987: 34.

7 Most of the petitioning communities were located in north-central Michoacán, in the regions around Morelia, Pátzcuaro, Zacapu, and Panindícuaro.

8 See Oikión Solano 1987. Many of the communities that petitioned for land in 1915 and 1916 would wait until the cristiada to see official action on their applications. Some de facto redistribution also took place under Rentería Luviano, as in the Cañada de los Once Pueblos, where peasants were granted permission to plant former communal lands; their occupation of these lands was later legalized by Cárdenas during his tenure as governor of Michoacán (1928–32), thus contributing to conflicts between the agrarista minority under the Prado family, and the smallholding peasants whose lands were among those adjudicated to the Pradistas (Ramírez 1986a: 128–29).

9 In Michoacán, the Zapatistas were never a political or military threat to the Carrancistas; the Villistas ceased being one after Villa's defeat in the Bajío in the spring of 1915 (Oikión Solano 1987: 95). Zapatistas attacked Michoacán from bases in the neighboring state of Mexico, operating in Maravatío, Zitácuaro, Tlalpujahua, Senguio, Irimbo, and Contepec (Pérez Escutia 1987: 43–45). Villista groups were more ubiquitous, in large part because the Villista label was adopted by or applied to a wide variety of rebels and activities, including banditry and local rebellion against Carrancista rule. See Knight 1986b: 273–74 and in the text that follows.

10 DS, 812.404/2, U.S. Vice Consul John P. Silliman, Tampico (Veracruz), to U.S. State Department, 27 July 1914.

11 On the emergence of the Catholic Action movement and Catholic congresses, see Bailey 1974; Ceballos Ramírez 1990; Olivera Sedano 1966; and Quirk 1973.

12 After the Maderista revolution, a new organization was created to coordinate Catholic Social Action projects aimed at improving the spiritual and material welfare of workers and peasants: the Catholic Association of Mexican Youth (Asociación Católica de la Juventud Mexicana; ACJM). This organization

would play a leading role in the National League for the Defense of Religious Liberty (Liga Nacional Defensora de la Libertad Religiosa; LNDLR), formed in 1925 in reaction to revolutionary anticlericalism; it would also provide much of the early and ill-fated leadership of the cristero rebellion. See chapter 4.

13   The law made no provision for expropriation, relying instead on the willingness of Catholic landowners to sell land, in keeping with the PCN's presumed vision of a good society as being organic and harmonious in nature.

14   DS, 812.404/2, U.S. Consul General, Mexico City, to U.S. State Department, 11 July 1914. Carranza intervened to nullify some of these restrictions.

15   DS, 812.404/18, Miguel de la Mora, Bishop of Zacatecas, San Antonio, to James Cardinal Gibbons, Archbishop of Baltimore, 14 August 1914.

16   One priest was permitted in towns of 500 to 10,000, two in towns of 10 to 30,000, and a maximum of four in towns of greater than 30,000. DS, 812.404/16, U.S. Consul, Veracruz, to U.S. State Department, 14 September 1914.

17   DS, 812.404/58, Antonio J. Paredes, Vicar General, Mexico City, to John P. Silliman, Special Representative, U.S. State Department, 22 January 1915.

18   See Knight 1986b: 206 and Oikión Solano 1987. Far more selectively, the commission also confiscated land and other properties belonging to landowners and merchants charged with supporting the Huerta administration.

19   The term *ejido* was based on the prerevolutionary communal lands of the same name, the pastures and woodlands used and owned in common by the Indian communities. The revolutionary *ejido* was quite distinct, however, in that peasants had only use rights, the distribution of which was controlled by the state rather than by the politico-religious authorities of the cabildo.

20   "Securing a restitution was justice," as Nugent (1993: 91) puts it with reference to Namiquipa, "while securing a *dotación* was an insult, a matter of the state posturing as a *patrón*."

21   ASRAM, San Pedro Caro, exp. 57 (dotación), Various San Pedro Caro residents to National Agrarian Commission, 8 November 1918.

22   ASRAM, San Pedro Caro, exp. 57 (dotación), "Breve exposición que formula todo el pueblo de San Pedro Caro a la honorable Comisión de Ingenieros encargada de ejecutar la ilegal resolución del Gobierno de este estado de Michoacán de Ocampo, declarando improcedente la restitución de tierras de ciénaga solicitada por este pueblo desde el veinte de enero de 1922," 30 March 1923. San Pedro Caro had the particular good fortune to be armed with irrefutable evidence of its ownership of communal lands in the Lake Chapala marshes, not the least of which were receipts for taxes paid on such land to the state as recently as 1922, documents related to the 1902 *reparto* that made it clear that the marshlands were not properly divided, and a survey carried out in 1916 by the juez de primera instancia de distrito de Jiquilpan that recognized the boundaries claimed by the community (AGN, CNA, Resoluciones Presidenciales, vol. 18, 3 April 1924).

23 AHPEM, Gobernación-Religión, caja 8/24, Jacinto Espinosa, Jacona, Michoacán, to Governor of Michoacán, Morelia, 26 August 1930. The Jacona peasants did well to worry about the government's reaction, should they have carried a saint's image into the fields. After Tarahumara Indians in western Chihuahua held an annual religious ceremony in 1927 with banners inscribed with the words "¡Viva Cristo Rey!" and with the images of Hidalgo and the Virgin of Guadalupe, state troops moved in to disperse the crowd, killing one person. The next day, three Tarahumara leaders were executed by a firing squad and 16 others were imprisoned (DS, 812.00/28324, U.S. Consul, Chihuahua to U.S. Secretary of State, 12 April 1927).

24 AHPEM, Gobernación-Religión, caja 8/24, Ministry of Government, Morelia, to Jacinto Espinosa, Jacona, 27 August 1930.

25 DS, 812.00/23686, U.S. Chargé d'Affaires to U.S. State Department, 13 April 1920. See also Benjamin (1990).

26 In addition to Múgica and Cárdenas of Michoacán, the most notable cases include Adalberto Tejeda of Veracruz, Tomás Garrido Canabal of Tabasco, Felipe Carrillo Puerto of Yucatán, Emilio Portes Gil of Tamaulipas, and José Guadalupe Zuno of Jalisco. The military rebellions of 1927 and 1929 are discussed in chapter 4.

27 DS, 812.00/23609, U.S. Chargé d'Affaires to U.S. State Department, 18 April 1920. AGN, Papeles Presidenciales, Obregón-Calles, 408-M-1, Memorandum by José Huerta, 15 December 1920.

28 DS, 812.00/23609, U.S. Chargé d'Affaires to U.S. State Department, 18 April 1920. AGN, Papeles Presidenciales, Obregón-Calles, 408-M-1, Special Commission of the Senate to the President, 7 June 1921; Memorandum by José Huerta, Former Interim Governor of Michoacán, 15 December 1920. Huerta notes that the state legislature did not support Obregón, "being composed in its majority of Bonillistas and Carrancistas." Ortiz Rubio therefore dissolved it, called for new elections, and handed over the governor's office to Rafael Alvarez, who shortly thereafter passed it on to General Lázaro Cárdenas, who called for elections in July. In the dispute following that election, Cárdenas once more assumed the governor's office; the legislature, acting as an electoral college, then split, with the supporters of the Liberal Party candidate Porfirio García León establishing themselves in the municipal palace and the Mugiquistas in the government palace. Under orders from de la Huerta, Cárdenas handed over the government to José Huerta on 21 September 1920. The following day, however, he allowed armed Mugiquistas to take over the state government by withdrawing the military guard at the government palace and disarming the civil guards protecting Huerta.

29 DS, 812.00/24677, U.S. Chargé d'Affaires to U.S. State Department, 29 September 1920. Obregón did not, however, formally recognize Múgica's government until the following April.

30 Regalado briefly considered running for governor in 1917 but deferred to Mú-

gica; he was assassinated in December of 1917 while surveying land for distribution to his own community of Atacheo. See Guzmán Avila 1986: 42–43.

31 As the first set of regulations attempting to implement the provisions of the 1917 Constitution with regard to agrarian reform, Obregón's 1920 Ejido Law was, according to Simpson (1937: 81), "notable chiefly for the confusion of its concepts, the vagueness of its language and its general incompleteness," complicating matters to such an extent that "not even the agrarian authorities could discover what it was they were supposed to do."

32 The institution of the local defense force was inherited from the previous decade. Huerta encouraged the formation of private armed groups to supplement the federal army in fighting the revolutionary armies; later, and with much greater popular support, local defenses were established to protect communities from bandits. Throughout the 1920s, both the state and national governments armed and attempted to disarm these local groups in accordance with military necessity. Control over the local defense forces became an important element of factional conflict within communities.

33 Large landowners also organized politically in response to Múgica's agrarian and labor reforms, forming the Union of Landowners of Michoacán in September 1921. The group urged Obregón to stop the distribution of land by the state's Local Agrarian Commission, given that it was "causing great wrongs and producing demoralization not only among the farmers but also among the other unions interested in solving the agrarian question" (AGN, Papeles Presidenciales, Obregón-Calles, 818-E-28, Union of Landowners of Michoacán to Obregón, 10 January 1922).

34 For example, federal troops assisted the owners of the Hacienda San Antonio in Puruándiro in preventing peasants from occupying hacienda lands they had been provisionally granted in October 1921 (AGN, Papeles Presidenciales, Obregón-Calles, 818-E-28, Anexo 1, CLA President to Obregón, 21 November 1921).

35 Many military leaders did oppose agrarian reform more generally, not the least because they had become major landowners themselves. See Tobler 1988 on the role of the federal army in opposing the agrarista movements of the 1920s.

36 AGN, Papeles Presidenciales, Obregón-Calles, 811-M-89, Chief of Military Operations to Obregón, 27 February 1922; 811-M-89, Anexo 1, Obregón to Subsecretary General of the National Revolutionary Confederation, 22 April 1922. Obregón refers to the death of two hacienda administrators in Curimeo in a letter explaining his attitude toward Múgica: the two were killed by the local defense force of Panindícuaro operating under orders from Múgica who was thus, according to Obregón, directing military operations in the state and thereby interfering with the prerogatives of the federal army.

37 DS, 812.00/25013 and 25027, U.S. Chargé d'Affaires to U.S. State Department, 27 and 28 May 1921.

38 AGN, Papeles Presidenciales, Obregón-Calles, E-28, National Agrarian Party to Obregón, 28 October 1921.

39 AGN, Papeles Presidenciales, Obregón-Calles, 811-M-89, Anexo 1, Representative of Santiago Undameo to the President of the National Agrarian Commission, n.d.

40 AGN, Papeles Presidenciales, Obregón-Calles, 811-M-89, Representative of Tiríndaro to the President of the Local Agrarian Commission, 10 November 1921; Memorandum of the National Agrarista Party, n.d. The second document includes summaries of other incidents involving federal troops' disarming of agrarista defense forces.

41 DS, 812.00/25023, U.S. Chargé d'Affaires to U.S. State Department, 27 May 1921. Santiago Slade controlled considerable areas of communal woodlands in the Purépecha highlands around Uruapan.

42 DS, 812.00/24992, 25019, and 25042, U.S. Chargé d'Affaires to U.S. State Department, 14 and 21 May and 3 June 1921.

43 AGN, Papeles Presidenciales, Obregón-Calles, 811-M-89, Anexo 1, Obregón to the Subsecretary General of the National Revolutionary Confederation, 22 April 1922. DS, 812.00/25517, U.S. Chargé d'Affaires to U.S. State Department, 1 April 1922. The latter letter cites Obregón as saying "In the case of Michoacán, I have consented to change the Military Chief five times on request of General Múgica. But this gentleman has not proceeded with the prudence and discretion due and has provoked unnecessary wrangling." The U.S. chargé d'affaires concludes that Múgica's troubles with Obregón lay in the former's "intolerant policies," particularly "his Down with Catholics and landowners" (DS, 812.00/25562, U.S. Chargé d'Affaires to U.S. State Department, 26 April 1922).

44 AGN, Papeles Presidenciales, Obregón-Calles, 811-M-89, Anexo 4, "Pedidos del C. Gral. Francisco J. Múgica," Memorandum of the Ministry of War, 17 November 1921.

45 Fowler-Salamini (1980: 179–81) argues that it was Múgica's attempt to arm and deploy the local defense forces in order to overcome army opposition to agrarian reform that led to his downfall.

46 DS, 812.00/25459, U.S. Chargé d'Affaires to U.S. State Department, 9 March 1922.

47 AHPEM, Guerra y Ejército, Chief of the 8th Sector of the Civil Defense, Pátzcuaro, to Múgica, 9 and 10 February 1922; State Secretary General to Civil Defense Chiefs, 13 February 1922.

48 AGN, Papeles Presidenciales, Obregón-Calles, 811-M-89, Anexo 1, Chief of Military Operations in Michoacán to Obregón, 5 March 1922; Obregón to Chief of Military Operations in Michoacán, 6 March 1922. DS, 812.00/25459, U.S. Chargé d'Affaires to U.S. State Department, 9 March 1922.

49 AGN, Papeles Presidenciales, Obregón-Calles, 811-M-89, Múgica to Obre-

gón, 10 March 1922. DS, 812.00/26264, U.S. Chargé d'Affaires to U.S. State Department, 15 March 1923. See also Fowler-Salamini 1980: 181. Múgica would subsequently attempt to return to office in the context of the de la Huerta rebellion of 1923 to 1924; he was promptly arrested and taken to Mexico City as a *delahuertista*. Although it is highly unlikely that Múgica could have thrown his support behind Estrada, the leading delahuertista in the region, he may well have been sympathetic to de la Huerta himself, given the latter's support during the crisis of February and March 1922. At that time, de la Huerta urged Múgica not to resign, but rather to appoint Lázaro Cárdenas as interim governor, thus "leaving a person who will sustain a revolutionary policy and who in no way can be taken as a triumph for the Reactionary Party." He further encouraged Múgica to come to Mexico City, writing that "[o]nce you find yourself among us, we'll arrange things in such a way that you will be happy and content with the situation in your state, as well as your personal situation" (AGN, Papeles Presidenciales, Obregón-Calles, 811-M-89, de la Huerta to Múgica, 8 March 1922).

50 AGN, Papeles Presidenciales, Obregón-Calles, 818-E-28, Anexo 3, 14 August 1922. Between January 1915 and April 1922, 25 Michoacán communities received presidential resolutions granting them 29,452 hectares in the form of dotaciones; one community received a restitution of 78 hectares. During Múgica's tenure in office alone (September 1920 to March 1922), 13 communities received presidential resolutions granting them 16,706 hectares, all in the form of dotaciones. As of April 1922, however, eight of the presidential resolutions issued during the Múgica administration, affecting 13,731 hectares, had not been executed, which is to say that the communities were unable to take possession of the land, often because they were prevented from doing so by federal troops and/or the affected landowners. These figures are for presidential resolutions only, and thus do not take into account the provisional resolutions made at the state level by Múgica himself. In 1921, for example, another 7,811 hectares were allocated in the form of provisional possessions, although peasants were not necessarily able to occupy much of this land either (Foglio Miramontes 1936: 194). The Zacapu cases are considered in chapter 5. See also Friedrich 1977 on this period.

51 "Crónica de los trabajos efectuados por la segunda gran convención de la Liga de Comunidades y Sindicatos Agraristas del Estado de Michoacán," 30 November 1924 (cited in Embriz Osorio and León García 1982). Agrarista delegates to this convention protested in particular the government's refusal to punish the private forces of the hacendados, which were often directly responsible for the assassination of agraristas.

52 Sánchez Pineda, for example, distributed more land (38,089 hectares to 24 ejidos) during his two-and-a-half-year interim administration (March 1922–September 1924) than had all of his predecessors combined (Embriz Osorio 1984: 111). In large part this was due to the need to draw peasant military

support during the de la Huerta rebellion of 1923 to 1924. Ramírez found himself in a similar position in 1927 and 1928, as he tried to win agrarista support to fight the growing cristero rebellion in Michoacán: 71,446 hectares were distributed between 1924 and 1928 under his administration (Embriz Osorio 1984: 115; Rivera Castro 1988: 82–83).

53 Although the Agrarista League was established after Múgica's ouster from office, the governor's support for peasant organization had been critical to its development (Fowler-Salamini 1980: 179). The Agrarista League continued to be one of Múgica's main bases of support: in early 1923, for example, it organized a contingent of thousands of peasants to meet with Obregón in Pátzcuaro to solicit Múgica's reinstallation as governor of Michoacán (Guzmán Avila 1986).

54 Both Article 27 of the Constitution and the Agrarian Regulatory Law of 1922 specified the necessary legal status of petitioning communities as including pueblos, rancherías, *congregaciones,* and *condueñazgos.* The latter are defined by Kourí (1996) as "private land-holding associations or companies in which each member or condueño (co-proprietor) owned a share of the lands in question. The shares or stocks (acciones) only represented percentages of ownership, and did not entail exclusive rights to specific plots of land." The 1922 law also included as eligible resident groups on abandoned haciendas but explicitly excluded resident peons on functioning haciendas. A CNA circular on 6 October 1920 partially counteracted this exclusion insofar as it urged state legislatures to "elevate" resident hacienda communities, which lacked independent political status, to "free" communities, which had it (Simpson 1937: 83). This was a common practice in Michoacán, although communities were not always successful in their petitions to change legal status. The landless peons of Cañada de la Magdalena (municipio of Morelia) were able to obtain the status of pueblo and thus to apply for land under the agrarian reform (AHPEM, Gobernación–División Territorial, caja 9, Residents of Cañada de la Magdalena to Governor of Michoacán, Morelia, 19 June 1928); those of Yurécuaro were denied the legal status that would have allowed them to petition for land from the Hacienda of Monteleón (Municipal President of Yurécuaro to Governor of Michoacán, 29 April 1926). More generally, many communities requested a change of status from rancho to congregación, because the former term included both politically dependent and independent communities whereas the latter included only independent communities; the communities of Matugeo, Cotiro, and Tunguitiro (municipio of Coeneo) all submitted a form letter making such a request in 1925 (Various letters from municipal presidents to Governor's Office, 1925). Legal status, like so much of the agrarian reform program of the 1920s, was often a question of politics rather than a matter of meeting certain technical criteria.

55 The first statewide Congress of such unions was held in Villa Jiménez in April 1924, organized by the agrarista leaders Primo Tapia and Ignacio Villegas and

with a focus on anticlericalism and temperance (Embriz Osorio and León García 1982: 119).

56 See the case studies for more detailed analyses of these factional conflicts.

57 DS, 812.00/26727, U.S. Chargé d'Affaires to U.S. State Department, 22 December 1923. As noted below, the Mugiquistas of Michoacán also initially supported de la Huerta. DS, 812.00/26467, U.S. Chargé d'Affaires to U.S. State Department, 12 October 1923.

58 Cedillo's agrarista followers, according to a U.S. War Department source, were "all peons, fairly well-mounted, badly disciplined, and armed with a variety of old rifles." According to the same source, "Cedillo is an old bandit chief, almost an illiterate peon who, in return for his support of the government and his supposed ability to rally the entire peon population of a large section of the state to his command when the occasion demanded, has been allowed to make himself 'dictator' or 'cacique' of the section under his control" (USMI, U.S. Military Attaché to U.S. War Department, Report on the Stability of the Government #4385, 5 January 1924).

59 In Yucatán, "the radical elements were greatly disappointed" by Carrillo's fate, "but the better class of people were greatly pleased" (DS, 812.00/26703, U.S. Vice Consul, Yucatán, to U.S. State Department, 24 December 1923).

60 USMI, U.S. Military Attaché to U.S. War Department, G-2 Report #4432, 8 December 1923; G-2 Report #4367, 29 December 1923. DS, 812.00/26767, U.S. Chargé d'Affaires to U.S. State Department, 22 December 1923.

61 See Friedrich 1977: 106–11. Naranja agraristas, for example, fought anti-agrarista peasants in Tiríndaro, massacring those who attempted to surrender; "most of the opposition to agrarian reform was thus broken in Tiríndaro," as Friedrich (1977: 107) rather laconically notes. Once the rebellion was over, the federal army attempted to disarm the agrarista militias, a process that led to considerable conflict and repression (AGN, Papeles Presidenciales, Obregón-Calles, 818-A-114, various letters reporting agrarista abuses of non-agrarista peasants and federal army abuses of agrarista peasants in the process of disarming militias).

62 AGN, Papeles Presidenciales, Obregón-Calles, 811-M-89, Sánchez Pineda to Obregón, 6 May 1924.

63 *El Universal*, 3 April 1927, p. 1.

64 AGN, Papeles Presidenciales, Obregón-Calles, 818-E-46. Although Calles's letter of 10 February 1927 is missing from the archives, the responses of the state governors were saved, and they use enough identical language to indicate the contents of the original letter. The governor of Zacatecas responded on 8 March 1927 by agreeing that the acceleration of the reform would be "the best way to counteract the slanderous agitation being carried out among the peasants." The Tlaxcala governor, in an undated letter, replied that he would "order whatever measures were necessary to continue responding with all possible speed to the communities demanding land, with the object of counter-

acting the agitation against the government." In the summer and fall of 1927, the *Periódico Oficial* of the state of Michoacán published a backlog of community petitions for land, such publication constituting the first step in the official agrarian reform procedure on petitions made up to twelve years previously. These cases, with the dates their petitions were filed, included Paricutín (1916), Capula (1915), El Rodeo (1915), Aporo (1916), Chucándiro (1918), Epunguio (1916), San Miguel Curínhuato (1915), and San Lucas Huaririapeo (1916).

65 AGN, Papeles Presidenciales, Obregón-Calles, 818-E-46, Ramírez to Calles, 24 February 1927.

66 *El Universal,* 2 February 1927, sec. 2, p. 2.

67 See Becker 1995 on the Cardenista period in Michoacán.

4   The *Cristiada*

1   DS, 812.00/27902, U.S. Department of Justice memorandum on de la Huerta's activities in the United States, transmitted to the U.S. State Department on 31 August 1926.

2   DS, 812.404/867.5, Ernest Lagarde, French Chargé d'Affaires, Mexico City, to French Foreign Office, Paris, "The Religious Crisis in Mexico," 18 September 1926. The "Lagarde Memorandum" (hereafter appearing in the notes as "Lagarde, 'The Religious Crisis in Mexico'") was widely distributed by the embassies of other countries as the French diplomat was viewed as a particularly knowledgeable and objective observer of church-state relations in Mexico.

3   Officially, Calles was president for the four-year term of 1924 to 1928. The period of 1928 to 1934, however, is known as the *maximato:* limited by the Constitution to one term as president, Calles declared himself to be the *jefe máximo* (highest chief, and hence the term *maximato*) and sole arbitrator of political power during the "provisional" presidential administrations of Emilio Portes Gil (1928–29), Pascual Ortiz Rubio (1930–32), and Adalberto Rodríguez (1932–34). These were provisional presidencies because Obregón, reelected in 1928, was assassinated before taking office.

4   Lagarde, "The Religious Crisis in Mexico."

5   DS, 812.404/327, U.S. Ambassador James Sheffield to U.S. State Department, 25 February 1925.

6   Lagarde, "The Religious Crisis in Mexico."

7   The initial leadership of the League included Rafael Ceniceros y Villareal, the former PCN governor of Zacatecas; René Capistrán Garza, president of the ACJM; and Luis Bustos, chief of the Knights of Columbus. The original name of the League was the National League for Religious Defense. It was changed to the National League for the Defense of Religious Liberty in September 1926.

8 Lagarde, "The Religious Crisis in Mexico."

9 DS, 812.404/327, U.S. Ambassador James Sheffield, Mexico City, to U.S. State Department, 25 February 1926.

10 Lagarde, "The Religious Crisis in Mexico."

11 Ibid.

12 DS, 812.404/424, U.S. Vice Consul Hernan C. Vogenitz, Progreso (Yucatán), to U.S. State Department, 25 April 1926.

13 DS, 812.404/374, U.S. Consul William P. Blocker, Mazatlán (Sinaloa), to State Department, 9 March 1926.

14 Ibid.

15 Lagarde, "The Religious Crisis in Mexico."

16 DS, 812.404/506, U.S. Consul General Alexander Weddell to U.S. State Department, 3 July 1926. USMI, U.S. Military Attaché to War Department, Freedom of Religious Belief and Practice #1033, 13 August 1926. Municipal presidents and neighborhood committees reported violations of the law (or lack thereof) on a regular basis to the state-level Ministries of Government (Gobernación) (AHPEM, Gobernación-Religión, caja 2, numerous letters).

17 DS, 812.404/519, U.S. Ambassador James Sheffield to U.S. Department of State, 20 July 1926.

18 DS, 812.404/535, U.S. Ambassador James Sheffield to U.S. Department of State, 25 July 1926. The churches would remain closed until the June 1929 accord between the Portes Gil administration and the episcopate.

19 DS, 812.404/581, U.S. Consul William Blocker, Mazatlán (Sinaloa), to U.S. State Department, 6 August 1926.

20 DS, 812.404/547, U.S. Consul Bartley F. Yost, Torreón (Coahuila), to U.S. State Department, 2 August 1926.

21 DS, 812.00/28000, U.S. Vice Consul Henry K. Pangburn, Acapulco (Guerrero), to U.S. State Department, 6 October 1927.

22 DS, 812.00/27889, U.S. Consul Dudley Dwyre, Guadalajara (Jalisco), to U.S. State Department, 18 August 1926.

23 In theory, Catholics were to refuse to pay taxes and buy nothing but essentials, in an attempt to wreak enough economic damage to force state officials to reform the Constitution. Contemporary accounts differ greatly on the economic impact of the boycott. In August 1926, the U.S. consul in Guadalajara reported that the boycott was "effective to an alarming degree," with merchants claiming that business was "paralyzed"; sales of meat were down by 60 percent and the markets were flooded with fruit, declared by the League to be a luxury item. In the city of Veracruz, in contrast, the boycott was barely observed; the U.S. vice consul's explanation was that "Veracruz is not a religious city, there being only three churches here." From Mexico City, U.S. consul general Weddell noted that the impact of the boycott was quite mixed, hurting business most in Mexico City, Puebla, and Guadalajara. By the end of Septem-

ber, however, the boycott had lost force even in Guadalajara, where its main impact "would seem to be the creation or intensifying of hatred for the wealthy classes by the laboring class and the very small merchants" (DS, 812.00/27889, U.S. Consul Dudley Dwyre, Guadalajara [Jalisco], to U.S. State Department, 18 August 1926; DS, 812.00/27922, U.S. Vice Consul Willys A. Meyers, Veracruz [Veracruz], to U.S. State Department, 1 September 1926; DS, 812.00/27922, U.S. Consul General Alexander Weddell to U.S. State Department, August 1926 Political Report; DS, 812.00/27966, U.S. Consul Dayle C. McDonough, Guadalajara [Jalisco], to U.S. State Department, September 1926 Political Report).

24 DS, 812.00/27891, Arthur Bliss Lane, Chief of Mexico Desk, U.S. State Department to U.S. State Department, 17 August 1926.

25 DS, 812.00/27922, Consul General Alexander Weddell to U.S. State Department, August 1926 Report on Political and Economic Conditions.

26 DS, 812.00/27940, Telegram from U.S. Consul William P. Blocker, Mazatlán (Sinaloa), to U.S. Secretary of State, 20 September 1926.

27 DS, 812.00/28000, U.S. Vice Consul Henry K. Pangburn, Acapulco (Guerrero) to U.S. Department of State, 6 October 1926. Similar uprisings were reported to have occurred in Tixtla and Ometepec, both in Guerrero.

28 DS, 812.00/27978, U.S. Vice Consul E. W. Eaton, Manzanillo (Colima), to U.S. State Department. The term *revolutionary* becomes a bit confusing at this point: consular officials usually used it with reference to rebels rather than the revolutionary state. League officials sometimes used it with reference to their own rebellion and sometimes with reference to the revolutionary state.

29 DS, 812.00/27987, U.S. Vice Consul Peter H. A. Flood, Tampico (Veracruz), to U.S. State Department, 2 October 1926.

30 DS, 812.00/28078, U.S. Consul Dudley Dwyre, Guadalajara (Jalisco), to U.S. State Department, 17 November 1926. Federal troops were concentrated in Sonora throughout much of 1926 and 1927, combating the Yaqui rebellion. See Hu-DeHart 1988.

31 DS, 812.00/28150, U.S. Consul Dudley Dwyre, Guadalajara (Jalisco), to U.S. State Department, 23 December 1926.

32 René Capistrán Garza was, by profession, a journalist. He never returned to Mexico to engage in any military activity, and he was removed from military command by the League in the spring of 1927, having earned himself the unfortunate nickname of "Sacristán Farsa" through his failure to do anything at all on behalf of the rebellion, except to raise expectations that huge sums of money from the United States would soon be pouring into Mexico (Meyer 1973/74a: 79). Capistrán Garza's activities are documented in detail in Quirk 1973 and Bailey 1974. Along with several other leaders of the League, he was permanently expelled from Mexico as part of the 1929 agreement between the episcopate and the Portes Gil administration.

33 In keeping with the social agenda of Catholic Action, however, much of Article 123, dealing with workers' rights, was to be retained, and some provision for land distribution was to be made, although private property rights were to receive constitutional protection. In the "Memorandum to the American People," issued at the same time as the manifesto, the League called for the support of U.S. Catholics in its fight against the "tyranny of Bolshevism" and requested that the U.S. government suspend its dealings with the Calles administration, refuse to recognize any other government "of revolutionary origin," deny all aid to the Calles government and any other rebellion against that government, establish regular channels of communication with the League and assist it in securing loans in the United States, protect the ecclesiastical hierarchy, recognize the belligerent status of the League, and, "in due time," grant it official recognition as the provisional government (DS, 812.00/28126, U.S. Ambassador James Sheffield to U.S. State Department, translated copies of "League Manifesto to the Nation" and "Memorandum to the American People," 10 December 1926).

34 DS, 812.00/28167 and 28176, U.S. Consul William E. Chapman, Torreón (Coahuila), to U.S. State Department, 6 and 13 January 1927; Olivera Sedano 1966: 169–70. Chapman placed the number of rebels at 9, whereas Olivera Sedano cites the sole survivor's account as claiming 35 rebels.

35 DS, 812.00/28165, U.S. Consul Thomas S. Horn, Saltillo (Coahuila), to U.S. State Department, 7 January 1927.

36 *El Universal*, 10 and 11 February 1927, pp. 1 and 8.

37 DS, 812.00/28156, U.S. Consul Thomas S. Horn, Saltillo (Coahuila), to U.S. State Department, 3 January 1927.

38 BFO, 371/A686/52/26, W. Whyte, General Mines Superintendent, Mazapil Copper Company, Aranzazu (Zacatecas), to British Vice Consul R. H. Jeffrey, Saltillo (Coahuila).

39 BFO, 371/A686/52/26, D. S. Williams, Storekeeper, Mazapil Copper Company, Concepción del Oro, to E. T. Woods, General Auditor, Mazapil Copper Company, Saltillo (Coahuila), 1 January 1927.

40 DS, 812.00/28156 and 28165, U.S. Consul Thomas S. Horn, Saltillo (Coahuila), to U.S. State Department, 3 and 7 January 1927.

41 DS, 812.00/28196, U.S. Consul William Blocker, Mazatlán (Sinaloa), to U.S. State Department, 11 January 1927.

42 *El Universal*, 10 and 11 February 1927, pp. 1, 8; USMI, U.S. Military Attaché to U.S. War Department, Distribution of Troops #1394, 18 February 1927; DS, 812.00/28229, U.S. Consul Arthur C. Frost, Tampico (Veracruz), to U.S. State Department, 4 February 1927; DS, 812.00/28170, U.S. Ambassador James R. Sheffield to U.S. State Department, 11 January 1927; Olivera Sedano 1966: 171–79; Meyer 1973/74a: 135–45.

43 *El Universal*, 10 February 1927, pp. 1, 8; 11 February 1927, pp. 1, 8. In

Yucatán and Campeche, several priests were arrested and deported to the United States for saying the mass.

44 DS, 812.00/27958, U.S. Consul Herbert S. Burley, Guaymas (Sonora), to U.S. State Department, 25 September 1926.

45 USMI, U.S. Military Attaché to U.S. War Department, Distribution of Troops #1334, 18 January 1927.

46 DS, 812.00/28225, U.S. Consul General Alexander Weddell to U.S. State Department, January 1927 Political Report.

47 DS, 812.00/28174, 28198, 28208, 28225, and 28256, U.S. Consul Dudley Dwyre, Guadalajara (Jalisco), to U.S. Department of State, 11, 18, and 25 January and 3 and 27 February 1927.

48 BFO, 371/A805/52/26, British Vice Consul P. G. Holmes, Guadalajara (Jalisco), to British Ambassador Sir Esmond Ovey, British Legation, Mexico City, 15 January 1927.

49 DS, 812.00/28201, U.S. Ambassador James Sheffield to U.S. State Department, translation of Calles memo, 20 January 1927; and U.S. Ambassador James Sheffield to U.S. State Department, 21 January 1927. In Jalisco, and possibly elsewhere, landowners were assessed a fee to pay for the cost of arming and maintaining the agrarista militias (DS, 812.00/28256, U.S. Consul Dudley Dwyre, Guadalajara (Jalisco) to U.S. State Department, 21 February 1927).

50 DS, 812.00/28236, U.S. Vice Consul E. W. Eaton, Manzanillo (Colima), to U.S. State Department, 5 February 1927; Olivera Sedano 1966: 162–65.

51 The League archives note "the entrance of the noble and Catholic state of Michoacán in the liberation movement" only in May of 1927, referring to the Cotija, Jiquilpan, and Coalcomán (INAH, CR, Reel 44, League War Bulletin #6, first week of May 1927). League records mention San Juan Parangaricutiro at least once (INAH, CR, Reel 16, "Boletín especial de acción militar," January 1928), but the residents of San Juan do not mention the League in their oral accounts of the rebellion, in contrast to the National Sinarquista Union of the 1930s and 1940s (see chapter 6 on San Juan's relationship with the Sinarquista movement).

52 INAH, CR, Reel 44, "Resumen de la situación política y militar," June 1927.

53 USMI, U.S. Military Attaché to U.S. War Department, Distribution of Troops #1710, 9 September 1927.

54 DS, 812.00/28886, U.S. Vice Consul E. W. Eaton, Manzanillo (Colima), to U.S. State Department, 6 October 1927.

55 Calculated by Olivera Sedano (1966: 185) from the League archives.

56 BFO 371/A2793/52/26, British Chargé d'Affaires David V. Kelly to British Foreign Office, 20 April 1927.

57 The U members took their vows of secrecy quite seriously, and as a result, we know little about how the society functioned. It is known to be distinct from

both the Popular Union and the League, although analysts sometimes confuse it with the former.

58 INAH, CR, Reel 43, "Informe de Jesús Degollado y Guízar," August 1929. The incident occurred in May 1927.

59 USMI, U.S. Military Attaché to U.S. War Department, Report on the Stability of the Government #2424, 6 June 1929.

60 The League convinced the Vatican to reprimand the Women's Brigades (Brigadas Femininas) that supplied the cristeros with ammunition, as well as the secret organization, the U, to which much of the regional leadership belonged. Neither organization would subordinate itself to League authority. League attacks on the Women's Brigades interrupted the supply of ammunition, which understandably infuriated Gorostieta.

61 DS, 812.00/28891, U.S. Chargé d'Affaires H. F. Shoenfield to U.S. State Department, 14 October 1927.

62 DS, 812.00/28883, U.S. Vice Consul Joseph C. Satterthwaite, Guadalajara (Jalisco), to U.S. State Department, 13 October 1927.

63 INAH, CR, Reel 15, "Telegramas recibidos," 9, 11, and 13 November 1927.

64 INAH, CR, Reel 16, "League resumen militar: boletín especial de acción militar," January 1928; "Telegramas recibidos," 11, 13/14, 16, and 22 March 1928; Reel 43, "Informe rendido por el C. Gral. de la División Luis Guízar Morfín," 18 February 1928.

65 DS, 812.00/28432 and 28440, U.S. Ambassador James Sheffield to U.S. State Department, 19 and 23 May 1927.

66 DS, 812.00/28776, 28786, and 28800, U.S. Chargé d'Affaires H. F. Shoenfield to U.S. State Department, 4, 5, and 7 October 1927; DS, 812.00/28948, U.S. Ambassador Dwight Morrow to U.S. State Department, 6 November 1927. Like Serrano, Gómez was captured and executed. Escobar would lead yet another unsuccessful rebellion against Calles in 1929.

67 DS, 812.00/28432, U.S. Ambassador James Sheffield to U.S. State Department, 19 May 1927.

68 DS, 812.00/29014 and 29215.5, U.S. Ambassador Dwight Morrow to U.S. State Department, 28 November 1927 and 16 July 1928.

69 DS, 812.00/29215.5, U.S. Ambassador Dwight Morrow to U.S. State Department. A memo from the U.S. military attaché is included in Morrow's report.

70 USMI, U.S. Military Attaché to U.S. War Department, Reports on the Stability of the Government #2405 and 2424, 21 May and 6 June 1929. USMI, U.S. Military Attaché in Mexico to U.S. War Department, Reports on the Stability of the Government dated 17 April, 22 May, 7 August, and 14 August 1928. At the same time, Gorostieta claimed to have 20,000 rebels under his command (INAH, CR, Reel 30, Enrique Gorostieta to "Val," 16 May 1929).

71 AGN, Papeles Presidenciales, Obregón-Calles, 818-A-114. This entire file deals with federal attempts to disarm agraristas from May of 1924 through the end of 1925.

72 AGN, Papeles Presidenciales, Obregón-Calles, 104-L-23, Chief of the Tenencia of San Juan Tumbio, Tingambato, Michoacán, to President Plutarco Calles, 26 October 1926; Reply of President Calles, 5 November 1926.

73 AGN, Papeles Presidenciales, Obregón-Calles, 104-C-23, Agrarian Communities of Maravatío to President Plutarco Calles, 2 August 1926; Anacleto Hernández, Secretary of the Agricultural Cooperative of Acuitzeo, to Calles, 5 August 1926; Josafat Rivera and other Ejidatarios, San Felipe de los Alzati, Zitácuaro, to Calles, 12 August 1926; Ejidatarios of Aguasalida, Zitácuaro, to Calles, 14 August 1926; Agrarian Community of Crecencio Morales, Zitácuaro to Calles, 16 August 1926; Agrarian Community of the Ranchería of Asoleadero, Angangueo to Calles, 17 August 1926.

74 BFO, 371/A686/52/26, D. S. Williams, Storekeeper, Mazapil Mining Company, Concepción del Oro, to E. T. Woods, General Auditor, Mazapil Mining Company, Saltillo (Coahuila), 1 January 1927.

75 DS, 812.00/27887, 27897, 27909, 27924, 27941, 27935, and 27978, U.S. Vice Consul E. W. Eaton, Manzanillo (Colima), to U.S. State Department, 14 and 18 August 1926 and 7 (letter and telegram), 9, 13, and 29 September 1926.

76 DS, 812.00/28208, U.S. Consul Dudley Dwyre, Guadalajara (Jalisco), to U.S. State Department, 25 January 1927.

77 *El Universal*, 3 April 1927, p. 1.

78 USMI, U.S. Military Attaché to U.S. War Department, Reports on the Stability of the Government #1751, 10 October 1927; #1773, 18 October 1927; DS, 812.00/28000, U.S. Chargé d'Affaires H. F. Shoenfield to U.S. State Department, 7 October 1927.

79 DS, 812.00/27987, U.S. Vice Consul Peter Flood, Tampico (Veracruz), to U.S. State Department, 2 October 1926.

80 On Michoacán, see Friedrich 1977: 87; 1986: 140.

81 Until 1929, the cristeros had never allied with a major dissident figure within the military or in exile, in spite of repeated attempts by the LNDLR to join forces with Félix Díaz or Adolfo de la Huerta, then in the United States. Gorostieta and the League negotiated an agreement with Escobar in February 1929 in which the latter somewhat vaguely promised to respect religious liberty should his rebellion succeed in overthrowing Calles. The military rebels were not very concerned with religion, however: Escobar, together with the military commanders of Sonora, Durango, and Veracruz, and the governors of Sonora, Durango, and Chihuahua, all opposed Calles's creation of a revolutionary party, viewing it as an attempt to institutionalize and perpetuate his rule.

82 On Morrow's negotiations and the June 1929 agreement, see Quirk 1973: 215–47.

83 INAH, CR, Reel 30, José González Romo, region of Coalcomán, to Francisco del Río, region of Coalcomán, 14 July 1929.

84 These explanations are compatible rather than competing. Tutino (1986), for example, cites both the institutional presence of the Church and the unique agrarian structure of the center-west in accounting for the regional character of the rebellion. Jrade (1980, 1985) focuses on class and the survival of small-holding communities in the center-west, and Knight (1990b) seems to attribute the regional character of the rebellion to the Church's institutional presence in the center-west.

85 The question of timing is explored at greater length in chapter 8, where the cristero rebellion is compared to other antistate popular movements.

86 One problem with the ratio of population to number of churches as an indicator of the institutional presence of the church is that in urban areas, where population density is high, churches might be numerous and yet have relatively large congregations. This partially explains the high ratios in the Federal District (which includes Mexico City), Jalisco (which includes the major provincial city of Guadalajara), and Veracruz (which includes the major port city of Veracruz). As in Table 4.2, the ratio of population to churches for the cristero center-west is calculated by dividing the total population of the region (3,663,443) by the total number of churches in the region (2,818).

87 The data in the following text were compiled from the Secretaría de Economía (1956). Data are not available for all of the states for the entire period, thus precluding the calculation of regional averages. With respect to the cristero center-west, there are no baseline data from 1878 for Michoacán, Zacatecas, or Guanajuato.

88 The Vatican neither approved nor condemned the cristero rebellion. Faced with the Calles Law of 1926, according to Ernest Lagarde, it "leaned towards a policy of temporization, for a tacit agreement [with the government], which would have left the points objected to unchanged but would have permitted leaving them in the field of theory, so that they would not actually be applied" (Ernest Lagarde, "The Religious Crisis in Mexico"). After an agreement was reached between Calles and the episcopate in June 1929, the Vatican ordered all Mexican Catholics to lay down their arms.

89 This analysis of the episcopate is based on J. Meyer 1973/74a: 19–24; Quirk 1973: 145–48; and the Lagarde memorandum. Meyer does not include Francisco Orozco y Jiménez, archbishop of Guadalajara, among the prorebellion prelates, but virtually all other accounts of the rebellion do.

90 See chapter 6.

91 INAH, CR, Reel 30, José González Romo to Father José Méndez. The priest in question was not Méndez himself.

92 According to reports made by the U.S. military attaché, 18 priests were executed and 22 "killed in action" during 1927, the latter category undoubtedly including summary executions, because priests were routinely and often falsely accused of being the military leadership of the rebellion. The number of deaths dropped to 11 during the first half of 1928, reflecting not a change of policy but

rather the fact that virtually all of the priests who were not in hiding or actively engaged in the rebellion had at that point found safer havens in the cities (USMI, U.S. Military Attaché to U.S. War Department, Freedom of Religious Belief and Practice #2077, 27 May 1928).

93 The League and the ACJM both had their roots in the Catholic Action movement that followed the 1891 encyclical letter *Rerum Novarum* and the National Catholic Party of the Maderista period, neither of which was limited to the cristero states of the center-west. Catholic Action Congresses were held in Morelia, Zamora, and Guadalajara, but they were also held in Tulancingo (Hidalgo) and Puebla. The National Catholic Party won majorities in the legislatures of Jalisco and Zacatecas, and the governorships of Jalisco, Zacatecas, Querétaro, and the state of Mexico. See chapter 3.

94 *David,* 8, 22 September 1966, pp. 30–31.

95 INAH, CR, Reel 17, Luis Navarro Orígel to José María Martínez, 13 July 1928.

96 INAH, CR, Reel 30, Jose González Romo to Maximiliano Barragán, 25 and 26 March 1929; Jose González Romo to Executive Committee of the League, 5 May 1927.

97 INAH, CR, Reel 16, League Special Committee to the League President, 25 March 1926.

98 Outside of the center-west, there were Brigades in the states of Mexico, Aguascalientes, Sinaloa, Durango, San Luis Potosí, and the Federal District. See J. Meyer 1973/74c: 120–30.

99 Ernest Lagarde, "The Religious Crisis in Mexico."

100 See, for example, Paige's (1975) analysis of hacienda peasants.

101 See Departamento de Estadísticas Nacional (1927). Most of the rural workers who did rebel in Michoacán were landless residents of cristero communities who worked on nearby haciendas. Although resident workers were technically excluded from the agrarian reform program, some of these workers did, in fact, successfully apply for ejidos. Political administrative categories could be changed: whether a settlement of landless peasants within the boundaries of a hacienda constituted part of that hacienda, or was a community in its own right divested of all its land by the hacienda, was a question of interpretation, and the interpretation depended on politics, not legal technicalities.

102 DS, 812.00/28237, U.S. Consul Thomas McEnelly, Chihuahua (Chihuahua), to U.S. State Department, 11 February 1927.

103 INAH, CR, Reel 13, Chief of the Division of the East, Liberation Army to the hacendados of Tlaxcala and Puebla, 1927, no day or month.

104 DS, 812.00/28266, U.S. Consul Dudley Dwyre, Guadalajara (Jalisco), to U.S. State Department, 5 March 1927.

105 BFO, 371/A2488/52/26, David V. Kelly, British Chargé d'Affaires, to British Foreign Office, 6 April 1927.

106 BFO, A2351/52/26, British Ambassador Sir Edmund Ovey to General Aaron Saenz, Mexican Minister of Foreign Affairs, 22 March 1927.

107 BFO, A5262/52/26, B. Johnson, Autlán (Jalisco), to British Vice Consul P. G. Holmes, Guadalajara, August 1927. These reports are drawn from U.S. and British diplomatic archives and hence focus on the property of U.S. and British citizens. The cristeros, however, attacked property belonging to both Mexicans and foreign nationals.

108 BFO, 371/A5503/52/26, British Vice Consul P. G. Holmes, Guadalajara (Jalisco), to British Consul General J. B. Brown, British Legation, Mexico City, 17 August 1927.

109 DS, 812.00/28135, U.S. Consul David Meyers to U.S. State Department, 14 December 1926.

110 DS, 812.00/28384, U.S. Consul William I. Jackson, Torreón (Coahuila), to U.S. State Department, 28 April 1927.

111 DS, 812.00/28266, U.S. Consul Dudley Dwyre, Guadalajara (Jalisco), to U.S. State Department, 14 March 1927.

112 INAH, CR, Reel 13, "Es una infamia," unsigned and n.d.

113 Tutino (1986), for example, argues that the rancheros of the center-west were threatened by the reform, insofar as state authorities might expropriate their property in lieu of that of more powerful landowners. By the 1930s, it was quite common for landowners cited as having affectable property to claim that they were smallholders (*pequeños propietarios*), but I found little evidence of this in the 1920s. The most common challenges were that agrarian censuses included ineligible people and that there was affectable land (i.e., another hacienda) closer to the petitioning community.

114 As discussed in chapter 8, Oaxacan peasants did participate in a "counter-revolutionary" rebellion (the Oaxacan Sovereignty Movement), but it occurred in the 1910s, when revolutionary state formation was at its most intrusive, and assumed a different political character.

5   The *Agraristas* of the Zacapu Region

1   The name Zacapu refers to the entire *municipio* (a political-administrative category including a *cabecera* or municipal seat and a number of politically subordinate units called *tenencias*), to the town (the municipal seat), and to the Indian community, a political, social, and historical unit within the town. The municipio of Zacapu includes the tenencias of Naranja, Tarejero, and Tiríndaro, among others.

2   One notable exception was Ramón Aguilar, the agrarista leader of Zacapu who later joined the cristeros.

3   The Purépecha region of Michoacán encompasses four distinct zones: Lake Pátzcuaro (comprised of what are now the municipios of Quiroga, Pátzcuaro, Erongarícuaro, and Tzinzuntzan), the Ciénega of Zacapu (the munici-

pios of Zacapu, Villa Jiménez, and Coeneo), the highlands around the city of Uruapan (the municipios of Paracho, Charapan, San Juan Parangaricutiro, Tingambato, Nahuatzen, Cherán, Tangancícuaro, and part of Uruapan), and the Cañada de los Once Pueblos (the municipio of Chilchota).

4 See Espín Díaz 1986a for a discussion of these different understandings of property rights within the communal property regime.

5 As a royal inspector discovered in 1775, "many Indian villages lacked any collective fund because their lands, capital and cattle had been absorbed by the confraternities and brotherhoods whose income was devoted to 'church ceremonies, dinners, fireworks and other useless and harmful things'" (Brading 1994: 131). This was of concern to the Crown because tribute came from communal funds, and the cofradías were not regulated by the state.

6 The individual nature of religious sponsorship undoubtedly increased during the nineteenth century as well in some communities, with the privatization of communal resources mandated by the liberal land reform.

7 Carrasco (1976: 88) considers the cabildo to be the central institution in defending popular culture and religious practice, writing "it was in a position to resist national attacks on popular culture, be they those that came from the priests, who wanted to change the religious fiestas, or those that came from the government, which wanted to suppress religious worship."

8 The image of the saint—usually a small statue—was sometimes considered to be the actual saint him or herself. This belief made the frequent desecration of saints' images during the revolution and 1920s, as well as the prohibition on carrying saints' images into the fields during times of scarcity, all the more devastating as attacks on peasant culture.

9 On Purépecha fiestas, see Brandes 1988.

10 AGN, CNA, Resoluciones Presidenciales, Zacapu, 8 October 1925. The título de composición is cited in the 1925 presidential resolution as being a response to a royal circular of 1836; given this error, the date of the document is uncertain. Beginning in 1591, the Spanish Crown began to require the confirmation of all colonial land titles. Because the document in question is the first to be cited in the resolution, the next document is dated 1661, and all of the other documents are cited in chronological order, it seems most likely that the royal title was issued at some point during the first half of the seventeenth century.

11 AGN, Tierras, Zacapu, vol. 854, exp. 2, 1759–67; vol. 1223, exp. 2, 1792–1802; vol. 2726, exp. 18, 1572–1791.

12 AHPEM, Hijuelas, District of Pátzcuaro, vol. 8, Community acta, 12 January 1869.

13 Ibid.; State Treasurer, Morelia to Secretary of Government, Morelia, 12 December 1887.

14 AHPEM, Hijuelas, District of Pátzcuaro, vol. 9, Felipe Atanacio, Legal Representative of Tiríndaro to Governor of Michoacán, Morelia, 17 January 1871. Both Naranja and Tiríndaro claimed to have carried out the reparto in accor-

dance with the state law of 1827, and although they may in fact have done so, they continued to pay taxes on the land as communal property. The claim of the earlier reparto was made after state officials raised taxes on communal property as an incentive to carry out the reform. As private property, the parcels for the most part would have been too small to be subject to property tax.

15 AHPEM, Hijuelas, District of Zacapu, vol. 4, Bruno Patiño to Governor of Michoacán, 15 January 1869; vol. 3, Sacramento Torres Yáñez and Eduvirgis Martínez to Ministry of Government, Morelia, 31 December 1893. Although conflicts between cabeceras and their subordinate tenencias were extremely common, none of the communities mentioned fell under the jurisdiction of the municipio of Zacapu.

16 As one community leader put it, "A large part of the land that should be privatized is not under the control of the Indians, because the usufructaries of these lands have alienated them to various mestizos, pawning them or through long-term rental agreements with the rent paid in advance" (AHPEM, Hijuelas, District of Zacapu, vol. 4, Benito Martínez to Ministry of Government, Morelia, 30 June 1879). The peasants' proposal that they simply evict the occupants of such land was rejected by the government, which insisted on the use of legal channels to resolve all conflicts.

17 AHPEM, Hijuelas, District of Zacapu, vol. 4, Municipal President, Zacapu, to Ministry of Government, Morelia, 15 July 1870.

18 In the community of Zacapu, for example, Luis Obregón, a government appointee, charged almost 1,800 pesos for his work in preparing the survey of the community's lands (AHPEM, Hijuelas, District of Zacapu, vol. 3, unsigned statement on fees charged by Luis Obregón, 15 June 1898). Each individual was charged a fee of 75 centavos by the state for the titles; almost half of the comuneros in Zacapu declared themselves unable to pay it (AHPEM, Hijuelas, District of Pátzcuaro, vol. 5, memorandum of the Ministry of Government, Morelia, 17 March 1903).

19 The same may have been true in Tiríndaro, but the much sparser archival record with respect to the liberal reparto does not reflect it. Tarejero was more likely to have been united, given that it was engaged with numerous conflicts with outside landowners who had seized almost all of the community's land, including part of the fundo legal.

20 The cabildo's control over communal property implied neither community democracy nor the egalitarian allocation of resources. Politico-religious authorities and their allies and families certainly enjoyed access to a disproportionate share of land, particularly cultivated land, and they sometimes took advantage of opportunities for personal enrichment in the reparto, as when one leader arranged to rent 100 parcels of land from other members of the community prior to the completion of the reform (AHPEM, Hijuelas, District of Zacapu, vol. 3, Dionisio Orozco to the Governor of Michoacán, 13 October

1902; Ministry of Government, Morelia, to Dionisio Ochoa, 7 November 1902). But the members of the cabildo generally did not alienate communal land to outsiders, as did the leaders of the other faction, thus protecting the landed base of the community from disintegration, and maintaining communal usage of village pasture, woodlands, and marshland.

21 AHPEM, Hijuelas, District of Zacapu, vol. 3, Agustín Pérez to the Governor of Michoacán, 4 February 1894.

22 AHPEM, Hijuelas, District of Pátzcuaro, vol. 8, Residents of Naranja to Governor of Michoacán, Morelia, 1 April 1899.

23 AHPEM, Hijuelas, District of Pátzcuaro, vol. 8, memorandum of the Ministry of Government, 4 August 1902. In subsequent documents, Mauricio Mata is referred to as Manuel Mata.

24 AGN, Papeles Presidenciales, Obregón-Calles, Eduardo and Alfredo Noriega, Hacienda of Cantabría, "La Desecación de la Ciénaga de Zacapu y las Leyes Agrarias: Caso Especial, Unico en el País," 1923. The Noriegas refer to contracts with the *hacendados,* not the communities.

25 AHPEM, Hijuelas, District of Pátzcuaro, vol. 10, Miguel Cupa, Felipe Aparicio, and Agustín Regalado and others to Governor of Michoacán, Morelia, 9 February 1897. Some 300 community members petitioned the government to nullify the sales contracts, on the grounds that "the aforementioned comuneros have no legal rights, either in their numbers or in any authorized powers."

26 AHPEM, Hijuelas, District of Pátzcuaro, vol. 10, Gustavo Roth to Ministry of Government, Morelia, 13 October 1896; vol. 5, Teódulo Torres to Governor of Michoacán, Morelia, 27 November 1899; Treasurer's Office to Ministry of Government, Morelia, 6 December 1899; Ministry of Government, Morelia, to Teódulo Torres, 17 January 1900; AGN, CNA, Resoluciones Presidenciales, vol. 28, Zacapu, 8 October 1925.

27 AHPEM, Hijuelas, District of Zacapu, vol. 6, Sixto Mayo and Buenaventura Telles, Legal Representatives of Tarejero to Governor of Michoacán, Morelia, 25 April 1896.

28 AHPEM, Hijuelas, District of Zacapu, vol. 6, Francisco Elguero to Governor of Michoacán, Morelia, 29 April 1896.

29 AHPEM, Hijuelas, District of Zacapu, vol. 6, Francisco Elguero to Governor of Michoacán, 24 August 1896.

30 AHPEM, Hijuelas, District of Zacapu, vol. 6, Ministry of Government to Governor of Michoacán, Morelia, 18 September 1896; District Prefect, Zacapu to Ministry of Government, 21 October 1896; Ministry of Government to District Prefect, Zacapu, 24 October 1896.

31 AHPEM, Hijuelas, District of Zacapu, vol. 6, Sixto Mayo and Jorge Santa Ana, Legal Representatives of Tarejero, to Governor of Michoacán, 18 December 1896. The auction was temporarily suspended, although the lands remained impounded, and it is not clear from the archival record how much was eventually auctioned off. An unspecified amount of land was distributed

to community members in a reparto approved in 1906 (AHPEM, Hijuelas, District of Huetamo, vol. 1, Ministry of Government, Morelia, to District Prefect, Zacapu, 30 November 1906).

32 Primo Tapia's full name was Primo Tapia de la Cruz; he was a grandson of Ambrosio, and the son of the sister of the prerevolutionary agrarian leader Joaquín de la Cruz.

33 AHPEM, Gobernación-Religión, caja 2/45, Ministry of Government to Governor's Office, Transmission of a copy of a letter received from Naranja Residents, 20 December 1927.

34 AGN, Papeles Presidenciales, Obregón-Calles, 818-N-12, Anexo 3, Primo Tapia, Crispín Serrato, and Tomás Cruz to President Plutarco Elías Calles, 4 September 1925. The reference to the Noriegas being Carrancistas against Obregón refers to the rebellion of Agua Prieta in 1920, in which Calles, Obregón, and de la Huerta overthrew Carranza.

35 The Chavistas never attacked the Zacapu communities, but they did operate in the surrounding area, leading residents to flee their villages on several occasions (Friedrich 1977: 51).

36 The most notable incident, described in detail by Friedrich (1977: 50–51) occurred in Naranja in 1912, when local residents attacked and killed a group of mestizo hacienda workers who became inebriated and fired shots into the air while visiting a store owned by the Torres family. Hostilities between Naranja comuneros and mestizo hacienda workers ran high, because landowners, having dispossessed the comuneros of the communal holdings, tended to hire mestizo workers, leaving the comuneros both landless and unemployed.

37 AGN, CNA, Resoluciones Presidenciales, vol. 17, Tiríndaro and Tarejero, 20 February 1924. According to an agrarian census undertaken in Tarejero, Tarejero had a population of 1,044, with 316 heads of household, most of them "poor farmers" given that the community only had 313 hectares of land, only 183 of which was cultivable, the rest being suitable only for pasture. Tiríndaro had a population of 1,304, with 396 heads of household, here too the majority being poor farmers, given that the community had 1,253 hectares of land, 37 of which were occupied by the town itself, with another 157 suitable for rainfed agriculture, 20 in the ciénaga, and the remaining 1,037 unsuitable for cultivation.

38 AGN, CNA, Resoluciones Presidenciales, vol. 17, Naranja, 20 February 1924. The requisite fieldwork following the petition for a dotación indicated that Naranja had a population of 1,071, with 358 heads of household. The total amount of land possessed by the community was 985 hectares: 19 taken up by the fundo legal, 176 suitable for rainfed agriculture, and the remainder unsuitable for cultivation.

39 Naranja resident quoted in Friedrich 1977: 91–92. Friedrich argues that about half would have willingly signed a petition for land whereas the other half would have opposed it.

40 AGN, Papeles Presidenciales, Obregón-Calles, 818-N-12, Primo Tapia, Tomás M. Cruz, Crispín Serrato, and other residents of Naranja and Tiríndaro to President Plutarco Elías Calles, 4 September 1925.

41 AGN, Papeles Presidenciales, Obregón-Calles, 818-N-12, Félix Espinosa to the CLA. The letter is undated, but another document in the same file refers to it as having been written on 10 November 1921.

42 AGN, Papeles Presidenciales, Obregón-Calles, 818-N-12, Telegram from Casa Obrero Mundial to President Alvaro Obregón, 12 November 1921. The telegram states that the defense forces of Naranja and Tiríndaro were attacked by federal soldiers in an attempt to disarm them, and, in failing that mission, soldiers attacked the families and houses of the agraristas.

43 AGN, Papeles Presidenciales, Obregón-Calles, 818-N-12, Jesús Corral, Secretary of the CLA to President Alvaro Obregón, 28 October 1921.

44 Provisional possessions were granted by the governors upon the recommendation of the state-level Local Agrarian Commissions. These were then reviewed by the National Agrarian Commission, and, if approved, sent to the president who granted definitive possession. Peasants, in theory, had the right to use the land once the provisional possession was granted.

45 AGN, CNA, Resoluciones Presidenciales, vol. 17, Naranja, Tarejero, and Tiríndaro, 20 February 1924. Zacapu did not receive provisional possession of its ejido until 27 August 1924 (vol. 28, 8 October 1925). The amounts of land granted were all raised in the definitive presidential resolutions of 20 February 1924: Tiríndaro received 792, Tarejero, 632, and Naranja, 716 hectares.

46 AGN, CNA, Resoluciones Presidenciales, vol. 28, Zacapu, 8 October 1925. Although the hacendados protested the provisional grant on the usual grounds that the agrarian census was faulty and that their lands were more than seven kilometers from Zacapu and hence legally not affectable, they won the injunction on the basis of Zacapu's legal status as a villa, the second highest of the political-administrative categories, the highest being ciudad, or city. Residents of villas were only eligible to apply for land if the town had lost population or sources of employment. The conservative municipal president of Zacapu, allied with the hacendados, reported that Zacapu had, in fact, grown by 50 percent in recent years and had by no means witnessed a loss of industry, mining, or commerce. Zacapu was actually about the same size as the other major towns of the region and had acquired the status of villa as an honorary recognition of some past military victory, rather than as a result of its actual characteristics as a town. The CNA ultimately decided that the villa status was irrelevant, that the town had, in fact, lost its weaving and fishing industries through the drainage of the marshlands, and that the report of the municipal president should be discounted because "it is a document that lacks validity and one can see an absolute partiality toward the hacendados."

47 AGN, Papeles Presidenciales, Obregón-Calles, 818-N-12, Ministry of Government, Morelia, to President Alvaro Obregón. The letter from the governor's

office included the reports from the Municipal President of Zacapu and the Jefe de Tenencia of Naranja on the incident. For the local versions of this incident, and Tapia's own description of it, see Friedrich 1977: 102–3. Tapia was reported to have said: "In Naranja . . . the eighteenth of the past month . . . there passed to a better life the celebrated leader for the hacienda, J. Natividad Torres, dead by the hands of our buddy (*cuate*), who gave him a bullet in the heart for the road that leads to glory" (cited in Friedrich 1977: 103).

48 Cited in Domínguez 1989: 199. The cristeros often played on the word *agrarrar,* in this context meaning to grab or seize, referring to agrarista peasants as "agrarristas."

49 AGN, Papeles Presidenciales, Obregón-Calles, 818-N-12, Anexo 3, Primo Tapia, Crispín Serrato, and Tomás Cruz to President Plutarco Elías Calles, 4 September 1925.

50 Primo Tapia's actions during and after the delahuertista rebellion earned him the enmity of Sánchez Pineda, who requested that Obregón have him arrested, writing "Tapia has been and is a divisive element, and was recently among the Agraristas of this state who took part with arms in hand in the rebellion led by Estrada" (AGN, Papeles Presidenciales, Obregón-Calles, 811-M-89, Sánchez Pineda to Obregón, 6 May 1924).

51 AGN, Papeles Presidenciales, Obregón-Calles, 818-N-12, Anexo 3, Primo Tapia, Crispín Serrato, and Tomás Cruz to President Plutarco Elías Calles, 4 September 1925; Senator Luis G. Monzón, Morelia, to President Plutarco Elías Calles, 21 January 1925; Primo Tapia, Crispín Serrato, Tomás M. Cruz, and others of Naranja and Tiríndaro to President Alvaro Obregón, 4 September 1925; 818-N-12, J. Natividad C. Espinosa, Severo Espinosa, and other residents of Tiríndaro to Luis G. Monzón, Camara de Senadores, 8 February 1925. These letters also report the 10 January 1925 assassination of two peons from the Hacienda Copándaro (also owned by the Noriegas) by federal soldiers, allegedly because they began to collect signatures for an agrarian petition. The "ombudsman" (*procurado*) was charged with investigating complaints by the villagers of abuses by public officials.

52 AGN, Papeles Presidenciales, Obregón-Calles, 818-N-12, Ramón Aguilar, Zacapu, to President Plutarco Elías Calles, 19 October 1925. The agraristas took formal possession of the ejido on 17 October 1925.

53 Ibid.

54 AHPEM, Gobernación-Religión, caja 9/18, Residents of Tiríndaro to President of Republic, 17 May 1930. In another letter, residents wrote: "By tradition we have conserved our religious beliefs, without knowing if they are good or bad, and we have taken refuge in that belief and have remained faithful to it. Now one of our neighbors, named Severo Espinosa, has tried, in the company of some other residents, to obstruct and change our beliefs" (AHPEM, Gobernación-Religión, caja 9/18, residents of Tiríndaro to Ministry of Government, Morelia, 5 May 1930).

55 AGN, Papeles Presidenciales, Obregón-Calles, 818-N-12, Chief of Staff, Mexico City, to Personal Secretary of President Plutarco Elías Calles, 9 June 1926; Ramón Aguilar to Luis León, Ministry of Agriculture and Development, 11 December 1926.

56 AGN, Papeles Presidenciales, Lázaro Cárdenas, 559.3/14, Carlos Reyes Aviles to President Lázaro Cárdenas, 28 May 1935. The letter relates attempts to capture the "bandits" led by the "ex-cristero" Ramón Aguilar around Zacapu and Cherán.

6 Catholics, *Cristeros,* and *Agraristas* in the Purépecha Highlands

1 See the oral histories collected by Plá (1989: 283–84, 286). Plá notes that these political explanations, advanced in the 1940s, gave way to accounts that emphasized God's anger with the amount of drinking and other sinful behavior that occurred in the context of the fiestas. Other oral histories of San Juan Parangaricutiro can be found in Moheno 1985 and Plá and Moheno 1981. See also Celedonio Gutiérrez's (1972) account of the volcano and subsequent relocation of the community. A San Juan peasant, Gutiérrez kept a series of diaries during the 1940s that were combined into a single manuscript in 1949 (Nolan 1972).

2 Oral history recorded by Moheno (1985: 139). The prevolcano community is referred to as San Juan, San Juan Parangaricutiro, and Parangaricutiro. The relocated community is known as Nuevo San Juan and Nuevo San Juan Parangaricutiro. The residents of Paricutín were moved to a new location called Caltzontzin by state authorities. They continued to use the name Paricutín, however, and sometimes the Indian Community of Paricutín.

3 Outside of the Itzcuaro valley, the highland communities were established by Franciscans, under the leadership of Fray Juan de San Miguel, who founded the new town of Uruapan in 1540. See Bishop 1977; Ricard 1966; and Romero 1860.

4 All of the quotations from this source were translated by the volume's editor, Mary Lee Nolan. As is common in histories of the region, Gutiérrez attributed the foundation of San Juan Parangaricutiro to Fray Juan de San Miguel and the Franciscan order.

5 Oral histories related by Celedonio Gutiérrez and other residents of Nuevo San Juan to Plá (1989: 272).

6 AN, District of Uruapan, vol. 16, record 2038, 30 April 1909; vol. 13, records 1748 and 1756, 19 and 21 January 1909. Land was often registered as private property many years after it was claimed as such. Anguiano claimed to have purchased land in 1895, Ortiz in 1898. Small proprietors and comuneros continue to dispute the ownership of land in Pantzingo. See documents in ASRAU, San Juan Parangaricutiro, exps. 1973 (dotación) and 108-A (bienes comunales), and in ASRAMC, San Juan Parangaricutiro, exp. 276.1/443 (bienes comunales).

7   Plá (1989) notes that local histories differ as to when the Lord of the Miracles arrived in San Juan: some residents say it was the late nineteenth century, but most agree it was at some point in the sixteenth century, not long after San Juan Parangaricutiro was founded by the bachiller Fuenllana. The icon, according to Plá (1989: 276–77), is made of a maize paste, in a technique common in the Purépecha region in the late sixteenth century. Lumholtz (1902: 376), traveling through the region between 1894 and 1897, claimed that the feast of the Lord of the Miracles was of recent origin, having been inaugurated by a local priest. Given the amount of conflict between the community and the Church hierarchy over the cult of the Lord of the Miracles, it seems more likely that a local priest tried to steer worship along more orthodox lines.

8   In their description of the arrival of the Lord of the Miracles, the residents of San Juan are in keeping with Purépecha oral tradition, which holds that icons (of Christ or of different saints) were often transported by muleteers; when they reached the appropriate community, they then made themselves too heavy to move (Plá 1989: 276–77).

9   These institutions are described at length in Bishop 1977; Carrasco 1976; and Moheno 1985. Moheno argues that the cabildo had lost control over San Juan's communal land by the end of the nineteenth century, the land having been appropriated and privatized by local mestizo elites. Extensive archival evidence (and much of Moheno's own analysis in his discussion of twentieth-century San Juan) indicates that the bulk of San Juan's land remained under communal control until the revolution itself and was alienated only when local mestizo elites formed alliances with revolutionary state officials. In her study of the cargo system in San Juan, Bishop argues that communal land remained under the control of the cabildo until the early 1930s, after the defeat of the cristeros and the consolidation of revolutionary state authority at the local level.

10 ASRAU, San Juan Parangaricutiro, exp. 108A (bienes comunales), paleographic study, 28 March 1977; ASRAMC, San Juan Parangaricutiro, exp. 276.1/443 (bienes comunales), "Resolución sobre el reconocimiento y titulación de bienes comunales del Pueblo denominado Nuevo San Juan Parangaricutiro, Municipio de Nuevo San Juan Parangaricutiro, Michoacán," 22 November 1991.

11 AHPEM, Materia Agraria, caja 1, Gabriel Avila to the Governor's Office, 26 March 1927.

12 *Periódico Oficial,* 23 October 1927.

13 AHPEM, Gobernación–Distrito Territorial, caja 9, J. Jesús Camilo, Chief of Tenencia, and J. Cruz Sánchez, Representative of the Indigenous Community to Governor of Michoacán, 13 September 1928; AGN, CNA, Resoluciones Presidenciales, vol. 13, San Angel Zurumucapio, 14 June 1923.

14 AHPEM, Materia Agraria, caja 1, Gabriel Avila to Ministry of Government, Morelia, 24 March 1907.

15 AHPEM, Hijuelas, District of Uruapan, vol. 18, Community acta, 12 January
    1869.

16 AHPEM, Hijuelas, District of Uruapan, vol. 21, Representatives of Zacán,
    Zirostro, Paracho, Cherán, Nahuatzen, Tancítaro, Apo, Peribán, Paricutín,
    Pamatácuaro, Angahuan, Aranza, Sevina, Corupo, Parangaricutiro, and Tin-
    güíndín to the Governor of Michoacán, Morelia, 12 June 1869.

17 AHPEM, Hijuelas, District of Uruapan, vol. 18, Juan Nepo Guerrero and
    others to District Prefect, Uruapan, 30 June 1869.

18 The 1894 law allowed individuals to "denounce" undivided communal land as
    being without legal title and to purchase it over the opposition of the commu-
    nity. In many cases, communities had initiated and suspended the reparto,
    often decades earlier, and such denunciations triggered the resumption and
    sometimes completion of the process. In addition, state officials encouraged
    communities to carry out the reparto in order to avoid such denunciations.
    They were quite aware that communities sometimes arranged denunciations
    themselves, in order to title land under the name of an individual while retain-
    ing de facto communal control over it.

19 RPP, District of Uruapan, vols. 1886–1912, 1912–55; AHPEM, Hijuelas, Dis-
    trict of Uruapan, vol. 18, Pedro Rodríguez and others to Governor of Michoa-
    cán, 31 May 1892; Treasury Office, Morelia, to Ministry of Government,
    Morelia, 1 August 1892. Bishop (1972) notes that mestizos controlled the
    ayuntamiento offices by the end of the nineteenth century, but generally did not
    participate in either the cargo system or the cabildo.

20 AHPEM, Hijuelas, District of Uruapan, vol. 23, Community acta, 2 Novem-
    ber 1902; District Prefect, Uruapan, to Ministry of Government, Morelia,
    13 December 1902.

21 Given that outright opposition to the reform was never expressed in public
    assemblies or letters written to state authorities, the specific identities of the
    leadership of the anti-*reparto* faction are difficult to identify. The cabildo re-
    tained de facto control over the bulk of communal resources at this time, and it
    seems likely that it was the principales who led resistance to the reparto, the
    implementation of which would, after all, deprive them of a key source of their
    power within the community.

22 AHPEM, Hijuelas, District of Uruapan, vol. 23, Gonzalo Chávez, San Juan
    Parangaricutiro, to Governor of Michoacán, Morelia, 24 December 1895.
    There is some confusion as to which law was in question here: all of the parties
    to the dispute refer to the Lerdo Law of 1856, which allowed for the denuncia-
    tion of corporate properties not claimed by tenants or occupants after a period
    of three months; Chávez and others, however, also referred to the lands in
    question as terrenos baldíos, which, together with the timing of the case, sug-
    gests that the denunciation was in accordance with the law of 1894, which
    specified that undivided communal lands might be denounced and claimed as
    being without legal titles. Chávez's case would have been much stronger had he

cited the 1894 law, given that a number of clarificatory circulars prohibited such denunciations under the 1856 law.

23 AHPEM, Hijuelas, District of Uruapan, vol. 23, Felipe Cuara, San Juan Parangaricutiro, to District Prefect, Uruapan, 12 November 1895.

24 AHPEM, Hijuelas, District of Uruapan, vol. 23, District Prefect, Uruapan, to Ministry of Government, Morelia, 7 October 1895; Municipal President, San Juan Parangaricutiro, to District Prefect, Uruapan, 25 March 1896; RPP, District of Uruapan, vols. 1886–1912, 1912–1955.

25 AHPEM, Hijuelas, District of Uruapan, vol. 23, Municipal President, San Juan Parangaricutiro, to District Prefect, Uruapan, 20 March 1896.

26 AHPEM, Hijuelas, District of Uruapan, vol. 23, District Prefect, Uruapan, to Ministry of Government, Morelia, 4 July 1899.

27 AHPEM, Hijuelas, District of Uruapan, vol. 23, Ministry of Government, Morelia, to District Prefect, Uruapan, 31 May 1899. Elsewhere, a state official noted that such arranged denunciations were a common tactic to secure claims to lands disputed with other communities or landowners; the government did not object, he continued, because the Indians owned the lands in question and it was up to them to arrange matters as best suited their interests (AHPEM, Hijuelas, District of Uruapan, vol. 23, Gabriel Avila, Ministry of Government, Morelia, to the Governor of Michoacán, Morelia, 17 October 1899).

28 AHPEM, Hijuelas, District of Uruapan, vol. 23, Ministry of Government, Morelia, to the Ministry of Finance and Public Credit, Mexico City, 21 March 1900. As state officials wrote in this letter: "Some commentators on the disentailment laws consider the former Indian communities to be civil corporations and they believe that their property should be adjudicated to whoever denounces it in accordance with the . . . law of 1856; but other people argue to the contrary, there being, therefore, no generally accepted rule about the matter."

29 AHPEM, Hijuelas, District of Uruapan, vol. 23, Ministry of Finance and Public Credit, Mexico City, to Governor of Michoacán, Morelia, 3 August 1902.

30 Stevens (1982) argues that Díaz at least occasionally supported village land claims against encroachments by outsiders in his discussion of the municipio of San Juan Tamazunchale in the Huasteca region of San Luis Potosí.

31 AHPEM, Hijuelas, District of Uruapan, vol. 23, Ministry of Finance and Public Credit, Mexico City, to Governor of Michoacán, Morelia, 3 August 1902.

32 AHPEM, Hijuelas, District of Uruapan, vol. 23, Felipe Cuara, San Juan Parangaricutiro, to Governor of Michoacán, Morelia, 29 December 1900; District Prefect, Uruapan, to Ministry of Government, Morelia, 21 January 1901; Ministry of Government to Criminal Court Judge, 19 November 1901; Ministry of Government, Morelia, to District Prefect, Uruapan, 29 July 1902; District Prefect, Uruapan, to Ministry of Government, Morelia, 13 December 1902.

33 It seems highly unlikely, for example, that the majority of San Juan residents could have successfully resisted attempts by the mestizo families to lease the community's woodlands in 1907, had they been so firmly under the political

and economic domination of those families. Nor does it seem likely that the community could have rebelled en masse during the cristiada, fighting agraristas led by members of the Anguiano and Equihua families, had the latter exercised the kind of hegemonic control suggested by Moheno. Moheno's own analysis of twentieth-century land conflicts doesn't support his assessment of late-nineteenth-century San Juan, given that he stresses how much communal land was privatized and alienated after the revolution rather than before it.

34 ASRAU, San Juan Parangaricutiro, exp. 108-A (bienes comunales), Anselmo Martínez Angeles, Bertha Cuara Murguia, and Carolota Campoverde Anguiano, San Juan Parangaricutiro, to President Carlos Salinas de Gortari, Mexico City, 31 January 1992.

35 ASRAU, Paricutín, exp. 1640 (restitución), DAAC memorandum, 29 October 1942; paleographic study, date illegible.

36 AHPEM, Hijuelas, District of Uruapan, vol. 20, "Escritura de arrendamiento del monte de Parangaricutiro," Luis Cuara, representative of the community and Santiago Slade, 26 November 1907. Slade established contracts with 21 highland communities between 1903 and 1913, two of which were never ratified for a variety of reasons.

37 ASRAMC, San Juan Parangaricutiro, exp. 276.1/443 (bienes comunales), "Resolución sobre el reconocimiento y titulación de bienes comunales del Pueblo denominado Nuevo San Juan Parangaricutiro," Municipio de Nuevo San Juan Parangaricutiro, Michoacán, 22 November 1991; ASRAU, San Juan Parangaricutiro, exp. 108-A (bienes comunales), paleographic study, SRA, 28 March 1977; AHPEM, Hijuelas, District of Uruapan, vol. 23, José Guido, San Juan Parangaricutiro to Governor of Michoacán, Morelia, 12 November 1902; Luis Cuara, San Juan Parangaricutiro, to Governor of Michoacán, Morelia, 19 November 1903.

38 AHPEM, Hijuelas, District of Uruapan, vol. 23, Rafael Bernabé, Representative of San Lorenzo to Governor of Michoacán, Morelia, 9 July 1899.

39 AHPEM, Hijuelas, District of Uruapan, vol. 23, Rafael Urtiz to Ministry of Government, Morelia, 26 August 1896.

40 Oral accounts of the three sambenitos are recorded in Moheno 1985: 124–27.

41 Espín Díaz 1986b; García Mora 1976; Hernández 1982.

42 This account of Charapan is based on García Mora 1981.

43 The terms "from below" and "from the center and above" refer to the geographic location of the four barrios.

44 In writing to revolutionary state officials, peasants (and others) routinely referred to their personal and political enemies as Chavistas, delahuertistas, counterrevolutionaries, fanatics, Catholics, and cristeros.

45 Whereas J. Meyer (1973/74c: 32) claims that Cherán was a cristero stronghold, Beals (1946: 12), who conducted extensive fieldwork in the community in the 1940s, argues that it was not. Meyer's assertions of partisanship in Michoacán are generally inaccurate: although he claims that San Juan Pa-

rangaricutiro, Nahuatzen, Cherán, Paricutín, and the communities of the Cañada de los Once Pueblos were cristero, Nahuatzen and Cherán were strongly Catholic but did not rebel during the cristiada, and Paricutín and the Cañada de los Once Pueblos were predominantly agrarista.

46 AHPEM, Gobernación-Religión, caja 2, Municipal President, Cherán, to Governor of Michoacán, Morelia, 12 March 1928; Chief of the Civil Defense, Cherán, to Governor of Michoacán, Morelia, 15 January 1928. The revolutionary credentials of Nahuatzen's civil authorities were also called into question in a letter from an unnamed resident of that community, who claimed that religious worship was being conducted in private houses. The municipal president denied the charge (AHPEM, Gobernación-Religión, caja 2/13, Ministry of Government to Governor of Michoacán, Morelia, 22 July 1928).

47 These are place-names used to identify the location of property within the boundaries of the community (AN, District of Uruapan, vol. 6, record 753 from year 1908; vol. 9, record 1139 from year 1908; vol. 16, record 2038 from year 1909; vol. 17, record 2002 from year 1909; vol. 28, record 2924 from year 1910; vol. 29, record 2890 from year 1911; and vol. 34, records 3333–35 from year 1912; RPP, District of Uruapan, 1912–55).

48 AN, District of Uruapan, vol. 10, records 1370, 1384, 1385, 1400, 1401, 1402 from year 1908; vol. 11, records 1605, 1610 from year 1908; vol. 27, records 2781, 2782, 2783 from year 1910; vol. 30, record 3116 from year 1911; vol. 32, records 3170, 3234 from year 1911; vol. 34, records 3314, 3315, 3316, 3317 from year 1912; vol. 5, record 3324 from year 1912; RPP, District of Uruapan, 1912–55.

49 AN, District of Uruapan, vol. 13, records 1747–50, 1756, 1758, 1769, 1778, and 1791 from year 1909.

50 ASRAU, Paricutín, exp. 1640 (restitución), Julián Rodríguez, Secretary General, DAAC, Mexico City, to DAAC Delegation, 29 October 1942.

51 As a representative from San Juan Parangaricutiro would later write of this history of conflict with Paricutín: "The properties that the residents of Paricutín attempt to make their own belong to us, because although it's true that for hundreds of years these gentlemen have tried to take our communal land from us, they have always failed because they have never been able to prove ownership of it" (ASRAU, Paricutín, exp. 1640 [restitución], Toribio Sandoval Martínez, San Juan Parangaricutiro to DAAC delegation, Morelia, 27 Sept. 1935).

52 Disputes between cabeceras and their politically subordinate tenencias were extremely common in Michoacán, and they helped to define partisanship throughout the revolutionary period and beyond. See the records contained in AHPEM, Gobernación–División Territorial, for detailed documentation of these disputes in the 1920s and 1930s.

53 On the initial uprising in San Juan Parangaricutiro, see *David*, 22 June 1955, p. 179. See also J. Meyer 1973/74a: 189 and Moheno 1985: 142–43.

54 AHPEM, Gobernación–División Territorial, caja 10, Residents of Corupo to Governor of Michoacán, 9 July 1930. Likewise, Zirosto residents requested a transfer to the municipio of Los Reyes, citing the "apathy and indifference" with which they had been treated by San Juan Parangaricutiro, San Juan's rebelliousness, and their own loyalty to the Supreme Government (AHPEM, Gobernación–División Territorial, caja 9, Residents of Zirosto to Michoacán state legislature, 9 June 1928).

55 ASRAU, Paricutín, exp. 1640 (restitución), Representatives of the Indian Community of Paricutín, to Governor of Michoacán, 9 November 1935; Julián Rodríguez, Secretary General of DAAC, Mexico City to DAAC Delegation, Morelia, 30 June 1943. No action was taken on the petition until 1933, when a paleographic study of Paricutín's supporting documents was ordered. The community's titles were deemed invalid, and the restitution was denied. Paricutín eventually achieved a "Reconocimiento y Titulación de Bienes Comunales" in 1980, recognizing the rights of 344 comuneros to 6,732 hectares of communal property.

56 Oral history related to Eliseo Aguilar in 1982 (Moheno 1985: 145). Moheno notes that the Zacán peasants never did accept the juridical status of their lands as an ejido. In 1965, they submitted a petition for the "Recognition and Titling of Communal Lands," only to be informed, in 1981, that they already had an ejido and could not have communal property. They continued to elect a "representative of communal property" rather than the ejido officials stipulated by law.

57 Ibid.

58 AHPEM, Gobernación-Religión, caja 2/14, Father José García Morfín, Uruapan, to Ministry of Government, Morelia, 10 September 1928.

59 ASRAU, Paricutín, exp. 1640 (restitución), Porfirio García de León, Comisión Mixta Agraria, to Municipal President, San Juan Parangaricutiro, 27 November 1939.

60 Crosses were frequently used as boundary markers during the colonial period.

61 ASRAU, San Juan Parangaricutiro, exp. 1640 (dotación), DAAC report, 4 July 1944.

62 Bishop 1977; L. Gutiérrez 1972; Plá 1989.

63 Ibid. State officials granted the community about 1,800 hectares of land, which, in addition to the town site, provided some arable land for 170 residents. In 1948, agrarian authorities began to pressure the community to apply for an ejido (to be composed of the lands acquired through the relocation) in order to "regularize" the situation. A group within the community did so and received a presidential resolution in 1968 that recognized the rights of only 70 families to ejido lands, the best arable land being assigned to only nine families. This decision generated conflicts between those who considered themselves to be ejidatarios, those who claimed land as comuneros, and several of those who

claimed land as small proprietors. Some residents claimed all three types of property rights. The dotación also caused considerable conflict with the ejidatarios of San Francisco, who lost land both through state action and subsequent invasions by residents of Nuevo San Juan Parangaricutiro. Documents related to the ejido can be found in ASRAU, San Juan Parangaricutiro, exps. 1640 and 1973 (dotación).

64   ASRAMC, San Juan Parangaricutiro, exp. 276.1/443, "Resolución sobre el reconocimiento y titulación de bienes comunales del poblado denominado Nuevo San Juan Parangaricutiro, Municipio de Nuevo Parangaricutiro, Michoacán," 22 November 1991. According to the resolution, the comuneros first submitted a petition for the Recognition and Titling of Communal Property in 1949. No action was taken until 1972, however, after the regulations for such a procedure had been implemented and the agrarian code amended to recognize the comunidad agraria as a legal corporate entity.

7   The *Cristeros* of Northwestern Michoacán

1   For general descriptions of the Chapala region, see, in addition to L. González 1968, 1974, 1979; Moreno García 1988, 1994; Ochoa Serrano 1978; and Vargas González 1989.

2   The Chapala region was one of the main centers of military activity during the independence wars of 1810 to 1821. Some of the plateau tenants fought in the insurgent armies led by José Antonio Torres, a hacienda overseer from Guanajuato, Luis Macías, owner of the nearby hacienda La Palma, and Marcos Castellanos, a priest from Sahuayo. Torres led a march from Guanajuato to Guadalajara, drawing considerable popular support along the way, particularly from the Indian communities along Lake Chapala. Remnants of this army fended off royalist forces from 1811 to 1816 on the lake island of Mezcala, with support from the shoreline villagers (Taylor 1988: 216–23).

3   On the subdivision of Cojumatlán, see L. González 1979: 107–11, 1974: 35–41; Ochoa Serrano 1978: 104; and Zepeda Patterson 1989: 66–67. Chevalier (1982: 66–67) also discusses Cojumatlán in his more general treatment of hacienda fragmentation as the origins of smallholdings in several center-west states.

4   AGN, CNA, Resoluciones Presidenciales, vol. 18, San Pedro Caro, 3 April 1924.

5   AHPEM, Hijuelas, District of Jiquilpan, Wenceslao del Toro, Cojumatlán to Governor of Michoacán, Morelia, 16 February 1903; District Prefect, Jiquilpan to Ministry of Government, Morelia, 1 July 1903; Municipal President, Sahuayo, to District Prefect, Jiquilpan, 18 September 1903.

6   AGN, CNA, Resoluciones Presidenciales, vol. 7, Presidential resolution denying restitution to the ex-community of Sahuayo, 16 March 1920.

7   AHPEM, Hijuelas, District of Jiquilpan, vol. 5, José Martínez Ramírez and

other residents of San Pedro Caro, to the Governor of Michoacán, Morelia, 20 June 1902.

8   L. González 1974: 40–43, 106–9; Vargas González 1989: 88; Zepeda Patterson 1989: 67–69.

9   In the late 1870s, for example, the crops planted by residents of San Pedro Caro in their holdings in the marshes were destroyed by floods three years in a row. State authorities refused to reduce or defer the community's property taxes because of the flooding (AHPEM, Hijuelas, District of Jiquilpan, vol. 9, José María Carlos Rodríguez to Ministry of Government, Morelia, 21 April 1879; Ministry of Government to State Treasury, 2 August 1879).

10 Conflicts between the community of San Pedro Caro, Cuesta Gallardo, the Compañía Hidroeléctrica e Irrigadora de Chapala, and the federal government are detailed in the 1924 presidential resolution granting San Pedro the restitution of its communal lands (AGN, CNA, Resoluciones Presidenciales, vol. 18, San Pedro Caro, 3 April 1924).

11 This account of social and political organization within San José de Gracia and Cojumatlán is based largely on L. González 1968, 1974.

12 In 1968, the tenencia of Ornelas was elevated to the status of an independent municipio, named Marcos Castellanos after the priest who led local peasants during the independence wars, at which point San José de Gracia became the cabecera or municipal seat.

13 AHPEM, Gobernación-Religión, caja 7, Municipal President, Cotija to Ministry of Government, Morelia, 17 February 1930.

14 AGN, CNA, Resoluciones Presidenciales, vol. 7, Sahuayo, 3 March 1920. Restitution was denied on the grounds that petitioners could prove neither ownership nor dispossession of the land. The case did not proceed as a dotación because Sahuayo had the politico-administrative status of villa, and thus its residents were not eligible to apply for a land grant.

15 AGN, CNA, Resoluciones Presidenciales, vol. 14, Pajacuarán and La Palma, 25 October 1923; vol. 18, San Pedro Caro, 3 April 1924; vol. 30, Ixtlán, 4 February 1926.

16 ASRAM, Cojumatlán, exp. 225 (dotación), Julián Sandoval, Cojumatlán to CNA, Mexico City, 28 January 1927; DAAC memorandum, Michoacán Delegation, 16 March 1934; Memorandum of the Tax Collector, Jiquilpan, 12 June 1934.

17 AGN, Papeles Presidenciales, Obregón-Calles, 408-M-1, residents of San José de Gracia to President Obregón, Mexico City, 25 June 1921.

18 Degollado y Guízar 1957: 21; J. Meyer 1973/74a; Zepeda Patterson 1989: 77–78.

19 AGN, Papeles Presidenciales, Obregón-Calles, exp. 104-L-23, Rafael and José Pérez, Pajacuarán to President Plutarco Elías Calles, Mexico City, 24 October 1926.

20 ASRAM, San Pedro Caro, exp. 57 (dotación), Municipal President, Sahuayo to the CNA Delegate, Morelia, 28 February 1928. The letter accuses the nearby community of La Palma of much the same thing.

21 Rebel activity around Cotija was reported in the Mexico City newspaper *El Universal* on 19 March 1927, sec. 2, p. 3, but as in all such reports dating from the first few months of sustained rebellion, it was deemed to be insignificant.

22 AHPEM, Gobernación-Religión, caja 7, Municipal president, Cotija, to Ministry of Government, Morelia, 17 February 1930.

23 INAH, CR, Reel 44, "Boletín de Guerra," num. 6, first week of May 1927.

24 On the military's counterinsurgency strategy in northwestern Michoacán and the Altos region of Jalisco, see *El Universal,* 16 March 1927, p. 1.

25 USMI, U.S. Military Attaché to U.S. War Department, Report on the Stability of the Government #1831, 2 December 1927; INAH, CR, Reel 15, summaries of telegrams received, 9 November 1927.

26 DS, 812.00/Jalisco/9, U.S. Vice Consul, Guadalajara to U.S. State Department, "Revolutionary and Political Situation in the Lake Chapala District," 17 May 1928; "Revolutionary and Political Situation in Eastern Jalisco," 15 August 1928; USMI, U.S. Military Attaché to U.S. War Department, Reports on the Stability of the Government, #1878 and 2028, 6 January and 17 April 1928.

27 AHPEM, Gobernación-Religión, caja 9/2, Lázaro Cárdenas to Luis Martínez, 28 September 1929.

28 ASRAM, Cojumatlán, exp. 225 (dotación), Benjamín Sánchez, Cojumatlán to DAAC Delegation, Morelia, 20 October 1951.

29 The relevant documents can be found in ASRAM, San José de Gracia, exp. 790 (dotación and new population center [*nuevo centro de población*]).

8 Popular Groups, Political Identities, and the State in Mexico

1 AGN, Papeles Presidenciales, Obregón-Calles, 818-N-12, Anexo 3, Ramón Aguilar to President Plutarco Elías Calles, 19 October 1925.

2 AGN, Papeles Presidenciales, Obregón-Calles, 818-N-12, Anexo 3, Primo Tapia, Crispín Serrato, and Tomás Cruz to President Plutarco Elías Calles, 4 September 1925.

3 In addition to Garner 1990, see Ruiz Cervantes 1986, 1993 on the social bases and political dynamics of the Oaxacan Sovereignty Movement.

4 This paragraph and the next are based on Knight 1986b: 240–51, 375–92.

5 Unless otherwise noted, this discussion of the Yaquis is based on Hu-DeHart 1988. Given the centrality of land, Yaqui resistance fits Knight's (1986a) category of agrarian, rather than serrano rebellion, but in keeping with the latter category, concerns with cultural and political autonomy were also paramount.

6 DS, 812.00/27980, U.S. Consul William P. Blocker, Mazatlán (Sinaloa) to U.S. State Department, 21 September 1926.

7   DS, 812.00/26727, U.S. Chargé d'Affaires to U.S. State Department, 22 December 1923.

8   USMI, U.S. Military Attaché to U.S. War Department, G-2 Report #4432, 8 December 1923; Report on the Stability of the Government #4367, 29 December 1923. DS, 812.00/26767, U.S. Chargé d'Affaires to U.S. State Department, 22 December 1923.

9   Benjamin (1990: 77) describes Zuno as "a ruthless opportunist who built an impressive regional *cacicazgo* in Jalisco, Colima, and Nayarit," in part through establishing alliances with radical labor and pleasant organizations created during the previous gubernatorial administration.

10 See Roseberry's (1994) discussion of hegemonic discourses and the use (and misuse) of names.

11 See documents dated after 1943 in ASRAU, Paricutín, esp. 1640 (restitución).

12 ASRAU, Paricutín, exp. 1640 (restitución), Julián Rodríguez, Secretary General, DAAC, Mexico City, to DAAC Delegation, Morelia, 29 October 1942.

13 On the sinarquista movement, see Meyer 1979; Vaca 1981; and Whettan 1948.

14 On the agrarian reforms initiated by the Salinas administration, particularly the (voluntary) privatization of ejido land, see Stephen 1994, 1997.

15 ASRAMC, San Juan Parangaricutiro, exp. 276.1/443, "Resolución sobre el reconocimiento y titulación de bienes comunales del poblado denominado Nuevo San Juan Parangaricutiro, Municipio de Nuevo Parangaricutiro, Michoacán," 22 November 1991.

16 The most in-depth study of the history and internal workings of the UCEZ is Zepeda Patterson 1986.

Bibliography

Archives

Archivo General de la Nación (AGN)
    Comisión Nacional Agraria (CNA): Resoluciones Presidenciales
    Hemeroteca: *El Universal*
    Papeles Presidenciales
        Obregón-Calles
        Lázaro Cárdenas
    Tierras
Archivo Histórico del Poder Ejecutivo de Michoacán (AHPEM)
    Gobernación–División Territorial
    Gobernación-Religión
    Guerra y Ejército
    Hijuelas
    Materia Agraria
    Periódico Oficial del Estado
Archivo de Notarías–Morelia (AN)
Archivo de la Secretaría de la Reforma Agraria—Delegación Agraria–Morelia
    (ASRAM)
    Ampliación
    Bienes Comunales
    Dotación
    Nuevo Centro de Población
Archivo de la Secretaría de la Reforma Agraria—Delegación Agraria–Uruapan
    (ASRAU)
Archivo de la Secretaría de la Reforma Agraria—Mexico City (ASRAMC)
British Foreign Office (BFO)
    Consular Reports from Mexico
Hemeroteca Nacional
    David

Instituto Nacional de Antropología e Historia (INAH)
  Conflicto Religioso (CR)
Registro Público de la Propiedad–Morelia (RPP)
United States Department of State (DS)
  Dispatches from Consulates, Mexico, 1910–29, Record Group 29, National
  Archives
    812.00 Political Affairs
    812.404 Religion and Church
United States War Department, Military Intelligence (USMI)
  U.S. Military Intelligence Reports, Mexico, 1919–41, Record Group 165, National Archives

Government Documents

Departamento de Estadísticas Nacional. 1927. *Censo general de habitantes, 1921: Estado de Michoacán.* Mexico City: Talleres Gráficos de la Nación.
Estado de Michoacán. 1958. *Proyecto de Programa de Gobierno del Estado de Michoacán.* Mexico City: Talleres Gráficos de la Nación.
Estado de Oaxaca. 1869. *Memoria que el Gobernador del Estado de Oaxaca presenta al H. Legislatura del mismo.* Oaxaca: Gobierno del Estado.
Estado de Oaxaca. 1872. *Memoria que el ejecutivo del estado presenta al Congreso del mismo.* Oaxaca: Gobierno del Estado.
Secretaría de la Economía Nacional, Dirección General de Estadísticas. 1937. *Primer censo agrícola y ganadero, 1930: resumen general* and *El Estado de Michoacán.* Mexico City: Secretaría de la Economía Nacional.
——. 1956. *Estadísticas sociales del porfiriato, 1877–1910.* Mexico City: Secretaría de la Economía Nacional.
Secretaría de Fomento, Colonización e Industría. 1905a. *Censo y división territorial del Estado de Michoacán, 1900.* Mexico City: Secretaría de Fomento.
——. 1905b. *Censo general de la República Mexicana y División Territorial, 1900.* Mexico City: Secretaría de Fomento.

Published Sources

Aguilar Ferreira, Melisio. 1974. *Los gobernadores de Michoacán.* Morelia: Gobierno del Estado.
Aguirre Beltrán, Gonzalo. 1952. *Problemas de la población indígena de la cuenca de Tepalcatepec.* Mexico City: Ediciones del Instituto Nacional Indigenista.
Ankerson, Dudley. 1980. "Saturnino Cedillo: A Traditional Caudillo in San Luis Potosí, 1890–1938." In *Caudillo and Peasant in the Mexican Revolution.* See Brading 1980.
Arreola Cortés, Raúl. 1980. *Coalcomán.* Morelia: Monografías Municipales del Estado de Michoacán, Gobierno del Estado.

Bailey, David C. 1974. ¡Viva Cristo Rey! The Cristero Rebellion and Church-State Conflict in Mexico. Austin: University of Texas Press.

———. 1978. "Revisionism and the Recent Historiography of the Mexican Revolution." Hispanic American Historical Review 58(1): 62–79.

Barragán López, Esteban. 1990. Más allá de los caminos: los rancheros del Potrero de Herrera. Zamora: Colegio de Michoacán.

Barragán López, Esteban, et al., eds. 1994. Rancheros y sociedades rancheras. Zamora: Colegio de Michoacán.

Bartra, Armando. 1985. Los herederos de Zapata: movimientos campesinos posrevolucionarios en México. Mexico City: Ediciones Era.

Bazant, Jan. 1971. Alienation of Church Wealth in Mexico: Social and Economic Aspects of the Liberal Revolution, 1856–1875. Cambridge: Cambridge University Press.

Beals, Ralph. 1946. Cherán: A Sierra Tarascan Village. Washington, D.C.: Smithsonian Institute of Social Anthropology.

Bechtloff, Dagmar. 1993. "La formación de una sociedad intercultural: las cofradías en el Michoacán colonial." Historia Mexicana 43(2): 251–63.

Becker, Marjorie. 1995. Setting the Virgin on Fire: Lázaro Cárdenas, Michoacán Peasants, and the Redemption of the Mexican Revolution. Berkeley: University of California Press.

Benjamin, Thomas. 1984. "Introduction: Approaching the Porfiriato." In Other Mexicos: Essays on Regional Mexican History, 1876–1911. See Benjamin and McNellie 1984.

———. 1985. "The Leviathan on the Zócalo: Recent Historiography of the Postrevolutionary Mexican State." Latin American Research Review 20(3): 195–217.

———. 1990. "Laboratories of the New State, 1920–1929: Regional Social Reform and Experiments in Mass Politics." In Provinces of the Revolution: Essays on Regional Mexican History, 1910–1929. See Benjamin and Wasserman 1990.

Benjamin, Thomas, and William McNellie, eds. 1984. Other Mexicos: Essays on Regional Mexican History, 1876–1911. Albuquerque: University of New Mexico Press.

Benjamin, Thomas, and Mark Wasserman, eds. 1990. Provinces of the Revolution: Essays on Regional Mexican History, 1910–1929. Albuquerque: University of New Mexico Press.

Berry, Charles R. 1970. "The Fiction and Fact of the Reform: The Case of the Central District of Oaxaca, 1856–1867." The Americas 26: 277–90.

Betanzos Piñón, Oscar. 1988. "Las raíces agrarias del movimiento cristero." In Historia de la cuestión agraria mexicana. Vol. 4: Modernización, lucha agraria y poder político, 1920–1934. See Montalvo 1988.

Betanzos Piñón, Oscar, and Enrique Montalvo Ortega. 1988. "Campesinado, control político y crisis económico durante el maximato (1928–1934)." In Historia de la cuestión agraria mexicana. Vol. 4: Modernización, lucha agraria y poder político, 1920–1934. See Montalvo 1988.

Bethell, Leslie, ed. 1991. *Mexico since Independence.* Cambridge: Cambridge University Press.

Bishop, Joyce M. 1977. "El Corazón del Pueblo: A Study of the Religious Cargo System of San Juan Nuevo Parangaricutiro, Michoacán, México." Ph.D. dissertation, University of California, Berkeley.

Boschi, Renato. 1984. "On Social Movements and Democratization: Theoretical Issues." *Stanford Occasional Papers in Latin American Studies* no. 9. Stanford: Stanford-Berkeley Joint Center for Latin American Studies, Stanford University.

Boyer, Christopher. 1997. "Old Loves and New Loyalties in the Construction of Revolutionary Peasant Culture in Michoacán, Mexico." Paper presented at the Conference on Latin American History of the American Historical Society, New York, 5 January.

Brading, D. A., ed. 1980. *Caudillo and Peasant in the Mexican Revolution.* Cambridge: Cambridge University Press.

———. 1994. *Church and State in Bourbon Mexico: The Diocese of Michoacán, 1749–1810.* Cambridge: Cambridge University Press.

Brand, Donald. 1960. *Coalcomán and Motines del Oro: An Ex-distrito of Michoacán, Mexico.* The Hague: Martious Nijhoff.

Brandes, Stanley H. 1988. *Power and Persuasion: Fiestas and Social Control in Rural Mexico.* Philadelphia: University of Pennsylvania Press.

Bravo Ugarte, José. 1960. *Inspección ocular en Michoacán: regiones Central y Sudoeste.* Mexico City: Editorial Jus.

———. 1962. *Historia succinta de Michoacán.* 3 vols. Mexico City: Editorial Jus.

Brenner, Anita. 1943. *The Wind That Swept Mexico: The History of the Mexican Revolution, 1910–1942.* New York: Harper and Brothers.

Buve, Raymond. 1980. "State Governors and Peasant Mobilization in Tlaxcala." In *Caudillo and Peasant in the Mexican Revolution.* See Brading 1980.

Cárdenas de la Peña, Enrique. 1970. *Tierra Caliente.* Mexico City: Secretaría de Asentamientos Humanos y Obras Públicas.

Carr, Barry. 1980. "Recent Regional Studies of the Mexican Revolution." *Latin American Research Review* 15(1): 3–14.

Carrasco, Pedro. 1976. *El catolicismo popular de los Tarascos.* Mexico City: Secretaría de Educación Pública.

———, ed. 1986. *La sociedad indígena en el centro y occidente de México.* Zamora: Colegio de Michoacán.

Ceballos Ramírez, Manuel. 1990. *Política, trabajo, y religión: la alternativa católico en el mundo y la Iglesia de "Rerum novarum" (1822–1931).* Mexico City: Instituto Mexicana de Doctrina Social Cristiana.

Centro de Estudios de la Revolución Mexicana "Lázaro Cárdenas." 1981. *Jornadas de Historia de Occidente.* Jiquilpan, Mexico: Centro de Estudios de la Revolución Mexicana "Lázaro Cárdenas."

Chance, John K. 1990. "Changes in Twentieth Century Mesoamerican *Cargo Sys-*

tems." In *Class, Politics, and Popular Religion in Mexico and Central America.* See Stephen and Dow 1990a.

Chevalier, François. 1982. "Acerca de los orígenes de la pequeña propiedad en el occidente de México: historia comparada." In *Después de los latifundios.* See Moreno García 1982.

Chowning, Margaret. 1984. "A Mexican Provincial Elite: Michoacán, 1810–1910." Ph.D. dissertation, Stanford University, Stanford, California.

———. 1990. "The Management of Church Wealth in Michoacán, Mexico, 1810–1856: Economic Motivations and Political Implications." *Journal of Latin American Studies* 22(3): 459–96.

———. 1992. "The Contours of the Post-1810 Depression in Mexico: A Reappraisal from a Regional Perspective." *Latin American Research Review* 27(2): 119–50.

Cochet, Hubert. 1988. "Ganadería y aparcería en la sierra de Coalcomán." In *Paisajes agrarios de Michoacán.* See Cochet, Léonard, and de Surgy 1988.

Cochet, Hubert, Eric Léonard, and Jean Damien de Surgy. 1988. *Paisajes agrarios de Michoacán.* Zamora, Mexico: Colegio de Michoacán, pp. 217–80.

Cohen, Jean L. 1985. "Strategy or Identity: New Theoretical Paradigms and Contemporary Social Movements." *Social Research* 52(4): 663–716.

Córdova, Arnaldo. 1989. *La revolución y el estado en México.* Mexico City: Ediciones Era.

Corona Núñez, José. 1938. *Rincones michoacanos: leyendas y breves datos históricos de algunos pueblos de Michoacán.* Pátzcuaro: n.p.

Costeloe, Michael. 1967. *Church Wealth in Mexico: A Study of the Juzgado de Capellanías in the Archbishopric of Mexico, 1800–1856.* Cambridge: Cambridge University Press.

———. 1978. *Church and State in Independent Mexico: A Study of the Patronage Debate, 1821–1857.* London: Royal Historical Society.

Craig, Ann L. 1983. *The First Agraristas: An Oral History of a Mexican Reform Movement.* Berkeley: University of California Press.

———. 1990. "Legal Constraints and Mobilization Strategies in the Countryside." In *Popular Movements and Political Change in Mexico.* See Foweraker and Craig 1990.

Cuevas, P. Mariano. 1928. *Historia de la iglesia en México.* El Paso, Tex.: Editorial "Revista Católico."

Degollado y Guízar, Jesús. 1957. *Memorias de Jesús Degollado y Guízar: Ultimo general en jefe del ejército cristero.* Mexico City: Editorial Jus.

De la Peña, Guillermo. 1981. "Los estudios regionales y la antropología social en México." *Relaciones* 2(8): 43–93.

Dennis, Philip A. 1987. *Intervillage Conflict in Oaxaca.* New Brunswick, N.J.: Rutgers University Press.

Díaz, José, and Ramón Rodríguez. 1979. *El movimiento cristero: sociedad y conflicto en los Altos de Jalisco.* Mexico City: Nueva Imagen.

Di Tella, Torcuato S. 1996. *National Popular Politics in Early Independent Mexico, 1820–1847*. Albuquerque: University of New Mexico Press.

Domínguez, José Luis. 1989. "Zacapu: Un pueblo que trabaja." In *Estudios michoacanos III*. See Zendejas Romero 1989.

Domínguez, Reinaldo Lucas. 1991. "La tenencia de la tierra." *México Indígena* 16/17: 45–46.

Durand, Jorge. 1989. "Tierra de volcanes: movimientos sociales en Michoacán (1976–1986)." In *Estudios michoacanos III*. See Zendejas Romero 1989.

Embriz Osorio, Arnulfo. 1984. *La Liga de Comunidades y Sindicatos Agraristas en Michoacán: práctica político-sindical, 1919–1929*. Mexico City: Centro de Estudios Históricos del Agrarismo en México, Colección Investigadores.

Embriz Osorio, Arnulfo, and Ricardo León García. 1982. *Documentos para el estudio de la historia del agrarismo en Michoacán*. Mexico City: Centro de Estudios Históricos del Agrarismo en México, Colección Investigadores.

Escárcega López, Everardo. 1990a. "El principio de la reforma agraria." In *Historia de la cuestión agraria mexicana*. Vol. 5: *El cardenismo: un parteaguas histórico en el proceso agrario nacional, 1934–1940 (primera parte)*. See Escárcega López 1990b.

———, ed. 1990b. *Historia de la cuestión agraria mexicana*. Vol. 5: *El cardenismo: un parteaguas histórico en el proceso agrario nacional, 1934–1940 (primera parte)*. Mexico City: Siglo XXI.

Escárcega López, Everardo, ed. 1990c. *Historia de la cuestión agraria mexicana*. Vol. 5: *El cardenismo: un parteaguas histórico en el proceso agrario nacional, 1934–1940 (segunda parte)*. Mexico City: Siglo XXI.

Escobar, Arturo, and Sonia E. Alvarez, eds. 1992. *The Making of Social Movements in Latin America: Identity, Strategy, and Democracy*. Boulder, Colo.: Westview Press.

Escobar Toledo, Saúl. 1990a. "El cardenismo más allá del reparto: acciones y resultados." In *Historia de la cuestión agraria mexicana*. Vol. 5: *El cardenismo: un parteaguas histórico en el proceso agrario nacional, 1934–1940 (segunda parte)*. See Escárcega López 1990c.

———. 1990b. "La ruptura cardenista." In *Historia de la cuestión agraria mexicana*. Vol. 5: *El cardenismo: un parteaguas histórico en el proceso agrario nacional, 1934–1940 (segunda parte)*. See Escárcega López 1990c.

Espín Díaz, Jaime. 1983. "La región de Uruapan: criterios de definición y características ecológicas." *Relaciones* 4(14): 5–30.

———. 1986a. "Ecología y política: el impacto del reparto agrario en la meseta y la secularización del poder." In *La sociedad indígena en el centro y occidente de México*. See Carrasco 1986.

———. 1986b. *Tierra fría: tierra de conflictos en Michoacán*. Zamora, Mexico: Colegio de Michoacán.

Espinosa, Fr. Isidro Félix de. ([1751] 1945). *Crónica de la Provincia Franciscana de*

los Apostles San Pedro y San Pablo de Michoacán. Mexico City: Editorial Santiago.

Fábregas, Andrés. 1979. "Los Altos de Jalisco: características generales." Introduction to *El movimiento cristero: sociedad y conflicto en los Altos de Jalisco.* See Díaz and Rodríguez 1979.

Falcón, Romana. 1988. "Charisma, Tradition, and Caciquismo: Revolution in San Luis Potosí." In *Riot, Rebellion, and Revolution: Rural Social Conflict in Mexico.* See Katz 1988b.

——. 1990. "San Luis Potosí: Confiscated Estates—Revolutionary Conquest or Spoils?" In *Provinces of the Revolution: Essays on Regional Mexican History, 1910–1929.* See Benjamin and Wasserman 1990.

——. 1994. "Force and the Search for Consent: The Role of the *Jefaturas Políticas* of Coahuila in National State Formation." In *Everyday Forms of State Formation: Revolution and the Negotiation of Rule in Modern Mexico.* See Joseph and Nugent 1994b.

Farriss, Nancy. 1968. *Crown and Clergy in Colonial Mexico, 1759: The Crisis of Ecclesiastical Privilege.* London: Athlone Publishers.

Foglio Miramontes, Fernando. 1936. *Geografía económico agrícola del estado de Michoacán.* 3 vols. Mexico City: Secretaría de Agricultura y Fomento.

Foley, John. 1979. "Colima, Mexico and the Cristero Rebellion." Ph.D. dissertation, University of Chicago.

Foweraker, Joe. 1990. "Popular Organization and Institutional Change." In *Popular Movements and Political Change in Mexico.* See Foweraker and Craig 1990.

Foweraker, Joe and Ann L. Craig, eds. 1990. *Popular Movements and Political Change in Mexico.* Boulder, Colo.: Lynn Rienner Publishers.

Fowler-Salamini, Heather. 1971. *Agrarian Radicalism in Veracruz, 1920–38.* Lincoln: University of Nebraska Press.

——. 1980. "Revolutionary Caudillos in the 1920s: Francisco Múgica and Adalberto Tejeda." In *Caudillo and Peasant in the Mexican Revolution.* See Brading 1980.

——. 1990. "Tamaulipas: Land Reform and the State." In *Provinces of the Revolution: Essays on Regional Mexican History, 1910–1929.* See Benjamin and Wasserman 1990.

——. 1993. "The Boom in Regional Studies of the Mexican Revolution: Where Is It Leading?" *Latin American Research Review* 28(2): 175–90.

Fraser, Donald. 1972. "La política de desamortización en las comunidades indígenas, 1856–1872." *Historia Mexicana* 21(4): 615–52.

Friedrich, Paul. 1977. *Agrarian Revolt in a Mexican Village.* Chicago: University of Chicago Press.

——. 1986. *The Princes of Naranja: An Essay in Anthrohistorical Method.* Austin: University of Texas Press.

Galván Campos, Fausto. 1940. "El problema agraria entre los Tarascos." In *Los Tarascos*. See Mendieta y Núñez 1940.

García Avila, Sergio. 1987. "El Dr. Miguel Silva y el primer gobierno maderista en Michoacán." In *La revolución en Michoacán, 1900–1926*. See Sánchez Díaz 1987.

García López, Lucía. 1984. *Nahuatzen: agricultura y comercio en una comunidad serrana*. Zamora, Mexico: Colegio de Michoacán.

García Mora, Carlos. 1976. "El conflicto agrario-religioso en la Sierra Tarasca." *América Indígena* 36(1): 115–28.

———. 1981. "Tierra y movimiento agrarista en la Sierra Purépecha." In *Jornadas de historia de occidente*. See Centro de Estudios de la Revolución Mexicana "Lázaro Cárdenas" 1981.

García Ugarte, Marta Eugenia. 1995. "Los católicos y el presidente Calles." *Revista Mexicana de Sociología* 57(3): 131–55.

Garner, Paul. 1990. "Oaxaca: The Rise and Fall of State Sovereignty." In *Provinces of the Revolution: Essays on Regional Mexican History, 1910–1929*. See Benjamin and Wasserman 1990.

Gledhill, John. 1988. "Agrarian Social Movements and Forms of Consciousness." *Bulletin of Latin American Research* 7(2): 257–76.

———. 1991. *Casi Nada: A Study of Agrarian Reform in the Homeland of Cardenismo*. Austin: University of Texas Press.

González, J. 1930. *Los cristeros*. Mexico City: privately printed.

González, Luis. 1968. *Pueblo en vilo*. Mexico City: Secretaría de Educación Pública, Fundo de Cultura Económica.

———. 1971. "Tierra Caliente." In *Extremos de México: homenaje a Don Daniel Cosío Villegas*. Mexico City: Colegio de México.

———. 1974. *San José de Gracia: Mexican Village in Transition*. Austin: University of Texas Press.

———. 1979. *Sahuayo*. Monografías Municipales del Estado. Morelia: Gobierno del Estado de Michoacán.

———. 1982. "Comentario." In *Después de los latifundios*. See Moreno García 1982.

Greenberg, James B. 1990. "Sanctity and Resistance in Closed Corporate Indigenous Communities: Coffee Money, Violence, and Ritual Organization in Chatino Communities in Oaxaca." In *Class, Politics, and Popular Religion in Mexico and Central America*. See Stephen and Dow 1990b.

Gruening, Ernest. 1928. *Mexico and Its Heritage*. New York: Century Company.

Guardino, Peter. 1996. *Peasants, Politics, and the Formation of Mexico's National State: Guerrero, 1800–1857*. Stanford, Calif.: Stanford University Press.

Gutiérrez, Angel. 1984. "Investigación histórica y lucha ideológica: el caso de las comunidades michoacanas." In *La cuestión agraria: revolución y contrarrevolución en Michoacán*. See Gutiérrez, Guzmán Avila, and Sánchez Díaz 1984.

——. 1989. "Las comunidades agrarias michoacanas: historia y política." *Tzintzun* 10:37–55.

Gutiérrez, Angel, José Napoleón Guzmán Avila, and Gerardo Sánchez Díaz, eds. 1984. *La cuestión agraria: revolución y contrarrevolución en Michoacán.* Morelia: Universidad Michoacán.

Gutiérrez, Celedonio. 1972. *Narrative of Human Response to Natural Disasters: The Eruption of Paricutín: San Juan Parangaricutiro: Memories of Past Years.* College Station: Texas A&M University.

Guzmán Avila, José Napoleón. 1984. "Movimiento campesino y empresas extranjeras: la ciénega de Zacapu, 1870–1910." In *La cuestión agraria: revolución y contrarrevolución en Michoacán.* See Gutiérrez, Guzmán Avila, and Sánchez Díaz 1984.

——. 1986. "Agrarismo y contrarrevolución en Michoacán." *Tzintzun* 7:42–47.

Haber, Paul Lawrence. 1996. "Identity and Political Process: Recent Trends in the Study of Latin American Social Movements." *Latin American Research Review* 31(1): 171–88.

Hale, Charles A. 1968. *Mexican Liberalism in the Age of Mora, 1821–1853.* New Haven, Conn.: Yale University Press.

——. 1989. *Transformation of Liberalism in Late Nineteenth-Century Mexico.* Princeton, N.J.: Princeton University Press.

Hall, Stuart. 1981. "Notes on Deconstructing 'The Popular.' " In *People's History and Socialist Theory.* See Samuel 1981.

Hamnett, Brian. 1996. "Liberalism Divided: Regional Politics and the National Republic during the Mexican Restored Republic." *Hispanic American Historical Review* 76(4): 659–89.

Hellman, Judith Adler. 1983. *Mexico in Crisis.* New York: Holmes and Meier Publishers.

Hernández, Luis, and Pilar López. 1990. "Campesinos y Poder: 1934–1940." In *Historia de la cuestión agraria mexicana.* Vol. 5: *El cardenismo: un parteaguas histórico en el proceso agrario nacional, 1934–1940 (segunda parte).* See Escárcega López 1990c.

Hernández, Manuel Diego. 1982. *La Confederación Revolucionaria Michoacana del Trabajo.* Jiquilpan, Mexico: Centro de Estudios de la Revolución Mexicana "Lázaro Cárdenas."

Herrejón Peredo, Carlos, ed. 1986a. *Estudios Michoacanos I.* Zamora, Mexico: Colegio de Michoacán.

——, ed. 1986b. *Estudios michoacanos II.* Zamora, Mexico: Colegio de Michoacán.

Hindess, Barry. 1983. "Rational Choice Theory and the Analysis of Political Action." *Economy and Society* 13 (3): 255–77.

Hobsbawm, Eric. 1984. *Workers: Worlds of Labor.* New York: Pantheon Books.

Holden, Robert. 1994. *Mexico and the Survey of Public Lands: The Management of Modernization, 1876–1911.* DeKalb: Northern Illinois University Press.

Horowitz, Irving L., ed. 1970. *Masses in Latin America.* New York: Oxford University Press.

Hu-DeHart, Evelyn. 1988. "Peasant Rebellion in the Northwest: The Yaqui Indians of Sonora, 1740–1976." In *Riot, Rebellion, and Revolution: Rural Social Conflict in Mexico.* See Katz 1988b.

Huizer, Gerrit. 1970. "Peasant Organization in Agrarian Reform in Mexico." In *Masses in Latin America.* See Horowitz 1970.

Huntington, Samuel P. 1968. *Political Order in Changing Societies.* New Haven: Conn.: Yale University Press.

Jacobs, Ian. 1982. *Ranchero Revolt: The Mexican Revolution in Guerrero.* Austin: University of Texas Press.

Jiménez Castillo, Manuel. 1986. "La organización social de los purépechas." *México Indígena,* nos. 10 and 11:26–36, 31–36.

Joseph, Gilbert M. 1988. *Revolution from Without: Yucatán, Mexico, and the United States, 1880–1924.* Durham, N.C.: Duke University Press.

Joseph, Gilbert, M., and Daniel Nugent. 1994a. "Popular Culture and State Formation in Revolutionary Mexico." In *Everyday Forms of State Formation: Revolution and the Negotiation of Rule in Modern Mexico.* See Joseph and Nugent 1994b.

——, eds. 1994b. *Everyday Forms of State Formation: Revolution and the Negotiation of Rule in Modern Mexico.* Durham, N.C.: Duke University Press.

Joseph, Gilbert M., and Allen Wells. 1990. "Yucatán: Elite Politics and Rural Insurgency." In *Provinces of the Revolution: Essays on Regional Mexican History, 1910–1929.* See Benjamin and Wasserman 1990.

Jrade, Ramón. 1980. "Counter-revolution in Mexico: The Cristero Movement in Sociological and Historical Perspective." Ph.D. dissertation, Brown University, Providence, Rhode Island.

——. 1985. "Inquiries into the Cristero Insurrection against the Mexican Revolution." *Latin American Research Review* 20(2): 53–69.

Katz, Friedrich. 1981. *The Secret War in Mexico: Europe, the United States, and the Mexican Revolution.* Chicago: University of Chicago Press.

——. 1988a. "Introduction: Rural Revolts in Mexico." In *Riot, Rebellion, and Revolution: Rural Social Conflict in Mexico.* See Katz 1988b.

——. 1991. "The Liberal Republic and the Porfiriato, 1867–1910." In *Mexico since Independence.* See Bethell 1991.

——, ed. 1988b. *Riot, Rebellion, and Revolution: Rural Social Conflict in Mexico.* Princeton, N.J.: Princeton University Press.

Knight, Alan. 1980. "Peasant and Caudillo in Revolutionary Mexico, 1910–1917." In *Caudillo and Peasant in the Mexican Revolution.* See Brading 1980.

——. 1985. "The Mexican Revolution: Bourgeois? Nationalist? Or just a 'Great Rebellion'?" *Bulletin of Latin American Research* 4(2): 1–37.

——. 1986a. *The Mexican Revolution: Porfirians, Liberals and Peasants,* vol. 1. Lincoln: University of Nebraska Press.

———. 1986b. *The Mexican Revolution: Counter-revolution and Reconstruction*, vol. 2. Lincoln: University of Nebraska Press.

———. 1990a. "Historical Continuities in Social Movements." In *Popular Movements and Political Change in Mexico*. See Foweraker and Craig 1990.

———. 1990b. "Revolutionary Project, Recalcitrant People: Mexico, 1910–1940." In *The Revolutionary Process in Mexico: Essays on Political and Social Change, 1880–1940.* See Rodríguez 1990.

———. 1991. "Land and Society in Revolutionary Mexico: The Destruction of the Great Haciendas." *Mexican Studies/Estudios Mexicanos* 7(1): 73–104.

———. 1994. "Weapons and Arches in the Mexican Revolutionary Landscape." In *Everyday Forms of State Formation: Revolution and the Negotiation of Rule in Modern Mexico*. See Joseph and Nugent 1994b.

Knowlton, Robert J. 1965. "Clerical Responses to the Mexican Reform, 1855–1875." *Catholic Historical Review* 50(4): 509–28.

———. 1976. *Church Property and the Mexican Reform, 1856–1910.* DeKalb: Northern Illinois University Press.

———. 1990. "La división de las tierras de los pueblos durante el siglo XIX: el caso de Michoacán." *Historia Mexicana* 40(1): 3–25.

Kourí, Emilio. 1996. "The Business of Land: Agrarian Tenure and Enterprise in Papantla, Mexico, 1800–1910." Ph.D. diss., Harvard University, Cambridge.

LaFrance, David. 1990. "Many Causes, Movements, Failures, 1910–1913: The Regional Nature of Maderismo." In *Provinces of the Revolution: Essays on Regional Mexican History, 1910–1929.* See Benjamin and Wasserman 1990.

Lee, James H. 1980. "Bishop Clemente Munguía and Clerical Resistance to the Mexican Reform, 1855–1857." *Catholic Historical Review* 66(3): 374–91.

López Lara, Ramón. 1973. Introduction to *El Obispado de Michoacán en el siglo XVII: informe inédito de beneficios, pueblos y lenguas*. Morelia: Fimax Publicistas.

Lumholtz, Carl. 1902. *Unknown Mexico.* New York: C. Scribner's Sons.

Mallon, Florencia. 1994. "Reflections on the Ruins: Everyday Forms of State Formation in Nineteenth Century Mexico." In *Everyday Forms of State Formation: Revolution and the Negotiation of Rule in Modern Mexico.* See Joseph and Nugent 1994b.

———. 1995. *Peasant and Nation: The Making of Postcolonial Mexico and Peru.* Berkeley: University of California Press.

Martínez de Lejarza, Juan José. 1974 [1824]. *Análisis estadístico de la Provincia de Michoacán en 1822.* Morelia: FIMAX Publicistas.

Martínez Vázquez, Víctor Raúl, ed. 1993. *La revolución en Oaxaca (1900–1930).* Mexico City: Consejo Nacional para la Cultura y las Artes.

Maturana Medina, Sergio, and José Sánchez Cortés. 1970. *Las comunidades de la Meseta Tarasca.* Mexico City: Centro de Investigaciones Agrarias.

McBride, George McCutchen. 1923. *Land Systems of Mexico*. New York: American Geographical Society.

Mendieta y Núñez, Lucio. 1966. *El problema agrario de México*. Mexico City: Editorial Porrúa.

———, ed. 1940. *Los tarascos*. Mexico City: Universidad Nacional Autónoma de México.

Mendoza, Moisés Franco. 1986. "La desamortización de bienes de comunidades indígenas en Michoacán." In *La sociedad indígena en el centro y occidente de México*. See Carrasco 1986.

Meyer, Jean. 1973/74a. *La Cristiada. La guerra de los cristeros*, vol. 1. Mexico City: Siglo XXI.

———. 1973/74b. *La Cristiada. El conflicto entre la iglesia y el estado, 1926–1929*, vol. 2. Mexico City: Siglo XXI.

———. 1973/74c. *La Cristiada. Los cristeros*, vol. 3. Mexico City: Siglo XXI.

———. 1976. *The Cristero Rebellion: Mexican People between Church and State*. Cambridge: Cambridge University Press.

———. 1977. *Historia de la revolución mexicana: período 1924–1928*. Vol. 11: *Estado y sociedad con Calles*. Mexico City: Colegio de México.

———. 1979. *El sinarquismo: ¿un fascismo mexicano?* Mexico City: Editorial Joaquín Morfín.

———. 1981. *El coraje cristero: testimonios*. Mexico City: Universidad Autónoma Metropolitana.

———. 1984. *Esperando a Lozada*. Zamora, Mexico: Colegio de Michoacán.

———. 1986. "La Ley Lerdo y la desamortización de las comunidades en Jalisco." In *La sociedad indígena en el centro y occidente de México*. See Carrasco 1986.

———. 1987. "Los 'kulaks' del ejido (los años 30)." *Relaciones* 8(29): 23–44.

———. 1991. "Revolution and Reconstruction in the 1920s." In *Mexico since Independence*. See Bethell 1991.

Meyer, Lorenzo. 1978. *Historia de la Revolución Mexicana*. Vol. 13: *El conflicto social y los gobiernos del maximato, período 1928–34*. Mexico City: Colegio de México.

Meyer, Michael C., and William Sherman. 1987. *The Course of Mexican History*. 3rd ed. New York: Oxford University Press.

Migdal, Joel S. 1974. *Peasants, Politics and Revolution: Pressures toward Political and Social Change in the Third World*. Princeton, N.J.: Princeton University Press.

Miller, Robert Ryal. 1985. *Mexico: A History*. Norman: University of Oklahoma Press.

Moheno, César. 1985. *Las historias y los hombres de San Juan*. Zamora, Mexico: Colegio de Michoacán.

Montalvo, Enrique, ed. 1988. *Historia de la cuestión agraria mexicana*. Vol. 4: *Modernización, lucha agraria y poder político, 1920–1934*. Mexico City: Siglo XXI.

Moore, Barrington. 1966. *Social Origins of Dictatorship and Democracy: Lord and Peasant in the Making of the Modern World.* Boston: Beacon Press.

Moreno García, Heriberto. 1986. "Un documento sobre las comunidades indígenas del distrito de Zamora durante el Segundo Imperio." In *La sociedad indígena en el centro y occidente de México.* See Carrasco 1986.

———. 1988. *Geografía y paisaje de la antigua ciénega de Chapala.* Morelia: Instituto Michoacano de Cultura.

———. 1994. *Guaracha: tiempos viejos, tiempos nuevos.* Zamora, Mexico: Colegio de Michoacán.

———, ed. 1982. *Después de los latifundios.* Zamora, Mexico: Colegio de Michoacán.

Múgica Martínez, Jesús. 1982. *La Confederación Revolucionaria Michoacana del Trabajo.* Mexico City: Eddisa.

Munck, Gerardo. 1990. "Identity and Ambiguity in Democratic Struggles." In *Popular Movements and Political Change in Mexico.* See Foweraker and Craig 1990.

Needler, Martin C. 1982. *Mexican Politics: The Containment of Conflict.* New York: Praeger.

Nolan, Mary Lee. 1972. Introduction and epilogue to *Narrative of Human Response to Natural Disasters: The Eruption of Paricutín: San Juan Parangaricutiro: Memories of Past Years.* See C. Gutiérrez 1972.

Nugent, Daniel. 1993. *Spent Cartridges of the Revolution: An Anthropological History of Namiquipa, Chihuahua.* Chicago: University of Chicago Press.

Nugent, Daniel, and Ana María Alonso. 1994. "Multiple Selective Traditions in Agrarian Reform and Agrarian Struggle: Popular Culture and State Formation in the *Ejido* of Namiquipa, Chihuahua." In *Everyday Forms of State Formation: Revolution and the Negotiation of Rule in Modern Mexico.* See Joseph and Nugent 1994b.

O'Brien, Jay, and William Roseberry, eds. 1991. *Golden Ages, Dark Ages: Imagining the Past in Anthropology and History.* Berkeley: University of California Press.

Ochoa, Enrique (pseudonym "Spectator"). 1961. *Los cristeros del volcán del Colima.* Mexico: Editorial Jus.

Ochoa Serrano, Alvaro. 1978. *Jiquilpan.* Morelia: Gobierno del Estado de Michoacán.

———. 1987. "Miguel Regalado y la Sociedad Unificadora de la Raza Indígena." In *La Revolución en Michoacán, 1900–1926.* See Sánchez Díaz 1987.

———. 1989a. *Los agraristas de Atacheo.* Zamora: Colegio de Michoacán.

———. 1989b. "Michoacán: contento y descontento, 1906–1911." *Tzintzun* 10: 102–16.

———. 1992. "Política y un poco de agrarismo en la Bolsa de Guaracha." *Estudios michoacanos IV.* See Zendejas Romero 1992.

Oikión Solano, Verónica, 1986. "Huetamo: trinchera de la revolución." In *Estudios michoacanos I.* See Herrejón Peredo 1986a.

————. 1987. "La cuestión agraria y social en el proyecto constitucionalista; el caso de Michoacán." In *La revolución en Michoacán, 1900–1926*. See Sánchez Díaz 1987.

Olivera Sedano [de Bonfil], Alicia. 1966. *Aspectos del conflicto religioso de 1926 a 1929: sus antecedentes y consecuencias*. Mexico City: Instituto de Antropología e Historia.

————. 1970a. *La literatura cristera*. Mexico City: Instituto de Antropología e Historia.

————. 1970b. *Miguel Palomar y Vizcarra y su interpretación del conflicto religioso de 1926 a 1929*. Mexico City: Instituto de Antropología e Historia.

————. 1981. "José Inés Chávez García, 'El Indio': ¿Bandido, revolucionario o guerrillero?" In *Jornadas de historia del occidente*. See Centro de Estudios de la Revolución Mexicana "Lázaro Cárdenas" 1981.

Olmos Velázquez, Evaristo. 1991. *El conflicto religioso en México*. Mexico City: Ediciones Don Bosco.

Paige, Jeffrey M. 1975. *Agrarian Revolution: Social Movements and Export Agriculture in the Underdeveloped World*. New York: Free Press.

Pérez, Daniel. 1985. "Cuando los cristeros llegaron a Acachuén." Oral narration recorded by José Vaca Cristóbal. *México Indígena*. 4 (May–June): 63–64.

Pérez Escutia, Ramón Alonso. 1986. "Explotación, despojo, y resistencia en las comunidades campesinas de la región de Zinapecuaro en la época colonial." *Tzintzun* 7:3–25.

————. 1987. "Los movimientos revolucionarios en el oriente michoacano." In *La revolución en Michoacán, 1900–1926*. See Sánchez Díaz 1987.

Pinet, Alejandro. 1987. "Bandolerismo social y revolución maderista en el Bajío." In *La revolución en Michoacán, 1900–1926*. See Sánchez Díaz 1987.

Plá, Rosa. 1989. "Leyendas y tradición oral en San Juan Parangaricutiro: pueblo nuevo." In *Estudios michoacanos III*. See Zendejas Romero 1989.

Plá, Rosa, and César Moheno. 1981. "¿Milenarismo campesino? El sinarquismo en San Juan Parangaricutiro." *Relaciones* 2(6): 65–81.

Popkin, Samuel L. 1979. *The Rational Peasant: The Political Economy of Rural Society in Vietnam*. Berkeley: University of California Press.

Portes Gil, Emilio. [1934] 1983. *La lucha entre el poder civil y el clero*. Mexico City: El Día.

Powell, T. G. 1972. "Los liberales, el campesinado indígena y los problemas agrarios durante la reforma." *Historia mexicana* 21(4): 653–75.

————. 1974. "Priests and Peasants in Central Mexico: Social Conflict during La Reforma." *Hispanic America Historical Review* 57(2): 296–313.

Przeworski, Adam. 1985. "Marxism and Rational Choice." *Politics and Society* 14(4): 379–409.

Purnell, Jennie. 1997. "Citizens and Sons of the Pueblo: Property, Identity, and Political Discourse in Liberal Oaxaca." Paper presented at the annual meeting

of the New England Council on Latin American Studies, Mount Holyoke College, 18 October.

——. 1999. "With All Due Respect: Popular Resistance to the Privatization of Communal Lands in Nineteenth Century Michoacán." *Latin American Research Review* 34(1): 85–121.

Quirk, Robert E. 1973. *The Mexican Revolution and the Catholic Church, 1910–1929*. Bloomington: Indiana University Press.

Raat, W. Dirk, and William H. Beezley, eds. 1986. *Twentieth Century Mexico.* Lincoln: University of Nebraska Press.

Ramírez, Luis Alfonso. 1986a. "Cañada de los Once Pueblos." In *Estudios michoacanos II.* See Herrejón Peredo 1986b.

——. 1986b. *Chilchota: un pueblo al pie de la sierra.* Zamora, Mexico: Colegio de Michoacán.

Reséndiz Torres, Sergio. 1986. "San José de Gracia-Jiquilpan: un caso de economía ganadera." In *Estudios michoacanos II.* See Herrejón Peredo 1986b.

Restrepo, Iván, and José Sánchez Cortés. 1972. *La reforma agraria en cuatro regiones: el Bajío, Michoacán, la Laguna y Tlaxcala.* Mexico City: Secretaría de Educación Pública/Setenta.

Reyes, Cayetano. 1982. "Las tierras creadas del noroeste de Michoacán." *Relaciones* 3(9): 33–48.

Reyna, José Luis, and Richard S. Weinert, eds. 1977. *Authoritarianism in Mexico.* Philadelphia: Institute for the Study of Human Issues.

Ricard, Robert. 1966. *The Spiritual Conquest of Mexico.* Berkeley: University of California Press.

Rivera Castro, José. 1988. "Política agraria, organizaciones, luchas y resistencias campesinas entre 1920 y 1928." In *Historia de la cuestión agraria mexicana.* Vol. 4: *Modernización, lucha agraria y poder político, 1920–1924.* See Montalvo 1988.

Rockwell, Elsie. 1994. "Schools of the Revolution: Enacting and Contesting State Forms in Tlaxcala, 1910–1930." In *Everyday Forms of State Formation: Revolution and the Negotiation of Rule in Modern Mexico.* See Joseph and Nugent 1994b.

Rodríguez O., Jaime E., ed. 1990. *The Revolutionary Process in Mexico: Essays on Political and Social Change, 1880–1940.* Los Angeles: Latin American Center, University of California, Los Angeles.

Romero, José Guadalupe. 1860. *Noticias para formar la historia y la estadística del obispado de Michoacán.* Mexico City: Imprenta de Vicente García Torres.

Romero Flores, Jesús. 1946. *Historia de Michoacán.* 2 vols. Mexico City: Imprenta "Claridad."

Roseberry, William. 1991. "Potatoes, Sacks, and Enclosures in Early Modern England." In *Golden Ages, Dark Ages: Imagining the Past in Anthropology and History.* See O'Brien and Roseberry, 1991.

———. 1993. "Beyond the Agrarian Question in Latin America." In *Confronting Historical Paradigms: Peasants, Labor, and the Capitalist World System in Africa and Latin America,* ed. Frederick Cooper, Florencia Mallon, Steven J. Stern, Allen F. Isaacman, and William Roseberry. Madison: University of Wisconsin Press.

———. 1994. "Hegemony and the Language of Contention." In *Everyday Forms of State Formation.* See Joseph and Nugent, 1994b.

Roseberry, William, and Jay O'Brien. 1991. Introduction to *Golden Ages, Dark Ages: Imagining the Past in Anthropology and History.* See O'Brien and Roseberry 1991.

Rubin, Jeffrey W. 1990. "Popular Movements and the Myth of State Corporatism." In *Popular Movements and Political Change in Mexico.* See Foweraker and Craig 1990.

———. 1996. "De-centering the Regime: Culture and Regional Politics in Mexico." *Latin American Research Review* 31(3): 85–126.

———. 1997. *Decentering the Regime: Ethnicity, Radicalism, and Democracy in Juchitán, Mexico.* Durham, N.C.: Duke University Press.

Rueda, Smithers. 1981. "El movimiento cristero en los Altos de Jalisco: un caso atípico." In *Jornadas de historia de occidente.* See Centro de Estudios de la Revolución Mexicana "Lázaro Cárdenas" 1981.

Ruiz, Ramón E. 1980. *The Great Rebellion, Mexico 1905–1924.* New York: W. W. Norton.

Ruiz Cervantes, Francisco José. 1986. *La revolución en Oaxaca: el movimiento de la Soberanía (1915–1920).* Mexico City: Fondo de Cultura Económica.

———. 1993. "El movimiento de la Soberanía en Oaxaca (1915–1920)." In *La revolución en Oaxaca (1900–1930).* See Martínez Vázquez 1993.

Samuel, Raphael, ed. 1981. *People's History and Socialist Theory.* London: Routledge and Kegan Paul.

Sánchez Díaz, Geraldo. 1981. "Movimientos campesinos en la Tierra Caliente de Michoacán, 1869–1900." In *Jornadas de historia de occidente.* See Centro de Estudios de la Revolución Mexicana "Lázaro Cárdenas" 1981.

———. 1982. "La transformación del régimen de propiedad en un pueblo: conflictos agrarios en Churumuco, 1869–1900." In *Después de los latifundios.* See Moreno García 1982.

———. 1988. *El suroeste de Michoacán: economía y sociedad, 1852–1910.* Morelia: Universidad Michoacana de San Nicolás de Hidalgo.

———. 1989. "Desamortización y reforma liberal en Michoacán 1856–1875." *Tzintzun* 10:56–81.

———, ed. 1987. *La revolución en Michoacán, 1900–1926.* Morelia: Universidad Michoacana, Departamento de Historia, Coordinación de Investigación Científica.

Sánchez Díaz, Geraldo, and Gloria Carreño A. 1979. "El movimiento cristero en el

distrito de Coalcomán, 1927–1929." *Boletín del Centro de Estudios de la Revolución Mexicana "Lázaro Cárdenas"* 2(2): 99–120.

Sánchez Rodríguez, Martín. 1992. "Ixtlán: La desamortización de bienes indígenas en una comunidad michoacana y el ascenso de un arrendatario." *Estudios michoacanos IV.* Zamora, Mexico: Colegio de Michoacán.

Sanderson, Susan R. Walsh. 1984. *Land Reform in Mexico, 1910–1980.* Orlando, Fla.: Academic Press.

Savarino, Franco. 1995. "Catolicismo y formación del Estado en Yucatán, 1900–1914." *Revista Mexicana de Sociología* 57(3): 157–74.

Schryer, Frans J. 1980. *The Rancheros of Pisaflores: The History of a Peasant Bourgeoisie in Mexico.* Toronto: University of Toronto Press.

Scott, James C. 1976. *The Moral Economy of the Peasant: Rebellion and Subsistence in Southeast Asia.* New Haven, Conn.: Yale University Press.

———. 1985. *Weapons of the Weak: Everyday Forms of Peasant Resistance.* New Haven, Conn.: Yale University Press.

———. 1990. *Domination and the Arts of Resistance.* New Haven, Conn.: Yale University Press.

———. 1994. Foreword to *Everyday Forms of State Formation: Revolution and the Negotiation of Rule in Modern Mexico.* See Joseph and Nugent 1994b.

Shadow, Robert D. and María J. Rodríguez-Shadow. 1994. "Religión, economía, y política en la rebelión cristera: El caso de los gobiernistas de Villa Guerrero, Jalisco." *Historia Mexicana* 43(4): 657–99.

Simpson, Eyler. 1937. *The Ejido: Mexico's Way Out.* Chapel Hill: University of North Carolina Press.

Sinkin, Richard N. 1979. *The Mexican Reform, 1855–1876: A Study in Liberal Nation-Building.* Austin: University of Texas Press.

Skocpol, Theda. 1982. "What Makes Peasants Revolutionary?" In *Power and Protest in the Countryside: Rural Unrest in Asia, Europe, and Latin America.* See Weller and Guggenheim 1982.

Stanislawski, Dan. 1950. *Anatomy of Eleven Towns in Michoacán.* Austin: University of Texas Press.

Starn, Orin. 1992. " 'I Dreamed of Foxes and Hawks': Reflections on Peasant Protest, New Social Movements, and the *Rondas Campesinas* of Northern Peru." In *The Making of Social Movements in Latin America: Identity, Strategy, and Democracy.* See Escobar and Alvarez 1992.

Stephen, Lynn. 1994. *Viva Zapata! Generation, Gender, and Historical Consciousness in the Reception of Ejido Reform in Mexico.* Transformation of Rural Mexico Series no. 6. La Jolla: Center for U.S.-Mexican Studies, University of California, San Diego.

———. 1997. "Pro-Zapatista and Pro-PRI: Resolving the Contradictions of Zapatismo in Rural Oaxaca." *Latin American Research Review* 32(2): 41–70.

Stephen, Lynn, and James Dow. 1990a. "Introduction: Popular Religion in Mexico

and Central America." In *Class, Politics, and Popular Religion in Mexico and Central America*. See Stephen and Dow 1990b.

——, eds. 1990b. *Class, Politics, and Popular Religion in Mexico and Central America*. Washington, D.C.: American Anthropological Association.

Stern, Steve J. 1987a. "New Approaches to the Study of Peasant Rebellion and Consciousness: Implications of the Andean Experience." In *Resistance, Rebellion, and Consciousness in the Andean Peasant World, 18th to 20th Centuries*. See Stern 1987.

——, ed. 1987b. *Resistance, Rebellion, and Consciousness in the Andean Peasant World, 18th to 20th Centuries*. Madison: University of Wisconsin Press.

Stevens, Donald Fithian. 1982. "Agrarian Policy and Instability in Porfirian Mexico." *Americas* 39(2): 153–66.

Tamayo, Jaime, ed. 1986. *Perspectivas de los movimientos sociales en la región centro-occidente*. Mexico City: Editorial Línea.

Tannenbaum, Frank. [1933] 1966. *Peace by Revolution: Mexico after 1910*. New York: Columbia University Press.

——. [1929] 1968. *The Mexican Agrarian Revolution*. New York: Brookings Institute.

Tapia Santamaría, Jesús. 1986. *Campo religioso y evolución política en el Bajío zamoreño*. Zamora: Colegio de Michoacán.

Thomson, Guy P. C. 1991a. "Agrarian Conflict in the Municipality of Cuetzalán (Sierra de Puebla): The Rise and Fall of 'Pala' Agustín Dieguillo, 1861–1894." *Hispanic American Historical Review* 71(2): 205–58.

——. 1991b. "Popular Aspects of Liberalism in Mexico, 1848–1888." *Bulletin of Latin American Research* 10(3): 265–92.

Tobler, Hans Werner. 1980. "Conclusions: Peasant Mobilization and the Revolution." In *Caudillo and Peasant in the Mexican Revolution*. See Brading 1980.

——. 1988. "Peasants and the Shaping of the Revolutionary State." In *Riot, Rebellion, and Revolution: Rural Social Conflict in Mexico*. See Katz 1988b.

Toral, Ramón. 1989. "Problemas de tierra en la región p'urhépecha." *México Indígena*, no. 27:61–62.

Trueba, Alfonso (alias Martín Chowell). 1959. *Luis Navarro Origel: el primer cristero*. Mexico City: Editorial Jus.

Tutino, John. 1986. *From Insurrection to Revolution in Mexico: Social Bases of Agrarian Violence*. Princeton, N.J.: Princeton University Press.

——. 1988. "Agrarian Social Change and Peasant Rebellion in Nineteenth Century Mexico: The Example of Chalco." In *Riot, Rebellion, and Revolution: Rural Social Conflict in Mexico*. See Katz 1988b.

——. 1990. "Revolutionary Confrontation, 1913–1917: Regions, Classes, and the New National State." In *Provinces of the Revolution: Essays on Regional Mexican History, 1910–1929*. See Benjamin and Wasserman 1990.

Uribe Salas, José Alfredo. 1986. "Política ferrocarrilera y el capital extranjero en Michoacán 1877–1886." *Tzintzun* 7:26–41.

Vaca, Agustín. 1981. "Apunte sobre un movimiento contrarrevolucionario: el sinarquismo." In *Jornadas de Historia de Occidente*. See Centro de Estudios de la Revolución Mexicana "Lázaro Cárdenas" 1981.

Vanderwood, Paul. 1990. "Explaining the Mexican Revolution." In *The Revolutionary Process in Mexico: Essays on Political and Social Change, 1880–1940*. See Rodríguez 1990.

Van Young, Eric. 1988. "Moving toward Revolt: Agrarian Origins of the Hidalgo Rebellion in the Guadalajara Region." In *Riot, Rebellion, and Revolution: Rural Social Conflict in Mexico*. See Katz 1988b.

Vargas González, Pablo E. 1989. "Venustiano Carranza: el conflicto político en la constitución del municipio." *Estudios michoacanos III*. See Zendejas Romero 1989.

Vaughan, Mary Kay. 1997. *Cultural Politics in Revolution: Teachers, Peasants, and Schools in Mexico, 1930–40*. Tucson: University of Arizona Press.

Vázquez León, Luis. 1986a. *Antropología política de la comunidad indígena en Michoacán*. Morelia: Editorial SEP Michoacán.

———. 1986b. "La comunidad indígena tarasca, sus recursos naturales y su adaptación sociocultural: el caso de Santa Cruz Tanaco." In *La sociedad indígena en el centro y occidente de México*. See Carrasco 1986.

———. 1986c. "La meseta tarasca: los municipios 'indígenas.' " In *Estudios michoacanos I*. See Herrejón Peredo 1986a.

———. 1992. *Ser indio otra vez: la purepechización de los tarascos serranos*. Mexico: Consejo Nacional para la Cultura y las Artes.

Warman, Arturo. 1988. "The Political Project of Zapatismo." In *Riot, Rebellion, and Revolution: Rural Social Conflict in Mexico*. See Katz 1988b.

Wasserman, Mark. 1990a. "Chihuahua: Politics in an Era of Transition." In *Provinces of the Revolution: Essays on Regional Mexican History, 1910–1929*. See Benjamin and Wasserman 1990.

———. 1990b. "The Mexican Revolution: Region and Theory, Signifying Nothing?" *Latin American Research Review* 25(1): 231–42.

———. 1990c. "Provinces of the Revolution: An Introduction." In *Provinces of the Revolution: Essays on Regional Mexican History, 1910–1929*. See Benjamin and Wasserman 1990.

Waterbury, Ronald. 1975. "Non-revolutionary Peasants: Oaxaca Compared to Morelos in the Mexican Revolution." *Comparative Studies in Society and History* 17:410–42.

Welles, Robert P. and Scott E. Guggenheim, eds. 1982. *Power and Protest in the Countryside: Rural Unrest in Asia, Europe, and Latin America*. Durham, N.C.: Duke University Press.

Weyl, Sylvia and Nathanial Weyl. 1939. *The Reconquest of Mexico: The Years of Lázaro Cárdenas*. New York: Oxford University Press.

Whettan, Nathan L. 1948. *Rural Mexico*. Chicago: University of Chicago Press.

Womack, John. 1968. *Zapata and the Mexican Revolution.* New York: Vintage Books.

——. 1986. "The Mexican Economy during the Revolution, 1910–1920." In *Twentieth Century Mexico.* See Raat and Beezley 1986.

——. 1991. "The Mexican Revolution, 1910–1920." In *Mexico since Independence.* See Bethell 1991.

Zárate Hernández, José Eduardo. 1992. "Procesos políticos en la Cuenca Lacustre de Pátzcuaro." In *Estudios michoacanos IV.* See Zendejas Romero 1992.

Zendejas Romero, Sergio, ed. 1989. *Estudios michoacanos III.* Zamora, Mexico: Colegio de Michoacán.

——, ed. 1992. *Estudios michoacanos IV.* Zamora, Mexico: Colegio de Michoacán.

Zepeda Patterson, Jorge. 1986. "No es lo mismo agrario que agrio, ni comuneros que comunistas, pero se parecen." In *Perspectivas de los movimientos sociales en la región centro-occidente.* See Tamayo 1986.

——. 1989. "Sahuayo y Jiquilpan: génesis de la rivalidad por una región." In *Estudios michoacanos III.* See Zendejas Romero 1989.

Index

Mata family, 121, 123
Maximilian von Hapsburg, Ferdinand, 28–29
Mendoza, Prudencio, 82, 84, 99, 164, 170, 175
Mercado, Aristeo, 30, 51
Mexican Catholic Church (schismatic), 74
Mexican Revolution, 4, 25, 44, 167, 188; in Michoacán, 48–61; in northwestern Michoacán, 169–70, 178; orthodox interpretation of, 4–6, 198 n.8; in Purépecha highlands, 149–50; revisionist interpretation of, 4–7, 198 n.12; in Zacapu region, 124–25
Mexico (state), 56, 80, 89, 97
Meyer, Jean, 7
Mincítar, Juan, 1, 136, 155
Moheno, César, 146–47
Mora y del Río, Archbishop José, 74–75
Morelos, 80, 94
Moreno, Antonia, 43–44, 165–66
Moreno, Diego, 166–67
Morrow, Dwight W., 90
Múgica, Francisco, 21, 48–55, 58, 61–68, 112, 126–27, 129, 151, 174, 186, 189–90, 211 n.28
Munguía, Archbishop Clemente de Jesús, 28–29, 168

Namiquipa, Chihuahua, 12, 14
Naranja, 3, 9–10, 13, 52, 111–33, 180, 189, 205–6 n.25, 230 n.36. See also Zacapu (region)
National Agrarian Commission (CNA), 156
National Catholic Party (PCN), 51, 56–57, 74
National League for the Defense of Religious Liberty (LNDLR), 1, 90, 188, 190, 198 n.7, 217 n.7, 220 n.33; and

leadership role in cristiada, 72–85; in northwestern Michoacán, 174–75, 177; and partisanship in cristiada, 97–103
National Peasant Confederation, 151, 195
Navarro Orígel Luis, 98–99
Nayarit, 75, 77–80, 84, 105
New social movements theory, 15–17, 181–82
Noriega, Alfredo, and Eduardo, 66, 112, 122, 125–26, 130, 180
Nuevo Léon, 55, 57, 81, 97

Oaxaca, 19, 26, 33, 56, 72, 80, 97, 107, 109, 185, 190–91
Oaxacan Sovereignty Movement, 5, 185–86, 190–91
Obregón, Alvaro, 53, 57, 61–68, 73–74, 125, 128–29, 170, 174, 188–89
Ochoa, Crisóforo, 178
Ochoa, Eufemio, 173, 178
Ortiz, José María, 154
Ortiz family, 138, 144, 147

Pajacuarán, 165–66, 167, 174
Pantzingo, 138, 153–54
Paricutín, 2, 9, 18, 23, 69, 134, 136, 142, 145, 148, 153–58, 162, 192–94
Paricutín volcano, 134, 141, 147, 154, 159
Partido Católico Nacional (PCN). See National Catholic Party
PCN. See National Catholic Party
Peasant rebellion: theories of, 15–16, 102, 181–82, 201 n.39
Political identity, 8, 10, 91, 94, 96, 102; construction of, 14–20; in northwestern Michoacán, 164, 171–78; in Purépecha highlands, 133–37, 149–62; Zacapu region, 111–12, 128–31, 133
Popular Union (UP), 83, 99–101, 190

Jennie Purnell is Assistant Professor in the Department of Political
Science at Boston College.

Library of Congress Cataloging-in-Publication Data
Purnell, Jennie.
Popular movements and state formation in revolutionary Mexico :
the agraristas and cristeros of Michoacán / Jennie Purnell.
p. cm.
Includes bibliographical references and index.
ISBN 0-8223-2282-X (cloth : alk. paper). —
ISBN 0-8223-2314-1 (pbk. : alk. paper)
1. Peasantry — Mexico — Michoacán de Ocampo — Political activity.
2. Cristero Rebellion, 1926–1929. 3. Land reform — Mexico —
Michoacán de Ocampo — History — 20th century. I. Title.
HD1531.M6P87 1999
972'.37 — dc21 98-46237 CIP

Contents

To my sons, Eric Austin
and Jeremy Edward Flint,
and in memory of my father,
Edward Ward Purnell

© 1999 Duke University Press
All rights reserved
Printed in the United States of America on acid-free paper ∞
Typeset in Sabon by Keystone Typesetting, Inc.
Library of Congress Cataloging-in-Publication Data appear
on the last printed page of this book.
Material from chapters 2, 5, and 6 was first published as
"With All Due Respect: Popular Resistance to the
Privatization of Communal Lands in Nineteenth-Century
Michoacán," *Latin American Research Review* 34, no. 1
(1999): 85–121.

Popular Movements and State Formation in Revolutionary Mexico

The *Agraristas* and *Cristeros* of Michoacán

Jennie Purnell

DUKE UNIVERSITY PRESS   DURHAM AND LONDON   1999

Popular Movements and State Formation

in Revolutionary Mexico

To Heidi Berthiaume, an exceptional woman
of grace, vision, strength, and passion . . . I only wish Claire
could be half the hero you are, every day.

To Sarah Brooke, also a hero. *Literally.* In this book.

ACKNOWLEDGMENTS

To Sarah Weiss, for keeping me as sane and organized as it's possible for me to get . . . You seriously rock.

To the lovely crew of the *Azamara Journey*. There will never be a nicer place to be panicking over a deadline. Thanks for the support, the love, and the cheers.

To *you*, dear reader, for making Morganville a living place that continues to be (for me!) a joy to visit.

AUTHOR'S NOTE

You'll be seeing several points of view in this book. Claire's is our basic story, with Amelie, Oliver, Shane, Michael, and Myrnin adding their own points of view to what's happening. So be sure to note the chapter headings.

INTRODUCTION

Morganville, Texas, isn't like other towns. Oh, it's small, dusty, and ordinary, in most ways, but the thing is, there are these—well, let's not be shy about it. *Vampires.* They own the town. They run it. And until recently they were the unquestioned ruling class.

But the vampires' reputation for invulnerability has taken some hits lately. The troublesome underground human revolt, led by Captain Obvious, never seems to die; even though the Founder of Morganville and her vampire friends defeated their most dire enemies, the water-monster draug, they needed human help to do it.

Now Morganville is rebuilding, and it's a new day. . . . But without the threat of the much-feared draug to hold them back, what's to keep Morganville's vampires from regaining their iron hold on the town?

One thing's for sure: there's going to be trouble.

And where there's trouble, there's Claire Danvers.

PROLOGUE

AMELIE

)

"I have a surprise for you," Oliver said.

I—not without reason—expected him to perhaps present a velvet box cradling rare jewels, or even a new pet ... but instead he held out a piece of expensive, heavy paper marked with the Morganville seal in the corner in thick, still-warm wax.

"Read it."

He collapsed into one of my brocaded armchairs across from my desk, crossed one leg over the other, and gave me a long, slow smile that made me shiver. Not in dread—oh, no. In something far more complex, and far more terrifying. We had been enemies a long time, uncomfortable allies for the past few years, and now ... now, I hesitated to put a name on what we were.

In more-ancient days, the word would have been *intimates*, which meant everything or nothing, as the situation required.

I lowered my gaze from that knowing expression and read the words inscribed in gorgeous, flowing script—the hand of a trained clerk, obviously, who'd been given proper education in a time when that truly mattered.

WHEREAS the Elders' Council of Morganville, concerned for the safety and security of all within its borders of influence, has resolved to enact a law requiring the identification of all persons, whether mortal or immortal. Such identification shall further be carried upon the persons of residents at all times. Whereas such proof of identity is vital to the health of our community, we also are resolved that the violation of such requirements shall be considered a direct offense to the council, and as such may be punishable with the First, Second, and Final Actions as written within the codes formulated by the Founder from the earliest foundation of this great community.

In approval of these requirements, and of these punishments, the Founder of Morganville sets her signature hereupon.

I froze, pen at the ready, and frowned. "What's this?"

"As we discussed," he said. "The requirement for citizens of Morganville to carry appropriate identification. For the vampires, of course, the requirements are somewhat different, but they'll still carry a card. It wouldn't do to appear to be discriminatory."

"Indeed not," I said, a ripple of irritation gliding through my tone. "I thought we discussed waiting a year to implement such identification measures, until they could be properly explained."

"I would have believed it was possible to wait that long had I not heard a rumor that Captain Obvious was once again among us, and agitating against us." Oliver's voice carried a bitterly dark undertone now, and his distaste for the nom de guerre of our most bothersome human adversary showed in the expression on his sharp, angular face. Age is of no consequence to vampires, of course, save in what power it brings with it, but Oliver was a rarity—a vampire who had been turned in his later years, and retained that appearance in his immortality, with gray threading his brown hair and lines pinching his skin at the eyes and mouth. He could appear warm and friendly when he chose, but I had long ago learned that Oliver was first, last, and always a warrior.

And this . . . Captain Obvious, as the humans of Morganville now named him, was cut from the same cloth. A fighter, determined to bring us harm. We had killed him a dozen times in the past hundred years, and, mortal lives being what they are, we'd never expected at first for the problem to resurrect itself again, and again, and again; yet as soon as a Captain Obvious fell, another stepped forward, masked and hidden, to take his place.

And now, it seemed, we were forced to endure yet another would-be avenger.

I felt Oliver's gaze on me, warm and yet challenging; for all the barriers that had fallen between us, his ambition wasn't one of them. He demanded more of himself, and thus more of me. It was a dangerous dance, and that was part—if not most—of the attraction.

"Yes," I said. "If they feel confident enough in their own power to openly follow yet another rabble-rouser, then I suppose we must have our own answer." And I penned my elaborate signature, all loops and swirls and slashes, to the bottom of the formal document. In true modern-age fashion, this would be photographed, digitized, transferred to bland and simple words on a screen . . . but the effects were the same. The word of a ruler was law.

And I was now the uncontested ruler of Morganville. All my enemies had fallen; the sickness that had crippled vampires for so very long had been conquered at last, thanks to the intervention of humans, most notably that troublesome young Claire, apprentice to my oldest friend, Myrnin. We had likewise dispatched at last my father, Bishop, that blood-maddened beast. And just in the past few months, the cool, cruel draug, who had hunted us to the edge of extinction, had been destroyed and were no more.

Now, nothing stood between my people—the last of the vampires—and the power and status that were rightly due us.

Nothing, that was, but the too-confident pride of the humans in this town—humans I had chosen, brought together, allowed to grow and flourish and prosper in cooperation and under strict conditions; humans who had repaid me, in large part, with fear, spite, and resistance that grew stronger each year.

No more.

"No more," Oliver said aloud, and rose to take the decree from my hand. "No more will these vassals think they can slip away in secrecy from their crimes. It's our time, my queen. Our time to ensure our final survival." And he captured my hand in his, bent, and touched his cool lips to my equally cool skin.

I shivered.

"Yes," I said. "Yes, I believe it is."

His lips traveled up my arm, in slow and gentle kisses, and found my neck; he unpinned my hair from its heavy crown and let it fall loose. His strong hands went around me and pulled me to him. He was as irresistible as Newton's gravity, and I gave up politics and pride and status for the sheer, novel joy of being wanted.

And if there was a part of me, a small and hidden part, that questioned all this and understood that the more power I took for the vampires, the more the humans would rebel . . . well, I buried it with ruthless efficiency. I was tired of being alone, and what Oliver drew from me was pleasant, and in some measure necessary.

The old ways of Morganville . . . They were my past.

Oliver was my future.

ONE

CLAIRE

)

Claire Danvers was in a rare bad mood, and nearly getting arrested didn't improve it.

First, her university classes hadn't gone well at all, and then she'd had a humiliating argument with her "adviser" (she usually thought of him that way, in quotes, because he didn't "advise" her to do anything but take boring core subjects and not challenge herself), and then she'd gotten a completely unfair B on a physics paper she knew had been letter perfect. She would have grudgingly accepted a B on something unimportant, like history, but no, it had to be in her major. And of course Professor Carlyle wasn't in his office to talk about it.

So she wasn't fully paying attention when she stepped off the curb. Traffic in Morganville, Texas, wasn't exactly fast and furious, and here by Texas Prairie University, people were fully used to stopping for oblivious students.

Still, the screech of brakes surprised her and sent her stumbling back to the safety of the sidewalk, and it was only after a couple of fast breaths that she realized she'd nearly been run over by a police cruiser.

And a policeman was getting out of the car, looking grim.

As he stalked over to her she realized he was probably a vampire—he was too pale to be a human, and he had on sunglasses even here in the shade of the building. Glancing at the cruiser to confirm, she saw the extreme tinting job on the windows. Definitely vampire police. The official slogan of the police was *to protect and serve,* but her boyfriend called the vampire patrol the *to protect and serve up for dinner patrol.*

It was unusual to see one so close to the university, though. Normally, vampire cops worked at night, and closer to the center of town, where Founder's Square was located, along with the central vamp population. Only the regular residents would see them there, and not the transient—though pretty oblivious—students.

"I'm sorry," she said, and swallowed a rusty taste in her mouth that seemed composed of shock and entirely useless anger. "I wasn't looking where I was going."

"Obviously," he said. Like most vamps, he had an accent, but she'd long ago given up trying to identify it; if they lived long enough, vampires tended to pick up dozens of accents, and many of them were antique anyway. His facial features seemed . . . maybe Chinese? "Identification."

"For walking?"

"Identification."

Claire swallowed her protest and reached in her backpack for her wallet. She pulled out her student ID card and Texas driver's license and handed them over. He glanced at them and shoved the cards back.

"Not those," he said. "Your town identification."

"My . . . what?"

"You should have received it in the mail."

"Well, I haven't!"

He took off his sunglasses. Behind them, his eyes were very dark, but there were hints of red. He stared at her for a moment, then nodded.

"All right. When you get your card, carry it at all times. And next time, watch your step. You get yourself hit by a car, I'll consider you roadkill."

With that, he put the sunglasses back on, turned, and got back in his car. Before Claire could think about any way to respond, he'd put the cruiser in gear and whipped around the corner.

It did not improve her mood.

Before she could even think about going home, Claire had a mandatory stop to make, at her part-time job. She dreaded it today, because she knew she was in no shape to deal with the incredibly inconsistent moods of Myrnin, her vampire mad-scientist boss. He might be laser focused and super-rational; he might be talking to crockery and quoting *Alice in Wonderland* (that had been the scene during her last visit). But whatever he was doing, he'd have work for her, and probably too much of it.

But at least he was never, ever boring.

She'd made the walk so often that she did it on autopilot, hardly even noticing the streets and houses and the alley down which she had to pass; she checked her phone and read texts as she jogged down the long marble steps that led into the darkness of his lab, or lair, whichever mood he was in today. The lights were on, which was nice. As she put her phone away, she saw that

Myrnin was bent over a microscope—an ancient thing that she'd tried to put away a dozen times in favor of a newer electronic model, but he kept unearthing the thing. He stepped away from the eyepiece to scribble numbers frantically on a chalkboard. The board was *covered* in numbers, and to Claire's eyes they looked completely random—not just in terms of their numerical values, but in the way they'd been written, at all angles and in all areas of the available space. Some were even upside down. It wasn't a formula or an analysis. It was complete gibberish.

So. It was going to be one of those days. Lovely.

"Hey," Claire said with fatalistic resignation as she dumped her backpack on the floor and opened up a drawer to retrieve her lab coat. It was a good thing she looked first; Myrnin had dumped an assortment of scalpels in on top of the fabric. Any one of them could have sliced her to the bone. "What are you doing?"

"Did you know that certain types of coral qualify as immortal? The definition of scientific immortality is that if the mortality rate of a species doesn't increase after it reaches maturity, there is no such thing as aging . . . black coral, for instance. Or the Great Basin bristlecone pine. I'm trying to determine if there is any resemblance between the development of those cellular colonies with the replacement of human cells that takes place in a conversion to vampirism. . . ." He was talking a mile a minute, with a fever pitch that Claire always dreaded. It meant he was in need of medication, which he wouldn't take; she'd need to be stealthy about adding it to his blood supply, again, to bring him down a little into the rational zone. "Did you bring me a hamburger?"

"Did I— No, Myrnin, I didn't bring you a hamburger." Bizarre. He'd never asked for that before.

"Coffee?"

"It's late."

"Doughnuts?"

"No."

"What good are you, then?" He finally looked up from the microscope, made another note or two on the board, and stepped back to consider the chaos of chalk marks. "Oh dear. That's not very—is this where I started? Claire?" He pointed at a number somewhere near the top right corner.

"I wasn't here," Claire said, and buttoned up her lab coat. "Do you want me to keep working on the machine?"

"The what? Oh, yes, that thing. Do, please." He crossed his arms and stared at the board, frowning now. It was not a personal-grooming highlight day for him, either. His long, dark hair was in tangles and needed a wash; she was sure the oversized somewhat-white shirt he was wearing had been used as a rag to wipe up chemical spills at sometime in its long life. He'd had the presence of mind to put on some kind of pants, though she wasn't sure the baggy walking shorts were what she'd have chosen. At least the flip-flops kind of matched. "How was school?"

"Bad," she said.

"Good," he said absently, "very good . . . Ah, I think this is where I started. . . . Fibonacci sequence—I see what I did. . . ." He began drawing a spiral through the numbers, starting somewhere at the center. Of course, he'd be noting down results in a spiral. Why not?

Claire felt a headache coming on. The place was dirty again, grit on the floor that was a combination of sand blown in from the desert winds, and whatever Myrnin had been working with that he'd spilled liberally all over the place. She only hoped it wasn't too toxic. She'd have to schedule a day to get him out of here so she could get reorganized, sweep up the debris, stack the books back in some kind of order, shelve the lab equipment. . . . No, that wouldn't be a day. More like a week.

She gave up thinking about it, then went to the lab table on the right side of the room, which was covered by a dusty sheet. She pulled the cover off, coughed at the billows of grit that flew up, and looked at the machine she was building. It was definitely her own creation, this thing: it lacked most of the eccentric design elements that Myrnin would have put into it, though he'd sneaked in a few flywheels and glowing liquids along the way. It was oblong, practical, bell-shaped, and had oscillation controls along the sides. She thought it looked a bit like an old-fashioned science fiction ray gun, but it had a very different use . . . if it had ever worked.

Claire hooked up the device to the plug-in analyzing programs, and began to run simulations. It was a project Myrnin had proposed months ago, and it had taken her this long to get even close to a solution. . . . The vampires had an ability, so far mysterious and decidedly unscientific, to influence the minds and emotions of others—humans, mostly, but sometimes other vampires. Every vampire had a different set of strengths and weaknesses, but most shared some kind of emotional-control mechanism; it helped them calm their prey, or convince them to surrender their blood voluntarily.

What she was working on was a way to *cancel* that ability. To give humans—and even other vampires—a way to defend themselves against the manipulation.

Claire had gone from building a machine that could pinpoint and map emotions to one that could build feedback loops, heightening what was already there. It was a necessary step to get to the *control* stage—you had to be able to replicate the ability to negate it. If you thought of emotion as a wavelength, you could either amplify or cancel it with the flick of a switch.

"Myrnin?" She didn't look up from the analysis running on the laptop computer screen. "Did you mess with my project?"

"A little," he said. "Isn't it better?"

It was. She had no idea what he'd done to it, but adjusting the controls showed precise calibrations that she couldn't have done herself. "Did you maybe write down how you did it?"

"Probably," Myrnin said cheerfully. "But I don't think it will help. It's just hearing the cycles and tuning to them. I don't think you're capable, with your limited human senses. If you'd become a vampire, you'd have so much more potential, you know."

She didn't answer that. She'd found it was really best not to engage in that particular debate with him, and besides, in the next second he'd forgotten all about it, focused on his enthusiasm for black coral.

On paper, the device they'd developed—well, she'd developed, and Myrnin had tweaked—seemed to work. Now she'd have to figure out how to test it, make sure it exactly replicated the way the vampire ability worked . . . and then make sure she could cancel that ability, reliably.

It might even have other applications. If you could make an attacking vampire afraid, make him back off, you could end a fight without violence. That alone made the work worthwhile.

And what happens when someone uses it the other way? she wondered. *What happens if an attacker gets hold of it, then uses it to make you more afraid, as a victim?* She didn't have an answer for that. It was one of the things that made her feel, sometimes, that this was a bad idea—and that she ought to simply destroy the thing before it caused more trouble.

But maybe not quite yet.

Claire unhooked the machine—she didn't have any kind of cool name for it yet, or even a project designation—and tested the weight of it. Heavy. She'd built it from solid components, and it generated considerable waste heat, but it was a prototype; it'd improve, if it was worthwhile.

She tried aiming it at the wall. It was a little awkward, but if she added a grip up front, that would help stabilize it—

"Claire?"

Myrnin's voice came from *right behind her*, way too close. She whirled, and her finger accidentally hit the switch on top as she fumbled her hold on the machine, and suddenly there was a live trial in action . . . on him.

She saw it work.

Myrnin's eyes widened, turned very dark, and then began to shimmer with liquid hints of red. He took a step back from her. A large one. "Oh," he said. "Don't do that. Please don't do that."

She shut it off, fast, because she wasn't sure what exactly had just happened. *Something,* for sure, but as live trials went, it was . . . inconclusive. "Sorry, sorry," she said, and put the device down with a *clunk* on the marble top of the lab table. "I didn't mean to do that. Um . . . what did you feel?"

"More of what I already felt," he said, which was uninformative. He took another step backward, and the red didn't seem to be fading from his eyes. "I was going to ask you if you'd send over some type AB from the blood bank; I seem to be running low. And also, I wanted to ask if you'd seen my bag of gummi worms."

"You're hungry," Claire guessed. He nodded cautiously. "And it . . . made it *stronger?*"

"In a way," he said. Not helpful. "Never mind the delivery from the blood bank. I believe I shall . . . take a walk. Good night, Claire."

He was being awfully polite, she thought; with him, that was usually a cover for severe internal issues. Before she could try to figure out exactly what was going on in his head, though, he'd headed at vampire-speed for the stairs and was gone.

She shook her head and looked at the switched-off device in irritation. "Well, that was helpful," she told it, and then rolled her eyes. "And now I'm talking to equipment, like him. Great."

Claire threw a sheet over the machine, made notes in the logbook, turned off the lab's lights, and headed home.

Arriving home—on Lot Street—didn't do much for her mood, either, because as she stomped past the rusty, leaning mailbox on the outside of the picket fence, she saw that the door was open and mail was sticking out. It threatened to blow away in the ever-present desert wind. Perfect. She had three housemates, and all of them had somehow failed to pick up the mail. And that was not her job. At least today.

She glared up at the big, faded Victorian house, and wondered when Shane was going to get around to painting it as he'd promised he would. Never, most likely. Just like the mail.

Claire readjusted her heavy backpack on one shoulder, an automatic, thoughtless shift of weight, snatched the wadded-up paper out of the box, and flipped through the thick handfuls. Water bill (apparently, saving the town from water-dwelling draug monsters hadn't given them any utility credits), electric bill (high, again), flyers from the new pizza delivery place (whose pizza tasted like dog food on tomato sauce), and . . . four envelopes, embossed with the Founder's official seal.

She headed for the house. And then the day took one step further to the dark side, because pinned to the front door with a cheap pot-metal dagger was a hand-drawn note with four tombstones on it. Each headstone had one of their names. And below, it said, *Vampire lovers get what they deserve.*

Charming. It would have scared her except that it wasn't the first she'd seen over the past few weeks; there had been four other notes, one slipped under the door, two pinned on it (like this one), and one slipped into the mailbox. That, and a steady and growing number of rude storekeepers, deliberate insults from people on the street, and doors slammed in her face.

It was no longer popular being the friend of the only mixed-marriage vampire/human couple in Morganville.

Claire ripped the note off, shook her head over the cheap dagger, which would snap in a fight, and unlocked the front door. She hip-bumped it open, closed it, and locked it again—automatic caution, in Morganville. "Hey!" she yelled without looking up. "Who was supposed to get the mail?"

"Eve!" Shane yelled from down the hall, in the direction of the living room, at the same time that Eve shouted, "Michael!" from upstairs. Michael said nothing, probably because he wasn't home yet.

"We *really* need to talk about schedules! Again!" Claire called back. She briefly considered showing them the flyer, but then she balled it up and threw it, and the dagger, in the trash, along with the assorted junk mail offering discount crap and high-interest credit cards.

It's just talk, she told herself. It wasn't, but she thought that eventually, everyone—human and vampire—would just get their collective panties unbunched about Michael and Eve's getting married. It was nobody's business but their own, after all.

She focused instead on the four identical envelopes.

They were made of fancy, heavy paper that smelled musty and old, as if it had been stored somewhere for a hundred years and someone was just getting around to opening the box. The seal on the back of each was wax, deep crimson, and embossed with the Founder's symbol. Each of their names was written on the outside in flowing, elegant script, so even and perfect, it looked like computer printing until she looked closely and found the human imperfections.

Her instincts were tingling danger, but she tried to think positively. *C'mon, this could be a good thing,* she told herself. *Maybe it's just a thank-you card from Amelie for saving Morganville. Again. We deserve that.*

Sounded good, but Amelie, the Founder of Morganville, was a very old vampire, and vamps weren't in the business of thanking people. Amelie had grown up royalty, and having people do crazy, dangerous (and possibly fatal) things on her slightest whim was just . . . normal. It probably didn't even call for a smile, much less a note of gratitude. And, to be honest, Claire's once almost-friendly status with the Founder had gotten a bit . . . strained.

Morganville, Texas, was just about the last gathering place for vampires in the world; it was the spot that they'd chosen to make their last stand, to forget their old grudges, to band tightly together against common threats and enemies. When Claire had first arrived, the vampires had been battling illness; then they'd been after one another. And four months ago, they'd been fighting the draug, water creatures that preyed on vampires like delicious, tasty snacks . . . and the vampires had finally won.

That left them the undisputed champions of the world's food chain. In saving Morganville, Claire hadn't really stopped to consider what might happen when the vamps no longer had something to fear. Now she knew.

They didn't exactly feel grateful.

Oh, on the surface, Morganville was all good, or at least getting better. . . . The vamps had been fast on the trigger to start repairing the town, cleaning up after the demise of the draug, and getting all of their human population settled again in their homes, businesses, and schools. The official PR line had been that a dangerous chemical spill had forced evacuations, and that seemed to have satisfied everybody (along with generous cash payments, and automatic good grades to all of the students at Texas Prairie University who'd had their semesters cut short). Claire also suspected that the vampires had applied some psychic persuasion, where necessary—there were a few of them capable of doing that. On the surface, it looked like Morganville was not only recovering, but thriving.

But it didn't feel right. On the few occasions that she'd seen Amelie, the Founder hadn't seemed right, either. Her body language, her smile, the way she looked at people . . . all were different. And darker.

"Hey," her housemate Eve Rosser—*no*, it was Eve *Glass* now, after the wedding—said. "You going to open those or what?" She walked up beside Claire, set a glass down on the kitchen counter, and poured herself a tall glass of milk. Her ruby wedding ring winked at Claire as if inviting her to share a secret joke. "Because the last time I saw something looking that official, it was inviting me to a party. And you know how much I love those."

"You almost got killed at that party," Claire said absently. She passed over Eve's envelope and picked up her own.

"I almost get killed at most parties. Hence, you can tell that's how much I love them," Eve said, and ripped open the paper in a wide, tearing swath. Claire—who was by nature more of a neat gently-slice-the-thing-open kind of person—winced. "Huh. Another envelope inside the envelope. They do love to waste paper. Haven't they ever heard of tree-hugging?"

As Eve extracted the second layer, Claire had a chance to do the usual wardrobe scan of her best friend . . . and wasn't disappointed. Eve had suddenly taken a liking to aqua blue, and she'd added streaks of it in her black hair, which was worn today in cute, shiny ponytails on the sides of her head. Her Goth white face was brightened by aqua eye shadow and—where did she find this stuff?—matching lipstick, and she had on a tight black shirt with embossed crosses. The short, poufy skirt continued the blue theme. Then black tights with blue hearts. Then, combat boots.

So, a typical Wednesday, really.

Eve pulled the inner envelope free, opened the flap, and extracted a folded sheet of thick paper. Something fell out to bounce on the counter, and Claire caught it.

It was a card. A plastic card, like a credit card, but this one had the Founder's symbol screened on the back, and it had Eve's picture in the upper right corner—taken when she'd been without the full Goth war paint, which Eve would despise. It had Eve's name, address, phone number . . . and a box at the bottom that read *Blood Type: O Neg.* Across from it was a box saying *Protector: Glass, Michael.*

"What the . . . ?" *Oh,* Claire thought, even before she'd finished the question. This must have been what the vampire cop was asking her for. The identification card.

Eve plucked the card from her fingers, stared at it with a completely blank expression, and then turned her attention to the letter that had come with it. " 'Dear Mrs. Michael Glass,' " she read. "*Seriously?* Mrs. Michael? Like I don't even have a name of my own? And what the hell is this about his being my Protector? I never agreed to that!"

"And?" Claire reached for the letter, but Eve hip-checked her and continued reading.

" 'I have enclosed your new Morganville Resident Identification Card, which all human residents are now required to carry at all times so that, in the unlikely case of any emergency, we may

quickly contact your loved ones and Protector, and provide necessary medical information.'" Eve looked up and met Claire's eyes
squarely. "I call bullshit. *Human* residents. With blood type listed?
It's like a shopping list for vamps."

Claire nodded. "What else?"

Eve turned her attention back to the paper. "'Failure to carry
and provide this card upon request will result in fines of—' Oh,
screw this!" Eve wadded up the paper, dropped it on the floor, and
stomped on it with her boots, which were certainly made for
stomping. "I am *not* carrying around a Drink Me card, and they
can't ask for my papers. What is this, Naziland?" She picked up the
card and tried to bend it in half, but it was too flexible. "Where
did you put the scissors . . . ?"

Claire rescued the card and looked at it again. She turned it
over, held it under the strongest light available—the window—
and frowned. "Better not," she said. "I think this is chipped."

"Chipped? Can I eat it?"

"Microchipped. It's got some kind of tech in it, anyway. I'd
have to take a look to see what kind, but it's pretty safe to say
they'd know if you went all paper dolls with it."

"Oh great, so it's not just a Drink Me card; it's a tracking device, like those ear things they put on lions on Animal Planet?
Yeah, there's no way that can go wrong—like, say, vampires being
issued receivers so they can just shop online for who they want to
target tonight."

Eve was right about that, Claire thought. She *really* didn't feel
good about this. On the surface, it was just an ID card, perfectly
normal—she already carried a student ID and a driver's license—
but it *felt* like something else. Something more sinister.

Eve stopped rummaging in drawers and just stared at her.
"Hey. We *each* got one. Four envelopes."

"I thought they were only for human residents," Claire said. "So what's in Michael's?" Because Michael Glass was definitely *not* human these days. He'd been bitten well before Claire had met him, but the full-on vampire thing had been slow-building; she saw it more and more now, but deep down she thought he was still the same strong, sweet, no-nonsense guy she'd met when she'd first arrived on the Glass House doorstep. He was definitely still strong. It was the sweetness that was in some danger of fading away, over time.

Before Claire could warn Eve that maybe it wasn't the greatest idea, Eve shredded open Michael's envelope, too, yanked out the inner one, and pulled out his letter. Another card fell out. This one was gold. Shiny, shiny gold. It didn't have any info on it at all. Just a gold card, with the Founder's symbol embossed on it.

Eve went for the letter. " 'Dear Michael,' " she said. "Oh, sure, he gets *Michael*, not *Mr. Glass*. . . . 'Dear Michael, I have enclosed your card of privilege, as has been discussed in our community meetings.' " She stopped again, reread that silently, and looked down at the card she was holding in her fingers. "*Card of privilege?* He doesn't get the same treatment we do."

"Community meetings," Claire said. "Which we weren't invited to, right? And what kind of privileges, exactly?"

"You'd better believe it's a whole lot better than a free mocha at Common Grounds," Eve said grimly. She kept reading, silently, then handed the paper stiff-armed to Claire, not saying another word.

Claire took it, feeling a bit ill now. It read:

Dear Michael,

I have enclosed your card of privilege, as has been discussed in our community meetings. Please keep this card close, and you are welcome

*to use it at any time at the blood bank, Bloodmobile, or Common
Grounds for up to ten pints monthly.*

Wow, it really was good for free drinks. But that wasn't all.

*This card also entitles you to one legal hunt per year without
advance declaration of intent. Additional hunts must be preapproved
through the Elders' Council. Failure to seek preapproval will result in
fines of up to five thousand dollars per occurrence, payable to the
family's Protector, if applicable, or to the City of Morganville, if there
is no Protector on file.*
    Best wishes from the Founder,
    Amelie

For a moment, Claire couldn't quite understand what she was
reading. Her eyes kept going over it, and over it, and finally it all
snapped into clear, razor-sharp focus, and she pulled in a deep,
shaking breath. The paper creased as her grip tensed up.

"Yeah," Eve said. Claire met her gaze wordlessly. "It's telling
him he gets a free pass to kill one person a year, just on a whim. Or
more if he plans it out. You know, like a special treat. *Privilege.*"
There was nothing in her tone, or her face, or her eyes. Just . . .
blank. Locked down.

Eve took the paper from Claire's unresisting hand, folded it,
and put it back in the envelope with the gold card.

"What—what are you going to say to him?" Claire couldn't
quite get her head adjusted. This was wrong, just . . . wrong.

"Nothing good," Eve said.

And that was the precise moment when the kitchen door
opened, and Michael stepped inside. He was wearing a thick black
canvas cowboy-style duster coat, broad-brimmed hat, and black

gloves. Eve had teased him earlier that he looked like an animé superhero, but it was all practical vampire sun-resistant gear. Michael was relatively still newborn as a vampire, which meant he
was especially vulnerable to the sun, and to burning up.

Now, he whipped off his hat and gave the two of them an elaborate bow he'd probably copied from a movie (or, Claire thought,
learned from one of the older vamps), and rose from that with a
broad, sweet smile. "Hey, Claire. And *hello*, Mrs. Glass." There was
a special gentleness when he said *Mrs. Glass*—a private kind of
thing, and it was both breathtaking and heartbreaking.

Heartbreaking, because in the next second, he knew something was wrong. The smile faltered, and Michael glanced from
Eve to Claire, then back to Eve. "What?" He dumped the hat and
his gloves on the table, and shed the coat without looking away
from Eve's face. "Baby? What's wrong?" He walked to her and put
his hands on her shoulders. His wedding ring matched hers, even
down to the ruby inset, and it caught the light the way Eve's had
earlier.

Bloodred.

It was terrible, Claire thought, that he was still so much *Michael*—
still exactly as he'd been when she first met him—eighteen, though
they were all catching up to him now in age. It wasn't fair to call
him pretty, but he was gorgeous—tumbles of blond curls that
somehow always looked perfect; clear, direct blue eyes the color of
a morning sky. His pallor gave him the perfect look of ivory, and
when he stood still, as he was now, he looked like some fabulous
lost statue direct from Greece or Rome.

It wasn't fair.

Eve held the gaze between herself and her husband, and said,
"This is for you." She held up the inner envelope with his name
written on it in flowing script.

For a second, Michael clearly didn't know what it was ... and then Claire saw him realize. His eyes widened, and something like horror passed over his expression and was quickly hidden underneath a blank, carefully composed mask. He didn't say anything, but just took his hands from her shoulders and accepted the envelope. He stuck it in his pocket.

"You're not even pretending to be curious?" Eve said. Her voice had gone deep in her throat and had taken on a dangerous edge. "Great."

"You read it?" he asked, and took it out again to open it up. The card fell out, again, but he deftly snatched it out of the air without any effort. "Huh. It's shinier than I thought it'd be."

"That's all you have to say?"

He unfolded the letter. Claire was no good at reading those micro-expressions people on TV were always talking about on crime shows, but she thought he looked guilty as he read it. Guilty as hell.

"It's not what you think," he said, which was exactly the wrong thing to say, because it made Claire (and almost certainly Eve) think about every guy ever caught cheating. Luckily, he didn't stop there. "Eve, all vampires get the hunting privilege; it's just part of living in Morganville—it's always been the rule, even when nobody in the human community knew. Look, I don't want it. I opposed the whole idea at the meetings—"

"Which you didn't tell us about at all, jerk," Eve broke in. "We're *community!*"

Michael took a deep breath and continued. "I told Amelie and Oliver I wouldn't ever use it, but they didn't care."

"Doesn't matter. You have a free pass for murder."

"No," he said, and took her hands in his, a gesture so quick she couldn't avoid it, but gentle enough that she could have pulled away if she'd wanted. "No, Eve. You know me better than that. I'm trying to change it."

Her eyes filled with tears, suddenly, and she collapsed against his chest. Michael put his arms around her and held her tightly, his head resting against hers. He was whispering. Claire couldn't hear what he was saying, but it really wasn't any of her business.

She took the glass of milk Eve had poured for herself, seeing as how it was sitting there unwanted, and drank it. *He still should have told us,* she thought, and slit her envelope open with a steak knife to take out her own letter and ID card. It felt weird, seeing her information on there. Even though the vampires had always known what her blood type was, where she lived . . . it felt different, somehow.

Official.

As if she were some kind of commodity. Worse: with the chip in it, it meant she couldn't hide, couldn't run. She now, as Eve had said, *had papers,* just as they demanded in those old black-and-white war movies; she had to carry the card or get arrested (today's encounter had proven that), and it meant that they could round her up whenever they wanted . . . for questioning. Or for sticking her in some kind of prison camp.

Or worse.

One thing was certain: Shane Collins was not going to like this at all . . . and just as she thought about that, Shane banged in the swinging door of the kitchen, headed straight for the refrigerator, and snagged himself a cold soft drink, which he popped open and chugged three swallows of before he stopped, looked at Eve and Michael, and said, "Oh, come on. Don't tell me you guys are fighting again. Seriously, isn't there supposed to be a honeymoon period or something?"

"We're not fighting," Michael said. There was something in

his voice that warned this was a bad time for Shane to get snarky. "We're making up. We'll be upstairs."

Shane actually opened his mouth to say something else, but he suddenly shivered and took a step back. "Hey!" he said, and looked up at the ceiling. "Stop it, Miranda! Brat."

Miranda was . . . well, the Glass House teen ghost. A real, official one. She'd died here, in the house—sacrificed herself, in the battle with the draug—and now she was part of it, but invisible during the day.

She could still make herself felt, when she wanted to; the cold spot she'd just formed around Shane was proof of how she felt about his impulse to harass Michael and Eve just now. Miranda couldn't be heard or seen during the daytime, but she could sure make her displeasure known.

And they'd probably hear about it tonight, in detail, when she materialized.

Claire sighed as Michael led Eve out of the room with an arm around her shoulders. "Here," she said, and passed Shane the envelope with his name on it. "You should sit down. You're really not going to like this."

Sitting Shane down to discuss things didn't help, because all it accomplished was an overturned chair, and Shane stalking the kitchen in dangerously black silence. He tried to throw his ID card in the trash, but Claire quietly retrieved it and put it back on the table, along with hers. Eve's still sat abandoned on the counter.

"You're going along with this?" he finally asked. She'd been watching him as he paced; there was a lot to learn about her boyfriend when he wasn't saying anything, just from the tenseness of his muscles, and the way he held himself. How he looked right now was telling her that he was on the verge of punching something—preferably something with a set of fangs. Shane had gotten better about controlling his impulses to fight, but they never really went away. They couldn't, she supposed. Now he stopped, put his back to the wall, and used both hands to push his shaggy, longish hair back from his face. His eyes were wide and dark and full of challenge as he looked at her.

"No," she said. She felt steady, almost calm, really. "I'm not going along with it. None of us is—we *can't*. Are you coming with me to talk to Amelie about it?"

"Hell yes, I'm coming with you. Did you think I'd let you go alone?"

"Do you promise to keep your cool?"

"I promise I won't go starting any fights. But I'm taking a little insurance, and you're carrying, too. No arguments. I know you don't think Amelie's exactly on our side anymore, so trusting her's off the table." He pushed off the wall and opened the cabinets under the sink; under there were several black canvas bags of equipment, all of it damaging to vampires in some way.

Claire wanted to be brave and say that she didn't need any kind of defenses, but she was no longer sure of that. Morganville, since the defeat of the draug, was . . . different. Different in small, indefinable ways, but definitely not the same, and she wasn't sure that the rules she'd learned about interacting with Amelie, the vampire Founder, were the same, either. The old Amelie, the one she'd gotten almost comfortable knowing . . . that woman would not have hurt her just for disagreeing.

But this new, more powerful Amelie seemed different. More remote. More dangerous.

So Claire looked at the contents of the bag he'd opened, and took out two vials of liquid silver nitrate, which she put in the pockets of her blue jeans. She wasn't exactly dressed for vampire fighting—not that there was a real dress code for that—but she was prepared to sacrifice the cute sky blue top she had on, in an emergency. Pity she hadn't picked the black one this morning.

Ah, Morganville. Where dressing to hide bloodstains was just good daily planning.

"We should talk to Hannah first," she said as Shane picked out a thin-bladed knife that had been coated with silver. He checked the edge on it, nodded, and jammed it back in the leather sheath before he stuck it in the inside pocket of his leather jacket.

"If you think that'll help," he said. Hannah Moses was the newly minted mayor of Morganville—she'd been the police chief, but with the death of Richard Morrell, she'd ended up being appointed the First Human of the town. It wasn't a job Hannah wanted, but it was one she'd accepted like the soldier she'd once been. "Though I figure if Hannah could have done anything about this, it would have already been done. She doesn't need us to bring her the news."

That was true enough, but still, Claire couldn't shake the feeling that they needed allies at their side before dropping in on Amelie. Strength in numbers, and all that; she couldn't ask Michael, not without asking Eve, and Eve was a hot button for the vampires right now. Michael and Eve were married, really, legally married, and that had cheesed off a good portion of the plasma-challenged in their screwed-up community. Apparently, prejudices didn't die, even when people did.

Not that the humans seemed all that happy about it, either.

"Still," she said aloud, "let's go talk to her and see what she can do. Even if she just comes with us . . ."

"Yeah, I know—she'd be harder to make disappear." Shane stepped in and bent his head and kissed her, a sudden and warm and sweet thing that made her pull her attention away from her worries and focus utterly on him for a moment. "Mmmm," he murmured, not moving back farther than strictly required for the words to form between their lips. "Been missing that."

"Me, too," she whispered, and leaned into the kiss. It had been a busy few months, rebuilding Morganville, finding their lives and place in things again. Then she'd been focusing on getting caught up at school again—once Texas Prairie University had reopened, she'd been determined not to have to repeat any credit hours she'd missed during the general emergency. Her boyfriend had been through some rough times—more than rough, really—but they'd come out of it okay, she thought. They understood each other. Best of all, they actually liked each other. It wasn't just hormones (though right now, hers were fizzing like a shaken soda; Shane just had that effect on her); it was something else. Something deeper.

Something special that she thought was actually going to last. Maybe even forever.

Shane pulled back and kissed the tip of her nose, which made her laugh just a little. "Gear up, Warrior Princess. We've got some adventuring to do."

She was still smiling when they left the house, hand in hand, walking through the blazing hot midafternoon. Lot Street, their street, was mostly intact from all the troubles Morganville had seen; it even had most of its former residents back in place. As they passed, Mrs. Morgan waved at them as she watered her flowers. She was wearing a bathing suit that was—in Claire's opinion— way too small, especially at her age, which had to be at least thirty. "Hello, Shane!" Mrs. Morgan said. Shane waved back, and gave her a dazzling grin.

Claire elbowed him. "Don't bait the cougars."

"You just don't want me to have any fun, do you?"

"Not that kind of fun."

"Oh, come on—she's not serious. She just likes to flirt. Gives her a thrill."

"*I'm* not thrilled."

Shane's smile this time was positively predatory. "Jealous?"

She was, surprisingly, and hid it under a glare. "Disgusted, more like."

"C'mon, you think that actor guy is hot, and he's probably as old as Mrs. Morgan."

"He's on TV. She's modeling a bikini for you two doors down from us."

"Oh, so it's about access. In other words, if he lived two doors down and was walking around in his Joe Boxers . . ."

She elbowed him again, because this was not turning out to be an easy win of a conversation. He grunted a little, as if she'd hurt him (which she hadn't, at all), and he put his arm around her shoulders. "Okay, I surrender," he said. "No more cougar baiting. I won't even go outside without a shirt on when I mow the lawn. But you have to make the same promise."

"Not to go outside without a shirt? Sure."

"No," he said, and suddenly he was completely serious. "No flirting with older guys. Especially the really old ones."

He meant Myrnin, her vampire boss, friend, mentor, and sometimes the bane of her existence. Crazy, wildly sentimental Myrnin, who seemed to like her more than was good for either of them.

And she sometimes hadn't done a very good job of handling that, she had to admit.

"I promise," she said. "No flirting."

He sent her a sidelong look that was a little doubtful, but he nodded. "Thanks."

Other than Mrs. Morgan's bright orange bikini, it was an un-
eventful walk. Morganville wasn't a huge place, and from Lot
Street to the mayor's office was about ten minutes at a stroll—in
the current late-spring temperatures, just about enough time to
really start to feel the burn of the sun beating down. Claire was a
little grateful when Shane opened the door and she stepped into
the cooler, darker space of the Morganville City Hall lobby. It had
been rebuilt, mostly, but one thing about the vampires: they demanded high standards on their civic buildings. The place looked
great, with new marble floors and columns and fancy-looking
light fixtures overhead. Old-world elegance in the middle of Nowhere, Texas.

A round wooden information desk was situated in the center of
the lobby, staffed by a good-looking lady probably only a few years
out of college. The nameplate in front of her said she was Annabelle Lange. Looking up as Claire and Shane stopped in front of
her, she gave them a warm, welcoming smile. She had chestnut
brown hair worn long and glossy, and big blue eyes . . . entirely too
pretty, and all her attention focused on Shane immediately.

This was worse than Mrs. Morgan by a whole lot. Annabelle
wasn't old. And she didn't have to wear a Day-Glo bikini to get attention.

"We're here to see the mayor," Claire said before Annabelle
could speak or ask Shane for his phone number. "Claire Danvers
and—"

"Shane Collins," Annabelle interrupted her, still smiling.
"Yes, I know. Just a moment; I'll see if Mayor Moses is available."

She turned away and got on a telephone. While she was busy,
Claire sent Shane a look—a significant one. He raised his eyebrows, clearly amused. "I didn't do anything," he said. "Totally
not my fault."

"Stop being so . . ."

"Charming? Attractive? Irresistible?"

"I'm going with arrogant."

"Ow." Before he could defend himself, the receptionist was back, all smiles and dimples.

"Mayor Moses is in a meeting, but she says she can work you in immediately after. If you'd like to go upstairs and wait in her office . . ."

"Thanks," Shane said. And the girl actually did that lip-biting shorthand for *I'm available* and gave him the under-the-lashes look. Textbook. Claire couldn't help but roll her eyes, not that she actually existed on Annabelle Lange's planet at all.

Shane noticed, though. Definitely. He hustled Claire on, fast, to the elevators. "C'mon, that wasn't worth all that effort at a reaction. She's just . . . friendly."

"If she were any friendlier, she'd be giving you a lap dance right now."

"Wow. Who turned you into the Green-Eyed Monster? And don't tell me you got bitten by a radioactive spider. There's no superhero of jealousy." When she didn't reply before they reached the elevators, he punched the button, then turned toward her. It wasn't just a casual kind of look; it was a level stare, very direct, and it caught Claire a little off guard. "Seriously. Are you really thinking I'm into Mrs. Morgan? Or what's-her-name back there?"

"Annabelle," Claire said, and wished she hadn't remembered the girl's name quite that fast. "No. But—"

"But what?" It wasn't like Shane to be so serious. "You know I was just kidding about Mrs. Morgan, right? I wouldn't go there. Or anywhere. I mean, I look at girls, because c'mon, that's biology. But I love you." He said it so matter-of-factly that it sent a shiver through her, deep down to her toes. When Shane was serious, when he got that steady, calm look in his eyes, it made her hot and cold all over. She felt as if she were floating someplace very high, where the air was terribly thin but intoxicating.

"I know," she whispered, and stepped closer to him. "That's why I'm jealous."

"You know that doesn't make sense, right?"

"It does. Because now I have so much more to lose, and more every time you kiss me. I think about losing you, and it hurts."

He smiled. It occurred to her that Shane didn't smile much with other people, only with her, and certainly not *that* way. It was so...hot, having that all to herself. "You're not losing me," he said. "I straight-out promise that."

Whatever else he was going to say—she would have managed to think about it in the ringing, happy silence of the afterglow—was interrupted by the soft bell of the elevator. Shane offered his arm, and she took it, feeling stupid and a little bit giggly, and let him escort her into the elevator.

As soon as the doors slid shut, Shane pushed the button for the third floor (it had a boldly lettered MAYOR'S OFFICE sign on it) and then backed her up against the wall, bent his head, and kissed her for real. A lot. Deeply. His lips felt soft and damp and sweet and more than a little too hot for being in public, and she made a protesting little sound that was half a warning that the door was going to open *any second*. The other half of her was begging him to completely disregard the warning and just keep going...but then he pulled back, took in a deep breath, and stepped away as the doors opened.

He was still smiling, and she couldn't stop staring at him. In profile, those lips were just...yeah. Delicious.

"Claire," he said, and gave her an after-you gesture.

"Oh," she said brilliantly, and pulled her head together with an effort. "Right. Thanks."

The warm spell of the elevator was broken, because as she and Shane stepped out into the hallway, a door slammed hard down the hall, and a tall girl in a short skirt and designer heels came striding around the corner. The season's color was hot pink, and she was practically glowing in the dark with it ... the skirt, the shoes, the nail polish, the lipstick.

The lips took a particularly bitter curl when Monica Morrell spotted the two of them. Her steps slowed for a second, and then she tossed her glossy hair over her shoulders and kept coming. "Somebody call security—vagrants are getting in again," she said. "Oh, never mind. It's just *you*. Here visiting your parole officer, Shane?"

It sounded classically Monica, Mean Girl, Deluxe Edition, but there was something different about her, Claire thought. Monica's heart didn't seem quite in it anymore. She looked a little pale under her must-have spray tan, and despite the up-to-the-minute makeup and clothes, she seemed a little lost. The world had finally and decisively knocked the props out from under Monica Morrell, and Claire wished she could have more satisfaction in that. She still felt the pulse of dull anger and resentment, sure; that was pretty much hardwired inside, after the years of abuse Monica had heaped on her since she'd arrived.

But, knowing what she knew, there was not nearly enough delicious revenge to be had in seeing Monica off-balance.

"Monica," Shane said. Nothing else. He watched her the way you'd watch a potentially hostile pit bull, ready for anything, but he wasn't reacting to her jibe. Monica didn't return the greeting.

"Nice dress," Claire said. She meant that. The hot pink looked particularly good on Monica, and she'd obviously taken a lot of time with the whole look.

Monica punched the elevator button, since the doors had already shut, and said, "That's it? *Nice dress?* You're not even going to ask me if I mugged a dead hooker for it or something? Lame, Danvers. You need to step up your efforts if you want to make an impression."

"How are you?" Claire asked. Shane made a sound of protest in the back of his throat, a low warning she disregarded; maybe this was useless, trying to be empathetic with Monica, but it wasn't really in Claire's nature not to try.

"How am I?" Monica sounded puzzled, and for a moment, she looked directly at Claire. Her eyes were expertly made up, but under the covering layers they looked tired and a little puffy. "My brother's dead, and you jackasses just stood there and let it happen. That's how I am."

"Monica—" Shane's voice was gentler than Claire expected. "You know that's not what happened."

"Do I?" Monica smiled slightly, her eyes never leaving Claire's. "I know what people *tell* me happened."

"You were talking to Hannah," Claire guessed. "Didn't she tell you . . ."

"None of your business what we talked about," Monica interrupted. The elevator dinged for her, and she stepped inside as it opened. "I don't believe *any* of you. Why should I? You've all hated me since forever. As far as I'm concerned, you all thought this was payback. Guess what? Payback's a bitch. And so am I."

Monica looked . . . alone, Claire thought, as the doors slid closed on her. Alone and a little scared. She'd always been insulated from the real world—first by her father, the former mayor of Morganville, and by her faithful mean-girl companions. Her brother, Richard, hadn't coddled her, but he'd protected her, too, when he thought it was necessary. Now that Richard was gone, killed by the savage draug, she had . . . well, nothing. Her power was pretty much gone, and with it, her friends. She was just another pretty girl now, and one thing Monica wasn't used to being . . . was ordinary.

"I thought she'd be less . . ."

"Bitchy?" Shane supplied. "Yeah, good luck. She's not the re-forming type."

Claire elbowed him. "Like you? Because as I remember it, you were all bad-boy slacker bad attitude when I met you. So you've what, forgiven her? That's not like you, Shane."

Shane shrugged, a slow roll of his shoulders seeming to be more about getting rid of tension than expressing an emotion. "Could have been wrong about some things she did before," he said. "Doesn't mean she isn't a waste of general air space, though."

Well, he was right about that, and since Monica was gone, there was no point in spending time discussing her, anyway. They had an appointment, and when they rounded the corner toward the mayor's office, they found the door open, with the receptionist at her desk.

"Yes?" The receptionist here, unlike the one downstairs, was all business . . . matronly, chilly, with X-ray blue eyes that scanned the two of them up and down and rendered a verdict of *not very im-portant.* "Can I help you?"

"We're here to see Mayor Moses," Claire said. "Uh—Claire Danvers and Shane Collins. We called up."

"Have a seat." The receptionist went back to her computer screen, completely uninterested in them even before they moved to the waiting area. It was comfortable enough, but the magazines were ages old, and within a few seconds Claire found herself itch-ing to do something, so she pulled out her phone and began scroll-ing through texts and e-mails. There weren't very many, but then her circle of tech-savvy friends wasn't very large. Most of the vampire residents of Morganville hadn't mastered the knack and didn't want to ever try. Most of the humans were too wary of network monitoring to commit much to pixels.

However, Eve had linked her to a funny cat video, which was a nice break from the usual vampire-related mayhem. Claire watched it twice while Shane flipped through a decade-old *Sports Illustrated* before the receptionist finally said, "The mayor will—" She was probably going to frostily pronounce that the mayor would see them now, but she was interrupted by the door opening to the mayor's inner office, and Hannah Moses herself stepping out.

"Claire, Shane, come in," she said, and cut a glance at her assistant. "We're not that formal here."

The receptionist's mouth tightened into a lemon-sucking pucker, and she stabbed at the keys on her computer as if she intended to sink her fingerprints into them.

Mayor Moses—that sounded so strange, honestly—closed the door behind the two of them and said, "Sorry about Olive. She's inherited from two previous administrations. So. What was so urgent?" She indicated the two chairs sitting across from her desk as she took her own seat and leaned forward, elbows on the smooth wood surface. There was something elegant and composed about her, and something intimidating, too. . . . Hannah was a tall woman, angular, with skin the color of very dark chocolate. She was attractive, and somehow the scar (a souvenir of Afghanistan and her military career) just worked to make her more interesting. She'd changed her hair; the neat cornrows were gone now, and she'd shaved it close to her head in a way that made her look like a beautiful, scary piece of sculpture.

She'd exchanged her police uniform for sharply tailored jackets and pants, but the look was still somehow official . . . even to

the Morganville pin in her lapel. She might not have a gun anymore, but she still looked completely competent and dangerous.

"Here," Shane said, and handed over his ID card. "What the
hell is up with these things?"

He certainly wasn't wasting any time.

Hannah glanced at it and handed it back without a smile.
"Don't like your picture?"

"C'mon, Hannah."

"There are certain . . . compromises I've had to make," she
said. "And no, I'm not happy about them. But carrying ID cards
isn't going to kill you."

"Hunting licenses might," Claire said. "Michael's letter said
they were back in force. Each vampire can kill one human a year,
free and clear. Did you know that?"

That got her a sharp, unreadable look from the mayor, and after a moment, Hannah said, "I'm aware of it. And working on it.
We have a special session this afternoon to discuss it."

"Discuss it?" Shane said. "We're talking about licenses to murder, Hannah. How can you sign up for this?"

"I *didn't* sign up for it. I was outvoted," she said. "Oliver's got . . .
influence over Amelie now. In defeating the draug—which we had
to do, for the safety of the human population—we also removed
the only thing that vampires really feared. They certainly aren't
afraid of humans anymore."

"They'd better be," Shane said grimly. "We've never taken any
of this lying down. That's not going to change."

"But—Amelie promised that things would change," Claire
said. "After we defeated her father, Bishop. She said humans would
have an equal place in Morganville, that all this hunting would
stop! You heard her."

"I did. And now she's changed her mind," Hannah said. "Believe me, I tried to stop the whole thing, but Oliver's in charge of the day-to-day business. He's put two more vampires on the Elders' Council, which makes it three to one if we vote along vampire versus human lines. In short, they can just ignore my votes." She looked calm, mostly, but Claire noticed the tight muscles in her jaw, and the way she glanced away as if reliving a bad memory.

Claire followed her gaze and saw a lone cardboard moving box in the corner. Hannah hadn't had the job very long, so it could have just been unpacking left to do . . . but from what she knew of her, Mayor Moses wasn't one to just let things sit around undone.

"Hannah?"

The mayor focused on her, and for a second Claire thought she might talk about what was bothering her, but then she shook her head. "Never mind," she said. "Claire, please take my advice. Drop this. There's nothing you can do or say that will change her mind, and Amelie's not the person you knew before. She's not reasonable. And she's not safe. If I could have put a stop to this, I would have; seven generations of my family come from Morganville, and I don't want to see things go south any more than you do."

"But—if we don't talk to Amelie, what are we supposed to do to stop it?"

"I don't know," Hannah said. She seemed angry, and deeply troubled. "I just don't know."

At times like these, Claire was sharply reminded that Hannah wasn't just some small-town sheriff upgraded to mayor. She had been a soldier, and she'd fought for her country. Hannah had taken up arms in Morganville before, and in a fight there wasn't anybody Claire wanted at her back more (except Shane).

"That's not an answer," Shane said. He tapped the identification card again. "You're not serious about really carrying these things."

"That's the new law of the land, Shane. Carry it or get fined the first time. Second time, it's jail. I can't advise you to do anything else but comply."

"What do we get the third time, stocks and public mockery?"

"There wouldn't be a third time," she said. "I'm sorry. I really am."

He looked at her for a long moment, then silently put it back in his pocket. Claire knew that look, and she saw the muscle jumping uneasily along his jawline. He was counting to ten, silently, letting go of the impulse to say something crazy and suicidal.

When he let his breath out, slowly, she knew it was okay, and she felt tension she didn't even know she had start to unbraid along her spine.

"Thanks for seeing us," Claire said, and Hannah stood to offer her hand. Claire accepted, though she still felt awkward shaking hands. Trying to be professional always made her seem like a fraud, like a kid playing dress-up. But she tried to hold Hannah's gaze as she returned the firm, dry grip. "Are you sure you won't come with us?"

"You're intent on going to see Amelie?"

"We have to try," Claire said. "Don't we? As you said, she used to listen to me, a little. Maybe she still will."

Hannah shook her head. "Kid, you've got guts, but I'm telling you, it's not going to work."

"Will you make an appointment for me, though? That way there's a record."

"I will." Hannah looked to Shane. "You're going to let her do this?"

"Not alone."

"Good."

Ten seconds later, they were out in the waiting area, under the judging gaze of the assistant, and then in the hallway. Claire took in a deep breath. "Did we actually accomplish anything?"

"Yeah," Shane said. "We figured out that Hannah wasn't going to help us much. Go figure, a Morganville mayor whose hands are tied? Who saw that coming?" He stopped Claire and put his hand on her shoulder. "I'll go with you to see Amelie."

"That's sweet, but having you with me is kind of a walking invitation to trouble."

"Just because they know I prefer my vampires extra-crispy . . ."

"Exactly." Claire covered the hand on her shoulder with her own. "I'll be careful."

"I meant what I said. You're not going in there alone," he said. "Take Michael. Or—and I can't believe I'm actually saying this— take Myrnin. Just have somebody at your back, okay?"

It was really something if Shane suggested she go anywhere at all with Myrnin, and for pretty good reasons. . . . Myrnin had feelings for her, and he had feelings for Shane, too, but in the opposite way entirely. As in, Myrnin probably thought about the death of her boyfriend, and Shane had the same fantasies. It was a mutual, weirdly cheerful loathing, even if it didn't come to outright conflict.

"Okay," Claire said. She didn't mean it, but it touched her that he was so genuinely concerned about her safety. She'd survived a lot in Morganville—not as much as Shane, granted—and she thought of herself as pretty tough these days. Not indestructible, but . . . sturdy.

One of these days, she'd have to sit him down and explain that she wasn't the fragile little sixteen-year-old he'd met; she was an adult now (she *so* didn't feel that status yet, despite the birthdays) and she'd proven she could meet the challenges of survival around here. And while it was sweet and lovely that he wanted to protect her, at a certain point he really needed to understand it wasn't his job to do it, twenty-four/seven.

He linked his arm with hers and walked her to the elevator. There was no repeat of the kissing, which was a little disappointing, but he outright ignored his would-be stalker Annabelle down in the outer lobby. That was better.

After the chill of the lobby, walking into the sun was like hitting a furnace face-first, and Claire blinked and grabbed her sunglasses. They were cheap and fun, blinged all to heaven—a gift from Eve, of course. As she adjusted them, she saw something odd.

Monica Morrell was still here. Standing at the bottom of the steps, leaning against a forbidding granite pillar (the courthouse was built in a style Claire liked to call Early American Mausoleum) and shading her eyes to peer out at the street. The hot wind stirred her long, glossy, dark hair like a sheet of silk, and that dress—as ever—was dangerously close to violating decency laws when the breeze inched the hem up.

Shane saw her, too, and slowed down, shooting Claire a sideways glance. She silently agreed. It was odd. Monica didn't just *stand* places, at least not unless she was making a statement of some kind. She was always on the move, like a shark.

"Huh," Monica said. "That's weird. Don't you think that's weird?" She addressed the remark to the air, but Claire supposed she intended it for her and Shane. Kind of.

"What?" she asked.

"The van," Monica said, and tilted her head toward the street. "Parked on the corner."

"Sweet," Shane said. "Somebody got new wheels."

"*This* year's model," Monica said. "I know for a fact that our lame-ass car lot doesn't even have *last* year's model. I had to go all the way to Odessa to buy my convertible. Morganville doesn't exactly keep up with the cutting edge."

"Okay." Shane shrugged. "Somebody went to Odessa and bought a new van. Why's that weird?"

"Because I'd know about it if they did, stupid. Nobody in Morganville's bought a new van in years." She sounded confident. Monica was the queen of town gossip, and Claire had to admit, she had a point. She *would* know. She'd probably know the serial numbers of each purchase, and how many times it had driven through town, and what the driver had been wearing on each occasion. "Besides, that shine? That's so *town*, not country. And check out the tinting."

"So?" Claire asked. Most glossy cars in Morganville had superdark windows, because they were owned by people who were— to put it mildly—allergic to the sun.

"That's not vampire shades," Shane said. "Dark, but not *that* dark. Custom stuff. Huh. And there's a logo on the side. Can't really see it, though, and . . ." His voice trailed off as the doors opened on the van. Three people got out.

"Oh," Monica said. "Oh. My. God. *Look* at him."

There were two men who'd exited the van, but Claire knew exactly what she meant. . . . There was only one *him*, even at a distance. Tall, dark, Latin, *hot*.

"That," Monica continued, in a voice that sounded very much like awe, "is some serious man candy." Shane made a throwing-up sound in the back of his throat, which brought out a leisurely smile on Monica's lips. "I'll bet if I licked him, he'd even taste like fruit. Passion fruit."

There was a woman, too—tall, leggy, with blond hair pulled

back in a bouncy, glossy ponytail. She seemed pretty, too, but Claire had to admit, her attention was on Mr. Man Candy. Even at a distance, Monica had nailed the description.

Monica pushed away from the pillar and set off in a runway stride, high heels clicking on the hot concrete sidewalk.

"Come on," Shane said, and tugged Claire after her. "This, I've got to see. And maybe get on the Internet."

TWO

CLAIRE

)

As they got closer to the van, Claire realized it was big—Texas-style big, with a high roof. It looked more like something to haul equipment than people. The logo on the side of the van was on a magnet backing, and it was red on black. There was some kind of skull with a microphone and hard-to-read letters, not that she was paying a lot of attention.

Monica's target was clearly Mr. Man Candy, who, Claire had to admit, did not suffer from closer inspection. He was tall (as tall as Shane), and broad-shouldered (like Shane) . . . but with an expensive-looking style to his thick dark hair, and perfect golden brown skin. Whether it was airbrushed or natural, it looked good on him. He had on a tight knit shirt that showed off his washboard abs, and his face was just . . . perfect.

"Hi," Monica said, and held out her hand to him as she came

to a stop about a foot away from him. "Welcome to Morganville."

He smiled at her with dazzlingly white teeth. "Well," he said, and even his voice was perfect, with just a little hint of a Spanish accent to give it spice. "Morganville gets points for having the loveliest welcoming committee yet. What's your name, lovely?"

Monica was not used to being one-upped in the flattery game, Claire guessed, because she blinked and actually looked a little taken aback. But it lasted only an instant, and then she smiled her biggest, brightest smile and said, "Monica. Monica Morrell. And what's *your* name?"

His smile lost a little of its luster, and those sparkling dark eyes dimmed a bit. "Ah, I thought you knew."

Monica froze. Shane muttered, "Thank you, God," and took out his cell phone to start recording. "It's like arrogant matter meets arrogant antimatter."

Monica unfroze long enough to snap, "Put that away, Shane. *God*, are you six?" before focusing back on Mr. Man Candy. "Don't mind him—he's the village idiot. And she's the village Einstein, which is nearly as bad."

He accepted that as an apology, Claire guessed, because he took the girl's hand and bent over it to plant his lips on her knuckles. Monica looked dazzled. And a little scared. Her lips parted, her eyes widened, and for a moment she looked like a normal, regular girl of nineteen who'd been knocked off her feet by an older, slicker man. "My name is Angel Salvador," he said. "I am the host of the show *After Death*. Perhaps you know it?"

It sounded vaguely familiar—one of those ghost-hunting shows Claire never watched.

Shane pivoted and focused on the girl. "And you are . . ."

"His cohost," the woman standing a few feet away said. She

was just as pretty as Angel, but she was frosty.... Even her hair was a pale, watery blond, and her eyes were very light blue. Unlike Angel, she looked uncomfortable in the harsh sunlight. "Jenna Clark."

The other guy snorted and said, "Since nobody's going to ask my name, it's Tyler, thanks. I'm just the one who does all the work and hauls all the equipment and—"

Jenna and Angel said, in perfect, bored synchronicity, "Shut up, Tyler." Then they threw each other poisonous looks. Clearly, there was no love lost there. Or maybe some gone bad.

"*After Death*?" Shane asked. "Don't you guys do some kind of spirit-hunting thing?"

"Yes, exactly," Jenna said, and seemed to focus on Shane as an actual human being for the first time. She smiled, but to Claire's relief it was more of a professional kind of attention, not a *Wow, you're hot* kind of thing. "We're looking for the permits office."

"Permits?" Monica had recovered her composure, at least a little. Angel had stopped kissing her fingers, but he hadn't let her hand go, and Claire thought her voice sounded a little higher than usual. She was also a little more blushy than normal. "Permits for what? Are you moving your business here?"

Angel laughed, low in his throat—a sexy laugh, of course. "Alas, no, my lovely. Our studio is out of Atlanta. But we are interested in filming some local sights here. Perhaps conducting a nighttime investigation of your graveyard, for instance. We always pay a visit to the local offices for our filming permits. It avoids so many problems."

Claire could not even count how many ways this was a bad idea.... Television people. In Morganville. Filming at night. She was mesmerized by the flood of horrible possibilities that ran through her brain.

Luckily, Monica wasn't one for deep thought. "Oh," she said, and smiled so warmly that Claire was almost fooled. "I see. Well, I wouldn't waste my time. Morganville doesn't have anything special for you. Not even a decent ghost to hunt. We're just really . . . boring."

"But it's so scenic!" Angel protested. "Look at this courthouse. Pure Texas Gothic Renaissance. We passed a cemetery that was perfect—elaborate tombstones, wrought iron, and that big dead white tree—such a striking color, very photogenic. I'm sure we'll find something."

Shane muttered to Claire, "If they hang around there at night, they definitely will, but I don't think it's what they're hoping for."

"Sssshhh!"

He cleared his throat and raised his voice. "Monica's right— it's very boring." He sounded like he was still struggling not to laugh. "Unless you want the world's least interesting reality show. The weirdest thing that happens around here is old Mr. Evans running around naked at midnight and howling, and he only does that on special occasions."

"That's unfortunate," Jenna said. "It does seem perfect."

"Well, it won't hurt to get the permits. At least we'll contribute to your local economy, yes?" Angel said, and flashed them all an impartial movie-star smile. "*Adios.* I'm sure we'll meet again." He gave Monica's hand another brief kiss, and then he and Jenna were striding up the walk toward City Hall, with Tyler scrambling in their wake while carrying a small camcorder—though what kind of filmable drama there'd be in applying for a permit, Claire couldn't imagine.

"Crap," Shane said. He still sounded *way* too amused. "So. Any bets on how long they last before the vamps make them go away?"

"No bet," Monica said. "They won't last long." Looking dreamy-eyed, she sighed and cradled her hand. "Too bad. *So* pretty. And totally manscaped under that shirt, I'll bet."

Shane sent her a revolted look, then put his arm around Claire. "And on that note, we're out."

"Really?" Claire said, and couldn't help but smile. "That's what creeps you out. Waxing. You can take on vampires and draug and killers, but you're afraid of a little chest-hair pulling?"

"Yes," he said, "because I am sane."

They walked on a bit, and it took a few minutes for Claire to realize that although they'd left behind the ghost hunters, they still had an unwanted visitor: Monica. She was keeping pace with them. Uninvited. "Yes?" Claire asked her, pointedly. "Something we can help you with?"

"Maybe," Monica said. "Look, I know I've been historically kind of a bitch to you, but I was wondering . . ."

"Spit it out, Monica," Shane said.

"Teach me how to do that stuff you do."

"What, be awesome? Can't do it."

"Shut up, Collins. I mean . . ." She hesitated, then lowered her voice as she brushed her hair back from her face. She slowed down and stopped on the sidewalk, and Claire stopped, facing her. Shane tried to keep going, but eventually he looped back, defeated. "I mean that I want to learn how to fight. In case I need to do that. I always sort of thought—my father always said we didn't need to worry about the vampires, because we worked for them. But Richard never trusted that. And now I know I shouldn't, either. So I want to learn how to make weapons. Fight. That kind of thing."

"Oh *hell* no," Shane said. "And we're walking."

He started to, but Claire stayed put. She was studying Monica with a frown, feeling conflicted but oddly compelled, too. Monica looked serious. Not defiant, or arrogant, or any of her usual poses. Her brother had told Claire before he'd died that he thought Monica could change—and had to change.

Maybe she was starting to understand that.

"How do we know you won't sell us out at the first possible opportunity?" she asked.

Monica smiled. "Shortcake, I probably *would* if it got me any-where, but these days, it wouldn't do squat. The vampires aren't looking at us like collaborators and enemies anymore. We're all just . . . snack foods. So. I understand what a stake is for, but you guys seem to have all the killer toys. What do you say we work out a sharing arrangement?"

"We'll take it under advisement," Shane said, and grabbed Claire's elbow. "We're going. Now."

They left her, and when Claire looked back, she thought Monica had really never looked lonelier. The other girl finally walked to her red convertible, got in, and drove away.

"We are *not* getting cozy with her," Shane said. "She's got vamp problems? Boo hoo. She spent her whole life siccing them on any-body who pissed her off. Smells like justice to me."

"Shane."

"C'mon, this is a girl who tormented me most of my life. Who beat you up and tormented *you*. She's a bully. Screw her."

Claire gave him a long look. "You're the one who was nice to her when Richard died. And she saved your life."

"Yeah, don't remind me," he said, but after a moment or two, he sighed. "Fine. She'll always be an ass, but I guess it doesn't hurt to teach her to use a stake or something. Basic self-defense."

"That's my guy." She squeezed his arm. "Besides, if you teach her self-defense, you get to smash her into the floor when you tackle her."

"Suddenly, I am all about this plan."

They got about half a block before Shane stopped in front of the used-parts store to talk to the guy who ran it—something about needing a new hose for Eve's always-being-rebuilt hearse. Claire lost interest after the conversation began sounding like a foreign language, and she ended up staring into a store two windows down. It was a junk store, really, full of discarded stuff (some of it actually good), and she got on the creepy track of wondering if people had actually brought it here to resell, or if it had been scavenged from abandoned houses after the owners' disappearances. Maybe both.

The storefront was blessedly in dark shade, and so was the narrow brick alley next to it . . . which was why she didn't see the attack coming. It happened so fast, she saw nothing but a blur out of the corner of her eye, and then felt the sensation of hands crushing her shoulders, and then a rush of dizzy motion. When she caught her breath to scream, she was slammed up against the brick wall, and a cold hand pressed over her mouth to seal in the sound.

"Hush!" Myrnin said urgently. "Hush, now. Promise me."

Claire didn't want to promise anything, because there was a manic gleam in her vampire boss's dark eyes, and he looked . . . especially disheveled today. Myrnin was prone to eccentric dressing, but this outfit looked as if he'd picked it out in pitch-darkness by feel—some kind of moth-eaten velvet trousers that would have been deemed too out-there for the 1970s, a loose-fitting lemon yellow shirt that was buttoned up wrong, and a vest with cartoon characters. He'd matched it up with a hat that a Pilgrim might have worn and, just to top it all off, neon Mardi Gras beads—three strands.

He was also—she cringed to see it—totally barefoot. In an alley. That was disturbing.

She nodded, which wasn't so much a promise really, but he accepted it as one and took his hand away. She finished drawing in the breath, but held off on the scream, just in case he wasn't crazy at the moment, bare feet aside.

"I heard that you spoke with Mayor Moses?" he asked.

"You forgot your shoes."

"Bother my feet! Moses?"

"Yes, we talked to her."

"Did she tell you that Amelie has just announced an election?"

Claire blinked. "For what?"

"For *mayor*, of course. She has removed Hannah from office, effective tomorrow, since Hannah has refused to agree to sign some of her more-aggressive new decrees. The election will be held next week to appoint someone more . . . friendly to the new agenda." Myrnin seemed not just agitated, but really worried. "You see why I object."

"Uh . . ." *Not really.* "You do remember you're a vampire, right?"

He gave her an utterly sane and baffled look. "The fangs and the fact I crave blood do give me a general clue, yes. And being a vampire, I am naturally interested in the survival of my species. Therefore I feel I ought to stop Amelie and that damn Roundhead from ruining everything we've accomplished of value here."

"Myrnin, you're not making any sense."

"Oh, aren't I?" He let go and stepped back from her, and she had to admit, despite the haphazard wardrobe, he looked a whole lot more together than he often did. His eyes were steady, dark, and focused; he held himself still, with no more than a minimum of fidgeting. "I came to Morganville to create something unique in the history of the world . . . a place where humans and vampires could coexist in relative safety, if not always peace. I will not allow Oliver to pervert that achievement into nothing more than his own personal . . . hunting preserve! It's a perversion of what Amelie intended here. And if she won't recognize it, I must do it for her."

Shane must have just noticed she'd gone missing, because she heard him call her name, a sharp and urgent note of alarm in his voice. He knew how easily people could vanish here, even in broad daylight. It didn't take him more than a few seconds to identify the alley as the most likely peril, and she saw his broad shoulders block out about half the murky light.

"Bother, it's your overprotective young man." Myrnin sighed. "Remember this: we must have a plan of how to counter Oliver's influence. Perhaps another human on the council. If not Hannah Moses, then someone in opposition to Amelie's agenda. Preferably someone sane, of course. Work on that. I'll be in touch soon." He sent a blistering look down the alley as Shane approached, then briefly bared thin, razor-sharp eyeteeth before just . . . vanishing. He didn't actually disappear in a mist, Claire knew; he just moved faster than her eye could track, so the human brain filled in something similar for reference.

And then Shane was there, staring first at her, then around at the shadows. "What the hell, Claire?"

She pulled in a deep breath, and wished she hadn't. Alleys. Disgusting. She thought of Myrnin's bare feet, and shuddered. "Let's get out of here."

A phone call to Michael sorted out her vampire escort problem for her upcoming audience with Morganville's Founder; he was willing—in fact, eager—to talk to Amelie along with her. Claire was especially grateful, since if she hadn't been able to land his support, Shane would have insisted on going with her, and she could foresee how *that* would turn out. She didn't need to be a psychic to know Shane's mouth would get them both in trouble, especially with Amelie's own attitude these days.

Michael brought his car and picked Claire up on the street in front of the Glass House. It was a standard-issue vampire sedan; having fangs in Morganville came with wheels, for free, as well as a membership on the withdrawal side of the town's blood bank. The downside of riding in Michael's car was that Claire couldn't see anything out the windows, since it was vampire custom-tinted.

"So," she said after they'd driven a couple of blocks in silence, "are you guys okay? Eve seemed . . ."

"She's okay," he said in a tone that meant he wasn't going to go over the details with her. "She's not happy with me for not telling you guys about the cards, but having a heads-up wouldn't have done anything but given you room to complain more. I was trying to keep the peace as long as I could." He shot her a look, eyebrows up. "Was I wrong?"

She shrugged. "I don't know, honestly. Everything's so weird these days, maybe you were right. At least we got to have some nice argument-free evenings out of it."

"Yeah," he agreed. "But those days are over."

Claire thought he was probably right.

Hannah might have called ahead, but that didn't mean word had gotten down to the level of the guards on duty near Founder's Square—two vampires, both wearing police uniforms, only this time they were female . . . a tall one and a short one. The taller one wore her white-blond hair in a thick braid down her back. The shorter one wore hers cropped close to the skull.

ID cards were the first thing they asked to see. Michael silently produced his gold card, but the two cops hardly even glanced at it. They wanted Claire's.

The taller one smiled as she looked it over. "Good blood type," she said, and handed it to her partner, who admired it in turn. "You take care of yourself. Wouldn't want to see it wasted."

Claire felt particularly weird about that. It was like being exposed, as if she'd had some kind of privacy taken away. Michael must have felt it, too, because he said, in a dangerously soft voice, "You've checked her out. Knock it off."

"You're no fun," the shorter one said, and winked at him. "Just like your grandfather. And look where that got him."

"Dead," the taller cop agreed. "All for trying to treat humans like equals. Seems like the Glass family members just never learn their lessons."

Michael's eyes flickered a sudden, bright crimson, and he said, "I'll take any comparison to my grandfather as a compliment. And you really need to stop screwing with us now."

"Or?"

"Viv, dial it down," the other cop said, and handed Claire's ID back to her. "We're done. They're cleared for the Founder's office."

"I'm sure we'll see you again," Viv said, and grinned, showing fangs. "Both of you. Hunting season starts soon."

Michael rolled up the window and put the car in gear. Claire let out a breath she hadn't realized she was holding, and finally said, "That was completely creepy."

"Yeah," Michael agreed. "I'm sorry. It was." He seemed to be almost apologizing for the two women, or maybe for vampires in general. "This might not have been such a great idea, coming out here. It's not like it was before."

"I have to try."

"Keep this short, then. I don't want you out here once the sun sets. Not even if I'm with you."

That was very unusual to hear from him, and unsettling, too. Claire looked straight ahead—at nothing, because the view was pretty much pitch-darkness. Michael's pale face and golden hair were tinged a little with blue from the dashboard light, and he glowed like a ghost in the corner of her eye. "What's happening to us?" she asked. She didn't mean to; it just came out, and it revealed way too much of the growing dread she was feeling. "They looked at me like meat in a supermarket. I know there have always been a few vampires like that, but . . . they were *police*. That means they're supposed to be the best at holding back their instincts."

Michael didn't answer her. Maybe he didn't know how. The dig they'd thrown about Sam Glass, his grandfather, had hit home, and she knew it. Michael's grandfather had physically looked about like Michael did now, only with more reddish hair. He'd been a sweet man, probably the most human of all of the vamps Claire had ever met. Sam had been a force for good in Morganville, and he'd paid for it with his life. Michael hadn't forgotten that. Claire wondered whether he thought about what might happen to his own life, if he kept trying to stay in the middle, squarely between humans and vampires, and whether he thought about being killed.

Of course he did. Especially now that he'd married Eve, against the wishes of both sides. They both had everything to lose.

Michael eased the car down, following the curve of the ramp as it led below Founder's Square. The vampires had excellent parking, all covered. When he'd pulled to a stop and turned off the engine, he finally said, "It's going to get bad, Claire. I know it. I feel it. We've got to do everything we can to stop it."

"I know," she said, and held out her hand. He took it and held it lightly—a good thing, because he could have easily shattered bones. "Glass House gang forever."

"Forever," he said. "If we're going to be a gang, we need a good sign to flash. Something intimidating."

They tried a few silly, strange attempts at flashing signs, but the efforts looked awkward. "We," Claire said, "are the worst gang *ever.*"

"Bad idea," Michael agreed, straight-faced. "Shane's the only one of us with real street cred anyway."

They got out of the car, and Claire was watchful of the shadows; so was Michael, but he must not have spotted anything out of the ordinary, because he nodded and escorted her to the elevator. While they waited for it to descend, Claire kept looking behind them, just to ensure that nobody had decided to stalk them.

Nobody did.

Someone had decided the elevator music had needed a change, so this time up, Claire was treated to an orchestral version of "Thriller," an oddly appropriate choice. Even vampires had a sense of humor, though it was mostly atrophied. Either Michael didn't think it was funny, or he was too focused to notice— probably the latter, because he seemed very self-contained just now. He must have been gearing up for whatever would be waiting for them.

The doors opened on a dead-white vampire, bald as a cue ball and dressed in formal black. Claire didn't know if he was security or just a very intimidating greeter, but she took a step back, and Michael tensed beside her.

The man looked them both over in silence, then abruptly turned his back on them and walked away. As he did, one hand snapped up to give them a follow-me gesture.

"Do you know him?" Claire asked as they trailed their black-suited guide into the paneled hallways. Vampires seemed to deliberately design all their buildings to confuse people, but the two of them didn't really need a personal escort; they'd spent a lot of time here, over the past couple of years. "And is he always this friendly?"

"Yes, and yes." Michael put his finger to his lips, asking her for silence, and she complied. They were passing closed, unmarked doors and watchful portraits of people she recognized as still walking the streets of Morganville, even though they'd been painted in ancient styles of clothes. Their escort moved fast, and Claire realized that even though it was tough for her to keep up, it was probably just standard vampire walking speed. It was oddly telling that the vamps no longer felt they needed to slow down to accommodate mere mortals.

She saved her breath and hurried, while Michael strode along beside her, matching her speed but not pushing her. He was watching the doorways, she realized. She'd never seen him quite this alert before, at least not here, in what should have been a safe place for them both.

It all became clear when a vampire slid out of the shadows ahead, lowered his chin, and bared his teeth. Claire knew him slightly, but he'd never looked quite so . . . inhuman. He was bone white, and his eyes were flaring crimson, and he gave off waves of menace that made her slow down and look at Michael in alarm.

Because that menace wasn't (for a change) aimed at her.

It was directed purely at her friend.

"You're not welcome here," the vampire said in a low, silky voice that was somehow worse than a growl. "Those who consort with humans use the servants' entrance."

"Ignore him," Michael said to her, and kept going. "Henrik's not going to hurt you."

"What's this one? Another little wife-pet you're planning to marry when you tire of the one you have?" Henrik's grin was full of cruel amusement. "Or won't you bother with the church's blessing next time? It's perfectly fine to eat them, you know. You don't need to sanctify them first. They still taste delicious."

Michael's eyes fixed on the other vampire, and his own eyes started turning red. Claire saw his hands flexing, trying to knot into fists. "Shut up," he said. "Claire, keep walking. He'll move."

This time there was something like a growl, or a rattling hiss, and Henrik's eyes turned even darker red. "Will I? Not for you, boy. Certainly not for your pet."

Claire kept walking, but she also reached into her pocket and pulled out a small glass vial. It had an easy-open pop-top, and she flicked it with her thumbnail, never taking her eyes off Henrik. "I'm not a pet," she said. "And I bite." She held up the vial. "Silver nitrate. Unless you want to spend a couple of hours nursing your burns, back off. We're here to see Amelie, not you."

His eyes fixed on her for the first time, and she felt a shock of fear; there was something really violent inside him, something she could only barely understand. It was a blind, unreasoning instinct to hurt—to kill.

But his teeth folded up into his mouth, like a snake's, and his smile took on more human proportions ... though it remained intimidating. Serial-killer intimidating. "By all means," he said. "Pass. I'm sure we'll meet again, flower."

He made an elaborate bow and retreated into the shadows. Claire kept her eyes on him as she edged through, but he didn't move at all.

When Michael followed, though, there was a sudden burst of movement, a blur punctuated by a soft outcry from Michael ... and then the other vamp was walking calmly away in the other direction.

"Michael?" Claire turned toward him, crying out when she saw the damage to his face. The blood was bad, but it was flowing from claw marks down the side of his face from temple to jawline. They were deep gouges—nothing that wouldn't heal, but still ...

Michael stumbled and caught himself against the wall, shut his eyes, and said, "Maybe you'd better go on without me. I'm going to need a minute." His voice was shaking, both from pain and—she assumed—from shock. "It's okay. I'll be fine."

"I know." Claire put away the silver nitrate and rummaged in her pockets, coming up with a pack of tissues, which she handed over. "Here."

He looked at her, gave her a weak flash of a smile, and took the packet from her. One after another, the tissues soaked red, but each successive one did so more slowly. By the time he'd used most of them, the wounds were sealed over—gruesome still, but steadily better.

"This isn't the first time, is it?" she asked. "You were expecting this. I could see how tense you were. It's about your marrying Eve. They're bullying you because of it."

Michael shrugged and scrubbed the last of the damp stains off his skin. "We all knew how they felt about it. Pretty much like Captain Obvious and his crew of humans-only believers feel, too. Everybody sees us as traitors to whatever their cause is."

"That's stupid. You two—you've been together for years!"

"Not *married* together. They're funny about that. In vampire circles, marrying someone is a huge deal . . . vampires being immortal and all. It hardly ever happens, and when it does, there's— power involved. The lesser partner gets elevated up to the status of the greater. So now Eve's technically got all the rights and powers and privileges that I do. And being Amelie's direct bloodline, that's kind of a big deal." He stuffed all the bloody tissues in his pocket and nodded to her. "Let's keep going. I don't like being a sitting duck around here."

Their escort hadn't waited for them, but he was standing in front of Amelie's office when they arrived, and he opened the door to shoo them inside. He didn't follow, and Claire heard the latch click shut with a finality that made her wonder if they were, in fact, locked in.

If they were, the receptionist inside gave no sign of it. Her name was Bizzie, and she'd been with Amelie a long time. She gave Claire a cool, impartial nod, and ignored Michael almost completely, though her gaze flicked quickly to the wounds on his face. She didn't ask what had happened. In fact, she didn't speak at all, which in Claire's experience was a little unusual; Bizzie had always been cordial in the past.

Things had changed.

Claire and Michael waited silently in the armchairs lining the small wood-paneled room, and Claire spent her time studying the portraits hanging high on the walls. Amelie was in one of them, looking just as she did now but with a more elaborate hairstyle that reminded Claire of movies she'd seen in high school about the French Revolution. Elegant in white satin, Amelie was shown lit by candles, and in her right hand was a mirror dangling negligently by her side. The fingers of her left hand rested on top of a skull.

Creepy and beautiful.

"The Founder will see you," Bizzie said, though Claire hadn't heard any phone or intercom. As Claire rose to her feet, the inner door swung open without a sound.

Deep breaths, Claire told herself. She didn't know why she was so nervous; she'd met with Amelie dozens of times, probably nearly a hundred by now. But somehow, this felt strongly like walking into a trap. She glanced back at Michael, and their eyes met and held.

He felt it, too.

Deep breaths, Claire thought again, and took the plunge.

*   *   *

The office looked eerily the same: high bookcases, big picture windows treated with anti-UV tinting to reduce damage from the sunlight, candles burning here and there. Amelie's desk was massive and orderly, and behind it, the Founder of Morganville sat with her hands folded on the leather blotter.

Behind her stood Oliver.

The two vampires couldn't have been more different. Amelie was polished, silky, pale haired, every inch a born ruler. Oliver, on the other hand, had the angular toughness of a warrior, and with his graying hair and ruthless smile, he might as well have been wearing armor as a turtleneck and jacket. Amelie's pantsuit was a pristine white silk, and it contrasted completely with his all-black—deliberately; Claire was certain of it.

Amelie was also wearing her hair down in flowing, gorgeous waves. Very *not* the old Founder.

Oliver had his hand on Amelie's shoulder, a gesture of easy familiarity that would have been odd in the time before the arrival, battle, and defeat of the draug. He and Amelie had been enemies, then unwilling allies, and then, finally—something else.

Something more dangerous, obviously.

Claire looked around, but the chairs that had once been in front of Amelie's desk, the ones for visitors, were gone. She and Michael would be expected to stand.

But first, apparently, they were expected to do something else, because Oliver watched the two of them for a moment, then frowned and said, "Pay proper respect, if you wish to speak with the Founder."

Amelie said nothing. She'd always been a bit of an ice queen, but now she was unreadable, all pale, perfect skin and cool, assessing eyes. There was no telling what she felt, if she felt anything at all.

Michael inclined his head. "Founder."

"I see you've been recently injured," she said. "How?"

"It's nothing."

"That doesn't answer my question."

"It's my problem. I'll handle it."

Amelie sat back in her chair and cast a glance upward at Oliver. "See to it that Henrik understands I do not condone this kind of behavior within these walls. Michael, you'd do well to answer my questions when I ask them next time."

"Since you already knew the answer, I don't see the point." He was almost as good at hiding emotions as Amelie. "If you really cared about stopping him and the others like him, you'd publicly acknowledge our marriage and put a stop to it."

"You didn't obtain permission from me, and it's my right as your blood sire to give or withhold it," she said. "I don't have to acknowledge anything you do without my blessing. And we've traveled this road before, to no good purpose. What brings you here, then?"

Claire cleared her throat and took a step forward. "I—"

Oliver interrupted her. "Greet the Founder properly, or you'll not utter another word."

Amelie could have quelled that; she could have just waved it away as she normally would have . . . but she didn't. She waited, her gaze on Claire's face, until Claire swallowed hard and bent her head forward just a little. "Founder," she said.

"You may speak, Claire."

Gee, thanks, Claire wanted to say with a liberal dose of sarcasm, but she managed to choke it back. Shane would have said it, which was why she hadn't let him come along on this little venture. "Thank you," she said, and tried to make herself sound truly grateful. "I came to talk to you about the identification cards."

Amelie's face did show emotion after all—anger. "I have heard all of the arguments that I am prepared to endure," she said. "The measure ensures that all Morganville residents have proper care in case of emergency, that their Protectors are properly identified, that they can be found in case they go missing. Whatever resentments you have come from a false sense that you are free to do as you will. You are not, Claire. No one is in this world."

"I thought you took Sam's goals seriously. You told me you'd make humans equal partners in Morganville, that we had rights just like vampires. You *told* me that!"

"I did," Amelie said. "And yet I find that where humans are allowed a little freedom, they will take more, until their very freedom destroys our way of life. If it comes to a choice, I must choose the survival of my own. Yours are certainly far too numerous as it stands. What is the count now, seven billion? You'll excuse me if I believe we might be at a slight numerical disadvantage."

"Is that why you're allowing hunting again?"

Oliver laughed. "A tempting side benefit, but no. Hunting is buried as deep in the vampire nature as the need to reproduce is in humans. It is not simply a thing we can turn off. For some, hunting allows them to control a dark and violent side that would be much more damaging. Think of a dammed-up river, with a flaw in the structure. Sooner or later, that torrent of water will break free, and the damage it does will be considerably worse than a slow and controlled release."

"You're talking about water! I'm talking about people's lives!"

"Enough," Amelie said flatly. "This is not a human concern. You and your friends need have no fear; the law does not touch you. The things you've done in Morganville have ensured my personal patronage for you, as you can see on your cards. And any vampire is free to refuse to hunt. Michael has done it. No doubt many will do so."

Somehow, relying on the goodwill of individual vampires wasn't what Claire could see as a positive solution, but it was pretty clear that Amelie wasn't interested in her opinions. "Then the humans need to know," Claire said. "They need to understand that going without a Protector means they're being hunted again. Let them at least have a chance to defend themselves!"

"Tell them if you wish," Oliver said, and smiled. "If it makes you feel safer to be prepared, tell them to go armed. Tell them to stay in groups. Tell them whatever you wish. It will not make any difference but to make the hunt more challenging."

"This is your doing, isn't it?" He just watched her without replying. Claire turned her attention back to Amelie. "You're going to let him destroy everything," Claire said, and locked her gaze on the Founder's. That was dangerous; Amelie had power, a lot of it, and even when she wasn't trying to project it, there was something truly frightening about looking deep into her eyes. "You're really going to let him turn this town into his own personal hunting preserve."

"You're always free to leave town, Claire," Amelie said. "I've said so before, and I've given you more than generous terms. I urge you to take the opportunity before you make me regret having given you so much . . . consideration. Remember, I can always withdraw Protection."

"Maybe I will leave! And what are you going to do then? Because I don't think Myrnin really likes any of your new ideas, and you can't control him, can you? But anyway, they're not really *your* ideas." Claire transferred her stare to Oliver. "Are they?"

Oliver went from standing still as a statue—if statues could smirk—to rushing at her full speed, a blur she instinctively flinched away from.

Michael got in the way, and shoved Oliver violently off course, into a side table, destroying a probably priceless antique vase. Oliver rolled to his feet, hardly slowed at all by the fall, and came at him.

"Enough," Amelie said, and Oliver just . . . froze. So did Michael. Claire felt a crushing sense of pressure in the room and realized that Amelie had just *made* them stop. It must have hurt, because even Oliver's face contorted in pain for a second. "I've had quite enough peasant-style brawling in my presence. Michael, your loyalty is misguided, and I've had enough of your thinking that your personal choices outweigh your duty to me. You owe me your *life*. If a choice is to be made, be very careful how you make it. A vampire alone is vulnerable to many things."

"I know," Michael said. "You can quit trying to threaten me. I'm not giving up the people I love, no matter what you do. And in the words of my best friend, bite me. Come on, Claire. We're not getting any favors from her."

She reached out to him, but in the next instant, his blue eyes went wide and desperately blank, and he went straight to his knees—driven there by the force of Amelie's fury. It felt like a storm, lashing over Claire as an afterthought, and she found herself on her knees next to him, reaching for his hand and holding it with shaking strength. He was trying not to crush hers, but it still hurt.

Amelie rose from behind her desk, took an elegant silver-coated letter opener from her desk, and walked to look down on Michael. As she turned the knife in her hand, thin wisps of smoke escaped; she wasn't invulnerable to the silver, just stronger than most.

"Don't test me," she whispered. "I have survived my father. Survived the draug. I will survive *you*. Learn your place, or die where you kneel, right now."

Michael somehow managed to laugh and turn his face up toward her. For the first time, Claire thought, he really looked like one of them.

Like a vampire.

"I know who I am, and I'm not one of *you*," he said. "Screw you."

She drove the letter opener down, and Claire had time to gasp in horror; she had a terrible, vivid flashback to the time she'd seen someone else stab Michael—in the earliest days of their friendship. He'd survived that. Not this. Not with silver. *No, I can't tell Eve this. No, please . . .*

Amelie drove the silver knife into the floor, to the hilt, an inch from Michael's knee. She rose gracefully, turned her back, and walked away, dismissing them both with a flip of her hand.

Oliver, after a long look at her that Claire couldn't read, said, "Count yourself lucky. Both of you, get out. Now."

Claire stumbled to her feet, still holding Michael's hand, and managed to get him up. He leaned heavily on her. He looked dazed, but his eyes were as crimson as the blood dripping from his nose and ears. He was, Claire thought, ready to go for Oliver's throat, so it was lucky he was too weak to try it. "Come on," she whispered to him. "*Michael!* Come on! You're supposed to be the calm one, remember?"

He closed his eyes, which was about all she sensed she was going to get from him in terms of agreement, so she half carried him to the door.

Which remained closed.

Behind her, Oliver said, "If you come here, you come as supplicants. Anything else, and next time, the knife won't miss."

Claire was smart enough to keep her *Screw you* to herself.

THREE

CLAIRE

G etting out of Founder's Square wasn't quite as bad as getting in, but with Michael staggering and only really able
to stand halfway through, Claire was worried that Henrik, or someone else with similar feelings, would step out to finish
the job Amelie and Oliver had started. He was hurt . . . maybe not
in terms of the obvious wounds, but she was convinced that the
blood that still stained his face near his nose and ears was a sign of
some kind of internal hemorrhage. She had no idea what to do for
him, but vampires could heal from most things without help.

Still, he probably was going to need blood, and she didn't want
to be the only source standing nearby if a sudden craving came
down hard. She'd seen that happen, and the aftermath. It might
not ruin their friendship, unless he actually killed her, but it would
make things very awkward around the dinner table.

"Can you drive?" she asked him anxiously as they arrived at the garage level. She kept a hand on his arm, though he was moving under his own power now; he hadn't said much at all, but now he nodded. "Are you okay?"

"No," he said. His voice sounded hoarse, as if he'd been screaming. "Not yet. Will be."

"You probably need a drink." She said it the matter-of-fact way she'd heard Eve phrase it, and he seemed relieved that he didn't have to bring it up. "I don't mind waiting in the car if you want to stop at the blood bank. Michael . . . I'm sorry. I didn't think it would go so . . ." *Wrong. Violent. Crazy.* But Shane somehow had intuited that, or he wouldn't have insisted on someone else going with her. Someone strong enough to fight off Oliver and Amelie . . . or who'd be willing to try.

If I'd had the machine finished, I could have used it. Canceled out her power. Maybe it would have worked. Maybe it would have even canceled out Oliver's influence on Amelie, made her go back to the old Founder, the one Claire sorely missed.

And maybe it would have only made things worse.

It humbled her to think how much danger Michael had put himself in, for her. And it showed just how much danger there was for all of them. Hannah had been right after all. There wasn't any point in trying.

In the car, finally, Claire felt safe enough to broach the subject she'd been frantically turning over in her mind during the long walk. "What's happened to Amelie? She wasn't like this. Could the draug have, I don't know, infected her? Done something to her?"

"Maybe," Michael said. He coughed, and it was a wet sound. Claire cringed. "Maybe it's got something to do with Oliver; he has the ability to influence people. She always kept him at a distance before. Now it's as though they're channeling Sid and Nancy."

"Who?"

Michael groaned. "It's sad how much you don't know about music, Claire. Sid Vicious? The Sex Pistols?"

"Oh, him."

"You have no idea who I'm talking about, do you?"

She smiled a little. "Not the least little bit."

"Remind me to play you some songs later. But anyway, if Myrnin said things were spinning out of control, he's not wrong. Amelie doesn't use that power she just pulled out on me, not unless things are really critical. Never just for her own personal amusement." He shuddered, and finally said, in a quiet voice, "She could have killed me, Claire. At least the part of me that isn't pure vampire. She could have made me into—I don't know, her meat puppet or something. She's got power like nobody else."

Claire swallowed, suddenly and sharply uneasy again. "But she didn't do it."

"This time," he said. "What if she decides that's the only way to make me obey the way she wants? I don't want to live like that, if she crushes everything in me that's *me*. Promise me, you and Shane, you'll . . . take care of it. If it happens."

"It won't."

"Promise."

"God, Michael!"

He was silent for a second, then said, "I'll ask Shane." Because they both knew Shane would understand that request, probably far too well.

And that he'd say yes.

"It's not going to happen," Claire said. "No way in hell, Michael. We won't let it happen."

He didn't tell her that it probably wouldn't be a thing she could control, but she already knew it anyway. She just felt better, and more in control, for saying it.

The drive to the blood bank was quiet, and Claire faced toward the blacked-out passenger window. In the aftermath of all the adrenaline, she felt numb, and exhausted, and—weirdly enough—really hungry. Michael went inside the back of the blood bank, through the vamps-only entrance, and came back with a small handheld cooler, which he handed her. She put it on the floor between her feet. "Blood supply's running low," he said. "They'll be sending out the Bloodmobile to collect tomorrow. Is Shane paid up?"

"Is he ever?" Claire rolled her eyes. "I'll get him in voluntarily in the morning. I'll donate, too." Claire, by Amelie's decree, had historically been free of the responsibility of giving blood, which was the tax humans paid in Morganville from age eighteen up; she'd been underage before, but even now that she was legal, she didn't have to contribute. She still did, mainly because the hospitals, not the vampires, were the ones that ran short in an emergency.

Shane had pointedly *not* been excluded from the tax rolls. Probably because of how much trouble he'd historically been in, in Morganville.

Michael sighed. "Do you mind if I . . . ?"

Claire opened the cooler and took out one of the blood bags. It was slightly warm, and heavy, and she tried to pretend it was a bag of colored water, one of those prop things they used in television shows.

But she still looked away when he bit into it.

It took only about a minute for him to drain it dry, and he looked around for a place to put the empty, then let her take it and return it to the cooler. "Sorry," he said. His apology sounded genuine. "I know that's probably not what you needed to see right now."

"All eating is gross," Claire said, "but we all have to do it. Anyway, I'm starving. Is Chico's still open?"

"You know if I get you Chico's, I have to get it for the house, right?"

"I'll pitch in."

Chico's Tacos was a relative newcomer to town, opened by a Morganville resident who'd taken a liking to something he'd tasted out of town in El Paso: delicious rolled tacos, soaked and floating in hot sauce, then topped with shredded cheese. Messy, yeah. Unhealthy, probably. But in taco terms, it was crack. Extra orders were mandatory.

Michael handled drive-through duties, forking over cash and receiving all of the goodies to hand off to Claire. It was still new for them to count *five* housemates; Miranda was only half-time, in that during the day she was insubstantial, but at night she was very much flesh and blood, able to walk around, talk, do chores, eat dinner. . . . It made very little sense to Claire, but the Glass House (like all the remaining Founder Houses original to the town) was capable of doing things that her science couldn't explain, no matter how far out of shape she stretched the boundaries.

When Michael had been killed within its walls, drained by Oliver, the house had preserved him—saved him, literally, like a file, only as a ghost. The Glass home was more powerful at night than during the day, so at night it could create a real flesh-and-blood form he could use to have half a life . . . but when dawn came, it melted away. It wasn't *real*, exactly, though Michael had said he could feel, eat, drink, do everything as if it were real, between dusk and dawn.

But to make that half-life truly permanent, he'd had to make a deal with Amelie and become fully vampire.

Miranda seemed to have inherited the same pluses and minuses. And she had no wish to become a vampire. In life, Miranda had been a lost little girl, cursed with a psychic gift that was as much creepy as it was informative; she'd been shunned all her life by most of the town, and even Eve—her best friend, maybe—hadn't been able to handle her some of the time.

Ghost-Miranda was blooming into a happy young lady, now that she no longer had the psychic powers and was able to have real friends. So Miranda got tacos, too.

"What are we going to tell Shane about what happened? Or Eve?" Claire asked as the familiar crunch of the car's wheels on gravel signaled they'd arrived home.

Michael parked, killed the engine, and spent a moment in thought before he said, "We're going to tell them everything. Anything else wouldn't be fair. And it could put them in a lot of danger if they think Amelie's still somehow got our backs."

It would upset Eve, and it would anger Shane, but he was right; keeping them in the dark was a sure path to disaster. You could protect people from harm, but not from *knowing*.

"Well," Claire said, "at least we have tacos. Everything goes better with tacos."

And the tacos did help. Even Shane, who met them at the door and glared at the cooler in Michael's hand, brightened up at the sight of the grease-stained paper bags Claire held. "You really know the way to a man's heart," he said, and grabbed them out of her hands.

"Between the ribs and angle up?" she said, and gave him a sweet, fast kiss when he looked shocked. "Hey, it's your joke. Don't blame me if I remember it."

"And you look like such a nice girl."

"Fine, if you're not into it, I'll just take those tacos back. . . ."

It devolved into keep-away with taco bags, which Shane of course would have won by virtue of sheer size and agility, except that Miranda sneaked up behind him and stole a couple by surprise, which sent him yelling in pursuit as she dashed off through the kitchen and into the living room. And then Eve was into it, and Claire had to fight to hang on to the two bags she had left.

In the end, it all somehow made it to the dining table. Eve broke out thick paper plates and forks and spoons, and Michael and Shane organized the drinks while Claire and Miranda put little taco boats at each of their place settings. It was all really warm and sweet and *home*, and Claire made sure as they were eating that Miranda got a couple of extra tacos that normally Shane would have grabbed as they passed. He pouted, but in a cute way.

It was when they were finishing up that Shane said, fauxcasually, "So I guess everything went okay today?"

Miranda licked the last of the hot sauce out of the bottom of the paper boat and raised her eyebrows. "What happened today? I never get to know anything." She was still physically a frail little thing, and Claire supposed that the girl's delicate, breakable look would never change now; ghosts didn't age, and no matter how many tacos she ate or Coca-Colas she guzzled, she'd never grow an inch or gain a pound. That was something a lot of girls dreamed of, Claire thought. Of course, those girls probably never thought about having to live their eternity trapped inside one house, living half a life, not even being able to shop or see a movie that wasn't brought in, or go out to eat . . . or date.

Miranda was never, ever going to date. That was probably the saddest thing of all. She probably hadn't ever even been kissed. Not once. And what was worse, she was living in a house with two *couples.*

Yeah. Living hell, Claire decided, and she elbowed Shane and gave Miranda the last taco. It seemed the least she could do.

Then she realized that Michael hadn't even started answering the question. Somehow, Claire had expected him to take the lead on it, but since he hadn't, suddenly everyone was staring at her, waiting.

Claire cleared her throat, took a drink of water, and said, "I guess I'll just get it over with. Hannah can't help about getting rid of the ID cards, or the hunting licenses. She's being thrown out of office. Oliver's a jerk. Amelie's turned into a Vampire with a capital V, and she nearly killed Michael to prove how badass she is now. Does that cover it, Michael?"

"Pretty much," he said.

That . . . didn't go over as well as she'd hoped. For a second, nobody said a word, and then everyone was trying to talk at once. Michael tried to put some kind of polish on what she'd said, but there was no changing the truth of it. Eve was sharply demanding to know what was meant by *nearly killed.* Shane was cursing and saying that he'd known it would be like this.

Even Miranda was timidly asking something that was lost in the general chaos.

"One at a time," Claire finally yelled, and that surprised them enough that they all fell silent. Surprisingly, it was Miranda who plunged ahead first.

"Are you feeling all right?" she asked Michael, and there was an edge of anxiety in her voice that surprised Claire . . . and then, didn't. After all, Miranda had never been kissed, and Michael couldn't help being a girl magnet. Claire felt a little relieved, really, because at least the girl didn't moon about Shane. Not that Shane would have noticed, or cared, but still.

Eve, on the other hand, seemed to ignore Miranda altogether; her gaze focused wholly on Michael's face. Her dark eyes were huge, and she'd gripped his left hand tightly with her right.

"I'm okay," he said, not to Miranda, but to Eve, and brought her hand to his lips to kiss it. "Claire might have been exaggerating a little."

"Not much," Claire muttered, but she ate a bite of taco and didn't object any louder.

"She's right, though," Michael continued. "Definitely, there's something wrong with Amelie and how she's handling things. It's not the Founder we've known; this is more the way Bishop acted. Maybe it's something to do with her near miss with the draug."

"Or maybe it's just that Oliver's in her pocket all the time," Shane said. "I'm saying *pocket* because there's a deceased minor present, but by pocket I mean pants."

Claire smacked him under the table on the side of the leg, hard, but she didn't disagree with the substance—just the presentation. "Oliver's a bad boyfriend," she agreed. "And she's listening to him way too much. That's why he's getting rid of Hannah; he doesn't want any disagreements on the Elders' Council. He just wants some rubber-stamping human body sitting at the table, to keep people in line by pretending they still have a voice."

"Can we go back to the issue of Michael nearly being killed?" Eve said. "Because I'm really not okay with that. What happened?"

"I didn't agree with Amelie on something." Michael shrugged. "It's not the first time, right? Eve, seriously, don't fuss."

Eve gazed at him a moment longer, then shifted her attention to Shane. "You buying this no-big-deal crap?"

"Nope."

"Then what are we going to do about it?"

"Oh, I don't know. Kill 'em all; feed their carcasses to chickens? Hell, Eve, what *can* we do? We got by this long because we're lucky and we've had the right vampires on our side. Now the same vamps are on the other side of the line. What've we got going for us?"

"Well, we're all smart, strong, and fashion forward," Eve said. "Except for you."

He saluted her with a fork full of dripping taco and shoveled it into his mouth. "You forgot handsome," he said. "Plus thoughtful, kind, brave . . ."

"Shane, the closest you ever got to the Boy Scouts was when that whole troop of them beat you up in fourth grade," Eve shot back.

"Be fair—they were Brownies, and those girls were soccer-trained. Mean kickers." Shane took a sip of his drink and changed the subject. "We don't have a lot of things counting up in our favor right now, do we? No offense, Mike. You know I love you and Eve, but you two getting married hasn't made life around here any easier; most people avoid us, the pro-human side hates us, the pro-vampire side hates us, too. Now we don't have the Ice Queen on our side, either. Strategically, I guess our whole position boils down to *this sucks.*"

"We've got Myrnin," Claire said. "He doesn't like how things are heading, either. He'll help."

"Oh yeah, because Myrnin's always reliable," Eve said. "Yes, Shane, I said it for you."

"Thanks for reading my mind."

"Thanks for making it so simple."

Shane threw a napkin at her, she deflected it into Miranda's lap, and Miranda threw it to Michael, who didn't even look up as he snatched the wadded-up paper out of the air and lobbed it to Claire.

Who missed, of course.

"Loser does the dishes," Michael said. "New rule."

"Awesome," Shane agreed, and then got less cheerful about it. "Wait—it's all paper plates and stuff."

"Hey, you could have lost if you'd thought about it."

Miranda was the one who spoiled the moment by asking, in a very worried voice, "What *are* you going to do about stopping Amelie? I mean, if she's really dangerous now?"

Eve put her arm around the girl and hugged her. "Claire will have an awesome plan, and we'll all make it work. You'll see."

Yeah, Claire thought gloomily, as she gathered up the trash. *No pressure.*

She was mostly done when she found Miranda standing next to her, handing her stuff. Eve, Michael, and Shane had all moved off, and the younger girl gave her a quick, crooked smile. "I don't mind," she said. "I like to help. Is it okay?"

"Sure," Claire said. "Thanks."

"I wanted to ask you something, actually. I heard Shane say something about those people who came to town. Those people with the TV show."

"Oh, right. Angel and Jenna." And Tyler, who did all the work. "What about them?"

"You don't think they'll, ah, find anything, do you? What if they do? What if they get the word out on Morganville?"

"It won't happen," Claire said. "Even if they do find any-thing—which I really doubt—I don't think they'd be able to get it out of town. Why? Are you worried about their finding out about you?"

"Not—not really." Miranda looked oddly embarrassed. "I

just—they must have met other ghosts before. I just wondered if maybe I could talk to them about it. About what's normal."

"I'm not sure there's any such thing as normal, when it comes to ghosts, especially around here," Claire said doubtfully. "Mir, you're not thinking of trying to get them over here, are you?"

"Well, at night, they wouldn't see anything weird. . . ."

"No. No, definitely no. What if Myrnin comes popping in through a portal in the wall, or some random vamp decides to drop in for a visit? How do we explain that? And Michael? They'd notice something strange about him, wouldn't they?"

"Oh," Miranda said. "Right. I hadn't thought about that. Okay, then. I just—I just wish I could make more friends."

Claire hip-bumped her and grinned. "We're not enough for you?"

She got a smile in response, but it wasn't a very certain one. "Sure," Miranda said softly, and walked away.

Oh dear.

That, Claire thought, might be a problem.

The blood bank in Morganville had odd hours—for instance, they'd instituted twenty-four-hour donations, which meant that Claire was able to shove Shane out of bed and into pants, shoes, and shirt at four a.m., and drag him, half asleep, into the place to drain a pint of blood before he was too awake to protest. She gave a second pint, just to make things even, and took him home to pile back into bed. He refused to go to his own, which was just pure stubbornness, and curled his warm, strong body next to her under the covers for another two hours until she had to rise to go to school. It might have been more sexy, except that he fell asleep within about five minutes, and she held out for only a few ticks more.

Seven a.m. came way too early, but Claire dragged herself yawning through the morning routine: shower, dress, sleepwalk to Common Grounds for a mocha. That was where she picked up the news that Mayor Hannah Moses was "stepping down for personal reasons" and that a write-in election would be held over the weekend.

The college students were, of course, oblivious to what that meant, but there was a stack of the flyers about it near the register, and Claire grabbed one. The press release was boring and dry, and there was a write-in form right on the bottom of the flyer, with instructions to drop it off at City Hall in the appropriate ballot box.

Claire stuffed the flyer in her backpack, grabbed her coffee, and headed out for class. Luckily, she had a different schedule of professors today, ones she actually liked, and sailed through the morning high on caffeine and challenging discussions on condensed-matter physics, which was the study of exactly how atoms combined and recombined to make liquids, solids, and states that, theoretically, hadn't been seen. Except she *had* seen them. Myrnin had invented them, and he used them as transportation hubs around the town. He called them doors, whereas Claire called them portals, but it boiled down to one thing: traveling from *here* to *there* and skipping the in-between.

So she kind of had a head start on that concept, and calculations.

She had a break at noon, and went to the coffee shop on campus. It was Eve's day to work there, instead of at Common Grounds; she was a good-enough barista that she could work anywhere she wanted, and she liked to see different people on the other side of the counter. Plus, Eve always insisted, she liked these little weekly vacations away from Oliver's scowling.

She didn't look especially happy now, though, Claire thought, as she waited in line. As the guy ahead of her walked away with his coffee, Claire leaned her elbows on the counter and said, "Are you okay?" She put the back of her hand to Eve's forehead. "I think you must have a fever."

"What?" Eve looked tired under the makeup, as if she hadn't slept much. "What are you talking about?"

"Mr. Hottie McGorgeous just walking away. He was way into you, and you didn't even smile at him."

Eve held up her hand and tapped the ring on her finger. "Anti-flirting device," she said. "It works."

"Oh, come on—it wouldn't keep you from smiling!"

"I just wasn't feeling it." But that wasn't it, and Claire knew it. There was a piece of paper on the counter, turned facedown, but the water had soaked through in places, and she saw tombstones drawn on it. Before Eve could stop her, Claire reached over and took it.

They were the same four tombstones as on the flyers that kept appearing at the Glass House, only this one was more personal. It had an arrow pointing at Eve's grave, with the words, *Soon, bitch* written above it.

Eve shrugged. "It was on the counter when I got here for work."

"Sorry," Claire said. "People are asses."

"Mostly," Eve agreed. "Mocha, then?"

"Just hot cocoa." Claire took the flyer she'd grabbed at Common Grounds out of her bag and put it on the counter, avoiding the drips of spilled drinks. "Did you see this?"

Eve mixed the cocoa and read the paper at the same time, which was pretty impressive. "Write-in candidates. Well, that's an easy one. They'll just pick whoever they want and write the ballots the way they want them to come out. And we bother voting why?"

"We can't let that be the way things go," Claire said earnestly.

"We have to get people together to demand a free and fair election, counted by humans."

"You have an impressive amount of crazy in that head. How exactly would you do that? Because I guarantee you, if you set up a Facebook page, they'll kill it before you can refresh the screen. And don't even *think* about Twitter."

It was true; the vampires had a headlock on the electronic communications in town, and that stumped Claire for a moment. "Old school," she said finally. "Captain Obvious is still around, right?" Captain Obvious was a little like the Spartacus of Morganville. . . . He was the guy in charge of organizing and leading the human resistance, in whatever form it took. Captain Obvious as an individual usually didn't last long, but a new one was always waiting in the wings.

"Well, in theory, I guess," Eve said. "Last one ran for it before the barriers went back up around town. Last I heard, though, there was nobody in charge of the human underground anymore, so it's pretty much done for . . . not that it ever made any difference in the first place. Bunch of disorganized losers, mostly. Well, except for that one time they saved our lives. But if he's still around, maybe he's the one sending us the die-already notices, so maybe not an asset."

Claire blinked and sipped the hot cocoa Eve handed her. Nobody was in line behind her, so she lingered at the counter. "The old Captain Obvious was outed, anyway. Everybody knew who he was. What if there was a new one? A secret one?"

"Sweetie, I'm pretty sure I'd have heard. I hear *everything.*" But Claire wasn't listening now; her brain was firing off a chain of brilliant, random flashes, putting things together, planning—until Eve snapped fingers in front of her eyes and she realized Eve was saying something along the lines of *Earth to whatever planet you're circling.*

"Sorry," Claire said. She smiled slowly. "I think I've got it."

"Swine flu? The answer to cold fusion? An aneurysm?"

"How do we get vampires not to ignore the results of the election?"

"You can't."

"Unless the results are what they want to see," Claire said. "Then they'd just announce them, right? They wouldn't bother to fake anything."

"True." Eve was eyeing her doubtfully. Very doubtfully. "What the hell are you thinking, CB?"

"We write in someone who is exactly what they want: a human connected to an old Morganville family. But one who isn't afraid to get in the faces of the vamps."

"Okay, maybe we need to walk this backward, because you're not making any sense at all," Claire said, and held Eve's stare for long enough that she saw the light begin to—kind of dreadfully—dawn. "Shane?" her best friend said, and covered her ink blue lips with one pale hand. "You can't run *Shane* for mayor. Come on! Shane's the exact opposite of political!"

"I'm not talking about him," Claire interrupted. "But there's somebody else in this town who's perfectly qualified. And perfectly unqualified at the same time. And if anyone knows about causing chaos in this town, it's her."

Silence. Dead, utter silence. Eve blinked, blinked again, and finally said, "What?"

But Claire was already walking away, humming softly under her breath, feeling for the first time in months that she had something actually going the right way in Morganville.

Ironic, really.

FOUR

CLAIRE

)

True to her word, Monica came to the gym ready to work, which was a bit of a shocker; Claire hardly recognized her. No makeup. Dark hair tied back in a plain, thick ponytail. Okay, the tight workout gear was still name brand, and her athletic shoes had a basketball star's name on them, but this was definitely Monica unplugged.

And she was shockingly good at punching things. Even Shane was impressed, after about two minutes of watching her hit the heavy bag with a flurry of well-placed jabs, elbows, and kicks.

"She's not bad," Shane admitted as Monica continued to pummel the target. "Good form. Hell of a right."

"Yeah, she got it beating up other kids, didn't she?"

Shane sent her a slightly embarrassed look. "I'm all for peace and love, babe, but I'm just talking technique, here." He went back to studying Monica with calm assessment, arms folded. "She's been working on it."

She had, no doubt about it. When Monica finished on the heavy bag after the required five minutes, panting and sweating, she sent Shane a triumphant look as she swigged some water. "See?" she said. "Not bad, right?"

"Don't get cocky," he said. "Hey, Aliyah? Got a minute?" He gestured to a tall, rangy girl who was shadow punching in the corner. She turned, and her dark eyes fell on Monica, and widened. "Monica needs a sparring partner."

"Wait," Monica said, and turned to him. "I thought *you* were—"

"I'm the sensei here, and you fight who I say you'll fight," Shane said, with entirely too much relish.

"But she—"

"Problem, Monica?" His smile was brutal, and Monica pressed her lips into a thin line and shook her head. She walked to the roped-off sparring area as Aliyah took her place inside.

"Let me guess," Claire said. "Monica bullied Aliyah."

"You couldn't throw a rock in Morganville without hitting somebody who fits that description," Shane said. "But nobody's bullied Aliyah in, I don't know, at least five years—okay, let's have a clean fight, girls!"

It wasn't.

Aliyah took about ten seconds to lay Monica out. It was a violent ballet of fake, strike, fade—almost surgical, really. Two fast, accurate punches—face and midsection—and a leg sweep, and Monica was on her back, staring dazed at the ceiling while Aliyah danced backward without a mark on her. Aliyah dropped her defense and looked at Shane, who shrugged.

"Thanks," he said. "Tells me what I needed to know."

He climbed in the ring as Aliyah got out, and he crouched down next to Monica, who was making no effort at all toward getting up. "Something broken?" he asked. She shook her head. "Then stand up."

"Help?" She held out her hand, but he straightened up and backed off. Monica groaned. "You son of a—"

"C'mon, you whiner. Up."

She climbed clumsily back to her feet and braced herself against the ropes a moment. "That bitch sucker-punched me." She felt her lip. "If I swell up—"

"You'll deserve it," Shane said, "because your defense was crap. Are you complaining, or training?"

Claire leaned against the pole and watched, mostly; Shane was a good teacher, patient but not kind, and he showed Monica with brutal and cheerful efficiency that bullying didn't really equal fighting. It was a relatively short lesson—about an hour—but at the end of it Monica was a disheveled, staggering mess. When Shane finally said, "Okay, enough for today," she flopped backward onto the floor as if she might never get up under her own power again.

"You," she said between heaves for breath, "are a total *ass*, Collins. You enjoyed that."

"Absolutely," he said, and grinned, but the grin faded fast. "No bull, Monica: you're not bad, you've got strength, but you've never been pushed. Fighting the vamps isn't like taking Jimmy's lunch money in fourth grade. You need to be fast, fearless, and accurate, and you need to understand that there's no giving up, because if they even smell it on you, you're done."

"I can do it," she said. But she said it flat on the floor. "I'm not quitting."

"Good," he said. "Because the opportunity to hit you is pretty much every Morganville kid's dream job. Oh, and you're paying me."

"I'm *what?*" She lifted her head from the canvas and stared at him, and Claire had to choke back a laugh at the look on Monica's face.

"Paying," he said. "For training. What, you thought I'd do this for free? Are we friends?"

"Fine," she said, and dropped her head again. "How much?"

"Twenty an hour."

"You're *kidding* me. You make about seven an hour on your best day!"

"That's when I'm doing honest labor, like cleaning sewers. Working with you means charging a premium."

She wearily lifted a hand and flipped him off, but said, "Okay, fine. Twenty an hour."

"Twenty-five now that you were rude about it."

Monica sent him a filthy glare, rolled over, and limped slowly off to the showers. Shane watched her go with a smile of pure satisfaction. "Gold," he said. "Pure gold."

Claire kissed him. "Don't gloat too hard," she said. "She's going to get better."

"I know. But I can enjoy it while she's not."

Claire took off after Monica for the locker room.

She found the other girl stripping off her workout clothes and examining in the full-length mirror the discolored places that were going to form bruises. Claire immediately felt a surge of awkwardness and didn't know where to look; Monica had an almost perfect body, sculpted and waxed and tanned. Claire flashed back to her awkward early-admission high school years, where showering with the pretty girls had been an exercise in merciless mockery.

But she wasn't even on Monica's radar, except as a second pair of eyes. "Hey," Monica said, without even focusing on her. "Do you think this is going to leave a mark?" She pointed to a red area on her ribs, just under her left breast.

"Probably."

"Dammit. I was going to go to the pool. Now I have to wear a one-piece." She made it sound like a burka. "So, pre-school, did you follow me in here to confess your gay love, or what?"

"What? No. And never you."

"Oh yeah? You got a girl-crush on someone else?"

Claire smiled. "Well, I lost my heart to Aliyah back there when she put you on the floor. . . ."

"Bite me, Danvers. I need a shower." Monica grabbed her soap, shampoo, razor, and a towel, and headed for the open tiled area. Claire followed at a distance and sat out of the range of splashing on the teak bench. "Seriously, are you stalking me? Because you're not doing it right."

"I need to talk to you."

"It's not mutual."

Monica turned the spray on and stepped into the steaming water. Claire waited until she'd foamed up her hair, rinsed it, put in the conditioner, and propped her leg up on the step to run the razor over it before she tried again. "I have a proposition for you."

"Again with the girl love."

"I want you to run for mayor."

Monica jerked, yelped, and blood trickled down her leg. She hissed, rinsed it off, and glared at Claire. "Not funny."

"Not meant to be," Claire said. "I'm really serious. People like familiar names, and there's no name for mayor more familiar than Morrell. Your grandfather was the mayor, your dad, your brother. . . ."

"Look, much as I'd like to be thought of as political royalty, that's not how it works. People have to actually *like* you to vote for you. I'm not stupid enough to believe they do." But she was listening while she soaped her leg again and shaved. Claire had known she would, because there was nothing Monica craved more than power and popular acceptance—and those things came standard with the plaque on the mayor's door.

"I think I can make it work," Claire said. "We could put up signs asking people to write you in on the ballot. You've got people who owe you favors, right? And the vamps would like it. They think you're easy to control."

"Hey!"

"I said they *think* you are. But you wouldn't be here working with Shane if you were all that easy, would you?" Claire cocked her head. "Missed a spot."

"Would you just get to the point?"

"Morganville needs a new Captain Obvious," she said. "And Morganville needs a new mayor the vamps would approve. You could be both."

"What, like a secret identity?" Monica laughed, but it was a dry, bitter sound. "You're such an idiot."

"Shane is already teaching you how to fight," Claire pointed out. "You already know how to target people you don't like. Why not do it for the sake of the town for a change? Captain Obvious has always been kind of a bully, just a bully on the side of the humans."

Monica had nothing to say to that. She simply frowned as she rinsed the last of the soap from her right leg, did the left, and then cleared the conditioner out of her hair. When she shut off the water, Claire threw her the towel. Monica dried off and wrapped up, and finally shrugged. "It'd never work," she said.

"Maybe not," Claire said, "but you owe me. And you're going to run for office."

Monica studied herself in the mirror, then smiled as she met Claire's eyes. "Well," she said, "I *would* make an awesome mayor. I'm very photogenic."

"Yeah," Claire agreed, straight-faced. "Because that's what really counts."

Shane didn't take it well.

"Monica," he kept saying, all the way home. "Wait, let's back up. We're going to campaign for Monica. For mayor."

"Yes," Claire said. "I'm sorry, why is this so hard to understand?"

"Did you trip in the shower and hit your head or something? *Monica Morrell*. I'm pretty sure we still hate her. Let me check my notes—yep, still hate her."

"Well," Claire said, "you're taking money to teach her to fight, so you sort of don't *hate* hate her anymore. And I'm not sure I do, either. She's just sort of annoyingly pathetic now that she doesn't have her position and her posse."

"And you want to turn around and give her back, let's see, a position, with a title and a salary, and the power to make the life of everybody in this town a living hell? She's not that sad a case."

"Shane, I'm serious about this. We need to get someone on the Elders' Council the vampires can't control, and someone who's human, and someone people might vote for. She's a Morrell. She'd get the sympathy vote because of her brother."

He scrubbed his face with both hands as she unlocked the front door of the Glass House. "*Such* a bad idea," he said. "In so, so many ways. Tell me we're not actually helping her."

"Well, I did kind of promise to make signs."

She expected him to kick about that, too, but instead, he got a slow, evil smile on his face and said, "Oh please. Allow me."

"Shane—"

"Trust me."

She didn't.

And sure enough, two hours later, she heard Eve's outraged scream coming from downstairs. She rushed into the living room and saw Shane holding . . . a poster. It was a vivid neon blue thing that read, in block letters, WHY VOTE FOR THE LESSER OF TWO EVILS? VOTE MORRELL!, and it had the saintliest picture of Monica that she'd ever, ever seen beneath it. Honestly, it couldn't have looked more angelic if Shane had Photoshopped a halo on it.

It also had one of those bright yellow callout stars in the corner that read ENDORSED BY CAPTAIN OBVIOUS! HUMAN APPROVED!, plus a copy of the write-in ballot with Monica's name written boldly in marker.

It was simultaneously the funniest thing Claire had ever seen, and the most appalling.

Eve couldn't seem to think of anything to say. She just stared . . . first at the poster, then at Shane, then back to the poster, as if she couldn't imagine a world in which this had happened. Finally, she said, "I really, really hope this is a joke. If it isn't, Monica's going to kill you. And then she'll wrap you in that poster and bury you."

"What's wrong with it?" Shane asked, and looked down at the paper. "I know, blue wasn't my first choice, but I figured hot pink would be overkill."

"Okay, I need a recap. Why exactly are you making a poster to elect Monica for mayor? Did I miss a step, or wake up in Opposite World, or . . . ?"

"It's Claire's plan," he said. "I'm just the graphic designer. She's the campaign manager."

Eve collapsed on the couch and put her face in her hands. "You're insane. You've gone insane. Too much stress. I knew one of us would break someday. . . ."

"Monica's perfect," Claire said. "Eve, really, she is. Think about it. And hey, if you want, you could be Captain Obvious."

"Me," Eve repeated, and gave a dry, strangled laugh. "Yeah, sure. Sure."

"Hey," Shane said. He propped the poster in the corner, and—unexpectedly, at least to Claire—dropped to one knee in front of Eve. He took her hands and dragged them down so he could see her face. "Look at me. You're the original rebel around here, Eve. Hell, you were a malcontent before I was. Before Michael. Before Claire. Most of these Captain Obvious wannabes half assed it because in their hearts they were regular guys, pissed off at not having everything they wanted when they wanted it. That isn't rebellion; it's just selfishness. But you're not like that. If you wanted to be Captain Obvious, you'd be real."

He meant it. No mocking, no digs, no friendly banter; he sincerely meant that, and Eve took in a deep, ragged breath as she stared back. She shook her head, once. "I can't, Shane."

"Yeah," he said. "You could be. But only if you really want to." He said it without drama, without even any special emphasis, just stating a simple fact. "C'mon. Pizza's getting cold."

"Michael's going to kill you both," Eve said, and followed him as he stood up and walked to the table, where Claire remembered what she was doing and set down plates. "Kill you so very, very dead."

But she was wrong, because when Michael showed up—about fifteen minutes later, coming out of the kitchen in that silent vampire-stealthy way he sometimes did, when he forgot his company manners—he took a long look at the poster, cocked his head, and said, "Wrong picture."

Shane cast Eve a look of evil triumph. "Well, I would've used her senior yearbook pic, but she looked like a Spice Girls reject. Anything else?"

"There is no Captain Obvious."

"That's your objection?" Eve said, dropping her half-eaten pizza back to the plate. "Out of everything on the poster, including—oh, I don't know, Monica?—that's your problem with it?"

"He spelled her name right. I actually like the 'lesser of two evils' motto; it really captures the spirit." Michael had brought his own pizza, and one of his opaque sports bottles. Pizza and blood, a combo only a vampire could love; trying not to think about it much, Claire added some crushed red pepper to her slice. "And to be fair, I did object to the picture first. That one makes her look way too sweet."

"I think that was intentional," Claire said. "Everybody knows—"

"There's a new Captain Obvious," Shane interrupted.

"Yeah?" Michael took a giant bite of crust and cheese and meat, then mumbled, "Who?"

Shane silently pointed to Eve, who swatted his hand away. So did Claire. And Michael choked, coughed, grabbed his sports bottle and swigged.

Eve said, "I'm so very not. Ever."

"No," Michael said, and coughed again, so violently Claire wondered if vampires could actually choke to death. Probably not. They didn't really need to breathe, after all; they'd just have to stop talking until they could clear their throats. "Hell no. Not you."

And that, Claire thought, was his first mistake, because Eve, instead of being relieved that he was supporting her general objection, looked at him with a sudden frown. "No? *Por qué,* Miguelito?"

"Because, well . . ." Michael stumbled over putting it into words. "I mean, Captain Obvious . . ."

"Is what, always a guy? That's what you're going with?"

"No, not—it's just that you—uh . . ." Michael leaned back and looked at Shane. "Help me out."

Shane held up both hands in silent surrender. "On your own."

"Look, being Captain Obvious makes you a target, and I don't want you to be—"

Eve interrupted him again, rising her chin in challenge. "Don't want me to be in charge? Out front? Taking risks? Have you *seen* the tombstone flyers people keep leaving us?"

"Yes," he said. "And I'm scared, because I love you. And it's going to be dangerous. You know that without my telling you."

"She knows," Claire said, "but you shouldn't tell her she *can't.*"

Michael was starting to get really concerned. Eve reached over and took his hand.

"Relax," she said, and held his gaze. "I know I *could* do it. But I won't. I know it would put you in a bad position, for one thing. Props for not saying that, by the way."

"It wouldn't matter what happened to me," he said, and brushed the hair back from her face with gentle fingers. "You know that."

"Okay, you're making me lose my pizza," Shane said, and pitched a napkin at him, and a paper war began, flying on all sides until Claire waved the last surviving unthrown one in a sign of surrender.

So it was all okay, then. For now.

One thing about pizza was that it made for an easy cleanup,

again—paper plates and paper boxes, and some glasses dumped in the dishwasher. Miranda had stayed in her room, watching movies; she was still fascinated with their having so many of them, and it was shocking how many of the classics, such as *Star Wars*, she'd never seen before. Claire left Michael to cleaning up, since it was his turn, and considered joining Shane on the couch (he and Eve were bickering over which video game to play, because she was heartily sick of shooting zombies and he never was) but the lure of study was just too much.

That made her weird. She was aware of that.

After an hour or so, she became aware of a faint tapping, and for a moment she thought it was at the door of her bedroom (and that it might, miraculously, be Shane choosing her over zombies), but no, the sound was at her window, the one facing the big tree at the back of the house. It was full dark now, with stars set like diamonds in the dark blue velvety sky; here in the high desert it was so clear, she could even see the faint, cloudy swirls of galaxies. The sky seemed close enough to touch.

So was Myrnin, standing balanced on a tree limb that was far too slender for his weight. If she hadn't known better, she'd have thought he was floating in midair, but not even vampires could accomplish that. No, he was just being incredibly graceful, and ignoring laws of physics that were inevitably going to protest.

"Open," Myrnin said. "Hurry up, girl. Open the window. This branch won't"—he stopped as there was a sharp crack, and the branch sagged under his feet—"hold me for long!" He finished his sentence in a rush as she jerked up the window sash.

He lunged forward through the opening just as the branch broke free and crashed through the leaves to the ground below. Claire got out of his way. Vampires were nimble. He didn't need help, and just now, she wasn't feeling especially like helping him, anyway.

Myrnin hit the floor, rolled, and came with fluid grace back to a standing position. He struck a pose. "I suppose you are wondering what brings me here like this, in secret."

"Not really. But I see you found your shoes, thank God," Claire said. Glancing down at the bright white patent leather loafers on his feet, he shrugged.

"I think they belonged to a pastor, perhaps. All I could locate," he said. "No idea what's carried the rest of my shoes away. Perhaps Bob has developed a taste for footwear, which would be most interesting. Albeit alarming."

"Bob the Spider."

"Yes."

"That's . . . not too likely. Please tell me you washed them."

"The shoes?"

"Your feet. Do you know what kind of diseases are all over alleys?"

He gazed at her with perfect stillness for a second, then said, "I saw the campaign poster on the porch outside. I'm not sure whether to applaud you for your initiative or box your ears. *Monica Morrell?* Really?"

"I know it seems weird."

"Weird? It seems *insane,* and believe me, when I am telling you that, it's worth taking seriously, dear girl. I expected you to put forth a real candidate."

"Can you think of anybody who could really do the job? If Hannah Moses couldn't manage it, nobody else has a shot, anyway," Claire said. "Monica will get the votes, just because, well, her brother died in office. And her father. And she's a Morrell. People mostly just vote for what's familiar, even if it's wrong."

Myrnin gazed at her, and he just looked . . . miserable. Defeated, really. "Unfortunately, I cannot refute your logic. Then we're finished," he said. "The grand experiment is done, and all hope is lost. I suppose I must make preparations to go away, then."

"What?"

"Claire, attend: if this madness proceeds unchecked, there is only one way for this to end, and that is in blood, fire, and fury. Amelie and Oliver have formed what psychologists would call a *folie à deux*, and their indulgences will lead to cruelty, and cruelty will lead to slaughter, and worst of all, slaughter will lead to the discovery of vampires in this modern age. I've seen it before, and I won't be caught up in the inevitable aftermath. Best to flee now, before the pitchforks and torches and scientists come calling. That is, if the two of them don't have a bitter and blackened falling-out first, and destroy the town in their rage."

"Myrnin!"

"I mean it," he said. "There is a reason that I've tried to keep Amelie and Oliver apart. Opposites do not merely attract. A chemist of your skill should know that quite often, they violently explode. Go while you still can, Claire, and take all your friends. In a matter of weeks, it would not be a fit place for you to call home anyway." He seemed almost sad now. "I have liked this home. Very much. It grieves me to leave it behind, and I fear I will never find a place that is as tolerant of my . . . eccentricities."

He really did mean it, and it shocked her. He'd always been a little cavalier about danger, even his own; he wasn't someone who ran away easily. In fact, he'd persuaded the other vampires to stand their ground against the draug, to *protect* Morganville.

How could he want to run away now, from so little?

"Well," she said, "you can go if you want, I guess, but I can't."

"Won't," he corrected primly. "You can leave whenever you like. Amelie has said so, and as far as I am aware, she never countermanded that."

"She said I could go *alone*. As in she insists that Michael, Eve, and Shane stay here. I'm not leaving them behind, especially not if you think it's going to get dangerous. What kind of friend—what kind of *girlfriend*—would I be if I did that?"

"One with a sense of self-preservation," he said, and gave her an off-kilter, fond smile. "And that would be so unlike you. You're always caring about the strays and outcasts among us, myself in-cluded. You really are a very odd girl, you know; so little sense of what is good for *you*. Perhaps that's what I find fascinating about you. Vampires, you know, have such an iron-strong sense of self-preservation; we are the ultimate narcissists, I suppose, in that we see nothing wrong with others dying to save us. But you—you are our strange mirror opposite."

"Coming from you, I don't know how to take that, and on the subject of strange and not at all appropriate, could you *please* stop dropping into my bedroom in the middle of the night?"

"Oh, did I?" He looked around vaguely. "I suppose I did. Sorry. Well. If you won't leave this place, arm yourself heavily for as long as you stay," he said. "Don't go anywhere alone. And make alternate plans to flee when that becomes necessary."

"Myrnin—you're scaring me," Claire said, and reached out. "Please, tell me what's going on!"

He took her hand and raised it to his mouth in an old-fashioned gesture that made her skin tingle, especially when she felt the cool brush of his lips against her skin. His eyes were very dark in the dim light of her study lamp, and she didn't think he'd ever looked more . . . human. Crazy, maybe, but so very human.

"I hope I *am* scaring you," he said. "When things seem calm-est, that is the time you should fear the most; it's when you have the most to lose. It's not your enemies who are likeliest to hurt you. It is, always, those you trust. And you have trusted Amelie too far."

He hadn't let go of her hand, and she was starting to feel flushed and awkward about it. "I've trusted you, too," she said. And he gave her a sad, slightly manic smile.

"Yes, and that too is a mistake," he said. "As you've known from the first moment you met me, I am not reliable."

"I think you are," Claire said softly. "I really do. Myrnin— please. Please don't go away. You—you matter. To me."

There was just a flicker of warmth, *something*, and for a moment she thought . . . But then Myrnin's face shut down, and he let go of her hand. Where his fingers had touched hers, her skin felt ice-cold.

"Don't," he said. "It's dreadfully unfair to say things like that when this is likely the last time we will speak, and we both know you don't mean what you say. It's pure selfishness that you want to keep me here." His tone had a harder edge than she was used to hearing from him, and his expression was deathly still.

She felt an unexpected surge of anger. "Didn't you just accuse me of not being selfish enough?"

"Don't play at word games with me. I was a master of it before your country even existed."

"You can't just *go*! Where will you—"

"Blacke," he said, cutting her off. "For a start. Morley and I do not get along well, but he and the quite-frightening librarian woman have built a rough approximation of a town where vampires are welcome. It will do until I gather resources to settle elsewhere more congenial. You'd do better to think of yourself. Without me to help protect you, you are likely to end up dead, Claire. I should regret that. You've been the least useless apprentice I've ever had."

"That's it? That's all you're going to say? I'm the *least useless?*"

It burst out of him in a furious, low-voice rush. "Yes, of course that's all I'm going to say, because there's no point in it, no point at all in telling you that I'm *lonely,* that it's been so long since I could discuss books and theories and science and metaphor and alchemy and philosophy, and that is a desperately lonely thing, Claire. Even for someone who has killed to stay alive, there's a point where life— where existence—just seems . . . worthless, without some deeper connection. Do you understand?"

She was afraid to, really, but she gulped down a deep breath, and said, "You're saying that you care for me."

Myrnin froze, staring at her. He really was amazing, she thought; when he had that light in his eyes, it was possible to see past the crazy behavior and clothing chaos and recognize him as just . . . beautiful. The longing in his face was breathtaking.

But he said, in a low voice, "Not as you would understand it. What I admire in you is . . . intellectual. Spiritual."

She actually laughed a little. "You love me for my mind."

He sighed. "Yes. In a sense."

"Then stay."

"And watch you torn apart between Amelie, Oliver, and this town? Helpless to stop it?" He shook his head. "Better I go."

"No," she said, and grabbed at his sleeve. The old fabric of his jacket had an odd texture to it—cloth that had survived a hundred years or more past its makers. He could have avoided her, of course, but he didn't. He simply waited. "You can't go! You fought the draug to save the town!"

"I won't fight Amelie, and for as long as Oliver holds sway over her, she's dangerous to us all. So what do you propose I do? They'll come for me, sooner or later; I've always been a thorn in Oliver's side, and he'll want me dealt with before long. If I'm lucky, he'll do it before he comes after you and your friends, relieving me of the burden of standing by for that."

"Amelie won't let him hurt you."

"Won't she?" Myrnin's face set hard, and he seemed to be remembering something very unpleasant. "Oliver has a talent for corruption. He had the same skill in breathing life. The atrocities men committed in his name were legion and legendary, and those were mere mortals acting on his behalf. Vampires can be infinitely more cruel. Let enough of us lose our better instincts to that, and there will be a kind of—fever. A madness that sweeps us away, and we won't care about promises of good behavior, or even about our own survival. I've seen it happen to entire towns of vampires. They just . . . break." He snapped his fingers in front of her face in a sharp, dry motion, and the sound reminded her of bones shattering. "I don't wish to see it again. And I certainly don't wish to be part of it."

"Then make her listen to you. You're one of her oldest friends!"

"Friends count for little when they cross lovers," he said. "You're old enough to know that. And it is why I can't—" He shook his head. "Why I can't stay."

She felt she would choke on tears, suddenly. He stepped forward and took both her hands in his cool ones. For a moment, she thought he intended to kiss her, and for a panicked moment she wasn't sure if she ought to stop him, *wanted* to stop him . . . but then he just touched his forehead to hers and held it there.

"Hush, now," he said, and there was so much sweetness in his voice. "I don't want to see you cry. I'm nothing to cry over."

"I don't want you to go."

He pulled back, still close, very close, *too* close. There was a faint crimson flicker deep in his eyes, like a distant thunderstorm. "Take care," he said. "Promise me."

"I will," she said. "Myrnin—"

He kissed her. It was so fast that she couldn't move to prevent it, even if she'd wanted to; it was also quick, and light, and cool, and then . . .

Then he was gone.

Claire leaned out the window and saw him scrambling in a blur down the tree. He jumped the last ten feet, landed smoothly on his white patent leather shoes, and looked up at her in silence, then held up a pale, long-fingered hand.

She held hers up in response. Tears blurred her view of him, before they broke free of her eyes and rolled hot down her cheeks.

When she blinked, the yard was empty, except for the broken branch he'd been standing on when she'd first spotted him.

Claire gulped in several deep, cold breaths of night air, then slammed the window shut and sat down on her bed. She felt . . . She didn't know how she felt. Just wrong. She wanted to talk, but she couldn't to Shane, not about this; he wouldn't understand, not about this.

Eve. Maybe she could talk to Eve. . . . But she could hear the shouting from downstairs, and Eve's voice was gleefully announcing her victory over Shane in the game. Upstairs felt like a whole world away from that.

Claire stretched out on her bed, closed her eyes, almost ill with how wrong that had been, how guilty she was about that whole conversation. But she'd needed to have it with him; she knew that.

She flinched and bolted upright at a knock on the door, both arms instinctively crossing over her chest. "Who is it?"

"What do you mean, who is it?" Shane eased the door open and studied her. Oh. Of course, that was Shane's knock; she knew it very well. "What's up? You all right? You look scared."

She felt a surge of feeling so fierce that it burned in her cheeks and made her stomach churn, and for a second she didn't even know what it was, until her brain kicked back in.

It was shame.

"No," she said, and her voice sounded shaky. "No, I just—I had a dream. A bad one." *Liar.*

He gave her a grin that made the shame bite deeper, then sank down on the bed next to her. "Shouldn't have come up here and gone to sleep, then. Come on, sleepyhead. It's too early for you to crash out."

He kissed her, and he felt warm and sweet and strong and most of all, *alive*... and she fell into it eagerly, almost desperately. The kiss went on, and on, damp and slow, like something perfect in a dream, and she pressed close and into his arms, and all the storm inside her turned into peace, a peace so strong she could feel it glowing in her blood. She sighed onto his lips, into his mouth, and he was smiling, his hair brushing gently over her face like a ghost's caress.

"You make me happy," she whispered. She meant it literally— he'd just led her out of a strange, dark place and into sunlight, and the relief was so great that she felt tears in her eyes. "So happy."

Shane pulled back and looked at her with an expression of absolute focus. His smile was blinding. "I was about to tell you the same thing," he said, and brushed his fingers over her face. "Cheater."

For an awful second she thought he knew about Myrnin, standing here in her room, but then with a wave of icy relief she realized he was talking about her beating him to the punch. She gave him a shaky smile. "Got to be quick."

"Oh," he said, and kissed her very lightly, moving his lips down her throat, "I really don't think I do."

She laughed, because the joy just became a pinpoint of light inside her, bright and searing, and she rolled him over and sprawled on top of him and kissed him again, and again, and again, until everything was a burst of brightness, everywhere in the world.

And when it faded, when it was dark and quiet again, she listened to the strong, fast beat of his heart with her head on his chest, and thought, *I'm sorry.* She wasn't even sure what she was apologizing for, or even to whom it was directed. Myrnin? Herself? Shane? Maybe she'd let them all down, somehow.

But not again.

Never again.

Shane fell asleep next to her, out like a light, but Claire found herself humming with energy and too restless to try to close her eyes. She went out into the quiet hallway, closed the door, and sank down against the wall, turning her phone over and over in her hands. *Might as well,* she thought. It was late, but her parents were used to that, and they were always going on about how she didn't call enough.

Claire dialed before she could think better of it. Her mom answered on the second ring, her tone anxious. "Claire? Are you all right, honey?"

"Fine," Claire said. She felt a deep surge of guilt, because what did it say about her that her mom assumed she was in deep trouble every time she bothered to call? "Sorry I haven't been to see you lately. How's Dad? Is he doing all right?"

"Your dad's fine," her mom said firmly. "Except he worries about you, and so do I. He was hoping you could come home and visit soon. Any chance of that? If you want to bring your boyfriend, I suppose that's okay." She didn't sound so very enthused about *that.* It wasn't that she and Dad disapproved of Shane, exactly, but they were . . . cautious. Very cautious.

"I might do that," Claire said. "So, are you still doing that book club thing?"

"Oh yes; I just read the best mystery novel, *The Girl with the Dragon Tattoo*. Maybe you've heard of it . . . ?"

"Yes, Mom, I've heard of it. And there are movies."

"I didn't think there were any theaters in Morganville."

"There are a couple," Claire said. "But I watched it as a rental. You should do that."

"Oh, I have to do it over the Internet now; it seems so complicated."

"It's not. I could show you—"

"You know me and technology, sweetie. So, how's school?"

"Fine," Claire said. She knew she ought to say something more, something important, but she couldn't seem to come up with anything much. *My vampire boss, who would like to maybe be my boyfriend, just dropped in to tell me he was running away because Morganville's too dangerous.* That was a lot to dump on an unsuspecting parent, on so many levels. "Thanks for the lovely birthday gift." It had really been lovely—Claire had been expecting an out-of-fashion dress or a gift card or something, but instead she'd gotten a hand-bound book that had pictures of her from babyhood on, with space to add more. She'd already put in some photos of her and her friends, and her and Shane. Suddenly it reminded her that she'd never taken a picture of Myrnin . . . and now maybe she never would.

"That's a relief. You know, I think you work too hard at those classes. We'd be so happy to see you, honey. Do you think you might be able to come out this weekend?" Claire's parents lived only a few towns away, in a house that they wouldn't have been able to afford except that Morganville's Founder had bought it for them, in a fit of conscience over their daughter's contributions to vampire survival. Her parents had also once understood about the vampires, but not anymore. Those memories had faded almost to nothing—a deliberate action by the vamps, or by Amelie in particular. And that was okay. Claire preferred it that way—she liked them thinking she was in a safe place, with people who loved her. It was half true, anyway—the second half.

"Maybe I can try," she said. If Myrnin was right, she might not have much choice in getting out of town soon. "Mom—I know you were disappointed at me about not going to MIT when they called me, but . . ."

"I trust you, sweetie. I was just afraid you'd made that decision because of—well, because of Shane. If you really made it because you weren't ready to go, then that's all right. I want you to do things the way that's most comfortable for you. Your dad agrees." There was an indistinct mumble in the background that *might* have been her dad agreeing, but more likely it was just the opposite, and Claire smiled.

"Shane's not in charge of what I do," she said. "But I won't lie. I didn't want to leave him here, either. So maybe there's a little bit of that in there."

"I—honey, I know you don't want to hear this again, but are you sure you're not plunging into something too quickly with him?"

It was a familiar subject, and Claire felt a white-hot stab of annoyance. *Never thought of that, Mom. Wow, what insight!* She wouldn't say it. . . . She'd rarely been sarcastic to her parents, but that didn't stop her from thinking it. Older people so often thought they'd been through everything, experienced everything . . . but it wasn't true. Few of them had ever lived in Morganville, for instance. Or apprenticed to a vampire with poor impulse control.

"I'm not," Claire said. She'd learned that short answers worked best; they made her sound adult and certain. Overexplaining only opened the door for more lectures. "I know you're concerned, Mom, but Shane's a really good guy."

"I know you wouldn't stay with him if he wasn't—you're a very smart girl. But it does concern me, Claire. And your father. You're just eighteen. You're too young to be thinking about spending a lifetime with someone. You've hardly even dated anyone else."

Claire was just about fed up with the *You're too young* litany. She'd heard it from the time she was old enough to understand the words. The format might change, but the song remained the same: too young to do whatever it was she most wanted to do. And she couldn't resist saying, "If you hadn't said I was too young to go to MIT at sixteen, I would never have come to Morganville."

It was true, but it was a little cruel, and her mother fell silent in a way that told Claire she'd scored. *It's not a game,* she reminded herself, but she couldn't help a little surge of satisfaction, anyway.

When her mom restarted the conversation, it was about her new hobby, which had something to do with remodeling the house. Claire listened with half an ear as she flipped pages in her textbook that she'd opened on her lap. She still had another twenty pages of material to digest, and calling home was having the desired effect: it was making her forget all about Myrnin, and what he'd said, and focus back on her studies.

The door to her room opened unexpectedly, and Shane was standing there, bed-headed and yawning. He waved at her. She pointed to the phone and mouthed *Mom.* He nodded, stepped over her, and headed for his own room. Knowing him, he'd be face-down in dreamland in five minutes.

Claire grabbed her stuff and went back into her own room. Mom still hadn't paused for breath, and except for a few noncommittal uh-huhs, Claire was just a conversational spectator.

A second after she settled in on the bed, there was another

knock at the door—not Shane this time, because it was much more tentative. Claire covered the phone and called, "Come in!"

It was Miranda, who stepped inside and looked around with interest. Claire mouthed to her, *I'm on with my mom.* Miranda nodded and went to stare at the large bookcase in the corner of the room. She began pulling out titles.

"Mom, I've got to go," Claire said. "My friend Miranda's here. I told you about her. She's the new one in the house."

"Oh, okay. Love you, pumpkin. Your dad says he loves you, too. Can't wait for you to take a look at the carpet samples. I'm sure you can help us decide on that. Maybe this weekend?"

"Thanks, Mom. I love you, too. Yeah, maybe this weekend."

She hung up and dropped her cell back in her pocket as Miranda wandered over with a couple of books. "Do you mind if I borrow these?" she asked. "I don't sleep anymore."

"Any time," Claire said. "Did you like *Star Wars*?"

"Yes," she said. Miranda sat down on the bed next to her. She was a small-framed girl, and she seemed even more fragile than Claire, who'd at least put on some muscle these past few years, if she hadn't grown much taller. Miranda had the seeming physical strength of a stick insect. That was deceptive, of course; Miranda wasn't really alive in the same way Claire was, and she could draw on the considerable power of the Glass House when she had to, so she could probably break bricks with her hands if necessary.

It was hard not to feel protective, though. The kid just had that look of vulnerability.

"That's it? Yes? People usually have more to say than that."

"It was good?" Miranda tried tentatively, and then shrugged. "I guess I'm not really in the mood for movies after all. You know, I used to think that if I couldn't see the future, it would be terrible, but really, it feels pretty good, not knowing what's coming. It makes it more fun to watch movies and things when you can't guess the ending." She fell silent for a second, then pushed her hair behind her ear. "But it'd be more fun if I did it with you guys."

She'd been coming out of her shell slowly, but steadily; she hadn't quite joined the Glass House gang in full, but she was, at least, an adopted kid who was trying to fit into the family. Claire knew how that felt; she'd come into the house when Shane, Michael, and Eve had already been an established unit of old friends. She knew what it felt like to be an outsider.

Claire hugged her impulsively. "We'll do that," she said. "Movie night. Tomorrow. I've got a bunch of things I think you'd like."

"Michael and Eve are going to move out," Miranda said.

Claire almost fell off the bed as she twisted to get a look at Mir's face. The other girl was staring down, and she didn't look like she was making a bad joke; she seemed serious, and a little sad. *"What?"*

"I know I'm not supposed to eavesdrop, and I try not to, really, but it's hard when you're invisible during the daytime," Miranda said. "I mean, you're drifting around bored and there's nobody to talk to. You can't even watch TV unless someone else turns it on, and then you have to watch whatever they want—"

"Mir, focus. Why would you say they're moving out?"

"Because they're talking about it," she said. "Eve thinks that it's hard to feel married when they're just living the same life, you know? When it's here, with you and Shane. I know she moved into Michael's bedroom, but she doesn't feel like anything really changed. Like, they're married for reals."

Claire had honestly never thought about it. It had just seemed, in her mind, like marriage wouldn't change anything—wouldn't mean any difference at all in the way Michael and Eve felt around her and Shane. They'd already been, ah, together, after all. Why should it matter? "Maybe they just need some time."

"They need *space*," Miranda said. "That's what Michael said, anyway. Space and privacy and nobody listening to them all the time."

Well, Claire could understand the privacy part. She always felt odd about that, too. Even as big as the Glass House was, sometimes it felt very crowded with five people in it. "They shouldn't move out," Claire said. "It's Michael's house!"

"Well, *I* can't move, can I?" Miranda said, and kicked her feet. She was wearing cute sneakers, pink with an adorably weird brown bunny face on them. "I don't want them to go, though. Claire— what happens to me if you guys all leave? Do I just . . . stay here? Forever? Alone?"

"That's not going to happen," Claire said, and sighed. She grabbed a pillow and flopped backward, holding it tight against her chest. "God, this can't happen now. Like everything wasn't complicated enough!"

Miranda lay flat, too, staring up at the ceiling. "I don't feel right tonight. The house feels . . . It feels weird. Anxious, maybe." The Glass House had its own kind of rudimentary life force to it—something Claire didn't exactly understand but could feel all around her. And Miranda was right. The house was on edge. "I think it's worried about us. About what's going to happen to us all."

Claire remembered Myrnin's anxious, determined expression, his insistence that she leave town, and felt a chill.

"We'll be fine," Claire said, and hugged the pillow tighter. "We'll all be fine."

It was as if the universe had heard her, and responded, because all of a sudden she heard the crash of glass downstairs. Miranda stood bolt upright and closed her eyes, then opened them to say, "The front window. Something broke it."

Claire raced her downstairs, with Shane stumbling out of his room in a daze to follow. They found Michael and Eve already there.

The window in the parlor was broken out, and a brick was lying on the carpet in a spray of broken glass. Wrapped around it was another note. Nobody spoke as Michael unfastened the string that held it on and read it, then passed it to Eve, who passed it to Shane, who passed it to Claire.

"Wow," she said. "I didn't think they could spell *perverts.*"

"It's getting worse," Eve said. "They're not going to let this go, are they?"

Michael put his arms around her and hugged her tight. "I'm not going to let anything happen," he said. "Trust me."

She let out a sigh of relief and nodded.

Shane, ever practical, said, "I'll get the plywood and hammer."

FIVE

OLIVER

☽

When Amelie slept, she seemed little more than a child, small and defenseless, bathed in moonlight like a coating of ice. Her skin glowed with an eerie radiance, and lying next to her, I thought she might well be the most magnificent and beautiful thing I had ever seen.

It destroyed me to betray her, but I really had no choice.

I slipped quietly away through the darkness of this, her most secret of hideaways; it was where Amelie kept those treasures she had preserved through years, through wars, through every hardship that had fallen over her. Fine artworks, beautiful clothes, jewels, books of all descriptions. And letters. So many handwritten letters that seven massive ironbound chests couldn't contain them all. One or two, I thought, might have come from my own pen. They would not have been love poems. Likely they had been threats.

I moved silently through the rooms to the door, and out into the jasmine-scented garden. It was a small enclosure, but bursting with colorful flowers that glowed even in the darkness. A fountain played in the center, and beside it stood another woman. I'd have mistaken her for Amelie, at a glance; they were alike enough in coloring and height and form.

But Naomi was a very different kind of woman altogether. Vampire, yes; old, yes. And a blood sister to the Founder, through their common vampire maker, Bishop . . . but where Amelie had the power to command vampires, to force them to her will, Naomi had always wielded her power less like a queen and more like a se-ductress, though she had little interest in the flesh—or at least, in mine.

Amelie appeared to be made of ice, but inside was fire, hot and fierce and furious; inside Naomi, I knew, was nothing but cold ambition.

And yet . . . here I was.

"Oliver," she said, and placed a small, gentle hand on my chest, over my heart. "Kind of you to meet me here."

"I had no choice," I said. Which was true—she had taken all choices from me. I raged at it, inside; I was in a tearing frenzy of rage within, but none of it showed on my face or in my bearing. None could, unless she allowed it; she had control of me from the bones out.

"True," she said. "And how fares my much-beloved sister?"

"Well," I said. "She could wake at any time. It wouldn't do for her to see you here."

"Or at all, since my dear blood sister believes I'm safely dead and gone. Or do I have you to thank for the attempt on my life, Oliver? One of you must have wished me dead among the draug."

"I organized your assassination," I confessed immediately.

Again, no choice; I could feel her influence inside me, as irresistible as the hand of God. "Amelie had no part in it."

"Nor would she have; we've held our truce for a thousand years. I'll have to think of a suitable way to reward you for betraying that. What does she suspect?"

"Nothing."

"You've gained her trust?"

"Yes."

"You're certain of that?"

"I'm here," I said, and looked around at this, Amelie's most sheltered secret. "And now, you're here. So yes. She trusts me."

"I knew that bewitching you was an investment that would soon pay off," Naomi said, and gave me a sweet, charming smile that made the storm inside me thunder and fury. I hated her. If I'd had the ability to fight, I'd have ripped her to pieces for what she'd done to me, and was doing through me, to Amelie. "She hasn't detected your influence on her decisions?"

"Not as yet."

"Well, she will likely start to question it soon, if she hasn't already; my sister has a nasty streak of altruism that surfaces from time to time. Once the humans begin to complain of their treatment, she may think about placating them once again." She ran her fingers over my cheek, then parted my lips with cool fingers. "Let's see your fangs, my monster."

I had no choice. None. But I tried, dear God, I tried; I struggled against the darkness inside me, I fought, and I won a hesitation, just for a moment, in obeying Naomi's iron will.

And still, my fangs descended, sharp and white as a snake's. There was a single tiny tug of pain, always, as if some part of me even now refused to believe my damned state of being, but I had centuries ago grown well used to that.

The pain she was wringing from within me was much, much worse.

She let me go and stepped back, eyes narrowing. "Your reluctance doesn't please me," she said. "And I can't risk your tearing free even a bit from my side, now, can I? Hold still, Oliver."

And I did, to my shame; I held very still, eyes fixed on the calm flowing water of the fountain as it spilled tears to the stone. She raised my arm to her lips, bit, and drank. She was a true snake, this one, and poison ran from her bite into me; it corrupted, and it destroyed the tiny pulse of will I'd managed to raise. She licked the remains of my blood from her lips and smiled at me.

Defeated.

And then she put her lips close to my ear and said, "I owe you something for that bit of will, don't I? Very well. I want you to feel pain. I want you to *burn*."

It started slowly, a sensation of heat sweeping up from my hands, but it quickly turned into the familiar bite of sunlight beating down on me . . . but where age had given me armor against such pain, I had no defenses from Naomi's witchery. It was like being a newborn vampire again, tied down for the noontime glare, with my blood boiling and burning its way through my flesh, exploding in thin pale flames, flaking my skin to ash and roasting nerves. . . .

I clenched my teeth against the pain, then whimpered softly at the extreme of the agony. *Let me die*, something in me begged. *Just let me die!*

But that, of course, was not her plan. She had done me no physical harm, none at all. It was only the memory of fire, the sense of it; my blood was cool and intact, and my skin unmarked.

I only felt as if I were a torch set afire.

When she finally released me, I fell to my hands and knees on the soft grass, sucking down cold night air in panicked breaths as if I were no more than a human. I didn't need the air, but I craved the coolness; the dew of the grass felt like a balm on my still-sizzling nerves, and it was all I could do to stop myself from pitching facedown to its embrace.

But I would not give her that. Not until she demanded it.

She did not. I calmed myself and climbed to my feet, and wished to heaven I could rip her apart, but I knew better than to even attempt it. And I was rewarded with a slow, calm smile. Above it, Naomi's eyes continued to watch closely for any hint of rebellion.

"Now," she said. "I have a job for you. I wish you to find the vampire Myrnin, and kill him."

Not that I hadn't often wished to do just that, but I hated the thought now, knowing that it was her driving me to it, and not my own will. "Yes, my lady," I said. The response was automatic, but it was also wise.

"That's my lovely knight," she said, and her eyes flashed red. "And inevitably, you will have to do the same to my sister, for my own safety. When we're done, we'll rule Morganville together. You can take your sport where you wish; I care not. That's what you've always wanted."

"Yes," I whispered. *No.* Not at this cost. And not with her.

I had never expected, after all we had endured, to be undone at the lily-white hands of a maiden. Myrnin might possibly have been able to find a way to stop it, and her. That was why Naomi wished him gone, of course.

And why I'd have no choice, none, but to do her bidding, until she finally had no more use for me at all. All vampires had some measure of control of others; it was an instinct that made us effective hunters, but in some—like Amelie—that trait was very strong, a hammer blow that could be wielded against other vampires. Naomi's ability was a whisper, not a shout, but it was just as powerful. I had never suspected she possessed such skills. She had always seemed so . . . innocent. And kind. I ought to have known better; vampires are never kind, not unless that kindness buys us something.

"Tell me," I said. "Tell me why you're doing this. Why now?"

"I did not come after *you*," Naomi pointed out, and raised an eyebrow. "I am not my father, Bishop; I had no need to rule until it became plain that Amelie was . . . incapable. I would have been happy to see her healed and whole again, even then. But *you* had to come after me, Oliver. So it's entirely your fault that I am driven to this extreme."

Naomi's chin suddenly rose, and her eyes dimmed to a pale blue. "It seems I must leave you now, Oliver. She's awake," she said. "You know what to do. And remember, if you fight me, I'll make the punishments I've given you already seem like a caress."

She vanished like smoke. Surviving my attempt to destroy her, in the chaos of the final battle with the draug, had made this one stronger, faster, more coldhearted than ever.

I waited until I sensed Amelie's approach, and then I turned with a false but convincing smile; it ripped at me like razors to betray her so, because even after all our years of rivalry, I had finally come to realize her worth, and now . . . now the smile was no longer mine. It was a lure, a lie, and it sickened me to see her return it.

She walked on bare feet down the path, hands stroking the petals of flowers as she came; her thin white gown blew like mist in the moonlight. She was beautiful, and desirable, and I despaired inside as her hands touched the bare skin of my chest, because I was going to be the death of her.

And there was nothing I could do to stop it. Nothing at all. I wanted to warn her, to tell her how dangerous I was to her now. How destructive.

"You strayed," she said, and kissed me very lightly.

"Yes," I said, and felt myself smile that warm, challenging smile that had charmed her into trust. "But I'll never go far."

Until I kill you. God forgive me.

SIX

CLAIRE

)

Claire really wanted to confront Eve about what Miranda had overheard—she and Michael *couldn't* really be considering moving out, could they?—but in the morning, Eve was gone early, and Michael was sleeping late; she wasn't quite gutsy enough to go knock on his door and demand to know the truth. Michael was grouchy in the mornings.

Miranda, of course, had kept Claire up talking into the wee hours; she'd been getting more and more chatty since taking up residence, which was great in a way, because the kid had been so repressed and isolated before, but bad for Claire's sleep cycle. It also cut into the time she could spend with Shane; he tended to steer clear when Miranda was around, and although he wasn't above just moving the girl firmly out of the room when he felt it was necessary, he hadn't done it last night.

So Claire woke up short of sleep, yawning, and a little cranky. Not her best morning ever, but in a matter of minutes it got drastically better; she was still stretching and trying to wearily decide what to wear, when there was a thumping knock on her door, one very different from Miranda's tentative taps.

She grabbed her robe and threw it on as she answered. She didn't open up all the way, just peeked through. There was Shane, balancing one coffee cup precariously on top of another. He'd given her the giant Snoopy cup this morning, which was nice. "What's the password?" she asked him.

"Um, you look hot with your hair standing up?"

"Good enough." She stepped back and relieved Shane of the Snoopy cup as he came inside; then she set it hastily down when he stepped in to slide his free hand around her waist and kiss her. She had morning breath, but it didn't seem to matter to him; he tasted of mint toothpaste and coffee, but she forgot all that in seconds and then it was just all incredibly delicious. Her whole body tingled with warmth.

"Morning," he murmured, his lips close to hers. They were so tasty, she licked them, which made him smile and kiss her again. "Too bad you're dressed."

"I'm not dressed. I just have on a robe."

"Oh?"

"Hey," she said, and put a hand flat on his chest. "None of that, mister. A girl's got to have boundaries."

"You'll let me know when I get there," he said, and untied her robe. "You lied. You've got on jammies."

"Well, yeah, those, too." She was short of breath, and when his hands found their way under the flannel of her pajama top, the air in her lungs rushed away. "You really shouldn't . . ."

"Do this? Yeah, I know." He undid the first button on her pajama top and put a kiss in its place. "But I've been thinking about doing it all night."

So had she, actually, and all the logical objections to why this wasn't a good idea kind of vanished under the heat of his touch ... until Claire realized he'd left her bedroom door wide-open, and someone was standing in the doorway.

"Your coffee's getting cold," Eve said. She was clearly on her way to the bathroom, arms full of black clothes, hair untied and in a multicolored mess around her pale face. She blew the two of them a kiss.

Claire yelped and jumped away, rebuttoning her top and retying her robe at light speed. Shane hardly seemed bothered at all, but she could feel the hot blush staining her cheeks. "Um, hi, Eve," she said. "Sorry."

"*I'm* not sorry," Shane said, and gave Eve a mean glare. Eve gave Shane a wicked grin. "Don't you have better things to do?"

"Than mess up your morning sexytime? Nope, never. Dibs on the shower! And you might want to remember this thing actually swings shut. Pro tip." Eve slammed the door between them.

Shane picked up a handy book and started to throw it, but Claire grabbed it out of his hands. "Not the advanced calc book!" She searched around and found a history text instead. He shook his head sadly.

"Moment's over," he said, and he wasn't just talking about the opportunity to throw something. He retrieved his coffee and sipped it, and she tried to get her racing heartbeat under control as she tasted hers. It was good and strong, and although it wasn't as good as what *might* have been her morning wake-up, it wasn't shabby. "What was Miranda in here gabbing about last night?"

"Things." Claire shrugged. "You know. She's lonely."

"I know the feeling, believe me." He gave her a puppy-dog look, and she aimed a kick in his direction, which he dodged.

"But she did say something weird."

"Miranda? Go figure!"

"She said—" Should she even repeat this? Somehow, saying it aloud, to Shane, made it more . . . real. But he needed to know. "She said Michael and Eve were talking about moving."

"Moving," he repeated, as if he didn't know the word. "Moving what?"

"I guess out. To another house."

"Why would we move?"

"Not we, Shane. *Them*. Michael and Eve. As a couple. Moving."

"Oh," he said, as if he still didn't get it, and then he did. *"Oh."* He looked as if someone had shot his dog, and he sat down on the unmade bed and stared down into his coffee cup. It was one of Eve's, black with purple bats all over it. "You mean, leave us behind."

He'd just distilled it down to the sharp, hurting point: *leave us.* Because that was what it was, really: not that they needed space, but that Michael and Eve were leaving Claire and Shane behind, in their past.

"They need space, is what Miranda said. Y'know, together-type space."

"They're not the only ones," Shane said. He didn't look up. "Hell. Michael didn't say anything."

"Neither did Eve. So maybe it's just, you know . . ."

"Talk? Maybe. But if they're talking about it, it's real enough to matter." He pulled in a breath and let it out slowly. "I've been thinking about it myself."

"Michael and Eve moving out?" Was she the only one who hadn't seen this coming?

"No. Moving out myself."

Claire couldn't have been more stunned if he'd announced he'd decided to turn vampire. She sat down too fast and just managed not to slop coffee all over herself; even that barely registered as a blip, because her attention was suddenly and completely on her boyfriend, and there was a sick, hurting knot in her stomach. *"What?"*

"It's just—" He gestured vaguely at the door. "We're in one another's pockets around here. Sometimes it'd be nice to just have it be . . ."

"You want to move out," Claire said. "By yourself."

"No!" Shane finally glanced up, startled. "I mean—*we* could . . . find a place—"

The moment froze, with the two of them staring at each other; this was a conversation Claire had never expected to have, and certainly not in the early morning in her pajamas with her hair in a mess. It clearly wasn't something Shane had thought through, either. The whole thing suddenly felt raw, fragile, *wrong*. And she didn't know why. It made the aching lump in her guts hurt even worse.

"Anyway," Shane finally said, in that we're-going-to-pretend-that-never-happened kind of tone, "it's just that this is Michael's house. It ought to be Michael and Eve's, if it's anybody's. I could always—we could—" He couldn't seem to get his words together, either, and she saw the same growing panic in him that she was feeling. *Not ready for this*, she thought. *Really not ready.* It reminded her of what her mother had said, so prophetically, last night on the phone. *Are you sure you're not moving too fast?*

She hated it when her mom was right.

"Okay, clearly, this is crazy talk anyway," Shane said, in a deliberately blow-off tone. "Let us never speak of it again. Wrestle you for dibs on the shower after Eve gets done with it."

"You take it," Claire said. Her lips felt numb. She drank coffee, but that was just to have something to do; she didn't taste it, and her brain felt overwhelmed with all the surges of emotion. Too many things were happening too quickly, none of them in tune. "I'll wait."

"Okay." He wanted to say something else, and even opened his mouth to do it, but whatever it was, his courage failed. He covered up by drinking, and Claire stared at the purple cartoon bats on his cup and wondered if somehow she could reset the morning back to the kissing. The kissing had been so wonderful.

But as Shane had pointed out, that moment was gone, and it apparently wasn't coming back anytime soon.

After an awkward few moments, with the coffee cups drained, Shane finally ventured, "I made up more posters."

"Good," Claire said. "Let's get them up."

She thought they were both relieved to have something to do.

Shane must have made up twenty posters, which was definitely overkill in a town like Morganville. Claire and Eve both had giggle fits over the variety of pictures—mostly wildly unflattering—that Shane had chosen.

"Gotta give it up for Monica," he said, admiring his handiwork. "That girl has a Photobucket album you would not believe. I think it runs to fifteen pages of pics. Even the Kardashians would say it was too much. Lucky for me she likes taking drunk pics."

"Isn't the idea to actually get her elected?" Eve finally managed to wheeze out, then broke out into another uncontrolled burst of laughter. "Oh, my God, *this* one. *This* is my favorite." She tugged one poster out and set it on top. It had Monica in her trademark tight-and-short, standing posed with her hands on her hips, puckering her lips into a duckface. "So many things wrong with this."

"This won't stop her from getting elected," Shane said. "Stupider people get elected all the time. It's America. We love the sleazy. And the crazy."

"I would like to think better of us," Claire said, "but yeah. You're right."

He offered a high five, which she reluctantly accepted, and then they split up the posters between them. They were heavier than Claire had imagined, and she *oofed* a little under the weight. Shane, without asking, redistributed, taking on the rest, and winked at Eve. "Wanna go with?"

"Somebody has to work around here," she said. "I suppose that turns out to be me. Again."

"Have fun with that day-job thing."

"Slacker!"

"And proud of it, wage slave."

Out on the sidewalk, Shane juggled the heavy cardboard until Claire caught up, with her backpack settled on her shoulder. "Did you bring the stapler?"

"Got it," she said. The stapler in question was a giant, ancient, industrial kind of thing, heavy steel that probably could fire its fastener through a car if it had to. "Also brought some stakes in case we need to put things on lawns."

"Like, say, this one?" Shane gazed longingly at the front yard of the Glass House, and Claire laughed out loud. She opened up her backpack and handed him a stake (funny, these had *so* not been meant for putting up signs). He hammered it into the ground and stapled the poster to it, and they stepped back to admire the effect. "A thing of beauty."

Eve opened up the window in the front room and peered out suspiciously. "Hey! You crazy kids, what are you doing?"

"You forgot to say 'Get off my lawn!'" Shane called back.

"Oh no, you didn't put that thing out there!"

"Relax—I used your favorite photo." Shane said to Claire as she zipped up her backpack, "We'd better make a moving target."

The first three signs went up without incident. At the fourth telephone pole, in Morganville's very sparse shopping district, Claire was stapling the sign in place when she heard the squeal of brakes on the street, and then the blare of a car horn. She turned and saw a bright red convertible and a blur of movement as the driver bailed out. Objectively, it was impressive that Monica could maintain her balance on those heels while moving that fast.

"What in the hell are you doing?" she asked, and shoved Claire out of the way as she faced the bright neon poster, which was flapping a bit in the wind. Her face went blank. Not angry, just... blank. "What is this?"

"What does it look like?" Shane asked. He took the stapler from Claire and finished fastening the poster to the pole, then spun the thing like a very awkward six-gun as he admired the effect from a few feet back. "Looks like you're running for mayor."

Monica's glossy lips parted, and she just... stared. As if she couldn't think of a single thing to say. *Wait for it*, Claire thought, and readied herself for the inevitable attack. Monica was about to achieve thermonuclear critical mass, and she intended to get to minimum safe distance before she blew.

But instead, a soft, delighted smile curled around Monica's lips, and she said, "Wait a minute. *You* did this?"

"Claire did," Shane said. "I'm just the incredibly awesome graphic designer. Also, head of the entertainment committee. Every campaign needs one of those."

"That's... incredible," Monica said. "I don't know—okay, well, you know, nobody's probably voting for me. I mean, I'm not

Richard. I haven't gone out of my way to be responsible or anything."

"You're a Morrell," Shane said. "Lots of people figure that's in your blood. Three generations of mayors in your family, right?"

"Well, they'd be wrong."

"We know that," Shane said cheerfully. "But hey, you'll make a hell of a seat-filler, and I *know* you love a good photo op, being such a big fan of yourself." He lost his smile, and all the levity that went with it. "All this comes with one condition, you know," he said. "You do what's good for humans. Not what the vamps say."

Monica arched a single well-plucked eyebrow. "You have that backward, Collins. I don't do what *you* say. You do what *I* say. After all, I'll be the one with the fancy nameplate on the door."

"As long as you don't dance puppet for the vamps, I don't really care," Shane said. "But as to us doing what you say . . . Yeah. Good luck with that."

Monica's attention went back to the poster, and her eyes narrowed. "Wait a second. Is that one of my Facebook photos?"

"Maybe."

"Hmmm." She cocked her head, lips pursed. "Could have picked a better one."

"You always said you can't take a bad picture," he said, straight-faced.

"True." She gave the poster a slow, wicked smile, and said, "Okay, then. Just so long as I don't have to pay for anything, or show up for a lot of meetings. Oh, and make sure people know I can be bribed."

"Deal."

She stared at him for a second, then at Claire. "What exactly are you up to? Don't even pretend that you're into this, because you don't think that much of me."

"We're not," Claire said. "Don't worry about it. It doesn't concern you. All that concerns you is making sure you act nice and wave to people. Pretend it's a popularity contest, because that's what it is."

"You don't win popularity contests by being nice," Monica said. "You win them by making people scared to vote against you. So consider this one in the bag."

She walked back to her illegally parked car, climbed in, and was gone. Claire shook her head as she watched the red convertible screech around the corner, and said, "Only Monica could think *Vote for me or I'll break your leg* is a decent campaign slogan."

"In Morganville, it probably is."

They made another ten stops before grabbing a snack. Reaction had varied from place to place where they'd asked to put up the signs, from laughter to consternation to, at the last stop, outright rage.

Claire had never seen anyone tear a tough cardboard poster apart with such enthusiasm, but the dry cleaner four blocks away definitely wasn't a Morrell for Mayor fan.

"What was that dry cleaner guy so cheesed off about?" she asked Shane as they ate their breakfast burritos sitting outside at a rickety metal table. It was still cool enough outside to do that in relative comfort, though the flies and mosquitoes (new and unwelcome visitors, since the draug's watery arrival) were already dive-bombing them for snacks. They wisely kept the lids on their soft drinks.

"Him? His name's William Batiste. We used to call him Billy Bats. I think Monica might have kissed him once back in junior high. To be fair, she kissed most of the school who stood in one place long enough. Billy's kind of a hard-core resistance guy. Doesn't like the Morrells from way back."

"I suppose not everybody can be a *yes*," Claire said.

"I think we're lucky if she gets the terror and apathy vote," Shane said. "We've still got another ten to put up this afternoon. You still up for it?"

"Sure," Claire said. "It's my free day, anyway. If you don't mind, though, could we stop in at the lab? Just to check on Myrnin?"

Shane wasn't enthusiastic, but he shrugged; he probably figured it was a small price to pay, since he had her all day long. "We just need to be done before dark," he said. "I'm not *that* dedicated a campaign staffer. Especially for Monica."

The town seemed calm and back to normal, and the sounds of construction were everywhere—saws, grinders, hammers. It all sounded industrious and positive. There were more Protection signs visible, too; many shops were displaying them in the windows now, or at least at the counters, and she was seeing more Morganville residents wearing bracelets with their Protectors' symbols on them, too. Morganville was on its way back . . . but to what? Not the same town it had been before the draug. Maybe it was turning the clock all the way back to what it had been in the beginning, with the vampires in iron control.

Not if we have anything to say about it, she thought, and helped Shane staple another poster to a telephone pole outside Common Grounds. They stepped back to admire their work, and Claire became aware of someone standing in the shadow of the awning next to her. She hadn't felt him arrive, but suddenly Oliver was just . . . there.

He was a solid, daunting presence even though he was wearing what Claire thought of as his nice-hippie disguise—gray-threaded hair tied back in a ponytail, a dark T-shirt, and jeans under the long tie-dyed apron with the Common Grounds logo on it. He smelled like coffee, a warm and welcoming kind of scent even though under it he was cold as marble.

He was staring at the poster with an oddly blank expression. "I see," he finally said. "You've all lost your minds."

"Nope," Shane said, and tossed the stapler up in the air in a fine display of both bravado and stupidity; he could have lost a finger to that thing if it had gone off. "Found our calling. We're activists. And hey, Monica takes a decent picture. That's all you really need in a candidate, right?"

Shane got a full-on glare for that one, and Claire felt the burn even from the edges of it. "Don't test me, boy," Oliver said, velvet-soft. "I'm no one you should play games with these days. I've been too gentle with you; I've let you and your friends run riot. No more. You'll take that down."

Shane raised his eyebrows. "Why?"

Because I said so was the obvious answer, but Oliver smiled thinly and said, "It's against code."

Their poster wasn't the only one on the pole; there were flyers for lost pets, missing persons, a new band playing (probably badly) at Common Grounds over the weekend, cheap insurance, baby-sitting. . . . Claire said, "You never had a problem with it before."

"And now I do." Oliver stepped out in the sunlight, even though his skin immediately began to turn a little pink where the glare touched it, and he began ripping things off the pole without any regard for splinters. His fingernails left gouges in the wood half an inch deep. He shredded Monica's poster in half with a casual swipe, dropped the pieces to the ground, and kicked them back toward Shane. "And now you're littering as well. Pick it up."

Shane didn't move. He didn't speak. He just stood there, stapler in his hand, and it looked . . . dangerous.

"Pick it up or I'll have you arrested," Oliver said. "Both of you.

And no one will be coming to bail you out this time. If Eve tries, she'll join you."

"Michael—"

"I can handle Michael Glass." Oliver's words guillotined whatever Shane was going to say as he stepped back into the shadows. There was a faint wisp of smoke coming off his skin, but it stopped as soon as he was out of the sun, and the burn faded almost as quickly. On the other hand, the glow of his eyes was eerily specific. "Pick. It. Up."

Shane still didn't move, and Claire sensed, with fatal dismay, that he didn't intend to—so she did. She bent over and grabbed up the poster and the other shredded paper, walked over, and deposited it into the Common Grounds trash can next to the entry door. And it might have been okay, except that Oliver just had to purr, "Good girl," at her as if she were his personal pet, and Shane—

Shane punched him.

The vampire never saw it coming, because he was looking straight at Claire, enjoying his little moment of triumph; Shane's fist caught him on the side of the jaw, and the power behind it was massive enough that Oliver actually staggered before turning with supernatural litheness and springing on her boyfriend so fast, it was as if he'd been launched from a catapult. He slammed Shane back into the brick wall next to the window and pinned him there with an arm across his throat. When Shane tried to push him back, Oliver caught his hand and wrenched it hard to the side. Shane froze.

"Nothing's broken," Oliver said, "but it's half an inch away. So please, do that again, boy. I'll crush every bone you have, a handful at a time, and have you pleading for me to finish—"

He cut off abruptly because Claire made him shut up, by the simple expedient of putting the point of a thin-bladed silver knife against his back, just over where it needed to go to reach his heart. "Let go," she said. "I picked up the trash, just like you said. We're even."

They weren't, and she knew it without him even bothering to say it, but Oliver silently released Shane's hand. Claire stepped away, knife still drawn and ready, as Shane pushed Oliver back with a violent shove and picked up the stapler from where it had fallen on the pavement.

"You owe us for a poster," Shane said. "They cost me five bucks apiece. I'll expect a free drink in exchange."

"So will I," Oliver said, "from the vein, the next time I catch either of you in less . . . visible circumstances." He showed teeth, and walked back into the coffee shop.

"I guess that means Monica can't count on his vote, either," Shane said. It sounded like a joke, but he was trembling, and clenching the stapler way too hard. He knew, as Claire did, that they'd just passed over some kind of line. Maybe permanently.

"Why?" she asked him, a little plaintively. "Why did you do that?"

"Nobody talks to you that way," he said. "Not even him."

He draped his arm around her shoulders, picked up the other signs, and they continued on to the next stop.

At the next stop Claire and Shane made to put up Monica's poster, they found someone else there before them stapling notices: a serious-looking older woman and a younger man, probably her son. He was about Shane's height, but thin as a whip. He nodded to Claire as if he knew her (and she didn't think they'd ever met), then fixed his gaze on Shane. "Hey, man," he said, and offered his hand. "What's up?"

"Nothing much. How are you?"

"Good, good. You remember my mom, Flora Ramos, right?"

"Mrs. Ramos, sure, I remember the burritos you used to make for Enrique in grade school," Shane said. "He used to trade them to me if I gave up my M&Ms. I always made the deal; that's how good they were."

"You gave away my burritos, 'Rique?" Mrs. Ramos said, and raised her eyebrows at her son. He spread his hands and shrugged.

"You gave 'em to me every day," he said. "So yeah."

"They were delicious," Shane said. "Hey, he made a profit. He used to cut them in half and trade each separately."

"Enrique."

"I was an entrepreneur, Mama." Enrique gave her a devastating grin. "What, you want my M&Ms now?" In answer, she handed him a small letter-sized sheet of paper, and he held it against the telephone pole as she stapled it in place.

The flyer said, CAPTAIN OBVIOUS FOR MAYOR, and it had a big question mark underneath the caption where a picture ought to go. The slogan said, VOTE HUMAN. That was all.

"What the hell?" Shane asked, and pointed at the blank picture. "Mrs. Ramos, Captain Obvious left town. You can't ask people to vote for somebody who isn't even here."

"Maybe an empty seat is better than one filled by another useless bootlicker," she said, and as friendly as she seemed, her eyes were chilly and dark all of a sudden. "I've seen these Morrell posters. How can *you* of all people support such a thing, Shane? I know what that evil *bruja* did to you and your family!"

"It's not . . ." Shane took a step back, frowning. "It's not what it looks like. Look, Monica's a whole lot of things, but a bootlicker? Not so I've ever noticed. She's more likely to be wearing the boots, and kicking with them. Weak, she's not. And we need somebody on that council who will stand up to the vampires for us."

Anger flared in Mrs. Ramos's lined face. "She is part of the cancer that eats at this town. She and her whole disgusting family! I thank God that her father and brother are gone——"

"Wait a second," Shane interrupted, and it was his serious voice now, the one that meant he wasn't going to let it go. "Richard Morrell was okay. He tried. Don't——"

"He was a corrupt man from a corrupt family." Her voice had gone hard now, as unyielding as the flinty distance in her eyes. "Enough. I've finished talking with you."

Claire tried a different approach. Emotion clearly wasn't getting them anywhere. "But——they won't let you write in someone who doesn't even exist!"

"Captain Obvious does exist," Flora said. "He always has, always will. Until he stands up again, I'll stand for him."

"You," Claire said. "*You're* the new Captain Obvious?"

Enrique had gone quiet now, and when he wasn't smiling and being friendly, he looked a little bit dangerous. "Why? You got a problem with that? My mom's not good enough for you?"

"No, I just——" Claire didn't know how to finish that.

Shane did. "Dude, she's your *mom*. She used to throw bake sales. She made cookies. How can she be Captain Obvious?"

"How can any mother not want to be against the evil that lives here?" Flora said. "I raised kids in this town. Enrique, Hector, Donna, and Leticia. You tell me, Shane. You tell me what happened to three of my kids."

He just looked at her mutely for a long few seconds, and then away. "That wasn't anybody's fault. It was an accident."

"So they said."

Claire cleared her throat; she felt——as always——as though

someone had failed to fill her in, and here she was standing in the middle of a scene clearly full of tension, and she didn't understand any of it. "Uh, sorry, but . . . what happened?"

Mrs. Ramos didn't reply, and Shane didn't seem to want to, now that he'd tripped over the land mine. So Enrique finally sighed and dived in.

"My sister Donna was driving," he said. "She was seventeen, just got her license. She was taking my brother Hector to work—he was nineteen—and my sister Letty to school. It was the middle of winter, a little icy like it gets sometimes. Black ice, the kind you can't see. She hadn't ever driven on it before. They hit a pole." He didn't finish the story, but Claire guessed how it would end: in funerals. That was confirmed by a sideways glance at Shane. He had that quiet, closed-in look he got when people talked about their lost friends and relatives; he'd had so much of it himself, losing his sister, then his mom, and finally his dad. He always seemed to guard against emotion, even when it came from other people.

"That wasn't all of it," Flora Ramos said, with a suppressed anger that made the hair shiver at the nape of Claire's neck. "My children were out there lying hurt and alone, and *they* took their lives. I know they did."

"Mama, it was an accident. They bled out; you know what the doctors said."

"The doctors, the doctors, like they don't work for the monsters just as we all do? No, Enrique. It was the *vampiros*. It wasn't an accident. You should know that!" She sounded weary and furious at the same time; whenever it had happened, it was still fresh in her mind. "I have one child left they haven't taken from me. And they won't. Not while I have breath left in my body."

"You could leave town," Shane said quietly. "You had a chance."

"And our house? Our life? No. My husband is buried here, and my children. This is our *home*. The monsters must leave it before we do." She raised her chin, and Claire saw that despite the wrinkles, the gray hair, she was determined, and dangerous. "Don't play these games, Shane; politics here means our lives. I will not let you make it a joke."

Shane stared at her for a long moment. He felt sorry for her; Claire could see it. He knew how it felt, to blame the vamps for the loss of people he loved. But above all, Shane was practical. "You can't win," he said. "Don't do this. We've got a plan. Trust us."

"*You* two?" Flora laughed. "Your girlfriend, she's a vampire's pet—the Founder's pet. And you, you are too much in love to see it, and too much of a child. She's with *them*, not you." She dismissed them both with a flip of her hand. "Enough. Enrique. *Vámanos.*"

He sent Shane an apologetic look and lifted his hands in a what-can-you-do? kind of gesture. "She's my mother," he said. "Sorry."

"It's okay." Shane nodded back. "But you should talk her out of this. Seriously. It's dangerous."

"I know, man. I *know.*"

Enrique hurried to catch up. His mother was already half a block away.

Claire stood with Shane, staring at the poster promoting Captain Obvious, and Shane finally took Monica's bigger, brighter poster and firmly stapled it right over the top.

"Let's go," he said. "I guarantee this isn't over."

SEVEN

CLAIRE

)

It wasn't over, not by a long shot, but at least they were left
alone to put up the rest of the posters; that didn't mean people
weren't glaring at them, or saying mean things, but nobody
actively tried to hurt them. Claire did wonder if Mrs. Ramos
would be tearing down posters behind them—and if she'd approve of Oliver doing the same thing. Maybe they'd meet in the
middle. That would be an interesting thing to witness.

By the time they'd stapled the last cardboard to a pole, in front
of Morganville High ("Go Vipers!"), Claire was thoroughly worn
out. This, she thought, had to be the worst day off ever. . . . They
hadn't even stopped for much of a lunch, though they'd wolfed
down some cookies between stops and had a couple of Cokes.
Morganville wasn't a very big town, but they'd been down almost
every street of it, and that was just about enough for one day in her

opinion. She was going to voice it, but she didn't have to, because Shane gave her a look that told her he was just as tired, and said, "Can we skip the lab and go home?"

"Home," she said, and slipped her arm through his. The only weight now was the stapler dragging down her backpack (and the anti-vamp knife and extra stakes that she rarely left behind) but it still felt like a ton. Shane took it from her and slipped it on one shoulder, and she envied those muscles—and admired them, too. They felt so warm and firm beneath her fingers, and it made her a bit light-headed, never mind the exhaustion. "What do you think Monica's doing right now?"

"Bullying someone to make her a crappy Web site and some buttons?"

Claire groaned, because he was almost certainly right. "We created a monster."

"Well, no. But we're enabling one."

By common unspoken consent, they avoided the street Common Grounds was on, which put them on a different, less traveled avenue; it was one that held some bad memories, Claire realized, and wished they'd risked Oliver's wrath one more time.

This was the street where Shane's house had once stood. There was nothing in the spot now except a bare, weed-choked lot, a cracked foundation, and the crumbling remains of what would have once been a fireplace. Even the mailbox, which had been leaning before, had given up the ghost and fallen to pieces of random, rusted metal.

"We don't—maybe we should—" She couldn't think how to say it, or even if she should, but Shane just kept walking, eyes fixed on the pavement ahead.

"It's okay," he said. She might have even believed him, a little, except for the slight hunch to his shoulders, and the way he'd lowered his head to let his shaggy hair veil his expression. "It's just an empty lot."

It wasn't. It was full—full of grief and anger, anguish and terror. She could almost feel it like needles on her skin, an irresistible urge to slow down, to stop, to *look*. She wondered if Shane felt it, too. Maybe he did. He wasn't walking quite as quickly as they approached the silent empty spot, which was choked with trash, scattered fire-blackened bricks, and the snarled balls of tumbleweeds.

It was the spot where Shane's family home had once stood, before it had burned down, taking his sister away with it.

Just as they took their first steps in front of it, Shane stopped. Just . . . stopped, not moving at all, head still down, hands in his pockets. He slowly looked up, right into Claire's startled eyes, and said, "Did you hear that?"

She shook her head, confused. All she heard was the normal, constant background noise of daily life—TV sets whispering from distant houses, radios in passing cars, the rattle of blown tumbleweeds against chain-link fences.

And then she heard something that sounded like a very soft, but clear, whisper. She couldn't have said what it *meant*, couldn't make out the word, but it didn't sound like distant conversation, or TV dialogue, or anything like that. It sounded very . . . specific. And very close.

"Maybe . . . a cat?" she guessed. It could have been a cat. But she didn't see anything as she glanced over the ruins of Shane's childhood. The only things still recognizable about it having been a home was the foundation—cracked in places, but still there where it wasn't hidden by weeds—and the jumbled outline of what must have once been a brick fireplace.

Shane didn't look toward the lot at all. He kept looking at

her, and she saw his eyes widen just as she, too, heard what he was hearing.

A voice. A clear girl's voice, very, very soft, saying, *Shane.*

His face drained completely of color, and Claire thought for a second he was going to hit the pavement, but he managed to hold on, somehow, and turned toward the lot to say, "Lyss?" He took a tentative step toward it, but stopped at the edge of the sidewalk. "Alyssa?"

Shane.

It was very clear, and it did *not* sound like a real person's voice—there was something eerie and cold and distant about it. Claire remembered the draug, the vampires' enemies who lurked in water and lured with song; this held something of that quality to it—something just not right.

She grabbed Shane's sleeve as he started to step onto the lot's dirt. "No," she said. "Don't."

He stared at the tumbled wreckage of his house, and said, "I have to. She's here, Claire. It's Alyssa."

His sister, Claire knew, had died in the fire that had wrecked this house—and he hadn't been able to save her. It was the first, and maybe the biggest, trauma in a life that had since had way too many.

She didn't even try to argue that it was impossible for his sister to be here, talking to him. There were far crazier things in Morganville than that. Ghosts? Those were no more unusual than drunken frat boys on a Friday night.

But she was scared. Very scared. Because there was a vast difference between ghosts who manifested themselves in the Founder Houses—like the Glass House, in which they lived—and one who could talk from thin air, powered by nothing at all. The first kind she could explain, theoretically at least. This?

Not so much.

"I have to do this," Shane said again, and pulled free of her. He stepped into the weeds, into what had once been the carefully tended front lawn of a relatively stable family, and walked steadily forward. The broken remains of a sidewalk were hidden under those weeds, Claire realized; it was buckled and broken into raw chunks, but it was recognizable when she looked for it. Shane kept going forward, then stopped and said, "This used to be the front door."

Claire devoutly did *not* want to do it, but she couldn't leave him alone, not here, not like this. So she stepped forward, and instantly felt a chill close in over her—something that didn't want her here. The pins-and-needles feeling swept over her again, and she almost stopped and backed up . . . but she wasn't going to let it stop her.

Shane needed her.

She slipped her hand into his, and he squeezed it hard. His face was set, jawline tight, and whatever he was looking at, it was not the rubble in front of them. "She died upstairs," Shane said. "Lyss? Can you hear me?"

"I really don't know if this is a good—" Claire caught her breath as the pins and needles poked again, deeply. Painfully. She could almost see the tiny little stab marks on her arms, the beads of blood, though she knew there was no physical damage at all.

"Lyss?" Shane stepped forward, over the nonexistent threshold, into what would have been the house. "Alyssa—"

He got an answer. *Shane.* It was a sigh, full of something Claire couldn't really comprehend—maybe a sadness, maybe longing, maybe something darker. *You came back.*

He sucked in a deep, shaking breath, and let go of Claire's hand to reach forward, into empty air. "Oh God, Lyss, I thought— how can you still be—"

Always here, the whisper said. So much sadness; Claire could hear it now. The resentment she felt was that of a baby sister hating that someone else had taken her brother from her; it might be dangerous, but it was understandable, and the sadness brought a lump into Claire's throat. *Can't go. Help.*

"I can't," Shane whispered. "I can't help you. I couldn't then and I can't now, Lyss. . . . I don't know how, okay? I don't know what you need!"

Home.

There were tears shining in his eyes now, and he was shaking. "I can't," he said again. "Home's gone, Lyss. You have to—you have to move on. I have."

No.

There was a wisp of movement at the edge of Claire's vision, and then she felt a shove, a distinct shove, that made her take a step back toward the sidewalk. When she tried to move toward Shane again, the pins and needles came back, but it felt more like a pinch now, sudden and vicious. She hissed and grabbed her arm, and this time when she looked down, she saw she had a red mark, just as if someone had physically hurt her.

Alyssa really didn't care for the idea that her brother had found a girlfriend, and Claire found herself skipping backward, pushed and bullied back all the way to the sidewalk.

Shane stayed where he was. "Please, can I—can I see you?"

There was that faint hint of movement again, mists at the corners of her vision, and Claire thought that for a second she saw a ghostly shadow appear against the still-standing bricks of the fireplace . . . but it was gone in seconds, blown away.

Please help me, Alyssa's whisper said. *Shane, help me.*

"I don't know how!"

Don't leave me alone.

Claire suddenly didn't like where this was going. Maybe she'd seen too many Japanese horror movies, and maybe it was just a tingle of warning from generations of superstitious ancestors, but suddenly she *knew* that what Alyssa wanted was not to be saved, but for Shane to join her.

In death.

She didn't know what Shane might have done, because just as she came to that breath-stopping conclusion, she caught sight of a shiny black van pulling around the corner. For a second she didn't connect it to anything in particular, and then she recognized the logo on the van's door.

Great. "Shane—we've got company," she said. "Ghost-hunting company."

"What?" Shane turned and looked at her blankly, then at where she pointed. Not only had the ghost hunters arrived, but the two hosts—Angel and Jenna—were already out and walking toward them. Jenna had something in her hands that looked like an electronic metering device; it was making strange, weird noises like a frequency tuner. Angel had what looked like a tape recorder. And behind them, following with a bulky handheld camera on his shoulder, was Tyler.

"—Activity," Jenna was saying in an intense voice. "Definitely some significant signs here. I got a huge spike from the van, and it's even bigger now. Whatever's out here, it's definitely worth checking into."

"Where?" Angel sounded tired and more than a little irritated. "We've had a lot of false alarms already. If I didn't know better, I'd think the local residents were trying to screw us up—oh, hello. Look, it's the kids from the courthouse. Where's your pretty friend?"

Claire didn't know which to take offense at more—the implication that she wasn't pretty, or that Monica might be considered a friend. She was saved from answering by Shane, who walked up to her and kept walking until he was blocking the path to the vacant lot completely. "Get lost," he said flatly. "I'm not in the mood."

"Excuse me?" Jenna said, and tried to move around him. He got in her way. "Hey! This isn't private property. It's a public sidewalk! We are fully within our rights to be here."

While she and Shane were facing off, Claire heard Angel mutter to Tyler, "Make sure you're getting all this. It's great stuff. We can use it in the teasers. The town that didn't want to know."

"You," Shane said, and pointed past Angel, at Tyler and the camera. "Turn it off. Now."

"Can't do that, bro. We're working here," Tyler said. "Relax. Just let us do our job."

"Do it somewhere else. You don't do it here."

"Why?" Jenna was staring at him intently, and past him, at the empty lot. She held out her meter gadget, and Claire could hear the tones it gave off. She didn't need to be an expert in ghostology to know it was pinging like mad. "Something you don't want us to see, perhaps?"

"Just back the hell off, lady. I mean it—"

"We'll see about this," Angel said, and pulled out a cell phone. Theatrically, of course. "We *do* have a permit to film direct from the mayor's office!"

"Let's see it," Shane said. "Go ahead; call somebody. I'll wait." He stared Angel down until the other man put the phone away. "Yeah. Thought so. Look, just do us all a favor, okay? Call it a day, get in your van, and head to some other town where they don't mind your making fun of dead people, all right?"

"That's not what we're doing!" Jenna said sharply. "I'm very committed to trying to locate those who are lost and stuck, and finding a way to bring them some peace. How dare you say—"

"I don't know—because you arrange all this crap for ratings, advertisers, and money? Maybe that?" Shane stepped forward, and he was using all his size and attitude this time. "Just *go*. Get off this street."

The device that Jenna was holding gave a sudden shrill alarm; she jerked in surprise and stared at it, then turned it to Angel. Tyler angled in to get a close-up of the meter.

"What?" Shane snapped.

"We got a huge electromagnetic spike," Jenna said. "It's coming from that vacant lot behind you. I've never seen anything like it—"

Shane. It was a very clear, cold, longing whisper, and it came from right behind them. And it just froze everyone right in place. Claire had a vivid, clear snapshot of them: Tyler, mouth open behind his camera; Angel, stunned silent; Jenna, eyes wide.

And Shane.

Shane's lips parted, but he didn't speak. His face had gone blank and pale, and he actually took a long step backward, pulling Claire with him. She didn't mind. That voice had a scary, otherworldly quality that didn't sound human.

Angel almost dropped his recorder, but he gained his composure and moved in to the camera to get a close-up. "Did you hear that?" he asked Tyler, then turned to Jenna. "That was no EVP. That was a *voice.*"

"Someone's messing with us," Jenna said in annoyance. "Cut, Tyler."

"I don't think so," he said. "Rolling. Keep going."

"Tyler!"

"Rolling, Jenna, keep rolling!"

"I'm telling you, the locals are having us on. We'll probably find some kind of EM transmitter out here, and some giggling high schooler with a megaphone. . . ."

"*Rolling!*"

"Okay, okay, it's digital. At least you're not wasting film. . . ." She took in a deep breath and said, in her tense ghost-hunting voice, "We may have gotten an actual spirit contact! I can't even begin to describe how incredibly rare this is!"

"Can you speak to us again?" Angel said, and if possible, he got even more pompous. "You said a name. Can you say it again?"

Nothing.

"I think it said *shame*," Jenna said. "Is it a shame you're gone? Are you ashamed of something?"

"Oh, for the love of—" Claire couldn't bite back her exasperation. "Come on. We have to go, now." She very deliberately didn't use his name. They didn't seem bright enough to make the connection, but even so . . .

"That's Alyssa," Shane said. "I'm telling you, it's her. My sister is *right there*."

Dammit. Well, there went her entire *nothing to see here, move along* plan.

"No such thing as ghosts," she said, and pointedly looked at the camera. Shane, recovering from the shock, finally got back on script enough to nod. "I think someone's messing with you. Really. You need to just—chalk it up to locals being stupid."

"Or," Shane said, "you could poke around in the dark. That's fun. There might be fewer annoying visitors if you tried it."

"Excuse me?" Jenna said. "Are you threatening us?"

"No, just making an observation. I mean, wandering around in the dark isn't a good idea, lady. Ask anybody." He shrugged. "Meth. It's a cancer around here. So I've heard, anyway."

"Oh," she said, and seemed to take it seriously for the first time. "It is a problem in a lot of places. I should have thought of that. Guys, maybe we should pack it in until later."

"But we *heard that*," Angel protested. "We should at least do EVP in the vacant lot, just in case!"

Shane started to object, but Claire tugged at his arm, urgently. *Let them,* she mouthed, and he finally shrugged and stepped out of the way. "Knock yourself out," he said. "Try not to get bitten by any rattlesnakes or anything."

"Snakes?" Tyler suddenly sounded very, very nervous.

"Or, you know, scorpions," Claire said cheerfully. "And tarantulas. We have those. Oh, and black widows and brown recluse spiders—they love it out here. You'll find them all over the place. If you get bitten, just be sure to, you know, call 911. They can most always save you."

"Most always," Shane echoed.

They walked on, leaving the three visitors—no longer quite so eager to delve in—debating the risks. As they did, Shane pulled out his phone.

"What are you doing?" she asked.

"Texting Michael," he said. "He needs to get to somebody in the vamp hierarchy and get these idiots off the street before this becomes really, really public and a big PR problem. . . ." He paused and looked up. "Oh hell. Twice in one day? Who did I piss off upstairs to make that happen?"

He meant that Monica Morrell had just crossed their path, again. She was standing against the side of a big, trashy-looking van, tongue wrestling her current boy admirer, just around the corner from where Shane's home had once been. Like most of Monica's boyfriends, her current beau was a big side of beef, sporty, with an IQ of about room temperature, and she was climbing him like ivy up a tree.

"Excuse me, Dan," Shane said as they got closer. "I think you got something on you—oh, hey, Monica. Didn't see you there."

She broke off the kiss to glare at him. "Freak."

"Any particular reason you're hanging out here, exactly? Not your usual territory. I don't see any stores within credit-card distance."

Her boyfriend—Dan, apparently—looked like a varsity football jock; he had the muscles, the bulk, and the jarhead hairstyle. Monica tended to attract the big-but-dumb ones, and this one, from the questioning look he sent toward them, seemed to run to type. "She said this was the right place," he said, "to set up the—"

"Shut up," Monica said.

"Set up the what?" Shane asked. "Would you maybe be planning to mess with our ghost-hunting friends?"

"Aren't you?" she shot back. "Yeah. We've got this thing in the van, totally guaranteed to screw up their—what is it?"

"Screw up their shit," Dan said, earnestly. "You know, their monitoring shit. It's going to play Black Sabbath backward and really freak 'em out. I read it on the Internet."

"Jesus, Dan," Shane said. He almost sounded impressed. "You are just . . . landmark stupid, aren't you? Has Guinness called yet about that world record?"

Dan growled and came at him, and that was of course a mistake; Shane balanced lightly on the balls of his feet, avoided his rush, dodged back toward the van, and as Dan lined up to rush him again, sidestepped like a matador and sent Dan crashing like a bullet headfirst into the metal.

Dan didn't go down, but he definitely thought about it. He leaned heavily on the metal and stared blankly into the distance for a minute. His forehead had a vivid red mark on it, and Shane said, "You probably ought to get some ice on that, man."

"Yeah," Dan said. "Yeah, thanks, bro." He didn't dare come after Shane again, so he turned on Monica with a glare. "Well? Brilliant plan, *Mayor*. What else you got?"

"Oh, Dan, don't be like that—"

"Play your own stupid pranks for a change."

Monica gave him a searing glare of disappointment, and he shrugged and got in the van. In seconds, it fired up and drove away in a belch of smoke.

Leaving Monica behind. She shot Claire a look of fury mixed with outrage. "I was trying to help get those jackasses out of town. Being proactive and all mayorlike! What the hell were *you* two doing? Auditioning for starring roles in their stupid show?"

They'd attracted attention, of course. It wasn't from surrounding houses, since no one bothered to look outside at mysterious fighting in the streets for entirely sensible reasons, but from the team from *After Death* that had come charging over with cameras, microphones, and gadgets. Angel immediately fixed his model's smile straight on Monica. "Are these two bothering you, lovely lady?"

"Please," Claire muttered, but it was too late; Monica was batting her eyes and putting on her best wounded-butterfly act as she crowded up next to her newly arrived knight in shining leather shoes.

"Oh yes," she breathed. "Did you see? He beat up my boyfriend!"

"Call the police," Angel ordered Tyler, who was still recording, but Tyler was distracted by Jenna, who was whacking her electronic meter device in obvious irritation.

"Hey, hey, hey, it's technology, not a drum!" he said, and took it from her. "What? What's wrong with it?"

"I had a strong signal!" she said. "It was there, I swear it was, but it just vanished about thirty seconds ago. I think they scared it off."

"You were reading something wrong."

"I saw it! It was maxed out in that vacant lot—I'm telling you. . . ."

"Oh—um, that was my boyfriend," Monica said, and brought the overlapping chaos to a dead halt. "He had the van that just took off? He was broadcasting a signal to make you think it was some kind of ghost. He thought it was kind of funny."

Angel was looking at Monica with a heartbroken expression. "Why would you do that?"

"It was Dan, not—"

"Why do teenagers do anything?" Jenna snapped. She stepped into Monica's space, looking for the world as if she was feeling just as strong an impulse to slap the girl as Claire was. "Get lost, before I call the cops."

"It's not against the law!"

"You're right. Get lost before I do something that *is* against the law, like putting my fist in your face."

"Hey!" Monica stepped into *Jenna's* space now, cheeks flushing a bright, hectic pink. "Do you know who I am?"

"Last year's high school queen bee who's no longer relevant but still thinks she is?" Jenna shot back, and Claire's eyes widened at the accuracy of the thrust. So did Monica's. "Look, sweetie, I've seen a dozen one-stoplight towns just like this, and there's always somebody just like you who thinks you're . . . well, somebody."

Monica opened her mouth to reply, but didn't. She was remembering that she was, in fact, nobody, at least by her own standards; she was just another bully now, with nothing to back it up. She didn't even have her best friends to enable her. Even her Cro-Magnon boyfriend had bailed on her at the first sign of trouble.

And it hurt. In that moment, though she shouldn't have, Claire felt a little twinge of sympathy.

"I'm running for mayor!" Monica rallied enough to snap back. "So careful what you say, because my first official act would be running you three out of town on a rail!"

Jenna shrugged and glared at Angel, who was still looking gravely disappointed, and said, "Come on, let's retake that last bit over in the vacant lot. We can still save some of the footage." She set out at a rapid pace around the corner, heading for the vacant lot. After a hesitation, Tyler followed her.

Angel shrugged and said, "I'm sorry, but you see how it is. We have work to do." This time, there was no hand kissing, and not much flirting, either.

"Wait," Monica said as he started to walk off. "You're just going to leave me here? Alone? With *them*?"

Angel flashed her a perfect smile but kept walking. "I'm sure they'll see you get home safe."

"Oh yeah," Shane said. "On my to-do list, right after discovering Atlantis. Enjoy your walk, Princess Mayor." He put his arm around Claire and tipped her chin up to look into her eyes. "You okay? Not hurt?"

"No," she said. "You?"

"The only way Dan can actually hurt me is to try to have a conversation. He may be on the college football team, but trust me, he's just barely junior varsity on street fighting."

Monica looked from the departing television people back to the two of them, then at the empty street. Looking for some kind of third option, Claire thought. "You could just go it alone," Claire said, with a little too much sweetness. "I'm sure you'll be safe. After all, *everybody* knows who you are."

"Thanks to our posters," Shane put in.

"You know, it's your fault my life is such a hell, anyway, so spare me your little gestures!"

"So now you're blaming us for your life falling apart, after a lifetime of earning it? Interesting."

"My life was fine before you came here!" Monica spat.

Shane gave her a long, level look. "You know whose life wasn't so fine? Pretty much everybody else's. Including the vampires', not that I'm counting that for a plus, but you get the idea."

She ignored Shane. Oddly, because those two were almost always gasoline and a match. "I need an escort home," she announced to the air somewhere between the two of them. "Tell me you're going that way."

Shane shrugged when Claire glanced at him. "Well, I guess we'd better. How can she be mayor if she's dead in a ditch?"

"She just taunted you with the voice of your *dead sister!*"

"No," Monica said.

"What?" Claire snapped; she was getting really angry now, angry enough to do or say something she couldn't take back. And Shane, oddly, wasn't.

"I didn't do that," Monica said, and met Shane's eyes. "I wouldn't do that. Dan and I were messing with their electronics, and we were planning to sneak over and make some rattling noises. But I swear, I didn't pretend to be your *sister.*"

"She wouldn't," Shane said softly. "Not after Richard, anyway." There was, Claire realized, some kind of understanding between the two of them now, something she didn't quite get but could see; it wasn't affection, and it sure wasn't a crush, but a kind of mutual . . . caution. As if they understood each of them had a place that could be hurt, and neither was willing to go there anymore.

"Then what *was* that? Was it really—really—" She couldn't finish the thought. She was feeling a little unstuck now, as if the world were bending around her. . . . She thought she'd seen enough of Morganville that something like that would never happen again.

"I don't know," Shane said, "but I intend to find out."

Walking Monica home was just exactly as fun as Claire expected, which was not fun at all. She complained about having to walk in her heels (to which Shane, proving he was not *totally* off the Let's Hate Monica bandwagon, suggested she mount her broom and fly home); she complained about the hot weather, and sweat ruining her outfit; she complained about the lack of cab service (Claire had to agree she had a point there—Morganville desperately needed cabs).

Claire had begun to tune her out by that point, since they were within sight of Monica's luxury apartment complex (the only one in Morganville, in fact, with ten apartments that cost more than most of the town could even think about paying). Monica had sold the Morrell family home, which had mostly survived all the troubles of the past few years intact except for party damage, and made a tidy bank account to allow her to not work for at least a couple of years, though it probably wouldn't last at the rate Monica blew through designer shoes.

And then Monica said, "I heard people talking around town today. Your friends ought to be watching their backs, 'cause the knives are out."

That got Claire's attention, fast. Shane's, too. They both stopped walking, and Monica clomped on a few more steps before coming to a halt and saying, "What? Like you didn't know?"

"What are you talking about?" Shane closed the distance toward her, fast. "What did you hear? Spill it!"

"Hey, hey, hold on!" She tried to back up, but she overbalanced on her precarious heels and almost went down; Shane grabbed her arm and steadied her, and didn't let go. "Look, I don't know why you're so surprised and all! Let go!"

"Not until you answer the question. What about Michael and Eve?"

"Oh, come on. A vamp marrying a human gets the fanged ones all upset, and Eve made herself look like the ultimate fang-banger to all the humans by putting a ring on one, so what did you expect, exactly? Flowers and parades? This is Texas. We're still figuring out how to *spell* tolerance."

"I said, what do you know about it? Where? When? Who's involved?"

"Let go, jerk!"

He didn't say anything, but Claire was almost sure he squeezed, because Monica made a funny little sound and went very still. "Okay," she said. "Okay, jackass, you win. It's just general talk as far as I know, but some people are saying an example should be made. Michael and Eve are just handy targets standing in the middle of the war zone. Come to think of it, so's your girlfriend, what with all her cozying up to Amelie."

Shane let her go. "You're one to talk."

"Yeah, I am. I know what it's like to think you're secure and safe and all of a sudden be standing all alone. You think you and your friends are the only ones in the crosshairs? Do you have any idea how many people want to hurt *me*?"

Monica was more self-aware than Claire had ever given her credit for. She knew how things were—maybe better than Shane, surprisingly enough. She'd probably had to learn how to protect herself fast, once the town had stopped being cowed by her status as Self-Crowned Princess.

"Then you shouldn't be pissing off the only ones who might listen to you when you scream for help," Shane said. "Get me?"

Monica finally nodded, a little unwillingly. She shot a quick, unreadable look at Claire, and then turned and strode up the walk to her apartment. They watched as she produced a key (though where she'd kept it on that skintight dress was a mystery) and unlocked her door. Once she was inside, and the lights were on, Shane put his hands in his pockets and extended an elbow to Claire, who threaded her arm through his.

"You're super nice to her, all of a sudden," Claire said.

"Ha. If I was super nice to her, she wouldn't have bruises on her arm right now," he said. "But I'm willing to forget to hate her, every once in a while. She's had it rough these past couple of years."

"So have you."

He flashed her a smile. "I never did have much, so having it rough came with the territory. I was conditioned for it. And you're forgetting the most important thing that's different."

"You don't have a fashion addiction to skintight clothes?"

"I have you," he said, and the warmth in his voice took her breath away. She let go of his arm and crowded in close as they walked, and he hugged her close. It was awkward making progress that way, but it felt so sweet. "Okay, *and* I don't have a fashion addiction. Valid point."

"You don't think she knows something about a plot to hurt Michael and Eve, do you? The way she said that back there . . ."

"I don't know," Shane said. "I don't think she'd hide it; she'd really like teasing us with it, but she'd give it up. She'd want to, I think. It's not as if she wants Michael dead, anyway. She always had a little bit of a thing for him."

"And you," Claire said, and elbowed him. "More than a little bit."

"Ugh. Please don't say that or I'll lose my will to live."

"I love you." It came out of her spontaneously, and she felt a little jolt of adrenaline, then a little burst of fear right on the heels of it. There had been no reason to say it now, walking down the street, but it had just seemed . . . right. She was a little afraid that Shane would think it was clingy, or fake, but when she glanced over at him, she saw he was smiling—an easy, relaxed smile, uncomplicated and happy.

It wasn't something she saw very often, and it made her feel glorious.

"I love you, too," he said, and that felt like some kind of milestone to her, that they felt easy enough with each other to just say it whenever they wanted, without feeling awkward about it, or afraid.

We're growing up, she thought. *We're growing up together.*

He put his arm around her, and they walked close together, all the way home. The setting sun was lurid reds and golds, spilling into the vast and open sky, and it was as beautiful a thing as Claire had ever seen in Morganville.

Peaceful.

It was the last of that, though.

EIGHT

AMELIE

❨

I knew of no one, vampire or human, who could detour Myrnin from a course once he had decided on it, whether it was mad, manic, destructive, or simply single-minded. So when the guards informed me that he had refused to stop at the checkpoint to the hallway of my office, I did not bother to order them to try to detain him. It might have been possible for a few moments, an hour, a day, but Myrnin wouldn't forget. He would simply start again, and sooner or later, he'd succeed.

I pressed the button on my phone—still such an awkward and common device, to my mind, nothing attractive about it—and informed my assistant that upon his arrival she should not stand in his way. Poor thing, she had taken enough abuse lately, from humans as well as from vampires.

Only I could handle Myrnin with any measure of success.

He exploded through my doorway with the force of a tropical storm, and indeed the riot of colors about his person reminded me of that . . . so many shades, and none of them complementary. I did not bother to catalog all the offenses, but they began with the jacket he had chosen. I had no name for that particular hue of orange, other than *unfortunate.*

"This is my last attempt at making you see sense," he said. Shouted, actually. "Damn you, how long have we worked, how many sacrifices have we made? To see you throw that all away for *him . . .*"

I had already decided, well before his grand entrance, what my first move would be, and with an economy of motion, I slapped him full across the face. The force of it would have felled a strong mortal; it certainly made Myrnin pause, with the mark of the blow blushing a very faint pink in the shape of my fingers.

He blinked.

"You may save your well-rehearsed speech," I said. "I'll hear none of it. This ill-advised intrusion is at an end."

"Amelie, we have been friends for—"

"Don't presume to tell me how many years. I can count as well as you, or possibly better on the days when you're insane," I snapped back. "Sit down."

He did, looking oddly watchful. I paced. I'd been doing that more frequently than was my normal habit, but I put it down to raw nerves. Morganville lately had seemed exasperating, a broken toy that would never be put right no matter how much time and love I lavished on the repairs.

Myrnin said, "You even move like he does now."

"Silence!" I whirled on him, snarling, and knew my eyes had gone deep crimson.

"No," he said, with an eerie sort of calm. Myrnin was many

things, but he was rarely calm, and when he was, it was time to worry. "There are some people who may say this is a good match for you, that you needed a strong right arm to calm the fears of the vampires and subdue the human population. I am not one. Sam gentled you, Amelie. He made you feel more a part of the world you rule. Oliver will never do that. He feels no responsibility for those he crushes, and—"

"Foul his name again and we're finished," I interrupted. I meant it, and it dripped from every syllable I spoke.

Myrnin sat still for a moment, staring into my eyes, and then he nodded. "Then we are indeed," he said. "I just had to be certain that you were beyond my hope, and my help. But if he has you tied this close, he will have you do as he wishes. Whomever it hurts."

"Do you think I am so—so stupid? So utterly weak that I would allow any man to—"

"Not just a man," Myrnin said. "He swayed a nation to kill its king, once. He persuades. He influences. Perhaps he doesn't even intend to do so, but it's in his nature. And while you are more powerful than he by far, once he has your trust, there is no saying what he might be able to accomplish, through you."

His words left me cold inside, a chill I'd not felt since the moment I'd finally acknowledged the aching need for Oliver's regard, for his loyalty, for his attention. I had been alone for so long; Michael's grandfather Sam Glass and I had loved, but save for a few precious times, always carefully, and from afar. Oliver had come at me like a storm, and the fury of it was . . . cleansing.

But was Myrnin right? Could I be falling victim, as so many had, to Oliver's deadly charm? Was what I was doing here right, or simply convenient to his ambitions?

I slowly sat down in a chair across from my oldest living friend, the one who—in the end—I trusted more than any still walking the earth, and said, "I know my own mind, Myrnin. I am Amelie. I am the Founder of Morganville, and what I do here, I do for the good of all. You may trust that. You *must*."

He had a sadness in his eyes that I could not understand, but then, who ever had understood Myrnin fully? I couldn't make that claim, and neither could Claire, the girl he trusted so much. And then he stood, and with the ease of thousands of years of experience, he made a graceful, ages-old bow, took my hand in his, and kissed it with the greatest of love and respect.

"Farewell," he said.

And then he was gone.

I slowly drew my hand back to my chest, frowning, and became aware that I was cradling it, rubbing the spot where his lips had pressed as if they had burned me. *Farewell.* He'd thrown tantrums many times, threatened to leave, but this—this seemed different.

It was a calm, ordered, and above all *sad* departure.

"Myrnin?" I said softly into the silence, but it was too late.

Far too late.

NINE

CLAIRE

❯

Shane preceded Claire into the house by a couple of steps as she shut and locked the door behind them; apparently that was a lucky thing, because as she was turning the dead bolt, she heard him say, "Oh, crap," in a voice that was choked with laughter, and then a startled yelp from Eve, followed by the sound of scrambling and flailing. Shane backed up next to Claire and held her back when she would have moved forward.

"Trust me," he said. "Wait a second."

Michael and Eve were in the parlor, the front living area that was so rarely used, except for dropping coats and bags and miscellaneous stuff, and from the hasty whispers and rustles of clothes, Claire quickly figured out exactly why Shane was holding her back.

Oh.

"I guess I should have said, *Put your pants on*," Shane said, loudly enough that they could hear. "Alert, there's a barely legal girl out here."

"Hey!" Claire swiped a hand at him, which he easily avoided. "What were they doing?"

"What do you *think*?"

Pink-faced, Eve leaned around the frame of the doorway and said, "Um . . . hi. You're early."

"Nope," Shane said with merciless good cheer. "It's sundown. Not a bit early. You got clothes on?"

"Yes!" Eve said. Her cheeks burned brighter. "Of course! And you didn't see anything anyway." There was a bit of worry to her voice, though, and Shane made it worse with a big, utterly unsympathetic smile.

"Married people," he said to Claire. "They're a menace."

Eve eased out of the door, zipping up her blouse—it was one of those with a front zip—and cleared her throat. "Right," she said. "We really need to talk, you guys."

"You know, my dad sucked at most things, but he did give me the birds and bees Q&A when I was ten, so I'm good," Shane said. Man, he was enjoying this way too much. "Claire?"

She nodded soberly. "I think I understand the basics."

Eve, still blushing, rolled her eyes. "I'm serious!"

Michael finally appeared behind her. He was dressed, kind of; his shirt was unbuttoned, though he was doing it up as quickly as he could. "Eve's right," he said, and he wasn't kidding at all. "We need to talk, guys."

"No, we don't," Shane said. "Just text me or something next time. We could go grab a burger or a movie or—"

Michael shook his head and walked inside the parlor. Eve followed him. Shane sent Claire a look that had a little bit of alarm in it, and finally shrugged. "Guess we're talking," he said. "Whether we want to or not."

Michael and Eve hadn't taken seats, when the two of them came in; they were standing with their hands clasped, for solidarity, apparently.

"Uh-oh," Shane murmured, and then put on a cheerful smile. "So, Mikey, what up? Because this looks like more than just a 'how was your day' kind of discussion."

"We needed to talk about something," Eve said. She looked nervous, and—for Eve—she'd dressed super plainly, just a black shirt and jeans, not a single skull or shiny thing in evidence, except for the subtle glimmer of her wedding ring. "Sorry, guys. Sit down."

"You first," Shane said as Claire dumped her backpack with a heavy *clunk* by the wall. Michael exchanged a look with Eve, and then sat beside her on the old velvet sofa, while Claire settled in the armchair and Shane leaned on the top of it, his hand on her shoulder. "If we're playing guessing games, I'm going to go with— you're pregnant. Wait, can you be? I mean, can the two of you . . . ?"

Eve flinched and avoided looking at the two of them. "That's not it," she said, and bit her lip. She twisted her wedding ring in agitation, and then finally said, "We've been talking about getting our own place, guys. Not because we don't love you, we do, but—"

"But we need our own space," Michael said. "I know it seems weird, but for us to feel really together, married, we need to get some time to ourselves, and you know how it is here; we're all in one another's business here."

"And there's only one bathroom," Eve said mournfully. "I *really* need a bathroom."

Claire had suspected it was coming, but that didn't make it feel any better. She instinctively reached up for Shane's hand, and his fingers closing over hers made her feel a little steadier. She'd gotten so used to the idea of the four of them together, always together, that hearing Michael talk about moving stirred up feelings she'd thought she'd outgrown ... feelings that hadn't been on her radar since she'd first walked in the door of the Glass House.

She suddenly felt vulnerable, alone, and rejected. She felt homesick, even though she was home, because home wasn't the way she'd left it this morning.

"We want you to be happy," Claire managed to say. Her voice sounded small and a little hurt, and she didn't mean it that way, not at all. "But you can't move out—it's your house, Michael. I mean, it's the *Glass* House. And you two are ... Glass. We're not."

"Screw that," Shane said immediately. "Sure, I want you two crazy kids to be happy, but you're talking about busting up something that's good, really good, and I don't like it, and I'm not going to be all noble and pretend I do. Together, we're strong—you've said that yourself, Michael. Now all of a sudden you want more privacy? Dude, that's about as logical as *Let's split up* in a horror movie!"

Michael gave him a look as he finished buttoning his shirt. "I think it's pretty obvious privacy's an issue."

"Not if you don't decide to get crazy in a room without a locking door. Or, you know, a *door.*"

"It's just that we were waiting on you guys, and we were nervous, and ... it just happened," Eve said. "And we're *married.* We have the right to get crazy if we want to. Anywhere. At any time."

"Okay, I get that," Shane said. "Hell, I'd like a little spontaneous sexytime, too, but is it worth putting us all in danger? Because Morganville ain't safe, guys. You know that. You go out of this house, or make us leave it, and something is going to happen. Something bad."

"Have you taken up Miranda's fortune-telling?" Eve asked. "I could say something about crystal balls. . . ."

"Don't need a psychic friend to tell me it's nasty out there and bound to get worse. Michael, you're on Team Vampire. Are you saying you don't think it's going toxic with Amelie and Oliver in charge?"

Michael didn't try to answer that one, because he couldn't; they'd all agreed on it already.

Eve jumped in, instead. "We could get a house in the vampire quarter," she said. "Free. It's part of Michael's citizenship in town. It wouldn't be a problem except—"

"Except that you'd be living in Vamp Central, and the only thing with a pulse in a couple of square blocks, surrounded by people who think of you as an attractively shaped plasma container?" Shane asked. "Problem. Oh, another problem: Mikey, you said yourself that being around us, meaning *all* of us, helped you cope with your instincts. Now you're talking about isolating yourselves with a bunch of also-deads. Not smart, man. It'll make you more vamp, and it'll put Eve in more danger, too."

"I never said we were moving to the vampire quarter," Michael said. "Eve was just pointing out we could, not that we would. We could find something else, something close. The old Profit place is still for sale down the street. Amelie gave me a bequest, so I've got money to put down."

"Michael . . . We are *not* moving into that pit," Eve said. It sounded like an old argument. "It smells like cat urine and old-man clothes, and it's so ancient, it makes this place look like the house of the future. I don't think it has phone lines, never mind Internet. Might as well live in a cardboard box."

"Always an option," Shane said cheerfully. "And you'd have a huge bathroom. Like, the entire world."

"Ugh, gross."

"It's what you pay me for."

"Remind me to give you a negative raise."

"This isn't getting us anywhere," Michael interrupted, and shut them both down, hard. "Besides, it's not just the four of us anymore. It's Miranda."

The conversation came to a sudden and vivid halt, and they all waited to see what would happen. It was night; that meant Miranda had physical form.

But it didn't necessarily mean she could hear everything.

Claire lowered her voice to an instinctive, fierce whisper. "Hey! Don't be that way!"

"Look, I'm not saying I don't have sympathy for her; I do, a lot. I used to *be* her," Michael whispered back. "I know what it feels like being trapped in here. It drives you half crazy, and the only way you can survive it, the *only* way, is to be around people who think of you as . . . normal. But she doesn't have that. We know what she is. We know she's around all the time, and that means she tiptoes around us, and we tiptoe around her, and—it's just not good, okay? It's not."

"So, what do you want me to do?" Miranda asked. They all flinched and turned. She hadn't been there before, but now she'd appeared in the doorway to the hall, just like the spooky ghost she sometimes was. Claire was almost sure it was deliberate. "Leave?"

"You can't," Michael said. He did it gently, but there wasn't any doubt in it, either. "Mir, you knew when you came here that last time"—when she'd been killed here, he meant—"that there'd never be a way to leave again. The house saved you, and protects you, but you have to stay inside."

"Just because you did?" Miranda said. There was something different about her now, Claire realized; she was wearing a definitely not-Miranda outfit. No dowdy oversized dresses this time, or cheap fraying sweaters; she was wearing a skintight black sheer shirt with a black skull printed on it, and beneath that, a red scoop-neck that somehow managed to give her cleavage—just the suggestion, but still. For Miranda, that was . . . quite a change. "I'm not you, Michael."

"Maybe not, but do you have to become Eve?" Shane asked. "Because I'm pretty sure you raided her closet."

"I bought those for her!" Eve protested. "And anyway, she looks cute in them."

She did. Miranda had also gathered her hair up in two thick ponytails on either side of her head, and used a little of Eve's eyeliner. It was a little Goth, but not full-on, either. It suited her.

"It's me, isn't it?" Miranda said, ignoring both Eve and Shane this time. She was totally fixed on Michael, her eyes steady and wide. "It's about me, being here all the time. You feel like you can't hide from me. Well, that's true. You can't. I'm sorry, but that's just how it is, and you know it better than anyone. You can't just . . . turn off, like some kind of light. You're here, and you're bored."

"I know," Michael said. "Mir—"

"That's why you don't want to stay here. Because I'm here. It's not about them at all."

"No, honey, it's not really—" Eve bit her lip and glanced from Michael to Miranda and then back again. "It's not that, I swear. . . ."

"Don't swear," Miranda said, "because I know I'm right."

"She is," Michael said. When Eve turned toward him, he held up a hand to stop the outburst. "I'm sorry, but like I said, I've been there. I know how it feels. I can't just . . . ignore her. And I can't enjoy life in here knowing how miserable she is, or at least is going to be."

"You were miserable?" Eve said in a small voice. "Really? With us?"

"No—I didn't mean—" He made a frustrated sound and plumped down in one of the chairs, elbows on his knees. "It's hard to explain. Being around you, the three of you, was all that made things bearable, most days. The world just keeps getting smaller and smaller until it smothers you like a plastic bag over your face. With her here, I—I remember how that feels. I dream about it."

"So what am I supposed to do?" Miranda demanded. "I saved Claire's life, you know! I *died* for her!"

"I know that!" Michael snapped back. "I just wish you'd done it somewhere else!"

Even Shane sucked in a breath at that one and said, softly, "Bro—"

"No," Miranda said. Her chin was trembling, and she blinked back tears, but she didn't fall apart. Claire felt an aching urge to hug her, but Miranda looked as if she might break if anyone touched her. "It's not his fault. He's right. I made this happen, and it isn't fair. Not to him, not to me, not to anybody. It's a mess, and I did it. I thought—I just thought that it was perfect. That I'd finally have a real home, real family, people who—" Her voice broke and faded, and she shook her head. "I should have known. I don't get those things."

"I didn't mean that—," Michael said, but she turned and walked off.

None of them reacted at first. Claire thought nobody quite knew what to think, or to do, and then she saw Michael flinch and rise to his feet. She didn't know why until she heard the front door opening.

"No!" he shouted, and flashed at vampire-speed out of the room.

"The hell?" Shane blurted, and rushed after him, followed by Eve and Claire. "What—"

Claire pushed past him as he stopped, and she sucked in a deep, startled breath.

Because Miranda was *outside*. On the porch. And Michael was standing there, holding on to her arm as she fought to pull free. He was holding on to the doorframe, stretched fully out, and Miranda must have had a tiger's strength in that small body, because he was clearly having trouble keeping his grip. "Stop!" he yelled at her. "Miranda, I'm not letting you do this!"

"You can't stop me!" she screamed back, and there were tears streaking her face now in uneven trains of running eyeliner. She looked horrified and tragic and very, very upset. "Let go!"

"Come back inside. We can talk about it!"

"There's nothing to talk about. You don't want me here, so I just need to go!"

"You can't go—you'll die!" Claire blurted. She pushed past Michael and out onto the porch and grabbed Miranda in a bear hug. She could feel the girl's not-quite-real heart pounding against her forearm, out of terror, anger, or sheer adrenaline. "Miranda, *think*. Come back inside and we'll talk it over, all right? None of us wants you to die out here!"

"I'm dying in there, if you all leave! This way you can stay; you can be happy again—"

"It's not you; I never meant that!" Michael was afraid, Claire thought, really and starkly afraid that this was all his fault. "You can't do this. We'll work it out."

Miranda went very still for a second, though her heart continued to race uncontrollably fast, and she let out a deep, surrendering sigh. "All right," she said. "You can let go."

Michael said, "If you come inside, sure."

"I will."

Claire loosened her grip, just a little.

And it was just enough for Miranda to twist like a wild thing, ponytails whipping in Claire's face, and when Michael yelled and tried to pull her in, Miranda grabbed hold of his arm and bit him, hard enough to make him let go.

And then she stumbled backward, free, down the steps, and sprawled on the ground in the yard.

They all froze—Miranda, Claire, Michael, Eve, and Shane who had lunged out as well. The only thing moving was a single fluttering moth circling the yellow glow of the porch light.

Miranda slowly got up.

"Um . . . ," Shane said, when no one spoke. "Shouldn't she be, I don't know, dissolving?"

Michael took a step down toward her, and Miranda skipped backward. He held out his hand, palm out, as if she were a lost child who might bolt out into traffic. "Mir, wait. *Wait.* Look at yourself. Shane's right. You're not—going away."

"I'm still on the property."

"It doesn't work that way," he said. "I couldn't leave the doorway, let alone get down into the yard. Claire?" He looked at her as she stepped down next to him, because she'd had a brief period trapped in a ghostly state, too. She nodded.

"I couldn't leave, either," she said. "Miranda, how are you doing this?"

"I'm not!" She took another step backward down the sidewalk, toward the fence. "I'm just trying to—to get out of your hair, okay? If you'll just let me go!"

It seemed so quiet out tonight. The houses of Lot Street were sketched out in broad strokes of grays; the sky overhead had turned the color of lapis, and the stars were bright and cold. There were no clouds. The temperature had already fallen at least ten degrees, as was typical for the desert; it'd dip down almost to freezing before dawn.

"How did it feel? Going outside?" Michael asked.

Miranda gave a little shudder. "Like . . . pushing through some kind of plastic wrap, I guess. It felt cold, but it's colder out here. Much colder. Like I'm moving away from a fire."

"But you feel okay? Not coming to pieces?" Eve said. She was watching with wide, scared eyes. "Miranda, please, don't go any farther, okay? Just stay where you are. Let's—think about this. If you don't want us to go, we'll stay, okay? We'll all stay in the house. We'll all be friends and be a family for you. I promise. We won't let you down."

"It's better if I go." Miranda shuddered again. She looked pale now, but not exactly ghostly. Just cold. Claire wondered if she should get her a coat, but that was stupid; the idea was to get her back *in*, not help her stay out.

That plan didn't seem to be working so well, because as Claire tried to take a step closer, Miranda opened the front gate in the leaning picket fence, which was badly in need of paint.

"No!" the four of them said, in chorus, and Michael took a chance, a big one. He rushed the girl, at vampire-speed, hoping to get hold and pull her back inside before she stepped out onto the public sidewalk, off Glass House property altogether.

But he didn't make it.

Miranda ducked and ran all the way to the street.

To the *middle* of the street, where she stopped, shuddering almost constantly now, and looked up at the wide Texas sky, the moon, the stars.

"I'm okay," she said. "I'm going to be okay. See? I don't have to be inside all the time. I can go out. I'm fine. . . ."

But she wasn't fine; they could all see it. She was milky pale and her teeth were chattering. It wasn't that cold outside; Claire's breath wasn't even steaming, but from the way Miranda was shaking, it might as well have been below freezing.

"You're not fine," Eve said. "Mir, please, come back. You've proven your point. Yeah, you can leave—" She glanced at Michael and mouthed, *Why?*, but he only shrugged. "You can leave anytime you want. So let's go inside and celebrate, okay? Besides, it's dark. You're vamp bait in the middle of the street like this."

"What are they gonna do—bite her?" Shane asked. "She's *dead*, Eve. I don't even think she has blood."

"Yes, she does," Michael said. He was watching Miranda with a concerned expression now. "She's got a living body, for the night-time, just like I did. She can be hurt at night. And drained. It just wouldn't kill her permanently; at least I don't think it would. . . . I think she'd come back."

"Renewable blood resources," Eve said softly. "There's a nightmare for you. We can't let them find out about her. We need to get her back inside and figure out how she's able to do this."

"How? She won't let any of us get close!"

"Surround her," Eve said. "Michael, Shane, get on the other side. Claire and I will come in from this side. Box her in. Don't let her run. We'll just herd her back inside."

"She's strong," Michael warned. "Crazy strong."

"She won't hurt us," Eve said. Michael glanced down at his arm, which was still healing and showed bite marks. "Well, not much, anyway."

"You and your strays," he said, but Claire could tell there was love behind it. "All right, we'll do it your way. Shane?"

"On it."

Michael and Shane spread out, right and left, circling around

Miranda and leaving her a wide berth in the middle of the road as Eve and Claire closed the distance from the front. Claire supposed it looked weird, but if anyone was watching from the other houses, no one made a sound. Not a curtain twitched. Not only did the town of Morganville not care; it didn't even notice when a tweener was stalked by four older teens.

Even if they had good intentions.

Miranda wasn't trying to get away, though. She had wrapped her thin arms around her body and was shuddering in continuous spasms now, and her skin looked less real, more like glass with mist behind it.

"Miranda," Claire said softly, "we need to get you inside. Please."

"I can do this," Miranda said. She was staring down at herself with a blank expression, but there was a stubborn set to her chin, and she wiped her cheeks with the back of a hand and squared her shoulders. "I can live out here. I can. I don't need to be in there."

"You do," Eve said. "Maybe it's a gradual thing. You need to work on it a little at a time. So we can try again tomorrow night. Tonight, hey, come inside; we'll watch a movie. You get to pick."

"Can we watch the pirate movie? The first one?"

"Sure, honey. Just come inside."

Shane and Michael were making steady progress coming up from behind Miranda, and Michael nodded to Claire as she got into position. "Let's all go in," he said. Miranda shuffled awkwardly in place, as if her legs didn't want to move, and turned to look at him over her shoulder. "We don't want anything bad to happen to you, Mir."

"Well," she said, "it's a little late for that, but I appreciate the thought. Did you know? I can't tell the future anymore? It's as if all the power I had went somewhere else." She gestured down at herself. "Into this."

That . . . might make some weird kind of sense, Claire thought, that Miranda's powerful psychic gifts—the same ones that had led her to die inside the Glass House to save Claire's life—had become a kind of life-support system for her, after death.

"But it means I don't know anymore," Miranda said. Her voice was fainter now, almost like a whisper. "I don't know what's going to happen. I'm scared."

"You don't have to be," Claire said, and stretched out her hand. Miranda hesitated, then reached out.

But the second their skin touched, Miranda's cracked like the thinnest ice, and an icy fog spilled out, searing Claire's fingers with chill. She drew back with a cry, and there were cracks all over Miranda's body now, racing through in lace black lines, and then she just . . .

She just broke.

For a few seconds the fog held together in a vague girl shape, and Claire heard a cry, a real and surprised and scared cry . . .

And then she was gone. Just completely gone, except for empty clothes lying in the street.

"Mir!" Claire felt the pressure in her hand vanish, and lunged forward, scissoring the air, hoping for something, anything . . . but there was nothing—just empty space.

Miranda had vanished completely, and her last word seemed to echo over and over in Claire's mind.

Scared.

"Oh God," she said in a whisper, and felt tears sting her eyes. Miranda had been dealt raw deals her whole life, up to and including dying in the Glass House at the hands of the draug, but it had felt like, finally, she was getting *something* going her way. A place of safety. A life, however limited, that she could call her own.

It was just . . . very sad—so sad that Claire felt tears choking her, and she fell into Shane's arms, clinging to his solid warmth for a long few moments before he whispered in her ear, "We have to go back. It's not safe out here."

She didn't want to go, but there wasn't any point in risking their lives for someone who was already gone. So she let him guide her back toward the Glass House. Michael and Eve were already there. Eve, uncharacteristically, hadn't shed a tear, from the flawless state of her mascara; she was usually the one prone to bursting into tears, but not this time. She just looked blank and shocked.

"Maybe she's okay," Eve said. Michael put his arm around her. "Maybe—oh God, Michael, did we make this happen? We started this, with all the talk about moving. If we hadn't said that she was bothering us, maybe she wouldn't have . . . have . . ."

"It's not your fault," Shane said quietly. "She was bound to try it, sooner or later; once she figured out she could make it out the door, she was going to keep pressing her luck. And anyway, you could be right. She might still be okay. Maybe she's just not anchored anymore. It could be harder for her to get back or let us know she's still around. Maybe she'll be back tomorrow."

He was trying to put the best face on it, but no matter what, it was grim. They'd lost someone, out here in the dark—a scared little girl, left on her own. Maybe for good.

And from the look in his eyes, even Shane knew they were all to blame.

Claire had been looking forward to spending the night in Shane's company, in all the shades of meaning that might hold, but Miranda's disappearance had taken all the joy out of it for them both. Michael and Eve seemed to be just the same. They all ended up sitting on the couch together and watching a DVD that none of them particularly cared about—something about time travel and dinosaurs—just because Eve had mentioned that it had been Miranda's favorite out of their little store of home videos. Claire closed her eyes for most of it, leaning her head on Shane's chest, listening to his slow, strong heartbeat, and allowing his steady strokes of her hair to soothe the grief a little. When the movie ended and silence fell, Michael finally asked if anybody wanted to play a game, but nobody seemed willing to take up the controllers—not even Shane, who had, as far as Claire could remember, never turned it down. That split Michael and Eve upstairs to their room, and left Claire and Shane sitting by themselves.

It felt chilly. Claire found herself shivering, but she didn't want to move away from Shane's embrace; he solved that by taking the afghan from the back of the couch and wrapping it around them both. "Well," he finally said, "I guess the issue of moving is off the table, at least for right now."

"Guess so," Claire said. Tears threatened again, but she wiped her eyes with the back of her hand in an angry swipe. *Enough.* She knew she wasn't really crying for Miranda at the moment; she was just feeling sorry for herself, for losing another brick in the wall of her zone of safety, for more change when she just wanted everything to stay the same. "But the issue's not going away. And we can't let our friends just . . . leave, Shane. It's not right. It's not safe."

"It's Morganville," he said, and kissed her gently. "Safety isn't something we get guaranteed."

"They do." She really meant, *He does,* because Michael was the one with the exemption to human rules, but surely that extended to Eve now that she was his wife. *Wife*—what a weird word; it still didn't sound quite real to Claire's mental ears. Eve was a *wife.* And Shane had raised the even weirder possibility that someday Eve might be a *mother.* Maybe that shouldn't have been quite so strange to her, but she hadn't had any other friends who'd gotten married; it was still a foreign concept when applied to an actual person, and she didn't altogether understand why Michael and Eve, who'd been so easy with sharing a house when they were all single-but-committed, would be so weird about it now that there'd been an actual church ceremony.

"Well, you might have a point. The Glass family's had special consideration for a long time," Shane agreed. "Probably because as a rule they weren't douche bags. But Eve's family . . ." He hesitated, as though wondering whether this was something he should share. Then he must have decided it was, because he said, "Eve's family had a bad rep, going back generations."

"For . . . ?"

"Some people suck up and stomp down, if you know what I mean. Eve's family was like that: sucking up to the vamps at every opportunity, stomping on the heads of everybody they thought beneath them. Bullies. Kind of like the Morrells, only on a much smaller scale. That didn't get them respect from the vamps, or the humans; they didn't have money to buy people off, or the power to make them afraid. So I wouldn't say Eve was born with the immunity idol or anything. Not like Michael was, when he was human. Everybody liked the Glass family."

Claire had known Eve's dad was bad, and her mom was pretty much wallpaper, but the knowledge that it had gone on for generations was revolting. Generation after generation, pandering to the vampires for favors, and giving up their children when the vampires got interested—as Brandon, the Rossers' Protector, had ordered Eve to be given to him. Eve hadn't played along, which was part of why she'd ended up in the Glass House with Michael in the beginning. She'd been so willing to rebel that she'd risked death to do it.

"So, you're saying that Eve could be hit from both sides if she leaves this house."

"I'm saying I think it's pretty much certain. She's got nobody but Michael to look after her, and he can't be there all the time. She wouldn't want him to be. It just . . . makes me worry." Shane smiled a little and gave her a sideways glance. "Don't get jealous. You're still my number one girl."

"I'm not worried," she said. She really wasn't. "I'm scared, too. And what happens when Michael and Eve aren't there for *us*? Because we're in the same boat, right? I have some respect from the vamps, but your family . . ."

"Yeah, the Collins family went out of its way to make itself unwelcome around here. And vampires don't forget. Ever." He sighed and snuggled her closer against him. "You know, we really should get some sleep. It's almost three in the morning, and you've got class today, right?"

She did. Her heart wasn't in it, but she couldn't afford to blow off any more lectures; the old days of professorial indulgences were over. Her newly minted grade B was enough to prove that. "Just a little longer," she said. "Please?"

"Can't say no to that."

And they fell asleep, spooned together on the couch and wrapped in the afghan, until a crashing noise—shockingly loud— brought Claire awake with a flailing spasm.

She couldn't get her breath to ask, but Shane vaulted over her, landed cat-footed on the wood floor, and ran to the hallway. He was gone only a second before he came back at a dead run. "Fire!" he yelled, and slammed through the kitchen's swinging door as Claire fumbled on her shoes. He came back in seconds, toting the big red extinguisher. "Get Michael and Eve up, and get out of the house through the back door!"

"What happened?"

He didn't answer her; he was already gone, pelting back down the hall. As she flew up the stairs, she heard him opening the front door, and she smelled acrid smoke.

Michael, dressed and ready, already had the bedroom door open, and Eve was belting a red silk kimono around her body. She took one look at Claire's face and slipped her feet into untied Doc Martens. "Let's go," she said, and led the way down the steps. Michael split off from them at the bottom, heading for the front; he grabbed up a heavy rug, yanking it like a magician right out from under the couch, and ran to join Shane in fighting the fire.

Claire and Eve went out the back. "What happened?" Eve asked as she flipped the locks open. "We heard something, but—"

"I don't know," Claire said. "Whatever it was, it was loud."

She started to plunge outside, but Eve held her back, craned her head out the door, and took a careful survey of the dark yard before saying, "Okay, go."

It was a mistake. A bad one.

Because they didn't look *up*.

The vampire dropped down behind them, cutting them off from the house, and Claire didn't even notice his appearance until she heard Eve give a little surprised gasp. That was all she had time for, because in the next instant he was already right behind them, with his hands closed around Claire's shoulders . . .

But only to shove her violently out of the way.

She fell and rolled, fetching up with a painful slam against the bark of the old live oak tree that Myrnin had climbed to get into her bedroom. It wasn't Myrnin who'd dropped in this time. This was Pennyfeather, a pallid, long-faced friend of Oliver's who reminded her of a skeleton held together with string and a covering of flesh. He wasn't interested in Claire. Not at all.

He had hold of Eve, fingernails shredding the red silk of her robe. She screamed and tried to break free, but he was too strong; Claire could see the gouges in Eve's arms that his claws left as she struggled to get free.

"If you want to be one of us," Pennyfeather said with a dreadful grin, "one of us really should oblige you. Your husband seems incapable of doing his duty."

That sounded awful, and as the implication sank in, Claire gasped and tried to get up. She didn't have anything to fight him—no stakes, no knives, not even a blunt object—but she couldn't just let him . . . do whatever he was going to do. As she scrambled up, her hand fell on a tree branch—broken, with curled-up, dried leaves along its length.

It was sheared off in a sharp, angular point toward the thicker end. The break looked fresh, and it took Claire a moment to realize that it was this branch that had broken under Myrnin's feet as he launched himself through her window the night before.

She grabbed it and launched herself into a run at Pennyfeather, yelling at the top of her lungs. It was a war cry, coming from someplace deep and primal inside, and she should have been afraid, she should have felt awkward or tentative or stupid, but she just felt filled with red, red fury, and determination.

She'd already lost Miranda tonight. She wasn't losing Eve, too.

Eve saw her coming, and her dark eyes widened. Pennyfeather was too intent on pulling Eve's head to the side and prepping his fangs for the bite to notice, and Claire had an instant of clarity to realize that if she kept going, heading straight for them, she was likely to skewer Eve along with the vampire.

So Claire changed course, ran *past* them, whipped around, and lunged, full extension, just like Eve had taught her to do when they'd been messing around with fencing foils. She put her whole body into it, the straight line of her back continuing the same angle as her stiffened left leg, and her right arm extended up, out, and she slammed her weapon into Pennyfeather's back, neatly to the left of center.

The branch was too thick to make it completely through the ribs, but it shocked him, and he gave a shriek that made the hair stand up on Claire's arms. He let go of Eve, and she toppled forward in a heap of tattered red silk, crouched, and spun to face him with a look on her face so murderous that Claire was momentarily shocked. Pennyfeather didn't notice. He was too busy trying to claw the wood out of his back, but even when he grabbed hold, the springy wood bent, and he only managed to scrape it partly free before it snapped out of his hand.

"Get the bag," Eve snapped to Claire, and she nodded and dashed back into the kitchen. In seconds, she had hold of one of the black canvas totes they kept ready, but by the time she'd made it back outside, Pennyfeather had yanked the branch free, ripped it to pieces, and was stalking toward Eve with a low, furious growl and one piece still held as a club in his clawed hand.

There was no time to get to Eve. Claire did the next best thing; she spun around and flung the bag. It arced through the air and hit the grass at Eve's feet, spilling out a confusion of objects, but Eve didn't hesitate over choices. She grabbed a small bottle, popped the plastic cap, and threw the contents in Pennyfeather's face.

Silver nitrate.

His growl turned to a howl, rising in volume and pitch until it hurt Claire's ears, and he sheared off from making his run at Eve to claw at his face. The liquid silver clung like napalm, and burned about as fiercely. Claire grabbed the bag, stuffed items inside as fast as possible, and grabbed Eve's wrist. "Come on!" she yelled, and they ran around the side of the house, feet sliding on the loose white gravel.

Michael and Shane were at the front, and between the last blast of the fire extinguisher and smothering flaps of the rug, they'd put out a fire that had blackened a ten-foot section of the exterior of the house. Broken glass lay around the base of it, and as they got closer, Claire smelled the sharp, almost-sweet stench of gasoline.

There was something pinned to their front door, too, fluttering pale in the night breeze.

Michael dropped the rug and flashed at vampire-speed to catch Eve in his arms. He must have smelled the blood from her cuts, Claire thought; she could see the faint, iridescent shine of his eyes. "What happened?" he asked, and touched the claw slashes on her kimono. "Who did this?"

"Pennyfeather," Claire said. Now that the adrenaline rush was passing, she felt weirdly shaky, and she was beginning to realize how many things she'd done that could have gone badly wrong for her. For Eve, too. "It was Pennyfeather. He was—he was going to bite her."

Michael made a hissing noise, like a very angry and dangerous snake, and blurred out of sight toward the backyard. Shane's gaze followed him, but he didn't go along; he reached instead for the bag that Claire held and sorted through the contents. He handed Eve a knife, gave Claire another of the bottles of silver, and for himself, a baseball bat—a regular bat, except that the last six inches of the business end were coated with silver plate. "Been dying to try this out," he said, and gave them both a tight, wild smile. "Batter up." He swung it experimentally, nodded, and rested it on his right shoulder. "You good, Eve?"

"This was my favorite robe," she said. Her voice was unsteady, but it was from rage as much as from fear, Claire thought. "Dammit. It was *vintage!*"

Shane was still watching the side of the house, around which Michael had disappeared. He was clearly wondering if he ought to go back him up. Claire put a hand on his arm and drew his focus, just for a second. "Eve got Pennyfeather with a face full of this," she said, and held up her bottle. "He's got a handicap, and Michael's really pissed off."

That eased some of the tension in Shane's back and shoulders, at least. "I don't want to leave you two alone out here," he said. "The fire's out. Get back inside and lock the doors. Go."

"What about you guys?"

"If you hear us crying for our mommies, you can come rescue us, but hey, Eve's kinda half naked and bleeding out here."

Shane had a great point, and as Claire looked over at her, she saw that Eve was gripping the knife in a white-knuckled hand and shivering badly. It was cold out, and the shock was setting in.

Claire took her arm and steered her up the steps. Shane watched them until they reached the door, and then nodded to her and dashed away into the dark, bat held at the ready. She pushed open the door and hustled Eve inside, then paused and looked at what was pinned to the wood.

She supposed it was Pennyfeather's writing, because it was hard to read, spiky, and had a nasty brownish color to the ink that might well have been blood.

It said, *Done by Order of the Founder*, and it was pinned deeply into the wood by a giant knife, like a bowie knife on steroids.

Claire worked it back and forth until she could pull it out of the door's surface, folded the piece of paper, and locked up with trembling fingers.

Eve was standing there watching her, an unreadable expression on her face. She was still shaking. "It's a death sentence, isn't it?" she said. "Don't lie, Claire. You're not good at it."

Claire didn't even try. She held up the knife. "On the plus side," she said, "they left us another weapon. And it's sharp."

Truthfully, that was cold comfort indeed. And in the end, after Michael and Shane came back in without Pennyfeather, who'd managed to run for his life despite taking a pretty good battering from both of them, nobody much felt like celebrating.

Or sleeping.

Morning brought light and warmth, but not much in the way of reassurance; the cops came and took statements, looked over the damage to the house, and photographed the slashes on Eve's arms (which, upon inspection at the hospital, fortunately turned out not to be as deep as they'd looked).

The police declined to include the destruction of her vintage robe as a separate charge of vandalism. They also played dumb about who Pennyfeather was, or even that vampires existed at all, even though both men were plainly wearing Protection bracelets in full view. Typical. Once upon a time, Claire could have called on some Morganville police detectives who had reputations for impartiality . . . but they were all gone now. Richard Morrell had been police chief before he'd been mayor, and he'd been fair about it; Hannah had been great in the same role, but now Richard was dead, and Hannah was helpless to act.

Done by Order of the Founder. That said . . . everything, really. It meant that whatever tenuous claim the four of them had to safety in Morganville was officially cancelled.

Claire stayed with Eve as long as she could, but classes were calling, and so was her in-jeopardy grade point average; she grabbed her book bag, kissed Shane quickly, and dashed off at a jog to Texas Prairie University. Nothing was going to happen during the day, at least from the vamp quarter. Morning was well advanced over the horizon, and she had to skip her normal stop for coffee and flat-out race the last few hundred yards to make it into the science building, up the stairs, and down the long, featureless hall to her small-group advanced study class. Today was thermodynamics, a subject she normally loved, but she wasn't in the mood for theory today.

It was more of an applied sciences day—such as the amount of fuel required to burn down a house. Claire slipped into her classroom seat, earning a dirty look from Professor Carlyle, who didn't pause in his opening remarks.

Pennyfeather had been the one who'd attacked them, but that didn't mean he'd been acting alone; he *could* have thrown the Molotov cocktails at the front of the house and then jumped up on the roof to wait for them to exit the back, but somehow, Claire thought there was more to it. Someone in the front, and Pennyfeather waiting for Eve, specifically. And while it was a little bit of a relief not to be the main target, it was unsettling. Eve wasn't helpless, but somehow she was more vulnerable. Maybe it was just that Claire wanted desperately for Michael and Eve to somehow work out, and for the town to stop hating them, and . . .

"Danvers?"

She looked up from consideration of her closed textbook; she didn't even remember getting it out of her bag. She'd lost track of time, she guessed, and now Professor Carlyle—a severe older man with a close-cropped brush of gray hair and eyes the color of steel—was staring at her with a displeased expression, clearly waiting for something.

"Sorry?" she said blankly.

"Please provide the equation for the subject on the board."

She focused behind him. On the chalkboard, he'd written *Harmonic Oscillator Partition Function.*

"On the board?"

"Unless you'd like to perform it in interpretive dance."

There was a stir of laughter and smirking from the ten other students, most of whom were master's candidates; they were at least five years older than she was, every one of them, and she wasn't popular.

Even here, nobody liked a smart-ass.

Claire reluctantly rose from her desk, went to the chalkboard, and wrote $zHO = 1/(1-e-a/T)$.

"Where?" he asked, without a trace of satisfaction.

Claire dutifully wrote down *where* $a=hv/k$.

Carlyle stared at her in silence for a moment, then nodded. Apparently, that was supposed to make her feel insecure. It didn't. She knew she was right; she knew he'd have to accept it, and she waited for that to happen. Once he'd given her the signal, she put down the chalk and walked back to her desk.

But Carlyle wasn't done with her quite yet. "Since you did so well with that, Danvers, why don't you predict the following for me?" And he scribbled on the board another equation: $K_p=P_b/P_a-[B]/[A]$. "What happens if T is infinitely large?" T was completely missing from that equation, but it didn't really matter. T was an implied variable, but that was misleading. It was a trick question, and Claire saw many of the others open their books and begin flipping, but she didn't bother. She met Carlyle's eyes and said, "K_p equals two."

"Your reasoning?"

"If T is infinitely large, all the states of energy are equal and occupied. So there are twice as many states in B as A. K_p equals two. It's not really a calculation. It's just a logic exercise."

She was taking advanced thermodynamics purely to help her understand some of what Myrnin had accomplished in building his portal systems in Morganville. . . . They were doorways that warped space, and she knew there had to be *some* explanation for it in physics, but so far, she'd found only pieces here and there. Thermodynamics was a necessary component, because the energy produced in the transfer had to go somewhere. She just hadn't figured out where.

Carlyle raised his eyebrows and smiled at her thinly. "Someone ate her breakfast this morning," he said, and turned his laser focus on another hapless student. "Gregory. Explain to me the calculation if T equals zero."

"Uh—" Gregory was a page flipper, and Carlyle waited patiently while he looked for the answer. It was blindingly obvious, but Claire bit her tongue.

It took Gregory an excruciating four minutes to admit defeat. Carlyle went through three other students, then finally, and with a sigh, turned back to Claire. "Go ahead," he said, clearly irritated now.

"If there isn't any T, there isn't any B," she said. "So it has to be zero."

"Thank you." Carlyle glared at the others in the class. "I weep for the state of engineering, I truly do, if this is the best you can do with something so obvious. Danvers gets bonus credit. Gregory, Shandall, Schaefer, Reed, you all get failing pop quiz scores. If you'd like to solve extra-credit equations, see me afterward. Now. Chapter six, the residual entropy of imperfect crystals . . ."

It was a grim thing, Claire thought, that even when she got the high grade *and* dirty looks from her fellow students, she still felt bored and underchallenged. She wished she could go talk to Myrnin for a while. Myrnin was always unpredictable, and that was exciting. Granted, sometimes the problem was to just stay alive, but still; he was never boring. She also didn't have to sit through the incredibly dense (and wrong) explanations from other students when she was at his lab. If he'd ever had assistants that dumb, he'd have eaten them.

Somehow, she made it through the hour, and the next, and the next, and then it was time to run to the University Center and grab a Coke and a sandwich. It wasn't Eve's day to work the counter at the coffee shop, so after gulping down lunch, Claire—done at school for the day—walked to Common Grounds, just to check in on her.

It was only lightly occupied just now, thanks to the vagaries of college schedules; there were a few Morganville residents in the house, and a group of ten students very seriously arguing the merits of James Joyce. Claire claimed a comfortably battered armchair and dumped her bag in it; the chair and everything else smelled like warm espresso, with a hint of cinnamon. Common Grounds, for all its flaws, still had a homey, welcoming atmosphere.

But when she turned to the counter, she saw a sullen young man in a tie-dyed apron and red-dyed emo hair, who glared at her as she approached. He yawned.

"Hi," she said. "Um, where's Eve?"

"Fired," he said, and yawned again. "They called me in to take her shift. Man, I'm fried. Forty-eight hours without sleep—thank God for coffee. What's your poison?"

At Common Grounds, that *might* be literal, Claire thought. "Bottled water," she said, and forked over too much cash for it. Nobody drank Morganville's tap water. Not after the draug invasion. Sure, they'd cleared the pipes and everything, but Claire—like most of the residents—couldn't shake the idea that something had once been alive in there.

Better to pay a ridiculous amount for water bottled out of Midland.

"So, what happened this morning to get her fired? Because I know she was planning to come in."

Counter Guy wasn't chatty enough to come up with an answer; he just shrugged and grunted as he rang up her purchase and handed over the cold bottle. He had tattoos running up and down his arms, mostly Chinese symbols. Claire considered asking him what they meant, but in her experience he probably didn't have a clue. He did have one thing in common with Eve: black-painted fingernails.

"Is Oliver here?"

"Office," Counter Guy said. "But I wouldn't if I was you. Boss ain't in a good mood."

He was probably right, Claire thought, but she knocked anyway, and received a curt, "In," a command she followed. She shut the door behind her. Counter Guy and the other residents out there wouldn't come to her rescue if things went badly, and she didn't want the clueless students involved. They were having enough trouble with James Joyce.

Oliver didn't even glance up, but then he didn't need to, she thought; he'd probably identified her before she'd come anywhere near the office, just by her heartbeat or the smell of her blood or something. Vampires were an endless source of creepy. "Pennyfeather attacked Eve last night," she said. "Did you tell him to do it?"

He *still* didn't bother to look up from whatever piece of paper he was reading. He picked up a pen and scribbled down a note, then signed the bottom. "Why?"

"He left a note pinned to the door, 'Done by Order of the Founder.'"

"I am not the Founder," he said. "And Pennyfeather is no longer my creature. He does as he pleases. Though I would say his attitude is an accurate weather vane of public opinion among our kind, if that is what you're asking." Oliver didn't ask how Eve was, or what had happened, and that, Claire thought, was different. He'd kind of grown a bit more human since she'd first met him, but now he was back to the bad old vamp, unfeeling and utterly careless of human lives. He wouldn't go out of his way to hurt Eve, probably, but he wouldn't bother to help her, either, if it meant he had to make an effort. "Do you have some valid reason for disturbing me, or are you simply trying to annoy me?"

"I know what's happening," Claire said softly, and his pen stopped moving on the paper. The sudden silence made her feel breathless, as if she were standing at the edge of a bottomless pit full of darkness. "You've wanted to rule Morganville ever since you found out it existed. You came here wanting to get Amelie out of power and make yourself king or something. But she didn't let you, so you had to get . . . creative."

Now he looked up at her, and although his face was human, softened by loose, curling gray hair, the expression and the focus were purely those of a predator. He didn't say anything.

Claire plunged ahead. "Amelie trusted you. She let you get close. And now you're playing her to get what you always wanted. Well . . . it's not going to work. She may like you, but she's not stupid, and when she wakes up—and she will—you're going to be sorry you tried it."

"I don't see that my relationship with the Founder is any of your business."

"You can influence other vampires," she said. "You told me so before. And you're subtle about it. Whatever you're doing to her, stop it before this all goes bad. The humans won't stand for being cattle, and Amelie won't let you go as far as you think. Just . . . back off. Oliver—maybe I'm crazy for saying this, but you're not like this. Not anymore. I don't think you really want all this deep down."

He stared at her with empty, oddly bright eyes, and then went back to his paperwork.

"You may leave now," he said. "And count yourself lucky you are allowed to do so."

"Why did you fire Eve?" she asked. It was probably a mistake, but she couldn't help but ask it. And surprisingly, he answered.

"She accused me of trying to have her killed," he said. "Just as you did. Unfortunately, I'm unable to fire *you*. And my patience is now at an end. Begone."

"Not until you tell me—"

She never even saw him move, but suddenly he was around the desk and slamming the pen into the wood of the door behind her. It was just a simple ballpoint, but it sank an inch deep, vibrating an inch from her head. Claire flinched and came up hard against the barrier at her back. Oliver didn't move away. This close, he looked like bone and iron, and he smelled—ironically—like coffee. She was forcefully reminded that he'd been a warrior when he was alive, and he wasn't any less a killer now.

"Go," he said, very softly. "If you're wise, you will go very, very far from here, Claire. But in any case, go from my presence, *now*."

She opened the door.

And as she did so, she had the blurred impression of someone standing a few feet away on the other side, of people scrambling and exclaiming, of Counter Guy yelling "Hey!" Then she zeroed in not on the figure standing before her, but on what the tall, dark figure was holding.

It was a crossbow with a silver bolt.

And before Claire could take a breath or react, the crossbow was raised and fired.

Claire felt a burning brush against her cheek as the bolt zipped past, and she clapped a hand to the bleeding scrape as she turned to see what had happened.

The arrow had slammed home in Oliver's chest, but it was up and to the right of his heart. Claire stared at it with a feeling of unreality; the silver glint, the slowly spreading crimson circle around the shaft, the bright red feather fletching, and Oliver, pinned in place with surprise as much as pain.

Then he staggered back against his desk. Claire didn't think; she just acted, reaching out for the crossbow bolt.

He swatted her hand away with impatient fury, hard enough that he could have broken bones, and said through gritted teeth, "You can't pull it out from the front, fool. Take it through my back!"

He said it as if he had no doubt at all that she'd obey, and for a fraction of a second, Claire was tempted to obey him; that might have been her natural tendency to want to help, or it could have been Oliver exerting his will.

She paused, though, and looked through the still-open doorway.

The attacker was calmly loading up another bolt in the bow. She didn't—and couldn't—recognize the person; it was just a blank figure in some kind of black opaque mask, a zipped-up black hooded jacket, and plain, well-worn blue jeans. Black boots. Gloves. Nothing to betray any personal identification at all, not even gender.

The figure looked up and saw her standing there, and she felt a chill, unmistakable and indefinable. Then it pointed to her and jerked a thumb at the door. *You. Out.*

"Claire!" Oliver snapped. His voice sounded ragged now, and full of fury. "Pull the bolt out!"

"Did you have Pennyfeather try to kill Eve?"

The wound around the silver was starting to smoke and blacken, and it must have hurt a whole lot, even if not immediately fatal, because he tried to snarl at her, but it came out as more of a moan. He collapsed down to a sitting position on the floor, leaning one shoulder against the desk. She almost caved in, almost, because he really looked bad just then . . . vulnerable and damaged.

But then his eyes flickered bright red in fury, and he said in a poisonous hiss, "I'll have him kill *you* if you don't do as I say, girl. You're a pet, not a person."

"Funny," she said, "seeing as I'm the only thing standing between you and a guy with a crossbow." Literally. The masked figure was still standing behind her, ready to fire. She was just in the way. "Did you?"

"No!" he roared, and convulsed over on his side. The poison was working on him, and working fast.

Claire turned to face the would-be assassin, who was pointing the crossbow now at her. Directly.

Move, the figure gestured once again, impatiently. Claire shook her head.

"Can't." She didn't try to explain, and she wasn't sure she actually could; there was not a reason in the world why she shouldn't walk away from Oliver and leave him to whatever fate was bringing. Clearly the rest of the coffeehouse population had fled, including the students; Counter Guy's red hair and tats had left the building, too. It was just her, standing between Oliver and death.

She guessed that she was doing it because it didn't matter that it was Oliver, after all. She'd have done it for anyone. Even Monica.

She hated bullies. She hated anyone being kicked when he or she was down, and Oliver was most definitely down.

Whoever the figure holding the crossbow was, he or she considered taking her out to get to Oliver. She could see that, even if she couldn't see a face, and she knew that in this moment she was in as much danger as she'd ever been in Morganville. She was utterly at the mercy of whatever this person decided. No one could, or would, help.

She smelled the acrid tang of burning flesh behind her. Oliver was bad, and getting rapidly worse.

The masked head nodded, just a little, as if in acknowledgment of what she hadn't said. The figure lowered the crossbow, stowed it in a black canvas bag, and backed away toward the front of the store. She lost sight of it in the glare of daylight silhouetting the form, though she had the impression that the attacker had stripped off the mask before running out into the street.

Claire didn't try to follow. She stood there for a few seconds, then turned and looked at Oliver.

"If I do this for you," she said, "you're going to owe me. And I'm going to collect."

He was beyond making a bitter comeback. He just nodded, as if he couldn't summon up the strength to do more, and managed to roll a little farther over onto his stomach. The sharp, barbed end of the bolt was sticking out of his chest about three inches below his shoulder blade. The edges were wicked, like razors. That might actually be a good thing; it wouldn't have done quite as much damage that way.

But she needed to get it out before the silver poisoning got much worse—either that, or leave it in for good—which she could just hear Shane saying was still a perfectly valid option.

With gritted teeth, she wrapped the loose fabric of her shirt around the razor-sharp arrowhead, grabbed the shaft just below that, and pulled, hard and fast. She almost stopped when Oliver convulsed again, and his mouth opened wide in a silent scream—silent because he couldn't draw in breath to fuel it—but she didn't dare quit. Better it was painful now than deadly later.

It seemed to take forever, but it must have been just a few seconds before she yanked it completely free. She dropped the arrow to the floor with a ringing clang and tried not to think about the blood staining her shirt where she'd pulled it out of his body. Or whose blood it might have been, because it wasn't really *Oliver's* blood, was it? It was borrowed, or stolen, from others.

She stood up, breathing heavily and trying not to feel nauseated by what she'd just done—not just the blood, or the pain she'd caused, but the fact that she'd just saved Oliver's life. Shane would have been so angry with her, she realized; he'd have walked away and called it karma. Or justice, at least.

But right now, that wasn't the smart play. If Amelie was out to get them—if she really had sent Pennyfeather, and Oliver hadn't—then she needed Oliver on their side.

For now.

Oliver rolled over on his back, eyes tightly shut. The wound in his chest was still smoking, and clearly he was in pain, but he'd heal. Vampires always healed.

"You'd better not have lied to me," she said. "And remember, if you come after Eve, you come after all of us. That's going to be a lot more dangerous for you than some random dude with a mask and a crossbow."

He didn't move, and didn't speak, but his eyes flicked open and studied her with odd intensity. She couldn't really decide what he was feeling, but she did decide that she really, truly didn't care.

She shut the office door on her way out.

TEN

CLAIRE

)

"Well?" Shane demanded. "Who was it?" Claire was on the phone with him as she headed home. Wherever he was, it was machine-shop noisy, metal grinding and whining, and he had to shout to make himself heard. "Who tried to hit Oliver?"

"I don't know."

. "C'mon, Claire. Take a guess."

"No, really, I don't. Whoever it was had a mask and jacket and gloves and everything. Kind of tall, maybe a little on the skinny side. Good with a crossbow, though. Seriously good." She remembered the cut on her cheek and touched it with tentative fingers. It didn't really hurt, and the bleeding had stopped, but there was a definite slice. For the first time, she actually wondered how bad it looked, and whether it might leave a scar. "Um, anyway, I didn't get a look at him without the mask. It wasn't *you*, was it?" That last was teasing. She knew better; Shane wouldn't have fired with her in the way, not unless he had no choice. This was someone who wasn't quite as . . . involved.

"Hell, girl, if it had been me, he'd be dead on the floor right now, because I wouldn't have missed. Make my day. Tell me he's hurting."

"Oh yeah, he's definitely hurting," she said. "And I don't think he was behind Pennyfeather last night. But there's something weird about him, Shane."

"When isn't he weird?"

"No, I mean—" She couldn't put her finger on it, really. "Did Eve tell you what happened this morning?"

"What?" Shane instantly sounded on guard again, braced for the bad news. "What now? Damn, hang on . . ." He retreated from what sounded like a car being crushed in the background, until he found a relatively calm space. "Go on."

"Oliver fired her from Common Grounds. I guess he got kind of pissed when she accused him of trying to kill her. You know Eve. It probably wasn't subtle."

"Might have involved trying to hit him with something, like an espresso machine," Shane agreed. "She's home, but she's not talking. Went straight to her room. She had that look, like she was going to cry, so I didn't get in her way."

"Coward."

"*Crying*, so yeah. Are you on your way home?"

"Yes," she said. "I need to make a stop, though. See you in about an hour."

Shane knew her way too well. "You're going to see Myrnin, aren't you? Claire—"

"I need to see what he's doing," she said quickly. "He was strange the last time I saw him."

Her boyfriend mumbled something that might have been *He's always strange*, but he mostly kept his dissatisfaction to himself. "Say hi to my dad while you're there. You know, the brain in the jar? Frankenstein? That guy."

"You could come and—"

"No," Shane said flatly. There was a second's pause, as if he'd surprised himself by the vehemence of his reply, and when he spoke again it was in a softer tone. "Be careful out there. If you want me to come along . . ."

"To Myrnin's lab? That's just asking for trouble and you know it. I can manage. I've got resources." And silver-coated stakes, in her backpack. She had resolved to never leave home without them, after the events of last night. "If I'm not home before dark, though—"

"Yep, rescue has been calendared. Got it," he said. "Love you."

She heard the effort it took him to say it—not because he didn't mean it, but because boys just didn't like admitting it over the phone. He even lowered his voice, in case someone—Michael?—could overhear him.

Honestly.

"Love you, too," she said. "Watch out for Eve, will you? There's something funny about all this. I think Pennyfeather really did come for her, not for any of the rest of us. I think there's something going on in vampireland that has to do with her and Michael."

"Copy that," he said. "Collins out." He made a kissing sound into the phone before he hung up, which was way more embarrassing than saying *Love you*, but probably amused him more, and she smiled so much on her walk to Myrnin's lab that her face hurt—especially around the cut.

The street that held the entrance to Myrnin's lair—she always thought of it as a lair, as much as a lab—was a pretty much normal Morganville residential neighborhood; more run-down than some, better than others. The houses were mostly cheaply built clapboard, thrown up forty or fifty years ago, though there were a few standouts. Two houses had burned down or been otherwise trashed during the recent draug invasion, and those were busy with swarms of hard-hatted workers scrambling over piles of bricks, lumber, and tile. The skeletons of new houses were up already. Claire wondered what it might be like to move into a new place, one that had never had anyone else in it, one that was fresh and unhaunted. That would be odd, probably. She'd gotten so used to houses with history.

At the end of the street loomed the old Day House. It was a Founder House, built almost exactly like the Glass House where Claire lived; it had been freshly painted a blinding white, and the trim had been done in a dark blue. As always, there was a rocking chair on the porch. Claire expected to see Gramma Day's ancient little form there, rocking and knitting, but instead, the woman sitting there was tall, long-legged, and she wasn't knitting.

She was cleaning a gun.

Claire veered off from the alleyway that was the entrance to the lab, and paused respectfully at the gate that blocked the Day House sidewalk. "Hi, Hannah," she said.

Hannah Moses looked up, and the sunlight threw the scar on her face into sharp relief; it was hard to read her expression, but she said, "Howdy, Claire. Come on up."

Claire unfastened the gate and came up the steps to the porch. There was another chair sitting across from the rocking chair, and a low table in between where Hannah had laid out the parts of her weapon with straight-line military precision.

"Grab a seat," Hannah said, and blew dust off the part that she held in her hand. She examined it critically, buffed it with a cloth, and put it down in its place on the table. "Where you headed, Claire?"

"Myrnin."

"Ah." Hannah's gaze fastened on the cut on her cheek. "Something interesting happen?"

"Depends on how you feel about Oliver, I guess. Someone all in black tried to shoot a silver arrow into his heart."

Hannah paused in the act of sliding a piece onto the frame of the handgun. "Tried," she repeated. "I assume, not successfully?"

"It was pretty close."

"I can see that. Apparently, whoever tried didn't much care if you were in the way."

"Cared enough to miss, I guess."

Hannah nodded and went back to reassembling her gun with graceful, practiced efficiency. It took a breathtakingly short period of time, and then she loaded the weapon, chambered a round, and checked the safety before laying it back on the table. "Claire, we both know I'm sidelined by the vampires, and I won't have much opportunity to help in an official capacity. So I want you to do something for me."

"Sure!"

"I want you to leave Morganville."

Claire fell silent, watching her. "I can't just run away."

"Yes, you can. You always could have done it."

"Okay, then, I *won't* do it. My grades—"

"You can't use a good grade if they're carving it on your tombstone. Pack up and get out. Go find your folks, get *them* to pack up, and go somewhere else. Far away. An island, if you can manage it. But get the hell away from the vampires, and keep away."

"But you're staying?"

"Yes," Hannah agreed, "I'm staying. This house has been in my family for seven generations. My grandmother's too old to go, and they've still got my cousin locked up somewhere in their dungeons, if she's not dead and drained. I was like you. I wanted all this peace and love and cooperation to work, but it's not going to happen. The vampires are ripping up the agreements. That ain't on us. It's on them."

When Claire didn't speak, Hannah shook her head, leaned over, and picked up the weapon. She seated it in a holster under her arm. "There's a war coming," she said. "A real war. There's not going to be any room for people like you standing in the middle, trying to make peace. I'm trying to save your life."

"You always wanted peace."

"I did. But when you can't have peace, there's only one thing you can aim for, Claire, and that's winning the war the best and maybe the bloodiest way you can."

"I don't want to believe it. There has to be a way to make Amelie listen, to stop all this—"

"It's too late," Hannah said. "She set up the cage in Founder's Square again. It's a clear message. Cross the vampires, and you'll burn. Everything you worked for, everything I worked for, is going away. You pick a side, or you go. Nothing else to do."

Claire cleared her throat. "How's your grandmother?"

"Ancient," Hannah said, "but she's been that way as long as I can remember. She's a hundred and two years old this year. I'll give her your respects."

There wasn't anything else to say, so Claire nodded and left. She closed the gate behind her and glanced back to see Hannah stand up, lean against the porch pillar, and gaze out into the street like a sentry watching for trouble on the horizon.

Anybody who decided to go up against Hannah Moses had to

have a death wish. It wasn't just the gun she'd so expertly assembled and loaded—heck, gun toting in Texas was practically normal. It was in her body language: calm, centered, ready.

And deadly.

If there really was going to be a war, being on the side against Hannah would be a very dangerous place.

Claire headed down the alley, away from the normal world of construction and power tools and Hannah standing sentry. As the wooden walls rose on either side of her, and narrowed from a one-car street into a cart path into a claustrophobic little warren, she hardly noticed; she'd made this walk so many times that doing it in broad daylight held no terrors for her at all.

But something was different when she got to the end of the alley.

The shack, the ancient, leaning thing that had been there ever since Claire had first come here, was just . . . gone. There was no sign of wreckage, not even a scrap of wood or a rusty nail left in its place. There had been stairs going down into Myrnin's lab inside the shack itself.

Now, there was a slab of concrete. It was almost dry, but it had been poured only a day ago, Claire was certain of that; concrete dried fast in the Texas desert heat, and this was still just a tiny bit cool and damp to the touch. Someone had left a handprint at the corner of the slab. She put her own hand in the impression; it was a larger hand, longer fingers, but still slender.

Myrnin's hand, she thought.

He'd sealed up the lab.

Claire felt an odd wave of dizziness pass over her, and she lowered her head and breathed in deeply to combat it. He'd told her that he was going to leave, but she hadn't really believed it. Not like this. Not this fast.

But sealing your lab with concrete was a pretty definite sign of intent.

Claire left the alley at a run. She blew through the Day House gate and up the steps, and said breathlessly to Hannah, "I need to use your portal."

"Our what?"

"C'mon, Hannah. I know you've got a portal in your house. It's in the bathroom. I used it to get to Amelie before. I need to see if I can still get into the lab that way." Hannah's face remained tight and guarded. "Please!"

The front door creaked open, horror-movie style, and the tiny, wizened form of Gramma Day appeared in the gap. She studied Claire with faded brown eyes that still held the same sharp intelligence that Hannah's did, and held out a palsied, wrinkled hand. Claire took it. The old lady's skin was soft as old, fragile fabric, and burning hot, but beneath it was a wiry strength that almost pulled Claire off-balance. "You get in here," Gramma Day said. "Ain't no call for you to be standing out on the porch like some beggar. You, too, Hannah. Nobody's coming today for us."

"You don't know that, Gramma."

"Don't you tell me what I know or don't, girl." There was a firm tone of command in the old lady's voice as she led Claire down the hallway. There was an eerie sense of déjà vu to it—the same hall as the Glass House, the same parlor to the left, the same living room opening up ahead. Only the furniture was different, and the march of family portraits on the walls, some of them going back to the mid-1800s, of earnest-looking African American people in their Sunday best. As they shuffled down the hall, it got more modern. Color portrait photos of people with heavily lacquered bouffant hairdos, then thick, luxurious Afros. Toward the very end, Hannah Moses looking incredibly neat and imposing in her military uniform, and a framed set of medals beneath it.

There was one important difference between the Glass House and the Day House: there was a downstairs bath. It must have been added ages ago, but Claire envied it, anyway. Gramma swung open the door and shooed her inside.

"You going to see the queen?" Gramma asked her.

"No, ma'am. I'm going to see if I can find Myrnin."

Gramma snorted and shook her trembling head. "Ain't no good gonna come of that, girl. Trap-door spider's not a safe thing for you to be running after. You ought to go home, lock your doors, get ready for trouble."

"I'm always ready," Claire said, and grinned.

"Not like this," Gramma said. "Never seen a time when the vampires weren't scared of something, but now, they ain't afraid of anything, and it's gonna go hard for us. Well, you do as you like. Folks always do." She swung the door shut on Claire, and Claire hastily felt for the light switch, an old-fashioned dial thing on the wall. The overheads clicked on. From the look of the bulbs, they might have been original Edisons.

It was an altogether normal sort of bathroom, and although she kind of needed to go, Claire didn't dare use it. Only Myrnin would have ever been thoughtless enough to build a portal in a bathroom, she thought. The people in the Day House must have a lot more fortitude than she did, because she'd never be able to take down her pants in a room where anyone with the secret handshake could walk right out of the wall and stare at her. Granted, that was a smallish circle of people ... Amelie, Oliver, Myrnin, Claire herself, Michael, a few others (and even Shane had managed once or twice).

Oh, and a couple of would-be serial killers who'd gotten their hands on the secret. Ugh.

Claire cleared her mind, closed her eyes, and focused. She felt the answering tingle of the portal, lying dormant and invisible, and when she looked, she saw a thin film of darkness forming over the white-painted door. It was misty at first, then as dark as a velvet curtain hanging in midair, rippling gently in an unfelt breeze.

She built the image of Myrnin's lab in her mind: the granite worktables, the art deco lights on the walls, the chaotic mess of books and equipment. Then there was Bob the Spider's tank in the corner, larger than ever and thick inside with webs, along with the battered old armchair sitting next to it where Myrnin sat and read, when he was in the mood.

The image flickered in the darkness, ghostly, and then flared out. No, it was still there, Claire thought, but the lights themselves had been turned off. To keep her away?

Screw that. Claire reached into her backpack and pulled out a small, heavy flashlight. She switched it on and stepped through the portal into the dark.

It was not just dark in the lab. It was profoundly, elementally black. This far below ground, and with the entrance sealed anyway, it felt like being sealed into a tomb. Claire felt the portal snap shut behind her, and for a moment she was tempted to turn around and wish herself home, immediately, but that wouldn't help. She still wouldn't *know*.

There was a master switch to the power, and by carefully watching her footing (Myrnin hadn't bothered to clear up the leaning piles of books or the scattered trip hazards), she found her way to the far wall, next to a musty old mummy case she'd always assumed was a genuine thing—because it was Myrnin's. She'd never opened it. Knowing Myrnin, there could be anything inside, from a body he'd forgotten about to his dirty laundry.

She threw the master switch up, and lights flared on. Machines started up around the lab with a chorus of hums, pops, crackles, and musical tones. The laptop she'd bought for Myrnin booted up in the corner and glowed reassuringly. At least one beaker started bubbling, though she couldn't see why.

But there was absolutely no trace of Myrnin.

She stopped at the table where she'd left the device she'd been working on; it was still there, covered over with the sheet. Myrnin hadn't taken it with him, and he hadn't made any more of his suspiciously accurate adjustments to it, either. For a moment, Claire debated sticking it in her backpack—she couldn't leave it here, gathering dust, not when she was close to it actually starting to work—but the weight was pretty extreme, and she needed to look around more.

She'd come back, she decided, and flipped the sheet back into place.

Claire edged past a pile of boxes and crates in the corner and opened the door in the back—or tried to. Locked. She rooted around through drawers until she came up with a set of keys, which contained everything from ancient, rusty skeleton models to modern gleaming ones. She sorted through, eyeing the lock, and tried likely candidates until she found one that fit and turned. The door swung silently open on Myrnin's bedroom. She'd stayed in it before (without him, of course) when she'd been confined to the lab on punishment duty, so she was well familiar with the contents. Nothing seemed different. The bed had been mussed, pillows tossed to the floor, and drawers were hanging open, but she couldn't tell—as always—if it was normal, or some kind of panic-packing frenzy.

There was no note. Nothing to tell her whether Myrnin was just temporarily out, or gone for good. She couldn't believe that he'd just . . . leave. Just like that.

"Frank?" Claire walked out of the bedroom into the main lab. "Frank, can you hear me?" Frankenstein, Shane called him. Frank Collins had, once upon a time, been Shane's dad—maybe not a good one, but still. Then he'd been turned vampire, against his will. Then he had died, and Myrnin had decided to scavenge his brain and use it to power the town's master computer.

Maybe Frankenstein wasn't too bad a name for him, after all.

There was a buzzing sound that seemed to come from all around her, and it coalesced finally into a distorted, drunk-sounding voice. "Yes, Claire," it said.

"Are you okay?"

"No," it said, after a long pause. "Hungry."

Claire swallowed hard and clenched her fists. Frank—Frank Collins, or what was left of him—was hardwired into a computer downstairs, an area that Myrnin hadn't wanted her to venture into. "I thought your nutrients were delivered automatically."

"Tank dry," he said. He sounded terribly tired. "Need blood. Get blood, Claire."

"I—I can't do that!" What was she supposed to do—order up a gallon drum from the blood bank? Somehow magically haul it all the way down there herself? She had no idea how Myrnin did these things; he'd never included her on any of that maintenance activity. But she strongly suspected the only one who'd be able to manage it would be a vampire. "Is Myrnin gone?"

"Hungry," Frank said again, faintly, and then just . . . stopped talking. The buzz under his voice shut down. She thought he was the equivalent of offline, like a laptop drained of battery shutting down.

If she wanted him to survive, she really did have to figure this out. Clearly, Myrnin wasn't here to do it.

Claire went to the glass enclosure in the corner. It was hard to see under all the webs, but when she took the top off the tank, Bob the Spider crawled up eagerly to the top of his wispy multilevel construction. He was a big fuzzy spider, and somehow impossibly cute, although part of her still screamed like a little girl at the thought of touching him.

He bounced up and down in his web, all eight eyes staring right at her.

"You're hungry, too," she said. "Right? Myrnin didn't feed you, either?"

That was really strange. Myrnin might neglect Frank, because he and Frank really weren't a marriage made in heaven (and Frank could be faking it; he had a cruel and weird sense of humor), but leaving Bob on his own and starving wasn't like her boss at all. He was ridiculously fond of the thing. She still remembered Myrnin's utter panic the first time Bob had molted. It had been like a normal person freaking out over the birth of a child.

It was not like him to leave Bob behind if he was really leaving.

Something was wrong here. Very wrong.

Claire pulled out her phone and dialed Myrnin's speed dial. It rang on the phone, and suddenly she heard an echo in the lab, a ringtone composed of scary organ music. She'd given him the phone and had put the ringtone on it herself.

The phone was lying in the shadows next to a stack of books. It had a cracked screen, but it was still working. Claire picked it up and felt stickiness on her fingers.

Blood.

What had happened?

"You shouldn't have come," Pennyfeather said from behind

her. His voice, like the rest of him, was colorless, and his odd, lilting accent only made him seem less human, somehow. "But don't worry. You won't be leaving."

Claire stumbled backward in surprise, catching her heel on a pile of discarded volumes, which overbalanced and rained down dusty, heavy tomes on top of her. She yelped and ducked, and realized she had an opportunity as Pennyfeather paused to survey the chaos; she jumped, slid over the top of the nearest lab table, sending books and glass beakers flying, and hit the floor running. She heard soft noises behind her, and in her mind's eye she saw Pennyfeather leaping effortlessly onto the same table, touching down, and racing after her.

She felt human, solid, clumsy, and utterly outmatched against his eerie grace. Claire was accustomed enough to running from vampires not to be utterly terrified—she'd done it often enough here, in this lab—but Pennyfeather was different from the others. Oliver, Amelie, Myrnin . . . They all had some kind of humanity to them, some hints of mercy, however hidden. They could be reached.

Pennyfeather was pure vampire-fueled serial killer, and a human, any human, was no match for him.

Claire grabbed for the silver-coated stake in her backpack, but it had rolled to the side, and running and hunting around in a bag and watching treacherous footing weren't exactly complementary activities. It was inevitable that just as her fingertips brushed the cool metal, her foot would come down on a book that slid greasily to the side, and she'd tumble, off-balance, to the floor.

As she did.

She got a grip on the stake just as Pennyfeather landed on her chest, nimble and startlingly heavy. He easily pinned her arms down. All she could do was rattle the stake ineffectively against the tile. No way could she get leverage to stab him, or even scratch him. She bucked, trying to throw him off, but he rode it out easily.

It came to her, with cold clarity, that she wasn't getting out of this. No last-minute brainstorms. No clever little science applications to solve the problem. In the end, she was just going to be another Morganville statistic. Score another one for the vamps.

"Hey," a scratchy, electronic voice barked over Pennyfeather's shoulder, and a grayscale, two-dimensional image flickered into existence there. Frank Collins, Shane's absent/abusive dad, looking scarred and scary, was wielding a tire iron, which he swung at Pennyfeather's head.

Pennyfeather reacted to the thing coming at him from the corner of his eye, jerking out of the way and letting go of Claire to stop the swing of the blunt object . . . but his hands went right through Frank's insubstantial arm, and Pennyfeather pitched forward, off-balance. Claire seized the chance to roll away, and Frank flickered between her and Pennyfeather, confusing the issue.

"Out of my way, spirit!" Pennyfeather snarled, fangs out.

"I'm not a spirit," Frank countered, and his fangs descended, too, as he returned the snarl. "I'm your worst damn nightmare, Skeletor. I'm a vampire killer with fangs and a grudge."

That sounded so much like Shane that Claire was actually startled. So was Pennyfeather, as a sudden blaze of fire shot up from one of the Bunsen burners nearby. Claire barely glimpsed it before scooping up the rolling stake and her book bag, and lunging for the dark doorway of the portal. *Concentrate!* she begged herself, shaking all over with adrenaline. She had seconds, at most, before Pennyfeather reached her no matter what kind of distractions Frank might be trying; he didn't have any actual, physical force to wield on her behalf, even if he was inclined. She needed out of here, fast.

She couldn't mentally reconstruct the Day House bathroom under this kind of pressure, or anywhere else that Myrnin had established one of his teleportation thresholds. The only one that leaped clearly and instantly to her mind was home—the living room of the Glass House, with its comfy couch and armchair and barely controlled chaos. . . .

It formed in front of her as she plunged forward, trusting somehow, desperately, that she could make it happen.

Pennyfeather lunged forward and caught her foot just as she pushed through the plastic-wrap pressure of the doorway, and she was stuck, mostly out but with her left leg held in a grip so iron-strong, she knew he'd drag her back through.

Or worse. If she was stuck in the portal when it closed, she'd be cut apart.

"Help!" Claire shrieked.

Michael, Eve, and Shane were all in the living room. Michael and Shane dropped the game controllers they'd been holding and twisted around on the sofa to look blankly at her, as Eve—already facing her—clapped hands to her mouth in shock.

"Help me! Pull me out!"

All three of them broke out of their momentary freeze at the same time. Michael scrambled over the back of the sofa and got to her first, grabbing her arm just as Pennyfeather yanked backward, and although Michael held on, they both slid toward the portal.

Claire couldn't get her breath. "He's got me; he's got me; I can't—!" she shrieked as Pennyfeather yanked hard on her leg, and she felt the strain in her muscles. He was still playing with her. She'd seen an angry vampire rip limbs off a person, and it was frighteningly possible just now.

Shane took hold of Claire and wrapped his arms around her in a grip so tight it felt as if she'd be crushed. "Go, Mike. I'll hold her here! Get the bastard off her!"

"It's the lab!" Claire blurted, "He's in the lab!"

She wasn't sure Michael could make it through at all—there wasn't much room—but she twisted over to the side in hopes of making more space. At least Michael knew what he was doing. He paused for a moment, fixing the lab's location in his mind, then nodded at her and plunged through in a rush.

Claire felt the disturbance of the thin membrane still holding her leg at the knee like a strange tidal wave, and Pennyfeather's grip tightened. He started to yank her steadily backward, and all of Shane's strength wasn't enough to keep them from sliding forward. If anything, Pennyfeather just seemed to be more intent on taking her with him, not less.

Claire screamed and buried her face in Shane's chest as she felt the strain on her leg increase, going from painful to intensely agonizing, and in one more second she knew she'd feel muscles tearing loose. . . .

But then a second later, the crushing hold on her ankle released. Shane had braced himself and was pulling with all his strength to counterbalance, and when the pressure let go, they both went crashing to the wooden floor with her on top. She was breathless and frightened, but it was still nice to be body-to-body with him, and she saw the pleasure fire in his eyes, too, just for a moment. He brushed her hair back from her face and said, "Okay?"

She nodded.

"Then let's do this again later," he said, "but right now, Michael needs backup. Stay here." He rolled her off him, got to his feet, grabbed the black canvas bag that Eve threw to him from the kitchen door, and dived into the dark.

Eve hurried to her side as Claire tried to bend her leg, and winced at the shooting pains that went through it. "Don't," Eve ordered, and dropped down next to her to run her hands over Claire's knee. "Damn, I can't believe Myrnin did that to you. I'll stake his ass myself, if there's anything left when the boys get done teaching him manners."

"Myrnin?" Claire asked, and then realized what she'd done. *"It's not Myrnin!"*

With a horrible sense of doom, she realized that she hadn't told them it was Pennyfeather.

And neither of the boys was prepared for that.

ELEVEN

MYRNIN

)

It was so dark. Dark dark dark dark dark dark. *Darkdarkdark-darkdarkdarkdarkdarkcan'tbreathedarrrrrrrrrrkkkkkkkk . . .*

I gained control of my clattering, chattering mind with an effort that left me trembling. Had I been still human, still breathing—as I was sometimes in dreams—I thought I would have been drenched in the sweat of fear and gasping. I dreamed that sometimes, too, the sticky moisture on my skin, dripping and burning in my eyes, but in the dreams it wasn't dark; it was bright, so bright, and I was running for my life, running from the monster behind. . . .

So many years running blackness turning red nothing nothing safe no havens no friends lost all lost until Amelie until this place until home but home was gone gone dead and gone . . . I gagged on the taste in the back of my mouth, the excruciating spike of hunger, and sagged against the wet, slick wall. *Don't remember,* I told myself. *Don't think.*

But I couldn't stop thinking. Ever. My mother had beaten me for fancies when I watched the stars and drew their patterns and forgot the sheep while wolves ate the lambs and my sisters with their cruel and petty wounds when no one saw and my father penned up like an animal as he howled all the *thinking never stopped never never never a howling storm in my head until the heat burst through my skin and devoured me.*

Stop. I shouted it inside my head until I could feel the force of it hammering against bone, and for a blessed moment, I gained the space of silence against all the pressing weight of memory and terror that never, never went away for long.

There was time enough to think where I was and to remember my present situation . . . not my past.

The prison was familiar to me, familiar not from Morganville but from ancient and heavily unpleasant years past. . . . My enemy was still a great fan of the classics, because he had dropped me into an oubliette—a round, narrow hole in stone that was deep enough, and smooth enough, to thwart a vampire's attempts to jump or climb. In less civilized times, one would be dropped in to be forgotten entirely. Humans lasted only days, generally, before the confinement, darkness, hunger or thirst—or simple horror—took them. Vampires . . . well. We were hardy.

It's a sad thing for a vampire to confess, but I have always hated the bitter, choking dark. It's useful to us to hide and stalk, but only when there is a hint of light—a glimmer, something that will define the shadows and give them shape. A blood-hot body glows, and that, too, is a comfort and a convenience.

But here, there was no glimmer, no prey, nothing to relieve the inky and utter black. It reminded me of terrible, terrible things *like the grave I had dug my way out of more than once, the taste of dirt and screams in my mouth, vivid and sour, and that taste never went away, leaving me gagging on it, gagging and unable to fight past the choking, awful sense of burial only blood could wash out, blood and searing light....*

DarkdarkdarkdarkdarkdarkdarkdarkdarkdarkdarkohmyGodwhy . . .

When I came to myself, I was doubled over and retching, my hands flat against the wall. I was on my knees, which was even less pleasant than standing. I sagged back and found the cold, wet stone of the wall only a few inches behind me. I could sit, if I did not mind waist-high filthy water, and my knees to my chin. Well, it made for a change, at least.

It was my fault that I was here, entirely mine. Claire always chided me for my single-mindedness and she was right, right, always right, even Frank had told me to go but poor, surly Frank, starving for lack of nutrients no one to change out the tanks and care for him properly, and Bob, what to do about Bob, I couldn't leave him behind all on his own how would he catch his flies and crickets and the occasional juicy beetle without assistance he was so very much my responsibility and Claire Claire Claire vulnerable now without Amelie without pity kindness mercy no no no I could not go should not . . .

Chilly skeletal Pennyfeather, with his acid eyes and killer's smile . . .

Frank warned me warned me warned me . . .

Pennyfeather dragging heretics to the flames, hunting me, digging me out of my last safe nest and into burning sunlight where Oliver laughed and then the oubliette the darkness dark darkdarkdarkdarkdarkdark . . .

I opened my eyes again, eventually, with my screams still ringing back at me from the stone walls. What a noisy chorus I was. It was still complete and utter darkness—the rock I leaned on, the water, my hand in front of my face, all bleak and black, not even a spark of light, life, color.

That was because I was blind. I remembered it with a sudden, guilty shock; it was odd that one would forget something that significant. But in my defense, one doesn't tend to wish to remember such things (Pennyfeather's awful pale grin, the flash of the knife, the pain, the fall).

You've healed from worse, I told myself sternly. I pretended to be someone clear, someone practical. Ada, perhaps, in her better days. Or Claire. Yes, Claire would be quite practical at a time like this.

Blind blind three blind mice see how they run who holds the carving knife where is the cat Dear God in heaven the cat *and I am only a mouse, a blind and helpless mouse in a trap cheese if only someone would drop down a bite of cheese, or another mouse...*

The oubliette, I was not a mouse, I was a vampire, I was a blind vampire who would heal, of course, eventually, and see again. *Stop*, I told myself. I drew in a deep breath and smelled ancient death, crushed weeds, rotting metal, stone. I had no idea where the oubliette was located. I was simply at the bottom of it, standing in cold, filthy water and thinking that this time, my favorite slippers were well and truly ruined. Such a pity.

All the whimsy in the world won't help you now, fool. I could hear Pennyfeather saying it; I could feel the cold clench of his hands on my shoulders. *This town belongs to the strong.*

And then the fall.

Well. I was strong. I had survived. I always survived. *Not this time never no one to rescue me no one to know I was so alone alone alone darkkkkkkkkkkkkkkkkkkkkkkkkkkkkkkk.*

The panic took some time to subdue; it lasted longer each time, it seemed; from a purely scientific perspective, I supposed I ought to have been taking notes. *A monograph on the subject of terrors of the dark, with additions for the blind.* I could write volumes, should I ever see again to be able to write.

Your eyes will heal, the rational part of me—a tiny part, at best, and by no means the best of me—whispered. *Delicate tissues take longer to regenerate.* I knew this, but the animal, instinctual part of me still shrieked in panic, convinced that I'd be left in this, choking nothing forever, doubly blind, unable to even make out the blank walls that confined me.

The evil tide of panic rolled over me again, and when it finally passed and my screaming brain stilled, I was crouched low in the water, huddling to the chilly walls and shaking in a near fit. My throat felt odd. Ah. I'd been screaming, again. I swallowed a trickle of my own precious and scarce blood and wondered when Claire would seek me out. She would; she *must.* I desperately believed she would. Surely she was not so angry with me that she'd spurn me and leave me here, in this awful place.

Please. Please come. I can't survive this I can't alone no no no not alone not blind no . . .

I was not used to feeling this horror, which combined all the fears of my mortal life in a toxic elixir; the closeness of the walls, the darkness, the filthy water, the knowledge that I might never leave this place, that I'd starve here to rags and bones until thirst robbed me of all shreds of the mind I'd struggled so hard to preserve, gnawing my own flesh until it was drained dry.

I have become my father after all.

My father had gone mad when I was only a very young boy, and they'd confined him . . . not in a well like this, but in a hut, a lightless and chained hovel, with no hope or memory of daylight. When I had nightmares—daily—that was my hell, that I woke dressed in my father's filthy rags, chained and alone, abandoned to the screaming in my head.

In the dark.

And here it is, nightmare come real, in the dark, alone, abandoned.

Nonsense. Pennyfeather has always worked for Oliver. I tried to focus on logic, anything to prevent myself from sliding over that muddy slope down into the pit of despair again. *Ergo, Oliver wished that I be removed. Why would he wish it? Because Amelie trusts me?*

It did not feel right. Oliver was not randomly cruel; he enjoyed power, but mostly for what power could do. He'd had many opportunities to remake Morganville in his own image, but he'd refrained, over and over; I'd thought there was genuine respect, even an odd and grudging love, growing between him and Amelie. Yet he'd changed, and through him, so had Amelie. For the worse.

Amelie, my sweet lady, so small and shy and quiet in the beginning when your master and mine had met, when as fledgling vampires we had learned the joy of the hunt, the terror of being owned. I rescued you from your vile father, and lost you, and found you again. Do you remember me at all, as that young and tentative vampire, full of fear and vague notions?

Amelie wasn't herself. Oliver should not have done this to me; he should not have been able to, without her consent. There was something missing, something I did not yet understand.

It was a puzzle, and I liked puzzles; I clung to them, here in the dark, a shield against all the pieces falling apart, crashing together in my head, crashing and cutting. . . .

Another panic attack swept over me, hot as boiling lead and cold as the snows that piled waist high in my youth, and what little mind I had dissolved in an acidic frenzy, thoughts rushing as fast as modern trains crashing through stone, veering wildly from the tracks, turning and burning into chaos *closedarktoodarktooclose smoothwallsnonono*. . . .

It was harder this time, coming back. I ached. I trembled. I think I might have wept, but water dripped cold on me, and I wasn't sure. No shame in tears. No shame at all, since there was no one to see me, no one ever ever ever again.

Come for me. Please, the lonely and lost part of me wailed. But no one did.

Hours crawled slowly, and I began to feel something odd ... a pressure, a strange sensation that made me want to claw at my injured eyes ... but I held off, hands fisted into shaking lumps, and pounded the hard, smooth walls until I felt bones shifting beneath the skin. It healed faster than I would have liked; the distraction didn't last, and the pressure in my eyes built and built and suddenly, there was a breathtakingly lovely burst of *light.*

The glare burned so badly I cried out, but it didn't matter. I could see, and suddenly, the panic wasn't quite so desperate or overwhelming. I could manage this. I *would* manage it. As everything in my life, there was a way out, a single slender thread of hope, however insane. . . .

Because that was, in fact, my secret. In an insane world, sanity made very little sense. No one expected me to live, and therefore, I did. Always.

I looked up, and saw a depressingly narrow tunnel closing into a tiny, dim hole far, far above ... and the gleam of a silver grate above, a circle enclosing a cross. Pennyfeather hadn't just thrown me blinded into a pit; he'd thrown me into one of the levels of hell, and locked me in with silver, on the terribly unlikely chance I might scale the heights to crawl out. And who knew what lay beyond; nothing good, I was sure. If it had been Oliver giving the order, he'd left little to chance when he was determined in his course.

Still. At least it's not dark now, I consoled myself. I looked down, and in the faintest possible sliver of light I saw my legs—bare below the knees, since I had perhaps unwisely worn a pair of ancient velvet knee britches, and as pale as I had ever seen my skin. It was the color of dirty snow, and wrinkled to boot. I lifted one foot from the brackish water, and the bunny slippers were soaked and drooped pathetically. Even the fangs seemed robbed of any charm.

"Don't worry," I told it. "Someone will pay for your suffering. Heavily. With screaming."

I felt I should repeat it for the other slipper, in case there should be any bad feelings between the two. One should never create tension between one's footwear.

That duty done, I looked up again. Water dripped cold from the heights and hit my face in sharp, icy stabs. It was cruel, since it could only irritate me, not sustain me. Still, there must be rats. Every dungeon had rats; they came standard issue. Rat blood was not my favorite, but as the old saying goes, any port in a storm. And I was most definitely in a storm, a true tempest of trouble.

Water. Water water water falling cold in gray skies drowning the land gray dirt gray ashes gray bones of houses falling slowly into ruin gray eyes of a woman staring down with pity and tears so many tears mother so much disappointment in her face, and what I was now was not what I had been when she'd last seen me . . . the screams, the slamming door, no family left now, no one to care . . . my sisters, screaming at me to go away, go away . . .

I pulled myself sharply away from the memory. No. No, we do not think of those things. *You should think of them, think of your sisters, think of what you did,* something whispered in my ear, but it was a bad whisper, a vile and treacherous worm with the face of someone I had once loved, I was sure of that, but I didn't want to remember who might have warned me. I hadn't listened, in any case. I never listened.

I lifted up the right slipper again and addressed its soggy little head. "I'm afraid I might have to leave you behind. And you, too, twin. It will be difficult enough to climb without you hampering me. And your fangs aren't very sharp."

They didn't respond. A small bolt of ice-cold clarity swept

over me, and I felt ashamed for talking to my shoes, and especially for apologizing to them. Clarity confused me. It was far less forgiving and kind than the general state of disconnection in which I liked to live.

Nonetheless, sanity—however brief—did force me to look again at the walls. The surface wasn't perfect, after all; it was pocked with tiny imperfections. Not built, but bored out of solid stone, and while whatever drill had made it had polished the sides clean, it hadn't quite removed every hint of texture.

It wasn't much, but it was something, and I sighed at the prospect of just how unpleasant this was going to be.

Then I grimly jammed my fingernails into the wall and began to scrape tiny handholds.

Come and find me, I was still begging Claire, because I knew all too well that my nails—however sharp and sturdy—would be worn to nubs long before I reached the silver grate above. And said silver would be impossible for me to break from below, with no leverage and a chancy hold. And, of course, it would take days to scrape myself a ladder to the top, even assuming my nails could hold out so long.

But the least I could do would be to try. Pennyfeather might come back, after all; he might not be done with me. Perhaps I had been gifted to him as some macabre toy. If that was the case, I certainly needed to be ready to kill him, quickly, before he could invent new horrible things to do to me.

It might be the only chance I had to survive.

TWELVE

SHANE

J

At least the lights in the lab were on; that was something. I hadn't thought to ask Claire if I needed a flashlight—I mean, there was a lot going on, and no time for leisurely Q&A—but when I squeezed through that icy/hot darkness that Claire called a portal, and I called *wrong*, it was decently lit up on the other side.

Myrnin's lab was, as usual, a wreck, but I thought it was worse than before . . . probably because there were two vampires fighting the hell out of each other, and at the speed they were moving, it was hard to be sure which one was my friend. All I got was impressions as they shoved each other up and down the crowded aisles made tricky with spilled and slaughtered books. Claire would hate that—all the mutilated pages.

I was more worried about the blood, because there were smears of it here and there, and it looked like someone was getting the worst of the fight.

And my guess that it was Michael was confirmed when suddenly the fight ended. It went from speed of light to full stop in one cold second, and Michael was on the floor with the creepy, androgynous Pennyfeather kneeling on his chest, eyes red and claws dripping the same color.

Oh, holy crap. It wasn't Myrnin. In a straight-out fight, Michael could have probably taken Claire's boss, but Pennyfeather was something else—something worse.

Pennyfeather drew back for a blow that would probably have decapitated Michael, except that I leaped forward and planted a boot in his side, slammed him off-balance, and shot him with my newest, sweetest toy. It had been made to tranquilize big game animals, like lions and tigers, and I figured it would do just fine for vampires. Especially if, instead of using sedatives, the darts were filled up with silver in suspension.

And it worked. Pennyfeather thought he had me; he rolled up and focused his rage right in my face, and yeah, that was scary, but I saw the first flicker as it passed over his face. Confusion. Then pain. Then shock.

"What—?" he said, and then he collapsed to his knees. He grabbed the dart I'd buried in his neck and yanked it out. I saw a wisp of smoke curl out from the blackened hole in his skin. "What did you—"

"You tried to kill my girlfriend *and* my best friend," I said. "Suck it, fangboy."

There wasn't enough silver in the dart to kill him, but it was more than enough to make him deeply unhappy for a long time—and, most important, stuck right there, unable to move.

Just the way I wanted him.

I held out a hand to Michael, who hadn't moved from where he'd landed, and he took it and managed to stand. His leg was broken, and I winced when I saw how not-straight it was, but he just shook his head, hopped on one foot, and kicked out, hard. The bones slid back together. He managed not to scream. I would have. A lot. But he did clamp his hand on my shoulder and hold on with brutal strength.

"You good?" I asked, which was a weird thing to say, admittedly; he'd just reset a broken leg, vampire-style, which was gross and cool at the same time.

"Nothing that can't heal," he said. "Damn, he's fast. I mean, *really* fast. I was expecting Myrnin gone wild. Not him."

"Want to go kick him a few more times?"

"With a broken leg?"

"Okay, fair point." I made sure he could stand on his own, then went back to my dropped bag. It was full of interesting things. I sorted through, slowly, because I knew Pennyfeather was still conscious and watching me. "Hmmm. So, should I go with something fast, like the silver stake through the heart? It's a classic, I'll admit, but I was hoping for something he'd really appreciate. One thing I know about this jackhole is that he really likes his quality pain."

"He's not getting out of here again," Michael agreed. "But you don't have to go all Marquis de Sade on him, either. Just kill him. Or let me."

"You're not a killer," I told him. "Fangs aside, I know you, man. You've got a nice-guy streak a mile wide. Now me..." I pulled out a big silver-coated knife, suitable for skinning deer, presuming I ever hunted any vampire deer, and held it up so it caught the light. "Me, I'm more of a 'Welcome to the dark side' kind of person."

Michael's leg was fixed well enough that he hobbled over to me and took the knife away. I let him, of course. "You're not a stone-cold murderer," he said. "And Pennyfeather's just lying there waiting for it. You'll kill somebody in self-defense, or defending someone else, but not like this."

"And you will? Give me my knife."

"Are you going to use it, or just pose for pictures? Because you know we can't leave him alive." Those last words were said quietly, in a voice that was a whole lot darker than the Michael Glass I'd known most of my life, the one who'd always had my back and been ready to kick ass if necessary.

But neither one of us *killed*. Not in the sense of cold-blooded murdering.

"He tried to kill Claire," I said. "I guess—"

"He tried to kill Eve, too," Michael said, "and wife trumps girlfriend just a little. So it's my job." His blue eyes looked dark now, almost like a night-sky color, and I would have actually felt better if he'd been vamping out in some way. But he wasn't. It was just regular Michael, talking about murder, with my knife in his hand.

I didn't know what to say to that. I stood up slowly, watching his face, and he nodded.

"Guess I'll get it done."

"Dude—"

Ignoring me, he limped over to Pennyfeather, who was still lying prone on the floor where the tranquilizer had taken him out. I had to admit, that one had worked way better than I'd expected.

Which raised the important question of why it had worked better than expected—because nothing ever did. In fact, I was always surprised when any of the things I invented worked at all. And Pennyfeather was one hard-to-kill fanger.

All of a sudden, I had a black, sick feeling in the pit of my stomach.

"Michael—"

"I've got this," he said. He looked pale but determined. "He tried to kill Eve, and Claire, and if we let him go, he's going to do worse. You know that."

"Watch—"

Out, I was going to say, but I didn't get the chance, because Pennyfeather wasn't all that tranquilized after all. He wasn't fully healed, though, and that was all that saved Michael from having his arm ripped off as the other vamp came up off the floor, grabbed his wrist, and yanked hard enough to break the knife free. It clattered to the stone floor and bounced, and I scrambled after it as Michael punched Pennyfeather in the face a couple of times to try to break his grip, without success. Pennyfeather's eyes had gone full-on red, and his fangs were down; he was trying to pull Michael down into biting range, and managed to score a long red scrape down his forearm before Michael wrenched backward. I grabbed the knife and headed back, and Pennyfeather knew the rules had changed; maybe it was the look on my face, and the fact that however much I might hesitate at knifing a helpless enemy, I wasn't even going to hesitate when he was a threat to my friend.

He shoved Michael hard into a table behind him, but Mike was ready for it; he bounced *forward* again, directly into Penny-feather, and body-slammed him flat into the floor.

"Shane!" he yelled. "Hurry up. I can't hold him!"

I was hurrying, and that was a mistake, because one of Myrnin's stupid always-scattered books slid under my foot and threw me off-balance, and during the second or two it took me to grab my balance again, Pennyfeather heaved Michael off him and almost levitated up to a standing position. He was by no means well; he was swaying in place, but somehow that made him seem more menacing, more inhuman, like some sinister demonic puppet with glowing eyes.

Instead of coming for me, he leaped backward, up onto a table, where he sent glass crashing and flying to the ground, and full-on hissed at us. He was still woozy, and maybe he really would come down for good from the silver, but not yet. Obviously.

Attacking a vampire who had the higher ground wasn't smart, and I slowed my rush and stood shoulder to shoulder with Michael. If he decided to come at us from up there, we'd be fighting for our lives in earnest, and although the knife would help, it wasn't enough. Not nearly.

"You know," I said to Michael, "my girlfriend took him down with a broken tree branch."

"Too bad she isn't here," he said. "Watch—"

He was probably going to say *out*, but Pennyfeather did something neither of us was ready for: he backflipped off the table to the floor, and ran, zigzagging through the land mines of Myrnin's lab, off into the shadows.

"Dammit," I said. "What the hell do we do now? We can't leave him here, not if the portals still work. He could show up in our house. And where the hell is Myrnin?"

"I don't know," Michael said, "but definitely not here. We have to get him. Once and for all."

"We may not have much time." I pointed toward the black doorway, which was still shimmering. Maybe Claire was holding it open for us, but it was starting to get an uneven look to it. I looked toward the stairs, where the other, non-magical exit was, and for a long moment couldn't figure out why I was seeing a wall. "Um, Mikey?"

"What?"

"Where's the regular door out of here?"

He turned and looked, too, and saw exactly what I did: a rough-poured mass of concrete that filled and blocked the stairs that led up and out.

"What the——?" He didn't waste time on it, though, just turned back to the portal. "That's our way out. Our *only* way."

"Like I said, time's ticking, man." I was watching the portal nervously, because it seemed to be vibrating, rippling like silk in a strong wind. Not good, or at least I assumed it wasn't good. "Either we go now or we're stuck here, and my odds aren't so good with two hungry vampires and no blood bank."

"He's not going to be easy to catch with what we've got here. We need something else!"

I looked around. There was surely no shortage of crap here that could be dangerous, but it was all a hopeless jumble . . . and as I opened up the first drawer I came to, Pennyfeather glided out of the shadows about twenty feet away, and pounced.

I almost got the knife in place, but he slapped it away, and it took everything I had—and Michael leaping on the other vamp's back—to wrench free of his grip before he could start ripping pieces off me. I grabbed blindly and wrapped my hand around a heavy, solid piece of—well, something. It looked a little like a fancy camera, only really cumbersome. I didn't try to do anything clever with it, just whacked it into the side of Pennyfeather's albino head as hard as I could. It was substantial enough that it didn't even bend, and he weaved as if I'd done some damage, which I followed up with a kick that doubled him over.

And we *still* couldn't get him, because he dodged free of Michael and circled around, and Michael stalked after him, intent and focused and with his eyes glowing with vampire power. He was more concerned for me, and I appreciated that, but I got the distinct feeling that Pennyfeather wouldn't mind adding Michael's death to his scorecard, either.

I guess in trying to swing the thing I was holding at the attacking vampire again, I hit some kind of a switch, because I felt a heavy surge of energy crawl up my arm, and then I must have accidentally turned it on Michael, because he flinched as if something had hit him . . .

And then he just went *maniac*. He moved in a blur at Pennyfeather, screaming in fury, and Pennyfeather went down hard. Next thing I knew, Michael was holding him on the floor, punching him with vicious fury like I'd never known he was capable of feeling before. It was . . . scary.

I stared down at the machine humming in my hands and quickly, clumsily felt around for an off button. I pressed something that seemed switchlike, and the hum died.

Michael stopped, breathing hard, staring down at Pennyfeather with eyes that glowed so red they seemed to be swimming with hellfire. Pennyfeather wasn't moving.

"Jesus," I whispered, and put the weapon—because that was what it was, some kind of weapon—down fast on the nearest available table space. "Michael?"

"I—" His voice sounded rusty and strange, and he looked up at me with those fury-filled eyes, and I almost wished he hadn't. "Give me the knife."

"Um . . . dude . . ."

"Knife."

I shook my head and put it away. "It's not because I don't want him dead. It's because I don't trust what you're going to do with it right now."

"He tried to kill Eve." There was a kind of terrible eagerness to the way he said it that made me want to shudder.

"Okay, man, it's great you got in touch with your inner serial killer and all, but no way." I was serious. I wanted Pennyfeather dead; that was no problem at all. What I earnestly didn't want was for Michael to wake up from this—whatever it was—and have the memory of what he was about to do. Besides, in the event he suddenly took an unhealthy interest in me, I wanted to be the one holding the knife.

It took another few seconds, but finally the glow faded out of his eyes to a more-normal bloody color—I hated that I could say it was normal—and he sat back, shaking all over. "What the hell was that? I just—"

"Went all evil superhero? Yeah. I don't know. One of Myrnin's fun little gadgets, I guess." I poked at it, frowning, and it slid on top of a pile of books and nearly toppled to the floor until I grabbed it and settled it in place again.

Michael was still holding out his hand to me, and I realized he was still waiting for the knife. Calmly, now. Our eyes met and held, and I said, "Are you sure, man?"

"No," he said. "But it's got to be done."

I handed it to him. Pennyfeather's eyes were shut, and he looked lifeless already, stunned unconscious by Michael's furious attack. Lying there silent, he seemed a lot . . . smaller. And with that androgynous bone structure, he could have just as easily been a strong-featured woman as a man, and that made the whole thing even more unsettling. I wasn't sure I could have done it at all, honestly.

And just to make matters worse right then, the portal shimmered, shivered, and belched out Claire. My girlfriend was still running on adrenaline; it was obvious in her too-wide brown eyes, the color burning in her cheeks. She had a longbow in her hand that was almost as tall as she was, and an arrow nocked and ready to pull. The arrow had a barbed silver tip.

She skidded to a halt, but she didn't drop her guard. "Is Pennyfeather—" She spotted Michael kneeling over the fallen vamp, and the knife, and she sucked her breath in hard.

"Has to be done," I said. She bit her lip, but she didn't try to argue. "Look, we need to get out of here. Myrnin did something crazy and filled in the exit, so we're now relying on the goodwill of my Frankendad keeping this portal thing open, and I'm not feeling good about the plan."

"Feel worse," she said. "Frank's starving. I don't know if he can even keep this up at all. We need to get out of here, *now.*"

"Not if we leave Pennyfeather behind and he has a way out that leads through our house."

Eve burst through just then, having apparently stopped to load up a rapid-fire crossbow that she held with frightening competence. She checked the corners for threats, too, before letting her guard down and starting to head toward Michael.

"Wait," I said, and got in her way. "Just—give him a minute."

She took a step back and considered me silently a second, then said, "I'm the one Pennyfeather came after. It's my job, right?"

"No!" Claire and I both said at the same time, but Claire went on, earnestly. "Eve, it's not killing him in a fight. It's—murder."

"So?" Eve said. Her eyes had gone flint-hard. "How many murders has he committed? You don't think he has it coming?"

"I don't think that's something any of us should decide!"

"Oh, honey," Eve said, and smiled just a little. "You really aren't from Morganville yet." She looked at me. "What's your objection, Collins?"

I shrugged. "Michael can handle him if he wakes up. You can't. Logistics."

Claire seemed shocked, but hey, Eve was right; Morganville kids understood this better. It might seem cruel and harsh, but when it came down to living and dying, we knew which side we wanted to end up on. Having Pennyfeather continue to stalk us was not an option.

Eve nodded. She walked over to Michael and put a gentle hand on his shoulder, and he looked up at her and took in a deep, steadying breath.

"He can't," Claire said. "He *can't*, Shane——"

I stepped in, and she dropped the bow and arrow with a clatter as I wrapped my arms around her and turned her back to what was going to happen. "Hush," I said, and nodded to Michael over her shoulder. "It'll be fast."

"Stop."

The voice seemed to come from everywhere, all around us, from hidden speakers and the tiny little one on my phone, too. It was scratchy and pale, and sounded exhausted, but it was all too familiar.

"Frank," I said. Facing down my dad was something I'd done a lot over the past few years, but it always seemed to have a new sting in the tail, every time. I wondered what it would be today. I swallowed what felt like a mouthful of acid, and said, "Just leave us alone, okay?"

"You don't need his blood on your conscience," Frank said. "Trust me, kids, you don't. Let me do it."

"You? Dad, hate to break it to you, but downstairs there's a computer, and in the middle of it there's a brain floating in a jar with wires running into it, and that's *you*. As in, you're not doing jack to Pennyfeather, however badass you think you are."

"I only have to do one thing, Son," he said. "I just have to die. I'm dying anyway; the nutrient tanks are dry, and there's nothing left for me. If you leave him here, I'll hold the portals shut until I'm gone. He's not going anywhere."

I turned and looked at Michael and Eve, and they seemed just as surprised as I was. And a little bit relieved. "Well," Eve said, "maybe it's the best—"

"Think about what you're saying," Michael said. "Because if I put this in his chest right now, he's finished. If we walk away, what if your dad screws up and lets him out?"

"Worse," Claire said, "what if he doesn't? You don't want Pennyfeather's death on your conscience, but you have no problem with leaving him here to starve? How would that be, Michael? Fun? Easy?"

He looked away. He knew, and I knew, that vampires didn't go easy from starvation; they lived a long, long time. And suffered. "Maybe he deserves it."

"Maybe," I agreed. "But if he does, he damn sure deserves the knife, too. And I don't want to wake up thinking of him down here screaming, do you?"

Pennyfeather took the decision out of our hands, because he opened his eyes, and snarled, and lunged up, claws outstretched.

And Michael acted completely out of reflex, defending himself and Eve. Quick and smooth and deadly accurate.

Pennyfeather hit the floor hard, and the silver began eating through his skin. His eyes stayed open. I didn't know if he was still alive, but I hoped not; either way, it didn't take long.

Frank's voice came back, weaker this time. "Time to leave," he said. "You need to go, now."

Michael left the knife in Pennyfeather's chest, took Eve in his arms, and led her to the portal. It rippled as they passed through without pausing.

That left just Claire and me staring at each other.

"Hey, Dad," I said to Frank. My voice sounded unexpectedly husky, and I cleared it. "Maybe this is wrong, but I think you tried

to help me when the draug had me in their tanks. They were killing me and making me dream while they did it, only someone—
someone kept trying to make me wake up. Was that you?"

Nothing. Silence. I listened to the distant drip of water for a
while.

"Well, if it was, thanks, I guess. It made me fight."

That summed up me and my dad perfectly. He made me fight,
whether I wanted to or not, and whether it was for a cause I believed in or not. He'd made me tough, and strong, and a survivor,
and yeah, that was worthwhile, especially now that I had things to
really fight for. Claire had quoted a writer named Hemingway to
me, not so long ago: *The world breaks everyone, and afterward, some people
are strong at the broken places.* I don't think my dad ever read Hemingway, but he'd have liked him.

I spent another couple of seconds waiting for—I don't know,
something—and then I turned to go.

And a grainy, shadowy, two-dimensional figure formed in
front of me.

My father had chosen a younger version of himself than the
age he'd been when he'd died, but it was still him—him from the
last of the good times of my childhood. Relatively speaking. We
stared at each other for a moment, and then his lips moved. I
could just barely hear the scratchy words hissing out of an ancient
speaker on the side of the machine across the room.

"I knew this day would come, Shane. That's why I sent you
back here. To be here when everything went bad."

"The vampires," I said. It was always about the vampires with
him. He blamed them for everything—for my sister's probably ac-
cidental death, for my mom's probable suicide, for his own drinking and bitterness and anger. And yeah, okay, maybe he was right,
because Morganville was a toxic place. "They're out of control."

"Always were," he whispered. "Always will be. Stop it. No matter what it costs. Burn the town around them if you've got to."

That was my dad. Always kill-'em-all-let-God-sort-'em-out. If a few innocents got caught in the inferno, well, collateral damage.

"Claire, go," I said. She was crying, I realized, silent tears that ran in silver drops down her cheeks. I couldn't sometimes fathom all of the goodness inside of her, because who cried for my dad, for a brain in a jar who'd hardly ever been good for anybody?

Claire did. She was probably crying for Pennyfeather, too.

"Go," I said again, gently, and kissed her on the lips. "I'm right behind you."

She picked up her bow and arrow and—after a hesitation, grabbed the bulky machine thing that had affected Michael so strongly. Before I could wonder about that, she headed for the portal, but she paused there, looking back. "Come on," she said. "We go together."

I headed for the exit, walking right through Frank's image. It felt like a curtain of pins and needles, but I was used to pain, especially where it came to my dad.

He re-formed ahead of me, blocking the way to Claire. I kept walking, and he kept backing up, traveling smoothly as the ghost he was. "Son," he said, "I want to tell you one thing. Just one."

"So do it."

"I'm proud of you," he said.

I came to a sudden and complete halt, staring at him—at the man I'd never really known, because he'd never let me know him; he'd treated me like a useful tool and potential enemy my whole life.

"You're different," he said. "You're better than I ever was. And I'm proud of you for being so strong. That's all. I just needed to tell you, before the end."

He dissolved in electronic smoke. Gone.

"Dad?" I turned on my heel, my voice echoing through the cool, silent lab. "Dad?"

Nothing. Just . . . silence. That told me he had no further energy to spare, and we were out of time. The lights flickered, warning me of the same thing.

Claire suddenly said, "Oh no—Bob!"

"Bob?" I stared at her blankly, and she pointed across the lab.

Oh. The spider. I shook my head and jogged over to pick up the tank—which, except for the glass content, was light—and made damn sure the lid was on it tightly before carrying it to the portal. Claire waited anxiously as the lights continued to flicker, faster and faster.

I paused on the edge of the portal as she stepped through. I wanted to say something profound, but I'm not that guy, so I just said, awkwardly, "Okay, Dad. See you."

"See you." His voice sighed, and there was something wistful in his electronic voice.

I stepped through the portal into the cool, familiar air of the Glass House, and felt the thing snap shut—utterly shut—behind me. There was an almost physical sensation of disconnection, of the whole system just . . . dying.

I put my hand on the blank wall and concentrated, for a moment, on just breathing. *You've lost him before,* I told myself. *He wasn't really there anyway.*

But it had felt real to me when he'd said he was proud. Maybe I'd always craved that, needed it. Maybe he'd known it.

But despite the surge of sadness, there was something good about leaving him this time—something that felt final, and complete.

Maybe this was what all those TV psych doctors meant when they talked about closure.

I put Bob's tank down on the dining room table, to Eve's

muttered distress, and Claire quickly dumped the heavy, clunky machine on the coffee table, along with her bow and arrow. I noticed vaguely that it was pointed in my direction, but at the moment, that didn't mean anything—and neither did the prickly feeling that raced through me.

"You're all right?" Claire said, and stepped closer with an expression of pure concern. She looked . . . I can't explain it, exactly, but all of a sudden I felt a bolt of heat go through me like fire out of heaven, and, man, did I want her in all kinds of ways—right and wrong. She'd grown over the past year—filled out in curves that begged to be held and stroked, and this definitely wasn't the time, but all of a sudden I was considering not minding what was appropriate behavior.

"Fine," I said through a suddenly dry throat. "I mean, I will be, anyway."

"I'm so sorry," she said. "I wish we could've done something."

"That's why I love you," I said, and reached over to brush her hair back from her face. "Because you care so much." Her gaze came up and hit mine, and more heat exploded through me like a bomb. I saw the shock wave of it in her eyes. *Oh.*

I really could not explain what was going on in my head and ricocheting around my body, but it was . . . good. Great, in fact. I fitted my hand around Claire's cheek and bent to kiss her. Her lips tasted like cherries and salt, sweet and tart together, and I growled somewhere deep and leaned in, pulling her close. She was mine, *mine*, and that was all that mattered. Myrnin had gone, vanished, and he wasn't any threat now. Some traitorous little whisper told me I could have asked Frank about him, about what had happened, but I hadn't wanted to know. He was gone.

And I had Claire, body and soul, and *man*, did I want her, right now. In so many ways.

"Hey," Michael said from somewhere behind me. "That's really sweet and all, but we just killed a guy and your dad—are you sure you want to be doing this *now*?"

He was dead right about that, but I couldn't take my hands away from her—or my lips. I'd somehow worked my thumbs under the tight knit of her shirt and found skin beneath, and I didn't want to let that go. The sensation of her fine, soft flesh, even that much of it, made me feel as if my head were on fire.

And then Claire gasped, coughed, and fought her way free of me. I instinctively reached for her and got air, and stumbled after . . . and as soon as I did, I sucked in a sharp, cold breath of air and felt something like sanity start to come back.

Oh. *Oh.* The machine. It lay on the coffee table, glowing a faint green, and the business end was pointed toward where Claire and I had been standing. It had gotten turned on when she'd dumped it there, I supposed.

And then, ha ha not funny, it had turned *me* on.

Claire, blushing a furious and gorgeous shade of red, circled around the table and flipped some kind of switch on the back. The glowing died, and so did the humming, and I felt . . . not normal, but less crazed. "Sorry," she said, and bit her lip. They were still damp and swollen from our kissing, and I shook myself out of focusing on them with a real effort. "It's—kind of an experiment."

"Myrnin's making a lust ray," I said. Of course he was, because . . . why not? I had to admit, I'd probably see some value in that myself. Hell. I just *had.* "Wait a second. I accidentally pointed that at Michael, and it made him—"

"Angry," Michael said. "Hyper-angry. Ready to kill."

"No, no, it's not—" Claire swallowed and visibly tried to calm herself. "It's not a lust ray. It just magnifies what you're feeling. And it's not Myrnin's. It's mine. I was just—experimenting."

"I know I'm not a scientific peer review or anything, but I have to say I think it works. If that's what you were going for, anyway." I skipped over the whole issue of why it had decided to focus on that particular impulse in me. She'd take it as a compliment, hopefully, but I wasn't too sure about that. My track record of guessing what might offend girls wasn't exactly perfect. "What were you thinking of using it for? Because the way it sent Michael into rage overdrive ..."

The blush just wasn't getting any less red, or—even without the ray—any less interesting. "The idea is that once I can exactly amplify a feeling, I can also cancel it out," she said. "It was supposed to just work with vampires, not humans. I don't know why—why it worked on you, Shane. I'm so sorry."

"Well"—I shrugged—"I'm not, particularly. That was a little bit fun."

"I hate to admit it, but it was when it was pointed at me, too," Michael said. "Kind of like it took away all the inhibitions."

"A drunk gun," I said. "Awesome."

"Not," Claire said, and frowned. "It's dangerous." She picked it up and stuck it in her backpack, engaging some kind of safety switch I hadn't noticed before. "I'll find someplace to keep it where it won't hurt anybody until I can destroy it. It was probably a dumb idea, anyway."

Eve disappeared into the kitchen, ever practical, and came out with a blood bag that she tossed to Michael, who snatched it out of the air and bit into it with a frightening level of enthusiasm. He drained it in about, oh, ten seconds or less, the same way a human would chug water after a really aggressive workout. And it had about the same effect; he got a little weak-kneed and had to brace himself on a wall, but after the shock passed, he seemed almost immediately better. His eyes faded back to simple blue, and his skin coloring went from dead-guy pale to more like ivory. Wounds started shutting faster, too.

"Thanks," he said to Eve. She raised a cocky eyebrow.

"You'll make it up to me later," she said, and winked. That got a really different kind of smile from Michael, and I found something else to look at, fast. Now I was the one feeling like an intruder on something personal, like I guessed Mikey had earlier, what with all the passionate groping and tongues.

Funny how just the way they smiled at each other could be intimate. Or maybe I was just turning into a girl, living with two of them in the house. That was frightening. Not that I don't like girls. I just preferred to be plain old insensitive me.

"One down," I said. "But Frank gave me a warning. This town's really going to go crazy. We need to be ready."

"Always," Eve said, and high-fived me.

But I wondered if we really, truly were.

THIRTEEN

CLAIRE

☽

The portal system had gone completely, utterly dead. The next morning, Claire started trying each of the entrances she had mapped out, and she found each of them just as inactive as the ones in the Glass House. Even Amelie's emergency escape, the one upstairs in the secret attic room, was gone.

She had known that was coming, but it was still...weirdly sad. She shuddered, and tried not to think about Frank dying slowly in his silent tomb as she exited the abandoned warehouse—portal number twelve on the map—and headed back toward the center of town. This side of Morganville was mostly left to rot and rats—had been for years, slowly falling into ruin as the businesses closed or relocated. The porch had finally fallen down at the front of the old hospital building where she and Shane had once run from both his father and Oliver, blocking it to even the hardiest urban explorers. There were likely lots of other ways in, but nobody sane wanted to go in there. It was a great place to go permanently missing—not just because of the vampires, but because there were some serious drug trade people who had claimed it for their own property. They could have it, as far as Claire was concerned. The place wasn't just haunted; it was *evil*.

I could have spent the morning working on the machine—what am I going to call it? The Vampire Power Cancellation Device? VPCD, for short? Fine, how about the Magic Thingy? She was fantasizing too much about what it could do, she thought, but she couldn't shake the idea that if she could just get a perfect amplification signal to match what the vampires were sending out, she could somehow cancel it . . . and perfectly nullify the effect.

Not that it would have stopped Pennyfeather from trying to rip her throat out, of course. Drawbacks.

This area of town was *really* run-down. Claire cursed under her breath as she tripped over another fallen fence. The vampires really could have done some urban renewal around here, but they liked having some ruins around; maybe it suited their Gothic sensibilities, or maybe it was just practical, having places where they could stalk around after dark in private. She wondered why they hadn't shut down the meth trade, though. Maybe—likely—they just didn't care enough.

As Claire was walking away, she saw the black ghost-hunting *After Death* van turn the corner and pull to a stop right in front of the building. *Oh, no. No. Don't* . . . But there they were: Jenna, Angel, and Tyler, getting out of the van, pulling out all kinds of equipment, cables, boxes. They were clearly going to stage some kind of spirit investigation in there. *Such* a bad idea.

Claire took out her phone and dialed the Morganville police department's nonemergency number. They weren't fast responders, generally, and it took at least ten rings before someone finally picked up. "Hi, it's Claire Danvers," she said. "You know who I am?"

"Yes. What do you want?" The voice on the other end was professional and cold. No clues as to who it was she might be talking to, or how the individual really felt.

"I'm standing in front of the old hospital building, the abandoned one? And those stupid ghost-hunting people are here. I just thought—maybe you could send a car over, tell them to move on?" She hesitated for a second, then plunged on. "Why are they still here, anyway?"

"We're waiting for a decision as to how to handle them," the voice said. "Until then, we're letting them poke around. People know to avoid them. The hope is they'll just lose interest and leave."

People meaning, Claire assumed, *vampire people.* The cops seemed to have it handled. "Okay," she said. "But that hospital's not safe. You know that, right?"

"We'll send a car," he promised, and hung up on her.

So much for being civic-minded. Claire watched the activity over at the van for a while, until she saw them actually ducking through a cut in the chain-link fence around the building. They were going inside.

Not good. For them.

She crossed the street, hoping to hear an approaching siren, but there was nothing except the hissing, constant desert wind and the rattle of tumbleweeds against the fences. In places, there were so many of the balled, thorny plants tangled in that it looked like a barricade. One skipped across open ground and bumped against her pants leg, and she had to stop to pull the burred tips free; her fingertips tingled and itched afterward.

Tyler had already gone inside. Angel was sliding through the fence now, with Jenna holding it open.

"Hey," Claire said, and they both turned to look at her in surprise. "Sorry, didn't mean to scare you, but this isn't a good place. It's unstable in there. The floor's all rotten."

"Ah, it's—Claire, right?" When she nodded, Angel smiled—with far less wattage than he would have used for Monica, she thought. "Well, we thank you for the warning, but we're very used to working in dangerous spaces. Remember the asylum, Jenna? The one in Arkansas?"

"The floors were completely gone," Jenna said. "We had to walk on the beams or we'd have dropped at least three stories straight into the basement. Got some great stuff, though. It was a huge ratings winner." She pushed a box through to Angel, then a second one. "Don't worry, we're trained for this kind of thing."

"There are snakes in there," Claire said. "Rattlers. And black widow spiders. It's *really* not safe."

"And we're *really* okay with it," Jenna said. "You go on, Claire. We've got this." Jenna studied her with curious pale eyes. "You seem pretty eager to keep us out of there. What's your real reason?"

Claire shrugged and kicked a random rock. "Nothing," she said. "Just I hate to see you get in trouble in there, for nothing. You're wasting your time around here, anyway."

"You'd be surprised what we've picked up already around here," Jenna said. That sounded ominous. "My personal opinion is that this town is a hotbed of paranormal activity. I believe we'll get dramatic footage out of what we find inside. It's almost as if—as if we're being guided."

"Guided," Claire repeated. "By what?"

"By whom," Angel corrected. His smile held just a touch of

indulgent doubt. "Jenna believes that she's made contact with a lost spirit."

"I have," Jenna said, and it sounded like the embers of an old argument, flaring up again. "Maybe you might recognize her. It's a young girl—"

Not Alyssa, Claire thought, stricken. *Please don't say it's Shane's sister.* Because there was no doubt in her mind, now, that Alyssa's spirit lingered, trapped in the lot where she'd died, even though the house had tumbled down.

"Miranda," Jenna finished. "At least, that's what I've been able to make out from the EVP recordings. We have quite a lot of them. She's very talkative."

"Miranda," Claire repeated, and drew in a deep breath. She'd survived out here, somehow; she'd latched onto the ghost-hunting crew in the hopes of getting help. But that was *so* dangerous. "Um . . . no, I don't think I recognize that name. Probably before my time."

"Huh," Jenna said, but Claire didn't like the look in her eyes. It was far too shrewd. "Funny how she knows *your* name, then. And a whole lot more."

She was saved by the distant wail of a siren. It was coming closer. Jenna and Angel looked at each other, eyebrows raised, as it became clear it was heading into their area, and both called, at the same time, "Tyler!"

Tyler backed out of the tumbled, brick-strewn doorway of the hospital. "Yeah, what? I'm going to have to climb over all this crap to get in this way. Maybe we should check the side—"

"Did you clear the location with the PD?" Angel asked.

"Didn't you?"

Jenna sighed. "Dammit, Tyler—"

Claire made a quick, tactical retreat as the Morganville police cruiser pulled up behind the van, lights and siren still going, and left them to sort it out.

Miranda was still around, and she was working with the ghost hunters in some way. Well—that was good that she'd found a way to survive, but still, Claire had a terrible feeling that it was also a complication.

Maybe a big one.

Claire felt better after leaving the neighborhood and starting to see open businesses again, ragged as they were; most of them were scrap yards and places that repaired appliances, maybe a couple of "antique shops" that were where you took things a step above the scrap yard. A secondhand clothing store Claire sometimes visited, though it was mostly Morganville natives who shopped there; the store over by campus was the one with stuff in her size, and from out of town generally, because of the college students who shed their clothes by season. It was terrible to be thinking of clothing just now, though; she'd just eliminated any possibility of searching Myrnin's lab for clues to where he'd gone. It deeply sucked. Not to mention that it would take a jackhammer and a backhoe to dig through the concrete sealing the entrance if she ever intended to rescue Myrnin's books, which were mostly irreplaceable.

She saw the first mayoral campaign sign stapled to a light pole—one for Captain Obvious—and remembered, with a shock, that the election was *today*. She hadn't cast a ballot yet. Well, the day was still young; she had time. And it was kind of her duty, since it had been her brainstorm in the first place, to vote for Monica, though she'd have to hold her nose to do it.

So she headed to City Hall, and ran straight into a mob scene.

The noise was a dull roar about a block away, and she thought it was some kind of construction work, maybe a giant bulldozer or grinding machine or something . . . but as she got closer, she heard that it wasn't mechanical at all. It was voices—yelling voices, all blending into something that sounded like a collective insanity. People were running *toward* the noise, and she found she had the same impulse to go and see what was going on. Though there'd been some attempts, nothing that big had ever happened in Morganville, in her experience. People just didn't have the heart to riot in those numbers.

Until now.

As Claire turned the corner, she saw there was a flatbed tractor trailer parked on the curb in front of City Hall, decked out with some sad-looking patriotic streamers and ribbons, and on it stood Flora Ramos, with someone in a black leather jacket, black pants, gloves, and a motorcycle helmet with a dark, opaque faceplate. His—at least, Claire assumed it was a man—arms were crossed. Flora was at the microphone next to a big pair of speakers.

The posters that people had on poles and held up over their heads were the CAPTAIN OBVIOUS FOR MAYOR signs.

And clearly, the guy standing on the dais next to Flora was . . . the new Captain Obvious? It could have been the same guy who'd fired at Oliver in Common Grounds; he'd been wearing a black hood then, instead of the helmet, but the jacket looked similar.

Flora Ramos held up her hands and stilled to a dull mutter the approving roar of the thousand or so people crammed in the street.

"We've had enough," she was saying. "Enough of the oppression. Enough of the death. Enough of the inequality. Enough of losing our homes, our lives, our children, to things we don't control. And we won't be silent. If Mayor Moses couldn't make our voices heard, we will make them heard on every street, in every building, and on every corner of Morganville until things change! Until we *make* them change! We built this town with our sweat and blood and strength, and it is *our* town as much as that of those who pretend to own it!"

She was, Claire had to admit, a *great* speaker. She was angry, full of passion, and it arced out of her like lightning to sting the crowd into more yells, chants, and shouts. Claire slowed down. She was a little afraid, suddenly, of the power of that mob, and of Flora's eloquence. So were the Morganville cops, she realized. They were out in force, all twenty or so, forming a solid cordon between the crowd and City Hall.

No telling how the vampires felt about it, but Claire had no doubt, none at all, that they were well aware of this. And if they'd been unhappy about Monica seeking the office, how pissed off were they now? Plenty, she imagined. From the crowd that had gathered, Captain Obvious was going to win in a landslide, and if the vamps thought they could ignore the ballots and pick their own candidate, it was going to get very ugly, very quickly. Nobody would be fooled, and clearly, the humans were in no mood to take it lying down.

Flora was still talking, but it was hard to hear her over the constant, fevered applause and cheering. Claire stared hard at Captain Obvious. Hard to tell anything about him, underneath the disguise, but he had a hell of a lot of guts coming out here in public and standing as a free target after putting a crossbow bolt in *Oliver*.

So she could have predicted what came next.

It started calmly enough. Claire was used to looking for vampires, so she picked up the smooth, subtle movements from the shadows well before most other people. It started with one or two coming out, well swathed in long coats and scarves, hats and gloves, but it didn't stop there. Soon it was ten. Then twenty. Then too many for Claire to count.

And like the police, they fanned out, but not to cordon off the crowd.

They were making for the stage, and Captain Obvious.

He saw them coming about the time that most others did. Vampires didn't need protection, even in a crowd like this; Morganville natives had it bred into them to back up, get away, and that was exactly what they did. Cries of alarm went up, and little islands of space formed around the vamps as they pushed forward.

Captain Obvious's helmet turned toward Flora, and she nodded. He backed up to the edge of the trailer, dropped off and out of sight, and one second later Claire heard the roar of a motorcycle. He came roaring out from concealment on the other side of the truck, spraying smoke as he fishtailed around. The crowd cleared for him, too, or at least for the snarling bike, and he leaned into the handlebars and hit the thrust hard.

A lunging vampire tried to take him off the machine, but he ducked low and weaved expertly, and she went rolling. When another tried it ten feet later, someone in the crowd—more daring than the rest—ran forward and knocked the vampire's hat off. The vampire turned with a roar of fury and slapped the broad-brimmed coverage back over his smoking head, but his second was lost, and Captain Obvious accelerated away, leaning into a sharp turn with his knee almost on the ground. It was someone with training, Claire thought, someone with a lot of skill.

The vampires largely gave up on him, though a few tried chasing him; the rest bolted forward, swarmed onto the stage, and two grabbed Flora Ramos. A third cleanly severed the microphone cord with a single pull, robbing her of her soapbox.

But when they tried to take her down from the platform, people surged forward, shouting. They'd lost their fear, all of a sudden. It made sense. Flora was a popular lady, a widow, who'd lost kids to the vampires. She was everybody's mom, all of a sudden, being dragged off into the dark—not in the middle of the night, but in public, in broad daylight, in a blatant show of vampire force.

Amelie and Oliver must have approved this. They must be watching, Claire thought with a sudden twinge. She turned and looked behind her, and saw a long blacked-out sedan idling at the corner. She walked that way. Walked right up to the car and rapped on the backseat window.

It glided down to reveal the pale, sharp face of Oliver. He didn't speak. He just gazed at her with cool disinterest. Next to him, Amelie was looking straight ahead, a slight frown grooved between her brows. She looked flawless, as always, but Claire knew her well enough to think she was bothered by what she saw before her.

"Let Mrs. Ramos go," Claire told Oliver.

"She's preaching sedition and breaching the public peace," he said. "She's ours by law."

"Maybe. But if you take her off that stage, you lose. Not just now, but for a long time. People won't forget."

"I care not what they remember," he said. "The only way to stop a rebellion is to crush it with blood and fire, and to wound them so they'll never dare to raise a hand again."

He sounded as if he almost *liked* it. Claire shuddered, and looked past him, to Amelie. "Please," she said. "This isn't right. Stop it. Let Flora go."

It took forever for the Founder to speak, but when she did, her voice was soft, even, and decisive. "Let the old woman go," she said. "It gains us nothing to make her a martyr. Our goal is to find this new Captain Obvious. He can't hide for long. Once we have him, we make an example of him and make it clear that this kind of disruption won't be tolerated. Yes?"

Oliver scowled and sent Claire a murderous glance. "My queen, I think you are listening too much to your pets. The girl's softhearted. She'll lead us all to ruin." He lifted Amelie's pearl white hand to his lips and kissed it, lips lingering on her skin, and she finally looked at him. "Let me guide you in this. You know I have the best interests of Morganville at heart. And *you* are Morganville."

The frown between Amelie's perfectly arched brows relaxed, smoothed, and she kept her gaze fully focused on him. "I fear your way will bring us more trouble, Oliver."

"And this chit's way will bring us death," he said. "Mark me, compromise is no answer. We would compromise ourselves into a pyre of ashes. Humans have no pity for us, and never have; they'd kill every one of us. Have you forgotten that one of them just yesterday tried to put a silver arrow in my heart?"

"And I pulled it out," Claire said. "Or you'd be dead now, you jerk. What exactly is a *chit*?"

It was a rhetorical question, but Amelie's gaze tugged away from Oliver's for a moment, and Claire got the full force of the Founder's attention. "A disrespectful young woman," she said. "Something I was called more than once. Something every woman of quality is called, sooner or later, by a man who feels they do not know their place. As we do not, because our place is as lofty as we may aspire to climb. It is the language of men who fear women." There was something weird about Amelie's eyes; they seemed darker than normal, and Claire couldn't figure it out until she realized that the pupils were inordinately large, as if she'd had some kind of dilating drops in them. Was she being drugged? "Which brings up a good point, Oliver. I believe you've called me a chit, upon occasion. Yet suddenly you call me your queen."

"You've ever been queen in my heart," he said, which made Claire want to gag. His voice was smoky, soothing, and way too seductive. "Can we not agree on this one thing, my liege? That the survival of what few vampires remain must take precedence over the legions of humans who roam this earth in their billions? If we trust to their good graces, we will die."

"He is not wrong in that, Claire," Amelie said. "Mankind is not known for its charity toward those it fears. If we're not torn apart as demons, we'll be dissected in your laboratories, for science. Or worse, put on exhibition, no better than those ragged lions and exhausted bears in your zoos. Who will protect us, if we don't protect ourselves?"

Claire wanted to say that she was wrong, that it wouldn't be like that, but she'd read enough history and knew enough about the grudges and fears that people held close to their hearts to realize that Amelie was probably right, in principle.

"Let her go," Claire said. "And people will see you're not afraid to be part of this town and listen to them. Trust me. Please. I don't want this to explode, and neither do you, but it will. You make Mrs. Ramos disappear, and it'll never stop exploding. Vampires will take out humans, humans will take out vampires, and sooner or later, we're all dead or you're discovered."

"I cannot let her go. Not an option." But Amelie seemed to consider things, and suddenly she pulled her hand free of Oliver's hold, opened the other side of the limousine, and stepped out into the sun.

Unlike the other vampires, she didn't bother to try to cover herself; she was old enough that the sun wouldn't do more than give her a painful but mild burn. The sight of her in full daylight was startling. She wore a white silk suit, expertly tailored, and her short stature was concealed with tall white pumps. Her pale gold hair, wrapped in a coronet around her head, was almost the same shade. The only color on her was a bloodred ruby necklace and a matching ring, and as she walked off toward the mob, she looked every inch a queen.

Oliver slammed his door open, grabbed Claire by the arm, and shoved her back against a brick wall. "Stupid girl," he said, and ran after Amelie. She didn't seem to be moving fast—drifting, almost—but he had trouble catching her.

She reached the crowd before him, and it parted in front of her like smoke before a strong wind. The vampires paused on stage, suddenly aware of her presence, and silence swept over the chaos to the point that Claire imagined she could almost hear the click of Amelie's heels as she moved up the portable stairs to the stage.

Oliver scrambled behind her, impassive in expression, but she could see the anger and frustration in his body language. He was too late to stop whatever she intended to do.

"Release the woman," Amelie said to the two vamps holding Flora. They let go, immediately, and stepped away with their heads bowed. Amelie advanced to stand in front of her. "Are you injured?"

Flora shook her head no.

"Then you may leave this place, if you wish. Or you may stay here, on this stage, and accept the very difficult and thankless job of mayor, a position to which I believe you are uniquely suited."

Whatever Flora was expecting, it wasn't that. Neither were her supporters. A confused babble started up, and Claire jogged back over so she could hear more clearly over the confusion. The microphones were dead, so only the first few rows were likely to hear what was going on.

"I'm not running," Flora said. "It's Captain Obvious the people want."

"And Captain Obvious they will not get," Amelie replied with perfect calm. "One cannot elect a man too cowardly to show his face. You, Mrs. Ramos, have courage enough for both, quite clearly. And so *you* are my nominee. What say you? We have enough residents here to win you the day, simply by voice. Yes or no?"

"I can't——" It wasn't a refusal, though; it was a confused and reluctant argument. "I'm not a politician."

"Neither is Captain Obvious, else he would not have run away at the first sign of trouble," Amelie said coolly, and got a ripple of chuckles from a few in the crowd. "I come to stand before the people of Morganville as the Founder. Unafraid. Can he say as much? You stand before them as well. And I say you will uphold their trust. I ask you for nothing but honorable service. Will you accept?"

Claire didn't hear the answer, because the roar that went up from the crowd was deafening.

There really wasn't any question of refusing.

Amelie had outmaneuvered Captain Obvious *and* Oliver, and she had regained the equilibrium of Morganville, at least temporarily—all in a mere thirty seconds.

Claire shook her head in wonder, and went home to tell Shane that, despite their hard work—and glitter—Monica was off the ballot.

He'd be *so* disappointed.

Claire wasn't the first one to get the news to the Glass House, even though she called as she jogged away from City Hall. Eve answered on the first ring and said, "Are you at the riot?"

"It's not really a riot. More of a rally."

"Because the underground talk is that it's a riot. Are they beating people with signs? Is there pepper spray involved? Details!"

"Not that I saw," she said. "I really thought I had breaking news, but you beat me to it."

"Not so much, sugar pie. Is it true that they almost got Flora Ramos? Man, I wish they had. It would have just destroyed whatever high ground Amelie had left. I mean, *Flora Ramos*—everybody knows about her kids. . . ."

"They didn't take her in," Claire said, and talked fast, in case Eve was refreshing the Web page. "Amelie declared her mayor."

"Wait—*declared?* How is that fair? Wow, Monica is going to be *pissed* that she didn't even get to properly lose. . . . Okay, that's an upside, actually."

"She wouldn't have gotten much of a vote. There was about half the town rallying out there—you know, the half that breathes? And they weren't carrying any 'Monica Morrell' signs. Everybody was Team Obvious out there."

There was a rustle on the other end, and then a confused blur of voices arguing. "Hey!" Eve came into focus again. "Hell no, Shane, call her yourself. I got her first. . . . Oh, all right. Shane says to tell you he worked hard on those signs, and they were way better than Captain Obvious's signs." Eve covered up the speaker, but Claire still heard her muffled exchange with him. "Really? You had to try to steal my phone to say that? Loser!" Shane's comeback was indistinct, but probably insulting. Eve frostily ignored it and said, "You were saying, Claire?"

"No matter how great they were, all our posters got torn down or . . ."

"Or? Claire? Helllloooooooo?"

"Gotta go," Claire said hastily, and hung up, because Monica's red convertible was pulled in at the curb up ahead, and she was standing there, staring at one of her posters that *hadn't* been pulled down. Claire could see the blank expression on her face, which made her curious, and she hurried over to stand at an angle where she could see the poster.

She covered her mouth to hide an appalled gasp, because someone had gotten downright artistic on Monica's poster—more than one person, obviously, from the ink-color variations and styles. One had written, in bold Sharpie, *Burn in Hell*, which was really the nicest thing anyone had said. The additions to her half-drunk duckface picture were interesting, too, and mostly pornographic.

Not that Monica didn't deserve it. She did. This was nothing but retribution, but from the look on the girl's face, she hadn't seen it coming, not at all.

"They hate me," Monica said. Her voice was quiet and a little hushed, and her eyes were wide. There were spots of high color on her cheekbones under the spray tan. "Jesus, they really do hate me."

"Um . . . sorry. But what did you expect?"

"Respect," Monica said. "Fear. But they're not afraid of me. Not anymore." She reached out, took hold of the poster, and yanked it down. It ripped in the middle, and she tore the second half down with even more vicious fury. The cardboard was tough, but she managed to reduce it to vivid neon scraps and toss it defiantly to the sidewalk in a shattered heap. "Their mistake! And *yours*, bitch! I know you and Shane set this up. You always wanted to see me humiliated!" She advanced on Claire, fists clenched. Claire stood her ground calmly, and Monica stopped coming when she realized she wasn't going to make her back down, but rage still boiled through her whole body. At the slightest opportunity, the least little sign of weakness, she'd pounce.

"We thought you might pull it off," Claire said. "It's not our fault you have more baggage than an airport at Christmas. Maybe instead of getting even, you ought to be thinking how to improve what people think about you."

"I think *you* have about ten seconds to get out of my face!"

Claire shrugged. "Enjoy your outcast life, then. You'll get used to it. The rest of us do just fine."

"Bitch!" Monica yelled at her back, but it was just words, and it was a sign of just how much things had changed between the two of them that Monica didn't dare attack her with anything else, not even when her back was turned. "I'll get you for this—I swear!"

Claire just waved and kept walking, though the area right between her shoulder blades kept itching until she heard Monica's car door slam and heard the roar of the engine. Even then, she stayed ready to jump out of the way should the Mustang mysteriously jump the curb, but once it had flashed past her, burning rubber in a thin, bitter mist on the still air, she relaxed. A little.

But only for a moment.

It was a sunny morning, quiet; the sun hung warm in a cloudless sky the color of faded denim, and a couple of big hawks kited overhead, circling for prey. It wasn't the time or place that she would have expected to sense a threat, and yet . . .

Yet something was wrong. She could just . . . feel it.

It took her a few seconds of quick analysis to figure out that what had tripped her alarm switch was the dusty college bookstore she had just passed. Instead of opening up, someone had been sliding the curtains closed in the window . . . and now a hand reached through the curtain and turned the OPEN sign to CLOSED. That wasn't right. It was a regular workday, and the store wouldn't have been open for very long. *Well, he could have just wanted to grab breakfast. Or an early lunch.*

She couldn't be sure, because it happened very quickly, but she could have sworn that the hand flipping the sign had taken on a vivid red sunburn even in that brief exposure to the sun.

Vampire.

Claire slowly backed up, staring at the store. She thought back to what was happening while she'd been talking to—well, been taking abuse from—Monica. Had someone gone inside the place? Yes, one person; she'd seen him out of the corner of her eye. And, now that she thought of it, that person had been Professor Carlyle, he of the utterly unearned B on her physics paper, so obviously not a creature of the night, even if he was evil.

Someone had been in the store already, like a spider waiting in a web.

Not my problem, Claire told herself, but something deep down argued with her. Maybe she'd spent too much time around Shane, who was always throwing himself gleefully into one fight after another. Maybe she was just still angry at Amelie and Oliver's arrogant attitude toward the mostly defenseless human population of Morganville. Whatever.

She slipped her backpack off her shoulder, tugged free a silver stake, and tried the door, and despite the sign, it was still unlocked. She was committed then—the vampire would have heard her anyway, however distracted he might have been. So she charged inside, let the door bang shut behind her, and landed solidly on her feet, ready for the fight.

Good thing she was, because the vampire came at her fast out of the shadows, a white distorted face and a red snarl, and she struck out and got flesh, but not his heart. He screamed and darted off, clearly not prepared for a fight with someone who could hurt him, and in the brief respite Claire glanced around the shop. The lights were on, which was helpful. Typical college bookstore, with loads of shelves crammed with dog-eared, highlighted-over textbooks; the whole place had a run-down, cheap look to it that probably was exactly what the average TPU student liked about it—that, and the low, low prices. (Claire had tried it out once, but the book she'd bought at pennies on the dollar also had significant issues, such as missing about a dozen crucial pages in the middle.)

The shopkeeper, whose name she vaguely remembered as Sarah something—Sarah Brooke, that was it—was sitting on the floor. Her wrists and ankles had been tied together, and her eyes were so wide that she was likely screaming under the duct tape that covered her mouth.

Professor Carlyle was kneeling beside her. He'd been blitz-attacked, apparently; he had a cut on the side of his head that was bleeding freely in shocking red streams, and he was holding a trembling hand to his neck. More blood trickled out of that wound, but it wasn't gushing. "Danvers?" he said, in blank astonishment.

"You okay, sir?"

"He—he bit me—but I'm Protected!" He held up the hand that wasn't clamped over his throat, and Claire saw the silvery glint of a bracelet. "This can't happen!"

Sarah was Protected, too—she was wearing a similar bracelet that guaranteed her safety from vampire attack, at least theoretically. Obviously, it wasn't a magic shield.

The vampire, who'd backed away from Claire temporarily, took another run at her, and this time, she skipped backward and ripped down the curtains over the big front window, framing herself in bright daylight. "Come on, if you're coming," she said, but the vamp skidded to a halt right at the edge where shadow met sun.

And she got her first good look at him. "Jason?" she blurted in horror.

The vampire who was trying to kill her—and Sarah, and Professor Carlyle—was Jason Rosser, Eve's brother.

He'd wanted to be a vampire—had actively campaigned for it—and she'd been afraid he'd be even worse as a person if he grew fangs; here it was, proof positive, that if you had creepy violent tendencies as a human, you felt free to indulge them as a new vampire. The only good thing about the situation was that he was *really* new, and super allergic to the sun. In fact, today's attack might have been his first try at hunting.

If so, it wasn't going extremely well.

"Get out of here," Jason said. His voice was low, rough, and ugly with fury. "I don't want you. *Get out.*"

"Too bad, you've got me, jackass. What the hell are you doing?"

"What does it look like, bite bait?" He flashed his teeth at her, which might have scared her, oh, years ago.

"Failure? And don't drop fang at me, Jason. It's not polite. Ah! Watch it!" He'd made a move, and although she didn't think he'd charge into the sunlight to grab her, she wasn't assuming anything. She brought the stake to an easy-stabbing position. He already had a blackened, sizzling hole in his side that wasn't healing fast. He wasn't eager to take another hit. "These people are Protected, idiot. They're off the menu. Go to the blood bank if you need your fix of B positive or whatever it is you're jonesing for." *Besides causing pain and terror,* she thought, but didn't say. Clearly, that was a big part of it for Jason. Most of the other vampires were more clinical about their feeding, but he'd brought all his weird, twisted baggage over with him.

In some ways, he and Eve were mirror images of each other—both fascinated by the darkness. Only Eve had chosen to manifest hers outwardly, and Jason . . . Jason had taken it all deep inside. For a while, Claire had been convinced there was something in him more than that. Something better. But over time, he'd proven her wrong.

And now, here he was, bloody-mouthed, grinning at her like Batman's Joker, if the Joker had fangs.

"Protection's a joke," Jason told her. He prowled the line of shadow, staring at her with dark, angry eyes that looked unsettlingly like his sister's. "Always has been; it's a racket, and the vampires laugh about it over their drinks. You know what the penalty is for me draining these two? I have to pay a *fine*. It's like a note in your file at school. I can do what I want. Nobody's going to care. Nobody's going to stop me."

"Oliver might. Or Amelie. They kind of like vampires to stay in line around here. Makes things easier for everyone."

He made a harsh buzzer sound. "Sorry, wrong answer," he said. "Old pioneer days, Claire. You're not keeping up. We've got privileges now. You can't keep us walking around on leashes anymore like tame dogs."

His pacing reminded her of a caged animal, too. Creepy. "Don't make me stake you, Jason. I'd have to tell your sister, and I don't want to do that."

"As usual, it's all about Eve. Why is it her business what I do?"

"She still cares about you, you know."

"She never really cared. Don't try that on me. If she'd been any kind of a stand-up sister, she'd have watched out for me. She just ran off and left me behind to take my punishment and shacked up with her precious *Michael*." Jason singsonged the name like a grade-schooler. *He's just trying to scare you*, Claire told herself, somewhat unconvincingly. *You've dealt with Myrnin all this time; you can handle this stupid kid.*

But she wasn't so sure. She'd counted on a vampire who'd back down, not one who was the poster child for unbalanced. Time for a shift of strategy.

Claire put down the stake. She needed both hands as she unzipped her backpack and reached inside to the inner pocket.

Jason decided it was the perfect time to make his move. He was fast, she had to give him that, but so was she, and she'd known he'd take the bait; he wasn't the cautious sort. So when her hand came up out of the bag holding the canister, he laughed, and his hands closed on her shoulders with crushing force.

"What're you going to do? Perfume me?"

She sprayed liquid silver in his open mouth.

Jason's shriek almost burst her eardrums, and, coughing and gagging, he staggered backward, smoke pouring from between his lips. His skin was burning from the sunlight. Claire shoved him backward into the shadows, and he stumbled a few steps, kept gagging, and sank down to his hands and knees to cough convulsively.

"It's just a little," she told him. "Consider it breath freshener. The next time, I spray it in your eyes, Jason, so keep the hell off me if you like your face."

He was too busy retching to try to speak, even if he could have managed it. Claire bypassed him and went to Sarah, tugged the ropes free, and let her pull the tape off her mouth. It must have hurt. The skin beneath it looked red and abraded, and Sarah whooped in a deep breath of relief. She fixed a poisonous glare on Jason. "You just wait, you little piece of crap," she said. "My Protector's not going to stand for this."

"Neither will mine," Professor Carlyle said. He looked pale and shaky, but righteously angry. Claire found paper towels behind the bookstore's counter and folded some into a thick pad, which she gave him to apply to his head wound. "Thank you, Danvers."

"You're welcome," she said. "So . . . can we talk over that B on the last paper? Because it was really an A effort. I'd take a B if I deserved it, but—"

"Yes, yes, fine, A it is. As far as I'm concerned, you have an A for the rest of the class," he said. "Sarah, would you like me to call someone, or—"

"Nope," the woman said, and climbed to her feet. She was small but had a wiry strength that probably came from bench-pressing boxes of textbooks all day. "I'm calling the pound to see if they can come get this damn rabid dog—"

Before she could finish the thought, Jason had scrambled to his feet and was running for the back door. Alleys, Claire thought. Shaded alleys, with sewer access. He'd be gone before anyone could catch him.

"Might want to keep that back door locked from now on," she said to Sarah as she returned the silver canister to her backpack and picked up the stake to slide it into the holster next to it. "Professor."

They both nodded, clearly still off-balance from the encounter with their own mortality; Claire felt it, too, a hissing tension running through her body that made her realize how much she'd just taken on herself. Shane would have been livid that she'd tried it without backup.

She went outside and walked fast, all the way home.

Where she was going to have to tell Eve her brother had gone full-on Hannibal Lecter. Fun.

She spotted the shiny black van of the ghost hunters—clearly driven off from their targeted hospital visit, thankfully—cruising slowly down the street. Jenna and Angel were arguing (there was a shocker) and Jenna was consulting a street map. There weren't many maps of Morganville that the vampires hadn't, ah, edited, so if the team members were trying to find some "haunted" location, they wouldn't be finding anything more exotic along the way. Except maybe Jason, who could be on the rampage after not getting his afternoon snack.

Claire swallowed her pride, dialed Amelie's number, and got the brisk, Irish-accented voice of her assistant, Bizzie. "Please tell Amelie that Jason Rosser's out here biting people, in public. Protected people. And if she wants those ghost hunters to get a good story, he's a great way to do it." She didn't wait for an acknowledgment. Amelie would shut Jason up; she might shut him up permanently, but that wasn't Claire's concern. She was more worried about the ghost hunters.

Nobody had said so, but it had seemed obvious from her conversation with the police that the decision the vampires were considering about the strangers had two outcomes: wiping their memories and dumping them out of town somewhere, or planting them somewhere deep, where no one would ever find the bodies. If they were still here, it was almost as if Amelie (or Oliver) had decided to toy with them, with no intention of letting them ever leave town alive.

Despite herself, Claire admired the ghost hunters' determination, a little. She recognized the curiosity, and the blind stubbornness; she had loads of that in her own character. She hated to see them punished for it.

But that, like so much in Morganville, was probably out of her hands.

Claire's adrenaline had finally stopped buzzing in her ears by the time she walked up the steps to the front door of the Glass House, and luckily, it seemed there was no emergency in progress. There was lunch being contemplated, and as she walked into the kitchen, Eve, Michael, and Shane were arguing the relative merits of hot dogs versus grilling hamburgers outside.

"Hot dogs are faster," Michael pointed out. "Microwave."

"Ugh, that's disgusting. Also, we don't make mac and cheese in there, either. That's just wrong," Eve said, and poured herself a tall glass of Coke. "Hey, college girl. Drinky?"

"Yes." Claire collapsed into a chair at the kitchen table. Eve gave her a quick look that let her know she'd picked up on her tension, then got down another glass from the cabinet. "The Apocalypse must be near, because a guy is arguing against grilling. That's just un-Texan, Michael."

"Vampire," he pointed out. "If I went out there, the only thing barbecuing would be me. And hot dogs are all-American. All-American trumps Texan."

"You're brainwashed by commercials about cars and baseball," Eve shot back, and handed Claire a fizzing glass. "Hot dogs are made of pig butts and the parts nobody in his right mind would eat. Yes, I used to like them. Don't judge me, okay?"

Shane was clearly Team Grill; he'd already gotten out the burger-flipping utensils and put them on the counter, and now he was digging sauces out of the fridge. "We're not even having this discussion," he said. "Eve's unemployed. The least she can do is help me grill burgers. And you two can chop veg—" He paused, looking straight at Claire. "What the hell happened?"

"Monica got creamed in the election?"

"We'll throw the party later. And?"

She really didn't want to say it. "I saw Jason. He was kind of . . . attacking people. So I stopped him. By the way, the silver pepper spray? Works great."

Eve had gone completely still. She stared at Claire for a moment, then said quietly, "Is he okay?"

"I didn't get him too badly. He's okay. Just less bitey for a while. Eve—he's not, ah—"

"Not wound too tight," Eve supplied, and lowered her gaze to fix on the bubbles in her Coke. "Yeah, copy that. He's always been off. You know that."

Off didn't really describe the feeling she'd had with Jason today. "I think it's worse than that," she said, as gently as she could. "He's really—vicious."

Michael stepped in, then. "It's not unexpected that would happen," he said. "Look, becoming a vampire—it's complicated, what it does to you, but it does kind of amplify whatever bad impulses you already had. It's tough to hang on to the good stuff, but easy as hell to bring the bad with you. I knew he'd be . . ." Michael shook his head. "Anyway. I'll let Oliver know. He's in charge of Jason."

"From what Oliver's doing now, he won't really care," Claire said. "He's gone a little power crazy. You might have noticed."

"Okay, so Jason Rosser is evil, and Oliver's power hungry. This is not breaking news that should keep us from grilling burgers," Shane said. "Can I get an amen?"

Eve and Michael chimed in, but Claire kept her head down. She was feeling pretty low. She'd spent a lot of energy this morning running down the portals and coming up empty, and then there had been the excitement of the rally, and Jason. . . . She was drained—not even hungry, actually, which was surprising.

She was also worried, *really* worried, about Myrnin. She'd thought that by now she'd have gotten some word from him. Bob was sitting upstairs in her room, contentedly spinning webs around flies that she'd caught for him, and she couldn't believe that even at his craziest, Myrnin would have left his pet to starve. He was careless of assistants, but never of his spider.

So . . . where was he? And if he couldn't communicate, how was she supposed to even begin to find him? It made her head hurt, and her stomach churn, and suddenly all she wanted was to finish her cold, sweet soda and crawl upstairs to sleep.

"Hey," Michael said as he took out tomatoes, lettuce, onions and pickles from the refrigerator. "Hand me a knife, would you?"

She pulled one off the magnetic strip Shane had installed on the wall—easier access, he'd said, in case it came down to that kind of a fight. Shane always thought ahead that way. She gave the blade to Michael without comment and watched as he chopped stuff up. He was neat, fast, and accurate. Vampire senses apparently made for great prep cooks. "Michael," she said as he finished slicing pickles into quarters, "do you know what bloodline Myrnin comes from?"

"I'm guessing you don't mean Welsh," he said. "Vampire bloodline?"

She nodded.

"No. Why?"

"Because I need to track him, and I remember Naomi could, you know, drink a sample of another vampire's bloodline to find him. She did it with Theo. Maybe—maybe you could do it to find Myrnin?"

"Maybe," Michael said, but he sounded doubtful. "I heard there's a blood record somewhere, but I have no idea where it is. Or if Myrnin's in it. From what I heard, he's the only one still living out of his line. It's pretty ancient, and he didn't make any others who survived long, so there may not *be* a record."

"But could you ask? Maybe look around? I need to find him, Michael. I think—I think he's in trouble."

"Why?" He put down the knife and looked at her directly. "Did he say something?"

"Only that he didn't like the way things were going in town," she admitted. "And that he was planning to leave. But you know how he is. I don't think he really would have run away. Not like that. You saw the lab!"

He shrugged. "The lab's always a mess; you know that. It's impossible to tell whether there was a struggle, or he just didn't like the latest newspaper he read and decided to trash the place."

"He left Bob! And how did Pennyfeather get in? He didn't have authorization."

"You don't know that. And maybe he just forgot about Bob. It's not like he's an exciting pet."

"Bob's cool, and Myrnin loves him like any other pet. He'd never just abandon him to starve," Claire said. "But . . . I just have the feeling, okay? So would you? For me?"

Michael ruffled her hair. "Yeah, sure. For you. Here. Chop some onions."

"Hey!"

"Consider it prepayment."

Lunch cheered her up—as did Michael's promise—and Claire actually enjoyed the burgers, which Shane had cooked pretty much to perfection. Eve and Shane got into it over the age-old mustard versus mayonnaise debate, but they had a nice time, even with that controversy devolving to tossing packets of condiment at each other. Even better, since it was Shane's turn to clean up.

After lunch, Claire went upstairs to her room while Michael and Shane settled in to try out a new first-person shooter game, and Eve shopped online; she stretched out on the bed and fell immediately, deeply asleep.

For a while she was too tired to dream, but finally she dreamed, and it was . . . odd.

At first, she didn't really understand. She was someplace dark and very, very quiet, except for the steady hiss of water dripping. She was cold and felt a gnawing, desperate hunger.

Then she heard a voice out of that dark whisper, "Claire?" It was as if she were torn out of her body and thrown violently up through the dark in a blur, and everything in her wanted to scream but she didn't actually have lungs or a body to use to do that, only a pure, condensed feeling of real terror. . . .

And from a great height, she looked down into a very deep, narrow pit, and far below, a starkly pale face upturned to her in the moonlight.

The voice.

It had sounded like Myrnin's voice, but it couldn't have been; it couldn't. There was no sense to this dream, because what would Myrnin be doing at the bottom of a hole, and why wouldn't he just jump out?

"Help," he said, from very far below, very far away. "Help me."

"I don't know how!" she called down, at least in the dream, and because it was just a dream, it made sense that he could hear her, somehow, and that even though she was very far away, she could see the desperation in his expression.

"Come for me," Myrnin said, and it sounded like a ghost, like Shane's sister whispering out there in that eerie vacant lot, like Miranda being torn to shreds of fog.

It sounded like someone who was already gone.

She woke up with a pounding heart and a nauseating headache bad enough to drive her to the medicine cabinet for ibuprofen, which she washed down with handfuls of bottled water in frenzied gulps. Somewhere in there, she noticed she'd managed to sleep away the rest of the day; it was already approaching sunset. *What the hell was that?* she wondered. She'd had anxiety dreams before, lots of them, but they usually involved being naked in a crowd, or running in slow motion, or taking a test unprepared. Nothing like this.

This was awfully—suspiciously—specific. If she was going to dream about Myrnin, why have him stuck deep in a hole in the ground?

Trap-door spider, something whispered in the back of her mind. *Gramma Day always called him that. So did you, once.*

Yes, but she hadn't meant it literally.

Maybe you just want him to need you, that awful, calm voice said. *Maybe you just like it that he depends on you so much.*

The thought unsettled her. She decided to put it out of her mind, all of it, especially the dream, because it was just her imagination working out her anxieties, just as it ought to do.

Maybe.

She went downstairs and found the video game amazingly still in progress, but on pause, as Michael and Shane argued the finer points of how the weapons array worked, and which would be a smarter choice with which to attack some kind of fortified position. It was confusing, and she still felt weird and sick. Downing a glass of milk helped settle her stomach, though, and she was just rinsing out the glass when the doorbell rang. The ring was followed up by knocking.

Michael had gotten up from the sofa, but Shane, still locked in his game world, was not paying much attention to anything else. Claire came out of the kitchen and met Eve coming down the stairs.

"Mail call?" Eve guessed.

"Not unless the postal service is starting night runs," Michael

said. "I'll get it." The unspoken implication of that was that if it
was something bad, he'd at least have a decent shot at fighting it.
He went down the hall and opened the door. Beyond it, the sunset
was burning the horizon a bright orange, but it wasn't quite evening yet.

"Who is it?" Claire asked, and craned to look.

"Can't tell," Eve said. "Oh, wait—it's—" She didn't finish the
sentence. She broke free and raced down the hall.

Claire, instantly scared and imagining all kinds of mayhem,
pelted after her. She almost immediately skidded to a halt in the
suddenly crowded hallway; Shane had somehow managed to cut
in front of both her *and* Eve. Being shortest sucked; she couldn't
see over Eve's shoulder, never mind Shane's broad back.

But she heard a frantic, female voice say, "Close it—please
close it, fast!"

Miranda's voice. But Mir was *gone*—disappeared out in the
darkness. Dissolved into mist.

And now, apparently, she was back.

And, from the sound of it, very, very scared.

Eve turned, ran into Claire, and shooed her backward; Claire
took several steps down the hall, and the party spilled out after
her and into the living area. Between Shane and Michael came—
yes!—Miranda, but a different one than before. This Miranda
was translucently pale as a glass copy of herself, and she seemed
terrified.

Everybody was trying to talk at once, except her. Ghost-Girl
leaned up against a handy wall (why didn't she fall through?) and
closed her eyes as if she were exhausted (could ghosts even get
tired?). Eve finally got the upper hand, conversationally speaking.
"What happened to you? Where did you go?"

"Away," Miranda said faintly. "So tired. Need energy." But the fact she was visible at all, before sunset, was odd and impressive. "I feel better here." She was looking better, too—already taking on a bit more form and substance. It wasn't a real body, but it had faint traces of color in it now. "They were after me. I had to keep running, find a safe place."

"Who was?" Shane asked. She'd just said the magic words to make him really pay attention. "Vamps? Why would vamps want a ghost?"

"She's not a ghost all the time," Michael said. "Remember, when she has a body, it comes complete with blood. Just like mine did. And since she can't be killed . . ."

"Oh, right," Eve said faintly, and her eyes widened. "They could keep her and keep, ah, draining her dry. . . ."

"Not the vampires," Miranda said. "I can handle the vampires. It's the rest of them. They won't leave me alone. They keep—" She was interrupted by *another* doorbell chime, followed by knocking. "Don't!" she said, and grabbed at Michael's sleeve, but her hand swiped through him. "Don't answer it yet—not yet!"

"It'll be okay," he said. "I'm just going to look. Relax. You're safe now." He pointed to Shane. "Stay with them."

"You suck!" Shane called after him as Michael went back to the door. Underneath, though, he was taking it seriously. Miranda wasn't the most reliable source of information, but Shane never underestimated a warning. "If it's Jason out there, no problem. If it's somebody worse, I don't know if Michael can hold his own."

"Then we'll handle it if it gets by him," Claire said, and surprisingly, she meant it. Between the four of them, nothing was going to overwhelm them. Not like it used to.

She thought that right up until the freaking ghost-*army* arrived.

The first indication she had that something was very, very wrong was Michael's outcry; he wasn't that kind of boy, generally, much less that kind of vampire. It was surprise, and definite worry—the kind of cry you made when you found a spider on a doorknob, or a snake in the toilet. A that-shouldn't-happen kind of sound.

Claire exchanged a look with Shane, and Miranda said, wearily, "I'm sorry I brought them here, but it was the only place I could think of that might keep them out. Maybe . . . maybe the house won't let them in."

But it turned out that the house did.

The first ghost to drift past—no, *through*—Michael was an old man, no one Claire recognized. He was just barely a visible shape, more a trick of the eyes than an actual presence; she saw him better in her peripheral vision than straight on. He walked down their hallway in a zombielike state, staring straight ahead. Shane backed up, but then stood his ground and tried to wave the phantom off. It ignored him and flowed around him like smoke over glass, and Shane shuddered and moved away, fast. "Okay, that was—unpleasant."

And there were more. Lots more. Some were just shadows, ominous and strange; some were almost-visible people. Claire only caught a glimpse of them because Michael let only a couple of them inside before he stepped back and slammed and locked the door . . . and that, surprisingly, worked. No more came inside.

But the ones already in were bad enough. One was an almost-visible man, but Claire couldn't make out his face as he moved toward them, until suddenly a trick of the light and shadows came together and showed her it was Richard Morrell, Monica's dead brother. She gasped and grabbed Eve's arm, and Eve nodded as she bit her lip. Richard slowed and looked at them, and Claire saw his mouth open and close, but he couldn't seem to speak. After a few seconds, he flowed on, heading for . . .

For Miranda, who was retreating from the oncoming old man, and Richard following behind. She looked miserably terrified. "Make them stop," she said, and looked at Michael. "Michael, *make them stop!*"

"I don't know how!" he said. It was ominous and eerie how the old man had zeroed in on Miranda, as if the little girl were the last cupcake left in the world and he had a sweet tooth. "What do they want?"

"Me!" She looked more real now, and she'd taken on a faint blush of color in her face and clothes. Miranda, in fact, looked way more real than any of the other ghosts. "They want me!"

"Shane . . . ?" Claire looked for him, but he wasn't beside her. That was surprising, but then she saw him, and she knew, with a sickening sense of horror, why.

He was standing motionless a few feet away, facing a ghost—a small ghost in the shape of a girl barely into her teens, with her hair in two long braids.

Claire knew immediately who it was he was staring at, even before she heard the small, pallid voice whisper, "Shane."

"Lyss," he said. There was a world of emotion in that name— pain, guilt, longing, love, horror. "Oh, my God, Lyss."

She reached out for him, and Shane raised his hand.

"No!" Miranda yelled. "No, don't touch her! You can't touch her. Don't you know *anything?*" She scrambled around the barrier of the sofa, playing keep-away with the shambling old man who was still chasing her. Richard was stalking her, too, now, but at a distance, as if he were irresistibly drawn toward her but didn't want to be. It was more of a slow circling. *Like a shark,* Claire thought, and shuddered.

She took Miranda at her very urgent word, and launched herself at Shane, slapping his hand away as he tried to touch his dead sister. He let out a harsh sound of surprise, and she saw his hand clench into a fist, but it relaxed almost immediately, and he pulled in a deep breath.

"Don't," Claire said. "Please don't."

Alyssa was still holding out her ghostly hand, but she wasn't trying to come at Shane. She was just waiting. Maybe—whatever Miranda was afraid of, maybe it had to be his decision to touch her, and it wouldn't count if Alyssa touched him first.

Though what would happen if he did do it was an entirely different question, and Claire really didn't want to know the answer. Not even as a scientist.

"Lyss?" Shane asked. "Can you hear me?"

She didn't move or speak again. She just kept holding out that ghostly, smoking hand toward him. Shane stared at it, and Claire knew he wanted to try, wanted it with everything inside him.

"Don't," she whispered, and took his hand in hers. "Please stay away from her."

Shane sucked in a deep breath. There were tears shimmering in his eyes, but he blinked them back and nodded. "Sorry, Alyssa," he said. "I can't." His voice shook. His whole body shook. But he meant what he said, and Alyssa clearly understood, because she dropped her hand back to her side and drifted back a few feet, then turned and joined the old man in stalking Miranda.

"Help me!" Miranda screamed. With ghosts on three sides, she was rapidly being cornered. It was only a matter of a minute or so until one of them had hold of her. "Do something!"

"What?" Michael asked, and then his eyes widened, as if something had finally occurred to him. "Can I make them leave? As head of the house?"

Normally Shane would have chimed in with something like *Who says he's head of this house?* but Shane's attention was riveted completely on his little sister's ghost, and it was Eve who said, "Maybe. Try!"

Michael closed his eyes and leaned against the wall, as if drawing strength from the house itself, or at least trying to communicate with it. Claire felt a flicker of energy around her, as if the connection were *almost* there, and then it died.

"All of us!" she shouted, and waved Eve to the wall, too. She put her hands flat on the old wallpaper and concentrated. *Come on, house. I know you're there. I know you're still alive; I can feel you. . . . Come out, come out, wherever you are. . . .*

Shane didn't join them. Claire didn't think he could. He was almost as fixed on his sister as the ghosts who stalked Miranda were on her . . . but luckily, that didn't seem to matter. Three of them together seemed to complete some kind of circuit, and Claire felt a surge of raw power whip through the room. "Hold on, Miranda!" she said, and the ghost-girl took hold of the arm of the sofa as a wave of force swept through the room in an almost-liquid ripple. It passed over Claire, leaving her skin tingling and raw, and when it hit the nearest ghost—Richard—he blew apart into mist. Alyssa was next, and then the old man, just seconds away from touching Miranda with his outstretched hand.

Miranda wavered and went pale and smoky, but then she stabilized as the wave passed her by, into an almost-real transparent form. She slowly let go of the sofa and straightened to look around.

"What did you do?" Shane said. He turned in a circle, frantically looking. "Where's Lyss?"

"Outside," Miranda said. "She's okay, Shane. She just isn't welcome here anymore. The house put her out."

"This is insane," he said, and sank down on the couch with his head in his hands. "Insane."

Eve sat beside him and put her hand lightly on his back. "I know," she said. "I'm sorry. I'm so sorry."

Before Claire could go to him, too, there was a thundering volley of knocks on the door, loud as gunshots, and all of them jumped. "What the hell now?" Michael said.

"Whatever it is," Eve said, "just leave it outside. Please."

"No," Miranda said. She took a deep breath and pulled herself up to her full height—which wasn't very much, but she looked suddenly very adult. "The house is looking out for us now, looking out for *me*. And it isn't just ghosts out there, anyway. They can't make noise like that."

The knocks came again at the door, and Michael took a few steps in that direction before turning to look at her again. She nodded.

"Please," she said. "It's okay. Now that the house is paying attention, it's not as bad. I think I might be able to . . . able to help them. It was just so overwhelming, out there alone. In here, I don't feel as bad."

Michael didn't seem convinced, but he didn't seem to know what else to do, either. He flipped the locks on the door and swung it open during the third round of knocking, and outside there were dozens of ghosts, maybe hundreds, a mass of misty waving forms crowded together like zombies on the attack, and standing in the middle of them on the doorstep were Angel, Jenna, and Tyler.

The ghost hunters.

Who apparently couldn't see any of the ghosts. Ironic.

Angel Salvador stiff-armed a very surprised Michael Glass out of the doorway and rushed up the hallway, followed by Jenna Clark and Tyler, with his camcorder light glowing red. "Hey!" Michael said. "Hey, wait a minute. I didn't say—"

"Keep rolling, Tyler. We can cut that," Jenna said. "I know she's here; I can feel her. Angel, are you getting anything there?" She seemed almost frantic, and there were spots of color high on her cheeks. "Hello, little girl. Are you here? Anywhere?"

"Hey!" Michael shut the door, though for the moment the house itself seemed to be barring the ghosts from drifting inside the opening, and darted around them—not *quite* vampire fast—and got in their way again. "Hold up. What the hell, man? This is our house!"

"Congratulations," Angel said. He continued staring at the handheld device he was clutching. "The readings are remarkably strong. I think we've found her. It looks like this is her home location." He looked up at Shane, who was right in front of him, blocking the hallway, and said, "How long has your house been haunted?"

Shane looked past him, to the camera, and then at Michael. Claire would have given odds that he'd punch him out, but instead, Shane turned beet red and burst into uncontrollable laughter.

"Hey!" Eve said, and pushed him out of the way with an irritated glare. "You people, out! Out of our house, right now!" She tried to push Tyler, but he danced backward, clearly used to people going for that move.

Angel cut her off. "Wait, wait, not yet. Let us at least document these readings—do you know the history of this house? Was there anything violent that happened here, perhaps a famous murder? Who were the previous owners? How long have you lived here?"

The blizzard of questions was confusing, and all the time Angel was firing them off, he was moving relentlessly forward. It wasn't so much that Eve backed off as she was swept out of his way by the force of his momentum, and the rest of them just followed along.

Tyler focused on Eve, evidently liking her Goth look in connection with a haunted house, which Eve didn't approve. "Hey, get your camera out of my face before I put it in yours!"

"Easy, babe," Michael said, and grabbed her by the shoulders to pull her back. "We're fine. It's okay." He leaned over to Claire and whispered, "Find out what the hell Miranda wants us to do." Then he turned the full glare of his smile on the camera. "So, do you want me to show you around, or . . . ?"

"We just need you to get out of the way," Jenna said. "You kids are what, under twenty, all of you? You've got no idea how this kind of thing can turn bad. One careless session with a Ouija board, messing around with tarot cards, you're inviting spirits to contact you. Once they're here, you might not be able to get rid of them . . . even when they start hurting you. I know. It happened to me."

There was, Claire sensed, a backstory that the show's viewers would probably all know. Jenna's face was tight and sober, and there was a feverish believer's light in her eyes. Claire had an eerie memory of the vindictive ghost of the house's original owner, Hiram Glass, tearing at her with hatred, and wondered exactly what a younger Jenna might have gone through. She was right. Ghosts could be vicious.

Miranda knew that better than anyone, apparently.

Despite Michael's winning personality and movie-star smile, it wasn't working. Michael had a definite effect on girls, when he was really trying . . . and *boy*, was he trying. Claire could feel the tingle from five feet away, and it wasn't even directed at her. He'd always had charm, but lately she'd realized that as a vampire, he was fully capable of wielding it like a weapon—a kinder one, but powerful in its own right.

But Jenna seemed immune.

Claire couldn't see Miranda, and she had the sinking feeling that maybe she'd lost her nerve and run, but then she saw a ghostly face peeking out from behind the bookcases. Claire headed that way, trying not to look obvious about it. She leaned in next to her and muttered, "Michael needs to know what you're doing."

"Waiting," Miranda said.

"For what?"

Miranda was looking past her, Claire realized—looking at the window that faced west, toward twilight.

Toward the sun slipping steadily below the horizon.

"For sunset," she said, and stepped out from behind the bookcase. Clearly a ghost. Clearly a walking dead girl.

There was a sudden, vivid silence as Michael, Jenna, and Angel all stopped talking, and everyone focused right on Miranda. Claire could even hear the tiny mechanical whir of Tyler adjusting the focus on his camera.

"Hello," Miranda said. "My name is Miranda. I'm a ghost."

And then she vanished.

"No!" Jenna screamed. "No, please, come back! I want to help you. *We* want to help. Don't run!"

And that was the exact moment the sun completely set outside, and Miranda fell out of the ceiling, going from mist to solid in midair, and thumping flat on her face on the floor in the middle of the rug.

She said, in a muffled voice, "Ow."

No one said anything else for a moment. And then Jenna said, in a flat, odd voice, "Tyler? Please tell me you got that."

*   *   *

For what felt like minutes, nobody seemed able to move. The three ghost hunters looked like wax statues, frozen in their poses, unable to process what they'd just seen. Tyler finally moved the camera away from his eyes and blinked, as if not sure exactly what had gone wrong with his eyes.

"Well, that was awkward," Shane finally said, and crouched down next to Miranda. "You okay, kid?"

She wasn't. She stayed facedown for a long moment, shuddering, and Claire remembered with a shock that when Michael had been trapped as a ghost, he'd reexperienced how he'd died, every day. That was particularly awful for Miranda, who'd been killed by the draug—not a pleasant way to go.

Shane helped her sit up, and Miranda gave him a grateful, brave little smile. "Sorry," she said, "but I needed to get their attention."

"Well, you've got it," Jenna said, barking out a laugh. "We *can't* leave. We have the biggest thing that's ever been recorded in ghost hunting. Hell, not just ghost hunting. Science. This isn't just huge, it's—it's world-breaking! It changes everything!"

Angel clearly didn't know what to say. He was staring down at Miranda with a curiously blank expression, as if he really didn't know how to handle this at all. He was more of an actor than someone who really believed, Claire thought, and unlike Jenna, who saw it as vindication, he saw it as upheaval. When Miranda plunged out of the air, his world had definitely broken, and it looked as if he'd be a while trying to put it all back together again.

Tyler hadn't said a word. He was still recording, as if too frozen to stop, but Claire heard him muttering under his breath, "Holy crap, holy crap, holy crap, what the hell!"

She'd felt the same way, the first time she'd seen Michael coalesce out of thin air. But by then, she'd already known about vampires. Her world had already been spun off its axis; the ghost team was having to make a whole lot of adjustments pretty damn quickly.

Jenna leaned in toward Miranda as she climbed to her feet. "You've been speaking to me, haven't you? Trying to help us?"

"No, I—" Miranda looked tired, and very worried. "I wanted to warn you. You were getting them all upset. It was going to get you hurt."

"Who?"

"All the ghosts."

"But that's why we're here, to talk to—"

"Morganville isn't like any other town," Miranda said, cutting her off, and met her eyes with an intensity that made Jenna blink. "You came here looking for ghosts, and they heard you. And that's dangerous. There's—okay, I can't explain so much of it, but there's power here. Old power. And sometimes the dead can use it if you give them access. You opened up the tap, I guess. And now we need to shut it off before something worse happens."

"This is insane," Angel said, and stood next to Jenna. "Clearly, this is the most sophisticated hoax I've ever seen, but . . ."

"Shut up," Jenna said. She was staring intently at Miranda, and suddenly she reached out and took the girl's hand in hers. "You feel real. You look real."

"I am," Miranda said. "Half the time. But it's because I'm like you. I had power, and the house could use that to save me—not all the way, but this way. During the day, though, I'm mostly invisible. It was hard to make you see me just now, even inside the house. I'm getting better, though."

"You're—you're a real spirit."

"Yes," she said, and shook Jenna's hand. "Pleased to meet you."

Jenna burst out in a delighted laugh and kept shaking Miranda's hand until the girl finally pulled free.

"It's a hoax," Angel said again. "Jenna, you can't believe any of this. It's obviously . . ."

"It's okay," Miranda said to him. "It'll take time to sink in. I know."

"Shut up!" he growled at her.

"Hey!" Eve said, and took a step forward. "She's a *kid*. Watch your mouth. Miranda, you don't have to talk to them. If that's going to be their attitude, they can shove that camera up their—"

"Eve," Michael said, and shook his head. "Not helpful." He got behind Tyler and tapped him on the shoulder. "I'm going to need that thing."

Tyler jerked forward, crowding protectively shoulder to shoulder with Angel. "Oh *hell* no, man. You're not taking this away."

"You don't think so?" Michael's eyes had little random flickers of red showing. Claire waved at him behind their backs and pointed toward her own eyes, then at him. He caught the message, and she saw him calm down with an effort. "Look, whatever you think you saw, you just didn't understand. There's nothing supernatural going on here. It's a trapdoor. She came from the next floor up."

Tyler and Angel both craned their necks to look up at the totally smooth ceiling . . . and Michael, vampire fast, snatched the camera away and backpedaled when Tyler came after him. "Don't make me crush it," he said. "It looks expensive."

"It is, man. Give it back!"

"Sure. Hang on." Michael looked it over, ignoring Tyler's attempts to grab it away again, and found the memory chip, which he ejected. He held it up, and handed the camera back. "No problem."

"You can't keep that!"

"Not planning to," Michael agreed. He snapped it in half, then tore the halves into smaller pieces. Then he put the pieces in his jeans pocket. "Done. Sorry, Mir, but you know they can't walk out of here with that footage."

She nodded in agreement, but Claire sensed something was wrong, especially when Tyler exchanged a fast glance with Angel and Jenna. "You asshole," Tyler muttered, but it sounded like something he felt he ought to say, not that he deeply felt. He backed off. "Maybe we should go, guys. Next thing, they'll be breaking our necks. Angel's right. This is some hell of a hoax."

Jenna looked at Miranda again. "You can talk to me," she said gently. "You really can. I'm not afraid of you."

"No," Miranda said. "I know. But I'm afraid of you. And what you can do. You made them hungry, and now they're dangerous. Don't you understand that?"

"Maybe," Jenna said. "My twin sister died, and she stayed with me for the longest time. Not real, like you are, but—there. But she changed. Turned evil. I had to . . . I had to get rid of her, send her away."

"You don't understand," Miranda said. "It wasn't something else. It was *you*. You changed her. You made her see a way back, and that makes them—us . . . *ghosts*—desperate. Desperate enough to do anything. It's you that's making it happen."

"You're not one of them, those lost people. You're loved here. Loved. Protected. And that's good; that's really good. I just want to be sure you're protected from the things your friends can't see and fight." Jenna took in a deep breath and blew it out. "I think that you and I together could—could fix whatever it was I did wrong. You could show me how."

"You need to leave," Miranda said. "You need to go before it's too late and everything goes completely wrong. I'm sorry."

"But—"

"I'm going to need the rest of the recordings," Michael said to Tyler. "Sorry, man."

"We don't have anything else," Tyler said. "You just broke the crap out of our whole show."

Shane looked at Michael, eyebrows raised, and Michael shook his head. "Lying his ass off," he said. *Heartbeat,* Claire thought. He could hear them. He might not be able to always tell when one individual was lying, but it was easier for him if there were three people all in on the same falsehood. More people meant more data, like a triangulation of the truth.

And most likely, all three of the ghost hunters knew Tyler had backups.

"I read people really well," he said. It was an obvious lie, but he didn't give Tyler time to argue. "All right, all three of you, out the door. If you want me to take your whole van apart next, I'll be happy to do that, too."

"Or, you know, punch you," Shane said cheerfully. "This is Texas. We have the right to do that when you break into our house."

He left it to Eve to say, "Or worse," in a voice so low and dark, it qualified as Goth all by itself.

Jenna shot to her feet. "Fine. If you want to doom this little girl to an eternity of pain and torment, you're doing exactly the right things. You're not prepared for what's going to happen to her. I am!"

Maybe that was kind of true; it was very hard to tell. But in any case, Claire was fed up with half-truths and aggression, especially when her head was pounding so very hard. "Just get out," she said wearily. "She's our responsibility. We'll take care of her. If she's right, you've done enough damage already around here."

That was when Jenna turned and focused on her, really focused, and Claire saw something familiar in her cool, pale eyes. It
was the same distant look she'd seen so often in Miranda ... here
and not here at the same time. "You dreamed it," she said. "It's
true. I see ... water. A hole. A silver cross in a circle. Someone's
trying to reach you."

"Yeah, yeah, save the Vegas act, lady," Shane said, and pushed
her forward toward the door. Angel and Tyler were already making their way out ahead of her. "If we want professional help, we'll
call the Ghostbusters. At least they have matching uniforms.
Ciao."

Miranda followed them, looking anxious. "Claire," she said,
and caught her arm. "*Claire!* It's dark out there."

"It's okay. They have a van," she said. She wasn't feeling particularly charitable toward the *After Death* team just now. If Michael
was right—and she honestly figured he was—then Jenna's interest
in stirring up the dead had brought back Shane's sister, and that,
that was unforgivable. "They'll be fine. Don't worry about them."

"The ghosts know what she is. They'll follow her, eating little bits of her. She won't feel it at first, but then she'll get tired
and sick, and they could kill her, Claire. Worse: they could get
strong enough to do other things. Dangerous things. She's really
powerful."

"I think she's full of it," Claire said, but now that her anger
was fading a bit, she ran what Jenna had said to her through her
head. *Water. Hole. Silver cross in a circle.* That fit with her dream about
the hole in the ground, and the water around her legs. *Someone is
trying to reach you.* "I think she was just making it up, Mir. Listen,
you stay here. We're going to make sure they leave, okay?"

Miranda shuddered. "I can't go out there again."

Even so soon after sunset it was dark outside, darker than

Claire had expected; the orange bands on the horizon were already fading, being painted over by shades of purple and blue. The biggest, bravest stars had already made appearances overhead, but there was no moon, not yet.

The *After Death* van was parked on the street, two houses down; they'd probably had trouble finding the place. Claire remembered seeing them checking maps. They'd probably been looking for the Glass House already. *Ugh.* To think she'd thought Angel was kind of greasily charming in the beginning. Now, she never wanted to see him again.

There was no sign of the mass of ghosts she'd seen before when they'd been in the house, which seemed weird; she could feel something out here, an uneasy sensation on the back of her neck, a phantom whisper on the wind. On instinct, Claire stepped back over the threshold into the house, and as she did, she saw the mists come into focus again. All the ghosts crowded now around Jenna as she headed for the van.

Inside the house, the ghosts were visible. Out there, in the real world, there was nothing.

Shane was already down the steps, and Claire hurried down to join him. "They're leaving too easily," he said. "Didn't it seem to you like they just let that thing with the memory card go too fast?"

"What choice did they have?" she asked. "Michael had it and broke it before they could do much."

"Yeah, but . . ." Shane shook his head. "I expected more drama out of them. They're on TV. It's kind of what they do for a living."

"The camera was off."

"For people like them, the camera's never off. . . ." His eyes suddenly widened, and he dashed forward to take the camera out of Tyler's hands. Tyler resisted, yelling for help, and suddenly it was a tangle of guys—Angel, Tyler, Shane, and Michael, all wrestling for control of the thing. Not too surprisingly, given the players, Michael won and tossed it to Shane.

"You wanted this?" he asked.

"Hey, you can't do that!" Tyler shouted. "That's expensive pro equipment, man! I'll sue your ass!"

Shane jogged back up the steps and held it under the porch light. "Dammit," he said. "Michael—you got the memory card, but this thing was broadcasting straight on broadband, too. The memory card was just backup. They've rigged it so it can record without the light coming on."

Michael rounded on Tyler, whose face had gone pale. "Where did it broadcast to?"

"Dude, you're wrong. Yeah, sure it's got the capability, but I didn't even switch it on—"

"That's a lie," Michael said, and grabbed him by the collar. "Tell me another one; go ahead."

"Let him go." Jenna's voice was cool, calm, and focused, and they all looked at her. Michael let go of Tyler, because Jenna was holding a gun. It was something semiautomatic; Claire couldn't tell the caliber, but it didn't really matter. Michael wouldn't be scared of it, but getting holes put in him and healing up would be just as damning, if not more so, than what they already had recorded on Miranda. So he held his hands up and stepped back.

"That's not going to look so good on camera," Michael said. "Better rethink it."

"I'm just defending my friends from some scary people," Jenna said, "and besides, by the magic of editing, they'll never see I was armed, anyway. Now let's all just calm down, okay? This doesn't have to get any crazier." She jerked her head at Tyler. "Get the camera and get your ass to the van. We have editing to do."

"We could stream it live," Angel suggested.

"Don't be stupid, Angel; you don't waste a revelation like this on a couple of thousand people who stumble over it on the Web. This is a major TV event, maybe even pay-per-view. We're going to tease the hell out of it for weeks before we put a single frame of it out. Tyler!" She raised her voice to a whip crack, and the camera monkey scrambled up the steps and took the recorder out of Shane's unresisting hands. "You don't know what you've got here. Or what's coming. You're going to need us, trust me. *Miranda* needs us. This whole town is going to be famous."

She was probably going to say more, but she never got the chance, because a dark-clothed figure came out of the shadows behind the trees, and before Claire could draw a breath, the figure knocked Jenna out of the way, spinning her to the ground. The gun tumbled away, lost in the sparse, weedy grass.

The intruder showed a flash of a pale face, red eyes, a young woman's crimson smile, and in a heartbeat more, she had hold of her target.

Not Jenna, after all.

Angel. The vampire clapped a hand over his mouth when he tried to speak and said, "Hush, now, pretty. What will all the neighbors think if you make a fuss?"

Tyler mumbled out a curse, and ran for the van. He made it as far as the fence before another vampire ghosted out in front of him.

Jason.

Eve's brother looked just as demented as he had earlier, and Claire shuddered at the smile he turned first on Tyler, and then on his sister. "Hey, Eve. You don't write, you don't call . . . but at least you brought us dinner. That's nice."

"No!" Eve dashed forward and put herself between Tyler and

Jason. "No, Jase. What the hell are you doing? They're not from here! You can't just—"

"I hate that word. *Can't*. Fact is, I can, big sister. I can do anything I want. So can Marguerite, here. And Jerold, he's back there somewhere.... Wave to my nice sister, Jerold." Claire turned. There was a vampire crouched on the edge of the steep roof, staring down at them with a knowing smile. He waved. "See, we have privileges now. We get to hunt if we want. And we really do want. So if you don't choose to be on the menu, turn your ass around and walk back in the house and shut the door. Hell, you were just arguing with these fools. Why do you care?"

"I—" Eve didn't really have a comeback for that. "It's not about them. I don't want to see you ... be this. God, Jason. Is this how it's going to be? You weren't bad enough already?"

"No," he said, very rationally. "I've never been bad enough to keep the bad stuff from happening to me. Until now." He waited. Eve didn't move. "Okay then. I'm going to be kind this time. We can share just this one. You can keep the other ones." He snapped his fingers, and Marguerite, the one who had Angel, nodded. She picked Angel up in her arms—quite a feat, because the man was bigger, taller, and panicked—and before any of them could draw breath, she just ... disappeared.

Michael started to run after her, but he came up short when Jerold dropped off the roof into his path. In one gloved hand, he held a glass bottle that swirled with silver. "We learned this from you," Jerold said. "You started fighting your own kind, and we're going to fight back. You like this stranger enough to burn for him, Michael?"

"No!" Eve looked pleadingly at her brother—who, whether she liked it or not, clearly was in charge. "No, come on, please— Jason, don't. Don't hurt him."

"If he stays out of our way, he'll be fine," Jason said. "Ditto for you, and Claire, and Shane; I'll leave you alone. But it's a new day around here. Our day. And the sun's never coming up to spoil it for us."

Somewhere out in the darkness, there was a pained cry. Angel. Claire tried desperately to think what to do, but there was nothing. They had weapons but Michael had just been outflanked; Shane just had stakes, and although Eve had a crossbow, she didn't seem inclined to use it on her own brother.

I need to do something, Claire thought. *Anything. I need to save him.*

"Jason, if you let him go, I think we can make some kind of deal," she said, talking as fast as she could. She didn't even know what she was saying. "Look, I'll even let you bite me—two pints for the guy you just took. Come on, it's a good deal. I'll get it witnessed at Common Grounds, we can put it in writing, and—"

"Shut up," Jason said, still smiling. "I don't want a measly two pints, like I'm out for a beer with the guys. I want to *hunt*. Button it if you don't want to play the rabbit, little girl."

She shut her eyes and tried to think what to do. There were three vampires, and even though she and her friends outnumbered them, it would be a tough fight, and probably one of them would be badly hurt, maybe killed. She'd never hated math so much in her life.

Shane put his arm around her. "Don't," he said quietly. "You can't, Claire. You can't save everybody."

And God, he was right; he was right and she hated that, too.

"All right," she said. "Eve—call the cops. Hurry."

Eve nodded and ran into the house. Jason laughed out loud.

"Good call," he said. "And nice counter, but the cops ain't gonna catch us, and you know it. They know better than to try. Nice doing business with you folks." He touched a finger to his forehead in ironic salute. "Catch you later."

"Wait!" Jenna blurted. "Wait, what about Angel, what—"

"Pretty lady really doesn't get it, does she?" Jason said. "Explain it to her. I'm starving."

And then he and Jerold were just . . . gone. Like smoke on the wind. And Angel had stopped crying out, though whether that was due to being gagged or being dead, Claire couldn't tell and didn't want to imagine. Her whole body ached with strain, and she wanted to throw up. *What did I just do?* Nothing. She'd saved the life of one of her friends, probably. At the cost of Angel's.

When she tried to take a step, she staggered and almost went down. Shane caught her and held her up. "Hey," he said. "Hey, it's okay. We're okay. The cops will be on the case."

Claire knew he didn't believe that any more than she did. The cops wouldn't be on the case; they wouldn't dare, unless Amelie or Oliver directed them to stop the hunting. After all, Jason—like Michael—had *privileges.*

And Angel had technically been fair game . . . unProtected, a stranger.

It meant, though, that there'd be some necessary cover-up with Jenna and Tyler. Either their memories would be altered to explain away Angel's disappearance or death, or they'd face the same fate. *Ten minutes ago you were throwing them out of the house,* she reminded herself. *They were going to go public about Miranda. About Morganville.*

"Check the van," she said to Shane. "See if Tyler was telling the truth. If they streamed that video to a server in their van . . ."

"Got it," he said, and jogged away to the vehicle. It was unlocked—trusting bunch—and he slid back the cargo door to climb inside.

"Hey!" Tyler snapped out of his stunned trance, and color flooded his face. "Hey, get the hell out of there—there's delicate equipment in there!" He charged for the van, but Michael caught up and stopped him with nothing but a look. That didn't, however, stop Tyler from talking. "We have rights, you know. You touch anything in that van and I'll sue your asses off!" It was obviously something he could seize on, something real and reassuring in a world that had drunkenly upended on him. He had to know Miranda was the real thing, but that was at least partly in his comfort zone, or he wouldn't be doing the *After Death* show. But being stalked and preyed on by vampires—even if nobody had said they were vampires—was different. And there was a feverishly bright light in his eyes that reflected as much fear as it did anger.

"Easy," Michael said. "Wait." He kept a hand outstretched, palm out, to ward Tyler off if he continued his rush forward, but Tyler just paced, staring past Michael at the van.

And then at Shane, who stepped out of it about half a minute later. "Video's on their server, Mike. What do you want me to do?"

This time, when Michael focused on Tyler, he wasn't playing around. Red swirled in his irises, and Claire felt a force coming out of him—what it was, she couldn't say, but it was powerful. "Is that the only copy left?" he asked Tyler. Even his voice sounded different, somehow. Less human.

"Yes," Tyler said, and blinked. "I mean, no! It streamed to the Internet already. . . ."

"Yeah, that's a lie." Michael glanced back at Shane and nodded. "It's the only copy. Wipe it."

"No!" Tyler's cry was furious and agonized, but he didn't try to go up against Michael, either. He must have sensed how dangerous it was to try.

Jenna didn't even protest. She slumped down on the ground, sitting cross-legged, and put her head in her hands. "He didn't believe," she said. "Angel never really believed. God. I shouldn't have gotten him into this. I should have made him go home. . . ." She sounded tired, and Claire remembered with a chill what Miranda had said. All around her, invisible here in the real world beyond the Glass House, ghosts were crowded around Jenna, breaking off pieces of her in some strange psychic way and consuming the tasty strength she'd brought to town.

Making themselves stronger.

Silence. Profound silence, broken by the distant, frantic barking of a dog.

"Come on," Michael said, and took Tyler by the arm. "Let's get inside."

Claire went to Jenna and offered her a hand. She looked at it, then her, and finally nodded and rose. "This is crazy," Jenna told her.

"I know," she said. "Come inside."

She paused on the doorstep to watch as Shane jogged back to join them. Nothing loomed out of the darkness to menace him . . . this time. Once he was in, she closed and locked the door, and took a moment to lean her head against the wood.

I'm sorry, she told the vanished Angel. In his way, he'd been charming. *I wish . . .*

But she didn't even know how to finish the thought.

FOURTEEN

MYRNIN

The trick to doing the impossible, I've found, is to simply never think past what is at your fingertips. Do the thing in front of you. Then the next. Then the next. In such ways have men built the pyramids, or climbed mountains, or raced to the moon on rockets.

And that is how I had carved, inch by painful inch, the niches for my hands and feet in the stone wall of the oubliette. I did not look up; I did not look down. I looked only at the task before me, and ignored the pain as a side effect. I'd had enough practice at that, certainly.

With enough concentration, the panic attacks faded into a running babble at the back of my mind, like a fast-rushing river that became background noise I didn't feel the need to heed. In a way, it was a comforting sort of distraction. It was a bit like not being alone, even if my only real company was my own horribly distorted, screaming mind.

I found out just how far I'd ascended the hard way, when I lost my concentration, and losing my concentration was *not my fault*. I was remarkably centered, but when suddenly there was a sensation inside my mind that felt like cold, icy fingers shuffling through my thoughts, and . . . well. One does tend to get distracted when something like that happens.

My fingers slipped, then my bare toes, and as I fell—counting the feet on the way down, my goodness, nearly ten steps completed—I saw Claire's face. Just a flash of it, pale and worried. And another face, a woman's, with pale gold hair and light-colored eyes. It was not Amelie, though in some ways the resemblance was there. . . . It was someone I didn't know.

Someone human. More remarkably, a human whose mental fingerprints were clear on my mind. A seer, a true one, like the girl Miranda—someone who could see the future, but not only that; one who could reach and touch the minds of others. I doubted she had enjoyed the experience any more than I had, but I had the conviction that through her, Claire had been told *something* of me.

Come for me, I begged her again, just as my fall abruptly ended in ice-cold water, and the even-colder stone beneath. Bones broke, of course. I stayed there, jammed in awkward discomfort at the bottom of hell, until I had enough focus and strength to heal, and then to start considering the climb again.

Claire, I thought. *Come for me. Please.*

Because the doubt had begun to creep in to inform me that ten feet was barely a beginning, and I had a very, very, very long way to go . . . and hunger was already nipping my heels. Soon, the clarity and focus I had managed to achieve thus far would be difficult.

And then impossible.

You won't make it, some coldly logical part of me declared, which was just not at all helpful. I wanted to cut that part of my brain out and leave it floating in the water, but perhaps that might not have been a very sane response.

So I locked the logical part of me up in a prison made of mental bars, focused on the next thing in front of my nose, and began to climb.

FIFTEEN

CLAIRE

🌙

The police took notes, sounding professionally skeptical of the idea that a strong young man might have vanished in full view of his friends. *Because that never happens here,* Claire thought cynically, but she knew that in a way they were right to be doubtful.... The vampires picked off strays; they didn't run at the herd. It wasn't smart, and they'd always been very careful not to involve strangers who might have been easily missed.

Angel was as high-profile a visitor as Morganville ever got, if you didn't count a drive-through by the shiny-haired governor two years before. That guy hadn't even stopped for gas, just whipped through town in a whirlwind of blown sand and shiny cars, though he'd reportedly rolled down the window at a stoplight and waved to people who hadn't really cared.

Carrying off Angel was almost as likely as vampires stopping the governor's caravan, ripping off his sedan door, and dragging him off in the middle of the afternoon.

They'd all provided statements—Eve, Michael, Shane, Claire, Jenna, and Tyler. Miranda had sensibly stayed inside. Tyler's story had morphed itself into an attack by a gang of teens bent on robbing the van—*armed* teens—and Jenna had just said she hadn't seen much except for one of them grabbing Angel and taking him off.

Shane had straight-out asked Eve before the first sirens and lights pulled to a stop, "Do you want us to snitch on your brother, or not? Your call, Eve. Personally, I don't think the little monster needs any more breaks, but—"

"Yes," she'd interrupted him. "Do it. I'm going to tell them everything."

So the four of the Glass House residents had all identified Jason by name and provided the names of the other two vampires as well; Claire certainly felt a bitter sort of validation in doing that. She'd trusted Jason, for a while, but he'd spun wildly out of control, and he had to be stopped. Even Eve acknowledged that now.

The cops had called it in, and gone on their way; no one seemed to have much of a sense of urgency about the whole thing. Tyler and Jenna sat together on the front steps, clearly numb and unsure what to do next, so Claire asked them inside, organized coffee, and—after consultation with the others—bedded Jenna down on the sofa in the living room, and Tyler in the parlor. Nobody slept very well, and when Claire came downstairs before dawn to make coffee, she found that the two visitors were up and sitting together at the dinner table, holding hands.

Claire paused on the stairs, watching. It was an odd kind of scene, and there was something definitely weird about it. For a moment, Claire didn't catch what Jenna was saying . . . and then, with a chill, she did.

"... Close," Jenna said in a distant, drugged voice. "I can sense him out there; he's coming. ... Just a moment ... It's hard for him to get through the barriers around this place. ..."

Claire cautiously descended a step, then another. The room was dark, except for flickering candles on the dining table to add sinister mood lighting. *What are you doing?*

It became very clear in the next second, as Angel's pale, insubstantial ghost drifted through the walls.

Tyler stiffened in his chair, but Jenna held on to his hand and made him sit down again. Angel hovered there, glowing with the eerie dim light of phosphorescence. He looked lost and distressed.

Claire's legs felt numb. She sat down fast on the stairs, watching with her lips parted on a fast-drawn breath. *What the hell is going on?* Angel was clearly, well, dead—no doubt of that; you don't get to be that kind of ghost without going all the way over the line. There was a dark smudge around his throat, and Claire winced seeing it. No doubt it evidenced what Jason had done to him. Or his friends. Whether Angel's body had been recovered or not, he was a victim of Morganville's growing vampire problem.

And Jenna—Jenna had been able to summon him up, and even get him past the house's defenses to appear.

Jenna let go of Tyler's hands, and Claire expected the ghost-Angel to vanish, but he stayed, drifting closer and closer to Jenna as if some kind of gravity were pulling him toward her. "Angel," she said, "I am so sorry. So sorry."

Claire realized that she was reaching out toward the ghost, and she remembered Miranda's stark fear. "Wait!" she blurted, and came down the stairs at a run. "Wait, don't. Don't touch him."

But it was too late. Jenna had already done it, and when their hands connected, Angel took on form, weight, even a little color—almost a kind of reality.

And Jenna sagged back in her chair, clearly exhausted.

"It's true," Angel said. His voice sounded as if it came from the bottom of a deep well. "It's all true what you said. So many spirits here, Jenna. So lost. So angry."

"I'm so sorry we couldn't help you," Jenna whispered.

"I know." He included Tyler in that, with a sideways glance, and the younger man flinched. He'd probably hoped to be ignored completely. As Ghost-Angel's gaze moved past him to brush across Claire, she knew how Tyler felt. There was something really, truly terrifying in that empty gaze. "And you," Angel said to Claire. "Not your fault. I know you blame yourself."

Claire shivered. The air in the room was feeling icy cold, as Angel's spirit drew in energy from the world around him. "I'm sorry we lost you."

"Angel's not lost," Jenna said. "I've got him. He can help us."

"I don't——" Claire took in a deep breath, and it felt like breathing in winter. "I don't think it's a good idea, Jenna. You know what Miranda said. . . ."

"Miranda's not here, and I'm certainly not abandoning our friend."

"You should," said a soft voice from the kitchen door, and Claire turned to see Miranda standing there with a mug in her hand that steamed fiercely in the chill. "You need to let him go. The longer he stays here, the hungrier he will be. And after a while he won't be your friend anymore, Jenna. Just like your sister."

"Don't talk about her!"

"You have to let him go," Miranda said. She walked to the table and set down her mug—the contents smelled like hot chocolate— and took a deep breath. "I can show you how to make him go on to where he needs to be."

Jenna's eyes widened, then narrowed. "How do I know you can do that?"

"Because I was there, and I came back. He's confused and scared. I can take him there if you'll let me. But I can only do it in the morning." Miranda looked out the window. It was still dark, but there was a strong glow to the east. "And I can only do it if he wants to go with me. The more you make him want to be here, with you, the harder that is. You have to let go of his hand, right now."

Jenna frowned, but she pulled her hand away from Angel's, and he immediately began to lose color and substance, taking on the wispy, foggy character of a ghost just barely together. The change, along with the obvious pain and horror on Angel's face, was so alarming that Jenna immediately tried to reach out again for him.

Miranda pulled her hand away. "No," she said. "You can't. Understand? You just can't. He's okay. What he feels . . . It isn't pain like you know it. It's confusion. I'll take him once the sun comes up. It'll be okay."

"Mir?" Claire asked softly. "Is this—is this okay for you to do? Is it dangerous?"

The girl sighed and shrugged, just a little. "It's hard," she said. "But I'm not ready to go, so I can come back. Not everybody can. And not every time. You remember, don't you? That feeling?"

Claire *did* remember, though she earnestly tried not to. . . . She'd died here, briefly, in the Glass House, and there had been this sensation, when the house's protections had collapsed, that had given her the feeling of being sucked up somewhere, thrown into chaos. And maybe that would have turned out all right, but it was genuinely terrifying.

She nodded.

"I can do it," Miranda said quietly. "I just don't like it. That's why they were all following me, before. Because they know I can help. I just . . . I just don't want to."

"Can you talk to them?" Claire asked.

"I can," Jenna said, and Miranda nodded as well. "I guess we both can."

"I was thinking . . ." She really hesitated on this, because it seemed like such a selfish use of what she'd just learned. "I was thinking maybe, if it was possible, you could ask them to find out something for me."

"What?"

"About Myrnin," she said. "Jenna, you had a vision of him, before. I think he's being held somewhere against his will. I need to help him, but I need some idea where to look. Can you help me? Can *they* help me figure out where it is?" She was trying not to make the desperation in her voice sound obvious, but she probably failed hard in that. "Please?"

"It's too dangerous for her," Miranda said, and nodded toward Jenna. "She shouldn't be trying to talk to any more of them. I will, though. As long as she stops making them excited, I should be able to get out and see them. . . ." She looked toward the window suddenly. "The sun's coming up. Angel and I have to go now. Sorry."

Miranda walked to Angel and took his hand, and he seemed to give a sigh of deep relief that he wasn't alone anymore. They were both fading. Tyler, who had been sitting in silent, dumb amazement the whole time, jumped back from the table, sending his chair flying; Jenna scrambled away, too, as Miranda threw her head back, closed her eyes, and her very real body seemed to just . . . dissolve, along with Angel's.

Then they were both gone.

Claire gulped back the instinctive fear, and said, "Mir? You still around?" She got a cold pulse that moved through her, and she understood that to mean *yes*. "It's okay. She's still here; we just can't see her right now. She'll get Angel where he needs to go, I guess."

Tyler looked about to cry. "Who *are* you people?"

But Jenna wasn't looking like that at all. She seemed . . . focused. There was a light dawning in her eyes, and her shoulders went back and squared up. "This is why I was led here," she said. "This is what I was meant to do. Meet this girl. And help her."

"Yeah?" Tyler shot back. "What about *me*, Jenna? What am *I* supposed to do, exactly? How am I supposed to go back to having a normal life now? Jesus, this was just a job, a stupid *job*. I never was some true believer, not like you. . . ."

But now he was, clearly. And he didn't like it. He tugged at his messy hair as if he wanted to pull it all out, then flopped facedown on the table, utterly spent.

"I can never leave here, can I?" His muffled voice floated up, almost as ghostly as Angel's had been. "Dammit. I had season tickets to the Red Sox. Good seats."

Claire heard footsteps behind her, and Eve appeared, Doc Martens clunking heavily on the stairs. She paused, yawning. There was something weird about her hair—it was sticking up like a cockatoo's crest. Probably not on purpose. She still had on an adorable pair of pajama pants, a giant White Stripes concert T-shirt, and she hadn't put on her makeup yet. "What'd I miss?" she asked.

"You'd better sit down," Claire said, "and I'd better make coffee."

✳   ✳   ✳

The police finally called after breakfast—breakfast meaning Pop-Tarts and arguments over whether it would be a good idea to knock Jenna and Tyler over the head and lock them in a room until they could decide what to do with them, which was Shane's idea. Claire half expected the cops to want the two surviving *After Death* crew members, but no, they wanted Eve down at the station. Just Eve, which was good, because Claire had to head off to class; she was aching to talk to Miranda again, and see if her ghostly connections might be able to find Myrnin, but hanging around the house demanding answers wasn't going to get her anywhere. And neither would blowing off classes.

"I have a jam session in five minutes at Common Grounds," Michael said, shifting as he checked his watch. Eve was sitting at her dressing table, applying eyeliner.

"And?" she asked. Claire was fascinated, watching her; she had so much concentration and precision, it was eerie. Claire wasn't good with eyeliner. It took skill.

"And I need to get moving," he said. "Are you coming?"

"Sweetie, true beauty can't be rushed." Eve switched to mascara. "You go ahead. I'll be fine."

"Not on your own," Michael said. "New rules. None of you walks alone. Not even Shane."

"Gee, Overprotective Dad, you probably should have told him that before he left this morning."

"Where was he going?"

"Job interview—he didn't tell me what it was for, so maybe it was something embarrassing, like flower arranging or male stripping," Eve said. "Relax; he's fine. And anyway, I can drive. The Car of the Dead is finally ready to go again." She meant her custom hearse, which had seen so many repairs and replacements, it was almost a brand-new vehicle again. "Besides, I'm seeing the cops, not hunting for vamps in dark alleys. I've got all the vampire I need." She blew him a kiss.

Michael leaned over and kissed the top of her head—now that her hair was tamed again, not such a dangerous proposition—and said, "Be careful."

"Always am."

He left in a hurry, carrying both his acoustic and electric guitars. Eve smiled serenely and did her other eye with the mascara in careful, even strokes.

"Can you give me a lift?" Claire asked. "I've got classes. And what *are* we going to do about our visitors, anyway?"

"Nothing," Eve said. "It's not our business."

"But—what if Jenna decides to go public? Or Tyler? They know too much, way too much."

"They've got no proof now. And that's what I'm going to tell the cops," Eve said. "It's not a Glass House problem anymore. It's a Morganville problem, and it needs to be officially handled. Hell, Jason is the one who made all this happen, not us."

It still felt wrong; Claire was afraid the official Morganville solution would involve two more bodies in a car crash, the end of the *After Death* story. But she had to admit, she couldn't see any way out of it without telling the cops, or Oliver, or Amelie. Things had gone a little too far. And, she had to admit, she was carrying around a staggering load of guilt over Angel's death. She had the nagging feeling that she could have done something to stop it . . . even though, in practical terms, she knew she couldn't have.

It was a tangled mess, and it would take time to sort it out, but one thing was certain: they couldn't afford to let Jason get away with it. He was already dangerous. If he thought he had a free hand, who knew what he'd do? Well, Claire knew; she knew that eventually, he'd come after Eve. And there was no way she could let that happen.

Eve *did* look beautiful, in a very Eve-ish way; she'd toned down the skull-themed clothes but kept the Goth color scheme of black, black, and some accent color. Her jewelry remained edgy, and her makeup was something normally seen only on fashion ads and outer-space movies.

She kept the clunky work boots, though, and Claire had to admit that it suited her.

The Car of the Dead looked shiny and new again, and Eve had added a bobblehead Grim Reaper to the front dashboard, complete with scythe and glowing red eyes that flashed when his head bobbed. She'd also swapped stuff for a kickin' stereo that she cranked up to twelve and a half on a ten-point scale, the better to advertise for Florence + The Machine in a town that, Claire thought, had probably never heard of the band at all.

The music was too loud to talk, and that was okay; Claire was in a brooding mood anyway. She hadn't slept well, and she was increasingly anxious about Myrnin. The day, by contrast, was a typical hot Texas day, low on humidity and high on sunburn potential. She kept the window rolled down for the arid breeze, such as it was.

Heads turned as they cruised past. Some, mostly older people, of course, were annoyed by the noise; some seemed neutral until they spotted the hearse. It was easily recognizable as Eve's car; nobody else in Morganville, except the Ransom Funeral Home, owned anything even vaguely like it, certainly not with Death as a dash ornament. Claire, suddenly nervous, reached over and turned down the music.

"What?" Eve asked. She was in a surprisingly sunny mood, considering the events of the night before and her brother's suddenly murderous turn, but then, Claire imagined she was relieved to be taking some kind of positive action against him for a change. "C'mon, it's not *that* emo."

"No, it's cool. I just—" Claire couldn't explain what her unease was, really, except that she definitely had a weird feeling. Maybe it was just all the flyers that they'd seen, and the fact that their front window was still shattered and braced up with plywood.

But it definitely felt personal, the glares they had coming these days.

The car cruised past Common Grounds, and in a glimpse through the front window, she saw that Michael was setting up his guitars. He didn't get to play as much as he liked, so this was a special event for him. Becoming a vampire might have modified his rock-star ambitions a little, but there was no denying that he was really, really, really good. He'd even had an offer of a recording deal, but he'd turned it down, since touring seemed like a bad idea (and, of course, Amelie had forbidden it). After all, he had a substance problem that even major record labels wouldn't be able to keep quiet about.

He didn't say much about that, Claire realized; about how his whole life had been centered on music, and then it had changed without warning, and without his permission. He never complained about how unfair it was—at least not out loud. And not to her.

"He should have more people there," Eve said.

"What?"

"A crowd. Michael *always* draws a crowd, but—look back there. Do you see a line of people?" Eve sounded shocked at first, then angry. "Those idiots. They're not mad at him, are they? Why?"

Because he's a vampire married to a human, Claire thought, but didn't say. Eve knew that. She just couldn't accept that people could hate Michael on principle, without counting who he really was.

"It'll break his heart if they don't come to hear him play. It's all he ever wanted, to play and make people happy. If they take that away from him . . ." Eve bit her lip, and tears shimmered in her dark eyes. Claire reached over and grabbed her hand, and squeezed, and her best friend sucked in a deep breath and tried for a smile. "Yeah. He'll be okay. We'll be okay. Right?"

"Right," Claire said, and felt the hollow ring of saying something she didn't quite feel. She covered it with a big smile.

Eve paused at one of the town's few stoplights, waiting for a few beat-up pickup trucks to crawl through the intersection, and said, "You in a big hurry to get to TPU?"

Claire checked her watch. "My class is in twenty minutes."

"Oh. I was thinking maybe a coffee at Common Grounds . . ."

And making Michael feel better by their support, Claire guessed. She hated to do it, but she said, "Aren't the police waiting for you, though?"

"Yes. Like there's anything else I can tell them they don't already have in the five-inch-thick file on my brother."

"I guess they want to know who his friends are now, things like that."

"Like I'd know."

True. Jason and Eve had gone very separate ways from an early age. Claire wondered sometimes what it would be like, having brothers and sisters, but considering how bad Eve's experience with it was, maybe she ought to be grateful to be an only child. . . .

"Hey!" Eve said sharply. "What are you doing?"

Claire jumped, thinking she'd directed it at her, but no, Eve had rolled down the window and was yelling *out*. As Claire started to turn her head, she heard a high-pitched screeching sound, metal on metal, and Eve yelped, threw open her car door, and jumped out. Claire fumbled at her seat belt and finally got it loose, then exited after her. "What happened?" she asked, but it was immediately obvious, because a group of teens stood there on the sidewalk next to the intersection, and one of them had keys out and was scraping out *letters* into the paint of Eve's car. He had a B and an I already incised. Claire guessed the T-C-H were coming.

"God, it's like high school all over again!" Eve said, and shoved the boy away from the hearse. "Get your hands off my car, Aaron!"

"How about you get your hands off *me*, fang-banger?" he sneered, and shoved her back to slam hard against the scratched paint. "What goes around comes around."

"You know, you weren't the brightest crayon in the box even before you flunked out of school, but those were your glory days, weren't they? You really want to get into it with me, dumbass? Biggest mistake of your life!" Eve, color managing to burn bright in her cheeks even through the Goth makeup, was furious, her body tight and shaking, her fists clenched.

"You think you've got some kind of magic shield, what with your hot vampire boyfriend?" one of the girls said from the curb. "You don't."

"Not boyfriend. Husband," another one said, and made a retching sound. "God, don't you have any self-respect? *Marrying* him? That's just gross. It's like a cow marrying a butcher. They ought to throw you both in jail for being sickening."

Aaron laughed. "Oh, sure, you'd say that, Melanie. You dated the guy in junior high."

"Sure, before he turned into one of them!"

"My dad says you're a traitor," said another boy, and he had a very different tone—quiet, sure, dangerous. "My uncle Jake

disappeared the other night. Just another casualty in a town full
of them, right? And you helped. You helped put the vamps right
back on top where they've always been. Just like all the Founder
House families. You're nothing but whores giving it up to the
vamps for money."

Eve lunged at him. Claire darted around the end of the limo
with a sinking conviction that she'd never be fast enough to stop
her, and she was right: Eve landed a solid slap right across his face.
"Don't you *ever*, Roy Farmer!" Eve shouted at him. "Don't you—"

He hit her back, clocking her, hard, right on the point of her
jaw, and before Claire could even draw a breath. It was as if some
invisible signal had gone out to all the other kids—her age or just
a couple of years older—to attack.

"No!" Claire screamed as Eve was grabbed, dragged forward,
and thrown to the ground. It all happened so fast, and in such
chaos, that she didn't know where to aim a shove or a punch to get
to her friend's rescue. Everyone was moving all at once, and Eve
was in the middle of it, and it was all just *insane.*

It seemed as if it went on forever until Claire grabbed hold of
one girl by the hair and yanked. The girl, foot raised to deliver a
furious kick, lost her balance and fell backward, and Claire
dragged her a few feet away as she screamed and twisted and
clawed. Whatever the girl was screaming, it involved a lot of curse
words, and Claire wasn't paying attention. She shoved the girl into
a thorny shrub and lunged back toward the circle of attackers.
Stopping one hadn't put an end to the beating. The weapons she
had were for vampires, not humans, and she couldn't use them on
people who couldn't heal . . . though if this went on any longer, she
might have to inflict real and lasting damage to save Eve's life.

Deep breath. She let herself take a second's pause, and identified
the ringleader, the one Eve had slapped; he was the one laying into

her with real viciousness. Claire quickly stepped up behind him, tried to channel Shane as hard as she could, and did two moves he had taught her: first, a hard, fast punch to the kidneys; second, putting the toe of her shoe in the bend of his knee as he twisted in her direction.

It worked. He broke off the attack and fell to his knees; then he got up, staggering, and turned on her. The others were still going after Eve, but as he came after Claire, they began to break off and follow.

She danced backward, screamed for help (probably uselessly), and tore off, running.

They followed.

Everybody in Morganville was pretty good at running, of course, but Claire had motivation; she slowed down just enough to make them believe they could catch her, and still stayed out of easy grabbing range. The ringleader of the group—what was his name? Roy something?—Roy was fast, and she had to work to stay just a few inches past his lunges. If he caught up with her, she had no doubt he'd take out his rage on her just as he had with Eve.

Let her be okay. Please, let her be okay!

Her legs were starting to burn; Claire could run a fair distance, but adrenaline and fear were taking their toll, and she knew that the kids baying like hounds behind her weren't going to get tired as fast—they had mob mentality to urge them on. There was another intersection ahead, but she didn't see anyone on the street. No, wait—there was a car, cruising up to the stoplight.

A red, flirty sports car with an open roof.

Monica Morrell's car.

Monica had a scarf looped over her head to prevent the dry wind from blowing her glossy dark hair all over the place, and she was wearing big rock-star sunglasses; when she turned toward the noise of Claire's pursuit, it was impossible to read her expression.

Claire took a chance. Jumping over the door of the car and into the passenger seat, she narrowly missed flattening Monica's expensive designer purse.

Monica stared at her for a second in silence, then looked past her as Roy Farmer skidded to a stop a foot away from the car, breathing hard and crimson with fury.

"What?" Monica demanded. "Touch my car and die, Roy Toy." And then, without turning her head to even *look* at the light, or oncoming traffic, she gunned the convertible straight through the intersection with a burning squeal of rubber. The mob—well, it wasn't actually a mob, Claire realized, so much as six teens fired up with rage—fell behind fast, even though they took a couple of steps in pursuit. Monica watched in the rearview for a couple of seconds, speeding up to a limit-breaking sixty miles per hour and blasting through two more stop signs without slowing down, then said, "Any particular reason for that? Not that I care, except somehow trash blew into my passenger seat."

"Thanks," Claire said, because regardless of the insult, Monica really had just done her a solid. She was having trouble catching her breath both from the run and from real worry. "Right turn!"

"Not heading that way, sunshine. I'm going shopping."

Claire grabbed the wheel and forced it, and Monica swore— honestly, she knew words Claire had never heard of, in interesting and colorful combinations—and smacked Claire's hand away to manage the turn carefully. "I swear to God, if you make me dent this car, I will *end you!*"

"They got Eve," Claire said. "Right turn! Make the block!"

"Why should I?"

"They beat her up. She's hurt. They could go back!"

"And I care because . . . ?"

"Monica, they could kill her! Just do it!"

Monica hesitated just long enough to make Claire consider diving out of the car while it was speeding, but then she hit the brakes and fishtailed into a hard right, then another one, then U-turned to squeal to a halt in the intersection where Eve's hearse still idled.

Monica didn't say anything at all. Claire took one look at Eve lying on the pavement in a pool of her own blood, time just seemed to freeze into a block of ice for a long breath. Then it shattered, and Claire scrambled out to kneel beside her. Eve's eyes were closed. She was breathing, but her skin looked ashen, and she was bleeding freely from cuts on her head; Claire didn't dare move her, but she could see the livid red marks on her arms where she'd been kicked and stomped. There could be internal injuries, broken bones. . . .

Ambulance, she thought, but even as she reached for her phone, she heard Monica saying, "Yeah, 911? There's somebody bleeding all over the sidewalk at Fifth and Stillwater. Just look for the hearse."

Claire looked up at her as Monica shut off her cell phone and tossed it into her purse. Monica returned the glance, shrugged, and checked her lipstick in the mirror. "Hey," she said. "Never let it be said I'm not civic-minded. That sidewalk might stain."

Then she drove off with a roar of the convertible's engine.

Claire was right about Roy leading the others back, but by the time they arrived, half of his friends had come to their senses, and the ones still with him weren't enough to really work up a good frenzy. They were further held back by the sound of the ambulance siren piercing the air and moving closer. Claire sat back on her heels as she stared at Roy. He was a nondescript boy, nothing really—an okay kind of face, neutral hair, standard high school clothes. The only thing that really made him stand out at all was the blood on his hands, and even as she noticed, he must have, too, because he pulled out his shirttail and scrubbed the skin clean, then tucked the fabric back into his pants. Evidence gone, except for the bruises on his knuckles.

He pointed at Claire as the ambulance pulled to a stop, siren winding down, behind the hearse. "This ain't over," he said. "Captain Obvious says vamp lovers get what they deserve. You do, too, for sticking up for her."

She had an almost-uncontrollable desire to scream at him, but she could see it wouldn't do any good. They were all looking at her as if *she* were the monster and as if Eve were some kind of pervert that deserved to die. Shane might have known what to say, but Shane wasn't here. Michael wasn't here. It was just her, alone, holding the limp and bloody hand of her best friend.

She met his gaze squarely and said, "Bring it, Roy Toy."

"Later," he promised, and jerked his head at his posse. They headed out at a jog and split up.

It was only as the ambulance attendants asked her to move back and started evaluating Eve's condition that she realized exactly what Roy had said.

Captain Obvious says . . .

Captain Obvious.

Oh God. Claire remembered the flyers, the brick, the gasoline thrown on their house, and the paper with the tombstones on it, and their names.

All their names.

Maybe Pennyfeather hadn't used the gas at all; he'd just taken advantage of the distraction. Maybe *humans* had already tried to kill them all.

She tried Michael's phone, but of course it was turned off; it would be, if he was playing. She dialed Shane, instead. He picked up on the fifth ring. "Hey," he said, "kinda busy trying to get an actual job here...."

"Eve's been hurt," she said. "Get to Michael. Captain Obvious has us on some kind of hit list. And watch your back."

"Jesus." Shane was quiet for a second; then he said, "Is Eve okay?"

"I don't know." For the first time, the reality of it was hitting her as the adrenaline rush faded away, and she felt panic choke her up. "God, Shane, they were kicking her so hard—"

"Who?" She could read the fury in the single word.

"I don't know. Roy Farmer, some guy named Aaron, a girl named Melanie—three others. Shane, please, get to Michael. He's at Common Grounds...."

"On it," he said. "You safe right now?"

"I'm going to the hospital with her," Claire said. "Watch your back—I mean it."

"I will."

He hung up, and she had an insane wish to call him back, to hear his voice saying her name, telling her it would all somehow, impossibly, work out, that he loved her and she didn't have to be afraid of the humans of Morganville, too, instead of just the vampires. But Shane would never say that last thing.

Because he'd known better, and always had.

Eve had disappeared into an emergency room treatment area, and Claire wasn't allowed to follow; she ended up sitting on the edge of a hard plastic chair in the waiting room, rubbing her hands together. They felt sticky, even though she'd washed them twice. When she closed her eyes, she kept seeing the avid delight on the faces of the kids—people Eve knew—as they kicked her when she was down.

She'd faced down Monica and her friends, but that had been a cold, calculated kind of violence. This was ... This was sickeningly different. It was a blind, unreasoning hate that just wanted blood, and she didn't understand *why*. It left her feeling horrified and shaky.

The first she knew of Michael's arrival was Shane putting his hand on her shoulder and crouching down in front of her. When she looked up, she realized that Michael had just walked straight past her, past the nurse who'd tried to stop him, and stiff-armed open the emergency room PATIENTS ONLY BEYOND THIS POINT door.

Shane didn't say anything, and Claire couldn't find the words. She just collapsed against him, and let the tears boil out of her. It wasn't all grief; part of it was a sharp-edged ball of fury and frustration that kept bouncing around in her chest. First Myrnin had disappeared, and then Pennyfeather had come at them, and Jason, and Angel, and now *this*. It was as if everything they'd known was going wrong, all at the same time. Morganville's bricks and mortar were back together, but its people were coming apart.

Shane made boyfriend noises to her, things like *Hush* and *It's okay*, and it did soothe that deep, scared part of her that had felt so alone. She gulped back her sobs and got enough self-control that she asked, "Was everything all right with Michael?"

"Nah, not really," Shane said. "While we were leaving, some guy taunted Michael about Eve getting what she deserved. We might have trashed the place a little bit. Oliver's going to be pissed. That was a bonus, though. I had to keep Michael from ripping the idiot's head off. He had some kind of Human Pride thing going on, and you know I don't exactly disagree with that, but ..." He shrugged. "At least I got to hit somebody. I needed that."

She dug in her backpack and found a sad little crumpled-up ball of tissues, blew her nose, and wiped the worst of her tears away. "Shane, I couldn't stop them. They were just—all over her. I tried, but—"

"Knowing you, you did more than try," he said. "I heard a rumor that Captain Obvious had put out the word we were no longer off-limits, but I didn't take it too seriously; hell, he just got started up again, I didn't think he had real juice yet." He sat beside her and took her hand in his. "Eve's tough. She's okay."

"She wasn't," Claire said, and felt tears threaten again. "She couldn't even try to fight them. They just—"

He hushed her and tipped her head against his shoulder, and they sat together, in silence, until Michael came back. He was moving more slowly now, but his face was tense and marble-pale, and he wasn't bothering to try to keep the vampire grace out of the way he walked, like a prowling animal. His eyes looked purple at a distance, from the flickering red in them.

He stopped in front of them, and Claire started to ask about Eve, but something in him kept her quiet and very still.

"I need you," he said to Shane. Shane slowly rose to his feet. "You know who it was?"

Shane glanced at Claire, then nodded.

"Then let's go."

"Bro—," Shane said, and for him, his voice sounded almost tentative. "Man, you've got to tell us something. We love her, too."

"She has a concussion and a broken rib," Michael said. "I can't be here. I need to go, right now."

Shane gazed at him for a long few seconds before he said, "I'm not letting you kill anybody, man."

"I have the privilege to hunt. If you want to stop me from using it, you'd better come along."

Shane cast a quick look of apology at Claire, and she nodded; there was no doubt that Michael was in a mood to get more violent than she'd ever seen him, and having Shane as wingman might actually save lives. "Stay here," he said to her, and gave her a fast, warm kiss. "Do *not* leave without me."

"Don't let him do anything stupid," she whispered. "And don't *you* do anything stupid, either."

"Hey," he said with a cocky grin, "look who you're talking to!"

He left before she could tell him—as if he didn't know—that she loved him, so much, and Michael never even glanced back at her. Maybe he blamed her, she thought miserably. Maybe he figured she should have been able to stop it, to save Eve.

Maybe she ought to have been able to, after all.

She sat in silence, miserable and aching with guilt and grief, for hours. It was long enough that she got thirsty and bought a Coke, downed it, had to find the restroom, went through all the ancient magazines piled on the table, and actually napped a little.

It was almost eight o'clock when the doctor finally appeared from the treatment area. He looked around, frowned, and then came to her. "You're here for Eve Rosser?"

"Yes." She shot to her feet and almost stumbled; her legs had gone a little numb from sitting for so long. "Yes!"

"Where's her immediate family?"

"He's"—she tried to think of something more clever than blurting out *Getting his revenge*, and shifted uncomfortably from one foot to the other—"gone to tell her mom."

That seemed to do the trick, because the doctor looked more satisfied with that. "Well, when he comes back, tell him she's in recovery. We've got her stabilized, but we'll have to keep her for a couple of days and make sure there's no brain trauma. She's lucky. The surgery went well."

"Surgery?" Claire covered her mouth with her hand. "*She had surgery? For what?*"

He stared at her in silence for a moment, then said, "Just tell him she's stable. I don't anticipate more than one night here for her, unless there are complications we can't foresee right now. But the internal bleeding is under control."

He walked off before she could ask him if she could see Eve. He got all the way to the door, then turned back to see her settling miserably back into the plastic chair. "Oh," he said. "If you want to see her, she'll be waking up soon. I warn you, she'll be in some pain."

Claire climbed to her feet again and followed him to the recovery room.

He wasn't kidding about the pain, and Claire was in tears trying to soothe Eve as she moaned and tossed and whimpered, but they finally gave her some kind of a shot that quieted her a little. Claire followed as they wheeled her into a room and hooked her up to machines, and this time, when Claire dozed off in a chair, it was a little more comfortable, and she pulled up to Eve's bedside.

When she woke up, Morganville had gone still and dark, bathed here and there in the soft glow of porch lights and streetlamps. Car headlights crisscrossed the grid of streets. There were, as always, more out at night. Vampire vehicles.

She was still staring out at it when she heard a rustle of sheets, and Eve said, in a shockingly small voice, "Michael?"

Claire went to her side as Eve woke up. She had bruises on her face—red right now, but starting to turn purple at the edges. Both eyes were puffy. "Hey," she said in as soothing a voice as she could manage. She took Eve's hand, carefully, and held it. "Hey, you scared the hell out of me, sweetie."

"Claire?" Eve blinked and tried to open her lids wider, then winced from the effort. "Crap. What car hit me?"

"You don't remember?"

"Did someone run into us? Is my hearse—" Her voice faded off, and she was quiet for a moment, then said, "Oh. Right. They jumped me, didn't they?"

"Yeah," Claire said. "But you're okay. You're in the hospital. The doctor says you're going to be fine."

"Son of a—" Eve tried to lift her hand, but it had tubes coming out of it; she looked at it, then lowered it slowly back down. "Where's Michael?"

"Ah—"

"Please don't tell me he went after them."

"I won't," Claire said. "Look, you just need to rest, okay? Get your strength back after surgery."

"Surgery? For what?" Eve tried to sit up, but she groaned deeply and sank back down in the pillows. "Oh *God*, that hurts. What the hell . . . ?"

The nurse came in just then, saw Eve was awake, and came to lift the bed up to help her sit. "You can sit up for a while," the nurse said, "but if you start feeling sick, use this." She pressed a bowl into Eve's hands. "The anesthesia could make you vomit."

"Wow. Cheery," Eve said. "Wait—what kind of surgery did I have?"

The nurse hesitated, glanced at Claire, and said, "Are you sure you want me to tell you with your visitor present?"

"Claire? Sure. She's like—like a sister." Eve paled a little as she shifted. "It hurts."

"Well, it will," the nurse said, without much sympathy. "They had to remove your appendix. It was bleeding."

"*It what?*"

"You were kicked in the stomach," the nurse said. "Your appendix was badly damaged. They had to remove it. So it's best if you stay still for a while and let yourself heal. The police are coming to interview you about what happened."

"Good."

The nurse smiled. There was something a little ominous about it, a little disturbing. "I'd advise you to refuse to give a statement. Might be healthier for you, all things considered. The people who hurt you might have friends. And you don't have very many."

Claire blinked. "What did you just say?" The nurse turned away. "Hey!"

Eve put a hand on her arm as Claire tried to get up. "I understand," she said.

The nurse nodded, checked the readings on a couple of machines, and said, "Don't keep her awake long. I'll tell the police to come back later. Give you some time to think about what you're going to say to them. You're a smart girl. You know what's best."

The message, Claire thought, was chilling and clear: don't tell the cops the names of the people who attacked you. Or else. And an "or else" from a medical professional was pretty nasty. If Eve wasn't safe here . . .

Captain Obvious had always been a little bit of a joke, in most Morganville resident circles, but Claire was starting to think that this new, more aggressive Cap was something else entirely. He was inspiring people. And leading them into frightening extremes.

Like the vampires, with their identification cards and hunting licenses.

If both sides kept escalating, nobody could stand in the middle for long without having a price on his head—and it sounded as though that had already happened. Eve was the first, but any one of them could be next.

The nurse left. Eve watched her go, then closed her eyes and sighed. "Figured that would happen," she said. "Humans first, and all that crap. They've gotten stronger. And now Captain Obvious is back. It's a bad time to be us, Claire. I have to tell Michael to back off. . . ."

Eve tried to sit up, but the effort left her pale and exhausted. "He never should have gone after them. That's what they *want*; don't you get it? They came after me to get to him. I'm not important. He is. He's Amelie's blood—kind of like her son. If they can hurt him, kill him—Claire, go find him. Please. I'll be okay here. Just *go*. The worst thing they're going to do to me is give me crap Jell-O."

Claire hesitated a long moment, then leaned over and hugged Eve, giving her a gentle and awkward kind of embrace that made her aware of just how fragile the girl was—how fragile they all were.

"Love you," she said.

"Yeah, whatever, you, too," Eve said, but she smiled a little. "Go. Give him a call. He'll listen to you—or at least Shane will."

And for the love of her, Claire tried, but the phone kept ringing, and ringing, and ringing, straight to voice mail.

And the day slipped away as they anxiously waited.

SIXTEEN

MICHAEL

☽

The anger that had hold of me made me ache all over, especially in my eyeteeth; I'd rarely experienced the urge to bite somebody in pure rage, but *damn*, I wanted to sink my fangs deep in someone now. Roy Farmer, that little son of a bitch, to start, and then the rest of his murderous little crew.

Eve had looked so broken, lying in that bed. So unlike the bundle of strength and energy I loved. I really hadn't known, deep down, how much she meant to me until I'd seen her like that, and known, really and deeply *known*, that I could lose her.

Nobody hurt my girl and got away with it.

Shane was angry, too, but—and this was a reversal of our usual roles as friends—he was the cautious one, the one telling me to play it smart and not let anger drive the bus. He was right, of course, but right didn't matter so much just now. I wanted blood, and I wanted to taste it and feel the fear spicing it like pepper. I wanted them to know how *she'd* felt, helpless and terrified and alone.

And yeah, it probably wasn't fair, but I was angry at Claire for leaving her, even for a moment. I knew she'd done the right thing, drawing off the mob, but that had left Eve lying bleeding on a sidewalk. Alone. And I couldn't get that image out of my head. She could have died *alone.*

I understood how Shane felt when he drove his fist through a wall. Some things, only violence could erase.

"Roy lives over on College Street," Shane said, "but he won't be there. He lives with his parents. He's a punk, but not so much of one that he'd run home to his mommy."

"Where, then?" We were in Eve's hearse, and Shane was driving; I was sitting in the blacked-out back area. Shane had verbally kicked my ass about risking sunburn when I'd wanted to walk; he'd made me stop off and grab a long coat and hat and gloves, too, just in case. "You know the guy, right?"

"Kinda," he said. "Roy's one of those vampire-hunter-wannabe types, came to me a couple of times for pointers on things, and showed me things he was working on as weapons. He hero-worshipped my dad, which tells you a little bit about how screwed-up he is. I never thought he'd do this, though. Not coming out for Eve, or any of us. Didn't think he'd have the guts."

"It doesn't take guts to kick a girl half to death," I said. Shane said nothing to that, just gave me an uneasy look in the rearview and tightened his grip on the wheel. "Where would he be?"

"Probably at the 'Stro," Shane said. "He has a sick hand-built Cadillac he likes to show off there. He's probably getting back-slaps from his buddies about how awesome he is."

The Astro was an abandoned old drive-in on the outskirts of

Morganville, just barely within its borders; it had a graying movie screen that tilted more toward the desert floor every year, and the pavement had cracked and broken in the sun, letting sage and Joshua bushes push up through the gaps. The concession stand had fallen down a couple of years back, and somebody had touched off a bonfire there for high school graduation.

It went without saying that the place was a favorite of the underage drinking and drugging crew.

Shane drove out there. It was close to twilight now, and sunset had stacked itself in bands of color on the horizon; the leaning timbers of the Astro's screen loomed as the tallest thing around in the flatland, and Shane circled the peeling tin fence until he came to the entrance. The cops made periodic efforts to chain it shut, but that lasted only as long as it took for someone to cut the lock off—and most of those who hung out here had toolboxes built in the beds of their trucks.

Sure enough, the entrance stood gaping, one leaf of it creaking in the fierce, constant wind. Sand rattled the windshield as Shane made the turn, and he slowed down. "Got to watch out for bottles," he said. "The place is land-mined with them."

He was right. My eyes were better in the dark, and I could see the drifts of dark brown bottles, some intact, most broken into shards. The fence line was peppered with shotgun blasts, and I got the feeling that a lot of the empties had been used for target practice. Standard drunken-country-teen behavior; I couldn't say I hadn't done some of that myself, before I'd been forced to adapt to something different.

I didn't miss it, though.

Shane's headlights cut harsh across dusty green sage, the spiked limbs of mesquite pushing up out of the broken pavement, and, in the far corner of the lot, a gleam of metal. Cars, about six of them.

Most were pickups, the vehicle of choice out here in Nowhere, Texas, but one was a sharply gleaming Caddy, painted electric blue, with shimmering chrome rims. Shane was right. It *was* a sick car.

A bunch of kids—about twenty of them—were sitting on the hoods of the vehicles, passing bottles, cigs, pills, whatever else they had to share.

They watched the slow approach of the hearse with the wary attention of people who might have to run for it at any moment. The only reason they hadn't scurried already was that it wasn't a standard vampire sedan, or a cop car.

Roy Farmer was sitting on the hood of his Caddy with his arm around a plump blond girl. They were both wearing cowboy hats and boots. She must have been cold in her tank top and torn jeans shorts, but from the looks of her, she was too drunk to care. Roy watched as the hearse pulled to a stop, and he took a long pull out of the brown bottle in his hand.

"Mike," Shane said as I reached for the door. "Seriously, man, slow your roll. He wouldn't just be sitting there like this if he didn't have something up his sleeve. He has to know you'd be coming for him. Let me check it first."

I didn't bother to answer. I wasn't letting Shane, or anyone, do *this*. If Roy had come after Eve, he'd come after me, and I couldn't let him see it any other way. Maybe it was loyalty; maybe it was possessiveness. I don't know; Eve wasn't there to set me straight on the difference. But I knew that it was my job, not Shane's, to make Roy regret it.

Maybe that was part of being married. Or maybe it was just me, discovering for the first time that I really, truly wanted Eve to look up to me and believe that I could—and would—protect her. She'd probably laugh and call me a Neanderthal, but secretly, deep down, she'd be pleased.

I got out of the hearse and walked over toward the other cars. The teens fell silent, watching me. Nobody ran, nobody reacted overtly, but they were all ready; I could see it in the tension of their bodies. Even the stoners put down their drugs of choice to pay attention.

I knew how it was. I'd rarely been one to come hang out here, but I was a Morganville kid. We'd all been taught to watch vampires with complete attention when one was in the area.

"You," I said, and nodded at Roy. He stayed where he was, one arm draped over his girlfriend's shoulders. "Just you. Everybody else gets a free pass tonight."

"Hey, look; it's the big man off campus," he said. "I'm busy. Screw you."

I felt a growl building inside me, the beast clawing on its chain. Eve's smile flashed in front of my mind's eye, and I wanted so badly to wipe the grin off his face. "Careful," I said softly. Just that. His girlfriend must have sensed the menace coming off me, because she straightened up and cast Roy a worried look; the others were slipping quietly off the hoods of their own vehicles, stowing their drinks and smokes. No loyalty here. Nobody was willing to stand up for Roy, not even the girl he still held clamped under his arm as if he intended to use her as a human shield.

I waited until the other vehicles started their engines and began heading for less hostile places to get high. Once they were all gone, the Morganville night was cold, silent, and very, very heavy around us.

"Why Eve?" I asked him. I was aware of Shane standing somewhere behind me, ready and most likely armed; I didn't need him. Not for this. "Why did you go after my wife?" *Wife* still sounded strange in my mouth; she'd been *girlfriend* or *friend* for so many years. But it was a heavy word, an important one, and he must have heard it, because his grin got tighter and more predatory.

"'Cause it's evil," he said. "Anybody stupid enough to marry a vampire deserves to die before she contaminates other people."

"She wasn't hurting you."

"Man, it makes me want to vomit just looking at her, knowing *you* had your hands all over her. She's better off dead." That grin— I kept staring at it, wanting to rip it off his face. "Is she? Dead?"

"No," I said.

"Too bad. Maybe next time. 'Cause you know there's gonna be a next time, fanger. You can't get us all."

"Maybe not," I said, "but I can damn sure get you."

I moved, and he caught it and moved at the same time, shoving his girlfriend into my path. She screamed and rolled off the hood, tripping me, but I landed easily on the other side of her and grabbed Roy by the arm as he tried to jump behind the wheel. His shirt tore as he jerked free, and he backed up, still grinning, but it was more like a snarl now.

He had a spray can in his hand. I didn't need to ask to know it was silver. The downside of all the weapons that Shane and Eve had developed to help us survive was that now all of the humans of Morganville had the recipes; he'd made his own anti-vamp pepper spray, and if he nailed me with it, it wouldn't just hurt; it might blind me for days. It would certainly put me down hard enough that he could stake me with silver without breaking a sweat.

Except that I heard Shane, still standing behind me, pump a shotgun. Roy's eyes slid past me to focus on him, and his snarl faltered.

"Looks like somebody brought a can to a gunfight," Shane said. "Just to be clear, if you tag my friend, I get to spray you right back. Seems fair."

"You won't shoot me," Roy said. "I'm like you. I'm resistance."

"Then the resistance is scraping the bottom of the DNA barrel," Shane said. "And you're going after my friends. That trumps anything else." I wouldn't have doubted him, in that moment. Eve was like his adopted sister, and I knew how Shane felt about her.

So did Roy. He stepped back, eyes darting side to side. He finally dropped the spray can and held up his hands. "Okay. Okay, fine, you got me. What you gonna do now, vamp? Kill me?"

"I could," I said.

"He's got a card that says he can, and everything," Shane said. "But he's not going to." I sent him a look. Shane shrugged. "You're not, man. I know you. Anyway, it ain't the Roys of this thing you have to worry about. You need to talk to the head man."

"Captain Obvious," I said. Roy's face drained of color. "You're going to tell me where to find him."

"No way."

His girlfriend was getting to her feet behind me. I didn't even look at her, but I grabbed her and pulled her closer, my arm around her neck to hold her still as she struggled. "We'll start with her," I said. "And if she's not important to you, then I'm pretty sure saving your own neck will do the trick. You kicked my wife when she was down, Roy. You're not that brave."

"Michael," Shane said, very quietly.

"Shut up," I said, and let my fangs come down. "Captain Obvious. Now."

It took only about a minute for him to give it up, but for me to feel I was done with him, it took four more.

"You have something to say?" I asked Shane. I was in the front now, since it was no longer daylight. He cut his gaze toward me for a second, raised his eyebrows, and shook his head. "Too little or too much?"

"I'm not you, Michael. I don't know. It's really too bad about the car, though. That was a really nice car."

"If it were Claire—"

"It nearly *was* Claire." He paused for a moment, then shook his head. "I don't know. I'd want to kill the little bastard. Hell, I still want to."

"I could," I said. "And nobody would say a thing about it. Do you know how scary that is?"

"Yeah," he said. "And I think it was damn nice of you to just break his arm. But the next vampire, they'd kill somebody for staring at them too long, spilling their coffee, whatever. That's why it can't be like this, with every vampire getting some kind of free pass to murder. For every Michael, there are three Jasons. Get me?"

I nodded. I understood that better than he did, probably; I'd been around more vampires over the past year or two than he ever had. "We have to fix things," I said. "You're right about that. First Captain Obvious, and then—"

"Then Oliver," Shane said. "Because that crusty old bastard is getting his way, and if he does for much longer, we're not going to have a town left. The only way we're going to survive here is if we make everybody show respect."

The drive—like every drive inside the city limits—was short, and when we pulled to a halt in front of a plain, everyday house— it was a little weather-beaten, a little run-down—Shane and I sat for a moment, assessing it. "What do you think?" I asked him. He shrugged.

"Looks okay," he said. "But if Roy wasn't shining us on, and it *is* Captain Obvious's place, he's going to be prepared for the vampire apocalypse in there. You walk in there all fangs and red eyes, and you're done."

"You want me to let you go in by yourself."

"Seems safer," Shane said. "After all, I'm the poster child for anti-vamp, right? He's going to hear me out."

"Maybe," I said. "But the point isn't to talk, Shane. It's to kick ass and make sure he never comes after Eve again. Or you. Or Claire. If he wants to nail a target on me, fine, I've earned it along with the thirst for blood. But there's a line, and he's crossed it."

"I know," Shane said. "Believe me, I know."

"No, you don't. You haven't seen Eve yet."

Shane considered that, then nodded, opened his door, and got out. He left the shotgun behind, on the rack behind the seat. "You hear me yell, get in there," he said. "Otherwise, wait here. Promise me."

I didn't, and he didn't insist on it; after a second's hesitation, he shook his head and walked up the cracked steps to the front door. He tried the bell, then knocked, and after a few long moments, the curtains in the front window twitched, and the door swung open.

I sat very still, watching. Listening. And, I realized, I wasn't the only one. There was another vampire in the shadows, almost invisible except for a quick shimmer of red eyes. Vampires had no scent, unless they'd recently fed, and out here in the yard, with all the smells of grass, manure, dirt, wood, metal, there was no chance to detect one that way at all. I wondered who it was. No point in a confrontation, anyway; I needed to focus, in case Shane ended up needing me.

The vampire disappeared just seconds after I noticed his presence.

Shane didn't yell for help. He opened the front door and gestured; I got out and walked up toward him.

"Take it slow," he advised me. "Think of it as visiting the

Founder's office. He's just about as ready to kill you if you put a foot wrong."

I'd defied the hell out of Amelie already, I thought, but Shane didn't necessarily need to know that. I walked up to the door and . . . stopped, because the house had a barrier. Most Morganville houses didn't, unless they were really old or Founder Houses, but this one was different.

And it was strong.

"Come in," Shane said, but that didn't change anything. I was a vampire, and I wasn't getting inside until the house resident altered the rules.

Enrique Ramos appeared in the hall behind my friend, and stared at me for a moment before he said, "Yeah, come on in."

I passed a pile of black clothing, a mask, a leather jacket, and paused to look at them. There was also a motorcycle helmet. "Yours?"

"Sure," he said, and threw me a cold smile. "Everybody saw me in them at the rally."

"Then you're not Captain Obvious," I said.

"Why not?"

"Too obvious."

And I was right; he was probably one of three or four decoys out there, playing the captain, leading the vampires around on goose chases. This was his house, and a good place to hold a neutral headquarters, since it had been in his family a long time; his mother had moved to a new place and left it to her son, and he'd made it a kind of secured, fortified meeting place.

The war council of Captain Obvious was in session at the dinner table in the kitchen, and as Enrique and Shane walked me in, I realized just how much trouble we were in. There were several of Morganville's most prominent businessmen at the table, including the owner of the bank, but that wasn't the issue.

There was a vampire sitting at the Captain Obvious table. *Naomi*. A blood sister to Amelie, she was a pretty, delicate-seeming vampire who looked all of twenty, if that; she had a gentle manner and sweet smile, and it concealed depths that I hadn't understood for a long time. She wasn't just ambitious; she was calculating, backstabbing, and determined to win.

"I thought you were dead," I told her. I'd been informed she'd been killed by the draug, in the final battle; there'd been a whisper that it wasn't the draug who'd done it, but Amelie, by proxy, getting rid of a credible rival for leader of Morganville.

Naomi lifted her shoulders in a very French sort of shrug. "I have been before," she said in that lovely, silvery voice, and laughed a little. "As you know, Michael, I am hard to keep that way." She sent me a smile that invited me to share the joke, but I didn't smile back. For all her graces and kind manners, there was an ice-cold core to her that most didn't ever see. "Sit and be welcome."

"*You're* not Captain Obvious," I said, and stared at each of the human men at the table in turn. Then I turned to the woman seated across from her. "*You* are."

Hannah Moses nodded. Her scarred face was still and quiet, her dark eyes watchful. "I knew you'd be impossible to fool about this. Sit down, Michael."

I didn't want to sit down at the Captain Obvious table. I was still angry, yeah, but I was also more than a little bit shocked, and betrayed. Hannah had been a friend. An ally. She'd protected all of us, at one time or another; she was a solid, real person, with a solid set of values.

That made it so, so much worse.

But anyway, I sat, because the alternative was to go full throttle, and I wasn't quite there. Not yet. Shane kept standing, leaning against the wall, arms folded. He was watching Enrique, who was doing the same thing; bodyguards, I guessed, facing off in silence and ready for the other to make a move. There was muttering among the business leaders, and at least one of them got up to leave the room in protest.

"Sit down, Mr. Farmer," I said without looking at him. "We're going to have a conversation about your son and where he gets his funny ideas."

Roy Farmer's dad got an odd look on his face and sank back in his seat. "Is my son alive?"

"Yep," Shane said, with false cheer. I wouldn't have been quite so quick to reassure him. "Hope you don't mind the fix-up on his car. Oh, and his arm."

"You bloodsucking parasite son of a—"

I moved, then, slamming my palm on the table hard enough to leave a crack in the wood. "I didn't kill him," I said. "Shut up and take it as a gift."

He did, looking white around the mouth. Then I looked at Hannah. "You put us in the crosshairs. You put *Eve* in the crosshairs," I said to Hannah. "Why would you do that?"

"Why did you have to put her in the middle?" she asked me, in a frighteningly reasonable tone. "You know that the vampires won't let her stay there for long; they'll have her killed before they let humans gain power in this town through her status as a legal consort. You knew that when you married her. By putting pressure on her from the human side, we were hoping we could save her life and make her leave you. Get you to understand how dangerous this is for her, and for you. We don't hate you, Michael. But you're in the way."

"Wait," Shane said, turning his head toward her. "You had Roy Farmer beat her up to *help*? That's what you're telling us?"

"It's hardly our fault. Roy was never supposed to do more than frighten her," Naomi said, with that charming little way she had. "I assure you, he was never supposed to harm her badly. He was only to make it clear that she would not be accepted as Michael's wife. As the vampires have also made it clear. I have heard that Oliver sent Pennyfeather to make that same point."

"Eve's not a pawn you can move around the board," I said, spearing Naomi with a glare, then Hannah, then the others. "And neither am I."

"But that is exactly what you are, Michael. You, Shane, Claire, Eve—all of you. You are played for one side or the other at every turn, and you fail to see it." Naomi shook her head in what I was sure was fake sadness, but it was very convincing. "Mistakes have been made, but no one intended permanent harm to your lover. You may take my word for it."

"My *wife*," I said, pointedly. "Call her that."

Naomi inclined her head. *"D'accord."*

I looked at Hannah. She hadn't said much so far, and left Naomi to try to make the justifications. She watched me, and Shane, with calm and careful attention, hands loose and relaxed on the table in front of her.

But she was afraid. I could feel that, hear it in the rapid beat of her heart. All of the humans were afraid. *They ought to be,* I thought. They were allied now with a traitorous vampire, and they'd just made an enemy of someone who by all rights should have been their friend and supporter.

"You should never have touched Eve," I told Hannah.

"I'm sorry for what happened," she said. "But, Michael, you all made your choices, and your choices have consequences. If you want Eve to be safe, you should allow her to come back to her own side. With us."

"Why do there have to be sides? We're *people*, Hannah."

She shook her head. "You *were* people. You like to think you still are, but you're a killer at heart. And there are always sides. If you can't give her up just because you love her, then you're selfish, and you're the one putting her more at risk every day—from your own kind."

"So what am I supposed to do?" It burst out of me in anger, and all of a sudden I was on my feet, eyes blazing, rage bringing out my fangs and my fury. "*She's my wife!* This isn't you, Hannah. It's not like you at all, bringing innocent people into this, getting them hurt, maybe killed!"

Hannah didn't move, and she didn't reach for a weapon. Enrique pushed off the wall, and so did Shane in a match move, but I was the only one showing any threat.

Hannah said, "Gentlemen—could you leave me, Naomi, and Michael alone, please?"

The Morganville businessmen all got up and left the room without argument. Enrique stuck around.

"I will if he will," Enrique said, and nodded toward Shane, who nodded right back.

"Maybe you guys can go have a stare-off in the other room," I said, and got a challenging frown from Shane. "If something was going to go sideways, it already would have happened. Right?"

"Probably," Shane said. "But I don't like this."

"It's better if we do this alone," Hannah said. "You, me, and Naomi. There are things we need to keep private, even from our advisers."

I studied them, then jerked my head at Shane. He made an

after-you motion to Enrique, then followed the other man out of the room.

The door to the kitchen shut tightly behind them.

From the moment the door closed, Hannah said nothing. It was as if she'd just... powered off. It was Naomi who stood up and walked the perimeter of the kitchen, apparently fascinated by the countertops, the appliances, the drawer pulls.

"The solution to your problem is perfectly commonplace," Naomi said finally. "Let Eve think you have ceased to care for her, and her safety will be assured. Your marriage is the problem, and it's the marriage that must be ended. You may choose the timing of the legal actions, of course, but it's imperative that you make her leave you *now*."

"I can't do that." The anger wasn't helping me, and all too soon, it drained away, leaving me feeling empty and hollow. "I can't just push her away. Hannah—"

Hannah wasn't looking at me, or at anything. I had a visceral sense of sudden danger, and I turned on Naomi. "Why are you here? You're not Captain Obvious; you can't be. How did you get them to even let you in the door?"

"I was wondering when you'd ask that," she said, and smiled at me from under her long eyelashes. "I can be *very* persuasive. It's been my strength. Once I realized that Hannah Moses made such an excellent leader for the human resistance, it was clear I should ally myself to it. How else am I to bring down my sister?"

I glanced at Hannah again, eyes widening, because it wasn't right that she was sitting so quietly, like a doll that had been switched off... or a *puppet*.

The distraction was all Naomi needed. If my nerves hadn't been strung guitar-tight, I'd never have seen her move; even with that much warning, though I didn't understand what she was going to do. I thought she was going to stake me, and I raised my hands in defense, but she darted past me, behind me, grabbed me, and pulled me off-balance. I felt her hands snaking cold around my chest, then pushing my chin high—

And then she bit me before I could yell for help.

Her fangs slid into my throat, and it felt like being stabbed with ice; all the warmth began to flood away from me, into her, and in its place I felt a terrible dark influence sliding through my veins. Naomi, like Bishop, her vampire father, had the power to subvert other vampires—and now, she had me. Just as she'd taken control of Hannah, and through Hannah, the entire human resistance.

We were all just puppets now.

It didn't take long, and there was absolutely nothing I could do to fight it. When she let me go, I collapsed to my hands and knees on the tile, mouth open, fangs extended, and Naomi walked calmly back to take her seat again at the table. She looked at Hannah. "Then that's finished," she said, and tapped her fingers on the wood of the table in a complex, musical rhythm. "Michael. Stand."

I did. I wanted to lunge at her, kill her, rip her apart, but I knew that none of it was showing on my face or in my body language. Just as nothing showed in Hannah's. The reason it hadn't fit for Hannah to have put Eve at such deadly risk was that it hadn't been her choice. It was Naomi's decision—all of it, tracing back to Naomi. And it was way too late for me to do anything about it. I couldn't even try to warn people.

"This is what you will do, Michael," Naomi said. "You will go back to see your lovely wife and tell her you've had second thoughts. You'll do whatever is necessary to destroy all trust between you. And then you will pack your things and come back here, to me. You'll make an excellent soldier. Best of all, no one will suspect you. Amelie's bloodchild? You are a perfect little assassin."

"Yes," I said. *No, no, no,* I was screaming, but I couldn't do anything at all to stop myself. "What should I do about Shane? And Claire?"

"Shane's of no consequence, and neither is the girl, except as a tool to be used. I've taken Myrnin out of play; without the protection of her black knight, she is no more than a pawn. But..." She tapped pale fingers to her lips, looking momentarily thoughtful. "You make a good point. What *of* Claire? Even a pawn may take a queen, if played properly...."

She rose to her feet and paced for a moment, arms folded, head down. Hannah and I stared at each other. Her heart was hammering, and I recognized now that it wasn't fear she felt but rage. She was just as trapped as I was. If Myrnin's black knight was off the table, Hannah was Naomi's white castle, hiding secrets. And what was I?

"Ah," Naomi said, and turned back toward me, eyes shining in unholy delight. "*I* know how to play Claire. So, this is what you will do, and what you will tell her...."

I listened. I hated her with every fiber of my being and every tiny bit of my soul.

But I knew I'd do what she said, even though it was going to destroy every good thing in my life.

Because I didn't have a choice.

SEVENTEEN

CLAIRE

☾

Michael looked like the walking dead when he arrived back in the waiting room, where Claire was getting coffee for the eleven-millionth time from the machine; it ate her quarters, again, but she'd learned from one of the nurses—not the one who'd threatened Eve, thank God—how to kick the side of the dispenser in just the right spot to get the container to drop and produce about a half cup of oily, disgusting swill that kind of tasted like coffee.

It was better than nothing. But not much better.

She almost dropped the cup when she saw the boys arrive. Shane had a guarded, solemn expression, but Michael looked as though he'd been to the gates of hell and back and returned without the souvenir T-shirt.

"She's sleeping," Claire said, before either of them could speak. "Hey, are you all right? Michael?"

"Fine," he said. His blue eyes looked oddly stark and empty, and there were dark smudges under them, as if he'd been robbed of a week's sleep in just the past few hours. "I need to see her."

"Just be careful not to wake her," Claire said. "She's pretty woozy, and in some pain. The doctor said she'll probably be better in the morning. They're going to let her go then, so we can take her home. She just can't do much for a while."

"Good," he said. He hardly even glanced her way, but he took the coffee cup out of her hand and tossed back the near-boiling contents in a single gulp, crushed the paper, and dropped it on the floor as he stalked off, heading for Eve's room. Claire bent and picked up the trash.

"Wow," she said, looking after him. "What the hell, Shane?"

"Wish I knew," he said. "That was the weirdest couple of hours I've ever had. Roy—that was okay, fine, I get it. But then we went to see Cap—" By which she understood Captain Obvious, without it being spelled out. "They made me wait outside toward the end. Whatever they said in there, it was bad. He's looked like that ever since. Like somebody cut his guts out and made him swallow them."

"So you know who it is? Cap, I mean?" She kept it in a bare whisper, glancing around at the empty waiting room. Shane nodded. "Who?"

"Better you don't know," he said. "Trust me, I wish I didn't. I'm starting to wish I didn't know a lot of things."

They settled into the chairs in the waiting area, and Shane put his arm around her . . . and they were just getting comfortable when Shane turned his head and said, "Did you hear that?"

"What?" Claire felt drowsy and content nestled against his shoulder, but now that he'd woken her all the way up again, she did hear something—raised voices.

"That's Eve," Shane said, and stood up. "Something's wrong." Claire sighed and followed him on aching legs down the hall, past the empty nursing station, and arrived just as he pushed the door open.

Eve was crying. Not just crying a little, but crying in shocked, awful, painful sobs, even though she was holding her abdomen with both hands as if it were agony to even try to breathe. Michael was standing at the end of her bed, staring at her without any expression at all on his face. He'd always looked like an angel, Claire thought, but now he looked like one of those cold, remote, vengeful ones, the kind that carried swords.

It was terrifying.

"How can you say that?" Eve said, in between painful gulps for air. Crying was hurting her; Claire could hear it in the little hitching whimpers between the words. "God, Michael, don't— please—"

"What the hell is going on?" Shane demanded, and got in Michael's face. "What did you say to her?"

"The truth. Marrying her was a mistake from the beginning," he said. "And I want it over, Eve. I'll get the papers done, and you sign them, and we're finished. It's better for us both. The two of us together—Captain Obvious is right. Amelie is right. It's sick, and it shouldn't be allowed to continue. It's going to get innocent people killed."

"Dude, don't do this," Shane said, and reached out. Michael batted his hand away before it reached his shoulder. "Maybe you think this is going to keep her safe somehow, but it's not the right way, okay? And it's not the right time. I know you don't want to hurt her. I heard you back there, with Cap. I know you're just try-ing to protect her—"

"Do you?" Michael turned that empty look on Shane, and stopped him dead. "You don't know a damn thing about me, man."

Shane actually laughed. "You're kidding, right? I know every-thing about you. You're my best friend."

"Think so?" Michael said, and then before Claire was ready, before she was even aware he was moving, he had turned and grabbed hold of her.

Michael Glass, holding her in his arms.

And bending.

And kissing her.

With tongue.

Expertly.

It took her by so much surprise that Claire could only make a muffled sound of shock and surprise at first, and she didn't even try to resist; her body reported in sensations in a rush—the cold strength of him, the softness of his lips, the taste, the absolute *authority* of it . . . and then her rational brain kicked in and screamed in horror.

Michael Glass was kissing her *in front of Shane. And Eve.*

And he was doing a damn good job of groping her along with it, with his hands slipping beneath her shirt.

Shane yelled something, and Claire felt him trying to pull her free, but Michael held on with relentless strength. She was sud-denly terrified to be between the two of them, like a rag between two possessive pit bulls, and then Michael let go just as fast as he'd grabbed on. That sent her crashing back into Shane, and Shane into the wall, with his arms wrapped around her. Claire's mouth felt bruised and wet, and her shirt was bunched up just below her bra line; she frantically tugged it down and tried to wipe her lips at the same time, not doing a very good job of either. Michael was watching her, and the look in his eyes was awful. It wasn't love. It wasn't anything she could understand at all.

"I've been wanting to do that for years," he said. "Just so you know. Did you see *that* coming, best friend? Maybe it's been going on for a while. Maybe ever since she moved in. How do you know?"

"You son of a—" Shane pushed Claire out of the way and came at Michael, but Michael just shoved him back again against the wall and held him there, ignoring his blows. He was looking now at Eve, who was gasping and crying, curled in on herself on the bed as if he'd punched her in an open wound.

"We're done?" he asked her.

"Yes," she whispered. "Yes. Get *out.*" It would have been a scream, Claire thought, except that Eve couldn't get the breath to make that happen.

Michael let go of Shane and walked away, stiff-armed the hospital door open, and disappeared in less than five seconds.

But what he left behind felt like an explosion that was still happening, the shock waves rippling on and on and on. . . .

Shane turned on Claire. "What the *hell* was that?"

"Why are you asking me?" she shot back, shocked, and scrubbed her mouth again. "I didn't ask for it!"

"He wouldn't just—" Shane was the one looking terrible now, and almost as betrayed as Eve. "Is that the first time? Is it?"

"*What?* What are you saying?" She felt sick to her stomach. One minute ago, everything had been fragile, but okay; now the whole world seemed to be splintering around her, breaking into unrecognizable fragments. "I didn't do *anything wrong!*" She remembered, with a horrible wrench, that Shane had once secretly worried about that, about her and Michael having a thing behind

his back. It had never happened, but now—now it was back, all
that paranoia, and the anger. Michael had chosen exactly the right
spot to hit to break their trust apart. "How can you even think I
would—"

"God, get out," Eve said in a small, broken voice. "Just get out.
Both of you." She was crying still, but quietly now, and all her
monitors were beeping and flashing red lights. "Jesus, please, go!"

The nurses came in then, crowding around Eve's bed to adjust
machines and poke needles full of meds into the hanging saline
bags. As Shane pushed her out into the hall, Claire heard the frantic fast beating of Eve's pulse monitor slow down. They were putting her back to sleep. Maybe, if they were lucky, Eve would think
it was all a drug dream in the morning. *No. She won't be that lucky.*

Shane let go of her, and she rounded on him, still trying to
pull her shirt down to a decent level. "I didn't do anything," she
insisted, again. "And I never kissed him! He kissed *me*; you saw
that."

"He did it like he knew exactly what you liked," Shane said.
"Like he was used to doing it. And you weren't exactly struggling."

"I didn't know what to do! God, Shane—it was *fast*, and I
didn't know—I didn't want that! How can you think that he and
I were—"

"I don't know," Shane said, and stuck his hands in his pockets,
shoulders hunched tight. "Maybe because my best friend thought
it was perfectly okay to stick his tongue down your throat to make
his point? Because I'm pretty sure he didn't have to do that just to
break up with Eve. He didn't have to be that cruel."

"Shane—*Shane!* Wait!"

He was walking away from her, heading down the hallway
with his head down. Leaving her, too.

Claire stood there, shocked and alone, feeling like the only sane person left in the world, and when the enormity of it hit, really hit, she burst into tears and curled up in a ball on the worn old couch in the corner of the waiting room.

How did I feel about it? She didn't want to ask herself that. She didn't want to remember the warm rush of feelings underneath the confusion and horror of the moment, or the way her heart had speeded up, and her body betrayed her right down to the core. *I didn't want it. I didn't.*

Well, hadn't she always thought Michael was a hottie? Yes, she had. She'd always noticed, and every once in a while she'd had the occasional little fantasy—but that was *normal*; that was what happened when you were around someone a lot, not—not this. Never this.

He hadn't wanted her. He'd used her, viciously and with cold calculation, to drive Eve away, and Shane. Each of them was alone now, in a world that didn't want or need them.

Why would you do that, Michael? It didn't make any sense. Even if he'd decided not to stay with Eve, Michael was a good man, a nice man; he would have done it gently and with as much kindness as possible because he *did* love Eve; he *did*. She couldn't have been so wrong about that. And when he'd left here before, he'd been a knight on a mission, hell-bent on avenging her. When he'd come back . . .

Claire gulped back the horrible, hurtful tears, and wiped her face, and tried to think through the problem, as if it were happening to someone else. *What makes someone turn around like that, turn on his friends?*

No. That wasn't the question. The question was, what would make a vampire turn on his friends . . . and there was only one answer to that, really. Claire thought of Bishop, Amelie's vampire father, who could infect another vampire with his bite and command his absolute loyalty. Amelie had a measure of that same power, but hers came in a different form. Bishop was unquestionably dead, so could it be Amelie? Would Amelie have broken Michael, as she'd once threatened to do, and made him do this?

Claire shuddered. If Amelie had done it, if this wasn't Michael's real will, then there were four victims of his cruelty, not three. . . . Michael himself was the first, and the most badly wounded of them all.

And even if it was true, even if this was no real choice of Michael's, the problem was . . .

How was she going to prove it?

In the end, Claire slept in the hospital chapel—it was quiet, calm, deserted, and she needed the spiritual support just now. She wished that Father Joe would make an appearance. . . . He was a great listener, and she desperately needed to talk to someone.

But in the end, she fell asleep reading the Bible through tear-swollen eyes, and tried to find some kind of comfort. If she did, she didn't remember.

Claire tried to call Shane six times in the morning, but her calls went to voice mail; texts went unanswered. She was surprised to see him show up around noon, but he hadn't come to talk to her, though she had a moment's pitiful hope. . . . He walked straight past her with a plastic bag, ignoring her, and into Eve's room.

When he came back outside, he sat across the waiting room and stared at the floor.

"Shane?" She took some tentative steps toward him. She wanted to burst into tears, but she knew it would only make things worse if she did. "Please, please talk to me. Please—"

"I brought her clothes," he said. "Then I'm driving you both home. Then I'm getting the hell out for a while. You take care of Eve. You do that for me."

"But—"

"Michael's stuff's already gone," he said. "He packed up last night. I don't know where he went, so don't ask me."

"Shane, please look at me." She sank down on a chair next to him. He smelled like sweat, as if he'd gone to the gym and hadn't stopped to shower. He didn't shift his gaze away from a dedicated examination of the stained tile floor. "I've never had anything going with Michael, *ever*. I don't know why he did that, but it's not what you're thinking. I've never cheated on you. I wouldn't. I've been thinking that maybe—maybe Amelie made him do this. Because I really don't think this was Michael, not the real Michael, do you?"

He didn't answer her. They sat in silence for a few dark seconds, and then a nurse rounded the corner and said, "She's ready to go."

Shane shot to his feet as if the chair had a catapult built in, and was halfway to Eve's room before Claire managed to follow, feeling slow, clumsy, and achingly lost.

Eve looked terrible—no makeup, chalky skin, bruises discoloring her swollen face. She'd let her hair fall forward to hide the worst of it, but it also hid any trace of how she felt seeing Claire come around the corner.

That was probably a blessing, Claire thought, with a horrible surge of unearned guilt. *I didn't kiss him! He kissed me!* But she couldn't insist on that, not with Eve so torn up with grief, and so badly hurt.

And I left her lying there on the sidewalk, bleeding, she thought. *I can't forget that, either.*

Shane held a wheelchair still as Eve practically fell into it; she kept her head bowed, and her hands over her stomach as if she were afraid it might break open. Claire hurried forward and took a plastic bag of clothes from the nurse, and some paperwork and pills. "Give her two of these twice a day," the nurse said. "And let her sleep. She's going to need it. No lifting anything heavier than a book for at least two weeks. She's to see the doctor again on Thursday. Someone will have to bring her to and from the appointment. No driving at all until he lifts the restriction."

Claire nodded mutely, barely able to clock in the instructions; her heart was a mess of hurt, from worry for Eve, grief over Shane, anger at Michael. *Now we have to go home and pretend everything is okay,* she thought, and the concept was pretty appalling. But what choice did she have? Leave? She couldn't. Eve needed someone, and Shane had already made it clear he'd rather run away. Michael already had.

Shane pushed the wheelchair fast, not waiting for Claire; she hurried to catch up, but the elevator doors closed in her face. Neither of her housemates looked at her directly.

She took the stairs down a floor and met them as Shane put the brakes on the wheelchair and helped Eve move shakily into the front passenger seat of the hearse.

"I can drive," Claire offered. Shane ignored her, and walked to that side of the car. He got in and started the engine, and she hardly had time to run to the back and climb into what Eve had cheerfully named Dead Man's Corner before he hit the gas for home.

It was a terrible few minutes. Claire clutched the soft bag of clothing; it smelled of Eve's latest BPAL perfume and a metallic tang she thought had to be blood. She'd wash them herself, make sure they were nice and clean before she returned them. Shane wouldn't think of that. It was something she could do, a little act of love.

Shane was careful on the drive home, avoiding the bumpy spots, and pulling up to the front curb without any jerky sudden stops. He even picked Eve up and carried her inside, waiting impatiently as Claire opened the front door.

Once Eve was settled on the sofa, with the old afghan tucked around her and a pillow beneath her head, Shane said, "You can handle nurse duties, right?" He headed for the door, again.

"Where are you going?"

"None of your business," Shane said. Claire heard the door slam behind him and felt tears clawing at her throat; honestly, it was so incredibly painful, she wanted to throw herself facedown on her bed and cry herself into oblivion. It was worse when she looked around and saw that Michael's music things were missing. He'd even taken the leather armchair with him, the one he liked to sit in while he played.

The house felt cold, hard, and empty without Shane and Michael, and without the love among all of them that had made it home.

Claire sank down beside Eve, put her head on the sofa cushions, and tried not to think about it.

"It's not your fault," Eve said, very quietly. Claire jerked her head up, hope bolting through her, but Eve wasn't smiling, and there was nothing in her swollen face that Claire could interpret as forgiveness. "He had doubts all along; I knew that. I was just— stupid enough to think he was worried about me. So maybe it's better we get it over with. It just hurts so much."

She wasn't talking about the physical pain.

"I don't know why he did . . . what he did, or why he said those things, but it isn't true, Eve. Please believe me."

Eve closed her eyes and sighed as if almost too depressed to listen. "All right," she said in a very faint, flat voice. "Doesn't matter."

Claire held her friend's loose, cool hand, and the two of them sat in silence for a long time before Claire's cell rang.

"Hello?" Her voice sounded strangled and rough; she hardly recognized it herself.

"Honey?" It was her mother. "Oh, Claire, what's wrong?"

That did it. Claire could handle the rest of it, but not that, not the compassionate warmth of her mother's voice.

She cried, and it all came out, in hitching, halting bursts—Shane, Michael, Eve, her fear, all of it. But mostly Shane, and how she was afraid it was all ruined, forever, all that bright and beautiful future she'd thought was so perfectly laid out. Somehow, she even managed to blurt that she was worried about Myrnin, too, which led to a line of questions she'd rather not have answered, but the confessional dam had well and truly busted open, and there was no going back. The call lasted at least an hour, and at the end of it, Claire lay huddled on the parlor floor, wishing the world would just suck her down into its molten core and end her misery.

She finally got her mind back in place enough to say, "I'm sorry, Mom . . . Why did you call me?"

"I just felt you needed me," her mother said. "It's a mother's instinct, sweetheart. Come home, Claire. Just come home and let us take care of you. You'll get through this; I know you will. You're a very strong girl. It'll be okay."

"I'll come," Claire whispered. "As soon as I can." She didn't have anything left to stay for, did she?

She hung up and went to give Eve her medication.

Eve was well enough by nightfall to take some food, though

not a lot. Claire made her soup in a cup, and then put her back to bed with the TV softly playing a movie she knew Eve liked well enough to sleep through.

They didn't talk much.

Miranda came back about the time that Claire was rinsing out the soup cups.

"I'm sorry," Miranda said, and hugged her. Claire threw her arms around the girl and squeezed tightly; for the first time, she felt like someone had truly forgiven her and understood how she felt. "I couldn't do anything today. Michael left; he wouldn't say *anything* to me, and then Shane—he drank too much, you know. It scared me. I thought he was going to do something—something bad. But he didn't."

It would have scared Claire, if she'd known it. "But Eve's okay; that's the important thing," she said. "We'll—we'll fix this. Somehow."

"Is it true?" Miranda pulled back to hold her at arm's length. "Shane said—Shane said you were with Michael, behind his back. But you weren't, were you?"

"No. No, never!"

"I believe you." Miranda held her hands and sat her down at the kitchen table. "I did what you asked. I got out and tried to listen to what the other ghosts were saying. I didn't talk to them, exactly, because it's dangerous to get their attention; they were still following Jenna, trying to tell her things, so that's why I was able to hear so much."

For the first time, Claire felt a surge of something that might have been hope. "Did you hear anything about Myrnin?"

"No," Miranda said. "I'm sorry. But I did hear something weird; maybe it could mean something." The hope was just a pale flicker now, but Claire nodded anyway. "One of them said a spider was in a hole under the white tree. And another one said—Claire, I'm really not sure this is about him at all, you understand—that something was climbing up, but the sun would burn it away."

That didn't help at all. Claire felt a white-hot urge to break something in frustration, or punch a wall, Shane-style, but she knew it wouldn't help. Nothing would help, except figuring something out for a change.

Think, she told herself. *Breathe.* If she could find Myrnin, that would be *something*, at least. Something positive, in all this devastation. *Something climbing. Hole by the white tree.* Was he climbing up in a hole by a white tree? That didn't make any sense. There weren't any white trees in Morganville. Was he even here, in this town? If he wasn't, she couldn't help him at all.

No, he's here. Think. Think!

White tree. That had to mean something. It must be a landmark, so it had to be something she could remember. But what . . . ?

"The ghost who was talking about the white tree," Claire said. "Do you know where he came from?"

"I think he died at the Sleep Inne over near the edge of town. You know that one?" Claire did. It was bland and forgettable, and there were no trees of any kind that way. "I guess his body is buried in the cemetery."

The cemetery, Claire thought. They'd remarked on it from the first, how it all looked so photogenic. *That big dead tree*, Angel had said. *Such a striking color.*

Because it was dead, and it was . . .

Claire's eyes opened wide. "The tree. The cemetery tree, it's *white*, right?"

"I guess. It's dead and the bark is all peeled off and it looks white."

"So it's at the cemetery," Claire blurted, and opened her eyes.

"It's got to be there, whatever this—this hole is. That's where Myrnin is. He's in the hole, in water. And there's some kind of a grate on top, with a cross; Jenna said she saw that in a vision. Mir, I have to go, right now. Can you stay with Eve?"

"I—well, yes, but you can't go out there in the dark, all alone!"

"I have to. Myrnin may be the only one left who can help us get through this, and your other ghost said the sun will burn it away. If he's in a hole in the ground, and the sun comes up, he could burn in there. I can't let that happen."

"I can't go with you! If I did, the other ghosts—they'd be all over me. I have to stay in the house. And Eve's too sick."

"Then I'll call Shane," Claire shot back, and pulled out her phone. She paced as it rang, and rang, and rang, and went to voice mail. She hung up and texted him, with a 911. No details. And finally, after five long minutes, he called back.

"Don't hang up," she said. "I need your help."

"Is it Eve?"

"No," she said reluctantly.

"Then no."

"Wait! Wait, listen to me. I have to go to the cemetery. There's—someone's in trouble, Shane. If you don't go with me, I have to go alone. Please. I know you're angry at me, but—but be angry tomorrow. Tonight, just please, do this for me." He was silent on the other end, but she could hear the uneven hitch of his breathing. "Shane, please. One time."

"Who's in trouble?"

She'd been afraid he'd ask that. But she couldn't lie. Claire squeezed her eyes shut and said, "Myrnin."

Shane hung up. Claire screamed, a raw and wild sound, and threw the phone violently on the table. Miranda's eyes were round as saucers.

"Wow," she said. "So . . . you're not going?"

"No," Claire said grimly. "I *am* going. Alone."

Eve's hearse was still parked out on the curb. Miranda argued with Claire all the way out to the picket fence, but she wasn't listening anymore. She'd put on Eve's long leather coat over her jeans and plain black shirt, and brought along a heavy canvas bag full of weapons, plus her own backpack, which had all kinds of things she might need—even textbooks, if she got study time. At the very least, they were a kind of paper-based armor she could put between herself and something attacking her.

"But—what do I do if you don't come back?" Miranda asked frantically as Claire settled in the driver's seat. The Grim Reaper on the dash shivered and nodded its head, eye-lights flashing. "Claire! Who do I call?"

"Call Shane," she said. "Maybe he'll feel bad if I'm dead. But make sure Eve's okay, and give her the medication she needs just before sunrise. Do *not* let her get up and do anything, and if she starts to run a fever, call the hospital and get them to send the ambulance. Promise me."

"I will." Miranda looked on the verge of tears. "This is bad. This is a really bad idea. . . ."

"I'm open to suggestions." When the other girl didn't offer any, Claire shook her head. "Wish me luck."

"I—" Miranda sighed. "Good luck. I'll wait for you to come back, and if you're not back before sunrise, I'll call . . . *somebody.* Amelie. I'll call Amelie."

"Don't do that," Claire said. "Because it might *be* Amelie. Okay?"

"But—"

Claire didn't give her time to argue.

The hearse drove differently from any other car she'd tried in her very limited driving experience. . . . It was heavy, hard to manage, and had terrible stopping distance, as she found when she rolled through a stop light while pumping the brakes. Luckily, no Morganville police cruisers caught sight of her. She passed some custom-tinted vampire cars. No one tried to stop her.

Claire drove the mile, give or take, out to the cemetery, which brushed the limits of the Morganville township. The place was surrounded by a thick stone wall and had heavy wrought-iron gates; the lightning-struck dead white tree loomed high, all spiky branches and intimidating angles. The gates were locked, of course. Claire considered ramming them, but she knew Eve would never forgive her for it, so she strapped the canvas bag over her shoulders, on top of her backpack, and climbed. The iron was cold and slick under her fingers, but there were plenty of crossbars, and she managed to make it to the top, then slipped down the other side.

Morganville Cemetery was an old one, back to pioneer days, full of time-sanded headstones that were hardly readable anymore, thanks to the constant wind. What grass there was grew fitfully. Nobody visited here with any reliability; the newer cemetery, Redeemer, was closer to the center of town, and that was where present-day burials were done. This was mostly just here for historical value.

It wasn't a very likely spot for vampires to hang out, at least; there hadn't been anyone with a pulse visiting the place in years. But it was still plenty creepy, all right—shadows like black knives across the ground, harsh and sharp in the moonlight. Tree branches rattled like dry bones.

Claire was headed for the tree when she saw the vampires appear on top of the wall and drop easily down, landing without breaking their stride. There were two of them, moving together. One had pale hair; the other had graying locks.

Amelie and Oliver?

She dropped to the ground behind a large carved angel and hoped that it would be enough to hide her. She also hoped she hadn't landed on one of the huge fire ant mounds that dotted the grounds; if she had, this was going to be a very short and unpleasant adventure. If the fire ants didn't bite her into a coma, the vampires would.

They passed fairly close to where she was hiding, and luck was with her; the wind had shifted, carrying her human scent away from them. And it was *not* Amelie with the pale hair shifting in the breeze, Claire realized, as she caught sight of the girl's face, her smile, her dimples.

That was Naomi. Walking with Oliver. But Naomi was supposed to be dead. *Of course,* Claire thought in horror. *Bishop's other daughter. She might have the same powers, too.* If Naomi and Oliver were in it together, Naomi could have turned Michael against them.

And Amelie didn't know.

The two of them strolled through the weeds, through tombstones and tumbleweeds, and came to a halt under the white tree. Oliver dragged a fallen piece of marble away, and Claire heard it grate on metal.

She was also close enough to hear the voices, and she heard Oliver say, "No need to go down after him. Between this and the morning sun, he's finished." He reached into his pocket and came out with a bottle Claire recognized—one of the weapons that Shane had first developed. Then he shared it with Captain Obvious and his crew. And then with the vampires, to use against the draug . . . It was silver nitrate. Oliver had on gloves, but he still handled the bottle carefully as he opened the top, then poured it into the ground—no, not into the ground.

Through the metal grate on the ground.

Claire heard Myrnin's scream of raw pain and fury, and she had to press both hands to her mouth to keep quiet. There was a splashing sound, and scraping, as if he were clawing his way up from a great distance below.

"He won't get far," Naomi said. "No vampire's strong enough to make it all that way to the top before sunrise, and the silver in the grate will keep him in. If he falls, the silver in the water will finish him. Well done, Oliver. Now go back to Amelie. Our little chess pawns are almost all in place. We'll play our last moves soon."

"Yes," he said, "my queen."

"Your white queen," Naomi said, and laughed. "I like the sound of that. You're a useful blunt instrument, Oliver. I shall keep you in my court when I take my rightful place."

"Amelie," he said, and it seemed it was hard for him to get the words out. "What of Amelie?"

"What about her?" Naomi asked. She was staring down through the grate, to where she'd just condemned Myrnin to death. "A wise ruler never leaves a rival at her back. Though I might consider a merciful exile, if you beg hard enough on her behalf. Would you, Oliver? Beg?"

He said nothing. He stood with his hands locked behind his back, and from what Claire could see of him, his face was hard as stone and his eyes flaring red.

"Obviously not," Naomi said. "Your personal dignity was always more important to you than mere emotion, wasn't it? Very well." She leaned over the grate. "Myrnin? I leave you to your gods." She put her fingers to her mouth and blew him a delicate little kiss, and then she and Oliver turned away, drifting soundlessly through the deserted graveyard, then up and onto the wall.

Then Naomi turned and looked right at Claire's hiding place, and smiled. "Did you really think I wouldn't see that ridiculous car, or sense your presence? Since your friend Eve is indisposed, I assumed it would be you rushing to the rescue," she said. "I think our little friend has outlived her usefulness after all, though it would have been a nice finishing move to use her to plant a dagger in Amelie's back. Michael. Take her off the board."

Claire gasped, because Michael jumped up on the wall next to Naomi, scanned the graveyard, and fixed his gaze right where she was.

Naomi nodded. "Adieu, Claire. It's too bad there will be no place for you in the Morganville we are to create."

She left.

And then Michael jumped down and came at her.

Claire ran.

Michael wasn't even trying hard, Claire thought; there was no real reason he couldn't catch her within ten feet. He was very, very fast, and she wasn't; the heavy leather coat she'd decided to wear was weighing her down, and so was the weapons bag. She wanted to leave it, but she didn't dare.

Are you really going to try to kill him? she asked herself, and didn't have any idea of the answer. She tripped over a fallen, tilted grave marker and went flying, rolled, and the canvas bag ripped open on a jagged piece of broken marble. The fabric was tough, but it had weakened along the zipper, and things spilled out through the gap. . . . The first one she laid hands on was a plastic Baggie full of random silver chain links, scavenged from old jewelry Eve had bought through the Internet. It made a nice, heavy handful as Claire opened it, and as she stumbled to her feet, she twisted and threw it at Michael.

The silver hit him, and where it struck skin, she saw sparks; it was more surprising than painful, but it slowed him down, giving her a moment to sort through her other available choices. She passed over the silver nitrate; she didn't want to hurt him—she really didn't.

Her hands closed on Shane's silver-tipped baseball bat, which was the biggest thing in the canvas bag, and she yanked it out.

She didn't even have time to prepare a decent swing as Michael lunged forward, but she did manage to get the coated end of the wood into place so that his momentum took him chest-first into it; the silver scorched him hard, and he veered off with a cry of pain.

Then it was a temporary standoff as Claire set her feet and took up a batter's stance, ready and watching as he paced beyond her reach.

"Michael?"

He didn't answer. His face looked as immobile and frozen as that of the marble angel behind him.

"Michael, please don't do this. I know this isn't your fault; Naomi's using you. I don't want to hurt you. I swear. . . ."

"Good," he said. "That makes it easy."

"But I will!" she finished, and took a swing at his knees as he came into reach. He jumped over the bat, landed lightly, and sprang for her with hands outstretched.

Something hit him in the neck with a soft, coughing hiss, and Michael landed off-balance, staggered, and shook his head in confusion. There was something sticking out of his neck.

A dart.

He pulled it out, looked at it in confusion, and turned away from Claire, toward the wall . . . and sitting on top of it, with a heavy rifle in his hands, was Shane Collins.

"Sorry, man," Shane said. He kicked free and dropped off the wall, flexing his knees and loading another dart into the tranquilizer gun. He aimed as he walked toward them. "You're going to feel real damn bad for a while. Don't make me hit you again. I'm not sure it won't kill you."

Michael growled something, but he was already losing his ability to function; he went down to one knee, then pitched forward to his hands, and then slowly sank down on his side. His back arched in a silent scream.

Claire dropped the bat and tried to go to him, but Shane caught her by the waist and lifted her up to stop her. She kicked and twisted, but he held her. "You get close to him, he could finish the job," he said. He slung her around and sent her stumbling well away from Michael, and from himself. "You came to get Myrnin. Go get him. I'll cover you."

There was still no hint of forgiveness in him, either for Claire or—as he looked at his fallen, suffering friend—for Michael. He was here to fulfill a duty as he saw it, and that was all.

But it was more than she'd ever expected. It was *something*.

"Thank you," she whispered.

Shane nodded, not meeting her eyes, and racked the second tranquilizer dart into place as he watched Michael writhe painfully on the ground.

Claire raced over the uneven graves toward the white tree; even uncovered, the silver grate, circular with bars that formed a simple cross, was almost invisible until she nearly stepped onto it. That would have probably broken her ankle. The grate was locked in place with an old, rusted lock, and Claire whaled at it frantically with the silver-tipped bat until it broke in two.

She threw back the cold, tarnished metal and tried to see into the dark. Nothing. Not even a hint of life.

"Myrnin?" She shouted it down. She had to cover her nose from the smell that rose up from the narrow little hole—rot, sewage, mold, a toxic brew of the worst things she could imagine. "Myrnin! Can you hear me?"

Something thumped down on the ground next to her, and Claire looked up to see that Shane had tossed over a coil of nylon rope he'd retrieved from the weapons bag. She nodded and unwrapped it, tied off one end around the dead tree, and dropped the other down into the hole. "If you can hear me, grab the rope, Myrnin! Climb!"

She wasn't sure for long moments whether he was there, or even whether he *could* get out. Maybe it was too late. Maybe he was already gone.

But then she felt the rope suddenly pull taut, and in seconds, she saw something pale appear in the dark below, gradually becoming clearer as it moved up toward her.

Myrnin climbed as if he'd learned how from his pet spider, swarming up with frantic speed. He had burns on his face and hands and lower legs, silver burns, but that didn't slow him down, and when he reached the top of the hole, Claire grabbed his forearms and dragged him out on the side that wasn't blocked by the raised silver grate.

He collapsed on his back, foul water bleeding out of his soaked and ruined clothes, out of his matted black hair, and after a second of silence he whispered, "I knew you'd come, Claire. I knew you would. Dear God, you took your time."

She took his hand, and sat down next to him.

Shane was standing fifty feet away, beside Michael, but he

looked up and jerked his chin in a silent question. *Is he okay?* She nodded.

It wasn't much, she thought. It wasn't anything to build any kind of hope upon, just that he was willing to show up here, willing to fire a rifle, throw her a rope.

But she'd take it. It was horrifying to her how pitifully grateful she was just for that smallest hint of a smile he gave her, before he turned his back.

"You're very sad," Myrnin said. He sounded faint and distant, as if he'd been a long way off in more ways than one. "You smell like tears. Did he break your heart?"

"No," Claire said, in a very soft whisper that she hoped Shane couldn't hear from where he stood. "I broke his."

"Ah," Myrnin said. "Good for you." He sat up, and suddenly leaned over to throw up a horrifying amount of black water. "Pardon. Well, that was distressing. . . . Oh no . . ."

He collapsed back on the ground, as if too weak to rise, and shut his eyes tight. His whole body was shaking and twitching, and it went on for a horribly long time. She didn't know what to do for him, except put her hand on his shoulder. Beneath the slimy clothes, she could feel his muscles locked and straining as if he were having an epileptic seizure.

He finally relaxed and took in a deep, slow breath before he opened his eyes and said, "We have to go, Claire. Quickly."

"Where?" she asked, because she was cold and scared and couldn't think of any place, any place at all, that might be safe now.

"To safety," he said. "Before it's too late."

"But you—you're not well enough to—"

Before she could finish, he was off stalking barefoot through the weeds toward the exit. He tore the chain off the fence with one hard pull and shoved the gates open with a rusted shriek.

Then he looked back with a red glow in his eyes and said, "Bring Michael. None of this is his fault. I won't allow him to suffer for it."

Shane hadn't moved during all of this, but now he bent down and pulled the tranquilizer dart out of Michael's neck. "It's going to be a few minutes before he's well enough to stand up."

"Then drag him," Myrnin said. "Unless you'd like to enjoy the comfort of my little oubliette. I'm sure Naomi will be sending Pennyfeather in a moment to be certain all of us are dead, and I'd rather not be here to oblige her. *Now*, children."

He clapped his hands and disappeared beyond the gates, and in a moment, Claire heard Eve's car start up with a roar.

She went back to Shane and took one of Michael's arms as he grabbed the other. Their eyes met, briefly.

"I'm so sorry," she whispered.

"Yeah," he said. "Me, too."

But she wasn't sure if they were talking about the same things at all.

EIGHTEEN

CLAIRE

)

It took them a while to drag Michael's heavy, unresponsive body over the uneven ground and out to the hearse. Myrnin stuck his head out of the passenger window of the hearse to helpfully suggest that Michael could be dumped down the same hole he'd just crawled out of. Shane suggested that Myrnin bite him, hard. Myrnin declined.

And Claire drove, leaving Shane with Michael, by his own request. She was a little anxious about that; Shane held grudges, and it was going to be hard for him to see past what Michael had done to them, but it was at least a truce for now. Mortal danger trumped emotional pain. Temporarily.

Myrnin said, "Michael seems to be under Naomi's spell, just as Oliver and Pennyfeather must be. I have no idea how many she's suborned, but it's too bad she didn't try it on me." He smiled, and his expression was bleak and dark, and it wasn't only the streaks of black water staining his face. "Greater vampires have tried, including her black-hearted father. I believe my blood made Bishop sick for a month."

"Where should we go?" she asked. He sighed.

"I suppose we really have no choice," he said. "Retreating to the Glass House will simply give them an easy point to attack, and we cannot defend the place, not from a concerted attack. So we will have to take the fight to them."

"Where?"

He shrugged wearily. "To Amelie herself. Ultimately, she is Naomi's target. Oliver's seduction of her—or at least, part of it—was Naomi's effort to weaken her, to stir up trouble against her. She must be warned of what's to come or she'll be taken unawares, by those she trusts."

"How the hell are we supposed to get into Founder's Square?" Claire asked. "Do you have some secret passage or something?"

"They're all shut up, I'm afraid," Myrnin said. "Oh, and I'm ruining your friend's lovely upholstery. Sorry about the mess. Imagine if they'd left me down there for months. That did happen, once. I was dumped into a cell no larger than a doghouse for half a year. All they did was throw down the occasional chicken or hog . . . disgusting. I seem to have lost my slippers."

"I'll buy you new ones."

"I expect we're going to have to rely on Michael," Myrnin said, switching suddenly back to the original question. "The boy has an automatic entrance to Amelie's presence, as her offspring. The difficulty is that he's hardly in a position to voluntarily assist us, and by the way, Shame, why did you shoot him?"

"It's Shane, and if you call me that again, you'll be getting the next dart."

"The question still stands."

"Because he was going after Claire. Again." Shane didn't look at her, not even a glance in the rearview mirror; Claire knew, because she was waiting for it—for some sign that his anger was starting to wear off.

"Again?" Myrnin asked, and his eyebrows rose. "My. Things change so quickly with you young people. Claire, are you enemies now with Michael?"

"Not exactly," she said. Shane cut her off.

"Last time he just tongue-kissed her," Shane said. "This time it looked a little more extreme than that. So I didn't take the chance of being wrong."

That earned her a sharp, interested look from Myrnin. "Well. We'll have to have the full story, then."

"We really don't," she said. "Something's wrong with Michael, all right. And I saw Naomi, with Oliver. They're working together."

"That—is very, very unpleasant," Myrnin said. He frowned and pulled at a stray thread on his shirt, threatening to unravel an entire piece of it. "Naomi was killed in the attack on the draug, or so it was said. I had my doubts. It seemed too convenient, considering that Naomi had begun working to undermine Amelie. I imagine she wanted to take her place even then, but Amelie's not someone who fails to respond to a challenge."

"You mean Amelie had Naomi killed?"

"Possibly. Or possibly Oliver did, to protect her. But if so, he must have had a change of heart, since, or Naomi secured control of him. I've never trusted the Roundhead, myself. A man of low character and high ambition. Naomi wouldn't be above using him to achieve her dreams of ruling."

"Then we have to tell Amelie he's stabbing her in the back."

Claire took a deep breath. "*You* have to tell her. She won't believe me, or Shane, and Michael's not able to tell her anything, even if he wanted to."

"I can't," he said. "Look at me. I'm in no fit state to—"

"You're the official bearer of bad news," Shane said, and pointed the rifle at Myrnin. "End of discussion."

"Yes," Myrnin said instantly. "Of course. No problem at all."

There was quite a lot of animated debate about how to make it into the guarded area around Founder's Square. In the end, they propped Michael up in the passenger seat, next to Myrnin, who held him upright with a friendly arm around his shoulders; when Claire rolled down the passenger window, the Founder's Square vampire guard took one look inside, saw Michael and Myrnin, and nodded them through without any questions. "Amazing," Myrnin said, squeezing rank water out of his hair. "You'd think someone might notice my general appearance."

"Funny, I'd think you'd notice that it's not that different from how you usually look," Shane said. He hadn't lowered the rifle; he sat braced in the back, aiming it generally in Myrnin's direction.

"Really? I'll have to work on that, clearly. Tell me, are you really so angry at Claire that you're willing to fire that weapon in an enclosed vehicle, with a distinct chance of hitting her?"

"I'm not angry," Shane said. "I'm careful." That, Claire noticed, didn't really answer the question at all.

It did shut Myrnin up for a while, at least until they'd parked the hearse in the underground lot of Founder's Square. Shane was forced to leave the gun, but he grabbed Claire's backpack and filled it with a selection of the handiest possible weapons.

"We're not going to be able to fight our way in, or out again," Myrnin said. "You might keep that in mind during your packing frenzy."

"Shut up." Shane put the backpack over his shoulder, and for the first time, looked at Claire directly. "He's your responsibility. Keep him from doing anything too crazy."

"I'll try," she said. It was the first real conversation—brief and businesslike as it was—that they'd had in hours, and it made her feel just a tiny bit less awful . . . until he turned his back on her in the elevator, in preference to watching the numbers flicker until they'd arrived at the right floor. Myrnin led the way, which was a good thing, because the first intersection brought them face-to-face with two of Amelie's black-uniformed guards.

"We were told you left," one of them said to Myrnin.

"You were ill-informed, then," Myrnin said loftily, and drips of filthy water ran down his feet to leave stains on the carpet. "I'm here to see the Founder."

"Like that?" The guard gave him an up-and-down look, eyebrows raised.

"Would you like me to shower and change before warning her of potential disaster? Because of course one wouldn't like to deliver that news in a less-than-pristine state."

The guard accepted that, but then he turned the analysis on Claire and Shane. "And them?"

"With me," he said. "Entourage. You know."

"Backpack," the second guard said to Shane, and gestured. He hesitated. "Now."

"Oh, give it up. I told you we couldn't use those anyway," Myrnin said. "Do it. Quickly. We have little time left, for heaven's sake."

The guards were ignoring him now, focused on Shane and the potentially lethal contents of his bag, and as soon as they'd turned away from him, Myrnin reached out, grabbed each of the guards by the side of the head, and knocked them together, hard. Claire shuddered at the sound of bone crunching. Both men dropped to the carpet, twitching.

"Come on," Myrnin said. "They won't be down for long. But don't worry, their brains aren't complicated enough to be damaged."

"But—"

"Claire, we *do not have time.*" He grabbed her by the arm and dragged her along at a run, past closed doorways, painted portraits, flickering lights . . .

And into an open doorway.

Amelie's assistant rose to her feet in alarm at the sight of them and bared her teeth, and Myrnin bared his in turn. "Announce me," he said, and then shook his head. "Never mind; I'll do it myself."

He lowered his shoulder and ran at the inner door. The lock broke, and the door swung open . . .

On Amelie, held in Oliver's arms. Not as a hostage, as Claire originally thought, but in a position that could only be called, ah, intimate. That was one hell of a kiss in progress, and there were fewer clothes than might be strictly formal.

The kiss broke off as Myrnin came to a sliding halt in the remains of the door, with Shane and Claire close behind, and said, "Well, this is awkward. Beg pardon, but I believe Claire has something to tell you."

Then he shoved her forward as Oliver stepped away from the embrace and began buttoning up his shirt. Amelie glared at Claire, then at Myrnin, then at Shane, as if deciding which of them to kill first.

Myrnin seriously wasn't going to do anything, Claire realized. He was standing back, watching. She wasn't sure what he was watching *for,* but he'd left her deliberately hanging there, wriggling like a worm on a hook.

"Well?" Amelie's voice was a crack of sound, like a sheet of ice snapping. "What could possibly be so vital that you intrude here on my privacy, like some assassin?" She grabbed Shane by the collar and dragged him close, ripped the backpack from his hands, and shredded it open, spilling weapons across the floor. "You come to use these, then? Are you in league with your father again? I warn you, this time, the cage won't go unused. You'll burn for this, you little fool."

"Shane's just trying to protect us! Oliver's betraying you," Claire blurted. "He's working with—"

She didn't have time for more. Oliver was right on her, hand gripping her throat as he lifted her effortlessly off the carpet until her feet dangled and kicked uselessly. She clawed at his hand, but he wasn't going to let her breathe. Panic blinded her, smothered her, and all she knew for a few seconds was that she was going to die before she could make things right again with Shane.

Myrnin reached down, grabbed the silver-tipped bat, and hit Oliver right between the shoulder blades, hard enough to knock him off-balance. Claire was dropped to the carpet, where she whooped in a breath.

"Enough!" Amelie said. There was pale color high in her cheeks, and a furious red glitter in her eyes. "I've had *enough* of your foolish chatter and your betrayals. You come here unasked; you threaten my consort. I am *done* with you all. I've coddled you too long. I'll start with you, Collins."

She grabbed Shane by the shirt when he tried to dart out of her way, and pulled back her other hand, claws sharp and extended. In one more second, she'd do it. She'd kill him.

"No!" Claire shouted through her agonizingly sore throat. "He's working with Naomi; Oliver's going to kill you!"

The Founder froze, and for a second her eyes went entirely

back to gray as she stared into Claire's face, reading what Claire hoped was utterly the truth as she knew it.

And then Amelie let go of Shane and started to turn toward Oliver.

Oliver grabbed the bat out of Myrnin's hands and swung it at the Founder's head with deadly, blurring speed; even for a vampire, that blow would have been fatal if it had connected . . . but Amelie moved like water, flowing out of the way and taking Oliver's arm as it passed, then twisting until the bat flew out of his grip. It shattered the windows beyond in an earsplitting crash, sending glass flying out into the night. The baseball bat whipped end over end to land almost a hundred feet away on the grass of the park below.

Amelie shoved Oliver face-first into the wall, pinned his arm behind him, and said, "Tell me why. *Why?*" She didn't doubt it; Claire saw that. Oliver's attempt to kill her had been clear enough. He cried out, and she twisted harder, though it was obvious from the expression on her face that she was hurting herself by hurting him. "Oliver, *why do you betray me?*"

He laughed. It was an awful, empty sound. "I don't," he said. "I was never loyal to you, you foolish woman. I've made a lifetime of toppling rulers. You're only the latest, and the most rewarding."

Amelie turned her head toward Claire and Myrnin. "He cannot be working with Naomi," she said. "She's dead."

"Sadly, and convincingly, not," Myrnin said. "I saw her with my own eyes. I am fairly certain Claire has her facts straight."

"And where in God's name have you been, then?"

"At the bottom of a pit," he said. "Which accounts for my current state of dress. Although Shane assures me it is not so odd."

Shane hadn't made a sound, and he hadn't moved; he'd probably judged, very rightly, that it was time to make himself a smaller target. From the way his lips tightened, he wished Myrnin hadn't mentioned him at all.

But Amelie didn't seem to care. She bent, picked up a silver-coated stake, and pressed it against the skin of Oliver's neck, just above the spine—just enough to tint the skin and start it burning. "So go traitors," she said. "In the old days, your head would have ended up as a decoration for a spike. I suppose I will have to settle for something less . . . satisfying." There were tears in her eyes, then tears coursing down her pale, still face. "I trusted you, you traitor. I suppose I should have known better. I've never been lucky in love."

"I never loved you," he said. "Kill me. It changes nothing."

"It changes *everything*," she hissed. "You'll not die yet. Not until you help me find my wayward sister. *Then* I will allow you to die. But not yet. Not yet."

"Why wait?" said a low, sweet voice from the doorway, and they all turned—even Oliver—to see Naomi standing there, with Michael behind her. And Hannah Moses, carrying a crossbow with a heavy wooden bolt already in place. And more, behind her—humans and vampires alike. "Thank you, Claire. Sometimes a pawn is the very thing to use as a sacrifice to lure the queen from hiding."

At Naomi's regal nod, Hannah raised the crossbow and fired the bolt straight at Amelie.

It was impossible that it would miss, and it didn't, but . . . something happened, a blur of movement Claire couldn't understand until it was over, and Oliver was standing in Amelie's place, swaying. The wooden bolt was in his heart.

He dropped to his knees, then collapsed.

Amelie was a blur, heading for the broken windows. Hannah had a second bolt in the bow, and Naomi grabbed the crossbow, aimed, and fired just as Amelie leaped out into the night air.

It hit her cleanly in the chest. Claire gasped and watched her tumble gracelessly down to crumple on the grass below.

"Satisfactory," Naomi said. "Though I have no notion why Oliver chose to put himself in the way. Take them all to the cage. Now."

Not even Shane tried to fight, this time.

"Great," Shane said. Claire sensed he would have been pacing, if there had been room, but the steel cage in Founder's Square was just big enough to hold her, Myrnin, and the limp bodies of Oliver and Amelie without any room left over. "Just great. I'm still going to die in this cage, after everything that's happened. That's just perfect."

"Well," Myrnin said, and shoved Oliver's limp body over to stretch out his long, dirty legs, "at least we're dying in royal company. That's something." He reached out to pull the stake out of Amelie's chest, but as he did, a thin silver blade poked through the bars and cut his hand. He yelped and pulled back.

Hannah was standing outside the bars, watching them with calm concentration. "Don't try it," she said. "No use. You leave the stakes where they are."

"Worried?" Myrnin sucked at the cut on his hand, and spat flecks of silver that burned on the floor. "You should be, Hannah. If you think supporting Naomi will win your people freedom, you're a fool. She's worse than Oliver ever thought of being, because I think she honestly believes that what she is doing is for the best—well, for *her* best, in any case." He cocked his head, staring at her, and then suddenly lunged at the bags, wrapping his hands around them. She didn't flinch, though she took a tighter grip on the knife she held. "She's Bishop's daughter. His *spiritual* child as well as his bloodline, with all his gifts. She believes humans are her property, and the world is her larder. Don't be a fool. You can't believe that Claire and Shane should be in here with us, even if you hate vampires so desperately. What has either of them done to deserve it?"

She didn't answer. Myrnin waited, then nodded, as if she'd done exactly what he expected. "I see," he said, and his voice was unexpectedly gentle. "I am well aware how being under such control feels, my dear. All will be well."

"How?" Hannah asked. She sounded indifferent, but Claire thought she heard something new in her voice: pain.

He shrugged. "No idea," he said. "But I'm quite certain that it's unfolding *even now*."

It was the emphasis he put on the last two words that made Claire realize that by lunging forward, and drawing Hannah's full attention, he'd left Amelie partially obscured. Shane was the closest to the fallen vampire. Claire frantically gestured to the wooden stake in her heart, and Shane didn't hesitate. He pulled it out— but not all the way out. Just enough, Claire thought, to clear her heart.

Amelie didn't move. At this point, she probably couldn't.

If he'd done it right, though, maybe she *would*, when she was ready.

Founder's Square was as busy as a mall at Christmas. The big braziers surrounding the center of the square were being lit, bringing a barbaric splendor to the deep night; vampires were gathering, some looking sleepy and confused, some excited, some outright worried. There were humans, too—a group of them, herded together nearby. Claire recognized several of them, including the new mayor, Flora Ramos, and—incredibly—Gramma Day. One of them was complaining loudly. It was Monica Morrell. She certainly hadn't been rousted out of bed like the others; she was dressed to party. . . . Well, that might not be true. Claire wasn't sure she *didn't* wear tube dresses to bed.

Myrnin sank back from the bars and crossed his arms, glancing at Shane. "Well done," he said in an undertone. "Clever boy, taking it out only part of the way. I take back at least one bad thing I've ever said about you."

"What's happening?" Claire asked.

"Naomi prepares to declare her primacy," he said. "She'll have herself crowned, and then she'll spill blood—"

"Ours," Shane said.

"Oh no, not at all. It's a very old custom, one even Bishop respected. She'll kill the most influential residents of Morganville . . . Founder families, important business leaders, politicians. . . . I suppose Monica's there to represent her family; more's the pity for their memories."

"It's about more than ceremony," Shane said. "Most of those guys are on Captain Obvious's war council. I saw them. And Gramma Day is related to Hannah."

"Really?" Myrnin raised his eyebrows. "Interesting indeed. She's honoring the old customs *and* ensuring her own long-term survival. Masterful. Worthy of her father, in his better days."

"Could you maybe not admire the evil enemy quite so much, and focus more on how we're going to get out of this?" Claire asked. "Because I'm pretty sure we're going to die, too."

"Oh yes. But you and I are merely collateral damage; this is a pyre for Amelie. And I see they've made improvements. See the grates underneath us? Natural gas. It's all very fuel efficient, not like the old days with all the logs. . . ."

"Myrnin!"

He went suddenly very cool and sensible. "Bite marks," he said.

"Michael's got one on his neck. So does Hannah Moses. So, in fact, does Oliver. All a very distinctive bite distance. It takes a delicate mouth to make such marks, such as, say—" He pointed a finger, and Claire followed the line of it to Naomi, who was standing draped in silver and white a few feet away. "She's got the gift, you see. Not every vampire can compel like that. Amelie can, though she never does, and Naomi can—both of them inherited that trait from their vampire father, Bishop. So whatever's been done, you can rightly assume she's the one pulling the strings, and that no one had any choice in what's been done."

"Oh," Shane said, in a very different sort of tone. "Oh, *crap*. Michael—I left him alone with Naomi and Hannah. Hannah's Captain Obvious. I thought Naomi was just working with her, trying to get at Amelie. But its more than that. She was controlling the whole thing. And Michael."

Which, Claire realized with a sweet surge of relief, was why Michael had turned on them—and why he'd been so cruel to Eve, and to her, and to Shane. He'd had no choice. *Thank you.* She felt like kissing Shane in pure gratitude for having confirmed her suspicions, but Shane didn't look especially relieved himself; he looked disturbed. Maybe he'd just realized that he'd spent a whole day hating the guts of a friend who'd been innocent after all.

"She was controlling Oliver, too, though likely that wasn't quite so difficult," Myrnin said. "Oliver's influence on Amelie was a dark thing even without Naomi bending it to her uses. Once she had, though, she used Oliver to corrupt Amelie, agitate the town against her, create chaos and dissension ... and then used you, Claire, to unmask him, giving her the chance to act directly while Amelie was distracted. My, if I didn't loathe her so much, I'd admire her."

"So how are we going to stop her?" Claire asked.

"We can't. Perhaps I failed to mention that we're locked in a cage and about to be burned alive . . . ?"

"Does this cage have a *lock*?"

"A very good one," Myrnin said. "Right there, on the other side of the bars. I'm reasonably certain that neither of us is a certified locksmith, however."

"Well, we can *try*."

"It's silver," Myrnin said. "I won't be able to break it."

"If the lock's pure silver instead of just plated, it's soft," Shane said. "We could use one of these stakes as a lever, maybe."

"And that will sacrifice our element of surprise," Myrnin pointed out. "You always seem to have something secreted about your person of a dangerous nature. . . . Have you nothing to contribute?"

"They took it," Shane said, "including everything out of my pockets and my belt. Just like jail."

"Not like jail," Claire said thoughtfully. "They left you your shoes."

"And? I'm pretty sure a battered-up pair of kicks isn't going to get us anywhere. . . ." Shane's voice faded at the look on her face. "What?"

"Laces," she said, and bent forward to untie her own shoes and began to pull the cords out. "Give them to me."

"I hardly think we should consider hanging ourselves, Claire," Myrnin said, looking a little worried. "And it wouldn't kill me, you know."

Claire grabbed the laces from Shane as he held them out, tied them end to end, and began quickly braiding them together with those from her own shoes in a rough twisted rope, which she wrapped around the center of the bars at the back. "Cover me," she said to Myrnin. He watched her for a few long seconds, then nodded and moved toward the front of the cage, shoving the limp body of Oliver out of the way, and began to loudly sing something in French. It sounded rude.

Claire began twisting the rope as fast as she could, rapidly getting it to the tension point. "I need something to use as a fulcrum," she said to Shane. "Something that won't break easily."

"Only thing in here is one of the stakes," he said. "Once we pull those, I'm guessing Hannah's got orders not to wait around for the official barbecue."

God, all she needed was a *stick*. . . . Claire cast her eyes about, frantic to find something, anything she could adapt to the purpose, and her gaze fell on, of all things, the headband that Amelie was wearing to keep her long, loose hair back from her face. It was a nice, wide one, not made of plastic but covered in fabric.

Maybe.

Claire edged over, leaving the rope in Shane's hand, and pulled the headband from the vampire's head. She thought Amelie's eyes flickered, just a little, but the Founder didn't move. She looked . . . dead.

Claire flexed the headband in her grip. It had a metal core that bent side to side, but not back to front. And best of all, it didn't break.

She scooted back, slipped it into the rope, and began using it to twist the strands tighter and tighter around the bars. By the fifth round, she felt the tension; by the tenth, she saw the bars actually starting to bend in the middle, yielding to the slow but inevitable force.

I love you, physics.

"Hey," Shane said as she muscled another turn out of the makeshift device. "I probably should tell you that after thinking it over, I'm an ass. And I'm—sorry."

"That must have been hard," Claire said. It was getting really difficult to turn the thing. The edges of the headband were digging into her hand deeply. She gritted her teeth and turned it again.

"Let me," he said, and took hold of the headband. For him, the next three turns were pretty effortless, and the bars bent slowly, steadily inward around the rope. "Damn, this really works. No wonder they don't let you have shoelaces in jail."

"This isn't why."

"I hurt you," he said, in the same tone of voice, without looking at her. "I swore I'd never do that again, and I did. I fell right for Naomi's easiest trick, turning us against each other. I should have trusted you, trusted him, and I didn't. So I'm sorry. And you have every right not to——" He was still turning the headband as he talked, but just then he broke off with a hissing gasp, and Claire saw the flash of red in his hand. Blood soaked quickly through the white fabric of Amelie's headband, but after a second's pause, he turned it again. "Not to trust me, or forgive me. But I hope you do."

"Let me see."

"It's just a cut, and if I let go, we're dead," he said. "It's fine." He kept turning the ever-tighter knot of cloth, and now Claire could hear the creaking of the bars. They were bowing strongly in the middle, and the gap was widening fast. Not only that, but she thought the welds at the top of one of the bars had weakened. *This can work*, she thought. *It's going to work.*

Then, with a sharp, snapping sound, the headband came apart in Shane's hands as he tried to crank it again. "Damn," he whispered, and looked at her. "Is it enough?"

"Let me see your hand."

He held it out, and there was a deep cut across the palm, one that made her ache to see it. Claire grabbed the tail of her shirt and pressed it against the cut, then fished around for the broken edge of the headband. The sheared metal in it was sharp, and she frayed enough of the cloth to rip a piece free to wrap around his hand. As she tied it in place, she looked up into his face.

"Do you forgive me?" he asked her. His eyes were warm and steady, and he had a little, tentative hint of a smile.

"No," she said. It made her sick to have to hurt him like this . . . but it was also right. It was *necessary*. "I want to, I really do, but you didn't trust me, Shane. You didn't believe me when I needed it. And that hurt me, Shane. It really did. It's going to take a little time and a lot of work for me to forgive you for that."

The breath went out of him as if she'd punched him, and his eyes widened. He'd just assumed she'd forgive him, she realized; she'd done that so many times before without any thought or hesitation that she'd made him think it was automatic.

But it wasn't. Not this time. Much as she wanted things to go back to normal, she needed him to understand that he'd hurt her.

From the look on his face, he did.

In the next second, he dropped his gaze and took a deep breath. "I know," he said. "I deserve it. If we get out of here, I promise, I'll make it up to you."

"Take the rope off the bars," she said, and reached forward to tip his chin up and kiss him, very lightly. She wanted to fall into his arms, but it wasn't the time, and it wasn't the message she wanted to send him. "And be ready for anything."

"Always." The cocky grin he flashed her was *almost* right. Almost. But there was a scared, tentative look in his eyes, and she wondered if he was thinking, as she was, *We could die here, right now, and not be right with each other.*

But she couldn't help that. She needed him to understand what he'd done to her, and to himself.

It was the toughest thing in the world, but she turned away from him. Myrnin was still belting out an endless chorus of whatever obnoxious song he was performing; no one was paying attention, but it was annoying enough that they were likely not paying much attention to her and Shane. When she tapped him on the shoulder, he coughed and broke off to say, "Are the two of you quite done with your sweet nothings? Because I might vomit."

"That would be perfect," Claire said. "It's been just a great day so far." She reached up, grabbed his pointed chin, and turned it to show him the bent bars at the rear of the cage. His eyebrows went sharply up. "Maybe you should rest a minute."

"Perhaps I should," he agreed. "Your shirt is torn. And you're wearing a lovely perfume, by the way."

"It's blood," she said. "Thanks. That's ever so comforting."

Myrnin crawled to the back of the cage, coming close to Shane as he did so. The two of them exchanged a look that made the hair rise on the back of Claire's neck; they were like two tigers sizing each other up, with Myrnin then leaning past her boyfriend to inspect the state of the bars. He made a soft *hmmm* sound and nodded, then—to Claire's surprise—pulled Shane close and gave him an utterly unexpected kiss on the cheek.

"Hey!" Shane said, and tried to wriggle free, but then he paused, because Myrnin was whispering to him. Shane's gaze darted for Claire's, then quickly away, and when Myrnin finished, Shane nodded. When Myrnin let him go, Shane moved back—way back.

Claire mouthed, *What the hell?* But Shane just shook his head and looked away. Whatever Myrnin had just said to him, it was ... disturbing.

Myrnin didn't pause for questions. He crawled over to where Amelie was still lying very still, and pulled her into his lap as he kneeled. "My poor, lovely lady," he said, and gently eased her fallen white-gold hair back from her ivory face. "Would you rather die in fire, or in glory? Dead is dead, of course. But I feel you should choose, *now*."

Amelie hadn't moved at all. It was possible that something had gone wrong; maybe a splinter had broken off in her heart, freezing her in place, or something else had happened. A wooden stake wouldn't kill her, but it would paralyze her. And they needed her, Claire thought. Too many vampires. Even if the trick worked to loosen the bars, even if they could break them free . . .

"Something's happening out there," Shane said. "Heads up."

Naomi was moving forward at last, stilling the confused babble of the assembled vampires in the square. She was every bit a queen in her silver and black, and her voice was warm, sweet, and compelling; she didn't need to bite people to convince them, Claire thought. She was persuasive enough without it. She'd only bothered to control the key players, and only for as long as she needed them. She was cold, but smart.

And now, she said, "My friends, I come before you in sorrow and pain to tell you that Amelie, our Founder, has lost the right to rule."

No one doubted what was going on, Claire thought, but a number of vampires out in the crowd began to voice their objections. It wasn't a lot of them, but it was enough to make it clear Naomi wasn't a popular choice.

She held up a hand in a sharp, angry gesture. "Our laws are clear: the strongest rules. My sister was strong; the past is littered with those who stood against her, and lost. Her strength carried us here, to this town, to a place where we can finally begin to regain our rightful glory. But don't be mistaken: she hesitated. She corrupted herself by compromising with humans, with their laws and morals, until she forgot what it was to be a proper vampire."

There were more shouts of protest, louder now. That might not have been what Naomi expected, Claire thought; there was a growing tension in her shoulders, and the hand she still held raised seemed to shiver, just a little. "There will be no debate on this! My sister became weak and foolish, and she was brought down by treachery. Not mine, but the treachery of a lover she trusted. She is not fit any longer to rule. Fear not; I will burn the traitor with her, and we will start newborn."

This time, no one shouted. There was an eerie silence. Claire honestly couldn't tell whether Naomi had won them over, or whether something else was happening—something that didn't bode well for the would-be queen. Vampires weren't that easy to read, especially not in large groups.

The humans in their pen had gone very quiet and still—even Monica. Frail little Gramma Day was standing very tall, hardly leaning on her cane at all. But there was someone new standing near them, almost invisible behind Monica's tall, long-legged form . . . another human, not a vampire.

Jenna? What the hell was the ghost hunter doing *here*? Trying to get a story? Was she insane?

No. She was holding hands with someone else; a small, slight form that Claire spotted as Flora Ramos shifted to one side.

Jenna had hold of Miranda's hand.

Miranda shouldn't be solid. But she was, very solid, though clinging to Jenna's hand as if to a lifeline in a stormy ocean. Maybe Jenna's psychic ability was feeding Miranda's own power and holding her steady in her nighttime form outside the Glass House, but from the strained, scared looks on their faces, it wasn't easy.

What the hell were they *doing*?

Naomi hadn't seen them, or if she had, she didn't care. She

busy trying to charm her new subjects.

"Tomorrow marks our new age, and I will lead you int

continued. "You have been robbed of your rights for s

friends—subjected to indignities, to the constant cor

restrictions of those who are rightfully our propert

over. As a token of this, I give you the first blood o

is yours to take, as is your right as the rulers of

but all the world." She extended her white han

ple held off to the side—twenty people, incl

The vampires looked in that directio

and then Jason sauntered out of the cro

time somebody did the right thing."

He grabbed Monica and dragge

She shrieked and hit him, h

back a bit, and Claire lunged

crossbow bolt all the way ou

through the bars of the ca

Monica leaned over b

and saw the bolt tumbl

that was shockingly

repeated if she'd re

jammed it not

that!" she yell

ized, had sil

held them

Jason

when

hand.

"We hav

distraction, but it

"It doesn't need to," Amelie said. She pulled the last inch of wood free from her chest and smiled up at him. "I find that I choose glory, my dear Myrnin."

"Most excellent," he said. "Claire has loosened the bars, and—"

Shane held up his bleeding hand.

"And Shane helped," Myrnin amended grudgingly. "But I be-eve we should go *now*. Naomi is losing the respect of her peers. It ll not go well for her. She will burn us out of sheer desperation."

Amelie nodded and rolled to a crouch. She studied the bars at back of the cage, made a fist, and hit with surgical precision at oint at the top of one of the bars where the weld was weakest. napped.

hand was burned in a bright red stripe, but she ignored it, the loose metal, and bent it in toward them with shocking It, too, snapped cleanly off at the base.

ah!" Shane was yelling behind them. *"Hannah, no!"*

lanced back and saw that Hannah—probably still fol-mi's implanted instructions—was reaching for a but-ost certainly would turn the cage into a fry basket. em, the gas jets sputtered into pale blue flame.

ire screamed. "Get out *now!*"

hit the second bar twice without breaking it, and her, kicking it with his bare foot between her e seconds later, the whole thing bent and then y free.

opening, but it was enough.

t, and Myrnin after her. Shane went next and Claire.

oving.

yelled. Hannah's hand was hovering over

the button, shaking, as if she were trying desperately to fight for their lives, and losing. "Claire, come on, *now!*"

She couldn't, because Oliver opened his eyes and began to move.

Claire broke loose from Shane's grasp and lunged for the vampire.

Oliver opened his eyes as she started dragging him, and he reached out to grab the bars and hold himself in place. "No," he said. "I have to—I have to pay for what I did."

"Not like this," Claire said. "Come on!"

But he wouldn't let go. The idiot wouldn't *let go*. . . .

She saw Naomi's head turn; she saw her take in the fact that her prisoners were getting loose, and she glared sharply at Hannah—

Who lost the internal battle, and hit the button that turned on the gas burners.

"Let go!" Claire shrieked as the flames shot up. She rolled for the hole in the cage bars and felt Shane yank her free into his arms. Her shirt was burning. He slapped the flames out.

Amelie reached past them, grabbed Oliver's burning form, and yanked him out with all her strength. The bar he'd been holding snapped in half, but he slid free.

Still on fire.

Amelie stared down at him for a bare second with true horror written on her face, then threw herself down on him, smothering the fire with her body and her hands. He was scorched and smoldering, but alive.

Oliver's burned hands moved, caressing her shoulders, and he whispered, "Forgive me."

"Yes," she whispered. "Yes. Hush."

"Stop me before I hurt you again."

"I will." She sat up as he closed his hands around her neck, and she drove the wooden arrow that she'd pulled from her own chest into his heart. Oliver went limp.

But Michael and Hannah had just rounded the corner, armed and ready to kill, and there was nothing but Naomi's will in their expressions now.

They were puppets—deadly puppets.

Amelie didn't seem to know, or care. Myrnin grabbed Hannah, avoiding the silver-edged knife as she expertly sliced it at him, and tried to throw her off-balance. "Don't hurt her!" Claire cried. "It's not her fault!"

Michael was still coming. Shane let go of her and faced off with him. "Not gonna happen, bro," he said. Michael bared fangs at him, and Shane held up the stake in his hand. "Not in this lifetime. I already had a vamp kiss me today. Not going all the way—"

But the banter wasn't slowing Michael down, and before Claire could take a breath, Michael had rushed forward, grabbed Shane's arm, and was relentlessly bending it back until the stake rattled on the granite slab. It rolled toward the cage and caught on fire from the inferno raging inside.

At that moment, Claire saw Miranda and Jenna step into view behind them, and Jenna let go of Miranda . . . and the air turned darkly electric with the rush of whispers.

Even Michael paused. There was something terrifying in that sound, something *wrong*.

Claire blinked, because she could see shadows now in the glare of the fire—shadows that moved on their own. Human-formed, they rushed forward past Miranda. Some piled onto Hannah, and although Claire could hardly see them, they must have had an effect, because Hannah staggered and stopped trying to stab the hell out of Myrnin. He let go and backed away, and she swatted at the whirl of shadows around her, movements growing more and more frantic and erratic.

And weak.

And then she went to her knees, and fell.

The same was happening to Michael, a storm of ghost-fury around him, and as Shane backed away, Claire saw one of the shadows break loose from the angry swarm and come toward her boyfriend.

The small figure took on shape and a glassy kind of reality as it approached him.

"Lyss," Shane whispered, "thank you."

She held out her hand; just for a moment, Shane took it. Claire saw the power that ran between them, a burst that exploded like a star in Alyssa's shadow-body and gave her, just for a few seconds, reality.

"I love you," Alyssa said, still holding on. "I just had to tell you it wasn't your fault."

Then she let go and faded into starlight.

Gone.

Shane staggered backward, and Claire caught him. His heart was beating fast, and he felt cold despite the inferno-like temperature of the gas jets nearby.

Michael was down now, and the ghost-swarm buzzed on for a few seconds before Miranda—called them back? That was what it looked like, Claire thought. The ghosts gathered like a cloak around her, crowding and whispering, and Miranda shuddered and turned very, very pale, almost translucent.

Jenna grabbed her hand, and she stabilized again.

"Bring them," Amelie said, pointing to Hannah and Michael. She stared at Jenna and Miranda for a moment, as if trying to decide what to do with them, then inclined her head just a tiny bit. It was a bow of recognition, if not approval.

"What are we going to do?" Shane asked as he bent to grab Michael under the arms. Michael moaned, but he didn't move much on his own.

"Now," Amelie said with all of hell in her eyes, "we'll find out who plays this game better."

She was a mess, Claire thought—dress torn, smudged now with soot and blood from Oliver's scorched body, hair in a tangle around her face. But she'd never looked more savage, or more like a queen, than when she walked out from behind the cage and faced Naomi.

The whole crowd froze, a mass of a hundred or more vampires, all deciding what to do; the humans panicking in their sacrificial corral; Jason and Monica, locked in a fashionista battle stance. *Nobody* moved.

Not even Naomi, who looked utterly cool and perfect. But her smile looked stark and—just for a moment—false.

"It's fitting," she said then, "that you die at the hands of your successor. Try to do it with dignity, Amelie."

"I always loved you," Amelie said. "It's a pity you were never worthy of it." Her eyes flared bright silver white, and she nodded toward Claire, who was standing nearest. "Bring them."

Claire guessed she meant Michael and Hannah, and she gestured. Myrnin carried Hannah over, and Shane dragged Michael.

Naomi laughed. "This is your army, dear sister? Pathetic."

"Is it?" Amelie extended her hand toward Michael Glass. "I'll have my fledgling back now."

Whatever hold Naomi was keeping over him, it broke with an almost audible twist; Michael grabbed his head, and for a few seconds he looked as if he might collapse—but he pulled himself upright, wiped blood from his nose, and walked past Naomi to stand next to Amelie. Next to Shane, too. His eyes flashed over Claire, as well, and she read the horror and sorrow in them. *Oh, Michael.*

"And you, too, Hannah." Amelie moved her pointing finger to Hannah Moses. "I free you. Join your people."

Myrnin let her down, and Hannah blinked, staggered, and whipped her head around to glare at Naomi. The blind fury in her eyes was terrifying . . . but then she backed off from the vampires, and she went to where Monica was holding Jason at bay with her silver-capped shoe.

Hannah said, "Put those back on. This works better." And she handed Monica the silver knife.

"What about you?" Monica asked as Jason took a big step away.

Hannah shrugged. "If he wants to come at me, he'll find I don't need anything else. Not for the likes of him."

Jason backed all the way to the first rank of vampires behind him.

They shoved him *forward*, into no-man's-land.

"Now," Amelie said to Naomi, in the hiss of the burning torches and the roar of fire in the empty cage, "tell me again how you plan to rule in *my* town, Sister. Tell me how you will command the obedience of all these gathered here. *Show me.*"

Naomi didn't lack for guts, Claire thought. She turned to the assembled vampires of Morganville, raised her hands, and said, "You know what Amelie offers. I will give you freedom. I will give you glory. I will give you back the world that you deserve. All you need to do is take one step forward, just one, and you will be free!"

Amelie said nothing. Not one thing.

No one moved. Not even Jason, who, Claire guessed, was starting to realize just how badly he'd screwed up his newfound immortality.

Naomi's face went from impassioned to blank as the reality hit her that she had lost. Decisively.

"You missed the strong hint you were given before," Amelie said. "Many of these were present when you fell among the draug. No one bent to save you then. And none will follow you now." Her eyes blazed silver, an awful and beautiful color, and she didn't even have to raise her voice at all. "Kneel to me, Sister."

"No," Naomi said. She was shaking now, as if about to collapse, but she was grimly clinging to whatever it was that had driven her this far. "No. I was made to *rule.*"

"Kneel," Amelie whispered. "I won't forgive you, but I can spare you. And I will. But you must kneel."

"Never!"

But she did. It happened slowly as if she were being crushed under a huge, impossible weight, and Claire actually felt sorry for her as she finally collapsed to her knees, bent her head, and wept.

Amelie lifted Naomi's chin, placed a soft kiss on her forehead, and said, "We share the darkest of fathers, you and I. And I don't blame you. It's a bitter thing, this blood of ours. You'll have time to think on it. So much time, alone in the dark. A hundred years of it before your penance to me is done."

Naomi said nothing. Claire wasn't sure she actually *could* say anything. She covered her face with her hands, and Amelie turned away from her to look at the vampires.

"Naomi was not wrong," she said. "I have been weak. I've allowed you to be weak as well, to indulge your passions as I indulged mine, as if there were no consequences to come. But my sister's way is the old way, and it will destroy us. . . . You know the fever that hunting brings on us, and the destruction it will cause.

Morganville was built to allow us to live *without* such risk, and with the human world encroaching on us at every turn, we cannot be weak. We cannot be indulgent." She drew in a long, slow breath. "Tomorrow, you will learn to be stronger than you ever thought you could be. There will be *no* hunting. *No* killing. You will share my sister's penance, for as long as it pleases me. And I will share it, too." She turned to Hannah, and to the humans who stood there. "You're free to go. And you may carry my pledge to the rest of Morganville: we will not kill. And if we do, the penalty for us is death, just as it would be for you to kill us. Only as equals can we keep the peace. It is not in our nature, but it is the only way to survive."

Hannah nodded. So did Mayor Ramos. Monica finally slipped her high heels back on, flipped her hair back over her bare shoulders, and said, "You ruined a great party at my place, you know." And she walked off without another word.

Claire almost laughed. Almost . . . and then Amelie turned toward her and said, "Explain to me about these ghosts."

It was a very long conversation.

Claire, Myrnin, Shane, and Michael were taken out of Founder's Square and back to Amelie's office, where workers were already sweeping up the broken glass and boarding up the windows in preparation for morning. After a glance at the work in progress, Amelie moved them into the outer office, where her assistant cleared her desk for the Founder to sit down. A couple of Amelie's guards carried Oliver in and stretched him out on the floor. He was silent, eyes shut tightly. His burns were healing, but there were still red patches all over his face, and his clothes were more char than fabric.

"I'll give the edicts now. Bizzie, be sure they are filed tonight,"

Amelie said. She looked tired, and desperately pale, but there was nothing but surety in her voice. "Myrnin, I wish you to return to your work. There's much to be done to repair Morganville. We can't do it without you, and your chances of survival outside are . . . slender, at best."

Myrnin hesitated, then said, "I'll consider it."

"I could order you."

"Well," he said, and smiled a little. "You could certainly *try*, dear lady, but—"

Amelie shook her head and cast a look at her assistant. "Just put down that he agreed," she said. "Michael, although what you did was not of your free will, you raised arms against your ruling queen and your sire. How do you intend to repay me? Think carefully about your answer. There's only one that will satisfy the debt."

He shook his head. "You always get what you want." Michael sounded exhausted and kind of . . . well, broken. He hadn't really looked Claire in the eyes, or Shane. "Eve's not going to forgive me. Not for any of it."

"True," Amelie said. "Yet there is no betrayal so bitter as that of a child. But I am prepared to allow you to go unpunished, under one condition."

"Which is?"

She gave him a very cold look. "I warned you," she said. "Again and again. I withheld my permission for your marriage not out of spite, but to protect you, and to protect Eve. She has suffered much, Michael, and some of it at your own hands; this is what I warned you against. Humans are fragile things, and we cannot resist the urge to exploit weakness. Already, you have felt this. So for your own good, I will allow you to go unpunished if you will leave your wife. Let her go, Michael. Do the kind thing."

He looked stunned—and then there was a slow-burning anger inside him that caught fire in his eyes. "You can't," he said. "You can't order me to do that."

"I am not ordering you. I am offering you the chance to avoid a heavy and very public punishment."

"Hasn't she been hurt enough? Breaking us up was what *Naomi* wanted!"

"For reasons that have nothing to do with mine," Amelie said. "I share a view with Hannah Moses, and many others. I believe that humans and vampires are best kept separate, for the safety of both. You have taken it too far. I am not angry at the girl, Michael; I am *terrified* for her. Do you understand how much danger you put her in, daily?"

He had to be thinking about seeing Eve in the hospital, Claire thought, and for a second she was sure he was going to agree, to just . . . walk away. And that was appalling.

But instead, Michael met the Founder's eyes and said, "I love her." Just that, simple and sure. "So whatever punishment you have to give me, go ahead. I'm not hurting her again."

Across from him, Shane nodded and tapped his fist against his chest. Respect. Michael gave him a small, weary smile.

"Very well," Amelie said. She didn't look pleased. "Bizzie, please note that Michael Glass has accepted punishment as decreed by his sire."

Bizzie's pen scratched dryly on the paper. "And what is it?"

"I haven't decided," Amelie said. "But it will be very public."

And then it was her turn, as Amelie's cool eyes fixed on her. "Claire," she said. "Always in the middle. What shall I do with you?" Claire stayed silent. She really didn't know what Amelie was thinking, or feeling; there was a lot of anger inside her, a lot of sadness, and it was always easy to target weakness, as Amelie had pointed out to Michael. When she didn't move and didn't blink, Amelie turned to Myrnin. "Well?"

"I need her help," he said. "Frank's off-line." Meaning dead, Claire suspected. "Without her, I'll be ages getting all of the necessary protections back online. Oh, and I'll need a brain. Something relatively undamaged. Not Naomi; I shouldn't like to have her run Morganville's systems, would you?"

"I thought you were planning to use Claire's brain," Amelie said casually, and flicked a glance back at her to see if she would flinch. She didn't. "Very well. One will be located for you. Claire, you will—"

"No," Claire said. Just that. A very simple word, but it meant throwing herself off a very high cliff. "You said I could leave Morganville once. Did you mean it?"

"Claire?" Shane blinked and took a step toward her. "What are you doing?"

She ignored him, watching Amelie, who was just as intently watching her. "Did you?"

"Yes," Amelie said. "If you wish. I can arrange for you to enter the university you wished—MIT, yes?—and have advanced study with someone who is friendly to Morganville, though no longer a resident. Is that what you require of me, as payment for saving my life?"

"No," Claire said. "That's what you *owe* me for saving all your lives, a bunch of times. What I *require* now is that you let Shane go, too. If he wants."

"Claire, this is unwise," Myrnin said. "You should not—"

"I want," Shane said, interrupting him. "I definitely want."

Claire nodded. She and Amelie hadn't yet broken their stare. It was really hard to keep doing it; there was some kind of power in Amelie that affected people even when she wasn't really trying, and it was giving Claire the shakes, and the faint outline of a headache. "I want you to get me into MIT. And for Shane to be able to go anywhere he wants. And for you to keep your word about Morganville. No killing. Not even to get Myrnin his brain."

"No need," Myrnin said earnestly. "There are several in the morgue who will—"

Amelie raised her hand and cut him off instantly. "Agreed," she said. "Note it down, Bizzie." Bizzie did, without lifting her head as she wrote in quick, dry scratches on the paper. "Now. As to Oliver," she said. Her voice had taken on a softer note, with something almost tentative about it. "As to Oliver, I will be seen as weak if I forgive him as well as Naomi. He was my most visible adversary, and the most visible knife at my back. So he must go. He is exiled from Morganville, until such time as I decide he may return."

Oliver opened his eyes and turned his head. Amelie's gaze fell on him, and for a moment, there was something so painful between them, it made Claire want to look away. It was a kind of desperate, angry longing she knew all too well.

And then Oliver said, "Yes, my liege." And he closed his eyes. "As you wish. I accept your punishment."

"You're all dismissed," Amelie said. "Oliver, you may gather your things. You'll leave tomorrow."

She went back into her office.

And . . . that was it. It felt oddly empty to Claire, where there should have been some sense of . . . of triumph. Of *something*. But she wasn't sure of anything anymore. She just knew that she had to take control of her life, *now*, or it would never happen.

Michael stopped next to Claire and said, "So this is where I tell you how sorry I am. So, so sorry. Believe me, I—I can't explain."

"You don't need to," she said. "I was controlled by Bishop; I know how it felt."

Michael sighed and shook his head. "Dammit. It's not—I know you've got some issues with Shane, and that's on me, not on you. I'm sorry. Let me fix things, if I can."

She wasn't sure that was remotely possible, but she smiled at him. "Thanks," she said. It was the best she could manage. "But it's my life, Michael."

"I know," he said. "I—I just don't know what we are going to do without you."

"You and Eve? You'll be fine. You love her; everybody can see that now. I think you'd even give her up, if she asked you to, but not if *they* ask it. That's real love, I guess." On impulse, she stretched up and kissed him on the cheek. He flinched. So did she, a little. "I'll be back. But I need—I need to have my own life for a while. Out there. Away. You know?"

He did; she saw it in his smile. "That's what Eve and I were trying to explain to you guys," he said. "Sometimes you just ... need that. To be sure who you really are." His smile faded. "You didn't ask for Shane to go with you."

"I didn't," she agreed, and walked away.

Shane was waiting at the hearse. He still wasn't looking directly at her, or for that matter at Michael, as the two of them approached. He leaned against the side, arms folded, and said, "Shotgun."

"Sure," Michael said. "I'll drive. Shane—"

Shane held out a palm to stop him. "Not now," he said. "I'm not ready for any apologies. You fix it with Eve, then talk to me."

Michael nodded. That wasn't what he wanted to hear, obviously, but it was the best he could have hoped for, really. *We won,* she thought. Why didn't it feel any better?

"Sorry," Shane said. He seemed flushed and awkward, suddenly, as she headed for the back of the hearse. "I—look, you should take the front and—"

"You called shotgun," she said. "It's okay."

He stared after her, clearly trying to think what to say, and failing. For that matter, she wasn't sure, either.

The drive home was weirdly silent.

Miranda met them at the door, face alight. Jenna was standing behind her, looking almost as proud. "You're okay," she said. "I knew you were going to need our help."

"Actually," Jenna said, "that was me. I had a vision of you locked in that cage, and I didn't know what to do."

"I did," Miranda said. "Once I stopped being afraid of the others and really tried to talk to them, it was easier. I still have to be careful around them, but with Jenna holding on, they can't feed on me as they could before. She can help me get out of the house. It's perfect."

Jenna didn't seem to think so, but for the moment, at least she nodded.

"How's Eve?" Michael asked. Miranda's smile faded.

"She's awake," she said. "She's waiting on the couch. We told her what happened."

"Thanks. You saved our lives." Claire hugged Miranda, then followed her into the living room. Eve was sitting up on the couch, and already her bruises were loads better; the ice packs on the floor were probably part of that.

She was watching Michael with a fragile kind of hope in her eyes.

He was a few steps away, as if he didn't dare make a move. Shane came to a halt behind him and leaned against the wall, arms crossed. Claire knew that pose; it was his bodyguard look. He was, at the moment, guarding Eve, from Michael.

But Michael didn't try to come closer.

"I hurt you," he said. "I never wanted it, but that happened. I could tell you I didn't mean it, and that it wasn't me, and that's true, but it *was* me, and I know you can't forget it. I—" He spread his hands wide. "I hate myself, Eve. That's all I can say. I hate myself. And if you want me to go, I'll go. I'll do anything. *Anything.*"

There were tears glittering in her eyes. "Miranda told me," she said. "About Naomi. About her biting you. That you didn't have a choice in what you did. But it *felt* real. You know?"

"I know," he said. "It felt real to me, too. And it scared the hell out of me."

"Don't ever do it again."

He smiled. "I won't," he said. "I love you, Mrs. Glass."

She opened her arms, and he hugged her, as carefully as if she were a fragile piece of crystal.

Shane cleared his throat. "Um, you should know that Amelie tried to make him give you up," he said. "Because Michael's probably not going to tell you that. And he refused. So now he's on her bad side, again."

"Oh, baby," Eve said, and drew back to look at Michael's face. "How bad?"

He shrugged. "Doesn't matter."

And Eve's smile was full of delight as she laid her head on his shoulder. Claire met Eve's eyes and got a very small smile. It was a little thing, but it was a start.

"I love you, too, Eve," Claire said. "I'm sorry."

"Hush up," Eve said. "Who *wouldn't* want to kiss him? Forgiven and forgotten."

That was more charity than Claire thought she could ever earn. Then Michael whispered something to Eve that clearly wasn't meant to be overheard, and the sense of intruding on something so precious and private was more than she could take.

Shane must have felt it, too; he pushed off the wall and went up the stairs toward his room. Claire hesitated, then headed that way.

"Hey." It was Michael's voice, soft and a little rough, and she glanced over at him as he untangled just a bit from Eve. "That thing, the one you were working on for Myrnin. There's something to it. I felt it. I thought you should know."

She was—surprised, she guessed, and a little elated. "Thanks," she said. The thing was sitting like a particularly large engine part on the dining room table, and she went back, retrieved it, and wondered, again, what exactly it would be able to do if she could really, truly make it work.

Something wonderful, maybe.

Or something awful.

She carted it upstairs, and at the hallway, she hesitated. All the doors were shut, including Shane's. She took a deep breath, steadied herself, and began walking in that direction.

It felt a bit like going to her own funeral.

Shane's door was shut. She knocked and got silence for an answer. *He doesn't want to talk about it,* she thought, and even though she'd wanted to keep him at a distance for now, to let him understand how badly he'd hurt her when he'd failed to trust her . . . it ached.

So she went to her room, feeling lost and alone. She left the lights off. The exhaustion, the chill, the despair, were suddenly . . . too much. She just wanted to crawl into bed and cry until she died. Tomorrow, she'd have to think about how to leave Morganville behind, how to go off to a new town, a new school, a whole new world . . . and somehow do it without Michael, or Eve, or even Myrnin.

And maybe even without Shane.

But she just couldn't face it now.

She dumped the machine on the dresser and didn't even bother to take her clothes off, just stripped back the covers, kicked off her shoes, and crawled beneath . . . and instantly felt the warmth of a body beside her, moving closer.

Oh.

Shane's arms went around her. It was slow, and tentative, and done in complete silence. He pulled her closer, and closer, until she was pressed against him, back to front. His lips pressed a slow, soft, burning kiss on the soft, tender skin at the back of her neck.

"I know you didn't ask me," he said. "I know you may not want me to go. But I'm going to Boston, and I'll be there when you need me. You don't have to say anything. I know I have to earn your trust back. It's okay."

She caught her breath, sighed, and felt her heart break all over again, in a whole new and beautiful way.

TRACK LIST

Music is important to my process of writing. It's the first thing I do before I start writing ... pick at least ten songs for this track list. Then, as I go along, I search for more music to fill it out and keep the soundtrack in my head fresh. I think I got some particularly juicy songs for this one! Hope you enjoy them ... and *please*, remember that, like writers, musicians exist on the money you pay for their work. So please pay to help them play.

"Seven Devils"	Florence + The Machine
"Haunted"	Kelly Clarkson
"Cold Morning"	Kitty Kat Stew
"Sonata Rapidus Revamp"	b.hantoot
"I Disappear"	The Faint
"Big Wheel"	The Bridge
"Black"	Danger Mouse & Daniele Luppi (feat. Norah Jones)
"Fresh Blood"	Eels

"Killing My Dreams"	Elysion
"Good Idea"	Peter Himmelman
"Immigrant Song"	Karen O, Trent Reznor & Atticus Ross
"The Recluse"	Cursive
"Oblivion"	Winter In Eden
"Haunted"	Evanescence
"Things Have Changed"	Bob Dylan
"Afraid"	Sarah Fimm
"What If I Were Talkin' to Me"	Louise Goffin
"Victoria"	Krypteria
"Snow White Queen"	Evanescence
"Somebody That I Used to Know"	Gotye (feat. Kimbra)
"Young Blood"	The Naked and Famous
"Stare into the Sun"	Graffiti6
"Second Chance"	Peter Bjorn and John
"Who Wants to Live Forever"	Queen
"Bullet in My Hand"	Redlight King
"Dark Horses"	Switchfoot
"Soldiers"	Otherwise
"Strangeness and Charm"	Florence + The Machine
"Ease My Pain"	Declan Flynn
"Gold on the Ceiling"	The Black Keys
"In My Veins"	Andrew Belle (feat. Erin McCarley)
"Natives"	blink-182

Read on for an exciting excerpt from
Rachel Caine's next Morganville Vampires novel,

Fall of Night

Coming in May 2013 from New American Library

The billboard at the border of Morganville hadn't changed since Claire had first driven past it on the way into town at the tender age of sixteen. It seemed a lifetime ago, but here was the same old sign, faded and creaking in the dry desert wind. It had a 1950s-era couple (white, of course) next to a finned car as big as a boat, looking into the sunset. WELCOME TO MORGANVILLE. YOU'LL NEVER WANT TO LEAVE.

Yet here she was. Leaving. Actually *leaving*.

The weight of it felt suddenly unbearable, and the billboard dissolved into impressionistic swirls as tears formed hotly in her eyes. She was finding it hard to catch her breath. *I don't have to go,* she thought. *I can turn around, go home, go back where it's safe* . . . because as crazy and dangerous as Morganville was, at least she'd learned how to live there. How to adapt, and survive, and even thrive. It had become, well, home. Comfortable.

Out there . . . she wasn't sure what she'd be anymore.

It's time to find out, the more adult part of her said. *You have to see the world before you can give it up to be here.* She supposed that was right. Didn't the Amish send their kids on *rumspringa* to find out what life was like outside so the kids could make a decision on whether to stay in their community? So maybe she was on a kind of vampire *rumspringa.*

Because that was what she was leaving, even though she definitely was not one of the plasma-challenged: a vampire community, with almost everything in some way related to them—to protecting them, to making them money, to giving them blood. In turn, at least theoretically, the vampires protected the town and the people in it. That didn't always work, of course. But the surprising thing was that it *did* work more often than not. And she thought, from the way things were settling down now, that it might work lots better this time around, now that the town's Founder, Amelie, had her mojo back.

"Troubled?"

The voice made her gasp and turn, then blink away tears, because she'd actually forgotten that he was standing there. Not Shane. She'd left early, before he was awake; she'd actually sneaked away before dawn so that she could be off without good-byes she knew would rip her heart into pieces. Here she stood with her suitcases and her stuffed backpack, and *Myrnin.*

Her vampire boss, if you could call being a mad scientist a profession, was standing next to the big black sedan he occasionally— *very* occasionally, thankfully—drove. (He was not a good driver. Understatement.) He wasn't dressed crazily this morning, for a change. He'd left the Hawaiian shirts and floppy hats at home, and instead he looked as if he'd stepped out of an eighteenth-century drama—breeches that tucked into shiny black boots, a gold-colored satin waistcoat, a coat over it that had tails. He'd even tied his normally wild shoulder-length hair back in a sleek black ponytail.

Vampires could stand still better than humans, and just now he looked like a carved statue . . . alabaster and ebony and gold.

"No," she said, aware she'd hesitated way too long before answering him. She shivered a little. Here in the desert, at night, it was icy-cold, though it would warm up nicely by midday. *I won't be here then,* she realized.

But Morganville would go on without her. That seemed . . . weird.

"I am surprised you did not bring your friends to say good-bye," Myrnin offered. He sounded cautious, as if he was far from sure what the etiquette of this situation might be. "Surely it's customary that they see you off on such a journey. . . ."

"I don't care if it is," she said. A tumbleweed—a thorny, skeletal ball of nasty, scratching branches—rolled toward her, and she sidestepped it. It plowed into a tangle of its fellows that had piled up against the base of the billboard. "I don't want them to cry. I don't want to cry, either. I just— Look, it's hard enough, okay? Please don't."

Myrnin's shoulders lifted in a minute shrug. For the first time, as he turned his head away, she saw that he'd secured his ponytail with a big black bow. It fit what he was wearing, and it was weird that it didn't look out of place on him. *He looks like Mozart,* she thought—or at least how Mozart had been dressed in the paintings she'd seen.

"It must have been easier when people dressed like that," she said. "Being a vampire. People made their faces white with powder, didn't they? So you didn't stand out so much."

"Not just their faces," he said. "They powdered their wigs, too. One could choke on the arsenic and talcum. I can't imagine it was good for the lungs of the living, but one does what one must for fashion." He paused a moment, then said, "What made it easier for vampires was that we lived by candlelight, lamplight—it makes everyone look healthier, even the sick. These harsh lights you favor now . . . well. Difficult. I heard that a few vampires have taken to those spray-tanning salons to get the proper skin tones."

She almost laughed at that, at the image of a badass vampire like Oliver—ferocious and fearless—standing around in a Speedo to get himself painted. But Oliver was leaving Morganville, too . . . banished, now, from Amelie's side. That had probably been the right thing to do, but Claire felt bad for him . . . a little. He'd betrayed the Founder, but he hadn't meant it—and he hadn't had a choice.

If any vampire could survive in the human world, though, it would be Oliver. He was clever, ruthless, and mostly without a conscience. Mostly.

"You can still change your mind," Myrnin said. He was perfectly still, except for the wind ruffling his clothes and the bow on his ponytail; he didn't try to meet her eyes. "You know you don't have to leave here. No one wants you to go, truly."

"I know." That was all she'd been thinking about for hours. She hadn't slept, and her whole body ached with nervous tension. "You're not the only one to tell me so." Shane, for instance. Though he'd been quiet about it, and gentle. It wasn't that she was angry with him—God, no—but she needed desperately to make sure that he trusted her as much as she trusted him. She loved him— that was what made it so, so hard to do this. She *needed* him. But he'd screwed up, big-time, in believing a big lie about her told by one of their enemies. He'd actually believed that she'd been sneaking around behind his back with Michael.

She had to think about how she felt about that disappointment on her own, but all she could really think about right at this moment was how much she wanted to feel his warm, strong arms wrapped around her, his body shielding her from the cold. How much she wanted one more kiss, one more whisper, one more . . . everything.

"The world out there isn't like it is here," Myrnin said. "I know it hasn't been easy for you here—and I've been a significant part of your challenges, as well. But, Claire, I do know something of the world—I have been in it for hundreds of years, and although technology changes, people are little different, then or now. They are afraid, and they use that fear to excuse their own actions—whether it is theft or hatred, violence or murder. People bond themselves into families and groups for protection. Strangers are always at risk."

He was right. She'd come into Morganville a stranger, and she'd been at risk . . . until she'd found her group, her family, her place.

Claire took in a deep breath. She kicked sand with her sneaker and said, "Then I'll find my group there, where I'm going. You know I can do it. I did it here."

"Here, you are exceptional," he said. "There, who knows? They might not value you as much as we do."

He'd put his finger on her greatest fear—the fear of not being the best. Of being just . . . average, like everybody else. She'd always worked so hard to excel, worked at it with a passion that was close to fear; going to the Massachusetts Institute of Technology was the Holy Grail of that quest, but it also came with a double-edged risk. What if she wasn't good enough? What if everybody else was faster, better, smarter, stronger? She couldn't fail. She *couldn't.* "I'll be fine," she said, and forced a confident smile. "I can do this."

He sighed then, and shrugged. "Yes. Yes, I imagine that you can," he said. "I wish it were otherwise. I'd rather you stayed here, safe."

"Safe!" She burst out laughing, which made him give her a hurt look . . . but really, it was ridiculous. Nothing about Morganville, Texas, was *safe*—it took a vampire to even suggest it. "I— Never mind. Maybe being safe isn't the best thing all the time. I need to be sure who I am out there, Myrnin. I need to be *Claire* for a while, and find out who I am deep down. Not part of something else that's so much more . . . confident than I am."

He looked at her directly with those warm dark eyes that seemed so human, and yet, at the same time, were so very not. He'd seen so much—ages, generations, all kinds of horror and death, brilliance and beauty. "I will miss you; you know that."

"I know," she said, and couldn't look away. She wanted to, but Myrnin's gaze held hers like a magnet. "I'll miss you, too."

He flew at her and embraced her, a sudden and awkward kind of thing; he was too strong and too fast, and it drew a startled little squeak from her as her body remembered all too well how it felt to have fangs sinking into her neck . . . but then he was gone again, stepping away, turning toward the horizon, where pink was painting the hills and scrub brush of the desert. The wind was cold and picking up speed.

"You should go," Claire said, and got control of her pounding heart somehow. "My parents are on the way. They'll be here any minute."

"A very poor escort I'd be to leave you out here in the dark, prey for anything," he said. "Highwaymen, and all that."

"Myrnin, there haven't been highwaymen in at least a hundred years. Probably more."

"Robbers, then. Serial killers. The modern bogeyman under the bed, yes? Bad men, skulking in the darkness have always been there, and always will." He flashed a smile at her, which was made unsettling by the extralong eyeteeth, but he was still glancing uneasily at the horizon. Myrnin was old; he wouldn't burst into flames with the rise of the sun, but he'd be uncomfortably scorched. "I'm sure you're familiar with the concept."

"More than a little," she said with a sigh, and caught sight of car headlights speeding over the crest of the far hill. *Mom and Dad.* She felt a little surge of excitement, but it was quickly overwhelmed by a huge wave of sadness and longing. It felt different than she expected, leaving Morganville . . . leaving her friends behind. Leaving *Shane.* "They're coming. You should go."

"Should I not see you off?"

"In that getup?"

Myrnin looked down at himself, baffled. "It's most elegant!"

"When you were partying down with Beethoven, maybe, but today you look like you're on your way to a fancy dress ball."

"So I ought to have worn the casual shirt with it, then?"

Claire almost smiled at the idea of one of his loud Hawaiian shirts thrown on over breeches and boots. "God, no. You look great. Just not . . . period appropriate. So go on. I'll be fine, okay?"

He looked at the car that was coming toward them, and finally nodded. "All right," he said. "Professor Anderson will be expecting you. Don't forget: you can use the telephone to call me."

He seemed proud he'd remembered that—modern tech not being his strongest skill—and Claire struggled not to roll her eyes. "I won't forget," she said. "You'd better get in your car. Sun's coming up—I don't want you to get burned."

It was. She could see the hot gold edge of it just cresting the hill to the east, and the sky above had turned a dark indigo blue. In minutes, it'd be full daylight, and Myrnin needed to be under cover.

He nodded to her and gave her a formal, antiquated bow, which looked weirdly perfect in that outfit. "Be careful," he said. "Not all dangers have a vampire's fangs. Or a vampire's predictability." He moved quickly to the driver's side of his car, opened the door, and then hesitated for one second more to say, "I will miss you very much, Claire."

He slammed the door and turned the engine on before she could say, "I'll miss you, too, Myrnin." And then he was gone, roaring back into Morganville's town limits . . .

. . . Past another car coming out of Morganville, and that screeched to a halt just at the border, near the billboard. In fact, it fishtailed sideways as it stopped, and the passenger door flew open so hard that Claire was surprised it didn't break off . . . and then Shane was hurtling out of it, heading for her at a run.

"No," he blurted, and threw his arms around her. "You don't get to go like that."

She felt stiff for a moment, with shock and fear of the pain that was coming, but then the familiar lines and planes of his body made her relax against him. Two halves, fitting as if they'd been molded that way despite the fact he towered over her. And then she was kissing him, or he was kissing her, and it was wild and hot and desperate and agonizing and heartbreaking, and when they finally broke, gasping, she rested her forehead against his chest. She could feel him breathing too fast, hear his heartbeat pounding too loudly. *I'm doing this to him,* she thought. *He's hurting and it's my fault.*

But she knew she wasn't wrong about this. She loved Shane, loved him with so much certainty it was like sunrise, but she also knew that he had to see her differently—and she needed to see herself differently if they were going to last. When he'd met her she'd been helpless, defenseless, and now she needed to prove she was not just his equal, but his independent equal.

Whether he—or she—liked it or not.

Over at the car, Michael had gotten out of the driver's side and was leaning against the fender; he seemed content to wait, but he was also eyeing the horizon, where the sun was rising quickly. In minutes, he'd be bathed in light, and at his very young vampire age, that was not good.

Claire put her hand on Shane's cheek, a silent promise, and then dashed over to Michael to throw her arms around him. In the thin dawn light, he looked human again—skin tinted pink, eyes the endless clear blue of a summer sky. He kissed her cheek and hugged her with careful strength. "Come back," he whispered to her. "We love you."

"Love you, too," she said, and stepped back. "You'd better get inside."

He nodded and retreated to the car's blacked-out interior—vampire tinting was way better than anything on human cars, and it would keep him safe from the fierce Texas day—and then it was Eve's turn.

Michael's wife hadn't taken time to get properly dressed; she looked exactly as if she'd bounced out of bed in her cartoon-bat pajama bottoms and tank top, with her dyed-black hair in a messy scraped-together knot at the back of her head. She still had sleep wrinkles on her cheek, and without her Goth makeup, she looked ridiculously young. She was also wearing vampire bunny slippers. Myrnin had given them each a pair for Christmas, since they'd all found his so hilarious, and as Eve marched toward Claire, the rabbits' mouths flapped up and down, their red tongues flashing and plush teeth biting the ground.

Not outdoor wear, but Eve clearly didn't give a crap.

"Hey," she said, stopping a couple of feet away and crossing her arms. "So. There's this."

"Yeah," Claire said. "I just— I couldn't—"

"Couldn't woman up and say good-bye? Jesus, Claire Bear, you didn't even leave a *note!*"

There was no defense for that. It was true. She'd figured that the good-nights they'd said were also good-byes, but now . . . now she saw that they weren't. Shane's twisted anguish had told her that, and so did Eve's tears that gathered now in her eyes.

Claire moved forward, and Eve uncrossed her arms just in time to receive the embrace. "Idiot," Eve said. "Dork. Loser. So, you're just going to run off in the dark and . . . and leave us . . . and . . ." She was crying now, and Claire felt the hot tears on her shoulder, soaking through her sweater. "And we might never see you again, and I love you, Claire. You're like my little sister, and—"

"I'm coming back," Claire said. She hung on fiercely while Eve bawled and let it all out. "I swear, I'm coming back. You can't get rid of me like that."

"I don't *want* to get rid of you!" Eve's balled-up fists hit her back, but softly, lacking any force. "God!"

There was only one thing to do, and that was let her cry it out, and Claire did, fighting back a rising tide of tears herself. This was why she'd tried to sneak away—not because she didn't love all of them, but because the good-byes were so, so awful.

Her parents' minivan rolled up to the sign and pulled to the shoulder, and Claire heard the engine shut off. She patted Eve's back a few more times, until her best friend gave a shuddering nod and stepped away.

"Hello, pumpkin," Claire's father said, and smiled at her from the driver's-side window. He looked tired, she thought, and it shocked her how much more gray there was in his hair. He didn't look well, though her mother had assured her that he was doing much better. "Ready to go?"

"Almost," she said. "Couple of minutes?"

"Take your time." He looked as if he understood, but it was definitely the Dad Look that he leveled at Shane—the disapproving, not-good-enough, up-and-down assessment.

Shane didn't notice, and even if he had, he probably wouldn't have cared much at the moment. He closed the distance between them as Claire came back, and although he didn't put his arms around her, the feeling of an embrace settled around her.

Safe. Safe, with him.

"I don't like this," he said. "I don't like knowing you can't forgive me, Claire. Please, I said I was sorry. What do you want me to do? Beg? I will. I'll get on my knees right here if you want, in front of your parents—"

"No!" she blurted. "No, it's— I'm not angry, really. I'm not. But I need this. *I* need it. I don't ask for anything for myself, but this is mine, Shane. It won't be for long, but it gives us time to— to see if we're really strong apart, like we are together."

She also needed him to understand that he'd screwed up, and she couldn't be one of those doormat girls . . . ready to forgive him when he did unforgivable things. He hadn't trusted her word. He'd believed—despite what he knew about her—that she'd been sneaking around behind his back, with Michael, which, well, *never.*

And so she couldn't fall for the fast, easy apology. Not even here, on his knees, in front of her parents.

Rachel Caine is the *New York Times* bestselling author of more than thirty novels, including the Weather Warden series, the Outcast Season series, the Revivalist series, and the Morganville Vampires series. She was born at White Sands Missile Range, which people who know her say explains a lot. She has been an accountant, a professional musician, and an insurance investigator, and, until recently, still carried on a secret identity in the corporate world. She and her husband, fantasy artist R. Cat Conrad, live in Texas with their iguana, Popeye.

CONNECT ONLINE

www.rachelcaine.com
facebook.com/rachelcainefanpage
twitter.com/rachelcaine